VIRGINIA WOOLF
AND HER WORKS

VIRGINIA WOOLF
AND HER WORKS

By
JEAN GUIGUET

Translated by
Jean Stewart

A Harvest Book

Harcourt Brace Jovanovich
New York and London

Printed in the United States of America

Originally published in French under the title
Virginia Woolf et Son Oeuvre

Library of Congress Cataloging in Publication Data
Guiguet, Jean.
Virginia Woolf and her works.
(A Harvest book ; HB 342)
Bibliography: p.
Includes index.
1. Woolf, Virginia Stephen, 1882–1941.
I. Title.
PR6045.072Z673   1976   823'.9'12   [B]   76-14812
ISBN 0-15-693630-5 pbk.

First Harvest edition 1976
A B C D E F G H I J

A MON PÈRE

Our criticism is only a bird's eye view of the pinnacle of an iceberg. The rest under water.

Virginia Woolf, *A Writer's Diary*

CONTENTS

KEY TO ABBREVIATIONS
OF VIRGINIA WOOLF'S WORKS

AROO	A Room of One's Own	1929-1946
AWD	A Writer's Diary	1959
B the A	Between the Acts	1941
CDB	The Captain's Death Bed and other Essays	1950
CR I	The Common Reader, First Series	1925-1948
CR II	The Common Reader, Second Series	1932-1948
DM	The Death of the Moth and other Essays	1942
F	Flush	1933-1947
G & R	Granite and Rainbow	1958
Three G	Three Guineas	1938-1952
HH	A Haunted House and other Short Stories	1943-1947
JR	Jacob's Room	1945-1954
KG	Kew Gardens	See *A Haunted House*
To the L	To the Lighthouse	1927-1949
M on the W	The Mark on the Wall	See *A Haunted House*
M or T	Monday or Tuesday	1921
The M	The Moment and other Essays	1947
Mrs D	Mrs Dalloway	1942-1950
N & D	Night and Day	1919-1950
O	Orlando	1928-1949
RF	Roger Fry	1940
TLS	The Times Literary Supplement	
VO	The Voyage Out	1915-1929
The W	The Waves	1950
The Y	The Years	1937-1940

N.B.—In the footnotes the figures in parentheses refer to pages in American editions of the works; references to *A Room of One's Own*, *Three Guineas*, *Jacob's Room*, and *The Waves* are to paper-back editions. The dates of the English editions referred to in the footnotes are given above.

FOREWORD

Having at first envisaged a study of "The Treatment of the Subconscious in the Twentieth Century English Novel", with the approval of M. Louis Cazamian, I gave up this subject as being too vast and too complex, and confined myself to one single author among all those who had figured in my original project. Although it may seem premature to attempt a general study of Virginia Woolf, since neither her correspondence nor her complete diary are accessible, it seemed to me none the less that a revaluation of her work was not only possible but imperative.

On the one hand, no study on the scale I envisaged has appeared since the publication of *A Writer's Diary* and the *Letters* of Virginia Woolf and Lytton Strachey. These two volumes introduce a considerable number of new factors, even though in many cases our curiosity is aroused without really being satisfied. Furthermore, the publication of *Granite and Rainbow* and of B. J. Kirkpatrick's Bibliography has brought within the reach of all a number of texts which were not available to our predecessors.

On the other hand, I was convinced that the majority of critics had not done full justice to the special qualities of Virginia Woolf.

The best of these critics had, indeed, revealed certain of the author's characteristics with great perception and skill; but either because they had not all the requisite elements at their disposal, or because they had deliberately limited their studies to certain aspects, it often seemed that their very merits prevented them from attaining a well-balanced comprehensive view. A concern for balance and completeness, indeed, was one of my main considerations. If I have taken advantage of earlier studies, I hope in exchange to help possible readers to appreciate these more fully by enabling them to see these different points of view in perspective, when they will be found to complement, rather than conflict with, one another.

Even when I have had occasion to contradict my predecessors, indeed particularly in such cases, I must acknowledge my indebtedness to them; their adoption of certain attitudes impelled me to clarify my own; and the portraits drawn by them enabled me to fix the broad lines of the one I offer here.

VIRGINIA WOOLF AND HER WORKS

I should like to express my gratitude to those who have helped me in my task: to M. Maurice Le Breton, for his kind encouragement in addition to the valuable training I received from him at the University of Lille; to M. Jean-Jacques Mayoux in particular, who kindly consented to supervise my work: the excellence of his advice, the close attention with which he has followed my ideas, have provided me with that atmosphere of intellectual security without which I should have had to struggle against doubts and uncertainties.

I wish to thank Mr Leonard Woolf, who very kindly enlightened me on certain points concerning the literary activity of Virginia Woolf, entrusted me with some pages of the MS. of *Between the Acts*, and gave me access to the files of reviews published in the Press on the appearance of each of the novelist's books.

I am most grateful to Mr E. M. Forster for the obliging readiness with which he granted me an interview and answered my questions about his friend. M. Pierre Jonin, Professor at the Faculty of Letters of Aix, undertook the thankless task of revising part of my manuscript: for which I should like to express my gratitude.

Finally I cannot conclude without mentioning my students: those who, during a stay in England, were good enough to procure various documents for me; and also those on whom I was allowed to try out my theories, as well as those who, more actively, enabled me, during the preparation of their theses for the Diplôme d'Etudes Supérieures, to discuss and clarify certain aspects of my subject.

March, 1962

CHAPTER I

INTRODUCTION

(Virginia Woolf and the Critics. Outline of the proposed study)

THERE are already some dozen books devoted to Virginia Woolf.[1] If I have chosen to add to these the result of my research and my reflections, it is because it seemed to me that there was still room for a general study of this author's personality and work. These earlier works, indeed, whether because of their date or because of the point of view peculiar to each writer, or finally because of some other deliberately chosen limitation, remain fragmentary. I have none the less found my predecessors' efforts of great value. Thanks to them, the greater part of the problems has been not only defined but also made familiar to us; and the solutions they have proposed, whether I contest them or draw inspiration from them, have in either case provided a fruitful impulse.

A brief examination of these works will give me the opportunity to define my attitude, to indicate what I have striven to avoid and what I hope to contribute. The relatively limited number of books exclusively devoted to Virginia Woolf will enable me to consider them each in turn. As for the numerous articles and chapters forming part of wider studies, I shall merely indicate their tendencies, and this will lead me to formulate the principles I have endeavoured to respect and, at the same time, to sketch the orientation of my own study.

The first two books which appeared in 1932, Winifred Holtby's[2] in England and that of Floris Delattre[3] in France, each had the great merit of offering an interpretation of Virginia Woolf's work immediately after the publication of *The Waves*, which had revealed her as one of the most original and made her one of the most discussed novelists of her day. The attempt was timely, but difficult. Neither sensitivity nor sympathy can completely make up for the

[1] Only general studies are considered here. Among the twenty-one works mentioned in the second section of the Bibliography, several only deal with limited aspects of Virginia Woolf's work; I therefore thought it irrelevant to devote particular attention to them in this Introduction.

[2] Winifred Holtby, *Virginia Woolf*, Wishart, London, 1932

[3] Floris Delattre, *Le Roman Psychologique de Virginia Woolf*, J. Vrin, Paris, 1932

lack of distance, which falsifies perspective and proportion. And since, when an author's work is not yet complete, it is like an action whose meaning remains uncertain until the final gesture, these studies could obviously claim no finality. Winifred Holtby's observations on Virginia Woolf's cinematographic technique are interesting, no doubt, but remain purely descriptive; while the delicate analyses of Floris Delattre, faithful to the atmosphere and the shimmering surface of the novels, constitute excellent prefaces; but neither of these critics reveals to us the author's intentions, her meaning, the significance of her work. Moreover, if they had to request our indulgence for the hypothetical and sometimes superficial character of their criticism, these pioneers might quote Virginia Woolf's own comment, in her Diary, about Miss Holtby's admiring judgment on *The Waves*. "What it means I myself shan't know till I write another book."[4] And unquestionably the work that Floris Delattre was proposing to write on *Consciousness and Life in the Novels of Virginia Woolf*, of which unfortunately only a single chapter exists,[5] would not only have corrected his earlier study but above all would have given it greater depth.

In the twelve years that elapsed between our author's death and the publication, in 1953, of *A Writer's Diary*, which sets new conditions for the criticism of her work, we have had seven general studies of varying importance and value. Rather than examine these in chronological order, I have thought it preferable to take them in order of interest, that is to say according to the importance of their contribution to the knowledge and understanding of Virginia Woolf's personality and work—which implies no dogmatic judgment on their merits in other respects.

Deborah Newton's booklet[6] has no claims to be more than a succinct introduction to the author and her novels. Its general judgments reproduce fairly faithfully those of E. M. Forster, which his Rede Lecture of 1941 (published in 1942 by the Cambridge University Press) has the advantage of offering in a more concise and vigorous form. If I have not included this short work in the series now examined, it is because its author makes no pretensions to offer more than a thirty-page sketch.

[4] AWD p. 174 (170)
[5] "Virginia Woolf et le Monologue Intérieur", pp. 225-47, in *Feux d'Automne, Essais choisis* by Floris Delattre, Didier, Paris, 1950
[6] Deborah Newton, *Virginia Woolf*, Melbourne University Press, 1946

INTRODUCTION

The little book by Joan Bennett, *Virginia Woolf, her Art as a Novelist* (Cambridge University Press, 1945) has the merit of attempting the vertical study of certain problems. But while none of her chapters exhausts the subject it deals with, the whole neglects many essential aspects of the novelist's work. Quotations are abundant, but the analysis is confined to a somewhat superficial description; and above all, Mrs Bennett does not appear to have concerned herself much with Virginia Woolf's intentions, which, in my opinion, makes some of her discussions otiose and some of her judgments arbitrary. The neglect, not to say disregard of chronology further limits the significance of her work. Finally, in between two chapters whose actual tenor is hard to distinguish, *Stories and Sequences* and *The Form of the Novels*, we find a chapter on *Morals and Values* which, far from providing the key to Virginia Woolf's art as one might have expected, is merely an excursion into the realm of her favourite subjects, ideas and themes.

Although belonging essentially to a very different category from these two books, and despite its merits of thought and expression, we may mention here *La Philosophie de Virginia Woolf* by Maxime Chastaing (Presses Universitaires de Paris, 1951). The method deliberately adopted by this philosopher, legitimate from his own point of view no doubt, makes his study not a contribution to our knowledge of Virginia Woolf but a paraphenomenon to her work. As he warns us, M. Chastaing is in no way concerned with what Virginia Woolf may have thought, nor consequently with knowing when, how or why she thought this rather than that, but he is solely interested in the system that may be extracted from her work considered as a whole, instantaneous and closed. This, obviously, is carrying the suppression of time, space, movement and individuality to their extreme consequences, in conformity with Virginia Woolf's tendencies. But this takes us into the realm of completed and hypostatized thought, with which criticism, as I understand it, is not concerned.

The little book by R. L. Chambers, *The Novels of Virginia Woolf*,[7] devoted, like Mrs Bennett's, to the vertical study of a few problems, is far superior to the latter in depth of analysis and breadth of reflection. This critic examines successively, with varying degrees of felicity, the plan, style and method of the novelist, in order to

[7] Oliver & Boyd, London, 1947

distinguish the qualities and weaknesses which will enable him to attempt a general evaluation of her work, to which task he devotes the second half of his book. Some of his preliminary formulae are somewhat disconcerting; for instance, his statement that Virginia Woolf's "primary purpose was the exposition of human conduct, largely a moral purpose, the exposition of her theory of good and evil".[8] However, we must admit that his conclusions disregard this hypothesis and bring out, very justly, the permanence and unity of three major themes: the integrity of a human being, his loneliness, and the wish to suppress all the lines we arbitrarily trace to define objects, persons and categories. Whereas all critics agree in recognizing the poetic qualities of Virginia Woolf's prose—sometimes praising and sometimes blaming her for this—no one has analysed its characteristics so precisely and justly as Chambers. On the other hand, his study of her method is vitiated by the vagueness, indeed the inexactitude, of his concept of the interior monologue.[9] True, it is not easy to grasp the relationship of *The Years* and *Between the Acts* with the rest of her work; but to deny the continuity between *The Waves* and the two novels that preceded it, *To the Lighthouse* and *Mrs Dalloway*, as Chambers does[10] is symptomatic of the weakness of his analysis of Virginia Woolf's technique.

But it is chiefly, in my opinion, the moderation and the justness of the opinions set forth in the last four chapters which give this short study its permanent value. Chambers subscribes to the view that the absence of any universal faith, belief or ideology *ipso facto* deprives art in general, and literature in particular, of a starting-point, of a system of references entitling it to claim universality. I shall return later to this principle, which forms the dividing-line between those critics who are favourable to Virginia Woolf and those who condemn her. But just because he unhesitatingly belongs to the opposite camp, Chambers is particularly well placed to show how Virginia Woolf represents her period, through her limitations as well as through her achievements. In particular, unless I am mistaken, he is the only one of all the critics referred to in my Bibliography who ventures to use the word "humanism"

---

[8] Cf. *ibid.*, p. 3.

[9] "Stream of consciousness technique" and "stream of consciousness method" discussed throughout Ch. III, "Method".

[10] Cf. *ibid.*, p. 39

with reference to our novelist.[11] Even if one hesitates to follow him unreservedly when he puts Virginia Woolf at the head of the novelists of her decade, his reasoned arguments, free from either partisan exaggeration or gratuitous admiration, provide a favourable testimony, which is indispensable to counterbalance the severe verdict not merely of hostile critics but even of those who are well-disposed.

Among the latter we must include David Daiches, whose *Virginia Woolf*,[12] published immediately after the novelist's death, is the first general study, strictly speaking. (Daiches had already, three years earlier, allotted a large space to Virginia Woolf in his book *The Novel and the Modern World*.[13])

We recognize here again the interest taken by this critic in the form of the contemporary novel, whose experimental character and whose imperfections he ascribes to the instability of the period. This dominant preoccupation constitutes, as it were, the point of view from which he considers the work. After a biographical sketch which sums up the scanty data available at the time, he proceeds to examine the different works in chronological order. In spite of their liveliness these commentaries leave one with an uneasy feeling, due to a sort of uncertainty in the commentator's method and indeed in his whole position. Appreciative of Virginia Woolf's originality, convinced of the unique quality of her work, Daiches considers that to try and account for it by referring to traditional categories is to invite failure. "If we try to analyse the novel on traditional lines, tracing out the development, complication and resolution of the plot, we may find ourselves with a neat piece of analysis, but we shall certainly have missed the essential novel that Virginia Woolf was writing."[14] However, in spite of this assertion, made at the outset with reference to *The Voyage Out* and repeated in connection with *Jacob's Room*,[15] Daiches seems unable to bring himself to abandon the traditional viewpoint. The words

[11] Cf. R. L. Chambers, *The Novels of Virginia Woolf*, p. 74. Irma Rantavaara (cf. *infra*), discussing V. W.'s essay on Montaigne at length (pp. 78-80) stresses the relation between the two writers but does not utter the word.

[12] David Daiches, *Virginia Woolf*, The Makers of Modern Literature Series, New Directions, New York, 1942, 169 pp.; Nicholson and Watson, London, 1945, 151 pp.

[13] David Daiches, *The Novel and the Modern World*, University of Chicago Press, Chicago, 1939

[14] *Ibid.*, p. 14

[15] *Ibid.*, p. 61: "It would be possible, but scarcely profitable, to analyse the 'plot' of *Jacob's Room*. . . ."

"structure", "pattern" which recur constantly must not deceive us; what he studies is the plot, and with it the characters. Not only does he embody these factors in his "summaries", they form the very core of his discussion; so that in spite of the reserves, the appreciation of detail, which seem like reluctantly made concessions, one has the impression that the novelist has constantly failed except perhaps in *To the Lighthouse*.

What appears more serious is that on the one hand, in spite of all the attention he pays to technique, Daiches does not see beyond its most superficial aspects, so that, while he is conscious of its progress, he never discovers, or at least he never shows, the profound springs and fundamental principles which ensure the unity of her technique through all its variations, from the earliest gropings to the final works. On the other hand, we look in vain through the whole book for an account, let alone for an analysis or a commentary, of the content of Virginia Woolf's work. Apart from the statement that "the dissolution of experience into tenuous insights . . . is the real theme of the most important part of Virginia Woolf's work",[16] and in spite of the promising title of chapter V, "Time, Change and Personality", we find not a word on solitude, anguish, the multiplicity of being, life, or death. . . . As though Virginia Woolf's work was pure form without content: to such an extent that one is almost tempted to hold Daiches responsible for the reputation of Alexandrianism that hangs over her.

With these reservations, the special character of Daiches's critical position has a certain advantage from the general public's point of view, and one which was no doubt even more remarkable in 1942 than today. His book provides a means of access to Virginia Woolf by ways familiar to the readers of novels more traditional than hers. Too often critics who use Daiches's language are hostile to our author; he, on the contrary, being on the whole favourable, provides a helpful introduction.

The "commentary" of Bernard Blackstone[17] is to a large extent the antithesis and complement of Daiches's study. Whereas the latter is chiefly interested in technique, the former is above all preoccupied by the content of her work. He stresses her thematic unity, the progress of her quest for reality, by way of freedom and

---

[16] Cf. *ibid.*, p. 78
[17] Bernard Blackstone, *Virginia Woolf, A Commentary*, p. 256, The Hogarth Press, London, 1949

truth, and continuously subtended by the criticism of false values. A constant sympathy towards his subject allows the commentator to reveal beauties which many others have not seen or have denied. However, if Blackstone rightly considers Virginia Woolf's work as the slow conquest of those moments of vision in which the mystery of reality is solved, he neglects that other preliminary enigma, the obsession with which provides part of the substance of Virginia Woolf's novels and contributes to the originality of their form: the mystery of personality. This fault is due to Blackstone's critical position: its incompatibility with his subject is immediately patent, and prevents his analyses, for all their merits, from achieving success. Although in his Introduction he declares that the successive themes around which he has organized his study are only the outstanding ones, and that they will be found recurring throughout the work, his choice is somewhat disturbing: are love and liberty, marriage and truth, the universe and reality, really the fundamental problems which concerned Virginia Woolf? Are these the basic constituents of that "human life" which, as he asserts in his conclusion,[18] "was her theme"? "She did not want to scratch about on the surface, to glue incidents together into plots . . .," he goes on. But he adds: "She wanted to reveal the springs of action", and a little earlier he had spoken of her as "a master of characterisation".[19] These formulae define what we may describe as Blackstone's traditional realism. If he does not use it to attack Virginia Woolf, as do most of those who start from the same premises, there is none the less a danger of his good intentions leading him to read things into her work that she never put there, or at least to take the accidental for the essential. Finally, having to decide between chronological order and a synthetic presentation,[20] Blackstone, having chosen the former, does not wholly renounce certain of the latter's advantages. Not to speak of the confusion that may result therefrom for a reader who does not carry the whole work in his head, there is a considerable risk of giving the earlier works undue credit for the substance of the later ones, whereas the only legitimate course would have been to illuminate the later by the earlier.

In 1953, Leonard Woolf declared that Blackstone's study was

[18] Cf. *ibid.*, p. 244
[19] Cf. *ibid.*, p. 241
[20] Cf. *ibid.*, Introduction

the best that had appeared so far; let us grant that it was the most important. At that time, he had probably not read Irma Ranta-vaara's thesis on *Virginia Woolf and Bloomsbury*,[21] although he had given help to its author. The remarkable qualities of this work seem due to the way the critic has traced the roots of Virginia Woolf's work both in her personality and in the social and cultural atmosphere in which she developed. Whereas other studies too often leave an impression of artificiality and irrelevance, we feel that Irma Rantavaara is concerned with an actual creative achievement rather than with abstract constructions. True, she by no means exhausts her subject; but within the limits she has set herself, this critic provides the first really pertinent interpretation, for she takes into account the conditions of artistic creation. However, if her title justifies the large space allotted to consideration of the milieu, one is somewhat surprised by the cursoriness of the final chapter which, in less than ten pages, deals with the productions of Virginia Woolf's last ten years, including *The Waves*, and leaves the reader to formulate his own conclusions.

Published in 1954 but already completed the previous year, *The Glass Roof* by James Hafley was unable to take advantage of the revelations of the Diary which, without modifying the essence of his study, would doubtless have led the author to qualify some of his judgments. The work, however, is remarkable for the rigour of its method and the precision of its analyses. The continuity of the novelist's development from *The Voyage Out* to *Between the Acts*, and the profound relationship between the content and the technique of her work, are clearly brought out. We may disagree with the author about the importance of *Jacob's Room* in the evolution of the novel form, or with his assessment of the merits of *The Years*, but he has earned our gratitude by defining the nature of one capital element in Virginia Woolf's technique, which had hitherto been and which still is very vaguely and incorrectly classed as "interior monologue" or "stream of consciousness technique". His precise analysis enables one to discard many concepts lazily transmitted from one critic to another on the relationship between Virginia Woolf and Joyce, Dorothy Richardson and Proust. However, by stressing the philosophical element, indeed, more specifically, the Bergsonian element in Virginia Woolf's novels he runs the risk, as he himself admits in his conclusion, of altering not only the

[21] Irma Rantavaara, *Virginia Woolf and Bloomsbury*, Helsinki, 1953

INTRODUCTION

aspect of her work but even the deeper meaning which emanates from it as a whole. With this reservation, James Hafley's study has the great merit of providing a coherent interpretation of the novels which, contrasted with M. Chastaing's arbitrary philosophical construction on the one hand, and on the other Bernard Blackstone's treatment according to the subdivisions of traditional psychology, establishes the novelist's intellectual importance in a manner far more in keeping with her thought and temper.

In the same year as Irma Rantavaara's thesis, there appeared *A Writer's Diary*. This document, whose significance will be discussed elsewhere,[22] scarcely offered enough new material to justify an attempted biography of Virginia Woolf, yet what it revealed about her work and its relations with the artist certainly provided more substantial bases for criticism. The revaluation that might have been expected was not forthcoming. On the other hand, there appeared a large book claiming to be a biography, *The Moth and the Star* by Aileen Pippett.[23] One quotation will serve to show the hybrid nature of this compilation, in which authentic biographical elements are mingled with extracts from the novels, unquestionable facts with hypotheses: "But though it [*The Waves*] adds greatly to our appreciation of Virginia Woolf as an artist, it tells us very little about her as a woman. It is a writer's book, not a human document, it yields richer material to the critic than to the biographer."[24] One does not know whether to regret that Aileen Pippett found nothing for her purpose in *The Waves*, or that she found too much in the other novels. However, it must be pointed out that the book contains important quotations from the unpublished correspondence between Virginia Woolf and Vita Sackville-West, which form a valuable complement to *A Writer's Diary* and the correspondence with Lytton Strachey.

Finally, the last in date, Monique Nathan's little book: *Virginia Woolf par elle-même*.[25] "By herself", that is to say through a number of quotations which encourage one to read the rest of her work, but also by Monique Nathan. And Monique Nathan has been unable to resist the temptation of re-creating her subject's mind and sensibility, as Chastaing had re-created her philosophy. In this

22 Cf. infra, ch. III
23 Little, Brown & Co., Boston, Toronto, 1953
24 *Ibid.*, p. 290
25 Ed. du Seuil, Paris, 1956

23

case, too, the result is brilliant; but it is too impressionistic, in Virginia Woolf's own manner, to be a reliable basis for scrupulous criticism. Admittedly the model has been studied at length, but that scarcely protects her from the painter, who shows impartiality in her aim alone; the numerous photographs, however, are admirable.

Before considering partial studies, mention must be made of the fifty or so pages devoted to Virginia Woolf in *The Bloomsbury Group, A Study of E. M. Forster, Lytton Strachey, Virginia Woolf and their circle*, by J. K. Johnstone.[26] This book has been criticized for not fulfilling its title; actually, it corresponds more closely to its sub-title. I have already pointed out what Irma Rantavaara's study owes to the fact of having been conceived in relation to the milieu; the same attitude, no doubt, accounts for the accuracy and shrewd-ness of Johnstone's comments, particularly concerning questions of technique, time and personality.

In his article on "The Contemporary English Novel" published in the *Nouvelle Revue Française* of May 1927, T. S. Eliot, while pay-ing full tribute to Virginia Woolf's talent, describes her, even at that early date, before *To the Lighthouse*, *Orlando* or *The Waves*, as an authentic representative of contemporary fiction. But that is no praise from him. T. S. Eliot, indeed, condemns contemporary fiction; and it was to the theory on which this condemnation is based that I referred earlier, when distinguishing between various critics' attitudes to Virginia Woolf. Without developing his point of view, T. S. Eliot contrasts "the shallower psychology that afflicts us all" with the deeper psychology which was Henry James's object.[27] And he admits that according to a contrary "theory" to his own, this judgment might be reversed. It is immedi-ately obvious that we are dealing here not with a purely literary judgment, but with an actual philosophical position, implying a conception of personality and, behind it, a moral and meta-physical conception. This is a pre-Freudian, pre-Bergsonian world, divided into compartments, stable and closed; a clearly defined system of values, corresponding to a system of equally definite objects, confronted with individuals whose nature and limitations present no sort of problem for anyone. Such a set of beliefs is rooted

---

[26] The Noonday Press, New York, 1954
[27] T. S. Eliot, "Le Roman Anglais Contemporain", *NRF*, May 1927, CLXIV, p. 674

in a static, well-ordered universe; it constitutes a faith, according to Sean O'Faolain's definition: ". . . A faith, then, for literary purposes, means any feeling for life, or any way of seeing life which is coherent, persistent, inclusive and forceful enough to give organic form to the totality of a writer's work."[28] Clearly, whoever holds a theory of this sort must find Virginia Woolf's work unsatisfying. It suffers from an intolerable lack, it is "shallow", to echo Eliot's term, it is futile and therefore irritating. Such a point of view may explain why Daiches says nothing about its content, and also explains the more categorical judgments of Q. D. Leavis, D. S. Savage, Dorothy M. Hoare, Arnold Kettle, Gabriel Marcel, Wyndham Lewis, the reticences of David Cecil, Orlo Williams, Lodwick Hartley, even those of E. M. Forster. Yet one may question both the legitimacy and the interest of this critical position. What should we think of a criticism of Einstein's system based on Euclidean rules, or of Cézanne's painting based on the standards of Ingres? To blame Virginia Woolf for her failure to create characters, construct a plot, connect incidents in a dramatic curve, or provide an answer to the questions that torment us, seems just as futile, to say the least. Futile because essentially irrelevant. In such cases the critic, more concerned with excluding than with understanding, betrays his mission. He becomes a polemicist, and the urbanity or moderation of his tone does not alter the fact.

In "English Prose between 1918 and 1939" E. M. Forster, defining the state of affairs confronting writers in the inter-war period, simultaneously defined the attitude of the critic who claimed to deal with these writers: "The idea of relativity has got into the air and has favoured certain tendencies in novels. . . . You can't measure people up because the yard-measure itself keeps altering in length."[29] Moreover, it is not enough to have perceived this changed atmosphere; the critic must abandon the use of the old, standard measure. This requires either a certain daring, or a personal adherence to the new modes of thought. That so few of Virginia Woolf's critics have attained this point of view may seem surprising. J. W. Beach, J. J. Mayoux, Robert Peel are about the only ones, together with Rantavaara and J. K. Johnstone, whom I have already quoted. Several reasons may be given for this puzzling ratio.

[28] Sean O'Faolain, *The Vanishing Hero*, p. 172
[29] E. M. Forster, *Two Cheers for Democracy*, p. 283. (Article dated 1944.)

To begin with, one must doubtless blame a sort of intellectual inertia, manifest in every sphere; a certain thought-lag, corresponding roughly to a generation, which condemns all creators, of whatever sort, to be generally misunderstood by their contemporaries, who have been fed on the substance of the masters of their childhood. Secondly, if it be admitted that two broad classes of mind can be distinguished, dogmatists and sceptics, and that conflict between these is inevitable, the latter are, or appear to be, in the minority. Finally, and this is the point that concerns us particularly, a certain conception of criticism and its purpose may be called in question. The way Valéry puts the problem is particularly pertinent to the present case: "Whereas the *value* of a work is a singular and inconstant relation between this work and a few readers, the particular and intrinsic *merit* of the author is a relation between himself and his purpose; this merit is relative to the distance between them."[30] To allot to criticism the task of discussing "value" may seem normal to one who, believing himself in possession of the truth or of the knowledge of absolute rules, simultaneously sets up his own judgment as a universal and permanent relation between the work and the reader. Not to mention the arrogance or plain presumptuousness implied by such an attitude, it may be asked what, in this type of criticism, becomes of the author? What share is left him, what consideration is granted him, what role is ascribed to him? In fact, such criticism denies the author, or at best ignores him, and it merely provides an opportunity for the critic to express and assert himself. This may be a literary genre as legitimate and estimable as the novel with a thesis, or didactic poetry. I should like to make it clear forthwith that it is not in this spirit that I am undertaking to examine Virginia Woolf. My object is the study of her "particular and intrinsic merit", the analysis of that "relation between herself and her purpose" of which Valéry spoke, the exploration of that distance in which are contained the whole tension, drama and miracle of artistic creation.

The broad plan adopted here, and the method I have endeavoured to respect, have been dictated by these general considerations.

If a biography had seemed possible, the first section of this book

[30] Paul Valéry, *Tel Quel*, vol. I, p. 21. The whole section, beginning of ch. III, is worth quoting. (Gallimard, 29th edn., 1941.)

would undoubtedly have been devoted to it. However, I have sought to remedy this inevitable lacuna by recourse to a substitute which should provide the point of reference indispensable for the evaluation of that distance between intention and realization referred to above. First, a study of the *ambiance*, without claiming to add anything original to what has already been said by Ranta-vaara, Johnstone, Annan,[31] and in the many articles or surveys included in works devoted to various aspects of the thought or art of the period, will make it possible to demarcate, as it were, the periphery of Virginia Woolf's thought and sensibility. To define the world in which she developed and wrote, and to define it in relation to herself, will be a way of getting near her and sharing her point of view, thus preparing for the intimacy sought in the third chapter, "The Self, Life and Artistic Creation". This is where I hope to reach the centre, the very core of her being, and that aspect or mode of being which is of particular interest to us: the artist. Whereas a biography would have led me thither by way of events, along the course of a human destiny, it is (as though circumstances had condemned me to a Woolfian attitude) through isolated gestures and moments, fugitive glimpses, that Virginia Woolf's personality must be discovered.

Only then can her work itself be considered. The earlier chapters will have thrown light on its nature and orientation, by tracing its innermost sources. But here, as yet, only tendencies and potentialities were revealed. The Diary puts us in touch with the spontaneous springs of the inner life; essays and pamphlets provide a deliberate, rationalized complement to it. This will comprise the fourth chapter, half-way between the creator and her creation, properly so-called.

The examination of the latter will form the king-pin of this study. The discipline observed in this long chapter may seem austere; the genesis of each work, a summary and then a discussion of it follow one another in strict rhythm. My study, I hope, will gain in clarity from this strictness what it loses in variety. Above all, since it was part of my intention to trace the creative movement from its germ to the completed work of literature, I have eschewed that sleight-of-hand by which the future is invoked as well as the past to complete, explain and justify the present. The division of

---

[31] Noel Gilroy Annan, *Leslie Stephen, his Thought and Character in Relation to his Time*, Macgibbon and Kee, London, 1951; Harvard University Press, 1952

this chapter and the order adopted therein, novels first, then stories and sketches, finally biographies, may invite question. It was not so much the difference between these genres as the difference in the author's attitude towards the various categories of her work which decided me to deal with these separately. As for the order chosen, it may seem illogical to go from what is most important to what is less so. Would it not have been better to begin with the fragments which sometimes anticipate, or serve as studies for, the major works? It seemed to me that by their very nature these writings would offer material for a sort of commentary, completing those suggested by the novels. Similarly the biographies, works of secondary importance, throw light on certain aspects and almost serve as a transition to my final chapter, dealing with the general problems posed by the work of Virginia Woolf.

If certain particular aspects of these problems have already been touched on in the analyses devoted to particular works, I have been careful not only to limit the discussion to what is related solely to the work in question, but also to pursue it in terms of the work rather than of the problem. Most of these questions constitute the ground where friendly and hostile critics meet. I have striven to avoid either polemical zeal or the temptation, inherent in the synthetic method, to discuss abstractions. Here, as elsewhere, my first concern has been to retrace—coinciding as closely as possible with the author's thought—the living growth of the ideas, attitudes and artistic formulations which characterize the genius and the work of Virginia Woolf.

CHAPTER II

THE SETTING

1. THE POSITION AND PROBLEM OF THE NOVEL

I HAVE no intention of tracing, even briefly, the history of
literature or even that of the novel in the early years of this
century. Even a sketch would go beyond the scope of this work,
and could add nothing to the countless studies devoted to this
period. I merely propose, making full use of my predecessors' researches, to suggest the intellectual and artistic climate in which
Virginia Woolf developed at the start of her literary career.

In the twenty years between 1903, when she was introduced to
the editor of *The Speaker*—later *The Nation*—and the publication
of *Jacob's Room* in 1922, our novelist, in close contact with writers
and artists through her reading and through conversation, was
able to become acquainted in varying degrees, directly or through
their immediate or remote manifestations, with most of the trends
of thought whose interconnections, combinations or conflicts provide the essential sustenance of sensibility and intelligence. How
far and in what way these trends affected Virginia Woolf, what
she assimilated of them or, on the contrary, what reactions they
aroused in her, such are the problems I shall seek to clarify before
tackling, in the second half of this chapter, the still imperfectly
defined question of Bloomsbury.

At the beginning of *An Assessment of Twentieth Century Literature*,
J. Isaacs, faced with the difficulty familiar to all critics seeking to
divide time into sections and to isolate periods, eventually adopts
1903 as his starting-point.[1] If not absolutely satisfactory, this year,
which witnessed Shaw's *Man and Superman* and the belated publication of Samuel Butler's *Way of All Flesh*, takes on a less spectacular,
but a deeper and more precise significance if one also mentions
Principia Mathematica by Bertrand Russell, *Human Personality and
its Survival of Bodily Death* by F. W. H. Myers, and above all
Principia Ethica by G. E. Moore. Whereas aesthetes and decadents
had long ago begun to undermine the Victorian universe, Shaw's

[1] Cf. *ibid.*, p. 18

play and Butler's novel proclaimed open war on the old order. It is going too far, perhaps, to consider Moore's treatise as the Bible of those intellectuals somewhat hastily lumped together under the convenient label of Bloomsbury; but at any rate the book provided a basis for discussion, a cluster of directions to those former Cambridge scholars and their friends who, in the ensuing years, constituted the circle of Virginia Stephen and, later, of the Woolfs.

For the time being, we must note that the century opens under the banner of anti-Victorianism, to which attitude the author of *Orlando* was to remain fiercely loyal, even when such loyalty had no further point. And note, too, that the following year (1904) the death of Leslie Stephen set his daughter free from a tutelage which, though indefinite, was burdensome, and that Virginia thus attained her independence at the same time as her majority.

Nevertheless, this first decade was not merely a period of preparation for our authoress, and in other respects, despite Shaw's plays, Henry James's later novels and those of Conrad, the new spirit was still only a private phenomenon, limited, like G. E. Moore's popularity, to a restricted circle. But members of this circle, small indeed but active and enthusiastic, were to be responsible for preparing the event which was to bring visibly before the public the new concept of art, the result and the expression of that new concept of man which they accepted. Roger Fry and Desmond MacCarthy were the official organizers of the Post-Impressionist exhibition which, in December 1910, startled London; in fact Duncan Grant, Clive Bell and his wife, Virginia's sister, and all those who frequented the Bells' and the Stephens' homes in Gordon and Fitzroy Squares were in some way or another involved in this adventure and above all were aware that it marked an epoch, opened the way for a sort of renaissance.

It was from that moment, from that manifestation that (without mentioning it) Virginia Woolf was later to date a change undergone by human personality. According to her, it marked a break between Edwardians and Georgians, and in actual fact between an outworn literature and a truly living one.[2]

The layman, struck particularly by these painters' "modernism", by their revolt against the academicism and realism of pre-

[2] Cf. "Mr Bennett and Mrs Brown" in CDB p. 90 (94) ff.

vious art, tends to group under a single label Impressionists, Post-Impressionists and Expressionists, or at least to blur the difference between them, to merge them under a single general theory. This illegitimate confusion, however, is neither wholly arbitrary nor lacking in significance. These schools are at one in their rejection of the rules and conventions governing the art of their predecessors, in their feeling that these rules and conventions interposed a screen between art and the reality which art must express. Consequently they are at one, too, in their effort to attain that reality through new means. They all reveal awareness of the problem which dominates contemporary art, namely, that artistic creation is primarily the creation of a form, the invention of an original means of expression perfectly adapted to render the artist's vision. This being the case, the fact that the Impressionists considered light as the essence of all painting and applied, in their technique, scientific laws which, according to Clive Bell, "were imperfectly understood",[3] whereas the Post-Impressionists restored the outline to objects, mixed colours again and exalted distortion, does not seem, in retrospect, to constitute a basic opposition. We see therein nowadays only modalities of style, all directed towards a single goal: the integral expression of the artist's vision, of his impression —a formula which includes both impressionism and expressionism.

To appreciate the profound influence of these theories on Virginia Woolf's development we have merely to confront their exposé in Roger Fry's writings, particularly *Vision and Design* (1920), and in Clive Bell's *Since Cézanne* (1922) with the essays or the Diary of our novelist. Above all, we must not forget that these writings all represent personal conclusions independently reached by the three artists, and that any similarities of vocabulary, formulation or thought are the residuum of long discussions together, of an intercourse which was not simply an intellectual pastime but the contact and exchange of sympathy and friendship.

This integration of successive movements is moreover in perfect conformity with the keen sense of tradition which Virginia Woolf, like her friends, always retained. "Movements are nothing but the stuff of which tradition is made", wrote Clive Bell. "At any given moment tradition ends in the contemporary movement."[4] Having

[3] Clive Bell, *The French Impressionists*, p. 127
[4] Clive Bell, *Since Cézanne*, pp. 77-8

already gone back, with Clive Bell, as far as 1872 and the Impressionist movement, I may as well mention here the literary antecedents referred to by several critics as the source of that attitude which questions both the conception of the self and that of its relations with the outside world. In the first place, Symbolism,[5] and further back still what one might call the Presymbolism of Wordsworth and above all of Coleridge.[6]

I have deliberately stressed on the one hand the broad principles governing the new tendencies and their plastic, or concrete, manifestations, and on the other their remote origins, to counterbalance two impressions often derived from those critics who have sought to trace the source of Virginia Woolf's art and thought. Basing themselves on the novelist's own statements, often detached from their context, without always allowing for exaggeration and the tone of controversy, they make her out as far more radical and revolutionary than she really was. Her antagonism towards her immediate predecessors conceals her affinities with those who had come before them, and at a deeper level with a whole current that can be traced throughout the centuries in English literature, as will be shown in more detail when we consider her critical essays. And above all, critics have been fascinated by certain formulae which, whether in the novels or in the essays, condense in abstract fashion her vision of human beings, of the workings of their inner life, of their relations with each other or with the outside world. They have rightly seen in these the essence of her thought, as illustrated by the treatment and the tenor of her works. So they have quite naturally yielded to the temptation of referring to Bergsonism, its theory of memory, its distinction between time and duration,[7] to William James and the fringes of consciousness,[8] to Freud—excluding the libido, however—and still further back, to Hume's empiricism and Berkeley's idealism. Without denying that all this may be found in Virginia Woolf—and much else beside, as Maxime Chastaing has brilliantly shown—it must be said categorically that it is not to these philosophers that Virginia

---

[5] Cf. M. Le Breton, *Journal de Psychologie*, 40th year, Jan.-Mar. 1947, "Problème du Moi et Technique du Roman chez Virginia Woolf", p. 20; and Louis Gillet, *Stèle pour James Joyce*, p. 31.

[6] Cf. J. K. Johnstone, *The Bloomsbury Group*, p. 63, note

[7] Particularly Floris Delattre in *Le Roman Psychologique de Virginia Woolf* and most critics after him.

[8] J. Isaacs, *An Assessment of XXth Century Literature*

Woolf owes her "philosophy",[9] simply because Virginia Woolf is not a philosopher and has no philosophy.

"She turned to account not so much the dogmatic foundations of Bergson's philosophy as the vision that crowns it, and her interest was engaged less by its order, so precise and lucid that it sometimes seems impersonal, than by its singular power of inspiration (*jaillissement*)."[10] Thus Delattre attempts to qualify the filiation which he had asserted a few pages earlier.[11] To my mind, one should go much further. Virginia Woolf's contacts with Bergsonism were on the one hand indirect, and on the other, inconsiderable. Leonard Woolf has told me that she had not read Bertrand Russell's *The Philosophy of Bergson*, the first work published in England about the French philosopher (1914); and he was even doubtful whether she had read her sister-in-law Karin Stephen's *The Misuse of Mind*, published in 1922. Even allowing for the possible unreliability of such remote recollections, and for the understandable reaction of the novelist's husband towards anything that might give a false impression of her personality, we should bear in mind the spirit, if not the letter, of these assertions. The dates, too, argue in favour of this view. *Jacob's Room* appeared the same year as Karin Stephen's book; *Kew Gardens* and *Monday or Tuesday*, which contain in embryo the fundamental principles which the author of *The Waves* was only to develop further, had come out in 1919 and 1921. And what of William James's *Principles of Psychology*, published in 1890, which according to W. Allen she had in mind in 1919, when writing *Modern Fiction*? The similarity between certain words in the two books seems to justify the critic.[12] But these are nothing more than words, the inevitable landmarks met by two minds in their progress towards the same reality. William James or Bergson may have discovered this reality, may have provided the clearest expression of it which, passed on from author to reader, from the intelligentsia to broader social groups, gradually spread until it became the "way of looking at things" of a whole period—first that of cultured people, then, after a few decades, everybody else's. Of course, the young Stephens, the

[9] Cf. Delattre's change of attitude and V. W.'s letter quoted by him in *Feux d'Automne*, p. 239.

[10] Floris Delattre, *Le Roman Psychologique de Virginia Woolf*, p. 141

[11] *Ibid.*, p. 137

[12] Cf. W. Allen, *The English Novel*, p. 330. Also J. Isaacs, *An Assessment of Twentieth Century Literature*, p. 88

Bells, the Woolfs and their set talked about James's and Bergson's psychological views, as they talked about Moore's ethics. But in such cases what was important and effective was not the actual thought of these masters; it was the incarnation of that thought in some speaker who endowed it not only with his voice and his words but with his whole personality, concealing the system behind his own "vision" of it. Remember Virginia Woolf's essay on George Moore; its theme is clearly defined from the start: "The only criticism worth having at present is that which is spoken, not written—spoken over wine-glasses and coffee-cups late at night, flashed out on the spur of the moment by people passing who have no time to finish their sentences. . . ."[13] It was in this fashion that she absorbed Bergsonism and all other 'isms. And at the end of the same article, accepting the novelist's criterion of excellence, she confirms what she understands by "an author" and at the same time allows us a glimpse of what she conceives of as a system: "He [George Moore] has brought a new mind into the world; he has given us a new way of feeling and seeing."[14]

This "mind", this way of feeling and seeing, springing from affinity of temperaments as much as from shared intellectual experience, is what I have described as the climate or atmosphere of the period. From this Virginia Woolf drew those elements akin to her own nature which she could assimilate, rather than from any underlying systems. Systems did not interest her. We have only to glance through her essays to be convinced of that. Slowly, deliberately (as we shall see later)[15] she acquired a vision of man, of the universe, of reality, and it was that vision that interested her, indeed that absorbed her passionately, in living beings first of all, in her friends, then in those writers who spoke a language close enough to her own to enable her to recognize it.

What has been said of Bergsonism applies even more cogently to the theories of Freud. Undoubtedly these were in the air; the fact that the Woolfs were sufficiently interested to undertake, in 1922, the publication of *The International Psychoanalytical Library* by the Hogarth Press (founded in 1917) entitles us to assume that Virginia Woolf had come into direct contact with Freud's teach-

[13] DM p. 100 (156)
[14] Cf. DM p. 103 (160)
[15] Cf. *infra*, ch. III

George Moore—See Death of the Myth

ing.[16] But on the one hand, here again, such contact must have been belated and on the other, what need had she of Freud to write what she did write and as she wrote it? We may recall here her comment—made both in the Diary and in "Modern Fiction"[17] on *Ulysses*, the most Freudian novel of the period, namely that *Tristram Shandy* and *Pendennis* had taught her as much about the human soul.

With the influence of the Russian novel in general and of Tolstoy, Chekhov and Dostoevsky in particular, we enter another sphere. As with French painting, we are here faced not with theories and systems but with works of art. And we know for a certainty that she was not content merely to talk about them and hear them talked about. In 1912, on her honeymoon, she read *Crime and Punishment*.[18] The same year, at Twickenham, she read *War and Peace*[19]; between 1921 and 1923 she was collaborating with Koteliansky on translations of Dostoevsky and Tolstoy.[20] "The novels of Dostoevsky are seething whirlpools, gyrating sandstorms, waterspouts which hiss and boil and suck us in. They are composed purely and wholly of the stuff of the soul."[21] These sentences from "The Russian Point of View", even allowing for the exaggeration inherent in their context, tell us clearly enough what the experience of the Russian novel had been for Virginia Woolf. When in 1940 she re-read Goldenweiser's *Conversations with Tolstoy*, her impressions, as noted in her Diary, have the same quality, the same intensity: "Always the same reality—like touching an exposed electric wire. Even so imperfectly conveyed—his rugged short cut mind—to me the most, not sympathetic, but inspiring,

[16] Freud set forth the objects of psychoanalysis and sketched the development of his doctrine in the *American Journal of Psychoanalysis* in 1910; the English translation of *The Interpretation of Dreams* appeared in 1913, that of *Wit and the Unconscious* in 1918. There are only two references to reading Freud in the Diary: Dec. 1939 and Feb. 1940 (AWD pp. 321 (309) and 326 (314)). In an article in the *TLS* of March 25, 1920, p. 199, entitled "Freudian Fiction" (Review of *An Imperfect Mother* by J. D. Beresford), she asserts that it is not only legitimate but desirable for the novelist to turn to Freudian theories to explain the behaviour of his characters, but at the same time she points out the dangers inherent in too slavish or too exclusive an application of these theories. This article is characteristic of our novelist's attitude towards doctrines and systems.

[17] Cf. AWD p. 51 (49), "I said I had found Pendennis more illuminating in this way", and CR I p. 192 (156).

[18] Cf. V. W. & Lytton Strachey, *Letters*, p. 41

[19] Cf. AWD p. 329 (317)

[20] Cf. Bibliography: Translations

[21] CR I p. 226 (182)

rousing: genius in the raw. Thus more disturbing, more 'shocking', more of a thunderclap, even on art, even on literature, than any other writer. I remember that was my feeling about *War and Peace*, read in bed at Twickenham."[22] This revelation is described again in *Modern Fiction*, with more sobriety but also with more precision: Russian writers bring the sense of inconclusiveness, of the flux of life, of the anguished uncertainty of questions left unanswered.[23] On the whole, Helen Muchnic[24] gives a fairly just idea of the relation between the popularity of Russian novels and the doctrines then in favour: "They formed the background for all those intellectual ventures—the philosophy of Bergson, the critical doctrine of A. France, the dramas of Maeterlinck, the painting of the Impressionists and Expressionists—which proclaimed the right of the individual to respect his own intuitive beliefs as possessing general interest, and suggested the importance of that which lay beyond the grasp of scientific observation." Without a shadow of doubt, it is from this psychological treasurehouse of the Russian novel that Virginia Woolf drew her inspiration, rather than from the parallel systems to which it corresponds.[25]

Moreover, Russian novels, like the painting of Cézanne, Van Gogh or Picasso must be considered not only in themselves or as mere incidents in the history of the time. They are both signs and symbols. Wherever they appeared, in Paris or in London, they were recognized as something long expected, as the startling expression of common aspirations; they became manifestoes. Gide's enthusiasm for Dostoevsky was contemporary with Virginia Woolf's, and it is noteworthy that *Les Nourritures Terrestres* appeared in 1898, the very year in which G. E. Moore gave those Cambridge lectures which were to become *Principia Ethica*. It matters little that Gide's book shows affinities with Nietzsche and Moore's with Pater; both are the counter-offensive of a passionate neo-romantic individualism against those forces of order which the nineteenth century had exalted: science and society.

There remain to be mentioned two trends which are themselves

[22] AWD p. 329 (317)
[23] Cf. CR I pp. 193-4 (158)
[24] Helen Muchnic, *Dostoevsky's English Reputation, 1881-1936*, Northampton, Mass., 1939, p. 167
[25] Other landmarks in the history of the influence of Russian fiction: translation of *The Brothers Karamazov* by Constance Garnett (1912), *Biography of Dostoevsky* by Middleton Murry (1916).

derived from that same romanticism: Unanimism and Existential-ism. Although Jules Romains' work is diametrically opposite to Virginia Woolf's, certain pages showing a human being's consciousness dilated through space to integrate, by degrees, a whole town, a whole country, are astonishingly similar.[26] Two features of Existentialism which acquire increasing importance recur throughout her work: the Absurd, and the anguish of the moment.[27] True, in neither case can we speak of direct influence; even the inevitable labels must be handled with considerable reservations. I have spoken of trends, not of doctrine; and M. Le Breton's reference to the "latent unanimism" in Virginia Woolf's thought implies the sort of relation to be assumed between these aspects of her thought, or rather "vision", and contemporary movements. Moreover the doctrines, even when closely akin, are mutually exclusive; the fact that we find traces of such diverse origins in Virginia Woolf shows that hers is no systematic thought, but a living process of assimilation which is far more catholic than rational thinking, and which can carry variety to the point of inconsistency; in this, moreover, the novelist's artistic temperament asserts itself.

Novels are produced in such wide diversity, and such heterogeneous factors affect our appreciation of them, that contemporary judgments are infinitely precarious. Even a distance of ten years is not enough to ensure a proper sifting of works that will endure from those which are merely for today's consumption. In this connection it is instructive to consult such studies as Abel Chevalley's *Le Roman Anglais de Notre Temps* (published in 1921) or *Twentieth Century Literature* by A. C. Ward (published in 1928). The mistakes made by those who identify the "normal" or "good" with what is old[28] are as amusing as those of the critics who mistake novelty for excellence. At the present time, it seems that the novel of the beginning of this century, say up till the end of the First World War, the period that interests us here, allowing for the antagonisms and alienations between successive generations, is sufficiently remote for its outstanding trends and works to be clearly discernable. Nevertheless, without embarking on a general assessment

[26] Cf. M. Le Breton, *Journal de Psychologie*, 40th year, Jan.-Mar. 1947, "Problème du Moi et Technique du Roman chez Virginia Woolf", p. 26, and André Maurois, Preface to *Mrs Dalloway*, translated by S. David; Stock, Paris, 1929

[27] Cf. Jean Wahl, "L'angoisse et l'instant", *NRF*, April 1932, vol. 38

[28] Cf. A. G. Ward, *op. cit.*, p. 52

which would contribute nothing to the purpose, I shall simply try to picture the position of the novel as it appeared to Virginia Woolf as a young novelist, and the problems implied for her by this situation.

— We have relatively little evidence about what contemporary authors she read. If we add the names disclosed by the Diary to those appearing in the Essays, we can establish a fairly restricted list. Wells, Galsworthy, Bennett are the chief Edwardians, with whom she contrasts the Georgians: Conrad, D. H. Lawrence, E. M. Forster, James Joyce and herself. As precursors to the latter group she names three novelists: Henry James, Meredith and Hardy. These three groups constitute, in her view, not exactly three aspects of the genre, since they are not strictly contemporaneous, nor yet three phases of its evolution, since they overlap as well as succeed one another: rather two extreme formulae and one transitional formula. "Modern Fiction",[29] written in 1919, is the principal text to which one must refer to discover, on the one hand, the situation of the novel as it appeared to Virginia Woolf, and on the other the primary data of the problem posed by this situation. These elements were to be resumed and carried to their extreme conclusions in 1924, in "Mr Bennett and Mrs Brown".[30]

Wells, Galsworthy and Bennett are disappointing because life eludes them. "Whether we call it life or spirit, truth or reality, this, the essential thing, has moved off, or on, and refuses to be contained any longer in such ill-fitting vestments as we provide."[31] This sentence sums up the whole position. It implies that "metaphysical crisis which affects both the notion of personality and that of reality"[32] which Gabriel Marcel, together with many other critics, sees at the basis of the novel's evolution. A crisis of which these authors whom Virginia Woolf calls "materialists" are not aware, unless it be that they refuse to face or solve it. Her epithet, used in a very personal way, which by its vagueness and basic inadequacy shows that she had no claim to be a philosopher, merely means that "they are concerned not with the spirit but with the body",[33] with objects, with exterior circumstances, with

[29] CR I pp. 184-95 (150-58)
[30] CDB pp. 90-111 (94-119)
[31] CR I p. 188 (153)
[32] Quoted by René Tavernier in *Problèmes du Roman*, Confluences, July-Aug. 1943, nos. 21-24, 3rd year, p. 13
[33] CR I p. 185 (151)

an over-simple psychology, with appearances, with the unimportant, the transitory, and that they neglect "the true and the permanent". We might express the same opposition by echoing another formula of the same period, Maeterlinck's: they do not distinguish "the accident from the essence". And their technique, perfect though this may be, particularly Bennett's, no doubt marvellously adapted to this pseudo-reality, solid, well organized, but inert, is perfectly incapable of rendering the true reality, that to which we aspire. This novelistic failure thus shows Virginia Woolf what must not be done, what she will not do. Its weaknesses are obvious to anyone who has glanced at *Tristram Shandy* or even *Pendennis*. And closer to our own time, Hardy, Meredith, Conrad, Hudson[34] deserve our gratitude for the richness and the promise of development contained in their work. But it is Joyce and the Russians, with their "spirituality", their access to "the dark places of psychology", who really open the way to the novel of the future. In the article of 1924 the various groups are more clearly distinguished. Opposed to the sterile trio of Edwardians we have, first of all, the great novelistic tradition, more generously represented this time, with Jane Austen and Dickens side by side with Sterne and Thackeray, and in addition Flaubert and the Russians. Hardy alone represents the "precursors"; Meredith and Henry James seem only to meet with temperate admiration from Virginia Woolf and although, from what she says of them elsewhere, one may class them in this group, they are not mentioned here. Conrad, being a foreigner, is entitled to a place apart, analogous no doubt to that of the French or Russian novelists, whose lessons need to be assimilated and adapted before they can prove fertile. Finally the Georgians, amongst whom, although she does not name herself, she must evidently be included, those who began to write about 1910 and found themselves faced with a difficult situation: E. M. Forster, D. H. Lawrence, Lytton Strachey, James Joyce, T. S. Eliot. And in actual fact, amongst these, Forster and Lawrence—and Virginia Woolf herself—spoilt their earliest writings by trying to use the conventions and technique of the Edwardians instead of discarding these obsolete tools.

It is noteworthy that no other contemporary name appears in

---

[34] W. H. Hudson's *Far Away and Long Ago*, published in 1918, was reviewed by V. W. in the *TLS*, Sept. 28, 1918. *A Quiet Corner in a Library*, reviewed in the *TLS*, Nov. 23, 1916, was written by another W. H. Hudson.

these essays. We have to read through the Diary to find a single mention of Dorothy Richardson, here associated with Joyce and condemned with him for their common incapacity to get outside themselves.[35] It is significant that the same fault was ascribed to Virginia Woolf (and she realised how liable she was to lapse into it)[36] as if it were inherent in writers of this category. Of the twelve or fifteen novelists mentioned in the Diary, except for Maurice Baring[37] and Katherine Mansfield,[38] who are briefly and somewhat harshly judged, not a word about their works. Is this silence merely the effect of the cuts made by Leonard Woolf, who may have feared lest the somewhat summary and sharp judgments Virginia Woolf was apt to pass might compromise her reputation as critic? Or did certain reflections suggested to the novelist by her reading of her contemporaries seem, in her husband's opinion, to suggest an indebtedness incompatible with an originality which (mistakenly, to my mind) was held essential to her fame? In this respect, certain omissions from the latest collection, *Granite and Rainbow*, are disquieting. A desire to include in the first part, "The Art of Fiction", only studies of wide enough interest, does not seem entirely to justify the omission of Virginia Woolf's articles on Dorothy Richardson, J. Hergesheimer, J. G. Beresford, W. E. Norris, Elizabeth Robins or even André Maurois.[39] True, these pages destroy the myth of an ivory tower in which Virginia Woolf was supposed to have shut herself up with the authors of the Great Tradition for sole company; but the diverse interests, broader and more topical, which they display, far from compromising her reputation, reveal a personality which is both richer and more attractive. Moreover, if these articles underline the points in common between her own work and that of certain of her contemporaries, they seem to indicate not that her own conceptions were derived from these writers but that she was able to recognize in them the first manifestations of that spirit of renewal which inspired herself and which, during that second decade of the

[35] Cf. AWD p. 23 (22)

[36] Cf. AWD pp. 120-1 (118-9) (quoted *infra*, ch. III)

[37] Cf. AWD pp. 95-7 (94-5)

[38] Cf. AWD p. 2 (2)

[39] Cf. respectively: Dorothy Richardson, *TLS*, 13/2/1919, *Nation & Athenaeum*, 19/5/1923; Hergesheimer: *TLS*, 2/12/1918, 29/5/1919, 25/12/1919, 8/7/1920, 16/12/1920; Beresford, *TLS*, 25/3/1920, 27/1/1921; Norris, *TLS*, 1/5/1919, 4/3/1920, 10/2/1921; Robins: *TLS*, 17/6/1920; Maurois: "On not knowing French" re *Climats*, New Republic, N.Y., 13/2/1929

century, had led her gradually to formulate her theories while trying out new forms of writing. While certain pages of *The Voyage Out* give no foretaste of the ideal which guided Virginia Woolf's experiments, one would be tempted, from the similarity of the formulae found in the account of *The Tunnel* and the article on Modern Fiction,[40] published in February and April 1919 respectively, to conclude that her reading of Dorothy Richardson had played a determining role in our novelist's evolution. However, if Virginia Woolf recognized the elder writer's merits, and if a few years later, writing of *Revolving Lights*, she classed her among the pioneers,[41] she was none the less keenly aware of the weaknesses of Dorothy Richardson's novels, despite their merits; and these weaknesses, what is lacking in this disorderly flow of fragments—unity, meaning and structure—probably contributed more to Virginia Woolf's development than what was original in *Pilgrimage*. Basically, it was through their negative aspect, their inadequacy, that her contemporaries, even the innovators, stimulated Virginia Woolf, and their influence on her seems to be of the same order as that of the Edwardians and Victorians.

Although we have only fragmentary and intermittent information about the books read by our author, there is no doubt that she remained in constant contact with the literary production of her time. To limit her library to that suggested by the collected essays, even supplemented by the two hundred articles still scattered throughout various periodicals, would be to falsify the picture of her literary experience. In "Hours in a Library", written in 1916, after recalling the enthusiasm and eagerness aroused by a bookshop full of books fresh from the press, Leslie Stephen's daughter declares that "the living voices are, after all, the ones we understand the best . . ." and that they reveal to us "the mind and body of our time". And the "taste for bad books" which we acquire from them is neither so harmful nor so sterile as might be believed. "We owe a great deal to bad books; indeed,

[40] Included in *The Common Reader I* under the title "Modern Fiction".

[41] Cf. "Romance and the Heart", *Nation & Athenaeum*, May 19, 1923, p. 229: "There is no one word, such as romance or realism, to cover even roughly the works of Miss Dorothy Richardson. Their chief characteristic, if an intermittent student is qualified to speak, is one for which we still seek a name. She has *invented* or, if she has not invented, developed and applied to her own uses a sentence which we might call the psychological sentence of the feminine gender. . . . Her *discoveries* are concerned with states of being and not with states of doing." (My italics.)

we come to count their authors and their heroes among those figures who play so large a part in our silent life."[42] And, faithful to the laws of alternation which, as we shall see, were to govern her life, she shows how the reading of the classics and of contemporaries, of established authors and those amongst whom posterity will remember only a handful of names, complete and fertilize one another. It is highly probable that all her life she divided her attention between the two. In a list made on October 2, 1934, beside Shakespeare, Maupassant, Vigny and Saint-Simon we find Gide, Powys, Wells, Lady Brooke and Alice James.[43]

No doubt, with characteristic perspicacity, she immediately allotted the rank they deserved to such third-rate novelists as Compton Mackenzie, J. D. Beresford, Frank Swinnerton and Francis Brett Young. Her friendly relations with Hugh Walpole made her sensitive to his criticism,[44] but it would never have occurred to her to consider him as an artist of any importance, any more than he would have dreamed of hailing her as a great novelist.

It is rather surprising to find no mention of Rosamond Lehmann or of Mary Webb. The absence of any reference to the structural experiments of Clemence Dane or the impressionism of May Sinclair does not necessarily prove that Virginia Woolf had never read them, nor that she did not appreciate their attempts. Once again in "Hours in a Library" a characteristic image shows us the stimulating effect—rather than examples, rules or theories—that she sought from the literature of her time: "Whenever there is life in them [the work of our contemporaries] they will be casting their net out over some unknown abyss to snare new shapes, and we must throw our imagination after them if we are to accept with understanding the strange gifts they bring back to us."[45] This imaginative leap counts for more than the discoveries actually made; and so the gaps in our knowledge of what Virginia Woolf may have read or glanced at in the work of her contemporaries, whether more or less popular, more or less talented, traditionalist or avant-garde, seem no serious obstacle to our understanding of her formation or our appreciation of her originality. A true

---

[42] Cf. G & R p. 28 (28)
[43] Cf. AWD p. 227 (219). Cf. *infra*, ch. III
[44] Cf. AWD pp. 127 (125), 134 (131), 281 (271)
[45] G & R p. 29 (29-30)

artist is to be defined in relation to extreme manifestations, not in relation to middle-of-the-road works and half-tones. Critics who handle bits and pieces picked up here and there tend too much to imagine that creative artists work according to the same methods. But in fact the latter neither borrow nor receive; they assert themselves by contrast; and their contrast is the more important and significant the greater is their closeness. After all, Wells, Galsworthy and Bennett and all their rivals matter little; they go their own way and Virginia Woolf goes hers, without any danger of encountering them. The difficulty lies in asserting one's unique individuality as against Sterne, Joyce, Proust and Lawrence, in preserving one's integrity as against the temptations of the "more or less alike" which might lead one to be satisfied with something merely "more or less". Faced with his daily problem, if the artist happens to glance at the way his fellows have solved theirs, it is to avoid imitating them rather than to borrow from them; for what they have solved is *their* problem, and he is well aware that only *his* solution is valid for his own.

And so, convinced of these modalities of artistic creation, I have simply tried to define in the most general terms the situation of the novel during the formative years of Virginia Woolf's creative life, when she was becoming conscious of her potentialities and intentions. Most individual works are of small importance in themselves; only a few broad tendencies matter, which are particularly manifest in certain of these works, which then assume a representative value. I have shown where Virginia Woolf stood in relation to such landmarks, avoiding tempting but unprovable hypotheses and relying with prudent (if perhaps excessive) trust on the novelist's own statements. The various trends of fiction created a problem for Virginia Woolf, as for any young novelist seriously concerned about his art—a problem set in general terms as old as the genre itself: characters, plot, style, reality, life. But if these words were familiar, their content, and consequently the relations between these different ingredients, needed to be defined, redefined. All this, which had hitherto seemed a matter of course, was indeed called in question by the contemporary vision of reality, of life, and of human beings. We find that vision everywhere, and nowhere in particular: in bad books and in good books, in our way of reading the classics and of understanding the writers of our own period. It can be labelled Relativist, Bergsonian, Freudian.... But it is not from Einstein or Bergson or Freud—without seeking in any way to minimize their pioneering role—that the artist gets that vision which inspires his art; it is the anonymous assimilation of those theories, characteristic of the general thought of the period, a collective crystallization constituting the reality which the artist endeavours to reproduce. Such is the vision that Virginia Woolf defines in that passage quoted by all critics and by all historians of the contemporary novel:

The mind receives a myriad impressions—trivial, fantastic, evanescent, or engraved with the sharpness of steel. From all sides they come, an incessant shower of innumerable atoms; and as they fall, as they shape themselves into the life of Monday or Tuesday, the accent falls differently from of old. . . . Life is . . . a luminous halo, a semitransparent envelope surrounding us from the beginning of consciousness to the end.[46]

The continuous, the definite, the organized are replaced by the discontinuous, the indefinite, the unorganized, and obviously at the same time character and plot are profoundly altered, are even liable to melt away. In any case, it follows from these changes that the novelist's task must be considered in terms of this new conception: "Is it not the task of the novelist to convey this varying, this unknown and uncircumscribed spirit, whatever aberration or complexity it may display, with as little mixture of the alien and external as possible? "[47]

And a little later: "Let us record the atoms as they fall upon the mind in the order in which they fall, let us trace the pattern, however disconnected and incoherent in appearance, which each sight or incident scores upon the consciousness."[48]

But these recommendations are of a disconcertingly general character, like those of Henry James who, half a century before, had advised the young artist to write out of his own "experience". And if we compare the way James tried to make his thought explicit, to define what he means by "experience", we see how close he is to Virginia Woolf:

Experience is never limited, and it is never complete; it is an immense sensibility, a kind of huge spider's web, of the finest silken threads, suspended in the chamber of consciousness and catching every air-

[46] CR I p. 189 (154)
[47] CR I p. 189 (154)
[48] CR I p. 190 (155)

borne particle in its tissue. It is the very atmosphere of the mind. . . . I should feel that this was rather a tantalizing monition, if I were not careful immediately to add, "Try to be one of the people on whom nothing is lost".[49]

They are close to one another, too, in their keen sense of the difficulty of this task, which a few words have sufficed to suggest. A difficulty which eludes all advice, all prescriptions, all mechanical formulae, which demands effort and vigilance, unremittingly, for a work of art is a discovery, indeed, but one which can only be made fruitful by a continuous creative effort. And if James corrects the cruelly disappointing inadequacy of his admonitions by the conclusion, "Try to be one of the people on whom nothing is lost", Virginia Woolf, for her part, was to formulate in 1924 the rule which had been hers from the beginning and was always to remain hers:

. . . to go back and back; to experiment with one thing and another; to try this sentence and that, referring each word to my vision, matching it as exactly as possible, and knowing that somehow I had to find a common ground between us, a convention which would not seem to you too odd, unreal, and far-fetched to believe in.[50]

Suppression of the plot, suppression of full-length portraits and descriptions, interior monologue, stream of consciousness, poetry of style, exaltation of the moment, musical structure, cinema technique—in short, all the traits characteristic of Virginia Woolf's novels are in germ in these remarks. The author of *Mrs Dalloway*, when she wrote "Mr Bennett and Mrs Brown" had just discovered the process which would enable her to grasp her own truth, her Mrs Brown—the truth about the human being—in the person of Clarissa Dalloway. About the same time in France Gide, in *Les Faux Monnayeurs*, tackling the "*roman intégral*"—the novel in its entirety—the least codified of genres, the most lawless as he said, was in pursuit of the same reality.[51] Thirty years later a friend of Virginia Woolf's, Harold Nicolson, was asking the same question in *The Observer*: "Is the Novel dead?" And, surely thinking of

[49] Henry James, *The Art of Fiction*, Oxford University Press, New York, 1948, pp. 10-11

[50] CDB p. 105 (112)

[51] Cf. André Gide, "Les Faux Monnayeurs", *NRF*, p. 236 ff. Here we find the same contrast between "reality" and realism, the necessity of liberating the artist from current conventions, and of finding simpler and more stylized formulae, the desire to achieve that "erosion of outlines" of which Nietzsche speaks, the absurdity of always cutting "the slice of life" the same way, etc.

Joyce and of Virginia Woolf (for we find throughout his article echoes of the very discussion I have just analysed) he concludes: "The novel has fulfilled its mission by a massive analysis of human feelings and motives extending over two hundred years. I do not think it has much more to say."[52] Meanwhile Philip Toynbee in his answer, "The Defence Brief", far from considering that all the efforts of the Georgians have led only to an impasse, integrates their acquisitions, their achievements in a broader definition of the novel, which Virginia Woolf might readily have accepted: "A novel is a narrative in prose which is concerned with imaginary human beings. It borders on biography and history on one side, epic and dramatic poetry on the other, and it may legitimately swing anywhere between these two extremes."[53] Alan Pryce-Jones[54] is even more convincing; for him, novelists are justified by their intentions and their results, and on this he founds his hope in the future of the genre.

The thing which really matters is the primary impression, and the test of a novelist's technique is whether he can find and use the exact resources which will make his impressions vivid to the outside world. Virginia Woolf did it one way, Dickens did it another. But both of them were attempting a feat of skill which is no more likely to fall out of use than the art of painting in oils or writing symphonies. . . . All such writers (Camus, Sartre, Faulkner, Hemingway) have one thing in common. Each of them has his private vision to convey. Each is using the novel as a means of clarifying his own imagination.

It is not without interest to compare with this passage what the same critic wrote in 1931 in his review of *The Waves*, declaring that this novel communicated the poetic vision of what lies behind appearances. "No one before her has done anything like it. Her brilliant success is one of the most interesting events of our time."[55] From this recent controversy it may be concluded that, if the situation has evolved in so far as we could add to the list of "Georgians" as well as to that of "Edwardians", the problem is by no means solved; it is pretty much the same not only as in 1931, but even as in 1924 and 1919; perhaps we should say the same as it has always been, inviting solutions none of which has triumphed, or can triumph, since they correspond to the two broad

---

[52] Harold Nicolson, "Is the Novel Dead?" *The Observer*, Aug. 19, 1954.

[53] Philip Toynbee, "The Defence Brief", *The Observer*, Sept. 5, 1954.

[54] A. Pryce-Jones, "The Novelist's Fault", *The Observer*, Sept. 12, 1954.

[55] A. Pryce-Jones, *London Mercury*, Dec. 1931.

categories of mind into which humanity seems to be divided.

This division, which served to classify Virginia Woolf's critics, occurs again in the question of Bloomsbury, which must now be briefly examined.[56]

2. BLOOMSBURY

Bloomsbury is the name of the close group of friends who began to meet about 1906 and included, among others, John Maynard Keynes, Lytton Strachey, Virginia and Leonard Woolf, Vanessa and Clive Bell, Duncan Grant, E. M. Forster and Roger Fry. The term was applied derisively to the group before the First World War, because their hostesses, Virginia and Vanessa Stephen (who became Virginia Woolf and Vanessa Bell), lived in the London district of Bloomsbury. Bloomsbury meant a number of things—snobbish, "highbrow", "arty", "Bohemian"—all rolled into one word. It was intended to smack, all at once, of the British Museum, of untidy art studies, of an exclusive, "unconventional" life, of pale aesthetes who met to read esoteric papers in some ivory tower.[57]

With this definition J. K. Johnstone begins his book on the Bloomsbury group; and we need only read the chapter devoted to Bloomsbury in Clive Bell's *Old Friends*[58] to be convinced that he, a foundation member of the group, and those close friends who could claim to share with him the honour, or dishonour, of its name, would have subscribed to Johnstone's paragraph, as much for the facts as for the fiction which it contains.[59] It is however somewhat surprising that this definition should be followed by studies, as probing as they are pertinent, of the philosophy of G. E. Moore, of Roger Fry's aesthetics and the works of Forster, Lytton Strachey and Virginia Woolf in the light of that philosophy and those aesthetics. Although the book on the whole is very just, it may leave the impression that Bloomsbury was not only a group but a school with a doctrine, which is not implicit in the premises from which the author seems to start.

Without taking literally Clive Bell's declarations which, with their frequently caustic and occasionally acid tone, require certain

[56] For more details, we refer the reader to J. K. Johnstone's book, *The Bloomsbury Group*, which, although one may criticise its use and interpretation of facts and ideas, collects most of the evidence together.

[57] J. K. Johnstone, *The Bloomsbury Group*, p. ix.

[58] Clive Bell, *Old Friends*, pp. 126-37.

[59] Cf. also Desmond MacCarthy, *Memoirs*, p. 173: "Bloomsbury is neither a movement nor a push, but only a group of old friends whose affection and respect for each other has stood the test of nearly thirty years, and whose intellectual candour makes their company agreeable to each other. It never was a movement."

reservations, it seems reasonable none the less to take into account his opinion on the real nature of Bloomsbury; an opinion moreover confirmed by the reactions, or the testimony, of Virginia and Leonard Woolf, of MacCarthy and Maynard Keynes. "Bloomsbury" is above all a controversial label, indeed a journalists' invention which happened to catch on. The word ought to be left to the vocabulary of polemics, from which it has improperly been transferred to that of criticism. Would anyone seriously try to distinguish a Saint-Germain-des-Prés group having *L'Etre et le Néant* as its Bible and Sartre as its prophet? The only difference between Bloomsbury and Saint-Germain-des-Prés lies perhaps in the difference between the English and French temperaments; they are more reserved in London than in Paris, ideas are less widespread, adepts are fewer, because there is less philosophical discussion on the banks of the Thames than on the Rive Gauche— and because a seat in the Square is not the same as a café terrace. I shall therefore merely indicate the evolution of the relationship between the different personalities usually grouped under the label Bloomsbury, the hostility that some of these aroused, which underlies the Bloomsbury myth, and in conclusion I shall try to assess how far the fact of belonging to this group influenced Virginia Woolf.

The initial cell of the group may be found in the "Midnight Society"[60] founded at Cambridge in the autumn of 1899 by five friends, first-year undergraduates at Trinity. Thoby Stephen, Clive Bell, Leonard Woolf, Saxon Sydney Turner and Lytton Strachey decided to meet on Saturday evenings in Bell's rooms to read plays and poems and talk about literature, philosophy and politics. Merely a group of students bound together by friendship and enthusiasm. At the end of their university life these young men might have scattered, or at least the bonds between them might have slackened, as so often happens. Circumstances, on the contrary, knit them closer, and for several years encouraged the friends' meetings. Thoby Stephen could entertain his old friends at 46 Gordon Square, in the house where, since August 1904, he had lived with his brother Adrian and his sisters Virginia and

---

[60] J. K. Johnstone does not seem to distinguish between the "Midnight Society", an ephemeral club consisting almost exclusively of the Stephens' young friends from "The Society", or "Apostles' Society", founded between 1820 and 1830 by F. D. Maurice, Tennyson and Hallam, to which Strachey and Keynes belonged and which also held its meetings on Saturday evenings (see Clive Bell, *Old Friends*, p. 26).

Vanessa. All of the same generation, passionately interested in intellectual and artistic matters, they re-created there the atmosphere of the Midnight Society. Anyone who numbered kindred spirits among their friends brought them along: thus Strachey introduced Maynard Keynes and his own brothers and sisters, Oliver, James and Marjorie, and then his cousin Duncan Grant, who in his turn, in 1909, brought Roger Fry into the group, Thoby Stephen, who had in a way been its most important member, in that but for him the Midnight Society might have had no sequel, died in 1906; but by that time the little group was so united that this loss did not jeopardize its solidarity. Clive Bell, in fact, had just become engaged to Vanessa Stephen, whom he was to marry the following year. From that time on the friends decided to call one another by their first names. After their marriage the Bells kept on the Gordon Square house, while Virginia and Adrian Stephen set up house at 29 Fitzroy Square (in 1911 they moved to 38 Brunswick Square). This did not mean a split in the group; the discussion begun at Vanessa Bell's one evening might be carried on at Virginia Stephen's the following week. In 1909 Lytton Strachey asked Virginia to marry him; she accepted; next day Strachey changed his mind, but no ill feelings ensued. In 1911 Leonard Woolf came back from Ceylon, where he had been since 1904, and in the following year he married Virginia Stephen. To these names we must add those of Desmond MacCarthy and his wife, who had known the Stephens and Clive Bell since 1901, H. T. J. Norton, Gerald Shove, E. M. Forster, Goldsworthy Lowes Dickinson, David Garnett and Francis Birrell. After the war Raymond Mortimer, Ralph Partridge and his wife (*née* Frances Marshall) and Stephen Tomlin came to swell the group. This indeed was no longer as tight-knit as of old, not indeed because of any break in the personal relations between members of the group, but because the nature of these relations had altered. People were now more involved with life; they no longer enjoyed the boundless freedom, the uncommittedness which, when they were young and unmarried, had made possible the frequency and intensity of their pre-war gatherings.[61]

[61] A typical example of the insidious effect of the myth: Irma Rantavaara includes in a single paragraph (op. cit. p. 45) facts and quotations which are perfectly correct but which, through neglect of chronology, convey the misleading impression that from 1904 to 1925 or 1930 the "group" retained the same characteristics.

This restatement of the situation should surely be enough. But the mythical character of Bloomsbury is seen in striking fashion if we carry the enquiry further and consider in relation to these facts both the reasoned attempts of scholars to reconstitute, or indeed to constitute, the history of Bloomsbury, and the attacks launched against the "group".

Paradoxically, indeed, it was when the group no longer had any real material existence, at the end of the ten years that followed the war, that the most virulent attacks were made on Bloomsbury. Hunting the highbrow has always been an easy and a popular pastime. Gilbert Frankau and Robert Magill, to whom Leonard Woolf[62] took the trouble to reply in 1927, were insignificant adversaries no doubt. Wyndham Lewis,[63] Frank Swinnerton[64] and after them Q. D. Leavis[65] proved antagonists of a different stature. In default of substantial merits, their position in the world of letters, their activity and their virulence have conferred on them a prestige scarcely deserved by their writings, which are characterized chiefly by invective and confused thinking. A few sentences will serve to show the tone:

Bloomsbury was full of what Desmond MacCarthy [in *Bloomsbury, an unfinished Memoir*, 1933, quoted above] called "alert original men and women" and what I call ill-mannered and pretentious dilettanti. (Frank Swinnerton)[66]

Those most influential in the literary world, as far as the highbrow side of the racket was concerned, have mostly been minor personalities who were impelled to arrange a sort of bogus "time" to take the place of the real "time"—to bring into being an imaginary "time", small enough and pale enough to accommodate their not very robust talents. That has consistently been the so-called Bloomsbury technique both in the field of writing and of painting. (Wyndham Lewis).[67]

Writings of this temper might almost convince an uninstructed reader that Cézanne, Picasso, Proust, James Joyce and Dorothy Richardson all belonged to Bloomsbury, which serves to show how a myth is created. In a sense, the fact that J. K. Johnstone was impelled to write his study proves to what extent these hostile

---

[62] Cf. Leonard Woolf, *Hunting the Highbrow*, 1927

[63] Wyndham Lewis, *Men without Art*, 1934 (ch. V devoted to V. Woolf)

[64] Frank Swinnerton, *The Georgian Literary Scene, 1910-1935* (1935).

[65] Q. D. Leavis, articles in *Scrutiny*, esp. "Caterpillars of the Commonwealth Unite", *Scrutiny*, Sept. 1938.

[66] *Op. cit.*, pp. 273-4

[67] *Op. cit.*, pp. 186-7.

critics had succeeded. If it took articles and treatises to prove a point, it will take more articles and other treatises to disprove it. Clive Bell in his restatement gives the impression of tilting against windmills; actually his irritated protests are directed not only against ephemeral articles and pamphlets, but against the solid volumes which zealous scholars are liable to extract from these.

Virginia Woolf, the particular object of the "Bloomsbury baiters' " venom, tried to accept the inevitable, even pretended to be thick-skinned, but in fact was rather deeply wounded.[68] However paltry such attacks might be, the hatred, contempt and mockery they exuded were very real, and eventually drew from her a reply which her husband wisely withheld from publication until 1947.[69] "Middlebrow" is a fine sample of spirited wit, which would certainly have fed the flames without convincing anybody, for in such conflicts no antagonist has ever proved accessible to argument. It was infinitely more effective to leave pamphleteers and professors to their pastime of slaughter and wounded pride. Unfortunately, Strachey and Roger Fry were dead; they could contribute nothing which, by its quality, would serve to refute the muddled and virulent attacks aimed at them. *The Years*, massive and somewhat heavy, was a feeble reply[70]; but Virginia Woolf might simply have advised Swinnerton to re-read *The Waves*; beside the two "poetic somethings" which he had missed out on his first reading, he might perhaps have found other elements susceptible of modifying his first impression.[71]

To pursue this examination would be as sterile as the original quarrel. However, as far as our purpose is concerned, we are now in a position to define precisely Virginia Woolf's "Bloomsburyism"; it would of course have been easy to assess it quite apart from her share in the quarrel, but the aggressive position she takes up

[68] Cf. AWD p. 241 (233, 232): "Having just written a letter about Bloomsbury . . . only affected me as a robin affects a rhinoceros—except in the depths of the night." Cf. also *ibid.*, pp. 228 (220), 229 (221), 231 (223)

[69] Cf. AWD p. 241 (233) "L. advised me *not* to send the letter and after two seconds I see he is right." "Middlebrow" was published in *The Death of the Moth*, pp. 113-19 (176-86)

[70] Cf. AWD p. 240 (232): "Write them [the Bloomsbury baiters] down, that's the only way."

[71] Frank Swinnerton, p. 301 of *The Georgian Literary Scene*, criticizing the lack of characterization in *The Waves*, mentions "four poetic somethings"; as there are obviously six voices in the novel, this inaccuracy, which is more than just a slip, gives some idea of the quality of his criticism.

in "Middlebrow" enables one to consider with a certain scepticism the whole ideological content with which historians of the so-called movement endeavour to puff out their myth. She appeals to no philosophical or aesthetic doctrine; she merely claims the inalienable rights of the artist to intelligence, sensibility, sincerity and liberty, while asserting her rejection of mediocrity, dead conventions, demagogy and conformism.

True, Moore's *Principia Ethica* appears to be Helen Ambrose's bedside book in *The Voyage Out*, and undoubtedly the heroine and her creator, both confirmed individualists, endowed with keen sensitivity and lucid intelligence, believed in the supreme value of personal relations and also in that of the moment, apprehended with the full intensity of an inner life. But it hardly needed the authority of the Cambridge philosopher to teach them this. After all, Ibsen, Plato and Gibbon are also mentioned in the novel as masters of the art of living and thinking, equally rich, equally worthy of trust. Moreover, if Moore's ideas could enthral Keynes and Strachey—or St John Hirst in *The Voyage Out*, who reminds one of the latter—it is questionable, as Clive Bell points out, "whether either of the Miss Stephens gave much thought to the all-important distinction between 'good on the whole' and 'good as a whole' ".[72]

In another connection, we can see from Virginia Woolf's *Roger Fry* to what extent the author of *The Waves* and *To the Lighthouse* was able to assimilate her friend's aesthetic views; and indeed it must be admitted that she succeeded in transposing into the field of literature the theories of *Transformations* and *Vision and Design*.[73] But it would be wrong, in my opinion, to let oneself be impressed by similarities of vocabulary which are, after all, a social phenomenon of a superficial character. It is surely legitimate to assert Virginia Woolf's originality, as well as that of Roger Fry. A similarity of nature and temperament, a similarity of aesthetic and intellectual experience, made even more striking by the fact that they frequently, no doubt, reached their respective positions through the common ground of their conversations together, these are phenomena real enough to render pointless any search for "influences" or for a "Bloomsbury doctrine".

J. K. Johnstone's book, bringing out not only the affinities but

[72] Clive Bell, *Old Friends*, p. 133
[73] Cf. particularly J. K. Johnstone, *op. cit.*, pp. 82-3.

also the divergences between the three authors he chose to represent Bloomsbury, showed clearly enough the arbitrariness of any attempt to see in the "group" anything more than what is contained in the definition that opens this chapter.

The Bloomsbury of critics and literary professors, following on the Bloomsbury of journalists and jealous writers and anti-Cambridge Oxonians, is a false category. Its only interest has been to attract the attention of critics to a state of mind, a set of attitudes, within which certain artists developed—whether or not these belonged to Bloomsbury—and which extend far beyond these artists, seeming now the substance upon which they feed, now the actual emanation of their works. This state of mind, these attitudes, did not originate in Bloomsbury; they are not confined to the people and the place that the label "Bloomsbury" implies. Consequently, the use of so inadequate a term should be banned from any strict critical vocabulary.[74] And to return to Virginia Woolf, her debt towards Bloomsbury—the Bloomsbury whose reality I have attempted to circumscribe—is not of the kind usually attributed to her. It is not a sum of ideas, still less of literary prescriptions. It is merely a fertile climate of intellectual and artistic life (in fact of life, pure and simple) in which divergences, originality and discussion played as great a part as likenesses, affinities and sympathy.

[74] To assert, for instance, as does Noel Annan (*Leslie Stephen*, p. 270) that "Bloomsbury adapted, pruned and chiselled Stephen's prose and gave it a cutting edge" seems typical of the way the Bloomsbury myth is misused even by the most serious critics.

Chapter III

THE SELF, LIFE AND ARTISTIC CREATION

WHEN he published *A Writer's Diary*[1] in 1953, Leonard Woolf appeared to set strict limits to the studies that might be undertaken at the present day about Virginia Woolf's personality and still more about her life. "The Diary is too personal to be published as a whole during the lifetime of many people referred to in it,"[2] he declared in the Preface, thus establishing a separation, temporary no doubt but none the less categorical, between the public and the private domain. This distinction, which may irritate impatient scholars, disappoint the legitimate curiosity of amateur psychologists and the more dubious curiosity of gossip-collectors, not only corresponds to Virginia Woolf's innermost wishes[3] but is moreover justified in terms of her notion of human personality. Without examining this notion in detail here,[4] I may simply point out how arbitrary the traditional limits of a human being seemed to the author of *The Waves*. For one who will not admit that we are confined within our own bodies and within the moment, and who accepts a feeling that everything outside the self, animate and inanimate, somehow contributes to what one is, it is logical to conclude that through our own participation in the being of others, our life does not end with our death; its substance remains mingled in the texture of other lives; our departure does not remove it thence, and thus does not exempt us from the discretion with which each of us, following personal criteria, traces the manifold circles spreading from the most secret part of his being to the most public of his faces. Certain examples of excessive exhibitionism which, in the long run, do only a devious service to truth and bear a very different testimony to that intended by their authors, incline us to appreciate the scruples of Virginia Woolf and her literary executor.

---

[1] *A Writer's Diary: Being Extracts from the Diary of Virginia Woolf.* Edited by Leonard Woolf. The Hogarth Press, London 1953.

[2] AWD p. vii (vii)

[3] "I am trying to tell whichever self it is that reads this hereafter that I can write very much better . . . and forbid her to let the eye of man behold it . . . writing thus for my own eye only . . .", AWD p. 13 (13).

[4] Cf. *infra*, ch. VI

Moreover, apart from any reasons of a strictly private or of an ideological order which may have motivated such a decision, we find it justified by Proust in terms to which our author would fully have subscribed:

In reality, what one gives to the public is what one has written alone, for oneself, it is the work of one's real self. What one gives to one's intimate friends, that's to say in conversation (however highly refined, and the most refined is the worst of all, since it warps the life of the spirit by associating it with itself: Flaubert's conversations with his niece or the watchmender are harmless) and those productions meant for a private circle, that's to say cut down to suit the taste of a few persons, which are nothing more than written conversation, are the work of a far more external self, not of the deep-down self that can only be reached by leaving out of account other people and the self that knows other people—the deep-down self that lay waiting while one was with others, and that one feels to be one's only real self, the self for whose sake alone artists eventually live, as for some god to whom they cling more and more, and to whom they sacrifice a life whose sole purpose is to do him honour.[5]

By identifying the "deep-down self", the "only real self" of the artist, with the self at the centre of the work destined to the public rather than with the self of everyday life and of supposedly intimate relations, Proust sets a fresh value on the finished work, the work deliberately matured, composed and corrected, at the expense of all those biographical elements on which the criticism of Sainte-Beuve and his followers laid stress. No doubt such identification makes sense only from the Proustian point of view, where the unity of the self is dispersed through time and space before being recovered in the work of art. But this, surely, was the point of view adopted by Virginia Woolf, in her life and in her work, with a disciplined determination and in a solitude which recall, in many respects, Proust writing against death in his cork-lined room.[6]

[5] "Un pamphlet inédit de Proust contre Sainte-Beuve", *Le Figaro Littéraire*, March 6, 1954. Cf. also AWD p. 75 (74): "People have any number of states of consciousness, etc." *Ibid.*, p. 230 (223): ". . . the different strata of being: the upper, under . . ."

[6] Cf. AWD, Preface, ix (ix): "The diaries at least show the extraordinary energy, persistence, and concentration with which she devoted herself to the art of writing and the undeviating conscientiousness with which she wrote and rewrote and again rewrote her books." And p. 361 (347): "I walk over the marsh saying, I am I: and must follow that furrow, not copy another. That is the only justification for my writing, living." P. 365 (351): "I will go down with my colours flying . . ." (March 8, 1941, a few days before her death). P. 314 (303): "I sometimes feel it's [life] been an illusion—gone so fast; lived so quickly; and nothing to show for it, save these little books. But that makes me dig my feet in and squeeze the moment" (1939).

No doubt, the silences which interrupt the Diary, those eclipses lasting for weeks and even months which conceal the everyday or minor aspects of Virginia Woolf and substitute the after-glow, the echo of that major personality that the book intends to reveal to us, are due to Leonard Woolf. We may ask ourselves whether his viewpoint, as husband, fellow-worker and editor, coincides with that which the writer herself would have chosen. However, if this question is doomed to remain unanswered, we cannot emphasize too much the complete confidence with which Virginia Woolf relies on her husband's judgment:

But what is to become of all these diaries, I asked myself yesterday. If I died, what would Leo make of them? He would be disinclined to burn them; he could not publish them. Well, he should make up a book from them, I think; and then burn the body. I daresay there is a little book in them; if the scraps and scratchings were straightened out a little. God knows.[7]

The shade of doubt that qualifies every sentence here need not disturb us; it does not refer to Leonard Woolf. It is the doubt she always felt in the case of each of her books, as to its quality, its necessity.[8] And there seems no reason not to accept the judgment with which Elizabeth Bowen concludes her assessment of the value of the Diary in its present form: namely, that an unprejudiced reader cannot help realising that Mr Woolf has been wise, and that he was the person who knew Virginia Woolf best.[9]

"The book throws light upon Virginia Woolf's intentions, objects and methods as a writer. It gives an unusual psychological picture of artistic production from within."[10] Leonard Woolf's definition of the Diary, although precise and just, is obviously too succinct to reveal the whole import of the book. If on the one hand it implies too much, on the other it omits, as though out of discretion, the deeply personal secrets which Virginia Woolf entrusted to her "kindly blankfaced old confidante".[11] True, these pages enable us to survey the whole of her literary career, from her first childish efforts written in Leslie Stephen's shadow, as it were,

---

[7] AWD p. 87 (86-7)
[8] Cf. *infra*, p. 144
[9] E. Bowen, "The principle of her art was joy", *NYT* Feb. 21, 1954.
[10] AWD p. ix (ix)
[11] AWD p. 31 (30)

at Hyde Park Gate[12] or at St Ives,[13] to her premonitions of books which death was to prevent her from writing,[14] and the completion of her last work, *Between the Acts*.[15] We can see the idea of each book germinating, growing, blossoming; we can follow the intermittent progress of editorial work, the successive corrections, the stumbling-blocks presented, in each case, by particular problems, the doubt (amounting to anguish and despair) when the time comes for the work to face the public and the critics; the author's reaction to criticism and her own verdict, deeply imbued with the atmosphere of the passing moment, but always moving in their lucidity and sincerity. All of which shows a writer at work, tells the dramatic story, with its countless vicissitudes, of that long trial of endurance, an artist's calling. We are immediately reminded of Flaubert's letters—even before Virginia Woolf herself suggests the comparison.[16] This is indeed the "psychological picture" promised by the Preface. On the other hand, as we shall see on closer analysis, the light thrown by the book on "the intentions, objects and methods" is an intimate twilight, rather than the piercing beam of an X-ray. This criticism, indeed, is less valid as regards her "intentions"—her frame of mind, her attitude, her aspiration to possibilities as yet unclarified—which by their very nature are more readily adaptable to this style of confidential communion with oneself, closely bound up with one's being, subsisting on

[12] "I was then writing a long picturesque essay upon the Christian religion, I think; called Religio Laici, I believe, proving that man has need of a God; but the God was described in process of change; and I also wrote a history of Women; and a history of my own family—all very longwinded and Elizabethan in style", AWD p. 151 (147).

[13] "On the whole the art becomes absorbing—more? no, I think it's been absorbing ever since I was a little creature scribbling a story in the manner of Hawthorne on the green plush sofa in the drawingroom at St Ives while the grown ups dined", AWD p. 309 (297-8)

[14] (*a*) A new sort of critical book: "I want to explore a new criticism", AWD p. 283 (275); cf. also pp. 282 (272), 305 (294), 337 (324). (*b*) A book of new, undefined form: "Anyhow it will be a supported on fact book . . . I think of taking my mountain top—that persistent vision—as a starting point", AWD p. 360 (346); cf. also pp. 307 (296) and 359 (345).

[15] "Finished Pointz Hall, the Pageant: the play—finally *Between the Acts* this morning (Feb. 26, 1941)." This is the penultimate entry in the Diary, AWD p. 365 (351).

[16] "New emotions: humility; impersonal joy; literary despair. I am learning my craft in the most fierce conditions. Really reading Flaubert's letters I hear my own voice cry out Oh art! Patience: find him consoling, admonishing", AWD p. 269 (260). And a little later: "Few people can be so tortured by writing as I am. Only Flaubert I think", AWD p. 270 (260).

allusions and things unsaid. About her "objects" she shows the same reticence; more often than not we have the merest inkling of them. As for her "method", we see it only in its broad lines; throughout the book, hints and suggestions of analyses whet our curiosity without ever satisfying it. The final revelation about the deep springs of Virginia Woolf's art haunts the background of this book; it is not in the book itself.[17]

Nevertheless this Writer's Diary is also a diary, pure and simple. If it reveals the portrait of an artist, this is because her lively mind and vibrant sensibility convey the impression of an actual presence. The continuity of this presence is not affected by Leonard Woolf's cuts, any more than it would have been by the original gaps in the notebooks. For one thing, as Virginia Woolf more than anyone would have agreed, discontinuity is surely an essential part of life. To find it in the portrayal of life cannot affect the faithfulness of the portrait. Moreover, to use the concepts of a more traditional psychology rather than these personal reasons, it is surely true that our everyday gestures always express the same self; if a few examples suffice to define us, their accumulation would only overload the portrait they trace. In any case, in one's life, how many of these words and actions remain, so to speak, anonymous? Even if we accept responsibility for them to the point of paying some attention to them, of identifying ourselves with them during a moment's thought, or even in a few lines invited by a blank page, or dictated by a vague aspiration towards continuity, don't they notwithstanding remain on the outer fringes of our being, forming that accidental outline of personality which belongs as much, if not more, to the non-self as to the self, which consists of adaptation, resonance, reaction rather than of affirmation, individual tone, or action? One must really not regret too much the absence of everyday reality in the Diary. What it loses superficially thereby it gains in depth; by stripping off the anecdotal it gains access to the essential. And at the same time it finds its place, quite naturally, in the line of Virginia Woolf's books, and almost twenty years before

[17] This partial disappointment is expressed somewhat differently by Richard Hughes in "Virginia Woolf", *Spectator*, Nov. 20, 1953: "Now that we can see her mind from within, then, as well as from outside, are we any nearer to an answer whether she was essentially poet or novelist?—The fact is that in this book we find much light on the question but no answer: we find only what we ought to have known, that nature even in compounding genius shows no signs of appreciating these classifications we so love." Cf. also Clive Bell, *Old Friends*, pp. 95-6.

it appeared it was vindicated by two lines from "Mr Bennett and Mrs Brown": "But do not expect just at present a complete and satisfactory presentment of her [Mrs Brown]. Tolerate the spasmodic, the obscure, the fragmentary, the failure."[18] In the present case, indeed, the fact that no Mrs Brown is involved but that the author and her protagonist are identical, the spasmodic, the obscure and the fragmentary do not imply failure. Of course any choice in such matters is full of risks; it may throw the whole personality out of balance, to the point of altering its nature. Yet to emphasize the writer in Virginia Woolf, to show her whole being centred in her artist's calling, is surely not to betray her, but to respect her deepest reality. By keeping out of the Diary ordinary life and the outside world, and the various occasions which we should have been glad to find there as shadows to set off the highlights, Mr Woolf has solved a conflict which, occasionally, still crops up. "I think the effort to live in two spheres: the novel; and life; is a strain. Nefs almost break me because they strain me so far from the other world."[19] Or again: "The difficulty is the usual one —how to adjust the two worlds"[20]—the world of creation and the world in which one has to live. By confining her within that magic world of art which she wanted "to raise . . . all round [herself] . . . and live strongly and quietly there"[21] the Diary, as we have it, restores her to herself in all the integrity of her solitude, and if it somewhat upsets the balance of her personality, it inclines her in the direction that was naturally hers. It shows her engaged on that passionate pursuit of her essential being which was the true meaning of her life—her life as woman, merged in her life as writer. "I thought, driving through Richmond last night, something very profound about the synthesis of my being: how only writing composes it: how nothing makes a whole unless I am writing." And if she promptly adds, "now I have forgotten what seemed so profound,"[22] fourteen months later the same revelation recurs: "Odd how the creative power at once brings the whole universe to order".[23] Barely two months after that, the death of her friend Roger Fry brings her face to face with her own death, and the two

[18] "Mr Bennett and Mrs Brown" in *The Captain's Deathbed*, p. 111 (119)
[19] AWD p. 209 (203)
[20] AWD p. 215 (208)
[21] AWD p. 215 (208)
[22] AWD p. 208 (201)
[23] AWD p. 220 (213)

fugitive gleams become an illumination: "... the exalted sense of being above time and death which comes from being again in a writing mood. And this is not an illusion, so far as I can tell."[24]

By writing, to fulfil oneself and to fulfil the world in oneself and at the same time to transcend one's mortal being, such was her destiny, as she glimpsed it and affirmed it at that moment of acute experience—and as I shall endeavour to trace it, starting with that book which tells its story.

Although we lack precise details or anecdotes, or any of those childish sayings that tradition preserves piously, reading into them a promise confirmed by later events, we can picture her none the less from her photographs as a little girl of fragile appearance, her thin face framed by smooth hair.[25] Her universe was a divided one, fostering two contrary trends in her being. At times she would settle down in the immediate world, where sensations merged freely into fantasy, where human beings, her brothers and sisters, her mother, were so close to her that she felt at one with them in joy as in sadness, in speech as in silence; at other times, on the contrary, the presence of her father, that sometimes kindly, sometimes tyrannical, but always mysterious giant called up around her an unfamiliar country where gentlemen of a rather different stature from those one met every day—Meredith, James, Hardy— talked about books and the writers of books, and wrote books themselves. Their summer home was Talland House at St Ives in Cornwall, where the countryside, the spaciousness, the holiday atmosphere seemed, despite the presence of a few distinguished guests, to assert the supremacy of the former universe with its spontaneous intimacy. The rest of the year was spent at 22 Hyde Park Gate, London, and in the mysterious world that loomed around the great room where Leslie Stephen sat writing, while the rhythmical tap of his rocking-chair beat out time like the waves on the shores of the English Channel—a time which was different and yet the same.

If in the immediate world of childhood, play and affection, little Virginia led a natural child's life, which was to make a deep

[24] AWD p. 225 (217)
[25] Annan, *Leslie Stephen,* and Monique Nathan, *Virginia Woolf par elle-même*
[26] Annan, *Leslie Stephen,* London, 1951, p. 101 ff.
[27] CDB—"Leslie Stephen" p. 68 (69)

impression on her adult sensibility, she was none the less fascinated by that other mode of being, represented by her father. She might indeed have sat "scribbling a story in the manner of Hawthorne on the green plush sofa"[28] without this being a presage of her literary future, and even a few years later her "long picturesque essay upon the Christian religion", her history of Women and her history of her own family, "all very long-winded and Elizabethan",[29] might just as well have been the end as the beginning of her career as authoress. Nevertheless, what might have been merely a commonplace phenomenon of identification without further consequence, must surely be seen, in view of Virginia Woolf's later development, to display certain basic tendencies. Far more than the distant heredity of remarkable ancestors, the atmosphere of the Stephen family, if it does not explain what after all remains inexplicable, enables us to retrace the genesis of Virginia's personality. The tension between sensibility and intelligence, or to speak even more precisely between feeling and being on the one hand, understanding and expressing on the other, this was the reality that became part of her childish being; and in that living complex in which the threads of several lives and several temperaments were interwoven, she selected nothing, rejected nothing. She gave herself up entirely to these two currents, equally, according to a rhythm or a balance which enabled her to follow them both without their neutralizing one another. No doubt her own natural resources made possible this twofold allegiance. At the same time Leslie Stephen's real, though repressed, sensibility and his love for his wife, as well as Julia's wisdom and her indulgence towards her husband, settling the conflicts of their characters with compromise and understanding, may also have encouraged Virginia's harmonious development.

The term harmonious, nevertheless, is accurate only in the broadest sense; it refers rather to the abstract whole of her personality than to the concrete moments of her existence. I spoke earlier of tensions, of different worlds. The synthesis cannot be reached through flesh or spirit, nor through the gestures of everyday life; only art can realise it. And when at fifty-six Virginia Woolf noted in her Diary: "On the whole the art becomes absorbing—more? no, I think it's been absorbing ever since I was a little creature, scribbling a story in the manner of Hawthorne . . ."[30] one might accuse her of ascribing to a thirteen-year-old child preoccupations incompatible with her age. But breaking through the surface of this literal meaning there emerges the obscure need of the child to assert herself and achieve unity within herself. This patient exorcising of the reality that fascinates and destroys,[31] of the reality within oneself as well as of external reality, was to be the effort of her whole life and the reason for her being. And within this reality, one cannot too much stress the importance of Leslie and Julia Stephen, what they were and what they stood for. It seems that Virginia Woolf repeatedly practised on them the magic spells of art without, however, obtaining the deliverance she obscurely sought. Neither with Mr and Mrs Ambrose in *The Voyage Out*, Mr and Mrs Hilbery in *Night and Day* or even with Mrs Dalloway did she succeed in breaking free from them, whether because these characters failed to attain the requisite wholeness and autonomy of existence, or because they were too remote from the living context with which, in her own mind, her parents were inextricably involved. She had to wait for *To the Lighthouse*, which she thus envisaged shortly after the publication of *Mrs Dalloway*: "To have father's character done complete in it; and mother's; and St. Ives; and childhood; and all the usual things I try to put in—life, death, etc."[32]

In this book, these ghosts have exhausted their substance; in writing it, Virginia Woolf had at the same time detached them from herself, in so far as they were foreign and disturbing elements, and had absorbed them into her own being, in so far as this was compatible with its autonomy and integrity. On her father's birthday, November 11, 1928, she reviewed the situation and discovered herself freed from this uneasy obsession: "I used to think of him and mother daily; but writing the *Lighthouse* laid them in my mind. And now he comes back sometimes, but differently. (I believe this to be true—that I was obsessed by them both, unhealthily; and writing of them was a necessary act.) He comes back now more as a contemporary."[33]

Having lost her mother at the age of thirteen, she had through-

[30] AWD p. 309 (297-8)
[31] AWD p. 138 (135-6)
[32] AWD p. 76 (75)
[33] AWD p. 138 (135)

out her adolescence been subjected to the fascination of a personality which represented an ideal and one whole side of her nature, but which at the same time stifled its complementary aspect. She felt herself at once mutilated by the lack of intimate understanding and discouraged by her own admiration for an intelligence too like, and yet too different from, her own. As long as Leslie Stephen lived she could never be more than a little girl. She would never have had a "room of her own"[34] other than her father's study. The freedom he allowed her, the help he could give her were fruitful only in so far as she remained passive; he helped her to accumulate her capital; but his presence kept her in tutelage and prevented her from making use of that capital. "His life would have entirely ended mine. What would have happened? No writing, no books; —inconceivable."[35]

When she left Hyde Park Gate and settled in Bloomsbury[36] with Vanessa and her two brothers, Virginia Stephen, at twenty-two, really attained her majority. She was leaving a world dominated by a generation on the decline to spend her youth in the most youthful *milieu* in London. If the "Bloomsbury group" did not as yet exist—we have seen how the term should be interpreted[37]— these gatherings of young people enamoured of art and literature undoubtedly constituted an ideal ground for the unfolding of youthful talents. The set included such men as MacCarthy, Charles Tennyson, Clive Bell, Lytton Strachey, Hilton Young, J. M. Keynes. Sharing the same enthusiasms, they tested their ideas and sharpened their wits in discussion. They created their own world, an intense, exclusive world, where they flourished like hothouse plants. Here they acquired their characteristic delicacy, subtlety and independent boldness, but also the somewhat artificial qualities and the limitations to which any sect is liable. Perhaps they had no conscious intention of cutting themselves off from the rest of the world; but chance had surrounded them with so many treasures and had so amply satisfied their taste for excellence that they were unconsciously led to neglect any broader, more diffuse sort of experience.

These years—from 1904 to the war—were, so to speak, Vir-

---

[34] Cf. *A Room of One's Own*
[35] AWD p. 138 (135)
[36] 46 Gordon Square in 1904, then 29 Fitzroy Square in 1907
[37] Cf. *supra*, ch. II, 2

63

ginia's "voyage out", the cruise at the end of which, having traversed appearances, she was to find herself.[38] She listened and looked: no doubt she wrote in her room—really a room of her own, on the first floor; but she was still writing for herself alone.[39] She could not grow up overnight from the little girl she had so lately been, in Leslie Stephen's shadow. She had to create herself, and create her world, before she could think of projecting anything out of herself by artistic creation. This long-drawn-out ripening is significant in many respects. It bears witness, above all, to the integrity of the artist who was able to resist her personal facility as well as the demands of circumstances; an integrity uniting a high consciousness of the artist's duty and a self-mistrust that refused to indulge in illusions. These ten years of waiting, which were ten years of preparation for the craft of letters, prefigure in the alternation of contemplation and discussion one of the essential rhythms of the author's life. The exchange of ideas, vivified by the warmth of human contact, was indispensable to her nature, in which feeling predominated over intellect; it was through human beings that she sought to explore the world of ideas. She would let herself be carried passively through other minds. Then, in solitude and silence, she would ponder over herself while pondering over these others, absorbing them into herself while constructing and asserting her own personality. This process may not be entirely original, at any rate in its more superficial aspects, but it assumes in Virginia Woolf a rare quality which deserves to hold the attention. This is not the ordinary experience, the familiar taking of notes, mentally or otherwise, which are later used as literary material. With her friends, and more broadly with those beings and things that attract her sympathy, Virginia Woolf does not "secrete an envelope which connects [her] and protects [her] from others",[40] the outside world is not for her a conglomeration of "foreign bodies", she merges into it, is lost in it.[41] It is this intense receptivity of which Duncan Grant speaks[42] that makes her world

---

[38] *The Voyage Out* published Duckworth & Co., 1915; see V, i

[39] Stephen Spender asked her how to correct or rewrite a novel refused by the Hogarth Press; she replied: "Scrap it and write something completely different." Spender adds: "When she said *scrap it,* I had a glimpse of the years during which she had destroyed her own failures." Stephen Spender, *World within World,* p. 157.

[40] AWD p. 75 (74)

[41] AWD p. 97 (96)

[42] *Horizon,* June 1941

so quiveringly alive. But, against this, she needs solitude and silence to avoid total destruction.[43] Withdrawal and apparent coldness are the necessary antidote to the heat of self-abandonment; but they are only on the surface. Basically, she does not reject those things and those beings that she has merged into; they have become her very substance. This no doubt explains the criticism of one of her friends, G. W. Rylands: "He says I have no logical power and live and write in an opium dream. And the dream is too often about myself."[44] But that self is limitless; like existence, it includes all the moments of life, and all that they embrace. And this is no abstract theory of personality, derived from some philosophy or other. It is a profound, daily, personal experience which underlies not only long-matured expressions such as *Jacob's Room* or *The Waves*, but is the very fibre of her personality. Witness those passages in the Diary which tell how, at the death of a friend, one's own being rather than the outside world is diminished:

A curious feeling, when a writer like S. B. dies, that one's response is diminished: *Here and Now* won't be lit up by her: it's life lessened. My effusion—what I send out—less porous and radiant—as if the thinking stuff were a web that were fertilised only by other people's (her that is) thinking it too: now lacks life.[45]

The same note is sounded after the death of Lytton Strachey[46] and again after Roger Fry's.[47] We see thus that there is nothing arid about her solitude, for it is thronged with people, and the silence into which she retreats is shot through with dialogues. At times, nevertheless, when baited by critics, or in reaction to a friendly sally like Rylands', she realises the danger of being a recluse:

The dream is too often about myself. To correct this; and to forget one's own sharp absurd little personality, reputation and the rest of it, one should read; see outsiders, think more; write more logically; above all be full of work; and practise anonymity.[48]

Basically, however, she scarcely needed this treatment: if in everyday life she sometimes felt her personality contract into

[43] On V. W.'s need to alternate between solitude and contact with the outside world, see Johnstone, *The Bloomsbury Group*, pp. 142-3.
[44] AWD p. 120 (118)
[45] AWD p. 214 (207)
[46] AWD p. 180 (175)
[47] AWD p. 223 (216)
[48] AWD p. 121 (119)

something "absurd", this was only at minor moments and, above all, not those devoted to her art; moreover, she practised that mental therapy that consists of alternating contact with the outside world and deeply delving into oneself. And should she be blamed for not following literally a prescription which was not quite right for her? Surely she lost nothing by choosing what people she saw, what books she read, by not writing more academically, by not thinking more logically; and we ourselves have lost nothing thereby. Her writings are ample proof that she had the strength to be fully herself—and her Diary reveals the energy and determination she put into developing and exploiting her potentialities.

Whereas in childhood her life had been governed by the alternation between London and Cornwall, we see her, as a young woman, dividing her existence between the human contacts to which she devoted all her sensibility and her intelligence, and the dedicated seclusion in which she worked. No doubt still under her father's influence, and also out of modesty, probity and diffidence, she confined herself to critical essays.[49] It was not until 1908[50] that she was to attempt novel-writing and to start *The Voyage Out*, at which she worked for seven years before publishing it in 1915.

Her marriage to Leonard Woolf in 1912 seems not noticeably to have modified her way of life nor the course of her inner development. Love, although it takes a leading place in her two first novels, appears there less as a total upheaval, a profound revision of values, than as a particular experience in the field of human relations, an important one no doubt but essentially of the same nature as other personal contacts. It would be easy to conclude from this that the real nature of passion was alien to Virginia Woolf. The absence of any evidence to the contrary tempts one to accept this interpretation. However, the word passion should here be taken in a strictly limited sense: the storm of the senses, the absorption of one's whole being by the sexual instinct are things absent from Virginia Woolf's world; perhaps, indeed, she was unfamiliar with them. This hypothesis, though plausible, is far from certain. Her work itself is an ambiguous document, from which one might extract contrary evidence: the exclusion of sexuality from her art might just as well imply that it played so healthy and normal a part in her life as to require no sublimation.

[49] Cf. *infra*, ch. IV
[50] Cf. *infra*, ch. V

Her first reaction to Joyce's *Ulysses* may give some weight to this interpretation, particularly if we note the comment with which she justifies her disappointment and disgust. "But I think if you are anaemic, as Tom [T. S. Eliot] is, there is a glory in blood. Being fairly normal myself I am soon ready for the classics again."[51] None the less, there are certain reservations to be made about this leaning towards "classicism", this normality of temperament. Art is not solely nourished on repressed, perverted or sublimated instincts; it is not only an indirect, but also a direct expression. A certain sensual warmth is surely permissible, short of finding "glory in blood"; but this, too, is admittedly repugnant to Virginia Woolf. Certain aspects of physical life seem too violent for her over-sensitive nature. Thus she confesses: "I don't like the physicalness of having children of one's own. This occurred to me at Rodmell; but I never wrote it down. I can dramatise myself a parent, it is true. And perhaps I have killed the feeling instinctively; or perhaps nature does."[52]

Is this shrinking from motherhood part of that rejection of mere femininity, of passivity, of purely organic and instinctive creation, against which the virile traits of her nature asserted themselves, or is it one aspect of a more general denial of any physical relationship between human beings? I have already pointed out how little place the physical element takes in her pictures of love. The only book[53] in which it may be glimpsed—smuggled in, as it were, behind a screen of satire and fantasy—is *Orlando*. And it was precisely during the writing of *Orlando* that she made the comment just quoted, on December 20, 1927. In the following paragraph, on the same day, we read: "I am still writing the third chapter of *Orlando*"[54]—that third chapter in which truth breaks out to the sound of trumpets, where truth springs naked from its sleep in the shape of Orlando transformed into a woman. True, the subject here is Vita—V. Sackville-West—whose "form combined in one the strength of a man and a woman's grace".[55] But who can boast

---

[51] AWD p. 47 (46)

[52] AWD p. 119 (117)

[53] In *Jacob's Room*, Jacob's experiences are so discreetly treated that they can hardly be referred to in this connection. Cf. the letter she wrote to Lytton Strachey who had deplored the chastity of the heroes of *Night and Day*: V. W. & L. S., *Letters*, p. 84.

[54] AWD p. 119 (117)

[55] *Orlando*, p. 126 (138)

of being able to discern unhesitatingly in a portrait what belongs to the model and what is the painter's? Added to which, if these thoughts lay in the background of *Orlando*, they remained unembodied in words until she watched her sister's children in a play: "The little creatures acting moved my infinitely sentimental throat."[56] This emotion lends pathos to the lines in which Virginia Woolf assesses the two possible ways taken by her sister and herself: to be a mother or to be a writer.

The dilemma had not always appeared to her so clearly. Seven years earlier—in a moment of depression, it is true, that is to say when doubt and weariness seemed to undo her whole being and reduce it to a state of diffuse aspiration—she still put motherhood on the same plane as literary activity, amongst those realizations that might have given a meaning to her life: "I want to appear a success even to myself. Yet I don't get to the bottom of it. It's having no children, living away from friends, failing to write well, spending too much on food, growing old."[57] None the less, now that the die was cast, there was neither envy nor bitterness, far less contempt, for the solution she had rejected; but on the contrary, a sense of sharing, as if her sister had accomplished by proxy what the need for choice had forbidden her:

... (I always measure myself against her and find her much the largest, most humane of the two of us), think of her now with an admiration that has no envy in it; with some trace of the old childish feeling that we were in league together against the world; and how proud I am of her triumphant winning of all our battles; as she takes her way so nonchalantly, modestly, almost anonymously, past the goal, with her children round her.[58]

And in this choice, which made her "cling . . . to [her] one anchor",[59] buffeted by contrary winds in turn, we see Virginia Woolf herself incapable of probing her own deep motivation and of assigning responsibility to her will, or to an instinct which has impelled her in a certain direction, or else to something even more obscure which she calls "nature" and which would include both of these.[60] Faced with this delicate problem, to which the future may perhaps bring a solution, let us for a moment borrow

[56] AWD p. 119 (117)
[57] AWD p. 29 (28)
[58] AWD p. 120 (118)
[59] AWD p. 119 (117)
[60] AWD p. 119 (117). *Supra*, cf. note 52

her own detached wisdom, slightly mocking about the overween-ing and emphatic distinctions made by science, and let us say, as she herself says of Orlando's strange nature: "Let biologists and psychologists determine. . . ."[61]

As an artist, Virginia Stephen undeniably found in Leonard Woolf an ideal companion who, while leaving her complete intellectual liberty, knew how to share in her work, not merely with the sympathy and intelligence that she might have got from the best of friends, but that understanding, that persuasive and encouraging power that are only possible when two lives are as one. As soon as she had finished a book she would give him the manuscript and wait for his opinion, not really as she waited for someone else's opinion, for Lytton Strachey's or Forster's, but as though it emanated from some other chamber of her own mind, a sort of secret court kept in reserve for that first verdict which confirmed her own and was merged with it. Without being entirely reassured by what he said against her own doubts and against out-side criticism, she drew from it an encouragement which, if it did not go right to the depths, none the less left her calmer.[62] It is not my purpose to consider the tenor of these judgments; what interests us here is their tone, their quality, which we recognize by the way Virginia Woolf waited for them and accepted them.[63] The dominant and recurrent impression is that of deliverance. As long as Leonard has not given his opinion, invariably approving and above all encouraging, but subtly qualified and wise, she waits for it in anguish, as a mother waits to be told that her child, whom she has not yet seen, is alive and normal. Finally, these commentaries of her husband's reach far beyond the finished work that had given rise to them: they also refer, we feel, to the slowly matured intentions, the patient labour of which he alone, among her readers, would be aware. All this may be summed up in a formula which is perhaps as trite as marriage itself, but which implies all the strength of marriage too: she trusted him, he trusted her.

If this were all there were to say about their married life, it would be no small thing. Nevertheless we are entitled to assume

[61] *Orlando*, p. 127 (139)
[62] "The first symptoms of *Lighthouse* are unfavourable. . . . Anyhow I feel callous: L.'s opinion keeps me steady; I'm neither one thing nor the other" AWD p. 104 (103)
[63] AWD (JR) p. 47 (45-6), (Mrs D) p. 71 (70), (To the L) p. 103 (102), (O) p. 128 (125-6), (The W) p. 173 (168-9), (The Y) pp. 270-2 (261-3)

that its solid, but seemingly somewhat monochrome texture was lit up by more striking motifs which give it a quite different quality. In a series of reflections made at Rodmell in 1926 this is what we read:

The married relation.—Arnold Bennett says that the horror of marriage lies in its "dailiness". All acuteness of relationship is rubbed away by this. The truth is more like this: life—say 4 days out of 7,—becomes automatic; but on the 5th day a bead of sensation (between husband and wife) forms which is all the fuller and more sensitive because of the automatic customary unconscious days on either side. That is to say the year is marked by moments of great intensity. Hardy's "moments of vision". How can a relationship endure for any length of time except under these conditions?[64]

If this analysis destroys the myth of continuity and asserts the heart's intermittences, it none the less proclaims, without romanticism but firmly and with conviction, a certain richness and a certain intensity in her conjugal life.

Freed from the repressive influence of her father, after an interlude during which she became aware of herself and, so to speak, took her bearings at that cross-roads where one's destiny is mysteriously decided, Virginia Stephen, by becoming Virginia Woolf, escaped from solitude without renouncing independence, satisfied her sensibility and her intelligence, and asserted herself while dedicating herself to art. What strikes one most about this marriage is its balance. But is this not a feature of many aspects of Virginia Woolf's life and of her being?—the quest for balance, not as flatness or stagnation but as the crest where two opposite slopes meet.

Her life, henceforward inscribed within a solid framework, was now to assume a rhythm that lasted to its end. Sheltered from material cares, Virginia Woolf was able to dedicate herself to her vocation as writer without having to try and make a profit from it. This perfect independence as regards the public, which nothing, not even success, could affect, is a factor that must not be forgotten. No consideration alien to that aesthetic quest which was the central motive not only of her activity but of her life, was ever to make her deviate from the goal she had set herself. Even if the attraction of financial reward accounts for a considerable part of her critical writing, she would never consent to any limitation

[64] AWD p. 98 (96-7)

of her freedom.[65] At most, one can say that the economic value of such an activity led her from time to time to devote herself to it, outside her major work and with a certain reluctance.[66] Not that the Woolfs, particularly in the earlier years, had as much money as they would have liked to spend. In 1920 Virginia Woolf notes: "Nessa's children grow up, and I can't have them in to tea, or go to the Zoo. Pocket money doesn't allow of much."[67] Her books did not sell widely. It was only with *Mrs. Dalloway*[68] and the two *Common Readers*[69] that she began to consider them in terms of financial success. True, the Woolfs lived comfortably, had a flat in London[70] and a house in the country for week-ends and holidays.[71] They went to France for several weeks in 1925 and 1928. However, it was only with the success of *To the Lighthouse* (which enabled them to buy a car[72]) and *Orlando*, that the question of money—of pocket money at all events—ceased to be something at the back of her mind and became a matter of accountancy. "When we made up our 6 months accounts, we found I had made about £3,020 last year—the salary of a civil servant: a surprise to me, who was content with £200 for so many years."[73] In the same year the Hogarth Press, founded in 1917, entered an era of real prosperity; Virginia, feeling richer than she had ever been, bought herself a pair of earrings![74]

These gifts of fortune, this affluent Bohemianism proved favourable circumstances, but not wholly decisive ones. Without a doubt they provided the social elements in Virginia Woolf's work, but one can scarcely imagine that different material conditions, even far harsher ones, would have altered its substance or modified its texture. The mechanical relations between individuals, such as

---

[65] Cf. AWD pp. 26 (25), 41 (40), 74 (73), 100 (99)

[66] "I write every day about something and have deliberately set apart a few weeks to money-making, so that I may put £50 in each of our pockets by September. This will be the first money of my own since I married", AWD p. 109 (108).

[67] AWD p. 29 (28)

[68] AWD p. 71 (70)

[69] AWD pp. 78 (77), 83 (81)

[70] Hogarth House, Richmond till 1924, then 52 Tavistock Square, London; W.C. 1

[71] Asheham House near Lewes, Sussex, till 1919, then Monks House, Rodmell, Sussex

[72] AWD pp. 124 (121-2), 125 (123-4) (Mar. 18, April 17, 1928)

[73] AWD, Jan. 26, 1930, p. 152 (149). Cf. also AWD pp. 140 (137), 126 (124), 109 (108).

[74] AWD p. 147 (144)

are imposed by the social structure, dominated by concepts of class and wealth, although she is aware of these, are only on the surface, merely a veneer, even if that veneer may grow so hard and thick as to crush the being within and deny it a life of its own. Problems at that level are not her problem: as an artist, she refuses to consider them as within her competence, just as she refuses to handle ideas—in her novels, of course.[75] Instinctively at first, although still imprisoned within the traditional forms of the novel, she strives to reach to the very core of a human being, to that nucleus of pure reaction where the self and the non-self, whatever they may be, interact, merging into one another or asserting differentiation. Then, more and more clearly, with an increasingly lucid effort of will, she devotes her life to this twofold problem, the apprehension of that reality and the expression of it—a twofold problem admitting only one solution, the work of art.

I shall endeavour, still in the light of the Diary, to retrace the course of this quest.

Although her apprentice years are not without interest, it seems far more profitable—particularly since Virginia Woolf has told us nothing about the composition of her earliest books—to observe her when her individual genius had begun to make itself felt, and she had acquired, if not the full mastery of her craft, at any rate a clear consciousness of her purpose and potentialities. The youthful achievements of talent and even, sometimes, of genius are revealing only in retrospect, they are interesting historically, but often teach us less than is supposed, since we attribute far more to them than they actually provide.

The day after her thirty-eighth birthday, January 26, 1920, when she had already published *Kew Gardens*, *The Mark on the Wall* and her first two novels, and when *An Unwritten Novel* was already written, Virginia Woolf takes her bearings in her Diary. She has already, in the earlier notebooks, spoken of her books, confronted her own judgments with those of her friends or of the critics, told of her doubts and also of her self-confidence. But, in this page that must be quoted in full, she goes beyond the impression of the moment to analyse her own inner continuity, the impetus that is carrying her on and the direction in which she is moving:

[75] Cf. criticism of Huxley's *Point Counterpoint*, AWD pp. 238-9 (230)

The day after my birthday; in fact I'm 38, well, I've no doubt I'm a great deal happier than I was at 28; and happier today than I was yesterday having this afternoon arrived at some idea of a new form for a new novel. Suppose one thing should open out of another—as in an unwritten novel—only not for 10 pages but 200 or so—doesn't that give the looseness and lightness I want; doesn't that get closer and yet keep form and speed, and enclose everything, everything? My doubt is how far it will enclose the human heart—Am I sufficiently mistress of my dialogue to net it there? For I figure that the approach will be entirely different this time: no scaffolding: scarcely a brick to be seen; all crepuscular, but the heart, the passion, humour, everything as bright as fire in the mist. Then I'll find room for so much—a gaiety—an inconsequence—a light spirited stepping at my sweet will. Whether I'm sufficiently mistress of things—that's the doubt; but conceive (?) *Mark on the Wall*, *K.G.* and *Unwritten Novel* taking hands and dancing in unity. What the unity shall be I have yet to discover; the theme is a blank to me; but I see immense possibilities in the form I hit upon more or less by chance two weeks ago. I suppose the danger is the damned egotistical self; which ruins Joyce and Richardson to my mind: is one pliant and rich enough to provide a wall for the book from oneself without its becoming, as in Joyce and Richardson, narrowing and restricting? My hope is that I've learnt my business sufficiently now to provide all sorts of entertainments. Anyhow, I must still grope and experiment but this afternoon I had a gleam of light. Indeed, I think from the ease with which I'm developing the unwritten novel there must be a path for me there.[76]

I shall examine later[77] the theories on the technique of the novel which are implicit or directly expressed in this passage: what concerns us here is the intellectual process described. Virginia Woolf's thought is based on deep foundations. Beneath the level of consciousness, a stream of meditation, inarticulate but powerfully directed by dominating preoccupations, seems to proceed unremittingly, sheltered from all surface movements and distractions. It is at this level that invention is to be sought. The whole of the mind's activity is polarized round the vacuum created by an unsolved problem; then suddenly an idea is trapped there, the vacuum is filled, the prey is released and sent up into the light of consciousness. This unexpected upsurge is a form of inspiration, but one strictly directed; chance plays no part in it save through the circumstances of time and place. Even the matter, the content, is determined by the rulings of rational thought, which has passed on its orders to the subconscious and waits for this to play its part in due course. This process, which we can reconstruct from many

[76] AWD p. 23 (22)   [77] Cf. ch. V

passages in the Diary, accounts for one of the essential aspects of Virginia Woolf's originality: the combination of a spontaneity which seems entirely derived from feeling, and a lucid determination which seems dominated by pure intelligence. "Seems", I said: and this double illusion explains how certain critics have condemned her for renouncing the clear paths of rational thinking,[78] while others accuse her of excessive self-consciousness and artifice.[79] In reality the fusion of the two antagonistic elements is achieved below the level of consciousness; it is in the depths of the mind that, inextricably inter-mingled, they proceed together to assimilate experience and to elaborate what is, for Virginia Woolf, an indivisible substance—thought. In a word, it might be said that her intelligence informs her sensibility and that her sensibility embodies her intelligence.

The obscurity of the word "form" used by Virginia Woolf in the passage just quoted is due no doubt to this twofold nature of her inspiration. In its creative potentiality, this entity suggests Plato's Ideas, Pythagoras's numbers, Spinoza's *Natura naturans* and even more, an aspect of Bergson's *élan vital*. Two years later, when discussing Percy Lubbock's *Craft of Fiction*,[80] she was to emphasize the vague and metaphorical character of the term. But the substitute she was to propose seems scarcely more satisfactory: "Is there not something beyond emotion, something which though it is inspired by emotion, tranquillises it, orders it, composes it?—that which Mr Lubbock calls form, which, for simplicity's sake, we will call art?"[81]

The definition here sketched out, however, envisages form as comprising all the elements, all the forces which, applied to emotion—the material of the novel[82]—transform it, achieve a kind of transmutation of reality. Considered thus, form is the active principle of creation; as for the modalities of creation, they remain obscure, and only its results can be characterized: flexibility, lightness, completeness, absence of scaffolding, a misty crepuscular atmosphere shot through with fire.

No doubt one may wonder what is the practical use, for the writer, of so elusive a vision. It cannot be resolved into principles,

---

[78] Cf. Gabriel Marcel   [79] Cf. William Troy
[80] "On Re-reading Novels", *TLS*, July 20, 1922, pp. 465-6; in *The Moment*, esp. pp. 127-32 (157-62)
[81] The M p. 131 (161)
[82] Cf. The M p. 131 (161): "Emotion is our material . . ."

THE SELF, LIFE AND ARTISTIC CREATION

far less into precepts. It remains a metaphor, and can only be developed metaphorically.[83] But behind this metaphor we feel that the urge to write—of which all true writers have spoken—is felt as a void to be filled, a hunger to be assuaged. Its urgent demands are mysterious, yet precise: if the artist cannot tell exactly how the void is to be filled, he is aware, none the less, of qualities having a twofold power of rejection and acceptance, which thus trace out the limits of his quest and assign directions to his effort.

With the genesis of *The Waves*, the Diary enables us to follow all the stages—or more exactly all the moments, for their succession, far from constituting a normal progression, marks out a course where retrogression alternates with forward leaps—which the page just quoted about her premonitions of *Jacob's Room* summed up in a single analysis.

On September 30, 1926,[84] into the blankness induced by profound depression there creeps the feeling of a presence, of something which, in her deep solitude, Virginia Woolf recognizes as distinct from herself, "something in the universe that one's left with"—something glimpsed on the horizon which seems to awaken a sense of existence. She notes this "curious state of mind" and hazards "the guess that it may be the impulse behind another book".[85] Later, in October 1929, she adds a note: "Perhaps *The Waves* or *Moths*" (the first title of *The Waves*). Then the vision fades, the feeling passes off, carrying its secret like Proust's fugitive memory falling back into the shadows of the subconscious. Preoccupied by *To the Lighthouse*, which she was finishing in January 1927, she writes: "I have no new book",[86] but five weeks later, on February 21st, a form emerges: "Why not invent a new kind of play".[87] As with *Jacob's Room*, it is only a complex pattern of spaces to be filled in:

Woman thinks . . .
He does.
Organ plays.

[83] Cf. The M pp. 128-9 (158): "We do not raise the question in order to stickle for accuracy where most words are provisional, many metaphorical, and some on trial for the first time."
[84] AWD p. 101 (100)
[85] AWD p. 102 (100)
[86] AWD p. 103 (102)
[87] AWD p. 104 (103); cf. *infra*, ch. v, p. 281.

She writes.
They say:
She sings.
Night speaks
They miss
I think it must be something on this line—though I can't now see what. Away from facts; free; yet concentrated; prose yet poetry; a novel and a play.[88]

This clearly implies that a whole way of writing has to be invented too. The concept of a literary genre occurs to one, but this is too narrow, too specialized, defining only aesthetic, formal qualities, whereas here, as with *Jacob's Room*, we feel that matter is inseparable from form; indeed, we feel that the inward vision is full of a reality, seeking a body in which to incarnate itself: and that this body, this visible form cannot be conceived independently of it. A few lines written some ten days before this passage bear witness to this inseparableness of expression and content, and at the same time to the subterranean crystallization around the initial nucleus—that fleeting vision of September 30th. Reading a piece of fluent prose had awakened in Virginia Woolf her dormant antagonism. She is not yet conscious of her own purpose, even in the form of an aspiration, and yet it contradicts this way of expression, denies its validity: "The method of writing smooth narration can't be right; things don't happen in one's mind like that."[89] Meanwhile, however, she is still haunted by the lure of story-telling, perhaps influenced by the disfavour which seems to have greeted *To the Lighthouse*; and suddenly, the project of a novel-play having been discarded or postponed, the temptation takes precise form:

It struck me, vaguely, that I might write a Defoe narrative for fun. Suddenly between twelve and one I conceived a whole fantasy to be called "The Jessamy Brides"—why, I wonder?[90]

This is the first glimpse of *Orlando*, with some of its principal themes and above all its tone: mockery, satire and unbridled fantasy.[91] But Virginia Woolf is well aware that this is merely a

[88] AWD p. 104 (103)

[89] AWD p. 104 (103)

[90] AWD p. 105 (104). The title may have been suggested by *The History of Jemmy and Jenny Jessamy*, a novel published in 1753 by Mrs Eliza Haywood. Under the title "A Scribbling Dame", Virginia Woolf reviewed *The Life and Romances of Mrs Eliza Heywood* by George Frisbie Whicher (*TLS*, 17/2/1916).

[91] AWD p. 105 (104): "Satire is to be the main note—satire and wildness. . . . Everything mocked."

diversion, an escapade, a yielding to her facility, the acceptance of one side of herself and of her potentialities which is only her lightest and most superficial aspect. Carried away on this downward slope, she yet feels the pull of that other side of herself, her "ardour and lust of creation",[92] that other slope which, as Gide said, is always an uphill one. This fantasy provides her with a sort of holiday: "I think this will be great fun to write; and it will rest my head before starting the very serious, mystical poetical work which I want to come next."[93] And while feeling the need for such relaxation, she only half believes in it, so potent is her urge to realise an ideal, even at this uncertain stage when the ideal has not yet matured enough to dominate her exclusively. "I suppose I might dash off a page or two now and then by way of experiment. And it is possible that the idea will evaporate."[94] And she concludes with a striking description of the chaotic spontaneity, the flash-of-lightning character of those moments of vision that gave rise to her books:

Anyhow this records the odd horrid unexpected way in which these things suddenly create themselves—one thing on top of another in about an hour. So I made up *Jacob's Room* looking at the fire at Hogarth House; so I made up the *Lighthouse* one afternoon in the Square here.[94]

Let us leave for the moment *The Jessamy Brides*—alias *Orlando*—which may indeed have evaporated (which was, in fact, eclipsed in its turn by the play-novel, as it had for a brief moment eclipsed this) and follow the progress of her inspiration, the way its form grows richer, more precise and more full of matter each time it reappears. After lying dormant for three months—in a slumber lit up by the growing success of *To the Lighthouse*, as by the glow of dawn—the ghost of the book re-emerges, clearer and more substantial. Perhaps, too, the book had recovered its vigour and its urgency during the few weeks' enforced rest due to the writer's illness, which provided the relaxation and fresh spirits she had hoped to get from *The Jessamy Brides*. At all events, we meet it again, one lonely evening, and we recognize under its new garb the outline sketched on February 21st:

---

[92] AWD p. 105 (104). "And I shall be off again, feeling that extraordinary exhilaration, that ardour and lust of creation."
[93] AWD p. 105 (104)
[94] AWD p. 106 (105)

Slowly ideas began trickling in; and then suddenly I rhapsodized ...
and told over the story of the Moths, which I think I will write very
quickly, perhaps in between chapters of that long impending book on
fiction. Now the Moths will I think fill out the skeleton which I dashed
in here; the play-poem idea; the idea of some continuous stream, not
solely of human thought, but of the ship, the night etc., all flowing
together: intersected by the arrival of the bright moths. A man and a
woman are to be sitting at table talking. Or shall they remain silent?
It is to be a love story; she is finally to let the last great moth in. The
contrasts might be something of this sort; she might talk, or think,
about the age of the earth; the death of humanity; then the moths keep
on coming. Perhaps the man could be left absolutely dim. France:
hear the sea; at night; a garden under the window. But it needs
ripening. I do a little work on it in the evening when the gramophone
is playing late Beethoven sonatas. (The windows fidget at their
fastenings as if we were at sea.)[95]

I have quoted the whole passage—including the final parenthesis which may appear insignificant—since it marvellously
completes the one quoted earlier,[96] analysing the first suggestion
of *Jacob's Room.* Whereas there only the form was apprehended,
the theme being left a blank (as indeed was the case with the
original concept of *The Moths* on February 21st[97]), here we see the
form (in Virginia Woolf's sense) gaining precision while, at the
same time, acquiring fragments of content. On the one hand the
idea of a continuous stream carrying along not only the human
element but also objects, and whose movement is made more
perceptible by the interruptions which provide contrast and
rhythm, and on the other hand the protagonists: a woman, a man;
their relationship: love; an element of symbolic synthesis, combining form and matter, the rhythm and the characters: the
moths; finally, places and moments.

There are other things here which shed light on the life of her
mind, its oscillation between effort and facility, the closeness of
sensibility to thought. Weary of *To the Lighthouse*, she had almost
lost interest in it, and she yearned for an easy book: the idea of *The
Jessamy Brides* had taken shape from this longing. Now, encouraged
by success and rested after her illness, she sets aside the easy
spontaneous narrative, to attempt a deeper, more complex work:
but she retains her nostalgic longing for swift writing. She works a

---

[95] AWD p. 108 (107)
[96] Cf. *supra*, p. 73
[97] Cf. *supra*, p. 75

little in the evening, but this is, as it were, extrinsic to her day's work and to herself. Actually, she does not really begin this book, which has not acquired the maturity, the expansive force which would bring it forth as quickly as she had hoped. Finally, we see here the theme of the moths influenced and altered by that of the sea—internally and externally at once; the sound of the sea, which is merely part of the setting for the book, heard in a garden at night, and at the same time the feeling of being at sea which strikes her consciousness with each gust of wind against the windows. And who knows whether from this double sequence of imaginary waves, by some alchemical process affecting the whole of her being, the harmonies of Beethoven did not conjure up the rhythm of *The Waves*?[98]

Meanwhile, however, the pages scribbled of an evening remain a shadow-play. Summer passes, and in September we glimpse the reappearance, not of *The Moths*, but of the "Defoe narrative": *Jessamy Brides* at first, now titleless but bringing an unexpected element of personal experience into the historical fantasy. She thinks of writing the memoirs of her contemporaries. Vita becomes a young nobleman called Orlando, and around her are grouped all Virginia's friends.[99] For the time being all this is kept for the Diary; but a fortnight later the bubble has formed and floated off: *Orlando* is born. The manipulation of Time hinted at by the conjunction of "memoirs" and "one's own times" is completed by stretching the hero's biography over four centuries, and the major joke of the change of sex is invented.[100] Delighted and amused, Virginia Woolf allows herself a week "for a treat" to play at this masquerade. But she has reckoned without the charm and high spirits of Orlando, the fantastic Elizabethan setting, and above all the necessity, possibly deeper than she chose to admit to herself, of complete relaxation, the importance of that neglected side of herself, the mischievous, caustic, undisciplined side, which dreamed only of freedom and fancy and which had suggested that *The Moths* might be written "very quickly". The week's holiday stretches out into a fortnight: she is playing truant. She is so happy that she throws all her other projects overboard:

[98] It may be of interest to note that in his late sonatas Beethoven tends towards a fugal style which may have affected V. W. and indirectly influenced her search for a structure for her novel.

[99] AWD p. 114 (112)

[100] AWD p. 116 (114-5)

I walk making up phrases; sit, contriving scenes; am in short in the thick of the greatest rapture known to me; from which I have kept myself since last February, or earlier. . . . The relief of turning my mind that way was such that I felt happier than for months; as if put in the sun, or laid on a cushion; and after two days entirely gave up my time chart and abandoned myself to the pure delight of this farce; which I enjoy as much as I've ever enjoyed anything.[101]

This is at the end of October 1927. A month later, Virginia Woolf talks of finishing her book by the beginning of January[102]; in fact, she was not to write THE END until March, on the eve of her departure for France.[103] But she had accurately assessed her reserves of enthusiasm, qualitatively as well as quantitatively.[104]

Re-reading the work, correcting the manuscript and then the proofs had the usual effect: weariness, loss of interest verging on disgust; all accompanied by the detachment and objectivity that allowed her critical spirit free play. She speaks harshly of what seems now merely an extravaganza. However, despite outbursts of petulance, her clearsightedness prevails, and soon after the publication of *Orlando* she admits its genuineness, and that it sprang from an essential aspect of her being:

Orlando was the outcome of a perfectly definite, indeed overmastering, impulse. I want fun. I want fantasy. I want (and this was serious) to give things their caricature value. And still this mood hangs about me. . . . The vein is deep in me—at least sparkling, urgent.[105]

Yet, driven by a kind of asceticism or will to power—or maybe both at once—to seek the best in herself unremittingly, and to maintain the highest degree of tension, she cannot give up a sense of hierarchy, an order of values for her own tendencies, even when these are complementary:

My notion is that there are offices to be discharged by talent for the relief of genius: meaning that one has the play side; the gift when it is mere gift, unapplied gift; and the gift when it is serious, going to business. And one relieves the other.[106]

[101] AWD p. 117 (115). Cf. a similar phenomenon in 1933: "Ah but my writing *Flush* has been gradually shoved out, as by a cuckoo born in the nest, by *The Pargiters* (AWD p. 136 (187))

[102] AWD p. 118 (116)

[103] AWD p. 124 (122)

[104] ". . . [the fun] was so tremendously lively all October, November and December", AWD p. 123 (121)

[105] AWD p. 136 (134)

[106] AWD p. 136 (134)

This relieving of genius by talent, this alternation between spontaneous and tense writing is a therapeutic necessity for Virginia Woolf. But she seems to accept it reluctantly. This free, "unapplied" gift seems to her somewhat wasteful. Just as she will accept no compromise with taste, fashion, critics or the editors of periodicals, she dislikes any compromise even with her own nature. She contrasts the "play side" with the "uncompromising side" of herself [107] and sets the latter far higher. And yet, with a realism devoid of illusion or of complacency, with an astonishing mixture of humility and pride, of submission to the contradictory tendencies that divide her and of unshakable determination to exact and obtain the best from them, she reaches a conclusion which defines both her artist's temperament and the upward dialectic movement that characterises her work:

I rather think the upshot will be books that relieve other books: a variety of styles and subjects: for after all, that is my temperament, I think, to be very little persuaded of the truth of anything—what I say, what people say—always to follow, blindly, instinctively with a sense of leaping over a precipice—the call of—the call of—now, if I write *The Moths* I must come to terms with these mystical feelings.[108]

Basically, underlying judgment and will, the thing that dominates and calls forth even the maturest, most necessary book is an instinctive impulse; that impulse represents the judgment and the will of the moment, it is at the centre of the artist's being and it is the core of his book. We have seen how the wayward dance of *Orlando* mingled at first with the flight of the Moths, then drove them back into their night. But even when it had passed by and seemed forgotten, it left in its wake a gleam and a turbulence that kept them at a distance. There is something impersonal and cold in that brief allusion to "something abstract, poetic next time—I don't know".[109] We can hardly recognize here the novel-play or the play-poem envisaged in the previous spring. Other projects, critical and biographical, seem infinitely more urgent. It is not until two and a half months later (August 12, 1928) that something emerges which takes the colour of a precise wish: "All this criticism however may well be dislodged by the desire to write a story. *The Moths* hovers somewhere at the back of my brain."[110]

[107] AWD p. 137 (134)
[108] AWD p. 137 (134)
[109] AWD p. 128 (126)
[110] AWD p. 130 (128)

Five more weeks pass without the moths issuing from their hiding place to make their presence imperatively felt. Virginia Woolf still does not know when she will begin this book nor what it will be like.[111] Then five more weeks again before she makes any mention of the "abstract mystical eyeless book".[112] However, she ruminates over it in the evening, listening to records, just as she had done a year ago before the intrusion of *Orlando*: this is hardly the book as yet, but only a distant music, shadowy dream-figures with which she plays. The book, she feels, is still elusive, and she delays pursuing it.

As for my next book, I am going to hold myself from writing till I have it impending in me: grown heavy in my mind like a ripe pear; pendant, gravid, asking to be cut or it will fall. *The Moths* still haunts me, coming, as they always do, unbidden, between tea and dinner, while L. plays the gramophone. I shape a page or two; and make myself stop. Indeed I am up against some difficulties.[113]

The chief difficulty is how to realize the synthesis which she had already envisaged when the idea of the book first occurred to her,[114] but it is now enhanced by the way her project has developed. In the long analysis that follows to which I shall return when studying her technique,[115] we find the same fertile core from which everything else irradiates: "This appalling narrative business of the realist: getting on from lunch to dinner: it is false, unreal, merely conventional."[116] She is "up against" these prison walls; within these bounds the book accumulates its expansive force which, for several months more, remains at the stage of mere pressure against the obstacle of inadequate technique.[117] Nevertheless she makes considerable progress. By dint of playing with these shadows, of trying to halt them and catch them, casually, in her evening ruminations at first, then with greater determination in her morning writing,[118] Virginia Woolf eventually tames them. As they circle round, they become more than pure movement, more than pure

---

[111] "And when, I wonder, shall I begin *The Moths*? . . . Nor have I any notion what it is to be like . . .", AWD p. 133 (131).

[112] AWD p. 137 (134)

[113] AWD p. 138 (136)

[114] Cf. *supra*, p. 76

[115] Cf. *infra*, ch. V

[116] AWD p. 139 (136)

[117] "I feel no great impulse; no fever; only a great pressure of difficulty" (AWD p. 142 (139), May 28, 1929).

[118] "Every morning I write a little sketch, to amuse myself", AWD p. 142 (139)

potential; we recognize objects, groups (May 28th), then characters (June 23rd). The beginning is almost sketched out; the idea of the auditory, or rather cosmic, theme of the waves appears, joined to the visual and living theme of the moths.[119] And above all, even more important than the clarification of its lines and the enrichment of its material, is the appearance of a new feeling that accompanies each thought about this book: "Everything becomes green and vivified in me when I begin to think of *The Moths*".[120] It is like the termination of an agreement, the sign of some impending event, as the delight in writing surges up before its cause (a weightier thing, still delayed). And yet two months, July and August, elapse before Virginia Woolf ventures on a first start: September 10, 1929, still timid—so timid that on the 24th she begins again from the beginning.[121] In early October the work has definitely made a start. She feels neither the zest nor the pleasure she had expected,[122] nor a haunting presence as with *To the Lighthouse* or *Orlando*[123]; yet, though "this book is a very queer business",[124] it progresses unswerving from its original course[125] and on April 29, 1930, Virginia Woolf steps lightheartedly down Southampton Row: *The Waves* is finished.[126]

This first version—it cannot be called a first draft, for so many of its pages had been written so many times already!—represents seven months of work, following three years of maturation during which *Orlando* and *A Room of One's Own* were written and published. These seven months represent, too, the best part of creation, the most natural phase, when the writer's various faculties all function in a harmony which produces a feeling of plenitude and

[119] ". . . *Waves* or *Moths* or whatever it is to be called . . .", AWD p. 146 (143). By the end of September she realizes that *Moths* is the wrong title (cf. note 121), but only a month later she seems to have adopted the eventual title: "I think it is to be waves . . .", AWD p. 148 (145)

[120] AWD p. 144 (141)

[121] "Yesterday morning I made another start on *The Moths*, but that won't be its title", AWD p. 146 (143).

[122] "I'm not writing with gusto or pleasure . . .", AWD p. 146 (143).

[123] "I don't have it in my head all day like the *Lighthouse* and *Orlando*." AWD p. 151

[124] AWD p. 156 (153)

[125] "I think I have kept stoically to the original conception", AWD p. 157 (154) "And I think I have kept starkly and ascetically to the plan", AWD p. 158 (155).

[126] "I have just finished . . . the last sentence of *The Waves*. . . . And I think to myself as I walk down Southampton Row, 'And I have given you a new book'", AWD p. 158 (155).

achievement. The sensibility provides the material which the intelligence organizes. For a time they move at the same rhythm, maintaining the unity of the inner life. The tension which divides them and unites them generates movement rather than dis-equilibrium; writing is the immediate product of the whole being, and the writer, realizing herself therein in entirety, finds joy. Moments such as these enabled Virginia Woolf to declare how essential her art was to her.[127]

But this first version is still an unfinished product: its surface betrays now the roughness of the material, now the marks of the tool, and an unevenness due to uncertain planning; we see where her will or her inspiration have flagged, and where they have been violently asserted. At this point we must remember that Virginia Woolf learnt her writer's craft in criticism, and acquired there a perfectionism which is practised in her work all the more uncom-promisingly because of the precision with which she envisaged her goal.

That same April 29, 1930, she notes: "I have never written a book so full of holes and patches; that will need re-building, yes, not only re-modelling."[128] This comment, indeed, only repeats an impression that seems to have haunted her all through the period of composition: "my writing book is like a lunatic's dream."[129] "It is a litter of fragments so far . . .,"[130] ". . . it goes by fits and starts."[131] And from the very beginning, more than with any other of her books, she foresees the need for thorough reshaping. She counts on a sudden illumination: "It might come in a flash, on re-reading—some solvent",[132] but feels confident and doubtful in turns. "What I fear is that the re-writing will have to be so drastic that I may entirely muddle it somehow."[133] And when, a week from the end, she envisages a fresh period of effort whose immin-

---

[127] Cf. *supra*, pp. 59-60
[128] AWD p. 158 (155)
[129] AWD p. 151 (147)
[130] AWD p. 154 (151)
[131] AWD p. 157 (153)
[132] AWD p. 149 (146). Cf. also p. 151 (147)
[133] AWD p. 157 (154). Cf. also AWD p. 232 (225), an explicit expression of this alternation with reference to *The Years*: "A note; despair at the badness of the book: can't think how I ever could write such stuff—and with such excitement: that's yesterday: today I think it good again—A note, by way of advising other Virginias with other books that this is the way of the thing: up down up down—and Lord knows the truth."

ence betrays all its aridity, anticipated weariness seems to prevail over possible joy: "and then back again to this hideous shaping and moulding. There may be some joys in it all the same."[134]

Usually, when the first version was finished, Virginia Woolf allowed herself a space of rest before resuming her work; time to stand back a little, to shake off the spell, to recover a certain freshness of apprehension. She had originally planned to make such a break between the first and the second versions of *The Waves*.[135] But this time the first sketch has not exhausted the impetus of the book. She has at the same time disregarded so many difficulties and come up against so many problems that even as she frees her mind of its content she burdens it with fresh preoccupations:

... can't read and can't write and can't think. The truth is, of course, I want to be back at *The Waves*. Yes that is the truth. Unlike all my other books in every way, it is unlike them in this, that I begin to re-write it, or conceive it again with ardour, directly I have done. I begin to see what I had in my mind; and want to begin cutting out masses of irrelevance and clearing, sharpening and making the good phrases shine. One wave after another. No room.[136]

Her ardour, though derived from an inward impulse, is sustained by an effort of will. Nearly four months of tension and struggle to bring the expression to coincide with the vision bring Virginia Woolf to the point of exhaustion.[137] With an irony that does not preclude pathos, she calls those attacks of depression, some of which verged on mental breakdown, "these curious intervals in life" and adds: "I've had many—[they] are the most fruitful artistically—one becomes fertilized—think of my madness at Hogarth—and all the little illnesses."[138] It may seem a pity that those nearest her should have drawn a discreet veil over these moments, as though they were liable to diminish her stature. Surely they represent a vitally important experience, the knowledge of which would bring us closer to her vision of the world and,

[134] AWD p. 158 (154)

[135] "... no holiday, no interval if possible, till it is done. Then rest. Then re-write", AWD p. 152 (149).

[136] AWD p. 159 (155-6), May 1, 1930

[137] Cf. AWD pp. 159-60 (156-7), Monday, Sept. 8, 1930. Cf. also the two months' attack resulting from strain of writing the fourth version of *The Years*: "... after two months dismal and worse, almost catastrophic illness—never been so near the precipice to my own feeling since 1913—I'm again on top", AWD p. 268 (259). This attack was probably followed by a four months' relapse after ten days' work on proofs. Cf. *infra*, ch. V, p. 309.

[138] AWD p. 146 (143)

simultaneously, to the sources of her art. The precariousness of her inward stability is an essential feature of Virginia Woolf's personality, and to evaluate it, to see it in its right proportions, we need not only to note its waverings but, by contrast with its moments of strength, to define those moments at which it breaks down. All the bright side of her which, in the present state of our knowledge, is based upon a zone of darkness would acquire, if that other zone were illuminated, its true relief and its relative significance. Her impassive will-power would be seen as a defence mechanism; that arrogant determination to plan the future according to a strict time-table of projects[139] as a counter-charm to exorcise the uncertainties of the morrow and the stealthy thefts of time; the doggedness with which she worked, her obsession with what she was creating, would appear not as a restriction of her being but as the firm path, the "little strip of pavement"[140] that one must keep to in order to avoid the quagmires that lie in wait amid the mists of nonchalance and reverie.[141] And also, maybe, we might discover that truth that haunted Virginia Woolf and that she strove to express, those basic relations between the self and the non-self, between sensation and object, at the limits of consciousness and the unconscious, the dialogue between life and death in that timeless duration that makes the instant coincident with eternity. All these points that critics, quoting Bergson[142] or Hume,[143] approach by the open, direct paths of philosophy, which are not those of Virginia Woolf, might more profitably be reached by the path she herself followed, a dark and painful path in which she was in danger of being irretrievably lost.

About these descents into the abyss, which only represent the extreme point in that rhythmic oscillation that carried her constantly from enthusiasm to melancholy, from self-confidence to self-mistrust, we know but little. Barely, here and there, a sentence or two which show her surfacing again, "signalise my return to life".[144] Amongst the most revealing are those that refer to that

---

[139] Cf. AWD pp. 48-9 (46-7), 53 (51), 166 (162), 236 (228), 275 (265)

[140] AWD p. 29 (27)

[141] Cf. AWD p. 143 (140): "And so I pitched into my great lake of melancholy. . . . The only way I keep afloat is by working. A note for the summer—I must take more work than I can possibly get done."

[142] F. Delattre.

[143] Chastaing.

[144] AWD p. 159 (156)

attack of depression in 1925 which, coming between *Mrs Dalloway* and *To the Lighthouse*, was as it were the price paid for the one, the fecundation of the other:

... [I] have lain about here, in that odd amphibious life of headache, for a fortnight. This has rammed a big hole in my 8 weeks which were to be stuffed so full. Never mind. Arrange whatever pieces come your way. Never be unseated by the shying of that undependable brute, life, hag-ridden as she is by my own queer, difficult, nervous system. Even at 43 I don't know its workings, for I was saying to myself, all the summer, "I'm quite adamant now. I can go through a tussle of emotions peaceably that two years ago, even, would have raked me raw".[145]

A week later she had still not emerged:

I am writing this partly to test my poor bunch of nerves at the back of my neck—will they hold or give again, as they have done so often?—for I'm amphibious still, in bed and out of it; partly to glut my itch ("glut" an "itch"!) for writing. It is the great solace and scourge.[146]

Note the recurrence of the word "amphibious": beyond the two meanings it owes to its context it conveys obscurely both the idea of dissociation or duality, and the image of submarine explorations into zones forbidden to ordinary organisms. Apart from this, the lines are sufficiently charged with struggle and drama to speak for themselves; they fully justify the opinion of J. J. Mayoux, who in this connection as in many others regrets the cuts made in the Diary:

How can we fail to understand that the categories of health or insanity are not the important point, that Virginia Woolf's "absences" were the cruel price she had to pay with her body, her nerves, her mental balance, for that intensity which is what matters to us, the significant element, the thing that has gone into her work.[147]

The following summer (1926) a small paragraph entitled "Returning health", which refers no doubt to the "nervous breakdown in miniature" analysed a little earlier in the same set of notes, throws light on the "artistic fruitfulness" of those "curious intervals of existence":[148]

[145] AWD p. 82 (80)
[146] AWD p. 82 (81)
[147] Letter, 24/7/54
[148] AWD p. 95 (94)

Returning health.—This is shown by the power to make images; the suggestive power of every sight and word is enormously increased. Shakespeare must have had this to an extent which makes my normal state the state of a person blind, deaf, dumb, stone-stockish and fish-blooded. And I have it compared with poor Mrs. Bartholomew almost to the extent that Shakespeare has it compared with me.[149]

This hypertrophied sensitivity, which no longer reacts according to the normal and pragmatic ways of perception but is dispersed lyrically, so to speak, in the adjacent realm of imagination, in limitless reverberations of sound, colour and form: is not this the very world of *The Waves*? There can be no doubt that it was in these moments of extreme sensitiveness that she discovered it. They comprise the unique experience which she shares with no other writer. To try to understand her without referring to this would be as illusory as to approach Novalis without taking account of his madness, or Poe without mentioning opium or dipsomania.[150]

The attack which interrupted her while she was re-shaping *The Waves* was similar in every respect to those sketched above:

After coming out here I had the usual—oh how usual—headache; and lay, like a fibre of tired muscle on my bed in the sitting room, till yesterday. Now up again and on again; with one new picture in my mind; my defiance of death in the garden.[151]

As in the other cases, physical misery reveals on its reverse side the ineffaceable imprint of a spiritual adventure—one might even say a metaphysical one, but that some of that word's connotations are incompatible with Virginia Woolf's temperament. Meanwhile, however, she is back at work; but it needs only the slightest thing to blur the vision of her submerged worlds. One day, a conversation with Arnold Bennett,[152] another time a "word of slight snub" in the *Times Literary Supplement*,[153] or again, merely an attack of flu at Rodmell during the Christmas holidays, when she was counting on a "fortnight of exaltation and concentration" for her work.[154] Nevertheless, in spite of these interruptions she has moments of happiness. She has allowed herself a week's breathing

[149] AWD p. 97 (96). Cf. also AWD p. 153-4 (150-1)
[150] See I. Rantavaara's interesting analysis of the schizophrenia which presumably afflicted V. W. intermittently. *Op. cit.*, p. 151, note 2. See also Leonard Woolf's *Beginning Again.*
[151] AWD p. 159 (156)
[152] Cf. AWD p. 160 (157)
[153] AWD p. 162 (158)
[154] AWD p. 163 (159)

space, hoping maybe to forget the *Literary Supplement*'s criticism and the somewhat hasty decision she has taken to "alter the whole of *The Waves*"[155]; and, on the eve of starting again, she reckons the last stages to be gone through and already sees herself, in about three months' time—by the end of March—handing over the finished work to her husband.[156] Soon after, as on the earlier occasion, Beethoven's music[157] proves the catalytic influence that crystallises the final motive:

It occurred to me last night while listening to a Beethoven quartet that I would merge all the interjected passages into Bernard's final speech and end with the words O solitude: thus making him absorb all those scenes and having no further break. This is also to show that the theme effort, effort, dominates: not the waves: and personality: and defiance: but I am not sure of the effect artistically; because the proportions may need the intervention of the waves finally so as to make a conclusion.[158]

Although this passage might seem more in its place in a detailed study of *The Waves* itself, I have quoted it here in full, since it reveals the progress of the writer's thought and the progressive integration of those explorations in depth which I have been analysing. We have already seen how the waves drove out the moths; here, the theme of effort seeks to displace the waves. This is not the place to examine its degree of success. But it is surely not rash to suggest that her breakdown that summer was not unconnected with this attempt to shift the dominant theme. We have only to superimpose these lines over the little sentence: "my defiance of death in the garden"[159] for the aridly literary element, the forced intellectualism implied by these manipulations of form to melt away in face of this struggle of a living being, body and soul, against its fate. That defiance, which is the point of convergence of both passages, is the will to live, the act of assertion and cohesion of the personality; and the feeling, or rather the sensation that goes with it, is that of effort. The whole being, at that instant which is to decide its doom or its salvation, is identical with its effort; so that the three terms "effort", "personality" and "defiance" are synonymous—or rather were so, fused in the living crucible of one dramatic moment. A kind of *vis inertiae* in the processes of thought

[155] Cf. *supra*, note 153
[157] Cf. *supra*, p. 78-9
[159] Cf. *supra*, p. 88
[156] AWD p. 162 (158-9)
[158] AWD p. 162 (159)

introduced and subsequently retained the final note: "O solitude". True, that note is sustained by its connection with the
struggle against death; but it by no means expresses the whole of
that struggle; it is rather the echo of the waves on the empty
beaches facing the waste of waters. We hear it still in the last pages
of *The Waves*: "Heaven be praised for solitude. Let me be alone."
and a little further on: "I would willingly give all my money that
you should not disturb me but let me sit on and on, silent,
alone."[160] This, presumably, is where—on September 22, 1930—
Virginia Woolf considered setting down the final chord, "O
solitude". But it is clear that already by that date her vision implied
the ensuing paragraphs of the final version, with its last outburst of
proud courage: "Against you I will fling myself, unvanquished
and unyielding, O Death!"[161] Moreover, by February 4, 1931—
and possibly even earlier—that delay in integration, by which "O
solitude" had been thrust into a context that transcended it, had
been made good, and as her thoughts acquired unity this weak
note was replaced by the strong note of the final version.[162]

And, meanwhile, the work goes on, not indeed as fast as the
author had reckoned[163] but impetuously, with a sure sense of
achievement. Despite physical feverishness, mental excitement
ensures the equilibrium of her whole being, precarious and risky
no doubt, but stimulating.[164] The book has lost none of its freshness; it poses so many problems that this revision demands as much
invention as polishing, and the interest and exaltation inseparable
from the one neutralize the tedium and aridity of the other. Conditions, then, are highly favourable: the creative impulse is in
harmony with the easy discipline of technical requirements.[165]
Above all, as the work acquires unity and movement—the artist's
main preoccupations all the time she was reshaping it—Virginia

---

[160] *The Waves*, pp. 209 (381), 210 (382)

[161] *The Waves*, p. 211 (383)

[162] "B.[ernard] is within two days I think of saying O Death", AWD p. 167 (163).

[163] "I was to have finished it at Christmas" (Feb. 4, 1931), AWD p. 167 (163).

[164] "Now if it could be worked over with heat and currency, that's all it wants.
And I am getting my blood up (temp. 99) . . . and having got astride my saddle the
whole world falls into shape; it is this writing that gives me my proportions", AWD
p. 164 (160); cf. also *supra* p. 55, note 6.

[165] "Few books have interested me more to write than *The Waves*. Why even now,
at the end, I'm turning up a stone or two: no glibness, no assurance . . . Something
new goes into my pot every morning—something that's never been got at before.
The high wind can't blow, because I'm chopping and tacking all the time", AWD
p. 165 (161).

Woolf gradually grows aware of her achievement and, even if this should not coincide with success, it justifies her effort and raises her in her own estimation[166] and furthermore, brings her the confidence and strength that spring from the triumph of will and courage:

I think I have just done what I meant; of course I have altered the scheme considerably: but my feeling is that I have insisted upon saying, by hook or by crook, certain things I meant to say. I imagine that the hookedness may be so great that it will be a failure from a reader's point of view. Well, never mind: it is a brave attempt. I think, something struggled for.[167]

These feelings, indeed, are neither enduring nor unmixed. The passage I have just quoted is flanked by two exclamations full of weariness and longing for rest, or at least for liberty:

Oh Lord the relief when this week is over and I have at any rate the feeling that I have wound up and done with that long labour: ended that vision. . . . Oh and then the delight of skirmishing free again—the delight of being idle and not much minding what happens; and then I shall be able to read again, with all my mind—a thing I haven't done these four months I daresay.[168]

Here, compressed into one instant, we catch the oscillation of Virginia Woolf's unstable nature, so tense that it is constantly vibrating in the intervals of swinging to those extremes that have been described.[169] In fact, she is at the end of her tether; fever has sapped her strength; two days later, Wednesday, February 4th, her doctor fails to diagnose her illness. And when, at the end of the week, the ordeal is over at last, she emerges from it in a state of exhaustion whose menacing symptoms she knows only too well:

I wrote the words O Death fifteen minutes ago, having reeled across the last ten pages with some moments of such intensity and intoxication that I seemed only to stumble after my own voice, or almost, after some sort of speaker (as when I was mad) I was almost afraid, remembering the voices that used to fly ahead. Anyhow, it is done; and I have been sitting these 15 minutes in a state of glory, and calm, and some tears, thinking of Thoby and if I could write Julian Thoby Stephen 1881-1906 on the first page. I suppose not. How physical the sense of triumph and relief is![170]

---

[166] "I think this is the greatest opportunity I have yet been able to give myself; therefore I suppose the most complete failure. Yet I respect myself for writing this book—yes—even though it exhibits my congenital faults", AWD p. 159 (156).

[167] AWD p. 167 (163)
[168] AWD p. 167 (163)
[169] Cf. supra, p. 86
[170] AWD p. 169 (165)

When we read these lines we feel how baseless are the accusations levelled against her of being artificial, cold, over-intellectual, and how far on the contrary writing was a dangerous game which she played with her whole being at the risk of ruining herself. But she did not shun that risk, for it was the reverse side of the salvation she strove to win. We have traced the genesis of one book and its vicissitudes; or rather we have disconnectedly followed the author's struggle with shadows called Moths or Waves, Rhythm or Continuity; we have seen her excited or depressed, nonchalantly following her dreams or doggedly striving to render some specific effect, writing from inspiration or cut short by the evanescence of her vision. The book was *The Waves*, but if we had watched her writing *Mrs Dalloway* or *The Years* we should have found her just the same, and we should not know what she was pursuing thus, with so much fervent obstinacy. No doubt, with *To the Lighthouse* and *Orlando*, names, people, known to us from other sources, reveal part of the secret of that vision. For *The Waves*, during a brief moment, one word lifts a corner of the veil,[171] but the ultimate secret remains faceless. We have seen the work take shape around something of whose constant presence we were made aware, but which remained, just as constantly, invisible. The Diary, in its existing form, leaves the novel to its fate as a work of art exclusively, denying it the support of any actual human destiny: it infuses no extraneous warmth into the book, lends it no life and humanity from its own store. At most, it provides a sort of accompaniment, so distant and so indistinct that we can scarcely grasp its connection with the principal melody: we remain vaguely haunted by ghosts that hover on the fringe of reality without ever entering into it. And when we glimpse the figure of Thoby Stephen through his sister's tears, we are irresistibly tempted to embody in him some of the nameless shades that flit around the confines of *The Waves*. The dedication which the author found impossible to write was doubtless the key to the dream—that endless "dream about herself"[172] in which, through love, she included those beings whom neither space nor time could separate from her being. Thoby Stephen, her elder by one year, the companion of her childhood games, founder, with Leonard Woolf, Clive Bell and Lytton Strachey of that Midnight Society at Trinity whose meetings seem a prelude to those in Gordon

[171] Cf. *supra*, pp. 88-9, 91   [172] Cf. *supra*, p. 65

Square,[173] should by rights have assumed, like Vanessa, a share in her destiny. Death, by taking him away in his twenty-fifth year, confined him within childhood and youth, of which he thus became the sole complete representative. Like the unseen Percival he is the hero, symbol and myth of a life and a world that lie out of bounds. By his death, a continuity was broken, and his unfulfilled life created an emptiness in the lives with which he was involved, while the regions where those lives had been enriched by his became frozen over by his immobility. And the solitude which was originally to have spread over the final pages of *The Waves* seems, indeed, to be that which Virginia Woolf experienced at her brother's death, which overwhelmed her a few days after she had begun her novel: "How I suffer. And no one knows how I suffer, walking up this street, engaged with my anguish, as I was after Thoby died—alone; fighting something alone."[174] This twofold mention of Thoby, at an interval of sixteen months, enclosing the greater part of the composition of *The Waves*, allows us to glimpse, if not fully to measure and understand, the human values involved with and animating this long endeavour.

But if most of the work was done, the end had not yet been reached: the second version must be typed and profusely corrected; at a rate of seven or eight pages a day, this meant six weeks of uninterrupted work in order to maintain in the mind the unity of tone and movement that must be infused into the book. "It is like sweeping over an entire canvas with a wet brush."[175] Her intellectual concentration is so intense that it produces a sort of physical cramp in the brain which, about midday, forces her to stop writing.[176] Nevertheless, she finishes this third version a whole week sooner than she had expected. "Not that it is finished—" she writes, "oh dear no. For then I must correct the re-re-typing."[177]

---

[173] Annan, *Leslie Stephen*, p. 123

[174] AWD p. 147 (144)

[175] AWD p. 171 (166). Cf. also an earlier passage, p. 69 (68): "I am now galloping over *Mrs. Dalloway*, re-typing it entirely from the start, which is more or less what I did with the *V.O.*: a good method, I believe, as thus one works with a wet brush over the whole, and joins parts separately composed and gone dry."

[176] "No, I have just said, it being 12.45, I cannot write any more . . . how it rolls into a tight ball the muscles in my brain", AWD p. 171 (167), May 30th. "And to get away from this hard knot in which my brain has been so tight spun—I mean *The Waves*. Such are my sentiments at half past twelve on Tuesday July 7th", AWD p. 171 (167).

[177] AWD p. 171 (167)

At last, on July 17, 1931, the definitive typescript is ready to be given to Leonard Woolf. By way of summing up the last stages of this long journey in pursuit of perfection, this is what Virginia Woolf notes herself in her Diary, on July 14th:

> But my *Waves* account runs, I think, as follows:—
> I began it, seriously, about September 10th 1929.
> I finished the first version on April 10th 1930.
> I began the second version on May 1st 1930.
> I finished the second version on February 7th 1931.
> I began to correct the second version on May 1st 1931, finished 22nd June 1931.
> I began to correct the typescript on 25th June 1931. Shall finish (I hope) 18th July 1931. Then remain only the proofs.[178]

This account, for what she calls a "little 80,000 word" book[179] is impressive, to say the least. Before finally clearing it, let us consider for a moment the antagonistic forces that accumulate like a sort of residuum from creation and obscurely prepare a work of a different character, which by its very dissimilar demands will ensure the relief of her faculties, of that part of her personality more particularly laid under contribution by the work in progress.[180] *The Waves* indeed provides a characteristic example of that phenomenon which alone can explain the alternation in Virginia Woolf's work of different genres, not to be accounted for by any straightforward linear development.[181] Working "at high pressure"[182] at correcting the second version, she foresees the impulse that is to alter her course and send her off at an angle, as *Orlando* had done after *To the Lighthouse*: "But I shall fling off, like a cutter leaning on its side, on some swifter, slighter adventure—another *Orlando* perhaps."[183] Although she is merely glancing towards other horizons where nothing is yet to be seen, one can assume that she is obeying the magnetic force of some hidden presence; a fortnight

---

[178] AWD p. 172 (168)
[179] "Heaven help me if all my little 80,000 word books are going in future to cost me two years!", AWD p. 165 (161).
[180] Cf. *supra*, p. 80
[181] Cf. what V. W. says about the sequence-relation between *The Waves* and *The Years*, or between *The Waves* and *Flush*: "Dear me. I see why I fled, after *The Waves*, to *Flush*" (AWD p. 252 (243)). Also on the possibility of writing two different kinds of book at the same time: "some book or work for a book that's quite the other side of the brain between times", AWD p. 257 (248).
[182] "The Waves is written at such high pressure that . . .", AWD p. 165 (161).
[183] AWD p. 165 (161)

later, indeed, the new land is in sight: "I have this moment, while having my bath, conceived an entire new book—a sequel to *A Room of One's Own*—about the sexual life of women: to be called Professions for Women perhaps—Lord how exciting!"[184]

So exciting that she cannot work at *The Waves* for nearly a week[185] and when she gets down to it again, her plan for work for the next half-year includes both the completion of *The Waves* and a first draft of *Professions for Women*, which she already calls *The Open Door*. Leonard Woolf indicates in a note that this eventually became *Three Guineas*, and the characteristics set down by Virginia Woolf seem to confirm this interpretation. However, she adds in the margin in May 1934: "This is *Here and Now*, I think". *Here and Now* was one of the many provisional titles for *The Years*. The divergence of these indications is more superficial than real, since Virginia Woolf was later to consider the two books as one.[186] To begin with they were united in a general trend, which only took precise shape later when the initial cell had proliferated and gained sufficient sustenance from dreams and rough sketches, fugitive visions and meditations.

It is not my purpose to follow the course of this new venture. I merely wish to indicate its starting-point, recognizing once again the hidden accumulation of compensating energies, and a constant watchfulness ready to pick up the slightest message emanating thence. *Orlando* had carried her away, unexpectedly, on a long journey; here she was merely deviating; she came back to *The Waves*. That is where we find her, about to correct her proofs, barely a week's work, at the end of the first fortnight in August 1931.

This is Virginia Woolf's last farewell to a book that had dipped back into her past, and she dismisses it as one does a thing in which one has dwelt for a long time, creating oneself and asserting one's liberty even while confined within it, serving an irrevocable long-term sentence, made more so by the prison's perfection. "They [the proofs] shall go tomorrow—never, never to be looked at again by me, I imagine."[187] This attitude is quite normal. Few writers

---

[184] AWD p. 166 (161-2)
[185] Jan. 23rd: "Too much excited, alas, to get on with *The Waves*."; Jan. 26th: "Heaven be praised . . . I have shaken off the obsession of *Opening the Door*, and have returned to *Waves*", AWD p. 166 (162).
[186] Cf. AWD p. 295 (162), quoted *infra*, p. 104
[187] AWD p. 174 (169)

re-read their books. No doubt, for them, reading is a process too directly opposite to writing not to be profoundly unnatural. It must be like walking backwards over one's own tracks, an acrobatic feat impossible to keep up for longer than a few moments, a few pages. If, for a short spell, Virginia Woolf spends an hour every morning re-reading *The Voyage Out*, it seems to have been out of sheer professional curiosity,[188] and reading over *To the Lighthouse* seems to have been a hindrance rather than a pleasure.[189]

But even when she has put it aside, the book is not completely detached from her, any more than the act of writing. Actually its nature has changed; it had been intimate, it has become public, and in so doing has formed a zone of contact with other people which, at first, is as hyper-sensitive as a raw wound which, with time, will heal over and lose its vulnerability. Without neglecting the aphorism with which Virginia Woolf defines her emotional relationship to her works: "The truth is that writing is the profound pleasure and being read the superficial",[190] it is none the less true that as each one was published she reacted profoundly to the reception it got. After the appearance of the first *Common Reader*, which was met with general silence, ". . . a dull chill depressing reception",[191] she then writes in her Diary, quite sincerely no doubt but also somewhat prematurely, forestalling serenity as though she could induce it faster by asserting it: "I have just come through the hoping fearing stage and now see my disappointment floating like an old bottle in my wake and am off on fresh adventures."[192] In fact, three days later, we see "the temperature chart of a book"[193] being prolonged, and one cannot imagine the author not deeply involved in the ups and downs of that intermittent fever. Hope revives at praise from G. Lowes Dickinson, and fear, with a touch of irritation, at the incoherent sarcasms of reviews in *Country Life* and *The Star*. A few days later we are conscious that the appositeness of Fausset's praise in the *Manchester*

[188] "The mornings from 12 to 1 I spend reading *The Voyage Out*, I've not read it since July 1913", Feb. 4, 1920; AWD p. 24 (23).

[189] "Reading the *Lighthouse* does not make it easier to write [*The Waves*]", AWD p. 150 (146).

[190] AWD p. 76 (75). Cf. also: "Joy's life is in the doing—I murder, as usual, a quotation; I mean it's the writing, not the being read, that excites me", AWD p. 134 (131)

[191] AWD p. 75 (74)

[192] AWD p. 75 (74)

[193] AWD p. 75 (74)

Guardian—or rather the way it coincides with her own opinion[194]—has given her genuine pleasure, which vanishes when, a fortnight later, she learns from Desmond MacCarthy that Logan Pearsall Smith thinks "the *C. R.* well enough, but nothing more".[195] Fortunately, "now comes Mrs Hardy to say that Thomas reads, and hears the *C. R.* read, with 'great pleasure' ". And after all, Logan is only a "salt-veined American"![196]

This is a fairly typical example of the alternating hot and cold showers which she endured with more or less fortitude according to her state of mind at the time.[197] Yet we must distinguish two kinds of sensitivity, differing perhaps not only in degree but in nature. One belongs to the authoress, the other to the woman; the first reacts to success, to fame, the other to phenomena far more individual and more profound. And despite all the reckoning of orders, sales, numbers printed,[198] that reveal the publisher in Virginia Woolf, even more than the authoress, a few quotations will serve to show that the authoress in her was a character imposed by circumstances and that far from identifying herself with it, she submits to the role more than she plays it.

Undoubtedly during the early years the novelty of the experience and above all, lack of self confidence, the need to be reassured, to feel that her resolution and her effort had not been wasted, tended to unify her reaction; at first she was interested in the amount of attention paid to her, as much as in the verdicts she incurred. She needed encouragement—and what could be more natural? But she already strove to escape from this bondage by a kind of autosuggestion.

As Sydney Waterlow once said, the worst of writing is that one depends so much upon praise. I feel rather sure that I shall get none for this story [Kew Gardens]; and I shall mind a little. Unpraised, I find it hard to start writing in the morning; but the dejection lasts only 30 minutes, and once I start I forget all about it. One should aim, seriously, at disregarding ups and downs; a compliment here, silence

---

[194] "I was really pleased to open the *Manchester Guardian* this morning and read Mr. Fausset on the Art of V. W.; brilliance combined with integrity; profound as well as eccentric", AWD p. 76 (75).

[195] AWD p. 77 (76)

[196] AWD p. 78 (76)

[197] Cf. *infra*, p. 98, reference 199.

[198] Cf. AWD pp. 53 (52) (JR); 77 (76), 78 (77), 83 (81) (Mrs. D); 106 (105) (To the L); 133 (130), 139-40 (137) (O); 175-6-7 (171-2) (The W); 282 (272) (The Y); 342-3 (329-30) (RF)

there; Murry and Eliot ordered, and not me; the central fact remains stable, which is the fact of my own pleasure in the art. And these mists of the spirit have other causes, I expect; though they are deeply hidden. There is some ebb and flow of the tide of life which accounts for it; though what produces either ebb or flow I'm not sure.[199]

Meanwhile, however, in spite of her fears, orders flowed in: "success showered during those days"[200] and already the duality referred to above made itself felt. "I think the nerve of pleasure easily becomes numb. I like little sips, but the psychology of fame is worth considering at leisure. I fancy one's friends take the bloom off."[201] Success comes from the general public and the critics; "the bloom" comes from being understood, if not invariably admired, by her friends. Friendship, which is a human value, makes this precious; and after such profound emotion, other voices seem remote and superficial. A little later, after sending five copies of *Night and Day* to some friends, she awaits their verdict in a state of excitement in which delight and dread are mingled. She counts on their approval; she longs above all for that of Lytton Strachey and E. M. Forster, which would strengthen her own self-confidence. But, even beyond the reach of all this, she is conscious of a certainty and a determination which sustain her and lead her on irresistibly towards further creation. This deep-seated, autonomous confidence, to which she resorts as though she had irremissibly staked everything on herself, explains the whole of her attitude towards the public. Nothing has any real or lasting significance save what reaches that inner source of energy and fertility. At one pole there is the conventional praise of her acquaintance, at the other the lucid judgment of those friends whom she completely respects.[202] Underlying all the trivial reactions of literary vanity, we feel here, once more, the living reality of the work of art, that intimate expression of the artist's

---

[199] AWD p. 14 (14)
[200] AWD p. 15 (15)
[201] AWD p. 15 (15)
[202] Cf. "Am I nervous? Oddly little; more excited and pleased than nervous . . . I have a kind of confidence, that the people whose judgment I value will probably think well of it, [*N and D*] which is much reinforced by the knowledge that even if they don't, I shall pick up and start another story on my own. Of course, if Morgan and Lytton and the others should be enthusiastic, I should think the better of myself. The bore is meeting people who say the usual things.", AWD p. 19 (18). Cf. also "I have still, of course, to gather in all the private criticism, which is the real test", AWD p. 32 (31).

being, which demands an equally intimate understanding, and impels the artist to reject any self-satisfaction in the long run, even if she should yield to it momentarily.

Clive and Vanessa Bell, Lytton Strachey, Violet Dickinson greet *Night and Day* enthusiastically; but Forster likes it less than *The Voyage Out*:

> Though he spoke also of great admiration and had read in haste and proposed re-reading, this rubbed out all the pleasure of the rest. Yes, but to continue. About 3 in the afternoon I felt happier and easier on account of his blame than on account of the others' praise—as if one were in the human atmosphere again, after a blissful roll among elastic clouds and cushiony downs. Yet I suppose I value Morgan's opinion as much as anybody's.[203]

In this human atmosphere consists the integrity of reality, that truth which she seeks in the wake of her book as she had sought it during the writing—the rest is just a play of shadows. We live on several levels, and surface scratches, although they heal more quickly, may hurt just as much as deeper wounds. "I don't take praise or blame excessively to heart," she says a little later, still with reference to *Night and Day*, "but they interrupt, cast one's eyes backwards, make one wish to explain or investigate."[204] "To explain or investigate", that's to say, as ever, to go after truth—your own truth or other people's, confronting them with one another for the final verdict. But what's the use? what's done is done and cannot be changed, by deeds, far less by words. It's more to the point, then, to write another book, try and make it better, than to persist in vain in trying to justify those which, written in all honesty of conscience as they were, may be good or bad, but cannot become any different.

Once she has cast off the fear of being "dismissed as negligible"[205] and the reactions of startled vanity, now seen in their right proportion,[206] Virginia Woolf watches her own rise to fame in the literary world with a certain detachment, generally tinged with humour and sometimes with irritation. "I expect a slow silent increase of fame, such as has come about, rather miraculously,

---

[203] AWD p. 20 (19)

[204] AWD p. 22 (21)

[205] "But if I'm as plain as day, and negligible?", AWD p. 31 (30). "What I had feared was that I was dismissed as negligible", AWD p. 33 (32).

[206] "One must face the despicable vanity which is at the root of all this niggling and haggling", AWD p. 32 (31).

since *J's R.* was published,"[207] she writes after *Mrs Dalloway*. She is pleased with the quietness of her fame, which seems somehow more valuable than any noisy success—what she later calls "the sublime progress of my books".[208] Moreover she seems not quite to believe in it: "suppose I might become one of the interesting—I will not say great—but interesting novelists? Oddly, for all my vanity, I have not until now had much faith in my novels."[209] Three years later, secure in self-confidence confirmed by success, she flings a few taunts at her own vanity: "Yes, yes: since I wrote here I have become two inches and a half higher in the public view. I think I may say that I am now among the well known writers."[210] The next page, full of sarcastic and contemptuous comments on those in high society with whom, on account of that very fame, she is entitled to mingle, clearly indicates the tone in which this remark must be read. And the final condemnation of that "sordid, commonplace" world, "coarse and usual and dull", represented by the Cunards and Colefaxes, echoes the declaration of independence made three years before: "I want as usual to dig deep down into my new stories without having a looking glass flashed in my eyes—Todd, to wit; Colefax to wit et cetera."[211]

That world of outward show and false values—titles, fortune, fame—is utterly alien to her. It is surely not rash to suggest that many passages in the Diary, omitted "in order to protect the feelings or reputations of the living"[212] must constitute a lively and virulent indictment of the representatives of that world, their way of thinking and of living.

In 1933 she refused a degree of D.Litt from the University of Manchester. The doctorate might have served as a revenge for the author of *A Room of One's Own*, but one can scarcely imagine the woman who was to write *Three Guineas* accepting the "tuft of fur"[213] on her head. She does not repeat the whole discussion in which she justified her refusal, but her conclusions are rather significant. The arguments put forward against her made her "feel a little silly, priggish and perhaps extreme...".[214] But while

[207] AWD p. 74 (73)
[208] AWD p. 74 (73)
[209] AWD p. 74 (73)
[210] AWD p. 135 (132)
[211] AWD p. 74 (73). Cf. "I want to be writing unobserved", AWD p. 52 (51).
[212] AWD p. vii (vii)
[213] AWD p. 196 (190)
[214] "They made me feel a little silly, priggish and perhaps extreme: but only superficially. Nothing would induce me to connive at all that humbug. Nor would it give me, even illicitly, any pleasure. I really believe that Nessa and I . . . are without the publicity sense", AWD p. 196 (190). Cf. AWD p. 249 (240)

she correctly assesses the element of priggishness in her refusal and judges it superficial, she does not mention the basic pride revealed by the contempt she professes for conventional values and for publicity. Pride, here, is only another name for that trust in one-self, that ultimate reliance on what is deepest and best in oneself, in which we see her take refuge and recover strength after the slightest squall as after the worst tempest. But if pride is often the failing of the strong, in Virginia Woolf's case it is restrained by such lucidity, tempered by so many scruples, that it never degenerates into vanity. At most, we can hold her pride respons-ible—and this is not a reproach so much as an expression of awe-struck sympathy—for having chained her to her highest destiny, making her its victorious victim. No doubt, too, pride accounts for the scorn she felt for the Colefaxes and Cunards—and all the rest whom Leonard Woolf's tact has spared. The violence of her judgments, the harshness towards any sort of weakness which we discern in a thumbnail sketch here, a passing comment there, may wound the feelings or arouse the indignation of those whom she criticises. However, without denying the exaggeration, perhaps even the injustices to which she was occasionally liable,[215] one can hardly accuse Virginia Woolf of a lack of human understanding or sympathy. Her staunch friendships, her attitude in many more superficial relationships, dispose of that indictment. If pride often drove her to take refuge in the bleakest solitude, it never created solitude around her—at least none other than that inhabited by the chosen few, the "live interesting real people" with vibrant minds,[216] such as Nessa, Roger, Duncan, Lytton, Morgan. Perhaps we may even consider that pride, more openly displayed as the years pass, less as a fundamental trait of her nature (in other respects scrupulous and hesitant to the point of diffidence) than as a defensive reaction, the refuge of her sensibility, the "rock of self esteem untouched in me"[217] where she can and will take shelter from whatever in life is liable to wound her, diminish her and ultimately destroy her.

Six months before and six months after that refusal of the honorary degree which served as starting-point for this study of

---

[215] Cf. Clive Bell, *Old Friends*, pp. 97-9

[216] "Could one . . . find a live interesting real person, a Nessa, a Duncan, a Roger. Someone new, whose mind would begin vibrating", AWD p. 136 (133).

[217] "I felt the rock of self esteem untouched in me", AWD p. 134 (131).

pride, we find a couple of passages which assert the close relationship between self-will raised to the point of will-to-power, and the
refusal to take part in Vanity Fair:

... now, aged 50, I'm just poised to shoot forth quite free straight and
undeflected my bolts whatever they are. Therefore all this flitter
flutter of weekly newspapers interests me not at all. . . . I believe in
forever altering one's aspect to the sun. Hence my optimism. And to
alter now, cleanly and sanely, I want to shuffle off this loose living
randomness: people; reviews; fame; all the glittering scales; and be
withdrawn, and concentrated.[218]

We find the same dismissal of grandeur and fame, the same
enthusiasm for the freedom to be oneself and oneself alone, in the
other passage, which simply echoes the first and indeed refers to it
at one point:

But let me remember that fashion in literature is an inevitable thing;
also that one must grow and change; also that I have, at last, laid
hands upon my philosophy of anonymity. . . . How odd last winter's
revelation was! freedom . . . I will not be "famous", "great".[219]

This is in October 1933;[219] she has resolutely taken up the
attitude which she was still seeking for in the spring of 1932 without
being as yet able to shake off a certain passivity inherent in her
nature. She had always, or at any rate for a long time, refused any
compromise, any submission to external limitations while the
creative impulse was upon her, while the demands of her art were
dominant; and yet when she had handed over her work to the
public she would lose her self-assurance, would seem ready to submit. "The most important thing is not to think very much about
oneself. To investigate candidly the charge; but not fussily, not
very anxiously."[220] This recalls the earlier self-searchings.[221] But
this submission is more in intention than in effect, it comes from
the head rather than from the heart. Hasn't she just written that
after extracting the essence of a criticism one must "use the little
kick of energy which opposition supplies to be more vigorously
oneself".[222] Although she ascribes to "rashness and modesty"

[218] AWD p. 187 (181)

[219] AWD p. 213 (206). Cf. another assertion of independence, AWD p. 83 (81).

[220] "The most important thing is not to think very much about oneself. To
investigate candidly the charge; but not fussily, not very anxiously", AWD p. 180
(175).

[221] Cf. *supra*, p. 99

[222] ". . . to use the little kick of energy which opposition supplies to be more
vigorously oneself", AWD p. 180 (174-5).

her quick recovery from the shocks of praise and blame,[223] a mere glance at the Diary suggests that such methods are less effective than she implies. At this period her modesty was the very thing that made her vulnerable; and what she calls her rashness—or versatility—seems to offer little help on such occasions. As we have seen, it was her pride that was to save her. I associated her pride with her will to power; so, her modesty was bound up with her weakness. At the beginning of 1932, she had not yet recovered from the effort *The Waves* had demanded of her[224]; the death of Lytton Strachey had affected her deeply; through her flayed nerves, she saw life as all barrenness and unreason; her whole being and her world were out of gear.[225] We see her deep in the trough of the wave. Her semi-capitulation to the critics is part of a general capitulation. She gradually emerges from this during the summer, and when she returns from Rodmell we see her on the crest of life, on the crest of herself, her strength and energy restored, capable once again of pride and independence.

But with Virginia Woolf the rhythm of alternation was, as we have often noticed, inexorable. In October 1934, Wyndham Lewis's attacks in *Men Without Art* almost threw her off balance again; fortunately the "revelation" experienced in autumn 1932 stood her in good stead and "the W.L. illness lasted two days" only.[226] On the publication of *The Years*, in 1937, in spite of the 5,300 copies sold beforehand[227] and a humorous tone that smacks of the defensive, and that scarcely conceals the profound uneasiness that this book never ceased to awaken in her,[228] Virginia Woolf seems on the point of betraying her resolutions; the super-

[223] Cf. "with my odd mixture of extreme rashness and modesty (to analyse roughly) I very soon recover from praise and blame", AWD p. 180 (175).

[224] "My word, what a heaving *The Waves* was, that I still feel the strain", AWD p. 176 (173).

[225] The whole entry for May 25, 1932, might be quoted; here are some typical phrases: "Lord how I suffer! What a terrific capacity I possess for feeling with intensity. . . . All is surface hard; myself only an organ that takes blows, one after another. . . . Lytton's death; Carrington's . . . terror at night of things generally wrong in the universe. . . . worst of all is this dejected barrenness. . . . I saw all the violence and unreason crossing in the air; ourselves small; a tumult outside; something terrifying: unreason . . .", AWD pp. 180-1 (175-6).

[226] "And I think my revelation two years ago stands me in sublime stead. . . . Quite cured today. So the W. L. illness lasted two days", AWD p. 229 (221-2). Cf. *supra*, p. 102.

[227] "We have sold 5,300 before publication", AWD p. 277 (267)

[228] Cf. particularly a whole series of reflections, pp. 270-5 (261-266) (AWD).

ficial reactions of wounded vanity, though ephemeral, stifle the deeper reactions:

> Maynard thinks *The Years* my best book . . . and this opinion though from the centre, from a very fine mind, doesn't flutter me as much as Muir's blame; it sinks in slowly and deeply. It's not a vanity feeling; the other is; the other will die as soon as the week's number of the *Listener* is past.[229]

Trifling disturbances, surface scratches; true, but they are painful, like Hugh Walpole's silence, even if, underneath, there lies the immeasurable happiness of having achieved her destiny in spite of everyone.[230] Yet that happiness is not an empty word, nor is that destiny an illusion. We meet them again, stronger than ever, a year later, shortly before the publication of *Three Guineas*:

> But I now feel entirely free. Why? Have committed myself, am afraid of nothing. Can do anything I like. No longer famous, no longer on a pedestal: no longer hawked in by societies: on my own, forever. That's my feeling: a sense of expansion, like putting on slippers. Why this should be so, why I feel myself enfranchised till death, and quit of all humbug, when I daresay it's not a good book and will excite nothing but mild sneers; and how very inconsequent and egotistical V. W. is— why, why I can't analyse. . . .[231]

And when, on the very day of publication, she takes her bearings, or more precisely when she leaps forward from the past to the future, she expresses in simpler but equally intense language the fundamental aspiration that had guided her life ever since her "revelation":

> Anyhow that's the end of six years floundering, striving, much agony, some ecstasy: lumping the *Years* and *Three Guineas* together as one book—as indeed they are. And now I can be off again, as indeed I long to be. Oh to be private, alone, submerged.[232]

And the fact that the contradictory shocks of criticism can still make her wince,[233] that a "word of tepidity" depresses her "more

---

[229] AWD p. 281 (270-1)

[230] "My happiness isn't blind. That is the achievement . . . of my 55 years. . . . Of course it ruffles, in the day, but there it is. There it was yesterday when old Hugh came and said nothing about *The Years*", AWD p. 281 (271).

[231] AWD p. 291 (281)

[232] AWD p. 295 (284)

[233] Cf. "They [my emotions] are fitful: thus not very strong. . . . Still they twinge. . . . So why do I twinge? Knowing it almost by heart. But not quite", AWD p. 338 (325)

than a word of praise exalts",[234] affects neither the sincerity nor the significance of those moments in which she asserts her independence and her serenity. And if that serenity and independence have been won through the ordeal of vulnerability and anguish, they assuredly represent the goal, half real, half ideal, towards which—obscurely at first, then with ever increasing clear-sightedness—Virginia Woolf had impelled her nature.

In fact, an insurmountable contradiction between her deepest tendencies and the external demands of her vocation condemned her to painful conflict. Writing and then publishing means dedicating oneself to the public. For her, writing meant dedication to herself—or at most, lending herself to her friends. Almost at the end, surveying her twenty years' literary career, she defines her position and stresses the paradox:

I'm fundamentally, I think, an outsider. I do my best work and feel most braced with my back to the wall. It's an odd feeling though, writing against the current: difficult entirely to disregard the current. Yet of course I shall.[235]

But this is, at any rate seen from the outside, an intellectual and abstract assessment. Under the words "fundamentally", "braced", "odd feeling", "difficult", "disregard", . . . and that final *shall* which implies *will*, we must set the whole person, body and soul, with all its capacity for sensation, suffering, joy, weakness and strength.

And thus, in conclusion to the lengthy analysis whose results seem hopelessly elusive, since the fusion of diverse feelings, the co-existence of incompatible tendencies, the impulses and the withdrawals, confuse the guiding lines and blur the contours, I offer a graphic formula which may suggest a sort of imaginative synthesis of the problem. If we pictured the alternation of enthusiasm and doubt—or rather the moments of intense vitality and the moments of depression—as a wavy line, and then concentric zones going from the periphery to the centre, to represent the different levels or sectors of sensibility, from the authoress's susceptibility to that hard, unified core that is the very basis of her psyche, we should have a complex system of references which would allow us to "place" and evaluate Virginia Woolf's re-

[234] AWD p. 342 (329)
[235] AWD p. 308 (297)

actions to the impact of each of her books on the public. To hazard the slightest judgment which did not take into account these co-ordinates would be to risk misunderstanding everything she has told us on the subject—and most probably everything we might learn from other sources.

The arid, abstract character of this illustration suggests what a distorted picture the preceding pages may all unwillingly have given of her personality—body, mind and spirit. By focussing my attention on the process of artistic creation, I have deliberately isolated that process; and even if I have constantly tried to relate it to the other movements, activities and impulses which constitute the complete being, I have none the less, by my self-assigned limitations, created a monstrously simplified figure. True, my essential aim was to portray the artist—more precisely, the artist at work, and this, I maintain, is the most fundamental aspect of Virginia Woolf; yet to confine my study within these limits would wholly invalidate it. Without claiming to offer a complete portrait of Virginia Woolf—which might be attempted by biographers in possession of many documents at present unavailable—I must at least sketch in its outlines and its dominant features, so as to re-integrate that non-human freak, the pure artist, into the totality from which it was extracted. Virginia Woolf was human, all too human, and one cannot even for a moment consider reducing her to her superhuman centre. Authentic and heroic though this may be, it owes its truth and its heroism to what surrounds it. It can exist as a centre only if it has a circumference. All those moments of artistic creation, whose shape we have outlined, whose substance we have weighed, are lit up by moments which, although simply moments of life, were just as intense and just as fertile, and without these the others would have remained empty and sterile. This circumference, these moments are what I shall next try to suggest, solely in order to give my portrait its right proportions, so that what was a caricature of a writer may become the likeness of a woman.

I have pointed out two central features of Virginia Woolf's artistic activity: alternation or rhythm, and determination or will. Just as the act of creating synthesized these contradictory aspects, so the act of living, as we shall see, diminished their antagonisms.

I have stressed the place that art held in Virginia Woolf's life, the power which she attributed to it to "bring the whole universe" —and herself—"to order".[236] It may seem paradoxical to assert now that she was just as passionately interested in life itself, with its richness and intensity; but it was precisely her passion for life which made the function of art so essential to her. She constantly takes refuge from one in the other, and if her redemption through writing becomes something almost metaphysical, her self-abandonment to the stream of existence is not only a therapy, it is a fulfilment. If, in order to write, she concentrates herself, focussing her whole being on a single point, she is nevertheless also capable of indulging the "scattered and various" side of her character: "when I write I'm merely a sensibility. Sometimes I like being Virginia, but only when I'm scattered and various and gregarious."[237] The dividing line between Virginia Woolf and Virginia is here somewhat over-stressed. An untimely interruption makes the transition from one to the other come as a sudden jolt,[238] whereas usually it happens smoothly and imperceptibly. When inspiration fails, when the effort of creation becomes so intense that it threatens to shatter the machine, then the writer withdraws and Virginia appears, ready for travel, conversation, reading, in a word for passivity and entertainment. Sometimes she only feels a longing and lacks courage or strength to satisfy it. Suffering from headache or depression, she dreams of idly watching the picturesque activity of market-day in a small French town,[239] or of wandering through the pine woods around Cassis[240] to recover the perfect happiness she had known there in the spring of 1925 with her husband, that inexplicable happiness that the parsimonious gods grant one when one least expects it.[241]

[236] Cf. *supra*, p. 55, note 6; p. 57, notes 12 and 13; p. 59

[237] AWD p. 48 (47)

[238] "One must get out of life—yes, that's why I disliked so much the irruption of Sydney" (Sir Sydney Waterlow), AWD, p. 48 (47). A visit from Mrs. Nef exhausts her literally: cf. AWD p. 209 (202), and *supra*, p. 59.

[239] "But this slight depression—what is it? I think I could cure it by crossing the channel and writing nothing for a week. I want to see something going on busily without help from me: a French market town for example. Indeed, have I the energy, I'll cross to Dieppe; or compromise by exploring Sussex on a motor bus", AWD p. 63 (62)

[240] "As it is I half incline to insist upon a dash to Cassis; but perhaps this needs more determination than I possess; and we shall dwindle on here", AWD p. 153 (150). Cf. also: "I should like a holiday—a few days in France—or a run through the Cotswolds", AWD p. 313 (302)

[241] "But L. and I were too too happy, as they say; if it were now to die etc. Nobody shall say of me that I have not known perfect happiness, but few could put their

Besides the journeys that were never taken, there were all those that she made in the Easter or summer holidays on the Continent or in England. She would go off, casting aside books and thoughts,[242] escaping from engagements and the routine that belongs to "habitation and habits"[243] with a zest that made light of the discomfort of hotels reached late at night, where the weariness of a day's travel intensifies the hardness of the single chair, the dimness of the single lamp.[244] At noon there were picnics "by the river, among the ants" or under the poplars shivering alongside the Rhône.[245] In the evenings she would watch the people dining in the hotel or the card players, chat to the little servant-girl enviously admiring their Lanchester, enjoy the tipsiness induced by the local wine.[246] Then there are landscapes: Les Baux, like Dante's hell[247]; the Apennines, like the inside of a green umbrella[248]; and buildings—Chartres, "the snail, with its head straight, marching across the flat country . . .", its rose window "a jewel on black velvet"[249]; the Antiques de Saint-Rémy in the sunshine; the tower and the cloisters at Pisa, where she and Leonard had come before, in the year of their marriage[250]; and there are the people encountered casually, during the halts in a journey by car, with whom one exchanges a few remarks that will enshrine

---

finger on the moment, or say what made it. Even I myself, stirring occasionally in the pool of content, could only say But this is all I want; could not think of anything better; and had only my half superstitious feeling at the Gods who must when they have created happiness, grudge it. Not if you get it in unexpected ways, though", AWD, p. 73 (72).

[242] "I gave up reading and thinking on 26th September when I went to France", AWD, p. 133 (131).

[243] "This strange interval of travel, of sweeping away from habitation and habits", AWD p. 206 (199)

[244] ". . . Piacenza, at which we find ourselves now at 6 minutes to 9 p.m. This of course is the rub of travelling—this is the price paid for the sweep and the freedom. . . . It will be all over this day week—comfort—discomfort; and the zest and rush that no engagements, hours, habits give", AWD p. 205 (198). Cf. also AWD p. 204 (198), "Piacenza", Friday, May 19th.

[245] ". . . lunching by the river, among the ants . . .", AWD p. 202 (195). ". . . eating our lunch on a green plot beside a deep cold stream", AWD, p. 205 (198). ". . . when we come to poplars we get out and lunch by the river", AWD p. 206 (199).

[246] "Often I was bobbing up and down on my two glasses of vin du pays", AWD p. 125 (123).

[247] AWD p. 125 (123)

[248] AWD p. 205 (198)

[249] AWD p. 125 (123)

[250] AWD p. 201 (195)

them for ever: the stone breaker waiting for the inspector,[251] the melancholy fisherman with his gift of fish. . . .[252]

There is about all this a reassuring simplicity, a pure pleasure emanating from direct contact with the surface of things. Even if Virginia Woolf happens to read—skipping, moreover—Henry James,[253] while her husband writes business letters,[254] even if, by the sea at Lerici, she thinks of Shelley—not his poetry but his life and his death[255]—we feel that this is merely a faint residuum of habit, of the same order as the scruple that obliges her to brush her teeth in mineral water.[256]

None the less she soon tires of this state of uncommittedness, this readiness to welcome the present moment or the unknown to-morrow. After two or three weeks the creative artist in her, which had withdrawn into the depths of her being to gather fresh substance, begins to re-emerge, and as the time draws near for going home it displays itself with growing urgency: "... and mounting all the time steadily was my desire for words, till I envisaged a sheet of paper and pen and ink as something of miraculous desirability—could even relish the scratch as if it were a divine kind of relief to me".[257] But this resurgence of her creative side in no way cancels out those days during which it abdicated temporarily in favour of the other self that Virginia Woolf bore within her as we all do—the self that sought fun and irresponsibility, the excitement of unknown horizons and new faces. On one of the last stages of some journey, she is torn between the two delights, the one that is ending and the one that is beginning—but she indulges in both of them with equal zest:

And "home" becomes a magnet, for I can't stop making up the P's: can't live without that intoxicant—though this is the loveliest and most distracting alternative. But I'm full of holiday and want work—ungrateful that I am!—and yet I want the hills near Fabbria too and the hills near Siena—but no other hills—not these black and green violent monotonous southern hills.[258]

[251] AWD p. 203 (197) [252] AWD p. 202 (195)

[253] "Yes, I am reading—skipping—the *Sacred Fount* . . .", AWD, p. 202 (196)

[254] "L. is writing directions to the Press. I am about to read Goldoni", AWD, p. 204 (198).

[255] Cf. Pisa, Friday, May 12, 1933, AWD pp. 200-1 (194-5).

[256] ". . . and not have to ask for Eau Minerale, with which to brush our teeth!", AWD, p. 207 (200).

[257] AWD p. 125 (123). Cf. also ". . . I must get pen to paper again", AWD p. 249 (241). [258] AWD p. 205 (199)

ind by a revealing paradox this perfect moment is an absolute zero hung between two infinities, two inaccessible happinesses: that of the country she has left behind and that of this other region which she will reach only to lose it again, where the joy of creating turns so swiftly into suffering and despair. Here we surprise the secret of that over-sensitive nature, which could have found health and peace at this zero but which was constantly driven by a need for intensity and for total dedication from one pole to the other of her being.

And then the homecoming proves disastrous: everything seems worn out and meaningless. The setting, the habits one has left behind have grown cold, are a mere shell in which, instead of regaining warmth and life, body and soul contract and freeze.[259] Fortunately adaptation is only a matter of days. But the comment with which Virginia Woolf concludes the analysis of that drop of tension that accompanies the transition to that neutral position between vacation and vocation is pregnant with meaning: "It occurs to me that this state, my depressed state, is the state in which most people usually are."[260] Is she not attributing to herself the aristocratic privilege of intensity in contrast with the mass of people, who are lukewarm and apathetic? And do we not recognize here the same pride, not blatant and arrogant but deeply felt, which she displayed as a writer? The pride of driving oneself to the extreme limits of life, parallel to the pride of driving oneself to the extreme limits of art. But if they spring from the same source, they become antagonistic in process of fulfilment, in so far as the ascetic practice of art is incompatible with the fervent exploration of the richness of the universe. One might be tempted to believe, after considering Virginia Woolf the novelist at work, that she had made her choice. But this choice is more apparent than real. On the one hand it may be more spectacular and tempting for those who would like to see her as a heroine devoting herself to the sacred cause of art: a twopence-coloured picture of the literary warrior or the saint, winning a too-easy victory over temptation. In fact, if a choice was made, it was merely as an alternative. "I am surprised", she writes in 1928, "and a little disquieted by the remorseless severity of my mind: that it never stops reading and writing ... is too professional, too little any longer a dreamy amateur."[261]

[259] Cf. Tuesday, May 30, 1933, AWD p. 207 (200): also p. 250 (242)
[260] AWD p. 207 (201)   [261] AWD p. 139 (136-7)

Surprise and anxiety are warnings sent from the hidden depths by the essential self, seeking to safeguard its wholeness. Until the very end, and even more resolutely after her great success had incorporated her, willy nilly, into the world of literary people, she was to assert her independence. If she could no longer describe herself as an amateur, she was constantly to repeat that she was and wished to be an "outsider".[262] The declaration of independence implied by this term is much more radical than it seems at first glance; it goes far beyond the mere freedom to write as one likes and to ignore the praise and blame dealt out by professionals. In fact, she asserts hereby that for her literature is not a career, and if none the less it is an essential activity, it is governed by the laws of life, not the conventions of a craft.

We have seen[263] what her art meant to Virginia Woolf, what she expected from it and what she found in it. But in fact was it not rather a means than an end? an attitude, a set of gestures that put her on the way towards what her troubled nature was seeking so desperately? It was not so much her reason for living as her means of access to life, and this pursuit of the expression only made sense in so far as it brought her back, or indeed led her, to the impression. Expressionism and impressionism may be aesthetic aspects of her work[264]: if these terms are given their original meaning, we find in them the twofold orientation of her being, which made her pursue life and art with equal intensity. Conscious, after reading Beatrice Webb, of a lack of foundation for her own existence, she analyses herself with her customary lucidity:

Great excitability and search after something. Great content—almost always enjoying what I'm at, but with constant change of mood. I don't think I'm ever bored. Sometimes a little stale; but I have a power of recovery—which I have tested . . . I enjoy epicurean ways of society; sipping and then shutting my eyes to taste. I enjoy almost everything. Yet I have some restless searcher in me. Why is there not a discovery in life? Something one can lay hands on and say "This is it"? My depression is a harassed feeling. I'm looking: but that's not it—that's not it. What is it? And shall I die before I find it? Then (as I was walking through Russell Square last night) I see the mountains in the sky: the great clouds; and the moon which is risen over Persia; I have a great and astonishing sense of something there, which is "it". It is not exactly beauty that I mean. It is that the thing is in itself

---

[262] AWD pp. 292 (282), 308 (297)   [263] Cf. *supra*, p. 59
[264] Cf. E. Weidner, *Impressionismus und Expressionismus in den Romanen Virginia Woolfs*, Greifswald, 1934

enough: satisfactory; achieved. A sense of my own strangeness, walking on the earth is there too: of the infinite oddity of the human position; trotting along Russell Square with the moon up there and those mountain clouds. Who am I, what am I, and so on: these questions are always floating about in me: and then I bump against some exact fact—a letter, a person, and come to them again with a great sense of freshness. And so it goes on. But on this showing, which is true, I think, I do fairly frequently come upon this 'it'; and then feel quite at rest.[265]

In this page, which defines Virginia Woolf's attitude to life, we recognize all the characteristics revealed by an analysis of her attitude to art: restlessness, search, instability, fervour, a need for absoluteness, the sense of mystery and the climax of a pacifying illumination. And this peace, analogous to the peace she finds in artistic creation, springs from the revealing fecundity of such moments, the fact that in them she attains—not through intelligence but through sensibility, through "some nervous fibre, or fanlike membrane in my species",[266] indeed by a sort of Bergsonian intuition—to the essence of things. As she was to write a little later: "Life is, soberly and accurately, the oddest affair; has in it the essence of reality."[267] No doubt this membrane, so delicate that it has hitherto evaded the scalpel of all anatomists, seems to unfold itself only in solitude to pick up these essential waves:

Often down here [at Rodmell] I have entered into a sanctuary; a nunnery; had a religious retreat; of great agony once; and always some terror; so afraid one is of loneliness; of seeing to the bottom of the vessel. That is one of the experiences I have had here in some Augusts; and got then to a consciousness of what I call "reality": a thing I see before me: something abstract; but residing in the downs or sky; beside which nothing matters; in which I shall rest and continue to exist. Reality I call it. And I fancy sometimes this is the most necessary thing to me: that which I seek.[268]

[265] AWD p. 86 (85)

[266] AWD p. 131 (128)

[267] AWD p. 101 (100)

[268] AWD p. 132 (129-30). Cf. also, five years earlier, in 1923, an imprecise account of similar experiences: "Somehow, extraordinary emotions possessed me. I forget now what. Often now I have to control my excitement—as if I were pushing through a screen; or as if something beat fiercely close to me. What this portends I don't know. It is a general sense of the poetry of existence that overcomes me. Often it is connected with the sea and St. Ives", AWD p. 56 (55). Cf. also, the following summer, in 1929: "If I could catch the feeling, I would; the feeling of the singing of the real world, as one is driven by loneliness and silence from the habitable world; the sense that comes to me of being bound on an adventure . . . And this curious steed, life, is genuine", AWD p. 148 (144-5).

Let us leave aside the agony and the terror—those qualities of intensity which are the reverse of joy—to consider only that reality which is "abstract" but which resides "in the downs or sky". The contradiction in this definition might perplex a rationalist philosopher; in fact it vanishes when we consider the writer's psyche as a whole in which sensibility and intelligence are merely two sides of the way of knowledge. And this sentence suddenly gives their full significance to those weeks and months spent at Rodmell, of which so far we have only considered the hours devoted to work. The whole Sussex countryside takes its place in Virginia Woolf's life, not as a setting but as an infinite wealth of signs, of silent messages, seeking day after day to reveal to her the secret of mankind and of the universe.

With the intense, concentrated vision that nostalgia bestows on an inaccessible reality, Virginia Woolf, lying ill, confined to her room by the doctor and incapable of working, dreams of the day as it should have been, in contrast with her wasted day:

No one in the whole of Sussex is so miserable as I am; or so conscious of an infinite capacity of enjoyment hoarded in me, could I use it. The sun streams (no, never streams; floods rather) down upon all the yellow fields and the long low barns; and what wouldn't I give to be coming through Firle woods, dirty and hot, with my nose turned home, every muscle tired and the brain laid up in sweet lavender, so sane and cool, and ripe for the morrow's task. How I should notice everything—the phrase for it coming the moment after and fitting like a glove; and then on the dusty road, as I ground my pedals, so my story would begin telling itself; and then the sun would be down; and home, and some bout of poetry after dinner, half read, half lived, as if the flesh were dissolved and through it the flowers burst red and white.[269]

That day—August 18, 1921—was only a dream-day, but it was loaded with memories, and also with anticipation, of innumerable joys, whose recurrence we can trace throughout her Diary.[270]

And the day these lines describe is surely typical of all her many stays at Rodmell, even when she tells us nothing about them.[271] The need for direct contact with nature was so urgent that it sent her roaming daily through the countryside, in all weathers.[272] The

[269] AWD p. 38 (37)
[270] AWD p. 187 (182)
[271] AWD p. 215 (208)
[272] AWD pp. 64 (62-3), 222 (215), 245 (237)

meadows with their cattle,[273] the cornfields with their harvesters,[274] the fox entering the furze,[275] a weasel crossing the racecourse,[276] the mole gliding over the meadow,[277] the rooks "beating up against the wind, which is high",[278] an unfamiliar path leading her to a new farm in a fold of the downs[279] or to the river,[280] the opalescent clouds[281] wandering across the sky, "and that fading and rising of the light which so enraptures me in the downs"[282]; this is what she seeks, all this beauty which is "too much for one pair of eyes. Enough to float a whole population in happiness, if only they would look.[283] She revels in the countryside,[284] and summer seems "dominated by a feeling of washing in boundless warm fresh air".[285] And this sense of well-being, often intensified into joy, is surely the token and the gift of that reality which she felt throbbing in the heart of the Sussex downs. Seventeen years later, which proves that her sensibility was not dulled, that she had kept that physical contact with the landscape, a contact which she so often tried to render in her work but which before being the stuff of art was the stuff of life, she asserts the overwhelming intensity of her feeling:

Coming back the other evening from Charleston, again all my nerves stood upright, flushed, electrified (what's the word?) with the sheer beauty—beauty astounding and superabounding. So that one almost resents it, not being capable of catching it all and holding it all at the moment.[286]

And this final echo of that ecstatic emotion, to which her death some two months later gives the quality of a farewell:

All frost. Still frost. Burning white. Burning blue. The elms red. I did not mean to describe, once more, the downs in snow; but it came. And I can't help even now turning to look at Asheham down, red, purple, dove blue grey, with the cross so melodramatically against it. What is the phrase I always remember—or forget. Look your last on all things lovely.[287]

[273] AWD p. 66 (64-5)   [274] AWD p. 65 (64)
[275] AWD p. 152 (149)   [276] AWD p. 131 (129)
[277] AWD p. 245 (237)   [278] AWD p. 131 (128)
[279] AWD p. 222 (215)   [280] AWD p. 301 (290)
[281] AWD p. 132 (130)   [282] AWD p. 131 (129)
[283] AWD p. 279 (269)   [284] AWD p. 131 (129)
[285] AWD p. 99 (97)
[286] Aug. 15, 1924, AWD p. 65 (64)
[287] AWD p. 362 (348). Cf. also "the lyric mood of the winter . . .", AWD p. 325 (313).

No doubt this contact with the world is not always so pure; often Virginia Woolf instinctively wonders "What's the phrase for that?"[288] But she seeks that phrase not among words, which are remote from reality, but closer, deeper down, by intensifying her sensations: "and try to make more and more vivid the roughness of the air current and the tremor of the rook's wings slicing as if the air were full of ridges and ripples and roughnesses". And even if, while she walks, phrases for the book in progress rise to her lips,[289] even if she takes advantage of a visit to Kew Gardens to "verify certain details",[290] it would be wrong to ascribe a secondary character to this experience of nature, to see in it merely a preparation for artistic activity. It is a profound necessity, possibly more common and more urgent among English people of that generation than among their French contemporaries, but one which in Virginia Woolf assumes exceptional intensity and value. If we can trace therein the source of many pages of *Jacob's Room*, *To the Lighthouse* and *The Waves*, we must not forget that it had consisted in the first place of simple moments of almost physical delight.

This need for the countryside by no means excludes the need for city life, but rather complements it. She moves between Rodmell and London in maturity as she had once moved between St Ives and London. And she reacts to city life with as keen a sensitivity as to nature. "London is enchanting",[291] and she yields to its spell the more readily for having escaped it for a while. After the solitude and concentration of Rodmell she plunges with delight into the rushing stream that seems to take over her personal life and govern it without any effort on her part. With a fickleness which will shock only those who are unacquainted with the power of manifold loyalties, she asserts her love of London and more particularly of the City, intensified by the threat of aerial bombardment hanging over the town:

[288] AWD p. 131 (128).

[289] AWD p. 29 (27): "Two weeks ago I made up *Jacob* incessantly on my walks"; p. 117 (115): "I walk making up phrases"; p. 189 (184): "declaiming phrases, seeing scenes, as I walk up Southampton Row".

[290] "I verified certain details", AWD p. 243 (234). Cf. also the irony with which she considers those entries in her Diary which might be considered literary note-taking: "Asheham diary drains off my meticulous observations of flowers, clouds, beetles and the price of eggs", AWD p. 2 (2).

[291] "London is enchanting. . . . One of these days I will write about London, and how it takes up the private life and carries it on, without any effort. Faces passing lift up my mind; prevent it from settling, as it does in the stillness at Rodmell", AWD p. 62 (61).

Odd how often I think with what is love I suppose of the City: of the walk to the Tower: that is my England: I mean, if a bomb destroyed one of those little alleys with the brass bound curtains and the river smell and the old woman reading, I should feel—well, what the patriots feel.[292]

But London is more than the City and Bloomsbury, the Zoo and Regent's Park, the Serpentine, Oxford Street with its crowds and its shops, and the small streets where barrel organs play; it is also the seat of human contacts, as Rodmell is the seat of solitude. Whereas in the hollow of the Sussex downs and the shifting Sussex sky Virginia Woolf seemed to discover a cosmic reality, in the anonymous faces wearing their social mask[293] that she studies at some evening party, or in the open and yet mysterious faces of friends at more intimate gatherings, she pursues a human reality equally fascinating and equally elusive. But we must not forget that Virginia Woolf was by nature solitary, that she lived in her dream[294] or her imagination[295] and that consequently her faculty for sympathising with, understanding and knowing others was limited to those beings who shared in her inner life.[296]

We have already seen how she shrank from people who do not "vibrate"[297], and it comes as no surprise to read certain outbursts which might suggest hardness or misanthropy:

And I do not love my kind. I detest them. I pass them by. I let them break on me like dirty rain drops. No longer can I summon up that energy which, when it sees one of these dry little shapes floating past, or rather stuck on the rock, sweeps round them, steeps them, infuses them, nerves them, and so finally fills them and creates them. Once I had a gift for doing this, and a passion, and it made parties arduous and exciting.[298]

But it would be wrong to isolate this passage and use it as evidence of a lack of human sympathy in Virginia Woolf. Even the

---

[292] AWD p. 325 (313). See also Dorothy Brewster, *Virginia Woolf's London*, an anthology of the descriptions of London scattered throughout her works.

[293] See AWD p. 75 (74): "people secrete an envelope [at parties] which connects them and protects them from others, like myself, who am outside the envelope, foreign bodies".

[294] Cf. *supra*, p. 65

[295] Cf. "But how entirely I live in my imagination . . . things churning up in my mind and so making a perpetual pageant, which is to be my happiness", AWD p. 67 (66).

[296] "This brew can't sort with nondescript people", AWD p. 67 (66).

[297] Cf. *supra*, pp. 99-100.

[298] AWD p. 79 (78). Cf. also p. 121 (119)

evolution that it suggests, towards her fortieth year, is entirely superficial. The curiosity about people which she imagined she had once possessed was in fact rather an optimistic trustfulness. While she infused life and energy and reality into those she met, she had believed them capable of absorbing and assuming these qualities. When experience showed her that only a few were worthy of the gift and the welcome she offered them, she gave up this exhausting and fruitless quest. Her work may show the effects of this limitation of the field of human experience. But can it be said that her life was impoverished thereby? In this sphere, as in many others, is quantity to be set above quality? If she could not love her fellow men it was because she loved her friends too much; because superficial relations had no meaning for her. Such an attitude may be condemned from the social or humanitarian point of view; it is hardly to be criticised from the point of view of the individual.

I shall not refer yet again to Virginia Woolf's relations with her friends, the emotional depth of which I have already had occasion to mention.[299] I shall merely cite one example of her sensibility and her power of participating in another's life. When, shortly after the death of Roger Fry, she went to see Francis Birrell as he lay dying in a hotel bedroom, she had to steel herself in order not to succumb to the emotion that overwhelmed her; it was more than she could bear to associate herself with his death-agony and experience it fully. "I cannot go through that again."[300] But the face of the dying man haunted her, and as thoughts of her friend's death merged with thoughts of the dying year, she experienced once again pain and loneliness, and the desire to live vanishing into nothingness.[301] Sometimes she refers with regret to the friendships which circumstances nipped in the bud and which death cut off forever, those with Katherine Mansfield and Stella Benson for instance; she had barely time to have an inkling of their richness, and she almost blames herself for failing, or not knowing how, to recognize them sooner, more swiftly.[302] Indeed, she made room in her own life even for those for whom her sympathy and respect were not unmixed, provided they were genuine inside; divergences of nature and intelligence were disregarded. Arnold Bennett for

[299] Cf. *supra*, pp. 64-5
[300] AWD p. 233 (226)
[301] "The expression on his face is what I see . . .", AWD p. 235 (227).
[302] "There seems to be some sort of reproach to me in her death, as in K.M.'s", AWD p. 214 (206).

instance, whose death "leaves me sadder than I should have supposed".[303] The surprise accompanying this feeling guarantees its sincerity, should her own explanation be unconvincing: "Queer how one regrets the dispersal of anybody who seemed—as I say—genuine: who had direct contact with life."[304] She could not fail to respond to a certain quality in those who through their weight and solidity of being had become "elements" in her life.[305]

This interest in others was not restricted to people: it extended to their books—to all books. I may perhaps have conveyed the impression, at times, that Virginia Woolf's passion for writing was so exclusive, so deeply rooted in herself, so untouched by "literary" concerns, that she took no interest in what was not her own work. The importance of her critical writings is sufficient proof of the contrary. And in her account of each day's activities we see reading constantly alternating with writing, sometimes as a means of getting under way, sometimes as a form of relaxation. It would take too long to catalogue her library: we need only consider its extent. In 1932, full of youthful ardour (she has just declared she still sometimes thinks herself the youngest person in the bus) she sets herself no less a task than to go through the whole of English literature "from Chaucer to Lawrence".[306] Of course this is a piece of extravagance, but one that verges on the truth. We need only refer to the list of "books read or in reading" that she drew up on October 2, 1934:

Shakespeare: *Troilus; Pericles; Taming of Shrew; Cymbeline;*
Maupassant ⎫
de Vigny ⎪
St. Simon ⎬ only scraps
Gide ⎭
    Library books: Powys
               Wells
               Lady Brooke
               Prose. Dobree
               Alice James
Many MSS.
           none worth keeping.[307]

[303] AWD p. 169 (165)   [304] AWD p. 170 (166)
[305] "An element in life . . . taken away . . .", AWD p. 170 (166).
[306] Cf. "I want . . . to go through English literature, like a string through cheese, or rather like some industrious insect, eating its way from book to book, from Chaucer to Lawrence. This is a programme . . . to last out my 20 years, if I have them", AWD p. 178 (173).
[307] AWD p. 227 (219). For more details see *supra*, pp. 41-2 and *infra*, ch. IV, 1: p. 125.

And we see that to English literature we must add French literature: Racine, Pascal,[308] Mme de Sévigné, La Rochefoucauld,[309] Mme de Lafayette,[310] Flaubert,[311] Proust,[312] the Russians[313] and Freud[314] and Dante[315] and Ibsen.[316] . . . And when she declares that she hardly ever reads contemporary writers[317] we should clarify this contempt as we clarified her hatred for her fellows. When she speaks of "writing by living people" she means second rate works—just as when she spoke of her "kind" she meant people who are devoid of interest. Moreover, the criterion is the same: such writing "adds nothing to one's vision of life, perhaps".[318] For such books Virginia Woolf has no time, any more than for the people who do not enrich her life. Pride, egocentrism? Maybe, but, with a sense of proportion which makes up for all her exaggerations, she says "perhaps", and she concludes, "yet I feel this is important. And why?" Moreover, with books as with people she professes to be harsher and more exclusive than she really is: just as she can put up with a boring visitor for three hours and a half,[319] she will read through an awe-inspiring pile of MSS for the Hogarth Press, read them "carefully, too" and judge "much of it on the border and so needing thought".[320] Of course she hardly enjoyed such duties, but she fulfilled them, showing thereby that she was capable of a certain flexibility and self-sacrifice all the more creditable in that they were foreign to her nature.

To complete this portrait, one should add a few intimate traits that give it that element of ordinary humanity which exceptional beings are too frequently denied.

It is undoubtedly hard to imagine Virginia Woolf in other than

[308] Cf. AWD p. 314 (303)
[309] Cf. AWD p. 312 (301)
[310] Cf. AWD p. 45 (44)
[311] Cf. AWD pp. 269 (260), 270 (260)
[312] Cf. AWD pp. 52 (50), 81 (79)
[313] Cf. AWD p. 210 (203)
[314] Cf. AWD p. 321 (309)
[315] Cf. AWD p. 233 (225)
[316] Cf. AWD p. 139 (136)
[317] "Writing by living people. I scarcely ever read it", AWD p. 95 (94)
[318] "But what qualities does it lack? That it adds nothing to one's vision of life, perhaps . . . but it has some existence now . . . yet I feel this is important. And why?", AWD p. 95 (94)
[319] Cf. AWD p. 138 (135)
[320] "I read and read and finished I daresay 3 foot thick of MS. read carefully too", AWD p. 150 (146)

serious mood: her intensity seems to make laughter as alien to her as futility. She admits none the less that "on the whole it is good to have an unbuttoned laughing evening once in a way".[321] Although she had little feminine vanity we find her hunting for shoes in a sale,[322] buying silk,[323] wearing a new coat[324] and reproaching herself for spending too much money.[325] Although her books are "in a muddle", and she is always losing her pen[326], she is none the less sensitive to her everyday surroundings: she plans to repaint a room, to choose chintz for curtains.[327] After chopping wood or playing a game of bowls, she will make a cake[328] and at seven o'clock start cooking haddock and sausages for supper.[329] She may relegate all these details to the background, but she does not ignore them. The texture of her daily life is not so very different from that of most people of similar means. But this universal routine corresponds, in life, to the story in a novel. If the artist's liberty enables her to elude the latter, the pressure of facts constrains her to accept the former. It remains on the surface; it represents the impersonal trappings of her feminine condition. I have drawn attention to it simply lest it should be assumed that she was exempted from this common bondage.

It is not easy to try and confine Virginia Woolf within a few phrases: she is made up of movements and contrasts. Essentially "very rapid, excited, amused, intense"[330] at the very instant when we catch her in one attitude, she has already slipped on to another; she writes in a mood of joyful enthusiasm, but next day every line costs her superhuman efforts and drives her to despair; criticism leaves her raw and discouraged; a moment later, roused into self-confidence and resolution, she excitedly asserts her independence, her freedom, bent on being herself in spite of everyone. She adores London, and Sussex delights her. She revels in solitude, yet will

[321] AWD p. 237 (229). Cf. also Clive Bell, *Old Friends*, pp. 95 and 108, and Stephen Spender, *World within World*, p. 156.
[322] Cf. AWD p. 314 (303)
[323] Cf. AWD p. 331 (319)
[324] Cf. AWD p. 238 (230)
[325] Cf. AWD p. 140 (137)
[326] Cf. AWD pp. 304 (293) and 321 (309)
[327] Cf. AWD p. 253 (244)
[328] Cf. AWD p. 330 (318)
[329] Cf. AWD p. 365 (351)
[330] AWD p. 231 (224)

plunge passionately into endless discussions. She may appear withdrawn, lost in her private dream, and then the death of a friend creates a void within her that nothing can fill. She seems wholly dedicated to artistic creation, and yet longs for "the width and amusement of human life".[331] And in each of her aspects, in every action or desire, we find utter sincerity. As the whole weight of the pendulum is in each of its oscillations, so the whole weight of her being is in each of her moods, every impulse of will or desire. Are we to infer instability, to assume that her life was divided between nervous melancholia and the ephemeral triumphs of the will?[332] But whence was that will-power derived, and that happiness which she so often attains, and to such a supreme degree, whether through the completion of a book or in the splendour of a summer's day?

It is not in the swing of the pendulum that we shall find the secret law of her being; we must seek out the fixed point from which its movement emanates. Often, towards the end of the year, as if the last pages of the calendar roused her from the fluidity of timelessness, of duration, to make her aware of discontinuous time, she takes her bearings in her Diary, and forgetting or transcending the mood of the moment she sets out the formula that gives unity to her many-sidedness. The last she gives us, on December 29, 1940, is possibly the ultimate revelation which, in an obscure foreboding of her imminent end, her subconscious dictated:

There are moments when the sail flaps. Then, being a great amateur of the art of life, determined to suck my orange, off, like a wasp if the blossom I'm on fades, as it did yesterday—I ride across the downs to the cliffs.[333]

It is this passion for life, only to be lived with all sails set and spread to the wind, which makes her course so devious. It is that thirst for the best, which, combined with her physical frailness, made her shift constantly from art to life, from writing to reading,

---

[331] Cf. "I believe I want this more humane existence for my next—to spread carelessly among one's friends—to feel the width and amusement of human life: not to strain to make a pattern just yet; to be made supple, and to let the juice of usual things, talk, character, seep through me, quietly, involuntarily, before I say Stop and take out my pen", AWD p. 186 (180-1).

[332] Cf. "What a born melancholic I am! The only way to keep afloat is by working. A note for the summer—I must take more work than I can possibly get done", AWD p. 143 (140).

[333] AWD p. 360 (346)

from solitude to society, from London to Sussex, from travel to seclusion. In fact, it was not the fading of the flower that drove her towards another: it was her own exhaustion, the price she paid for the intensity of her quest, that forced her to give up. She was always seeking causes or justifications for her inconstancy: "free use of the faculties means happiness"[334] as she had said long ago. And if she knew how to turn her illnesses to account by exploring the borders of life and death, far from any morbid indulgence in these periods of forced abdication she always aspired to full health, "to be well and use strength to get more out of life is, surely, the greatest fun in the world".[335] The fact that she repeatedly contemplated suicide[336] and eventually yielded to that temptation only confirms her zest for life, carried to excess. The higher the peak one reaches, the more dizzy is one's fall. After such supreme moments as the completion of a book, or perfect contact with another human being, after "one of those days that I called 'potent' "[337] "there's nothing left of the people, of the ideas, of the strain, of the whole life in short that has been racing round my brain . . .".[338] And amid such emptiness how can one realise that some day one will feel, once again, "the splendour of this undertaking, life . . .".[339] Only hope, self-confidence, a sort of faith in one's strength and in the universe—when any other faith is absent, as was the case with Virginia Woolf[340]—can regenerate the will and restrain the individual on the brink of destruction. In the spring of 1941, these certainties, her only certainties, crumbled away. The war meant the unleashing of irrational forces in the universe: "We live without a future. That's what is queer: with our noses pressed to a closed door."[341] And her faith in herself, in her work, which had risen, with so many setbacks and uncertainties, to that "I am I"[342] which she would say to herself as much, perhaps in order to convince herself of it as in order to assert it, had reached a peak at which only a miracle could sustain

[334] AWD p. 58 (56)
[335] AWD p. 56 (55)
[336] Cf. AWD p. 229 (222)
[337] AWD p. 141 (138)
[338] AWD p. 229 (222)
[339] AWD p. 184 (179)
[340] Cf. ". . . there were causes in her life: prayer; principle. None in mine", AWD p. 86 (85)
[341] AWD p. 364 (350)
[342] "I walk over the marsh saying I am I", AWD p. 361 (347)

it. And on the contrary everything, from within and from without, now threatened it. The effort and tension which had brought it to such a height had, despite appearances, undermined it. The wall had thinned through which she saw "the pale disillusioned world",[343] since 1937, since Julian Bell was killed in Spain and now that so many others were dying every minute. She had strained her reason and her mind and her body to hold together the tortured universe, and wrest joy from it. But the universe was disintegrating in war, and she realised that she herself was losing her footing. She felt that she no longer had the vitality which, when she was younger, enabled her to shake off mental illness. She felt, too, that the universal delirium could only be an echo amplifying her own delirium beyond all hope: "I feel certain that I am going mad again. I feel we can't go through another of those terrible times. And I shan't recover this time."[344] This was her farewell message to Leonard Woolf. Her suicide, her will to die was only the reverse side of her will to live; in the paroxysm of its accomplishment, the act forms a counterpart to the intensity of the life which it brought to an end. It was the last swing of the pendulum, summing up all the rest, and to which her whole existence, made up of alternations, seemed destined by some ineluctable inner force of gravity.

[343] AWD p. 284 (274)
[344] Quoted by D. Daiches, *Virginia Woolf*, New Directions, 1942, p. 156, and Nicholson & Watson, London, p. 146.

CHAPTER IV

ANALYSIS AND ARGUMENT

VIRGINIA WOOLF'S critics, whether because they
reflect the tastes or interests of the public, or because the
originality and richness of her novels have led them to relegate
her essays to second place, have only allowed these a very restricted
place in their studies. Some indeed, considering her solely as a
novelist, have merely picked out from a few articles on general
aesthetic questions such quotations as might throw light on the
theories of which the novels represent the practice. Without prejudging either the absolute value of her six volumes of essays—to
which we should add the two pamphlets, *A Room of One's Own* and
Three Guineas—or their value relative to the main body of her
work, we must stress the interest of these writings. They have most
frequently been used either to clarify the novelist's aesthetic views
in order to justify the form of her creative work, or to facilitate or
deepen the interpretation of this; which represents only a very
limited aspect of her critical production. The popularity of certain
essays, *Modern Fiction*,[1] *The Art of Fiction*,[2] *Mr. Bennett and Mrs.
Brown*,[3] *The Russian Point of View*,[4] quoted by all the critics, is not
undeserved, indeed, but it has none the less had, in my view, two
undesirable consequences. On the one hand it has helped to spread
the opinion, or at any rate the impression or feeling, that Virginia
Woolf, primarily preoccupied by technical questions, was an
adept of art for art's sake, out of touch with the reality of the outside world and the living problems of her time, and that consequently her work was merely a literary curiosity whose interest
dwindled as its novelty became familiar and the doctrine of
"commitment" in literature gained ground. Thus both the work
itself and the author's personality were seen in a false perspective.
On the other hand, these few essays represent only a very minor
portion of Virginia Woolf's critical activity. To stress this aspect
to the detriment of all the rest results in breaking the harmony, in
destroying the balance of tendencies and interests so characteristic

---

[1] CR I pp. 184-95 (150-8)   [2] The M pp. 90-111 (106-12)
[3] CDB pp. 89-93 (94-119)   [4] CR I pp. 219-31 (177-87)

of our author. It means cutting her off from a tradition with which she never claimed to break, and of her indebtedness to which, indeed, these essays are an acknowledgment; it means, moreover, neglecting that "extraordinary catholicity of taste" ascribed to her by David Daiches[5]; it means, finally, emphasizing her sensibility and imagination and that intense self-centred dream that fostered her novel-writing at the expense of the vigour and vitality of her mind, which found in analysis and rational argument a form of activity and a means of expression. It is with the intention of restoring their complex fulness to both the work and the personality of Virginia Woolf that I shall study first her essays, then, in a second section, the two pamphlets; and in view of the importance of feminism in the latter, I shall take the opportunity to examine this question.

1. THE CRITICAL ESSAYS

On finishing a long essay about Hazlitt,[6] Virginia Woolf notes in her Diary:

And I am not sure that I have speared that little eel in the middle— that marrow—which is one's object in criticism. A very difficult business no doubt to find it, in all these essays; so many; so short; and on all subjects.[7]

Confronted with the six volumes of essays she has left us, I feel in the same dilemma as she was over Hazlitt. If my intention were merely to study Virginia Woolf's criticism on its own account, to mark the limits of the field it covers, to set forth its contents and assess its value, I should find it relatively easy to classify these essays according to their date or type. But I am anxious myself (due proportion being kept) to spear the elusive eel hidden in the folds of the text, and to orientate my study in function of the whole to which it belongs. I shall seek to extract from these writings what they reveal to us of Virginia Woolf's attitude to literature. I shall thus limit my analysis to four points.

In the first place, it seems indispensable to specify the place and the importance of this aspect of our author's activity within the

[5] D. Daiches, *Virginia Woolf* (New Directions, p. 139; Nicholson & Watson, London, p. 130): "From the two volumes of *The Common Reader* we get the impression of a wide range of reading and an extraordinary catholicity of taste."
[6] Cf. CR II pp. 173-85 (156-66)
[7] AWD p. 160 (156)

general setting of her work. Then I shall analyse her conception of criticism, and finally the evolution of this conception. The biographical data and the texts themselves enabling Virginia Woolf's relations with her contemporaries to be more clearly circumscribed than in the case of her novels, I shall try to estimate her possible debt to them; needless to say in this quest for possible influences Leslie Stephen will not be forgotten. Finally I shall consider the application she made of her critical theories, finding there traits which will complete the portrait of the artist sketched in the previous chapter. However, even in this last section, my analysis will be governed by the desire to probe more deeply into the thought, the sensibility and the literary experience of my subject, rather than to make an exhaustive study of her criticism or assess its merits. Incidentally, I shall not set out her theory of the novel, which may easily be gleaned from the general essays she devotes to the subject, or to some of its aspects, and from her studies of particular novelists. A consideration of the novels in the first place, then of the problems peculiar to her work, will provide a better opportunity to examine these theories and trace their development, with reference meanwhile to the essays which deal with them. As regards the essays which are not concerned with literary subjects, as for example "The Death of the Moth", "Three Pictures", "Street Haunting", "Royalty", which undoubtedly provide interesting evidence as to Virginia Woolf's personality, what they tell us will be dealt with in the course of this study, and to devote a special section to them would involve repetition.

The fact that Virginia Woolf began her literary career by writing criticism needs no special explanation: it was a normal step. Moreover, considering the circle of acquaintance of her father, her brothers and sister and her friends, her entry into literature by this back door was quite natural. About 1902 she was introduced to the editor of *The Speaker*, and a year or two later, in 1903 or 1904, she met Bruce Richmond,[8] editor of the *Times Literary Supplement*, to which she was to be a lifelong contributor.[9]

---

[8] Information provided by Leonard Woolf.

[9] In fact the first two published items in B. J. Kirkpatrick's bibliography are dated 1905, in the *TLS*. The only contribution to *The Speaker* is April 21, 1906. Not until 1908 (as the Diary implies, moreover) did V. W. become a regular contributor to the *TLS*. The last of the 215 articles published during her lifetime in the *TLS* is Sept. 25, 1937; cf. also AWD p. 293 (283).

Her articles are to be found in thirty-two other periodicals and a couple of daily papers,[10] among which the most important are *The New Statesman*, *The Criterion*, *The Nation and Athenaeum*, *The New Republic*, *The Yale Review* and *The New Statesman and Nation*. During her lifetime she published two volumes of collected essays, the first and second *Common Readers*, in 1925 and 1932. She was preparing a third volume, which she was hoping to publish at the end of 1941 or the beginning of 1942. *The Death of the Moth and Other Essays*, published by Leonard Woolf in 1942, while it fulfils this intention, does not necessarily correspond, either in its order or in the choice of articles, to the author's intentions, which were still too vague at the time of her death to guide her executor. Three other volumes of essays were still to appear: *The Moment* in 1947, *The Captain's Deathbed* in 1950, and *Granite and Rainbow* in 1958. Moreover these six volumes, comprising 162 essays, represent less than half[11] her achievement in a field which, although secondary, is none the less important enough to justify an even wider study than can be devoted to it here.

If Virginia Woolf's Diary in its existing form reveals to us the phases of her creative activity, that part of her life and thought which was dedicated to her art, it also displays her reactions as reader. Whether about contemporary writers such as Katherine Mansfield, Joyce or D. H. Lawrence, or about Shakespeare, Sophocles, Milton, Byron, Henry James or Pascal, we feel her always on the alert, "following the scent"[12] pen in hand. Her reactions are spontaneous and fruitful: "Whatever book I read bubbles up in my mind as part of an article I want to write."[13]

---

[10] List of periodicals in which we find articles by V. W. (date of appearance of first article): *TLS*, 1905; *The Speaker*, 1906; *The National Review*, 1905; *The Cornhill Magazine*, 1908; *Living Age* (N.Y.) 1908; *Athenaeum*, 1919; *New Statesman*, 1920; *London Mercury*, 1920; *Criterion*, 1923; *Broom* (N.Y.), 1923; *Nation & Athenaeum*, 1923; *Dial* (N.Y.), 1923; *Lit. Rev. of N.Y. Evening Post*, 1923; *New Republic* (N.Y.), 1924; *Vogue*, 1925; *Sat. Rev. of Lit.*, 1925; *New Criterion*, 1926; *Arts* (N.Y.), 1926; *Yale Review*, 1926; *N.Y. Herald Tribune*, 1926; *Forum* (N.Y.), 1927; *Atlantic Monthly* (Boston), 1927; *Time and Tide*, 1928; *Life and Letters*, 1928; *Bookman* (N.Y.), 1929; *Nineteenth Century and After*, 1929; *Listener*, 1929; *Harper's Magazine* (L. & N.Y.), 1929; *Harper's Bazaar*, 1930; *New Statesman & Nation*, 1931; *Fortnightly Review*, 1931; *Lysistrata* (Oxford), 1934; *Hearst's International combined with Cosmopolitan*, 1938; *Folios of New Writing* (London), 1940. Daily papers: *Daily Worker*, 1936; *The Times*, 1936.

[11] Cf. B. J. Kirkpatrick, *A Bibliography of Virginia Woolf*; section C, "Contributions to Periodicals", includes 375 articles.

[12] AWD p. 312 (301)   [13] AWD p. 38 (37)

Nearly ten years later, in 1929, we find the same sentiments, the same enthusiasm:

I am free to begin reading Elizabethans— . . . This thought fills me with joy—no overstatement. To begin reading with a pen in my hand, discovering, pouncing, thinking of phrases, when the ground is new, remains one of my great excitements.[14]

And right at the end of her life, in 1939, the same expressions recur, bearing witness to the constancy of her attitude and the consistency of her method: "That's the real point of my little brown book—that it makes me read—with a pen—following the scent; and read the great books: not the slither of MSS."[15] This concern for exactitude, this seriousness, are natural tendencies which the demands of journalism might have impaired; on the contrary, they fostered and developed these qualities. But journalism did not merely provide character-training; it was also a school of writing:

I learnt a lot of my craft writing for [TLS]: how to compress; how to enliven, and also was made to read with a pen and notebook, seriously.[16]

One comment by the author of "Reading" and "How should one read a book" sums up to perfection what reading meant to her: "What a vast fertility of pleasure books hold for me!"[17] This twofold aspect of pleasure and fertility, of relaxation and enrichment, characterizes the moments devoted by Virginia Woolf to essay writing; and it is to these two factors that we must refer, both to evaluate the place this activity held in her life and to bring out the principles which govern it.

In 1924, when she was working simultaneously on *Mrs Dalloway* and on the preparation of the first *Common Reader*, Virginia Woolf appears to have discovered the ideal rhythm" . . . my fiction before lunch and then essays after tea".[18] This alternation, sometimes rapid and daily, as here, and sometimes slower, corresponds to an inner compulsion. The writing of her novels made demands on only half of herself: on the creative spirit, the imagination, which called forth its own world, was confined within it, fed from it. An intense, excited world, in which the writer cannot dwell too

[14] AWD p. 150 (146-7)
[15] AWD p. 312 (301)
[16] AWD p. 293 (283)
[17] AWD p. 211 (204)
[18] AWD p. 65 (63)

long "Half my brain dries completely. . . ."[19] The regenerative power of criticism is due moreover as much to the reading it involves, the absorbing of fresh substances,[20] as to the refreshment provided by a change of mental attitude, the exercise of different faculties. This function of relief is none the less very important: it is a sort of physical necessity, as certain expressions in the Diary bear witness: "Always relieve pressure by a flight. Always violently turn the pillow: hack an outlet. Often a trifle does. A review offered of Marie Corelli by the *Listener*. . . ."[21]

But the relationship between the two activities—novel writing and criticism—like that between the two sides of the writer's nature, is sometimes more complex. Although most frequently these activities are complementary, and contribute—sometimes spontaneously, sometimes in a deliberate pursuit of mental health—to ensuring unbroken production and consequently physical equilibrium, there may, on the other hand, be a conflict.[22] While Virginia Woolf is writing a novel, we constantly find her being distracted by the thought of articles, by ideas or theories springing up, obsessing her until she has allotted them a small place in her time-table.[23] And inversely, hardly has she decided to devote a week or a month to essay writing, when the novel she has abandoned, or some new novel, suddenly matured and weighty, overturns all her plans.[24] Sometimes the mental attitude has lingered on, impeding a different form of activity: "After a dose of criticism I feel that I'm writing sideways, using only an angle of my mind."[25] Actually, this awareness of the opposition between the critic and the novelist in Virginia Woolf confronts us with the complex unity of reality, which no abstraction, however

[19] AWD p. 253 (244): "Half my brain dries completely, but I've only to turn over and there's the other half, I think, ready, quite happily to write a little article."
[20] Cf. AWD p. 80 (78): ". . . replenishing my cistern at night with Swift. I am going to write about Stella and Swift for Richmond" (*TLS*); or again, AWD p. 178 (174): "However a year spent—save for diversions in Greece and Russia—in reading through English literature will no doubt do good to my fictitious brain. Rest it anyhow."
[21] AWD p. 324 (312). Cf. AWD p. 46 (45): ". . . so that I can vary the side of the pillow as fortune inclines."
[22] Cf. AWD p. 181 (176): "I tried to analyse my depression: how my brain is jaded with the conflict within of two types of thought, the critical, the creative." Also AWD p. 246 (237).
[23] Cf. AWD pp. 320 (307), 321 (308), 329 (316)
[24] Cf. AWD p. 159 (155): "I want to be back at *The Waves*."
[25] AWD p. 58 (56)

handy, however apparently convincing, should make us forget. By trying too hard to distinguish between the author of *The Common Reader* and the author of *Mrs Dalloway*, we risk misjudging them both, for neither of them is ever wholly absent. If they seem to take it in turns to write now essays, now novels, it is less as one runner relieves another in a relay race than as one might simply change hands. And no doubt it is largely due to this unconscious collaboration between her analytical intellect, her critical lucidity, her logical powers on the one hand and, on the other, the autonomy of the imagination, nourished on sensibility and on private dreams, that Virginia Woolf's work owes certain characteristics which I shall try to bring out in the course of this book: something rather studied about her novels—some will call it art and others artifice—and the element of vision, of fantasy, of impressionism, of curiosity about the writer's personality and craft, in her criticism. The strict separation of genres is a classical principle which seems jeopardized by the polymorphous works of our own time. And of all genres the broadest and most flexible are certainly the novel and the essay. Virginia Woolf, from a sense of discipline, intellectual exactness and concern for art, attempted to keep them distinct; and yet she was liable to ask herself the significant question: "Do I write essays about myself?"[26] She dared not or could not answer. But when, nearly ten years later, in 1932, she conceived of *The Years* as an "essay-novel",[27] we may surely interpret this formula as the long-deferred acceptance of a synthesis to which, at the time of *Mrs Dalloway*, she was not ready to adhere.

Novels being, in spite of everything, her main work and preoccupation, one might be tempted to think that Virginia Woolf found criticism the easier task. If most frequently the Diary stresses the impression of relief, ease and rapidity,[28] it would be wrong to ascribe any general or absolute value to these comments. They express only relative and fleeting states of mind. A change of work after a long creative period of fiction writing provokes a lightheartedness and zest comparable to those which the writer experiences when she first starts on a novel, and equally short-lived. "I shall tire of Hazlitt and criticism after the first divine

[26] AWD p. 57 (56) (June 19, 1923).
[27] Cf. AWD p. 189 (183), and *infra*, ch. V, p. 303 ff
[28] E.g. AWD pp. 117-18 (115-6).

relief,"[29] she writes. Or again, when she is preparing her two critical collections, we find each time, after the first burst of energy, effort, weariness, discouragement, or disgust.[30]

The fact is that she exercises as much care over the slightest review as over any page of her novels.[31] She corrects, polishes, condenses, seeks for lightness, vigour, precision, going over each piece an incalculable number of times. And this concern with form is no superficial vanity; it represents the need, a fundamental one with Virginia Woolf, to express her every idea with the greatest possible precision and perfection. But this pursuit of perfection, these successive revisions that she compels herself to undertake, are just as exacting as the same patient efforts devoted, as we shall see, to her novels: "Oh I am so tired of correcting my own writing."[32] She feels her weaknesses, she is aware of them; she doubts her logical exactness,[33] she dreads the consequences both of her over-meticulousness and over-impetuosity:

I am horrified by my own looseness. This is partly that I don't think things out first; partly that I stretch my style to take in crumbs of meaning. But the result is a wobble and diffusity and breathlessness which I detest.[34]

She admits that she lacks the scholar's patience or the taste for scholarship.[35] But if, consequently, certain forms of criticism and certain fields are closed to her, she retains none the less a justified confidence in her own particular qualities, which I shall presently examine and assess.

Without attaching more importance to this detail than it deserves, one should note that her essays, critical articles and reviews were a form of commercial writing for Virginia Woolf, bringing in an immediate and unproblematical return. On June 22nd, 1927, for instance, she notes in her Diary: "I write every day

[29] AWD p. 158 (155)

[30] Cf. AWD p. 178 (173): "Why did I ever say I would produce another volume of *Common Reader?*"

[31] Cf. AWD p. 46 (45): ". . . when I write a review I write every sentence as if it were going to be tried before three Chief Justices."

[32] AWD p. 170 (166)

[33] Cf. AWD p. 246 (237): "I recognize my own limitation: not a good ratiocinator, Lytton used to say. " Also *ibid.*, pp. 83 (80), 120 (119), 314 (303)

[34] AWD p. 143 (140)

[35] In 1926, thinking of a general book on literature, she writes (AWD, p. 100 (99)): "One could spin a theory which would bring the chapters together. I don't feel that I can read seriously and exactly for it."

about something and have deliberately set apart a few weeks to money-making, so that I may put £50 in each of our pockets by September."[36] And the following year, in March: "And money making. I hope to settle in and write one nice little discreet article for £25 each month."[37] None the less, a month later, we find by way of corrective: "Once I get the wheels spinning in my head, I don't want money much, or dress, or even a cupboard, a bed at Rodmell or a sofa."[38] We should therefore not assume that financial considerations impelled her to exploit this aspect of her talent. These comments are of the same order as the balance-sheets we have seen her set out about her literary earnings.[39] They have been mentioned here only as evidence of a realistic sense too often ignored or even denied her.

Virginia Woolf's critical theory is relatively simple. At first sight, it is an art of reading, which she analyses in various articles,[40] but the essence of which is concentrated in two sentences of the brief introduction, "The Common Reader", which opens the collection of that name.

Above all, [the common reader] is guided by an instinct to create for himself, out of whatever odds and ends he can come by, some kind of whole—a portrait of a man, a sketch of an age, a theory of the art of writing. He never ceases, as he reads, to run up some rickety and ramshackle fabric which shall give him the temporary satisfaction of looking sufficiently like the real object to allow of affection, laughter, and argument.[41]

Without prejudging the justness of the epithet "common" or "average" with which she professes to make her reader represent a category broad enough to ensure for her criticism a universality which would be its justification, we see from the start that Virginia Woolf is opposed to learned, academic criticism. She does not intend to teach, correct or judge. She never misses an opportunity

[36] AWD p. 109 (108)
[37] AWD p. 125 (122)
[38] AWD p. 126 (124)
[39] Cf. *supra*, ch. III, pp. 71, 97n, 198
[40] "Hours in a Library" (1917) in G & R pp. 24-31 (24-31); "Reading" (1919, 1921) in CDB, pp. 140-65 (151-79); "On Re-reading Novels" (1926) in The M pp. 126-34 (155-66); "All about Books" (1931) in CDB pp. 112-17 (120-6); "How should one read a book?" (1932) in CR II pp. 258-70 (234-45)
[41] CR I p. 11 (1)

for some lively, ironic taunt at those "heavily furred and gowned" critics who claim to lay down the rules about literature and in the name of Aristotle or some Absolute of their own invention to codify genres and distribute praise or blame.[42] We recognize her inveterate antagonism towards authority of any sort, and the Universities in particular, whose teaching, in her view, leads away from reality and brings only sterile knowledge:

> Instead of knowing that the sun was in the sky and the bird on the branch, the young knew the whole course of English literature from one end to another; how one age follows another; and one influence cancels another; and one style is derived from another; and one phrase is better than another.[43]

The lover of books, the ideal reader who, being the author's chosen interlocutor, is also the only critic who matters, is not concerned with all those notions that proliferate on the fringe of literature. To classify, to affix labels is not his aim; to refer to categories, to judge according to so-called standards is not his method. He must approach a work with the same simplicity, the same sincerity with which he would approach the reality from which it has sprung, of which it is the token, and to which it must bring him back. To be oneself strongly and deeply, without prejudices or timidity, allowing the whole of one's being, sensibility and intellect, the free play of all its faculties, such is the basic attitude which makes the art of reading a worthy complement to the art of writing, and makes the reader a partner worthy of the author who addresses him. It is not merely a question of rejecting passivity[44] and following superficially, with self-complacent but misleading eagerness, the intricacies of a plot, the complexity of characters, the richness of the descriptions[45]; the reader who went

[42] Cf. CR II p. 258 (234): "To admit authorities, however heavily furred and gowned, into our libraries and let them tell us how to read, what to read, what value to place upon what we read, is to destroy the spirit of freedom which is the breath of those sanctuaries. Everywhere else we may be bound by laws and conventions—there we have none."

[43] CDB p. 116 (125). The occasion for this taunt was *Scrutinies*, two volumes of essays collected by Edgell Rickword, one of the editors of *The Calendar of Modern Letters* (1925-27). F. R. Leavis, an admirer of Rickword's, was to develop similar aims and theories in his review, *Scrutiny*, which V. W. was to consider her No. 1 enemy.

[44] Cf. The M p. 104 (165), "On Re-reading Novels": ". . . the common reader will refuse to sit any longer open-mouthed in passive expectation."

[45] Cf. The M p. 128 (157), *ibid*.

no further than this would no more grasp the essence of the book than some curious, interested observer, appreciating the splendour of a stage set and capable of noting its diversity and its nuances, grasps the essence of the play. Access to the heart of a book, like access to the heart of reality, requires a more total presence, a more complete mobilisation of one's whole being. Virginia Woolf's reader must be a creator, and it would be wrong to give the term a purely metaphorical meaning which would make it almost synonymous with active. If the preliminary definition quoted above leaves any doubt on the subject, and if, after the two volumes of essays, we are still uncertain, "How should one read a Book?", which concludes the second volume and clearly forms a counterpart to the introduction, should serve to dissipate any ambiguity:

Perhaps the quickest way to understand the elements of what a novelist is doing is not to read, but to write; to make your own experiment with the dangers and difficulties of words.[46]

Addressed as it originally was to schoolgirls, this remark may appear somewhat extravagant, yet it reveals an essential truth, namely that Virginia Woolf has fused—some might say confused —three activities which in her own case were so closely associated that she could not conceive of their being distinguished except as three aspects, each of which implied the other two. For her, writing, reading and criticism were one.

Two preliminary conclusions must be drawn: "If to read a book as it should be read calls for the rarest qualities of imagination, insight, and judgment"[47] obviously Virginia Woolf's "common reader" represents no statistical average, but an ideal one. In spite of that apparent deference towards a wide audience, which is the appropriate tone for a preface, Virginia Woolf is well aware that her reader is one of an elite, that he bears a likeness to herself and her friends: Forster, Strachey, Vita Sackville West, Desmond MacCarthy, Maynard Keynes, Harold Nicolson, all those whose verdict on each of her books she awaits with such anxiety.[48] Nowhere perhaps has she better defined that reader than when analysing Roger Fry's qualities as art critic:

[46] CR II p. 259 (235)
[47] CR II p. 269 (244)
[48] Cf. V. W.'s adversary, F. R. Leavis, in 1933 introducing extracts from the defunct *Calendar of Modern Letters*, speaks of "the Common Reader, who has to be created rather than addressed to" (quoted in *The Importance of Scrutiny*, p. 385).

He knew from his own experience what labours, joys, despairs, go to the making of pictures. A picture was to him not merely the finished canvas but the canvas in the making.[49]

And correspondingly, she condemns the criticism of such writers as Edmund Gosse or Walter Raleigh which, unlike that of Keats, Coleridge, Lamb or Flaubert, never goes to the heart of things.[50] All these judgments are based on the same postulate: "The critic who makes us love poetry is always sufficiently gifted to have had experiences of his own."[51] Such a critic, who is a writer rather than a reader, is interested above all in identifying himself with the artist by means of the work of art. With the artist, not simply with the man, but with the man in his creative capacity. And the totality towards which the critic is guided by instinct is not, as one might be tempted to interpret it,[52] now a character such as Goldsmith,[53] Defoe[54] or Crabbe,[55] now the outline of a period such as we find in "The Pastons and Chaucer"[56] or "The Leaning Tower",[57] now a literary theory as in "Modern Fiction"[58] or "A Letter to a Young Poet",[59] but all of these together: a character illustrating a literary theory within a given period. Undoubtedly, one or the other aspect is dominant in any particular article, casting the others into the background, but the sense of the complexity of the work of art, whose very substance consists of these three elements, is never absent. This exploration of the work, this attempt to rediscover, through its manifold revelations, the living forces which contributed to its origin, is the peculiar quality of Virginia Woolf's criticism at its best. "It is not merely that we are in the presence of a different person—Defoe, Jane Austen, or Thomas Hardy—but that we are living in a different world."[60] Any author worthy of the name bears within himself a whole world which he recreates with words, with all the resources of the art of writing. The keen awareness of that aim which she herself pursued in her work, is so constantly present within Virginia Woolf that

[49] The M p. 86 (103-4). Cf. her analysis of Gosse's weakness: "His criticism becomes more and more a criticism of the finished article, and not of the article in the making", The M p. 78 (91-2).

[50] CDB p. 87 (90)
[51] CDB p. 87 (90)
[52] Cf. I. Rantavaara, *op. cit.*, pp. 77-8
[53] CDB pp. 9-18 (3-14)
[54] CR I pp. 121-31 (89-97).
[55] CDB pp. 31-3 (28-30)
[56] CR I pp. 13-38 (3-23)
[57] The M pp. 105-25 (128-54)
[58] CR I pp. 184-95 (150-8)
[59] DM pp. 132-44 (208-26)
[60] CR II p. 260 (236)

she rightly estimates that access to this world is the only goal a reader is entitled to set himself, and that the critic, in so far as he can be distinguished from the reader, must have no other.

This project, both ambitious and precise, leads Virginia Woolf to contrast her sort of criticism with mere reviewing, or what might perhaps more accurately be described as criticism of contemporary writing. At first sight, there seems no reason why a book published yesterday should not have the same potentialities as a book published a century ago, and consequently deserve the same attention and respect. But it is precisely because it deserves them and because more often than not contemporary critics are incapable of awarding them that Virginia Woolf considers Lockhart,[61] Edmund Gosse,[62] Walter Raleigh[63] and their like as irritating and useless vermin.[64] There can be no doubt that the virulence of her attack, which indeed called forth violent reactions,[65] sprang basically from her hypersensitivity to the opinions expressed about her own books in the press and in reviews.[66] None the less the pamphlet of 1939, *Reviewing,* is based on ideas identical with those underlying the two articles of 1931 on Lockhart and Gosse, echoes of which are found in the Diary[67] as well as in other essays[68]:

To write about a new book the moment it comes out is a very different matter from writing about it fifty years afterwards. A new book is attached to life by a thousand minute filaments. Life goes on and the filaments break and disappear. But at the moment they ring and resound and set up all kinds of irrelevant responses.[69]

The network of associations through which any contemporary work is bound up with our own existence forms a screen as impenetrable as it is impossible to define, which prevents us from reaching the essential part of the work, the object of criticism. All these relations with ourselves, our habits, our conventions, our preoccupations, our tastes, constitute the immediate and

[61] The M pp. 60-4 (69-74)
[62] The M pp. 72-8 (84-92)
[63] CDB pp. 84-9 (87-93)
[64] Cf. "Reviewing", CDB pp. 118-33 (127-45), esp. p. 120 (129)
[65] Cf. AWD p. 320 (308).[11] "*Reviewing* came out last week: and was not let slip into obscurity as I expected. *Lit. Sup.* had a tart and peevish leader; the old tone of voice I know so well—rasped and injured. Then Y.Y. polite but aghast in the *N.S.*"
[66] Cf. *supra*, ch. III, pp. 96-100
[67] Cf. AWD p. 246 (237)
[68] Cf. particularly "Notes on D. H. Lawrence", The M p. 79 (93)
[69] The M p. 62 (72)

ephemeral quality of the book to which we respond too keenly to be able to reach the enduring elements beyond. Her penetrating analysis of the bias inherent in criticism of one's contemporaries gives further evidence of Virginia Woolf's clearsightedness and intellectual probity. If she attributes Lockhart's freakish opinions about novels to the fact that he was a novelist himself,[70] it is because she realises how much her own judgments on her fellow-writers are biased by her own experience as writer. And so, with the exception of E. M. Forster and George Moore,[71] she avoids including in her collections any articles about her contemporaries. Her essays on Henry James,[72] Thomas Hardy,[73] D. H. Lawrence,[74] Conrad[75] are as it were, obituary notices. And if the names of Bennett, Galsworthy, Wells and Joyce appear in her general studies, it is as representatives of some trend or theory rather than as subjects of critical study.

Is there not a contradiction between declaring, on the one hand, that Lockhart understood nothing about novels because he wrote them himself, or refusing to write about one's contemporaries because they are engaged on the same problems as oneself, and, on the other, challenging the judgments of Edmund Gosse and condemning the barrenness of Walter Raleigh's books because these critics were neither novelists, poets nor playwrights?[76] The contradiction is only on the surface, and it is resolved by the general condemnation of any criticism dealing with contemporary works. The writer who is only a critic, such as Gosse, is incapable of it because he knows nothing about literary creation, and equally incapable is the writer like Lockhart, who is an artist himself, because he cannot leave out of account the concepts and tastes that govern his own creative activity, and sets them up as criteria. It is not only her personal experience which induces Virginia Woolf to make these exclusions, in which, moreover, she is at one with academic criticism in its concern for objectivity: the countless errors of judgment that mark the course of literary history provided her with an argument that is hard to refute.[77]

One sentence in the article on Edmund Gosse which might

---

[70] The M p. 63 (72-3)

[71] DM, "George Moore", pp. 100-4 (156-61), "The Novels of E. M. Forster", pp. 104-12 (162-75)

[72] DM pp. 83-100 (129-55)

[73] CDB pp. 61-6 (62-8)

[74] The M pp. 79-82 (93-8)

[75] CR I pp. 282-91 (228-35)

[76] CDB pp. 86 (90), 87 (91)

[77] Cf. CR I, p. 294 (238)

stand as footnote to *Reviewing*, written eight years later, defines the trend of Virginia Woolf's criticism and confirms the reservations made here about the "common reader" to whom she claims to speak: "He is a critic for those who read rather than for those who write."[78] Starting from the postulate that the critic should be versed in the art which he is discussing, she would like him to give the writer the benefit of his wisdom, and instead of setting himself up as judge or merely taking on the role of publicity agent, he should assume that of technical adviser. The suggestion is an original one, but perhaps, as Leonard Woolf implies in the note he has appended to the pamphlet, neither very realistic nor in keeping with the economic and social conditions by which literature is bound. It chiefly reveals to what extent criticism, according to Virginia Woolf, is complementary to artistic creation. It is less a by-product than a phase of it. It is for the writer what a session in a master's studio is for a painter. It is neither more nor less than a discussion between specialists, such as took place at Bloomsbury gatherings, the fruitfulness of which, as difficult to define as to evaluate, is the justification of all literary coteries, particularly when each of their members has enough vigour and originality to develop along the lines of his own genius.

Virginia Woolf seems to have remained faithful throughout her career to that concept of criticism whose various aspects I have just examined; however, the constant need for self-renewal, the search for means of expression more perfectly adapted to the complexity of the realities she wishes to convey, repeatedly led her to envisage experiments comparable to the one she was to undertake in the sphere of fiction. As early as 1923, when she first contemplates a volume of collected articles, she is dissatisfied with mere juxtaposition and seeks some way of giving unity, movement and structure to these scattered fragments. Several possibilities occur to her mind: to integrate them into the continuity of a conversation, to give each of them a framework, to write an introductory chapter, to provide a dominant theme[79] ... Various attempts,[80] of

[78] The M p. 78 (92). Cf. also, five years earlier, AWD Dec. 2, 1934, p. 233 (225): "David Cecil on fiction: a good book for readers, not for writers ... I've done though with that sort of criticism."

[79] Cf. AWD p. 58 (57): "The brilliant idea has just come to me of embedding [my essays] in Otway conversation. The main advantage would be that I could then comment and add what I had to leave out, or failed to get in. . . . Also to have a setting for each would 'make a book'; and the collection of articles is in my view an

unknown nature, prove ineffective. But as soon as she contemplates a new collection, Virginia Woolf is seized with the same longing to find a better, more effective form of criticism, more in keeping with her vision of authors and their works:

I feel too, at the back of my brain, that I can devise a new critical method; something far less stiff and formal than these *Times* articles. But I must keep to the old style in this volume. And how, I wonder, could I do it? There must be some simpler, subtler, closer means of writing about books, as about people, could I hit upon it.[81]

She is clearly stirred by the spirit of adventure, stimulated by the success of *The Waves*,[82] which had appeared six weeks previously. However, apart from the lightness of its touch, the liveliness of its tone and the richness of its verve, the second *Common Reader* scarcely brings us that new criticism of which its author had once dreamed. But six years later, in the relief and euphoria induced by the success of *The Years*, as formerly by that of *The Waves*, the dream revives.[83] She wants to invent a new form of criticism. The dates show how far Virginia Woolf as critic has profited by the impetus given by Virginia Woolf the novelist. The close co-operation between them is confirmed when a few days later she writes in her Diary:

I saw the form of a new novel. It's to be first the statement of the theme: then the restatement: and so on: repeating the same story: singling out this and then that, until the central idea is stated.
This might also lend itself to my book of criticism.[84]

We shall see that this is perhaps not so much a clear conception as the formulation of certain characteristics already latent in earlier essays, and that this new form is, on the whole, only the hypostasis of an older attitude and style. And even if all the qual-

---

inartistic method. . . . There could be an introductory chapter. A family which reads the papers. The thing to do would be to envelope each essay in its own atmosphere. To get them into a current of life, and so shape the book; to get a stress upon some main line. . . ."

[80] Cf. AWD pp. 60 (59), 64 (63)

[81] AWD p. 177 (172). Cf. also AWD p. 182 (177): "I must find a quicker cut into books than this."

[82] After the above passage she comments, in brackets: "(*The Waves* has sold more than 7,000)."

[83] Cf. AWD p. 282 (272): "Were I another person, I would say to myself, Please write criticism; biography; invent a new form for both . . ."; and *ibid.*, p. 286 (275): "I want to explore a new criticism."

[84] AWD p. 287 (276)

ities of Shelley and Coleridge, whom she was then reading, and which she longed to express, make her too harsh on her own writing, the wish uttered in 1940 tells us that the dream was even then still only a dream:

I wish I could invent a new critical method—something swifter and lighter and more colloquial and yet intense: more to the point and less composed; more fluid and following the flight; than my *C.R.* essays. The old problem: how to keep the flight of the mind, yet be exact. All the difference between the sketch and the finished work.[85]

Do these ideas, these theories, these aspirations, reveal any precise influence? At the risk of applying to Virginia Woolf the methods which we have just seen her condemn, can we discover anything in her predecessors or in her contemporaries which may have helped to bring forth and foster that ideal towards which her critical work tended without ever, according to her own estimate, getting near enough to satisfy her?

For Virginia Woolf, the "great critics" are Dryden, Johnson, Coleridge, Arnold,[86] to whose names, in the same article, she adds those of Keats and Flaubert.[87] To conclude from her admiration for these masters that her criticism owes anything to them is a hypothesis which is of value and of interest only if strictly defined and circumscribed. Virginia Woolf certainly derives neither methods, nor certain forms of criticism, from them. They are as different from one another as she herself is from each of them. There can be no question of influence or even of inspiration. What she admires about them shows clearly that they simply served her as examples, in the broadest sense of the word: their general attitude towards literature, their power of penetration, the vigour and honesty of their judgments, the weight of personality and the quality of the outlook on life implicit in their writings. Their greatness as critics, as also their greatness as artists, is due to their conviction of the close and unbreakable relation between art and life, between art and man. These convictions are so commonly held that one cannot speak of a debt: let us merely say that these authors provided Virginia Woolf with examples from which she

[85] AWD p. 337 (324)

[86] Cf. CR I p. 294 (238). The three last also named in "Reviewing", CDB p. 119 (128)

[87] Cf. CR I p. 295 (239), and also in "Walter Raleigh" (CDB p. 87 (90)): "But it is the Keats, the Coleridge, the Lamb, the Flaubert who get to the heart of the matter."

derived her definition, not of such and such a kind of criticism, but of an order of criticism, the most ambitious, perhaps the highest of all, from which she was to make her ideal.

Are we to make an exception for Dr Johnson, who gave its name to the *Common Reader*? Apart from the phrase which she briefly develops at the beginning of her first collection and from which she derives that image of the ideal reader to which she repeatedly refers, she does not appear to owe very much to him. Whether Dr Johnson's misfortunes in his choice of a protector, and his letter to Lord Chesterfield sounding the knell of literary patronage, provided Virginia Woolf with the germ of "The Patron and the Crocus"[88] is a matter for conjecture. It may be noted that Leslie Stephen's *English Literature and Society in the Eighteenth Century*[89] contains a greater wealth of suggestions than the great lexicographer's misfortunes. If Virginia Woolf needed a precedent for her treatment of this theme, to which her verve and her point of view give complete originality, nothing entitles us to choose one source rather than the other. Similarly, as regards her fundamental opposition to sentimentality, an attitude which she shares with both Johnson and Leslie Stephen—and with many others, T. S. Eliot and Lytton Strachey, for instance—it seems more rational to consider it as a characteristic of her temperament than as the result of reading some particular author. We must not forget, finally, that the moral preoccupations which the author of *Rasselas* sets up as criteria in his discussion of books and writers are completely foreign to Virginia Woolf. If she often mentions Johnson, it is chiefly as a precursor to whose authority she can refer. She may have found him more readable than her father declared,[90] but we have no proof of this. She probably admired his general attitude and his personality more than she really loved his writing. "He is always a man of intuition rather than of discursive intellect; often keen of vision though wanting in analytical power",[91] wrote Leslie Stephen; such was the man with whom she felt herself to have certain affinities, and whose position in literature justified her own critical ambitions.

In point of fact, the immediate source of certain trends in Virginia Woolf's criticism should be sought not in the writings

[88] CR I pp. 261-6 (211-5)   [89] Cf. particularly *op. cit.*, pp. 35-65.
[90] Cf. Leslie Stephen, *Hours in a Library*, II, p. 9.
[91] *Ibid.*, p. 14

of Dr Johnson but in the influence of her father, author of *Hours in a Library*,[92] *Studies in Biography, Society and Literature in the Eighteenth Century*. Among the quotations appended to *Hours in a Library*, Leslie Stephen quotes Henry Sidgwick's remarks: "A library is itself a cheap university."[93] And such, indeed, was his own library for his daughter. Here it was that for lack of more formal education she made contact with English literature from Chaucer, Ford, Sir Thomas Browne to the Victorians. Virginia Woolf's love of the Elizabethans[94] being certainly as pronounced as her interest in the eighteenth century, if not actually more profound, it is difficult to estimate what seeds Leslie Stephen's opinions and preferences may have sown in her mind. They undoubtedly gave direction to her reading: "When I was 20 I liked 18th century prose; I liked Hakluyt, Mérimée. I read masses of Carlyle, Scott's life and letters, Gibbon, all sorts of two-volume biographies, and Shelley"[95]; and she tells us that it was her father who brought her back from the library the huge volumes of Hakluyt when she was fifteen or sixteen[96]; and those other authors whom she mentions were indeed favourites of Leslie Stephen's. But the fact that later on she chose to write about Geraldine and Jane rather than about Carlyle, Mary Wollstonecraft rather than Shelley, Dorothy Wordsworth rather than William, indicates how we should interpret Virginia Woolf's indebtedness to her father. He gave her access to Orlando's wonderful palace with its countless rooms, and indeed such an opportunity is offered only to a few; but he left her free to pass through certain chambers, linger in some and settle down in others. But if their tastes and interests sometimes coincide, any conclusion that might be drawn from this is invalidated by certain divergences. It is quite revealing, in this connection, to compare the articles on George Eliot written by father and daughter. The similarity of their methods of composition, the analogies between their opinions, only bring out more clearly the essential difference between the kinds of criticism the two texts represent.[97]

[92] She gives this title to one of her articles in 1916; (cf. G & R pp. 24-31 (24-31).
[93] Leslie Stephen, *Hours in a Library*, I, p. xiii.
[94] Cf. AWD p. 150 (147): "It was the Elizabethan prose writers I loved first and most wildly."
[95] Cf. AWD p. 65 (64)   [96] AWD p. 150 (147)
[97] Leslie Stephen, *Hours in a Library*, III, pp. 193-219, and V. W., CR I pp. 205-18 (166-76). It is particularly interesting to compare the following passages: L. S. pp. 210-12, with V. W. pp. 214-16; L. S. p. 219, with V. W. p. 217.

To begin with, an apparently superficial yet really basic difference: Virginia Woolf's thirteen small pages—the usual length of such articles—seem very slim beside Leslie Stephen's close-packed twenty-six.[98] Whereas he takes his time—and time was presumably more plentiful in the nineteenth century than it is in the twentieth—she keeps strictly to her purpose: whereas he digresses throughout a long paragraph about criticism of one's contemporaries,[99] or the limits of an artist's fertility, or the extent to which a novelist may legitimately intervene in his story, or the relationship between psychology and action . . . supporting his argument by references to Shakespeare, Dumas, Scott, Balzac and a score of others, Virginia Woolf confines herself to George Eliot, only deviating by a sentence here and there, often merely by a single clause, intended to give her portrait a frame or a background. Whereas Leslie Stephen quotes a whole paragraph or sums up a plot, Virginia Woolf makes do with a gesture, a name, an expression, a word in inverted commas. In point of fact, the scholar, the philosopher, the universal reader, the "Cambridge critic"[100] is constantly present beside his subject, whom he examines at leisure, dropping her, as one thought suggests another, to take us with him on a ramble through his literary reveries. Perhaps we should interpret these digressions as a compensation for the restrictions that weighed on the author of the *Dictionary of National Biography*, who had to be "content sometimes to toil for hours with the simple result of having to hold (his) tongue".[101] On the other hand, when he can let himself go, the result is somewhat uncertain: a swarm of ideas amidst which, by the end of the article, we are confused between Leslie Stephen and George Eliot, and it is by no means sure that the dominant impression we retain is not of the critic rather than of the author whom he has been discussing. Those asides to the reader, for which others criticize George Eliot and which Leslie Stephen, far from resenting,

---

[98] Cf. G & R pp. 151-2 (151-2): "But the diminution of size was only the outward token of an inward change."

[99] In the passage (*Hours in a Library*, III, p. 194) where he discusses the limitations of contemporary criticism, L. S. quotes Browning's title: "How it strikes a contemporary", which V. W. takes as title for her article on the subject (CR I pp. 292-305 (236-46)).

[100] Cf. Q. D. Leavis, "Leslie Stephen, Cambridge Critic", *Scrutiny*, March 1939, pp. 404-415

[101] L. Stephen, *Studies of a Biographer*, I, p. 22

admires,[102] are an essential feature of his own method where ideas are concerned.

Virginia Woolf proceeds in a very different fashion. The subject, George Eliot, stands alone in the centre of the picture, which is painted in broad vigorous strokes; her work forms an integral part of it, identified with her gestures and actions, her feelings, her thought; it is not a thing apart, the occasion for reflections and judgments. These, indeed, are present, but only to bring out the colour and outline, the intrinsic quality of all the elements presented to us. The conclusions of the two articles are, in this respect, characteristic. Whereas Leslie Stephen's consists of a long series of *I*'s and *we*'s,[103] Virginia Woolf's, beginning with the words: "Thus we behold her, a memorable figure . . ."[104] evokes a final synthetic portrait, independent of the critic sketching it.

Not that one should conclude that Virginia Woolf's criticism is more objective than her father's. The painter's discreet retirement behind her model is only apparent; it cannot even be called a matter of form or style, for both remain profoundly characteristic, but of technique. In point of fact, Virginia Woolf has more or less identified herself with her subject: the features she stresses are those which she recognizes as her own: the slow maturing, the conflict with her surroundings, the will to emancipation and independence, the championing of women's rights, the aspiration to learning and art. . . . And her criticisms, her reservations are naturally so many avowals of her personal tastes and ideas. But one only becomes aware of this symbiosis of painter and model by considering all the portraits in which, apart from the similarity of treatment and despite the diversity of faces and periods, one can recognize basic affinities of temperament between Virginia Woolf and her subject. Through the half-transparence of these faces her own is reflected, her features mingling with the features she observes through her reading and over the centuries. Moreover, is not this ambiguity inherent in the very nature of criticism, such as Virginia Woolf defines it in her article on the modern essay, just after contrasting Leslie Stephen with Max Beerbohm: "Never to be yourself and yet always—that is the problem."[105]

---

[102] Cf. L. Stephen, *Hours in a Library*, III, p. 197
[103] Cf. *ibid.*, p. 219
[104] Cf. *Common Reader* I, p. 218 (176)
[105] CR I p. 275 (222)

It was, of course, thanks to her father that Virginia Woolf was brought up in the midst of literature, nurtured on literature, and that thus she came not only to conceive of, but to feel as a living experience, the closeness, indeed the continuity of art and life, whence springs one of the basic principles of her criticism: that all works of art are deeply rooted in ordinary life. But it seems that we need not look to Leslie Stephen for the source of her concept of criticism, the aims and methods of her own essays.

If we turn to the critics who were her own contemporaries, we are struck rather by the hostile statements which have been quoted earlier[106] and the absence of any recognition of indebtedness or even of any expression of admiration. It is scarcely surprising that the criticism of I. A. Richards and C. K. Ogden, with its tendency towards semantic analysis and its research into interpretation, held no attraction for her and consequently had no influence on her essays.

Again, the metaphysical and religious orientation of T. S. Eliot, together with his intellectualism and his concern with general theoretical questions, place his criticism in a realm, if not on a level, foreign to Virginia Woolf. No doubt a certain parallelism can be found between her attempts to define the essence of the novel and Eliot's to define the essence of poetry. Nevertheless their profound ideological divergences are too obvious to need underlining.[107] Yet we must not forget that from their first meeting in 1916 the two writers, both at the outset of their careers, became firm friends.[108] Certain echoes conveyed by the Diary justify the assumption that literary discussions played an important part in their relationship. Both writers assert the complementary nature of the creative and critical activities, thus proposing as a general truth the fruits of their personal experience. Similarly, both hold that it is necessary for a critic to have himself practised the art he is discussing.[109] And her paradoxical union of the sense of tradition with the need for constant renewal of artistic forms may perhaps have been stimulated, although not directly inspired, by the example of Eliot. This sentence from "Tradition and the Individual Talent" might serve as a footnote to *Orlando*:

[106] Cf. *supra*, pp. 132-3; 136
[107] Cf. T. S. Eliot, "Le Roman anglais contemporain", *NRF* May 1927, CLXIV; despite moderation of tone and some praise, the final verdict is severe.
[108] Cf. Clive Bell, *Old Friends*, p. 119
[109] Cf. T. S. Eliot, *Selected Essays*, pp. 30-1

The historical sense involves a perception not only of the pastness of the past but of its presence; the historical sense compels a man to write not merely with his own generation in his bones, but with a feeling that the whole of the literature of Europe from Homer and within it the whole literature of his own country has a simultaneous existence and composes a simultaneous order.[110]

Detached from its context, this thought is too banal for the comparison to be significant, but the analysis of the relationship which Eliot pictured between the works of the past and those of the present day[111] is a justification of the aims which Virginia Woolf set herself as critic, namely that the elucidation of great masterpieces, their reinterpretation from a modern point of view, are necessitated by the change of outlook brought about by the appearance of new works. It may be said that to a certain extent Virginia Woolf puts into practice, at the "common reader's" level, one consequence of Eliot's aesthetic theory.

It may be asked, since she contributed to the *Athenaeum*, whether she shared the views of John Middleton Murry, who was its editor for a couple of years. Both display the same hostility towards Dr Leavis[112] and deplore the bondage involved in reviewing contemporary works.[113] More generally, the essential aim they assign to the critic seems indeed to be the same: to express the total and unique effect of the work under consideration. Both agree no doubt in discovering this unique quality of the work in the unique quality of the author's sensibility, whose nature and determinant factors the critic must analyse. "This symphonic movement of an ideal criticism",[114] described by Middleton Murry, is a formula which might have attracted Virginia Woolf; does she not suggest a similar art when she envisages "the statement of the theme: then the restatement"?[115] However, these analogies, like those pointed out between Virginia Woolf and Leslie Stephen, remain too

[110] T. S. Eliot, *Selected Essays*, p. 14

[111] Cf. T. S. Eliot, *Selected Essays*, p. 15: "The existing moments form an ideal order which is modified by the introduction of the new (the really new) work of art among them. The existing order is complete before the new work arrives; for order to persist after the supervention of novelty, the *whole* existing order must be, ever so slightly, altered; and so the relations, proportions, values of each work of art towards the whole are readjusted; and this is conformity between the old and the new."

[112] Cf. J. M. Murry, *Unprofessional Essays*: "In Defence of Fielding"

[113] Cf. J. M. Murry, *A Critical Credo*, p. 252

[114] Cf. J. M. Murry, *Countries of the Mind*: "A Critical Credo", in *Essays of Today* selected by F. H. Pritchard, p. 257

[115] Cf. AWD p. 287 (276), quoted *supra*, p. 139

general to be significant. Thus Virginia Woolf could never have accepted a principle like this one: "The critic's business is to express himself by expressing his opinion. . . ."[116] At any rate she would have made weightier reservations than Murry does. And above all she would have categorically rejected that fundamental declaration that "criticism should openly accept the fact that its final judgments are moral. . . ."[117] Apart from her dislike of mingling ethics with aesthetics, to subscribe to such views would mean being guilty of the typically masculine sin of pride which she condemns so sharply in Murry himself.[118] In short, despite all the esteem she may have had for Murry one may safely say that, in the sphere of literary criticism, the similarities that have been pointed out are unimportant compared to the divergences that separate them.

If we now consider the narrower circle of Virginia Woolf's intimate friends, we find certain preoccupations, certain tendencies which enable us to appreciate her position and define more precisely her true critical originality. Before embarking on the study of these connections, I must specify that they reflect chiefly the intellectual atmosphere in which she developed as a writer, and came, in the course of countless conversations rather than through reading books, either to modify her thought or to define it more precisely, or to consolidate her position. The similarities I shall point out, based on the written word, are merely landmarks; they are significant only as indices; and they are not proposed as sources, strictly speaking, but only as evidence of an intercourse more important for the intellectual stimulus it provided than in any actual contribution in the sphere of ideas or principles.

Four members of Virginia Woolf's circle may be considered: Desmond MacCarthy, Harold Nicolson, Lytton Strachey and Roger Fry. They had been close friends of Virginia Woolf's since the early years of the century, and the friendship was not broken even by death.

Amongst them, Desmond MacCarthy was the only literary

[116] J. M. Murry, "A Critical Credo", in *Essays of Today*, F. H. Pritchard, p. 254
[117] *Ibid.*, p. 258: "Criticism should openly accept the fact that its final judgments are moral. A critic should be conscious of his moral assumptions and take pains to put into them the highest morality of which he is capable." Cf. T. S. Eliot, "The Function of Criticism" (*Selected Essays*, p. 26), where the moralistic attitude is similar, although its foundations and modalities are different.
[118] Cf. AWD p. 12 (12)

critic, strictly speaking. Nevertheless, whereas in the case of the other three, despite the diversity of personal interests and idiosyncrasies, a certain community of tendencies and tastes seemed to foster fruitful human and intellectual contacts, we are more struck by the antagonism between Desmond MacCarthy and Virginia Woolf than by their similarity. Although according to Clive Bell[119] Mrs MacCarthy was the first to coin the name "Bloomsberries" for the habitués of Fitzroy and Gordon Squares, it is unlikely that she or her husband could ever have been accused of Bloomsburyism. One has only to read a few pages of *Criticism*,[120] or better still, the friendly but highly critical reviews of Virginia Woolf's novels written by Desmond MacCarthy,[121] to be convinced that he was far from sharing his friend's most cherished and most extreme ideas. When he wrote to her about *Jacob's Room*: "I marvel and am puzzled",[122] it is tempting to complete this declaration by his remarks about Proust:

Personally, nothing would induce me to live in Proust's world, but I like to visit it. And just as one can sharpen one's perceptions of certain aspects of things by gazing attentively at the pictures of some modern artist, without necessarily holding that he saw more beauty than some familiar master who ignored these aspects, so one can learn to observe and feel like Proust without believing that he has interpreted life better than writers who ignore what was to him so important. Proust's world is that of the searching, inquisitive, intellectual artist.[123]

Searching, inquisitive, intellectual: essentially the world of Virginia Woolf, which somehow lost its sap and its colour in contact with MacCarthy's balance and humour. It was indeed after a meeting when they had talked about the first *Common Reader* that Virginia Woolf gave vent to these disillusioned observations about their friendship:

Desmond has an abnormal power for depressing me. He takes the edge off life in some extraordinary way. I love him; but his balance and goodness and humour, all heavenly in themselves, somehow diminish lustre. I think I feel this not only about my work but about life.[124]

It may be suspected that the impression he made on her, in

[119] Cf. Clive Bell, *Old Friends*, pp. 129 and 131: it was about 1910 or 1911.
[120] Desmond MacCarthy, *Criticism*, Putnam, London, 1932
[121] E.g. D. MacCarthy, "Phantasmagoria", *Sunday Times*, Oct. 14, 1928
[122] AWD p. 53 (52)
[123] D. MacCarthy, *Criticism*, p. 186
[124] AWD p. 77 (76)

some respects, must have reminded her of her father.[125] In the short preface to his collected essays, *Criticism*,[126] where MacCarthy sets forth his conception of the subject, every sentence suggests phrases, ideas, themes of Virginia Woolf's, sometimes parallel, sometimes divergent, thus suggesting the hypothesis of a kind of dialogue, during which, over the years, each of them, without renouncing his fundamental convictions, might have come to understand and respect the other's vision.

Whereas Virginia Woolf identifies the critic with the common reader, MacCarthy sees in the critic a reader in a thousand, whose imagination and sensibility are particularly keen, and who can thus interpret the creative experience better than the ordinary reader. In the light of what has been said of Virginia Woolf's "common reader", we see that, under their different labels, the two critic-readers are akin. Some of their aims, too, are identical:

One of the main functions of the critic, when he is expounding the literature of the past, is to put the reader at the point of view from which *its* contemporaries saw that literature, at the same time, of course, judging it from his own.[127]

Even in the form in which it is expressed, the need for a revaluation of literature by each generation, which is part of MacCarthy's credo, is also characteristic of Virginia Woolf: "Each generation holds the butterfly to the light at a slightly different angle."[128]

And confronted with this assertion: "The psychology of the reader of a book is almost as much part of his subject as the book itself",[129] we may recall the importance that this field of study occupies in Virginia Woolf's criticism. No doubt she would also have subscribed to the identity of the critic's and writer's aims:

If asked what is the use of (criticism) he can only reply that it is another way of doing what the artist does: his work, too, intensifies and multiplies experiences worth having.[130]

Must one deduce from all this any decisive influence? It is only in her least original and most restrained aspect that Virginia Woolf comes close to MacCarthy. At most, one may suggest that he helped to maintain in her a certain classicism and discretion

---

[125] Of whom MacCarthy wrote a study: *Leslie Stephen*, Cambridge University Press, 1937.
[126] D. MacCarthy, *Criticism*, pp. vii–x
[127] *Ibid.*, p. vii   [128] *Ibid.*, p. viii   [129] *Ibid.*, p. viii   [130] *Ibid.*, p viii

which, although not foreign to her nature, were certainly jeopardized by the extreme and revolutionary tendencies that were dominant in her.

Although he was no bolder in his aesthetics and although, while recognizing the daring and importance of Virginia Woolf's novels, his reservations were of the same order as MacCarthy's,[131] Harold Nicolson probably had a greater influence on certain trends in her criticism. It would of course be untrue to suggest that he was responsible for her interest in biography, which can be more logically and more convincingly attributed to Leslie Stephen and Lytton Strachey. However, it is worth noting that on February 28, 1927, she writes in her diary:

If they—the respectables, my friends, advise me against the *Lighthouse*, I shall write memoirs; have a plan already to get historical manuscripts and write *Lives of the Obscure*; but why do I pretend I should take advice?[132]

while in the conclusion of *The Development of English Biography*, published that same year by Leonard and Virginia Woolf at the Hogarth Press, we read:

We shall continue to have second-rate reconstructional biographies, "life-and-times" biographies, biographies of gallantry and adventure, lives of the obscure, the intemperate and the good. We shall have floods of memoirs and diaries.[133]

Without forgetting that "Lives of the Obscure" was originally the title of an article published in the *London Mercury* of January 1924, or that it was used again for an essay in the first *Common Reader* in 1925, and that the project here suggested no doubt goes back to that earlier period,[134] it is tempting to ascribe to Harold Nicolson a certain influence on Virginia Woolf's plans. This temptation is further increased by the fact that, that very year, Virginia Woolf published in the *New York Herald Tribune* of October 30th a highly favourable review of *Some People*.[135] More-

---

[131] Cf. "The New Spirit in Literature, VII", *The Listener*, 18/11/1931.

[132] AWD p. 104 (103)

[133] Harold Nicolson, *The Development of English Biography*, p. 156

[134] Cf. AWD p. 81 (79): "I want to read voraciously and gather material for the *Lives of the Obscure*—which is to tell the whole history of England in one obscure life after another" (Monday, July 20, 1925).

[135] "The New Biography", review of *Some People*, by Harold Nicolson: in *Granite and Rainbow*, pp. 149-55.

over, if we remember that it was between these months of February and October 1927 that her ideas of writing memoirs, fantastic stories à la Defoe, historic tableaux and biographies, gradually merged to become, eventually, the project for *Orlando*, other sentences of Harold Nicolson's spring to one's mind:

But in general literary biography will, I suppose, wander off into the imaginative, leaving the strident streets of science for the open fields of fiction. The biographical form will be given to fiction, the fictional form will be given to biography.[136]

We know, moreover, that in June of that same year the Woolfs travelled to Yorkshire with the Nicolsons to watch an eclipse.[137] Virginia Woolf and Harold Nicolson were on excellent terms, saw one another frequently, and probably held long discussions on literary matters.

Although "The Art of Biography" did not appear until April 1938,[138] although it provides a commentary to the life of Roger Fry which she was then writing, and although a whole section is devoted to Lytton Strachey whereas Harold Nicolson is never mentioned, one can scarcely fail to recognize an echo of the guiding idea of *The Development of English Biography*. Moreover, the central problem of the conflict between facts and the freedom of the imagination had already been broached in "The New Biography". The difficulty of fusing the granitic solidity of truth and the immaterial, rainbow transparency of personality, a problem which is at the heart of this first essay, is a variation on the same theme.[139] It therefore seems fair to suggest that in this particular case, Virginia Woolf's thought and her line of argument won the approval of her friend. She seems indeed to start from data provided by Harold Nicolson's study, and to develop the analysis of this hybrid genre more deeply and more subtly, reaching identical conclusions as to its interest and its future. "The creative fact; the fertile fact; the fact that suggests and engenders"[140] which accord-

---

[136] Harold Nicolson, *The Development of English Biography*, pp. 155-6
[137] Cf. AWD pp. 109-13 (108-11)
[138] In the *Atlantic Monthly*, April 1939; cf. DM pp. 119-25 (187-97)
[139] Cf. G & R p. 149 (149): "And if we think of truth as something of granite-like solidity and of personality as something of rainbow-like intangibility and reflect that the aim of biography is to weld these into one seamless whole, we shall admit that the problem is a stiff one."
[140] Cf. DM p. 126 (197)

ing to her the biographer should give us, is identical with the substance of that impure, applied biography thanks to which literature, as Harold Nicolson says, "may well discover a new scope, an unexplored method of conveying human experience".[141]

With Lytton Strachey, we are confronted with a paradox: the certainty of extremely rich personal relations, of fruitful intellectual intercourse, and yet, apart from external—one might almost say circumstantial—evidence, we cannot quote a single sentence by one of them echoing a sentence of the other's or one principle, one rule which they have in common. So much so that one wonders whether the precise parallels noticed in the preceding cases are not an illusion, a play of words with no more substantial reality than the play of light; one is then tempted to assert that an authentic influence neither acts nor reveals itself on the plane of language, but lies hidden below it; that it is in fact an encounter in depth, where temperaments, tastes and vision meet and mingle.

I have referred elsewhere to the friendship between Virginia Woolf and Lytton Strachey.[142] The fact that they dedicated to one another *Queen Victoria* and *The Common Reader* is more than a gesture of affection or respect: it can be read as a sign of their mutual indebtedness. This is not the place to examine Lytton Strachey's "You influence me".[143] And whereas we have no such direct acknowledgment from Virginia Woolf, the presence of Strachey, although diffuse and elusive, is none the less constant throughout her work, whether in fiction or criticism. The precise, incisive wit of St John Hirst in *The Voyage Out* forms a continual counterpoise to the sensibility and imagination of Terence Hewett. In the everlasting conflict between these two tendencies within Virginia Woolf herself, it is highly probable that Lytton Strachey, not only by his comments and his literary example, but by the constant presence of his way of feeling and thinking, contributed to the endurance of the rationalist vein inherited from her father, which a certain longing for emancipation might have led her to reject. He is the antagonist who fascinates, as Peter Walsh was for Clarissa Dalloway, or Bonamy for Jacob.[144] "My dear old

---

[141] Cf. Harold Nicolson, *Development of English Biography*, p. 158

[142] Cf. *supra*, pp. 47-9, 65

[143] AWD p. 34 (33): " 'You influence me', he said" (long literary discussion between the two friends).

[144] Cf. V. W. & L. S., *Letters*, p. 103: "Of course you're very romantic—which alarms me slightly—I am such a Bonamy. . . ."

serpent,"[145] she says of him in the Diary, echoing more than eight years after his death an expression used in the last letter she had written to him.[146] He is undoubtedly, like Roger Fry, one of those "visionary figures" that "admonish" her, one of those "invisible censors" that keep watch over her writing.[147] He is there to affect her reactions, her thought, her very style:

And behold, when I come to write about old Mrs Gilbert, it runs of its own accord into two semi-colons, dash, note of exclamation, full stop. Do you recognize your style?[148]

She exaggerates, teasing him: none the less one has only to read their parallel evocations of Thomas Browne[149] or Walpole[150] to recognize in the general rhythm, the use of periods and short sentences, the unexpectedness of epithets or nouns, a turn and a tone which, underlying surface analogies, reveal two closely related modes of vision. Virginia Woolf had no doubt discovered Gibbon in her father's library before making Hirst give a copy to Rachel; but through Strachey, he becomes "The Historian and the Gibbon" of *The Death of the Moth*, closer, in treatment if not in substance, to the Gibbon in *Portraits in Miniature*[151] than the one in *Studies of a Biographer*.[152] The fondness and the feeling for vignettes, the choice of key gestures and events, the concentration of the narrative, the judgments suggested rather than formulated, the balanced proportion of sympathy and detachment,[153] are features common to both writers. True, each is faithful to his own nature, but one can scarcely dismiss the hypothesis that their intimacy and mutual admiration contributed to unite loyalty to one's friend with loyalty to oneself and to introduce into the writings of each of them touches and tones which make them far closer than any identity of theories or words.

[145] Cf. AWD p. 314 (303): "Still I see Lytton's point—my dear old serpent."
[146] Cf. V. W. & L. S., *Letters*, p. 117: "I can't help writing to the bearded serpent. . . ."
[147] Cf. AWD p. 315 (303): "How visionary figures admonish us. . . . All books now seem to me surrounded by a circle of invisible censors."
[148] V. W. & L. S., *Letters*, p. 95
[149] Cf. V. W., CDB pp. 157-61 (170-9) and L. S., *Books & Characters*, pp. 27-40
[150] Cf. V. W., DM pp. 45-51 (64-75) and L. S., *ibid.*, pp. 69-92
[151] Cf. V. W., DM pp. 55-62 (82-93) and L. S., *Portraits in Miniature*, pp. 154-68
[152] Cf. Leslie Stephen, *Studies of a Biographer*, I, pp. 147-87
[153] For Lytton Strachey's critical theories cf. his article on Johnson, "The Lives of the Poets", in *Books and Characters*, esp. p. 61.

I have already had occasion, when analysing the critical theories of Virginia Woolf, to mention Roger Fry.[154] Whether we consider the complete biography[155] or merely the speech made at the opening of the Memorial Exhibition at Bristol[156] we realise that something deeper is involved than coincidence of ideas or even identity of attitude. Here we have an agreement between temperaments which proved immensely stimulating. It matters little that Virginia Woolf's Roger Fry does not exactly represent the man as he was.[157] The influence of one personality on another depends more on the latter's inward vision than on the objective character which is its pretext and which has, so to speak, no real substance. In contrast with Lytton Strachey, in whom the rational intellect was dominant and who, after all, was not an artist, Roger Fry was infinitely closer to Virginia Woolf. She stresses his painter's vocation,[158] which was of primary importance to him, as her novelist's vocation was to herself. If he was actually greater as a theoretician and critic than as a creator, it does not matter; his strength in that field was only a consequence of his direct experience of painting. This intimate relation between theory and practice is precisely one of Virginia Woolf's critical dogmas. In Roger Fry she found her model, all the more attractive because in other respects his aesthetics resembled her own. The fact that she tried to make use in her literary technique of certain elements and values derived from that of painting is due no doubt to the nature of her sensibility, and also to the circle in which she grew up and lived; but it may be asserted that her close friendship with Roger Fry reinforced that tendency. On the one hand he contributed to clarifying what might have remained at the stage of mere impressions, providing her with a vocabulary, but above all he helped her, by his analytical method, to bring about the transposition from the pictorial to the literary which was to prove so fruitful for her. The relations between art and reality, the resources of composition with all its elements and their connections: structures, balances, motifs; in short, the three great themes indicated by the very titles

[154] Cf. *supra*, pp. 134-5
[155] Cf. *infra*, pp. 348-52
[156] Cf. The M pp. 83-8 (99-105), Roger Fry, an address given at the opening of the Roger Fry Memorial Exhibition, July 12, 1935.
[157] Cf. for instance the less flattering, but probably no truer, picture drawn by Clive Bell in *Old Friends*, pp. 62-91.
[158] Cf. particularly The M pp. 86-7 (103-4)

of Roger Fry's works, *Transformations*, *Vision and Design*, would not have been explored nor exploited with the same strictness and stubbornness had not a twenty-five-year-old friendship existed between the two artists. Not only did Roger enable Virginia Woolf to enrich her aesthetic experience, but through him the novelist and the critic in her acquired an acuter awareness of their intentions. When, at 29, she met him, she found in this man, sixteen years her senior, not only the sympathy and interest shown her by friends of her own generation, but the authority and force of conviction conferred by age and experience.[159] Whether consciously or not, she made him play the part of the father she would have liked to have. As in the case of Lytton Strachey, we recognize Leslie Stephen again behind a mask and an incarnation. This permanent presence is an essential element of Virginia Woolf's personality. But above all the different aspects under which we have met it enable us to evaluate the nature of the influences to which the author of *To the Lighthouse* was susceptible: not the influence of ideas or systems, but that of temperaments, of personalities, which may have brought her nothing essentially new, certainly nothing alien, but which was favourable to the growth and expansion of her profoundest tendencies and her innate gifts. Undoubtedly, without Lytton Strachey and Roger Fry her work as critic and novelist would not have been the same; but the difference would have been one of degree only, not of nature. And if Strachey provided her with discipline and Roger Fry with inspiration, these proved effective and fruitful only because they corresponded to fundamental needs.

Without losing sight of the autonomous character of Virginia Woolf's critical articles, which, called forth haphazard by what she had read, what had been published, by deaths or centenaries or other chance circumstances, correspond to no premeditated general plan, it would be a mistake in my opinion to ignore the guiding lines, which if not always clearly drawn are at least indicated by the choice and composition of the two collections which she herself prepared with great care and, it should be added, much effort and labour. More than any other arbitrary classification superimposed from outside, the analysis of the two

[159] Cf. AWD p. 303 (292): "His persuasiveness—a certain density—wished to persuade you to like what he liked."

Common Reader books will allow one to grasp the complex play of the different forces or trends which combine to ensure for Virginia Woolf's criticism an originality for which her theories on the subject do not adequately account.

"The collection of articles is in my view an inartistic method,"[160] declares Virginia Woolf when envisaging the publication of her first volume of essays, thus implicitly asserting the need for unity and structure that she was to endeavour to satisfy, despite the obvious resistance offered by these bits and pieces which were not originally conceived with such a purpose. Although the projects for integration which she considered at the time were to come to nothing, they left their mark on the general intentions of the *Common Reader* clearly enough to deserve examination. She states categorically what she would like to do:

To get [the essays] into a current of life, and so to shape the book; to get a stress upon some main line—but what the line is to be, I can only see by reading them through. No doubt fiction is the prevailing theme. Anyhow the book should end with modern literature.[161]

The two essential points in this declaration, the "current of life" and the "prevailing theme", the novel, characterise both the quality and the content not only of these two volumes but also of all Virginia Woolf's critical work.

The current of life into which the author wished to plunge her various articles, by a process of whose artificiality she was already vaguely conscious,[162] comprises, in fact, the atmosphere and movement of each article; it is the impression that emerges from a complex reality made up of historical and social as well as individual elements, and of which every work is the expression and every author an active centre. It is the evocation of all those worlds, apparently distinct and unconnected, separated by time, space, conditions of life, the quality of genius, the forms of thought or the peculiarities of temperament, and which nevertheless communicate with one another, sometimes in depth, sometimes on the surface, to constitute through time and space an organic, growing whole. Whether this organic whole is a fact, a reality in itself, or simply a reality of point of view, a synthesis realised in the reader's

---

[160] AWD p. 58 (57)
[161] AWD p. 59 (57)
[162] Cf. AWD p. 58 (57). Considering providing a setting for each article, she comments: "But then this might be too artistic; it might run away with me.. . ."

mind as he re-creates the world of Donne or Thomas Hardy, for instance, to make it his own world, is of little importance; the essential thing is that continuity, connectedness, and indeed unity should be apparent under the discontinuous, the heterogeneous and the diverse. The two collections follow the same pattern, tracing the course of literature downstream so to speak, and thus Virginia Woolf's critical work reveals the same vision which, as novelist, she was to integrate into the complex structure of *Orlando*.

If we compare the list, on page 158, drawn up in chronological order, which was originally to constitute the first *Common Reader*, with the final version of the book, we notice certain alterations which become clearer in the light of the guiding ideas set out above, and which at the same time confirm the importance of these.

The suppressions, at first, appear to have been dictated by the need for unity. Sheridan and Sterne, in any case only provisionally included in the first list, would have introduced, in the one case an alien theme—comedy—and in the other, a jarring note owing to its anticipations. Defoe and Jane Austen were to be the only two landmarks to be retained before the discussion of the modern novel which, it should be noted, instead of concluding the debate as originally planned, opens it, taking its place before the Brontës, George Eliot, the Russians and Conrad.[163] Similarly, the Americans would have interrupted the unity of historic, if not of literary, experience which the critic was anxious to evoke. It is harder to explain the rejection of "On re-reading Novels",[164] "a very laborious, yet rather gifted article . . ."[165] in its author's words. None the less, if we take into account that it was replaced by "The Patron and the Crocus", it is easy to see that this analysis of the relations between a writer and his public is a general commentary on all the articles which preceded it; whereas "On re-reading Novels", an attempt to elucidate the notion of form, useful though it is for clarifying the reader's aim—and above all the critic's—was

---

[163] The article on Conrad in this list is presumably, considering the date, the "Mr. Conrad: a conversation" mentioned by V. W. in her Diary, about a fortnight after drawing up her list (AWD p. 60 (59)) and only published later on in CDB, pp. 74-8 (76-81). In the CR I, it was replaced by the article written on the occasion of the novelist's death, in August 1924, which expresses the same ideas with greater firmness and precision.

[164] Published in The M pp. 126-34 (155-66).

[165] AWD, p. 46 (45)

VIRGINIA WOOLF AND HER WORKS

(*Note.* In the left-hand column I have combined the two parallel lists drawn up by Virginia Woolf on August 17, 1923 (AWD p. 59), putting in brackets the titles omitted in the chronological list, which I have placed by referring to the numbers attached to the first list, drawn up probably at random according to what articles she then had at her disposal. The right-hand list reproduces the Contents List of CR I.

	The Common Reader
	····The Pastons and Chaucer
(Greeks)	On not knowing Greek
1a. (Old Memoirs) . . . .···:	The Elizabethan Lumber Room
	Notes on an Elizabethan Play
Montaigne	Montaigne
	The Duchess of Newcastle
4. Evelyn	Rambling round Evelyn
2. Defoe	Defoe
3. Sheridan?	
2. Sterne?	
5. Addison	Addison
	Lives of the Obscure
	I. Taylors and Edgeworths
	II. Laetitia Pilkington
6. Jane Austen	Jane Austen
	····Modern Fiction
	"Jane Eyre" and "Wuthering
8. Charlotte Brontë . . .	Heights"
7. George Eliot	George Eliot
11. The Russians	The Russian Point of View
The Americans	
9. Thoreau	
Emerson	
10. Henry James	
12. Modern Fiction . . . .····	Outlines
	I. Miss Mitford
	II. Bentley
	III. Lady Dorothy Nevill
	IV. Archbishop Thomson
On re-reading novels . .	The Patron and the Crocus
13. Essays	The Modern Essay
14. (Conrad)	Joseph Conrad
How it strikes a contemporary	How it strikes a contemporary

(There is no no. 1; two no. 2; "Greeks", "Emerson", "Re-reading novels" are not numbered.)

both too technical and too special in character, thus jarring somewhat with the easy general nature of the other essays. "The Patron and the Crocus", with a lightness of touch that does not preclude seriousness, casts retrospective light on the whole composition of the volume. It enables us to understand why this book, which to begin with seemed devoted particularly to great names (with the exception of "Evelyn" and "Old Memoirs") eventually became a subtle composition where the Pastons set off Chaucer who, without them, would have lacked sustenance for his genius. "The Duchess of Newcastle", "Lives of the Obscure" and "Outlines" add to literature in the strict sense—the classics—that literature which is merely writing. This "rubbish heap", as Virginia Woolf calls it,[166] this residuum of daily life, doomed to oblivion, represents none the less the essential part of those who live that life and without which no enduring work could arise—and without which such work could not be understood.

The second collection, like the first, starts from the Elizabethans and Robinson Crusoe to lead us to perfect mastery of the art of reading by way of a sort of secondary itinerary. But let us make no mistake: just as the Pastons threw light on Chaucer, just as a glimpse of scholars, aristocrats or archbishops contributes to our understanding of books, or evokes types, conditions, habits of life and of thought which all have their bearing on literature, similarly James Woodforde and John Skinner[167] display the perfect balance of the eighteenth century; behind Mary Wollstonecraft we catch a glimpse of Godwin, Shelley and Byron, while through Dorothy Wordsworth her brother and Coleridge, without ceasing to be poets, take on a common humanity more accessible to the common reader. Sometimes one is tempted to call this an oblique method, a sort of ricochet. This hypothesis might find support in the concept of point of view or accent, which recurs constantly in those discussions on the novel, on biography or criticism so dear to Virginia Woolf. Just as the author of *Flush* sought to reveal Elizabeth Barrett Browning through the medium of her spaniel, so she appeals to these writers of diaries or letters, these friends, patrons, relatives of famous authors, like so many stage supers or members

---

[166] "Every literature, as it grows old, has its rubbish-heap, its record of vanished moments and forgotten lives told in faltering and feeble accents that have perished", CR II p. 263 (239).

[167] CR II pp. 93-9 (83-9) and 100-7 (90-6)

of the chorus, to create around them the world they expressed, to set flowing the current of life in which they were immersed.

No doubt we must hold these ideas in part responsible for the choice and arrangement of the essays collected in the two *Common Readers*. Yet this is merely a method, sometimes applied with a certain inflexibility which reduces it to a mechanical process: it is not an end. The end is undoubtedly an attempt to reconstitute the literary phenomenon in its full complexity, which eludes all partial apprehensions: literary history, dogmatic criticism or biography. It is in this general impression, where the trivial everyday facts of obscure lives are merged in historic happenings, where the story of Mercy Harvey[168] echoes the *Midsummer Night's Dream* or *Cymbeline*, like the sub-plot of a Shakespearean play, where some contemporary novelist's Mrs Brown takes over from an Elizabethan Soranzo,[169] or from Moll Flanders; it is in the evocation of that twofold and yet single adventure, life and literature mingled, that we must see the essential element in Virginia Woolf's criticism.

We can recognize here one aspect of the theories that I have already analysed. Their application, however, enables us, better than any abstract discussion on the level of principles, to judge their merits and discover their weaknesses. Thanks to her novelist's gift, Virginia Woolf succeeds perfectly in this task of re-creation. She plays on our imagination and sympathy, calling up a whole landscape with figures, defined by their everyday gestures, manias, typical expressions, obsessions, dreams and humours with a sharpness which precludes neither subtlety nor complexity. Some of her figures, Dorothy Nevill,[170] Jack Mytton,[171] or Beau Brummel[172] have, as she said of Strachey's sketches, "something of the overemphasis and the foreshortening of caricatures"[173]; but we also find a delicacy of detail and an integration of character with background which entitle us to use the term miniature. If "Dr Burney's Evening Party"[174] suggests Hogarth, "The Elizabethan Lumber Room"[175] and "The Countess of Pembroke's Arcadia"[176] recall

[168] Cf. CR II pp. 9-23 (3-16) "The Strange Elizabethans"
[169] Cf. CR I pp. 72-83 (49-58), "Notes on an Elizabethan Play"
[170] CR I pp. 248-53 (201-5)
[171] CR II pp. 126-31 (113-8)
[172] CR II pp. 148-55 (134-41)
[173] Cf. DM p. 122 (190)
[174] CR II pp. 108-25 (97-112)
[175] CR I pp. 60-71 (40-8)
[176] CR II pp. 40-50 (32-41)

the *Très Riches Heures du Duc de Berry*. But, it may be asked, what has become of literature? And what sort of criticism is this, where historical vignettes alternate with portraits of people of every sort and of every stature? In fact, literature is everywhere: great works and great authors intermingle constantly with these obscure writings, these unfamiliar names: they only appear to be lost among them; all that they lose, indeed, is that character of pure literature, of dehumanized and devitalized authorship, which generations of respect, of abstract discussion and erudite research have gradually conferred upon them. This return to common humanity and everyday life, which are within the reach of the common reader, explains the charm, the interest and also the weakness of Virginia Woolf's criticism.

It is the charm of direct contact with reality and life, analogous to that of the novel; instead of abstraction and argument, we have images, impressions, gestures and actions. It is easy to understand Virginia Woolf's quarrel with academics and professional critics. The interest of this attitude and this point of view prefigure that which we shall find in her novels: a reorganization of literary reality, analogous to the reorganization of psychological reality, or indeed just of reality. All those entities, categories, in a word all the "objects" which make up the traditional world of literature: genres, schools, matter and manner, background, sources, style, character, plot, message—the whole orthodox system of references is abolished. In all this there was a puerile and sterilizing simplicity which fails to satisfy a twentieth-century mind. Things do not happen like that; great works of art are not like that. They are so inextricably intermingled with everything else that one cannot possibly separate them from the whole world out of which they sprang and which, at the same time, they create. Outlines grow blurred: we are left with innumerable interconnections. Literature, as Virginia Woolf presents it, is made up, like the mind that apprehends it, of infinitely interlaced ramifications. If we are thus recalled to the too frequently forgotten truth that life and art are one, and if the vision communicated to us is a richer and more involved one, it loses at the same time the clarity of outline which was familiar to us. Whether the subject under discussion is a period, a single work or an author, the alteration of perspective and of proportion is disconcerting. Sidney or Swift or Jane Austen are no longer to be defined according to standards which may perhaps have restricted them, but which outlined them with convenient clarity. Caught up in the stream of the *Common Reader*, their "literary" outlines dissolve, consumed from within and from without by the life that stirs within them and by the life that surrounds them. We are left with an impression of them, rather than knowledge: a word, a motif, a phrase remain, the feeling of possible closeness and intimacy; perhaps we should say a sense of present reality which invites one to read them. But it is a matter of feeling rather than of knowledge, and it is fugitive and inexpressible.

Of course, such criticism lacks the precision and solidity of a specialist's work. Virginia Woolf is well aware of this and makes no claims to the contrary. In this field, just as with her novels, she accepts the authority of no school of thought, only that of her own instinct; she declares herself an outsider, an amateur. But we must not forget that this is a declaration of independence, not a confession of weakness.

From certain terms I have been obliged to use: instinct, feeling, impression, one might be tempted to label her criticism "impressionist".[177] However, if a certain degree of impressionism is not absent from these studies, the term by no means does them justice or characterises them fully. "To take a theme from the book and make his criticism an air played in variation on it"[178]—such is the method of the impressionist critic, which Virginia Woolf has no intention of practising.[179] She has both too much historic sense and too much respect for the author she is considering, she is too fascinated by people and things, to yield to this temptation. The originality and value of her studies lies rather in the sense of a concrete presence that they convey. Imagining the readers of Arcadia, whose "insight and blindness" vary in every century, she concludes:

Our reading will be equally partial. In 1930 we shall miss a great deal that was obvious in 1655; we shall see some things that the 18th century ignored. But let us keep up the long succession of readers; let us in our turn bring the insight and the blindness of our own generation

---

[177] Cf. also CR II p. 268 (243): ". . . our taste, the nerve of sensation that sends shocks through us, is our chief illuminant; we learn through feeling. . . ."

[178] CR II p. 132 (119)

[179] Cf. also what she says about a passage in Hazlitt, CR II p. 183 (165): "Needless to say that is not criticism. It is sitting in an armchair and gazing into the fire, and building up image after image of what one has seen in a book. . . . It is being Hazlitt."

to bear upon the "Countess of Pembroke's Arcadia", and so pass on it to our successors.[180]

If, side by side with this, we note her constant, and constantly asserted, preoccupation with crossing—or rather suppressing—the gap in time which divides us from the works of the past, we have the essence of Virginia Woolf's criticism. She achieves, in the realm of literature, what her novels achieve in that of psychology: the past is made present, and while retaining its own particular qualities, takes on the colour and movement, in a word the life of the present, and thus is integrated with it. Such criticism then appears as guardian of tradition, not in the name of any aesthetic or ethical principles or systems, but simply in the name of the organic continuity of life, of the life of human beings, the life of society, and also in the name of the development of the mind, adding to its own experience that of humanity.

As an accessory factor, such an attitude justifies the perpetual renewal of criticism: each generation needs to make its own journey round its library. And if the function of criticism is not to elucidate literature—a task for scholars—but to make it accessible to one's contemporaries, there can be no such thing as definitive criticism, and to a certain extent it must always be impressionistic. Without wishing to imply thereby that Virginia Woolf's kind of criticism is the ideal kind, within its accepted limits it is perfectly legitimate.

The guiding line of Virginia Woolf's criticism, her main theme as she says, is naturally the novel. This is what interests her most and also the sphere in which she feels surest of her own competency, according to the qualifications she requires of the critic.[181] Although she never carried out the project of collecting in one volume all her articles on the novel,[182] this may mean that, on closer consideration, she realised that most of her essays deal more or less directly with the subject. True, the *Common Reader* books do not include many articles already written when this idea occurred to her[183]; but, from the *Canterbury Tales* and the *Arcadia* to Hardy and

[180] CR II p. 40 (32)   [181] Cf. *supra*, pp. 133-6
[182] According to Leonard Woolf, the references to a book on the novel (*Fiction*) found in the Diary, on Oct. 22, 1927 (p. 117 (115)) Aug. 12, 1928 (p. 130 (128)), and Sept. 22, 1928 (p. 133 (130)), concern a proposed collection and re-writing of articles on the novel.
[183] Articles prior to 1928 include: three on Henry James, 1917-1920. (DM); "On Re-reading Novels", 1921 (The M); "Mr Bennett and Mrs Brown", 1924 (CDB); "American Fiction", 1925 (The M); "The Art of Fiction", 1927 (The M); "The Novels of E. M. Forster", 1927 (DM).

Conrad, by way of Defoe, Jane Austen, the Brontë sisters, Elizabeth Barrett Browning, George Eliot, Gissing, Meredith and the Russians, she surveys—although not confining herself within the narrow traditional limits of the genre—the evolution of written narrative, which, at first hesitantly, then more boldly, in the hands of one genius after another, seeks to express life through the synthesis of facts, human beings, and a vision.

The path taken by Virginia Woolf, the things she notes at every stage, are characteristic. What she says about Defoe, if it scarcely explains or justifies her omissions, tells us what she admires, what for her constitutes the only criterion of value in literature. "He deals with the important and lasting side of things, not with the passing and trivial . . ."[184] True, the formula is so general that it becomes tricky to apply. But we have only to glance through her essays to see these words acquire substance, and this antithesis define two contrary attitudes and temperaments, into which not only artists but all human beings may be divided: idealists and materialists, those who are concerned with "the soul", "Life", "reality", which they apprehend and make perceptible through flashes of vision; and those who lose themselves among objects and events, through which they wander and lead us blindly. The former sort bring her, as she says of the Russians, "such revelations as we are wont to get only from the press of life at its fullest".[185] She is peculiarly responsive to the moments of intensity which, in prose works, attain the level of poetry. Phrases such as these give the key to her interests and the quality of her literary intuition:

We read Charlotte Brontë . . . for her poetry.[186]
[Emily Brontë] could free life from its dependence on facts.[187]
It is possible to enjoy [Jane Austen's novels] as one enjoys poetry.[188]
[Montaigne's] essays are an attempt to communicate a soul.[189]
There are many passages of such pure poetry in Sterne.[190]
His [Hardy's] own word, "moments of vision", exactly describes those passages of astonishing beauty and force which are to be found in every book that he wrote.[191]

She finds such "moments of vision" in Conrad[192]; and what she

[184] CR I p. 129 (95-6)
[186] CR I p. 200 (162)
[188] CR I p. 125 (142)
[190] CR II p. 82 (72)
[192] Cf. CR I pp. 287 (232), 290 (235)

[185] CR I p. 226 (183)
[187] CR I p. 204 (165)
[189] CR I p. 92 (66)
[191] CR II p. 247 (224)

admires in *Aurora Leigh* is "a sense of life in general, of people who are unmistakably Victorian, wrestling with the problems of their own time, all brightened, intensified, and compacted by the fire of poetry",[193] just as she had admired it in Chaucer, where "everything happens... more quickly and more intensely, and with better order than in life or in prose".[194] Here we have what was to be the essential factor of her conception of the novel, and whose presence in certain authors she sometimes exaggerates or overstresses. But is not this distortion, after all, an inevitable part of the process of reinterpreting the masterpieces of the past?

Among other features that arouse her sympathy and admiration, for she considers them essential to the artist, are the spirit of enquiry, the love of independence and a pioneering quality. In Sidney she finds latent all the germs of the English novel.[195] Defoe, well before Richardson and Fielding, was "one of the first indeed to shape the novel and launch it on its way".[196] Addison "is the respectable ancestor of an innumerable progeny".[197] Not that the novel owes anything to Sir Roger de Coverley, but even our weekly journals show the influence of his essays' perfection. She imagines Jane Austen—had she lived long enough to write six more novels—creating for herself a method "clear and composed as ever, but deeper and more suggestive, for conveying not only what people say, but what they leave unsaid; not only what they are, but what life is.... She would have been the forerunner of Henry James and of Proust."[198] And of Virginia Woolf, one might add to round off her thought. This extrapolation, whose correctness we need not discuss, shows to what point Virginia Woolf traces back her aesthetic genealogy among the great masters. Later, she says of Meredith that he "deserves our gratitude and excites our interest as a great innovator".[199]

The lack of resonance in her article on George Eliot is revealing: her admiration lacks warmth and spontaneity. Similarly, if she admits the native creative power of Walter Scott and Dickens,[200] these authors, despite their genius, are too self-assured, too devoid

---

[193] CR II p. 212 (191) [194] CR I pp. 32-3 (19)

[195] Cf. CR II p. 49 (40) [196] CR I p. 123 (90)

[197] CR I p. 144 (108) [198] CR I p. 183 (149)

[199] CR II p. 234 (212)

[200] Cf. particularly The M p. 65 (76): "... he is of course Shakespearean; like Scott, a born creator; like Balzac, prodigious in his fecundity ...", and also The M p. 55 (66)

of the charm of restlessness and anxiety to please her. She reveres their power and sets them among the classics; they form part of the world in which she lives, like St Paul's Cathedral or the Downs, but they are not subjects for criticism nor teachers of art. These two examples suffice, in contrast with the names on which she chooses to dwell, to define the limits of Virginia Woolf's critical activity. She is only interested in those writers whose example can stimulate her, those who have opened the way that she is following, those in fact who are like her, or with whom she can imagine affinities. And we find here, too, another characteristic trait: her deliberate preoccupation with the art of writing. Not that she dissects the techniques of style or composition in order to discover secrets or recipes. She is too well aware that secrets, those that matter, are impenetrable, and that with recipes one can only make bad books. But she is constantly seeking to rediscover the inner and outer conditions which, for every writer, determine a whole system of forces and obstacles, gifts and deficiencies, and which constitute for him the problem of art. To put oneself in the artist's place, at the very moment and point when he comes to grips with all that has been granted him and all that has been denied him, and to see how he triumphs or stumbles: such is her aim. Nevertheless, this identification only interests her in cases where the problem, either in the manner of its solution or its result, corresponds with the questions she asks herself. She is as interested in what Defoe makes of facts as in what De Quincey makes of dreams, just because both of them triumph over their own limitations, the one to carry us into a world of unreality, the other to maintain us in the world of everyday.[201] She considers Jane Austen, imprisoned within her milieu, George Eliot shackled by Victorianism, Hazlitt the thinker in love with reason, at odds with Hazlitt the painter in love with sensation and emotion; Conrad-Whalley, the sea-dog, at grips with nature but at peace with himself, in contrast with Conrad-Marlow, the observer and commentator at grips with man. It is the struggle of the author who, from manifold inner and outer conflicts, endeavours to bring forth harmony and unity—a balance precariously maintained, but whose very tension means intensity, life. And it is her discovery, at the meeting-point of period, personality and work of art, of that drama of creation

[201] Cf. "Defoe", CR I pp. 121-31 (89-97); "Robinson Crusoe", CR II pp. 51-8 (42-9), and "De Quincey's Autobiography", CR II pp. 132-9 (119-26)

which is in fact her own, that gives Virginia Woolf's criticism its original quality.

We can understand thus why she denies the competence of critics who are not themselves creators. They can have no experience of this drama, and if it is indeed the essential part of the creative act, their comments can relate only to what is superficial and accidental. However, without denying the soundness of this point of view and the interest of the type of analysis to which it gives rise, it must be admitted that there is also room for a static criticism of the work itself, which allows more importance to its content—a criticism addressed more specially to the reader, whether "common" or belonging to an elite, rather than to the curious practician fascinated by the sight of a fellow-writer at work. Moreover, one may occasionally ask oneself whether Virginia Woolf does not generalize from her own experience to an excessive degree. This is a risk to which all vigorous personalities are liable, since their creative imagination tends to substitute interior data for objective realities. We frequently have the impression that we are confronted with Virginia Woolf herself, or at least with what there was within her of Defoe or Jane Austen, Donne or Elizabeth Barrett Browning.

2. PAMPHLETS AND FEMINISM

Virginia Woolf's two pamphlets are akin to one another not only in style and tone and to a large extent in subject, but also by the circumstances of their composition, which explain certain of their common features. Each was contemporary with a novel; written as it were in the margin of *Orlando* and *The Years*, *A Room of One's Own* and *Three Guineas* provide an ideological commentary to these books, contain things left over from them and at the same time bring out points that the artistic requirements of the novels had left blurred. If they are thus enriched by echoes from the major works alongside which they were written, at the same time they suffer from a certain subordinate character; owing to their original lack of autonomy they have neither the structure nor the concentration which would provide strength and exactness as well as sincerity and verve. Nevertheless they are works of capital importance, if only because they invalidate the legend of the ivory tower so often associated with the author of *The Waves*. It is especially for what they reveal about her contacts with the outside world and her broad human interests that I propose to study them.

A ROOM OF ONE'S OWN (1929)

The apparent point of departure of *A Room of One's Own* was a lecture on "Women and Fiction" which Virginia Woolf was to give to the Arts Society of Newnham in May 1928, and for which she had probably been asked in the February of that year.[202] Eventually she gave two lectures, one at Newnham, the other at Girton, and not in May but in October. The text was revised in February 1929[203] and the first version, completed on May 12th,[204] required further careful correction and was only finished on August 19th.[205] The book was finally published on October 24, 1929. Needless to say, during the year between the lectures and their publication, the text, even allowing for its original length,[206] was considerably recast. It none the less retains the tone of speech and, to a large extent, too, an oral form. The lecturer's "I" appears on every page, almost in every sentence; and with that "I" her personal interests and preoccupations, and as she herself suggests, her limitations, prejudices and idiosyncrasies.[207] We recognize the reader of Fanny Burney, Miss Mitford, Dorothy Osborne and the Duchess of Newcastle[208]; we are reminded of her visits, as a girl, to her brothers at Cambridge, of her delight in the life and movement of the London streets,[209] and of her indignation at the condescension shown by some critics towards her own novels.[210] But the

---

[202] Cf. AWD p. 123 (121): "My mind is wool-gathering away about *Women and Fiction*, which I am to read at Newnham in May."

[203] Cf. AWD p. 141 (138)

[204] Cf. AWD p. 142 (139): ". . . having just finished what I call the final revision of *Women and Fiction* . . ."

[205] Cf. AWD p. 145 (141): ". . . for good or bad I have just set the last correction to *Women and Fiction*, or *A Room of One's Own*."

[206] Cf. AROO p. 5 (v.) note: "The papers were too long to be read in full, and have since been altered and expanded."

[207] Cf. AROO p. 70 (4): "One can only give one's audience the chance of drawing their own conclusions as they observe the limitations, the prejudices, the idiosyncrasies of the speaker."

[208] Cf. "Dr Burney's Evening Party", *N.Y.H.T.*, 21/7/29, and CR II: "Fanny Burney's Half-sister", *TLS*, 28/8/30, and G & R; "Dorothy Osborne's Letters", *N.R.N.Y.*, 24/10/28 and CR I; "The Duke and Duchess of Newcastle-upon-Tyne", *TLS*, 2/2/11; "An Imperfect Lady", *TLS*, 6/5/20, and "The Wrong Way of Reading", *Athenaeum*, 28/5/20, both incorporated into "Miss Mitford", CR I.

[209] Cf. "Street Haunting: A London Adventure", *Yale Review*, Oct. 1927, and DM

[210] Cf. AROO p. 113 (78), and AWD p. 131 (129)

most striking feature is the violence of her polemic. True, the quarrel is fought on general grounds, but we feel how much it was a personal one for her. This demand for independence and security, made by one who apparently had always enjoyed both, may be surprising. But it was just because she knew how exceptional and how precarious these advantages were: personal privileges which, indeed, she owed to her birth, but which she had been forced to defend by an effort of will and a stubborn and unremitting resistance to adverse currents, and which remained continually in jeopardy.

Although the title of the lecture from which the book was to spring seemed scarcely to anticipate the attitude this was to take, the lecturer had from the start warned her audience of the limits she intended to set on her subject:

All I could do was to offer you an opinion upon one minor point—a woman must have money and a room of her own if she is to write fiction.[211]

And, thinly disguised as a fictitious character, the novelist Mary Seton, she tells how the reflections which are to follow have been suggested by a visit to Oxbridge and Fernham, by which, of course, we must understand Oxford and Cambridge, Girton and Newnham. The difference, here caricatured, between the old Universities reserved for men and the "colleges" recently created for women, reveals the shocking state of things which Virginia Woolf attacks:

. . . thinking of the safety and prosperity of the one sex and of the poverty and insecurity of the other and of the effect of tradition and of the lack of tradition upon the mind of a writer, I thought at last that it was time to roll up the crumpled skin of the day, with its arguments and its impressions and its anger and its laughter, and cast it into the hedge.[212]

In this passage we find, at the same time, the two main themes of the book and a hint of the way they are treated. Repeatedly, Virginia Woolf herself recognized that she was no sort of logician. She feels more at ease with the concrete than with the abstract, she associates images and scenes more readily than she marshals arguments, and is on surer ground stimulating the reader's intuition than leading him to accept her conclusions by formal reason-

[211] AROO p. 6 (4)   [212] AROO p. 37 (24)

ing. She knows herself to be better equipped to raise laughter than to convince, and she trusts to mockery to undermine the institutions, customs and prejudices that revolt her. Finally, like all hypersensitive and timid beings, when dealing with a question that brings her to grips with society, with an anonymous crowd, with forces which, although human, are too remote and diffuse for her to achieve any contact with them, she is driven by her sense of weakness and inferiority to assume an aggressive attitude. Her exaggeration and violence are the measure of her vulnerability, rather than proportionate to the evils she attacks. And so it would be vain to seek in this book for any strict method. It is rather a series of vignettes with commentary, illustrating her two chosen themes. Moreover, the very heterogeneity of these themes further confuses the general plan. The social problem and the literary problem contradict rather than illuminate one another. The feminist pamphleteer and the critic of feminine literature encroach on each other's field, and Virginia Woolf does not always alter her tone when she shifts from one to the other. It seems more profitable therefore to make separate studies of what one might describe as Virginia Woolf's social feminism and her literary feminism, as they are displayed in *A Room of One's Own*, rather than to follow the devious and tangled path of the author's impassioned pleading.

The basic complaint Virginia Woolf makes against men is that they consider women as inferior beings and that on the strength of this arbitrary postulate, whose only foundation is their own pride, vanity and egotism, they maintain women in a semi-servile state; at the same time, they keep them out of all important activities, particularly those that determine the course of society and civilization. History and the contemporary scene provide the author with many examples, amusing or shocking and most frequently both at once, of this attitude, the two most serious consequences of which are those that she particularly proposes to indict. Women are denied the possibility, on the one hand, of developing their personalities freely and fully, and on the other, of sharing equally in the life of society and thus of influencing it according to their own tastes and nature, instead of being obliged to fill the secondary, purely ornamental role assigned to them by men. Relegated to the background in that society, they have to submit to the laws and the mentality imposed by men during the centuries of their exclusive rule. In a word, England, and indeed the whole world, are subject to a "patriarchy"[213] as intolerable as it is unjustifiable. However, irritation and bitterness do not blind Virginia Woolf nor preclude broadmindedness and tolerance.[214] She knows that it is absurd to blame any class or either sex as a whole,[215] that after all a woman is better fitted to be a nursemaid than a coalheaver, and that if the weaker sex is a victim of discrimination, it enjoys certain advantages thereby. For in fact, hostile here as always to abstractions, Virginia Woolf does not lay claims to an equality which physiology renders utopian. Thus the right to vote seems to her less important than economic and financial independence.[216] Although she never utters the formula, what she is basically claiming is "equal opportunity for all"[217] which, allied to liberty, will secure for women the full enjoyment of social advantages and this world's goods and, at the same time, the chance to develop their individual personality. We recognize at the base of these demands, and in their very moderation, the androgynous character that underlies *Orlando*. Tradition, customs and laws are founded on an arbitrary generalization about the absolute distinction between the sexes. As soon as this is shown to be an illusion, the whole system appears grotesque and unjust.

From this clear conception of the origins of woman's inferior position, there follow the reforms proposed by Virginia Woolf, which bear chiefly on the destiny allotted to girls. From adolescence they are prepared for their future bondage by being kept at home, deprived of the privileges of education which are reserved for men, and trained exclusively for the roles of wife and mother to which they are to be confined for life. Let schools and universities be laid open for them as for boys, let them be allowed the same liberty of movement, the same free contact with the world, let their tastes and gifts be respected. Let that room of her own in which a girl can be by herself be the symbol of her autonomy, not only the protecting shell which will allow her to be herself, but her very substance, born of the fusion of her being with the outside world. This room, in fact, is identical with the one Virginia Woolf the novelist created for Jacob, a closed room yet an open one at the same time, attainable only by universal consent, and through the possession of enough money to live there without having

[213] Cf. AROO p. 50 (33) [214] Cf. AROO p. 59 (39)
[215] Cf. AROO p. 58 (38) [216] Cf. AROO p. 56 (37)
[217] The phrase "equal opportunity" occurs in *Three Guineas*, p. 182 (100).

recourse to men's generosity, which is seldom unconditional.

The verve and the occasional violence with which these modest claims are made may cause a smile today and appear disproportionate. When judging them, however, we need to go even further back in time than thirty-five years, to rediscover the personal experience which is at the back of these indignant outbursts.

In the very year when Virginia Woolf was giving her lectures, there appeared *The Cause, a Short History of the Women's Movement in Great Britain*, by Ray Strachey.[218] Despite its historical character, this work had a topical interest asserted in its opening sentence: "The organized women's movement is not yet at an end"[219] and stated more precisely in the closing pages: "Morals and economics are at the best but indirectly affected by Parliament and in these two directions the present position of women still falls far short of the ideal that has inspired their movement."[220] Virginia Woolf was to quote *The Cause*,[221] and the final title of her book may well have been suggested by a fusion of her own *Jacob's Room* and a sentence of Ray Strachey's: "a young lady never had a moment she could call her own".[222] If women students were admitted to Oxford on an equal footing with men as early as 1920, Cambridge was to maintain a distinction by conferring on them only "titular degrees". Not until 1925 were women admitted to the Civil Service competition, and not until 1928 was the age when women were allowed to vote dropped from thirty to twenty-one. We see from this that the attitude of a veteran militant such as Ray Strachey and of a sympathizer like Virginia Woolf was not as anachronistic as it may appear nowadays, when women can become doctors, members of Parliament and even soldiers.

For another thing, the power of tradition and of British respectability, with certain aristocratic survivals, contributed no doubt to the perpetuation of customs and ways of behaviour already outdated on the Continent.[223] And paradoxically, the mass of unmarried women which was one of the demographic characteristics of

[218] London, G. Bell & Sons, 1928, 429 pp.

[219] *Ibid.*, p. 11

[220] *Ibid.*, p. 396

[221] Cf. AROO p. 31 (21). The passage quoted is in *The Cause*, p. 250.

[222] Cf. *The Cause*, p. 19

[223] Not entirely outdated, to judge by François Mauriac's comment, reviewing a novel by Brigitte Gros in *Express*, 7/4/60: "Why does a politically-minded woman annoy one, even if she is a friend?"

England at this period, while providing forces and arguments for feminism, fostered an atmosphere of antagonism between the sexes which was not unlike the atmosphere of the class struggle.[224]

Finally, if the Universities, the liberal professions and the Civil Service were accessible to women by 1928, such progress, notable though it was, had not yet had time to effect a very tangible change in society in general or in its mental attitude. Moreover, if Virginia Woolf was originally speaking to women students of a later generation than her own, she superimposed her personal experience on that of her listeners to the point of mingling a more or less distant past with the present. The combative spirit of these pages is fired by memories of her own youth, contemporary with the beginnings of feminism and of what Ray Strachey calls the great days of the women's movement (1897-1906 and 1906-1911), and of her own fears and hesitations and moments of daring: "But what is amusing now, I recollected, ... had to be taken in desperate earnest once."[225] Looking back, she sees how many personal privileges and fortunate chances have enabled her to assert herself in spite of the hostile conspiracy of institutions and customs. Her very luck makes her measure and perhaps even exaggerate the dangers she had incurred—stimulating her indignation and her spirit of revenge. But this is not all. This book, in which humour constantly verges on irony and sarcasm, is also a characteristic outburst of temper. Although she was admired and respected as a writer by her men friends, she felt that her femininity divided her from them. Neither the freedom of their relations, nor her own independence, nor her intelligence, nor her success could totally abolish this difference in nature. To be a woman and yet to behave in many ways like a man, was in one sense something as shocking as Orlando's change of sex. And if Virginia Woolf was a jealous upholder of her femininity and refused to abdicate any portion of it, at the same time she was constantly on the defensive, for fear men should not treat her as an equal. It was moreover less with individuals than with groups that she felt vulnerable: the University, the Critics, the Administrative Council of the British Museum. She was afraid of their generalizing, she knew they would generalize, catalogue her under the label "woman". Long before *A Room*

---

[224] V. W. compares the crushing of genius in women with its repression among working class people, AROO pp. 73-4 (50-1).
[225] AROO p. 84 (57)

of One's Own, in 1920, she had already written in the *New Statesman* a defence of the intellectual status of women, which her friend Desmond MacCarthy appeared to question.[226] Such public assertions and attacks, shot through with scruples and doubts, are defensive manifestations, displays of aggressiveness which conceal, in the hope of stifling it, the fear of submitting to the influence of another's opinion. And if she takes the defence of Woman, it is in order to protect the woman novelist, and this indirect approach explains the unexpected conjunction of the two themes I have isolated, the second of which must now be considered.

Surveying women writers from the sixteenth century to the nineteenth, Virginia Woolf notes one constant feature, which she attributes to a sense of inferiority due to their position in society, as she has described it.[227] A woman writer, whose "mind must have been strained and her vitality lowered by the need of opposing this, of disproving that",[228] "harassed and distracted with hates and grievances",[229] could attain neither the lucid vision of reality nor the freedom of expression indispensable for artistic creation. Only in the eighteenth century, with Mrs Behn, can one glimpse the possibility of a future when, freed from her shackles, a woman could write what she liked.[230] Meanwhile, however, the translations and the bad novels left by eighteenth-century women display more diligence than genius. But this activity in itself implies a revolution:

For if *Pride and Prejudice* matters, and *Middlemarch* and *Villette* and *Wuthering Heights* matter, then it matters far more than I can prove in an hour's discourse that women generally, and not merely the lonely aristocrat shut up in her country house among her folios and her flatterers, took to writing. Without those forerunners, Jane Austen and the Brontës and George Eliot could no more have written than Shakespeare could have written without Marlowe, or Marlowe without Chaucer, or Chaucer without those forgotten poets who paved the ways and tamed the natural savagery of the tongue. For masterpieces are not single and solitary births; they are the outcome of many years of thinking in common, of thinking by the body of the people, so that the experience of the mass is behind the single voice.[231]

---

[226] Cf. "The Intellectual Status of Women", *New Statesman*, Oct. 9, and Oct. 15-16, 1920. Letters to the Editor: correspondence conducted with "Affable Hawk"; also "A Society" in *Monday or Tuesday*, 1921. A reference in AWD, 10/9/28, p. 131 (129), shows the persistence of the disagreement.

[227] AROO ch. IV   [228] AROO p. 83 (56-7)

[229] AROO p. 88 (62)   [230] Cf. AROO p. 95 (67)

[231] AROO pp. 97-8 (68-9)

The interest of this extract goes beyond the present discussion. It not only defines the tradition of feminine writing developing parallel to the tradition of masculine writing, but furthermore it asserts that these traditions are rooted in the whole society with which the artist is closely involved. And so this page refutes at one blow the two criticisms often made of Virginia Woolf: the reproach of pure aestheticism, unconcerned with contact with the masses, and that of a revolutionary radicalism as regards art. Even allowing for the circumstances in which *A Room of One's Own* was composed, and the ulterior motives which may have affected its expression, the sincerity of these statements cannot be questioned. They fit in with the tendencies we have noted in her critical essays, and to some extent they enable one to consider *A Room of One's Own* as a chapter of that book on the novel mentioned in the Diary in March 1927,[232] and which Virginia Woolf was never to write. The fact that on June 22nd in the same year, four days after having once more referred to that project,[233] she notes the depressing effect on her of "woman haters"[234] allows us to imagine how the two currents of thought, coexistent in her own mind, matured the twofold inspiration of this book.

Virginia Woolf does indeed, as we have seen,[235] refer to the whole tradition of literature, without distinction of sex; and Orlando, in his androgynous unity, symbolizes the unity of that tradition. None the less, the interest Virginia Woolf always showed in women writers shows an awareness—originally obscure but subsequently clarified and rationalized—of a fundamental difference between artists of the two sexes[236]: a difference hitherto neglected or made the pretext for an arbitrary hierarchy. From her long acquaintance with women's writing, Virginia Woolf brings out two principles which complement one another, confirmed moreover by her own experience as writer. From the mere

---

[232] Cf. AWD p. 105 (104): "I have to write my book on fiction and that won't be done till January I suppose."

[233] Cf. AWD, p. 108 (107): "I will write [The Moths] very quickly, perhaps in between chapters of that long impending book on fiction" (June 18, 1927).

[234] Cf. AWD p. 109 (107)

[235] Cf. *supra*, ch. IV, pp. 145-6; 155

[236] In her second article on Dorothy Richardson, she had already written this characteristic remark: "She has invented, or, if she has not invented, developed and applied to her own uses a sentence which we might call the psychological sentence of the feminine gender" ("Romance and the Heart", *Nation & Athenaeum*, May 19, 1923, p. 229).

fact of their natural difference, and from the dissimilarity of their daily lives, women have a vision of reality which is different from men's; their system of values is different too.[237] The deliberate refusal to take into consideration these differences, and the wish to conform to a masculine point of view and set of values, have imbued a large part of women's writing with artifice and conventionality. Jane Austen and Emily Brontë were able to escape this fatal temptation; they remained women in their writing, they did not try to write like men, submitting to men's precepts and judgments.[238] And so it is essential for a woman to turn for help to the great women writers.

Lamb, Browne, Thackeray, Newman, Sterne, Dickens, De Quincey— whoever it may be—never helped a woman yet, though she may have learnt a few tricks of them and adapted them to her use. The weight, the pace, the stride of a man's mind are too unlike her own for her to lift anything substantial from him successfully.[239]

From subject to sentence, by way of structure, a woman's work, if she wants to be authentic, to have that indisputable value that art acquires through the perfect adherence of form and substance, must be purely feminine. Apart from a few successful achievements among the women novelists of the nineteenth century, it is only in flashes that the woman writer of today can find among her predecessors a purely feminine literature on which she can base her own writing. All things considered, this search for a tradition leads to a negative rather than to a positive result; it is more useful through the dangers it reveals, through the lessons that can be learned from these mutilations and renunciations, than through the examples it provides. And we recognize the author of "Modern Fiction" and "Mr Bennett and Mrs Brown", and the novelist contemplating *The Waves* when we read:

. . . who shall say that even this most pliable of all forms is rightly shaped for her use? No doubt we shall find her knocking that into shape for herself when she has the free use of her limbs; and providing some new vehicle, not necessarily in verse, for the poetry in her.[240]

[237] Cf. AROO pp. 110-11 (76-7).
[238] Cf. AROO p. 112 (78): "They wrote as women write, not as men write. Of all the thousand women who wrote novels then, they alone entirely ignored the perpetual admonitions of the eternal pedagogue—write this, think that."
[239] AROO p. 114 (79)
[240] AROO p. 118 (80)

In her analysis of that imaginary novel, *Life's Adventure*, by one Mary Carmichael, no less fictitious than Mary Seton,[241] Virginia Woolf undoubtedly puts forward her own conception of the novel, except that for the antagonism between materialism and idealism she substitutes the antagonism between the masculine and feminine natures and points of view. By dint of sincerity and independence, this novelist of the new school triumphed at last:

Men were no longer to her "the opposing faction"; she need not waste her time railing against them; she need not climb on to the roof and ruin her peace of mind longing for travel, experience and a knowledge of the world and character that were denied her. Fear and hatred were almost gone, or traces of them showed only in a slight exaggeration of the joy of freedom, a tendency to the caustic and satirical, rather than to the romantic, in her treatment of the other sex. Then there could be no doubt that as a novelist she enjoyed some natural advantages of a high order. She had a sensibility that was very wide, eager and free. It responded to an almost imperceptible touch on it. It feasted like a plant newly stood in the air on every sight and sound that came its way. It ranged, too, very subtly and curiously, among almost unknown or unrecorded things. . . . It brought buried things to light and made one wonder what need there had been to bury them.[242]

Just as we should not attribute too literal a significance to the antagonism between materialism and idealism, to interpret the antagonism between the sexes as something absolute would be to betray Virginia Woolf's meaning. This antagonism is superficial and secondary, rather than profound and fundamental. It is more the result of prejudices and habits than a reality inherent in human nature. The author of *Orlando* here quotes Coleridge to assert her belief in our androgynous nature, and her conviction that it is a fruitful factor: "The androgynous mind is resonant and porous; . . . it transmits emotion without impediment; . . . it is naturally creative, incandescent and undivided."[243]

We may thus conclude that Virginia Woolf's literary feminism is as moderate and realistic as her social feminism. She merely desires the suppression of that sort of censorship which involves different criteria, special reservations, severities or indulgences where women's writings are concerned. Let these writings be

241 Cf. AROO p. 120 (84)
242 AROO p. 139 (96)
243 AROO p. 148 (102)

granted the same welcome, the same treatment, the same chances as men's, just as it is only fair to grant the same chances and openings to girls as to young men. In the solitude and independence of a room of one's own, the artist is neither man nor woman, but a bisexual spirit at grips with reality, in pursuit of truth.[244]

True, *A Room of One's Own* displays little of the serenity and impersonality its author recommends. But considering that it is a work of controversy, it would be futile to linger over this aspect. Mingling history, satire, literary criticism and self-confession, the book is, like *Orlando*, rich in revelations about its author. It is chiefly in this capacity that it holds its interest, particularly through the relations it establishes between the different lines of thought which we find scattered throughout her work. It provides the analysis of that "situation" which, according to Sartre, defines a writer. We perceive here in what way Virginia Woolf is the product of her reactions to her education, her social, historical and literary surroundings; how she asserted herself in opposition to all those adverse forces whose very resistance helped to steel her integrity.

As usual, Virginia Woolf passes clearsighted judgment on her own book: "It has much work in it, many opinions boiled down into a kind of jelly, which I have stained red as far as I can."[245] She is dissatisfied with its tone, even more than with its heterogeneous character: "Has an uneasy life in it I think: you feel the creature arching its back and galloping on, though as usual much is watery and flimsy and pitched in too high a voice."[246]: what a little later she calls "a shrill feminine tone".[247] On this point she cannot be contradicted; but the ardour and conviction which she admits having put into it[248] redeem that shrillness, giving the "highpitched voice" certain infinitely deeper resonances.

THREE GUINEAS (1938)

Rather more than a year after the publication of *A Room of One's Own*, on January 20, 1931, Virginia Woolf conceived of a sequel

---

[244] Cf. AROO pp. 171-2 (117-8)
[245] AWD p. 142 (139)
[246] AWD p. 145 (141-2)
[247] Cf. AWD p. 148 (145)
[248] Cf. AWD p. 149 (145)

to this book, which would deal with "the sexual life of women: to be called Professions for Women perhaps".[249] The various titles successively proposed by Virginia Woolf in the course of the seven years which elapsed between this first project and its final realization are so many landmarks in the development of the work. Failing any first drafts or author's notes, they enable us to imagine the emergence of dominant preoccupations and guiding ideas, which were to be fused, more or less, in a surge of eloquence rather than by any real logic.

About "sexual life", indeed, there is little left, unless we understand by this the repercussions of sex on life, the limits and restrictions which, from the past to our own day, have weighed on women's existence, and particularly the reduction of their activities to the domestic sphere and their exclusion from the liberal professions. It is from this angle that the book, reverting to the themes of women's education and economic independence, completes and often, it must be admitted, repeats *A Room of One's Own*. Early in 1932, the book is called *Tap on the Door*, or *A Knock on the Door*.[250] This title leads one to suppose that at this period Virginia Woolf had conceived the idea of an appeal from men for women's co-operation, an idea which was to provide the structure for the final work. Perhaps she was already thinking of those appeals for funds—two to begin with, in March 1936,[251] and then three at the end of the same year[252]—to which she was to contribute her three guineas, symbolic of her support of their causes. But at the same time the title might just as well have been "Men are like that",[253] for the male attitude in general is analysed there in all its manifestations and at every period: men at home and in public life, university men, ecclesiastics, politicians, statesmen, makers of tradition and civilization for their own use—namely, against

[249] Cf. AWD pp. 165-6 (162). A note, in 1934, identifies this book with *Here and Now*, alias *The Years*; this does not invalidate my hypothesis, since the two books had the same origin; cf. AWD p. 295 (284) and *infra* p. 302ff

[250] Cf. AWD pp. 178 (173), 179 (174): "My mind is set running upon *A Knock on the Door* (what's its name?) owing largely to reading *Wells on Woman*—how she must be ancillary and decorative in the world of the future, because she has been tried, in 10 years, and has not proved anything."

[251] Cf. AWD p. 268 (258). "And I'm so absorbed in *Two Guineas*—that's what I'm going to call it."

[252] Cf. AWD p. 274 (264)

[253] Cf. AWD p. 179 (174): "And I'm quivering and itching to write my—what's it to be called?—'Men are like that?'—no, that's too patently feminist."

women, whom they despise. And this suggested another possible title: "On being despised", which Virginia Woolf was considering at the beginning of 1935.[254] But now the rise of the totalitarian menace, Nazism in Germany, Fascism in Italy, and the Spanish war, deflected her thought, and she planned to write an anti-Fascist pamphlet.[255] This was eventually to find its place in *Three Guineas*, along with everything else. In the background, behind Fascism, the spectre haunting all minds was war. War as a product of existing society, the subject of discussion at the Labour Party Congress at Brighton in October 1935, became an obsession with Virginia Woolf, and in the following days she wrote *The Next War*.[256] At the end of that year and in the beginning of 1936 she gradually discovered the idea from which the final structure of *Three Guineas* was to emerge: a series of articles on all sorts of subjects, written at the request of editors of newspapers or reviews.[257] Then the titles *Answers to Correspondents*[258] and *Letter to an Englishman*[259] show that by the early months of 1936 she had at last found the form which would "give me the right to wander; also put me in the position of the one asked. And excuse the method: while giving continuity".[260] On March 24th the title *Two Guineas* appears for the first time, and the author is immersed in her book to the point of obsession, talking to herself in the street.[261] By the end of the year, *Two Guineas* has become *Three Guineas*—which Virginia Woolf "begins" on January 28, 1937.[262] By this we must understand that she takes up again all the material, all the drafts

[254] Cf. AWD p. 236 (228): "But now I want to write On Being Despised."

[255] Cf. AWD p. 239 (231): "And here I am plagued by the sudden wish to write an anti-Fascist pamphlet." Cf. also AWD p. 257 (248)

[256] Cf. AWD p. 257 (248): "Three days I got into wild excitement over *The Next War*. Did I say the result of the L.P. at Brighton was the breaking of that dam between me and the new book, so that I couldn't resist dashing off a chapter." Cf. also AWD p. 259 (250)

[257] Cf. AWD p. 262 (252-3): "I had an idea—I wish they'd sleep—while dressing—how to make my war book—to pretend it's all the articles editors have asked me to write during the past few years—on all sorts of subjects. . . ."

[258] Cf. AWD p. 263 (254): "The next book I think of calling *Answers to Correspondents*."

[259] Cf. AWD p. 267 (258): "And I can't concentrate this morning—must make up Letter to an Englishman. I think, once more, that is the final form it will take".

[260] Cf. AWD p. 262 (253)

[261] Cf. AWD p. 268 (258): "I must very nearly verge on insanity I think, I get so deep in this book I don't know what I'm doing. Find myself walking along the Strand talking aloud."

[262] Cf. AWD p. 275 (265)

and sketches accumulated during six years[263] and casts them in this final form, which has acquired precision during the year 1936. She was to finish on October 12, 1937.[264] From the fact that she announces yet again, on January 9, 1938, that she is finishing *Three Guineas*,[265] one may conclude that, as was her habit, Virginia Woolf has gone back to her first version and spent almost three months revising it.

"Answers to Correspondents", otherwise *Three Guineas*, puts in its opening pages the question which has suggested these answers and the explanations that justify them: "How in your opinion are we to prevent war?"[266] But before considering the purport of the question, the very fact that it is put to a woman by a middle-class man, a product of Public School and University, versed in business affairs and politics, deserves attention. Indeed, is not this the first time that a man enjoying the privileges of education has sought a woman's opinion on a point which hitherto seemed to be solely within his province? Such an unprecedented gesture implies a revolutionary change in the relations between the sexes. And in a retrospective survey which is already familiar to us from *A Room of One's Own*, Virginia Woolf recalls the underprivileged position of women until quite recent years; deprived of any real education, confined to the home, excluded from the liberal professions, dedicated to marriage and to financial dependence on a father and a husband, considered as inferior beings, they have hitherto been practically kept out of the life of society and of the nation, which are exclusively masculine creations, the expression and the result of masculine psychology. And is not war, which is inherent to this civilization, a product of essentially masculine instincts? History, biography, and the present state of affairs would seem to prove it so. "War is a profession; a source of happiness and excitement; and it is also an outlet for manly qualities, without which men would deteriorate."[267] Fascist theories are merely the extreme result of these ideas, which are upheld by politicians, famous professors, dignitaries of the Church and respectable bourgeois who justify them in the name of patriotism, whereas in reality they are only thinking of defending their own privileges and satis-

[263] Including, among others, the story "A Society" from *Monday or Tuesday*.
[264] Cf. AWD p. 286 (276)
[265] Cf. AWD p. 288 (278)
[266] Three G p. 7 (3)
[267] Three G p. 15 (8)

fying their own vanity. By depriving women of education, and thereby depriving them of the intellectual and economic independence which alone ensure the autonomy of thought, men have effectively excluded women from any share in the growth of society, in the direction of civilization, and thus have assured their own monopoly of power. And, in view of what they are, such power can only foster a warlike spirit.

The first step to be taken in order to prevent war, then, is to change the system that encourages war; to enable Englishwomen to become "full daughters" of their country[268] by providing the liberal education which would prepare them to play, in society, the peacemaker's role which is theirs by nature. The ideal feminine university sketched by Virginia Woolf[269] is undoubtedly closer to Thélème than to Cambridge. But this escape into dream does not preclude realism. Under present conditions, the essential, the most urgent thing is to ensure for women the possibility of influencing the destiny of society by allowing them to play an active part in it—that is to say by preparing them through a broad general education. So that the first guinea goes to the secretary of the Women's College, which "imperfect as it may be, is the only alternative to the education of the private house".[270] Such is the first "positive contribution to the prevention of war".[271]

But suppose the modern woman, equipped to become a doctor, a lawyer, a civil servant, finds herself excluded from these professions or kept in a subordinate rank, what progress can be expected? The hope of economic independence leading to independence of opinion and action will have been disappointed. The letter from the treasurer of a society to help women to find posts in the liberal professions leads Virginia Woolf to examine the *de facto* situation, which hardly corresponds to the situation *de jure*; from her enquiry it appears that the important posts are reserved for men, that nepotism[272] and the spirit of competition in the labour market[273] tend to neutralize the trend to women's emancipation, and that a sort of masculine dictatorship relegates women to the home.

[268] Cf. Three G p. 28 (14): ". . . the right to call herself, if not a full daughter, still a step-daughter of England."

[269] Cf. *ibid.*, pp. 61-4 (33-5)

[270] *Ibid.*, p. 72 (39)

[271] *Ibid.*, p. 72 (39)

[272] Cf. *ibid.*, p. 91 (50)

[273] Cf. *ibid.*, pp. 93-4 (50-1)

In the reigning atmosphere, this anticipates the success of the programme "Work, Family, Fatherland" of full-blown fascist regimes.[274] Enrolled as footsoldiers in the bourgeois army,[275] women are in great danger of being contaminated by the spirit of the system,[276] and thus, in spite of themselves, led to co-operate with capitalism[277] under the slogan "For God and Empire".[278] They would then be bound to lead the same existence and profess the same loyalties as their brothers.[279] This is clearly not the ideal envisaged by Virginia Woolf. The life of the middle class, as it appears in biographies, sermons, newspapers, with its routine of work, profit, activity, selfishness, is destructive of mind and soul.[280] But then we are in an impasse if, in order to acquire independence and influence, women must go into the liberal professions, and if, owing to existing structures and habits, the exercise of these professions is highly undesirable for them. How are they to take up such careers and yet remain civilized human beings?[281] The study of biography and history will, once again, give us the answer. In their struggle to emerge from their bondage, four guiding principles have sustained women and ensured their victory: poverty, chastity (of the mind even more than of the body), "derision and freedom from unreal loyalties . . .".[282] Let them retain these guides, and they will become an integral part of society, and thus pursue their struggle, not for themselves alone, but for humanity and peace—for civilization. Out of respect for Virginia Woolf's argument, her own terms have been retained here, although she herself realized that the demands of her demonstration obliged her to strain these key words beyond the limits of their elasticity. "By poverty is meant enough money to live upon. That is, you must earn enough to be independent of any other human being and to buy that modicum of health, leisure, knowledge and so on that is needed for the full development of body and mind. But no more. . . ."[283] This vital minimum corresponds to the ideal proposed by all socialist ideologies.[284] It should not be

[274] Cf. ibid., p. 97 (53)
[275] Cf. ibid., p. 115 (61)
[276] Ibid., p. 121 (66)
[277] Ibid., p. 123 (67)
[278] Ibid., p. 127 (70)
[279] Ibid., p. 128 (70)
[280] Ibid., p. 131 (72)
[281] Ibid., p. 137 (75)
[282] Ibid., p. 142 (78)
[283] Ibid., p. 145 (80)
[284] This, together with the image of a procession mentioned above, no doubt suggested to Q.D. Leavis the title of her critical article "Caterpillars of the Commonwealth Unite", Scrutiny, Sept. 1938.

forgotten that Leonard Woolf was a member of the Labour Party. We should also notice the bourgeois, individualist background implied by this independence and security which guarantee a harmonious material and moral development. Note, finally, a touch of asceticism—or relative asceticism—which reflects the simplicity and austerity natural to the author as much as the survival of a certain Anglo-Saxon puritanism. It is with the concept of chastity that Virginia Woolf takes the greatest liberties. This physical virtue, jealously protected by the male sex, in fact almost invented and imposed by them with hypocritical selfishness,[285] becomes what would more usually be called intellectual integrity.

By chastity is meant that when you have made enough to live on by your profession you must refuse to sell your brain for the sake of money. That is you must cease to practise your profession, or practise it for the sake of research or experiment; or, if you are an artist, for the sake of the art. . . .[286]

In this disinterestedness, this incitement to research, we recognize the accents of the Diary, with its rejection of any compromise or prostitution. Indeed, it is through the intermediary of this term that the word "chastity" can assume the sense which Virginia Woolf gives to it.

Derision, such as women endured in their conquest of independence, becomes, by an even more devious route, the refusal of "all methods of advertising merit", the belief that "ridicule, obscurity and censure are preferable, for psychological reasons, to fame and praise".[287] This is a profession of humility corresponding to her profession of asceticism but, above all, it is a repudiation of the vanity that she has satirized in men: the love of display, of dressing-up, of pomp, shown by academics and ecclesiastics, soldiers and statesmen; barbaric survivals, she says, unworthy of supposedly civilized men. Without attaining to the epic grandeur of *Sartor Resartus*, this attitude is none the less akin to Carlyle's. All these insignia, this purple and ermine are merely masks and disguises intended to impress the crowd and to introduce confusion into its sense of values. They are the auxiliaries, almost the creators of all

---

[285] Cf. Three G, long note on pp. 296-301 (166-9).
[286] *Ibid.*, p. 145 (80)
[287] *Ibid.*, p. 146 (80)

false values and false loyalties, which they maintain to the great detriment of true civilization.

Hence the fourth principle, which Virginia Woolf defines as follows:

By freedom from unreal loyalties is meant that you must rid yourself of pride of nationality in the first place; also of religious pride, college pride, school pride, family pride, sex pride, and those unreal loyalties that spring from them. Directly the seducers come with their seductions to bribe you into captivity, tear up the parchments; refuse to fill up the forms.[288]

And to illustrate these principles and give them a convincing force she evokes one of her favourite figures: Antigone. In her conflict with Creon, her rejection of laws in favour of The Law, she represents the heroine *par excellence*, struggling against tyranny. And the author of *Three Guineas* seems to be suggesting to Anouilh that play which was to awaken so much sympathy among the men of the Resistance movement when she writes of Sophocles' *Antigone*: "It could undoubtedly be made, if necessary, into anti-Fascist propaganda."[289]

This clearly shows how far the feminism of *Three Guineas* goes. It is a point of view, a method of analysis, not an end in itself. It provides the elements of a diagnosis, leading from particular symptoms to the sources of more general ills which imperil the whole of civilization. The guinea which the author decides to send to help women to enter the liberal professions is, like the first sum intended to improve their education, assigned to a wider cause to which these particular causes contribute:"

You can join the professions and yet remain uncontaminated by them; you can rid them of their possessiveness, their jealousy, their pugnacity, their greed. You can use them to have a mind of your own and a will of your own. And you can use that mind and will to abolish the inhumanity, the beastliness, the horror, the folly of war.[290]

The phrases "a mind of your own", "a will of your own", echoing *A Room of One's Own*, reveal both the continuity and the unity of Virginia Woolf's thought. The two books are a plea for the rights of the individual, the safeguarding of the individual's

[288] Three G p. 146 (80)
[289] *Ibid.*, p. 301 (169)
[290] *Ibid.*, p. 151 (83)

integrity. But whereas the first pamphlet was limited[291] by its personal and aesthetic aims, the second, while stressing the solidarity of the problems considered with its own cause, attains a general character which, whatever may be the faults of the book, entitles one to include Virginia Woolf in the great line of Humanists[292]—and also among "committed" writers, paradoxical as this epithet may appear when we consider the dominant aspect of her work. It should be enough to refer the reader to certain pages of *Mrs Dalloway*, *Orlando*, *The Years* (which she had just written) and above all *Between the Acts*, which had barely begun to take shape in her mind.[293]

At this point it may be asserted that this liberal individualism is neither so narrow nor so purely escapist as implied by Stephen Spender, who seemed to have had the author of *A Room of One's Own* particularly in mind when he wrote:

All the writers ask is a little annuity that will enable us to live as civilized people, to go to concerts, buy a piano, live in a room of one's own, take a holiday by the seaside, entertain our friends, be free from the anxiety of not knowing where the next revolution will come from, and they think that has nothing to do with politics, politics concerning just the life they want to escape.[294]

The third answer, by far the longest—106 pages as against 65 and 81 respectively for the first two—attempting to show how women can help to prevent war by protecting culture and intellectual liberty,[295] to some extent achieves the synthesis of the first two while developing their implications.

In the first place, does not this appeal to women bear witness to the failure of masculine education, its incapacity to prepare men to protect culture and intellectual liberty by themselves; is it not the sign, indeed, that the pretensions of the Universities and Public

[291] V. W. herself assessed the difference between the two books: she writes in her Diary on April 11, 1938 (AWD p. 289 (279)), referring to *Three Guineas*: "I think there's more to it than to a *Room*: which, on rereading, seems to me a little egotistic, flaunting, sketchy."

[292] The affinities between V. W. and Montaigne are analysed by Rantavaara, *V. W. and Bloomsbury*, pp. 78-80, with reference to the article on Montaigne in the first *Common Reader*.

[293] Cf. AWD p. 289 (279), a fortnight after the passage quoted n. 291.

[294] Stephen Spender, "Liberal Individualism", *New Masses*, Nov. 10, 1936. In his autobiography, Spender, while reasserting his disagreement with V. W.'s political attitude, pays tribute to her idealism and broadmindedness (*World Within World*, p. 154 ff.).

[295] Cf. Three G p. 154 (85)

Schools, in this sphere, are without foundation, and that these institutions, as their attitude towards women's rights has proved, are more concerned with defending their privileges and those of an out-of-date patriarchy than with promoting a better state of society? If the feminism of the previous century is old fashioned,[296] the fact remains none the less that this movement was the advance guard of today's mobilization, which appeals to all citizens of good will to unite against war: it stood for the same democratic ideals of justice, equality and liberty.[297] The discrimination of which women were victims then finds a parallel today in the discrimination to which totalitarian ideologies subject certain races.[298] The spirit of tyranny is the same, and Virginia Woolf declares herself ready to fight against it. Yet she is still reluctant to adhere to this society, even if she approves its aims and grants it her material support. The very notion of a society repels her. Her opposition to Society extends to all societies.

Is there not something in the conglomeration of people into societies that releases what is most selfish and violent, least rational and humane in the individuals themselves? Inevitably we look upon society, so kind to you, so harsh to us, as an ill-fitting form that distorts the truth; deforms the mind; fetters the will.[299]

This transition from societies to Society may seem logically dubious. But apart from this formal licence, her arguments are sound. Mass psychology plays its part in every case. And nothing is more characteristic of Virginia Woolf than this refusal to be enrolled, this mistrust of the herd spirit. It is the revenge of the individualist who, while consenting to commit herself in a common cause, is unwilling to compromise herself within it, and intends to safeguard her independence, to preserve her integrity. True, there is something paradoxical about that "Outsiders' Society" proposed by Virginia Woolf as the only possible alternative to the enrolment, or regimentation, asked of her. Lacking offices, committees, secretary or treasurer, meetings and membership—anonymous and elastic[300]—it is more suggestive of anarchism than of the socialism to which reference has been made. If we remember

[296] Cf. *ibid.*, p. 184 (101)

[297] Cf. *ibid.*, p. 185 (102): "It was a claim for the rights of all—all men and women —to the respect in their persons of the great principles of Justice and Equality and Liberty. The words are the same as yours; the claim is the same as yours."

[298] Cf. *ibid.*, p. 187 (102-3)

[299] *Ibid.*, p. 191 (105)

[300] *Ibid.*, p. 193 (106)

that about the same time Virginia Woolf was using the same term, outsider, to define her own literary position,[301] we are led to conclude that with her, individualism comes first. It is to her credit that honesty and generosity led her to come down into the arena, but we should not conclude therefrom that she had a particularly active political or social conscience. This need not, however, be held against her. Virginia Woolf shares this reserve with a great number of intellectuals who, out of their need for the absolute, resent the demands of dogma or militancy. This does not prevent them from taking part in the struggle in defence of their ideal, as is the case with *Three Guineas*, when their anger and indignation go beyond the limits of their patience and passivity.

The ultimate aims of these free-shooters, who refuse any weapon and any banner, despite—or perhaps because of—their basic individualism, coincide with those of all the ideologies that can be combined under the vague name of "progressive" or "left-wing". In the first place, the denial of patriotism. One's country is a society like any other: exclusive, possessive, arrogant. It is not merely a masculine concept, but a masculine fact. A woman has no country, since she may change her nationality on marriage. She wants none; she is a citizen of the world.[302] This intellectual internationalism does not, however, preclude a certain emotional patriotism. It would be unthinkable for the author of *Orlando* and *The Waves* to deny that integration of the ambience to the individual which binds us irrevocably to a certain corner of the world.[303] But instead of using this attachment as a pretext to renounce the rest of the planet, she was to make of this small circle traced around her by fate the model of what she sought for all that lay beyond it. And the most effective method of combating patriotism, which is essentially militaristic, is not only the refusal to participate or even to associate with its manifestations, but to meet them with serene indifference.

Then, "at the risk of some repetition"[304]—which in fact seemed

---

[301] Cf. *supra*, ch. III, p. 105; AWD p. 308 (297), passage quoted

[302] Cf. Three G p. 197 (109): ". . . as a woman, I have no country. As a woman I want no country. As a woman my country is the whole world."

[303] Cf. *ibid.*, pp. 197-8 (109): "And if, when reason has said its say, still some obstinate emotion remains, some love of England dropped into a child's ears by the cawing of rooks in an elm tree, by the splash of waves on a beach, or by English voices murmuring nursery rhymes. . . ."

[304] *Ibid.*, pp. 199-200 (110)

hardly necessary—the author surveys "rapidly" (less so than she asserts) the various other duties of the members of this Society of Outsiders. To ensure their economic independence by paid work, so as to preserve their freedom of opinion and action; to strive to win from the state a salary for housewives and mothers. But obviously, the vast size of the war budget rendering this prospect utopian, they had better bring their efforts to bear on more accessible objects, such as the defence of professional integrity, the refusal to take part in war preparations and in all activities, such as those at the Universities of Oxford and Cambridge or that of the Church, which tend to restrict liberty.[305] In short, to subject all institutions to critical analysis in order to indict false values, and to preserve oneself from false loyalties and the temptations of selfishness and vanity. Thus they are not to take part in official celebrations and they must refuse honours and distinctions.[306] They must oppose with passive resistance all the forces which help to perpetuate the barbaric spirit and structure of existing society, of which Fascism and Nazism are merely extreme forms. This Society of Outsiders exists; it has been functioning for a century, witness such women as Sophia Jex-Blake, Elizabeth Barrett, Miss Woodhouse, Miss Davies, Barbara Leigh Smith, and all those who fought privately or publicly for the advent of the reign of justice, equality and liberty.[307] And once again, behind these cohorts, Virginia Woolf recalls the figure of Antigone, whose integrity and whose uncompromising spirit make her the heroine and symbol of resistance against all forms of tyranny—a resistance which, after all, attacks the causes of war at their very source. Moreover, besides Antigone, Virginia Woolf appeals to other famous defenders of the democratic ideal: Coleridge, Rousseau, Whitman, George Sand, whom she quotes in a final note, as though by setting their signatures to her manifesto she were giving it the weight of their authority.[308]

If such is the thread of the ideas expressed in *Three Guineas*, it must be admitted that on a first reading the incessant return of the argument to its starting-point, the juxtaposition of the different periods under discussion, the obsessional recurrence of criticism

---

[305] Cf. Three G p. 204 (113)
[306] Cf. *ibid.*, pp. 206-7 (114-5)
[307] Cf. *ibid.*, p. 250 (138)
[308] Cf. *ibid.*, note 49, pp. 327-9 (187-8)

of the anti-feminist attitude of the Universities and the Church, break up the line of reasoning and obscure her fundamental intentions. The reader experiences the same uncertainties that the author must have gone through, to judge by the various provisional titles that occurred to her mind. This book, which she had carried too long within her, bears despite its recasting the marks of a multiplicity of intentions, awkwardly synthesized. The vigour noticeable in particular pages or paragraphs does not extend to the whole work. This weakness is doubtless not solely due to a prolonged gestation or a divided inspiration. It is to be accounted for by the way the author's mind worked, far more intuitively than logically. She visualized scenes or situations far better than she could deduce abstract connections, and in consequence she is more skilled at making one see things than at explaining and convincing. After having pointed out the complexity of the problem and the inextricable contradiction of opinions, she adds:

But besides these pictures of other people's lives and minds—these biographies and histories—there are also other pictures—pictures of actual facts; photographs. Photographs, of course, are not arguments addressed to the reason; they are simply statements of fact addressed to the eye. But in that very simplicity there may be some help.[309]

And basically, such is the method she has chosen, in accordance with the psychological concepts developed in her theory of the novel[310] and with her nature, which disliked abstractions. The photographs inserted in the work are not extrinsic to it. The general, the heralds, the university procession, the Judge, the Archbishop, like the sixty pages of notes in small print, help to make the reality, which the text attempts to evoke, more striking, more concrete, more present, and to set the reader's mind directly on the path along which Virginia Woolf hopes to lead him to her own conclusions. As a matter of fact, one may criticize the author not so much for having adopted this method as for not having followed it strictly enough. It is the effort to prove a point, the anxiety to attach an argument to these pictures, which weaken

[309] Three G p. 20 (10)
[310] These sentences from *Three Guineas* (p. 21 (11)), ". . . the eye is connected with the brain; the brain with the nervous system. That system sends its messages in a flash through every past memory and present feeling . . ." recall the famous passage in "Modern Fiction", CR I, p. 189 (154), "The mind receives a myriad impressions. . . ."

their satirical power and, above all, the whole effect. Why did she not remember her own precepts: not to preach; why did she not take into account her own self-confessed limitation, her lack of ratiocinative power?[311]

Although it does not save *Three Guineas* from such criticism, this incursion of Virginia Woolf's into a sphere which was not hers may be excused, if not entirely justified. It was a necessary gesture:

It has pressed and spurted out of me. If that's any proof of virtue, like a physical volcano. And my brain feels cool and quiet after the expulsion. I've had it sizzling now since—well I was thinking of it at Delphi I remember. And then I forced myself to put it into fiction first. No, the fiction came first. *The Years*.[312]

For one thing, the very words used here suggest a sort of boiling-point, that degree of revolt and indignation I spoke of earlier which impels one to make some passionate gesture, to go down into the street or to incite others to do so. There can be no question then of deliberating about one's aptitude or inaptitude for such behaviour. For another thing, the uncertainty, which is here merely a matter of imprecise memories, as to the priority of novel or pamphlet, bears witness more clearly than any other state-ment[313] to the unity of inspiration of the two works. The place of woman in the home, in society, in professional life; the atmosphere of the university, the conflict between the forces of emancipation and the forces of tradition in great families, the horror of war, the confusion and absurdity of the modern world, even the message of Antigone, emerge through the kaleidoscope of *The Years*. But at the point to which the world had come, with German rearmament, the arrogance of Italian Fascism, the Spanish revolution, these images by themselves, with their impassivity, the remoteness conferred on them by art, provided deliverance to the novelist in her but not to the simple human being. For that, something more explicit, more direct, was needed:

But I wanted—how violently—how persistently, pressingly, com-pulsorily I can't say—to write this book: and have a quiet composed feeling: as if I had said my say: take it or leave it: I'm quit of that.[314]

[311] Cf. AWD p. 188 (183), 245 and 246 (237)
[312] AWD p. 286 (276)
[313] Cf. AWD p. 295 (284)
[314] AWD p. 288 (278)

There is no thought here of art or achievement, but only of relief. *Three Guineas* can add nothing to Virginia Woolf's literary fame. Yet the fact that she was thus impelled to write almost in opposition to her own aesthetic belief, throws an unusual light on her personality. This abdication of the artist in her reveals a human being whom deliberate discipline had kept mute and hidden. And with that human element, too, a considerable degree of social consciousness. Even if, as we shall see when studying her novels, these tendencies crop up repeatedly, who knows whether their repression did not prove a disturbing factor which contributed to the tension and instability that constantly threatened her health. Among the different contradictions of her temperament have been mentioned her love of solitude and her sociability.[315] Should we not add to these, as secondary aspects, detachment and isolationism, together with a certain taste for commitment and militant action? *A Room of One's Own, Three Guineas* and many other essays, contrasted with *The Voyage Out* and *The Waves*, incline one to this hypothesis. And with all their faults, these two pamphlets deserve the place here allotted to them, if only to prepare us better to discover certain trends in the rest of her work, and not to neglect the whole background of contemporary preoccupations, of social and political problems, against which is contrasted the quest—apparently, but not really, a selfish one— for the absolute values of an individualistic philosophy.

[315] Cf. *supra*, ch. III, pp. 64-6

CHAPTER V

SYNTHESIS AND FICTION

THE study of Virginia Woolf's essays and critical works enabled us to acquire a clear picture of her conception of reading and writing, and to deduce from this her aesthetic theory, a solidly organized set of ideas and precepts. This led eventually to a precise definition of a work of literature and an analysis of the creative process. If her sense of reality and the richness of her sensibility invest her critical writings with a quality of life, a sensuous vibration that one is tempted to call feminine, lucidity and logic are none the less their dominant characteristic. In these essays the intellect explores and organizes a whole shadowy world in which it opens up a network of paths, where both reader and writer feel they may venture with the certainty of reaching their goal. To approach Virginia Woolf's novels by the way she herself suggests is a natural temptation. It is not without danger however. Travelling along these brightly lit paths we should risk neglecting the hidden processes of creation, and seduced by the brilliance of intellect we might remain blind to the dimmer light of spontaneity. Without rejecting the illumination brought by the critical works, I shall use these with great caution, so as not to ascribe a generative power to what is merely analysis *a posteriori*. The distinction will not always be easy to make. Chronology itself will not always be a valid criterion. An aesthetic principle is not necessarily a recipe. We shall have to bear constantly in mind a phrase of our author's which succinctly sums up the relations between theory and practice in the field of art: "One writes synthetically not analytically."[1]

Theories about the novel, ideas about style, even the vision of the aim to be reached merely define attitudes and tendencies. If they determine a certain trend in the work, its movement and its substance come from elsewhere. And if the work, once realized, seems at times to satisfy the requirements of certain principles

[1] Cf. letter from V. W. to J. J. Mayoux, 1930; cf. also "How my brain is jaded with the conflict within of two types of thought, the critical, the creative", AWD, p. 181 (176)

stated clearly elsewhere, it is often less as a direct consequence, less as a result of their conscious application, than by an obscure connection with some common source from which both emanate in different ways. It is above all in this unity of origin that I shall seek and consider the close relation between Virginia Woolf's criticism and her novels. And similarly, it is above all the unity of her being, bent on a single quest, that I shall endeavour to discover amidst the diversity of subjects and forms through which she tried to express it.

Between 1907 and 1941 Virginia Woolf wrote nine novels and a number of stories and sketches[2]; in the present chapter, I propose to study these works of imagination, dealing first with the novels and afterwards with those brief writings which bear the same relation to her main work as do studies of detail, or drawings, to the great compositions of a painter.[3]

1. THE NOVELS

Critics, concerned with classifying and labelling, or making a somewhat over-facile application of the principle of evolution, have distinguished either successive periods[4] in Virginia Woolf's novels, or a series of dominant preoccupations.[5] This dividing-up of her work may be a legitimate procedure, but it is surely based on superficial, indeed accidental, aspects of that work rather than on what is fundamental in it. Without seeking to ignore that variety which has struck and sometimes disconcerted critics and readers, I feel on the contrary that the real distinction and value of Virginia Woolf's work lies in the unity of its inspiration, the continuity of her unfailing effort in pursuit of a goal which she envisaged from the very beginning of her literary career.[6]

[2] *Kew Gardens* was published separately in 1919, followed in 1921 by *Monday or Tuesday*, which contained eight stories. It was only after the death of Virginia Woolf, in 1944, that Leonard Woolf published under the title of *A Haunted House* a collection of 18 stories and sketches, including *Kew Gardens*, those published in *Monday or Tuesday* (except for "A Society" and "Blue or Green"), 6 stories reprinted from various journals, and 6 unpublished ones.

[3] Cf. *infra*, 2, Stories and Sketches, pp. 329-43

[4] Daiches, Chambers.

[5] Blackstone.

[6] Of all V. W.'s critics, Johnstone has grasped this continuity most clearly. "*The Voyage Out* and *Night and Day*, as their titles indicate, are quests for reality; and the same is true of the rest of V. W.'s novels", *op. cit.*, p. 323. Cf. also particularly pp. 335-6. Yet his analysis is not always consistent with his thesis, especially when dealing with *The Years*, pp. 368-70.

Although from her earliest childhood she was surrounded by writers, and although she was not yet 20 when she was introduced to the editor of *The Speaker* (later *The Nation*) and barely 21 when she met Bruce Richmond, editor of the *Times Literary Supplement*, it was not until she was 25 that she started her first novel, on which she was to work for seven years. The exceptional length of this preparation, if contrasted with all the circumstances which could have and should have shortened it, is highly suggestive.

If it may be accounted for by a girl's shyness, together with an overscrupulous artistic temperament and a clear-sighted perfectionism which were to grow even more exacting, the fact remains that the product of such long labour, of such slow ripening, at a crucial period in the formation of a personality, cannot be considered solely as youthful or prentice work. If certain aspects of *The Voyage Out* display a certain inexperience and hesitancy, what one might call inadequate craftsmanship, these are the more superficial features of the book. Basically, the essence of this first novel, what it is seeking for, and what it is trying to express, is what Virginia Woolf seeks and tries to express in each of her books: "All the usual things I try to put in—life, death, etc. ....",[7] she was to say about *To the Lighthouse*; "Life itself going on",[8] about *The Waves*; "the whole of human life",[9] about *The Years*, and finally "We ... the composed of many different things ... we all life, all art, all waifs and strays—a rambling capricious but somehow unified whole—the present state of my mind?"[10] about *Between the Acts*.

No doubt the breadth and vagueness of such statements provide an easy argument for those who wish to see in them merely the great themes of literature (or even the sole theme of all literature)—common, in short, to all writers of any importance and to all great works. None the less, set in the context of the Diary from which they are taken, and beside the work which they define, these phrases can be referred to a strictly limited content, they acquire a significance which is perfectly definite and, so to speak, unique, peculiar to Virginia Woolf, and at the same time they affirm the profound unity of her work.

That *Jacob's Room*, in 1922, and its predecessors *Kew Gardens*.

[7] AWD pp. 76-7 (75)
[8] AWD p. 143 (140)
[9] AWD p. 192 (186)
[10] AWD pp. 289-90 (279)

An Unwritten Novel and *The Mark on the Wall* are different from *The Voyage Out* and *Night and Day* is too obvious for anyone to dream of denying it. But to conclude that this difference implies a fresh orientation, an altered vision, would be to displace the focus of interest of these books, and, to my mind mistakenly, to follow those critics—and they are the majority—who have stressed now the technique, now the apparent subject of Virginia Woolf's novels. After the turn taken with *Jacob's Room*, it becomes difficult if not impossible to account for the break made by *Orlando* between *To the Lighthouse* and *The Waves*; and *The Years* seems an incomprehensible harking-back to the objects and forms of *Night and Day*, twenty years earlier, while *Between the Acts*, which follows it, is odd and even more inexplicable.

Rather than to any idea of evolution represented by some curious broken line, it is to the concepts of depth and rhythm that I shall refer to establish the connection between Virginia Woolf's successive works.

These concepts have already proved adequate to explain the fluctuations of her inner life[11]; similarly we shall see that they account for the diversity or even the apparent divergences of her novels without breaking the flow of impulse and will that inspire these.

In the case of an artist like Virginia Woolf, who did not brave the public until after her thirtieth year, whose outward and inward life knew no upheaval, no extraordinary experience capable of disturbing her view of the world, and who concentrated her efforts, moreover, on a limited and clearly defined set of problems, it may fairly be said that each fresh work takes up the previous one to perfect it. Allowing for the exaggeration inherent in any paradox that may probe deeper into truth than the reality of experience would admit, one may say that Virginia Woolf, for whom the theme of a novel was unimportant,[12] spent her life re-writing the same book, of which she has given us nine different versions—just as she would spend months making seven versions of a novel of which she would only give us the last.

I propose to trace the progress of this unwritten novel, out of the various shapes it assumed.

[11] Cf. ch. III
[12] Cf. AWD p. 101 (100): "I doubt that any theme is in itself good or bad. It gives a chance to one's peculiar qualities—that's all."

THE VOYAGE OUT (1915)

"In 1915 Virginia Woolf began regularly to write a diary."[13] We do not know whether before this date she had noted down any of her impressions or the problems of a budding novelist. In fact we have no written information about the seven years' work which led up to the publication of *The Voyage Out* in 1915. The book must therefore be approached as it stands, lacking any of those asides or confidences which might make its purpose clearer or shed light on its obscurities.

If it is easy enough to define *The Voyage Out*, it is practically impossible to sum it up. This difficulty is a characteristic one and sets this novel, from the outset, in the same category as those that followed it. The texture of incidents on which it is embroidered is so slack, woven with such slender threads, that if one tries to analyse it one is caught between two dangers either to see it disintegrate, or to see it stiffen into a coarse, inflexible framework whose pattern confuses or even destroys the essential lines of the work. Nevertheless the distance between this "story" and the novel can be fully appreciated only by starting from the story itself, which we may therefore usefully recall.

Rachel Vinrace, a ship-owner's daughter, motherless, shy and withdrawn by nature and as a result of the loneliness and emptiness of her life with her father and her aunts, is sailing on one of her father's boats, the *Euphrosyne*, with her uncle and aunt, Ridley and Helen Ambrose. A twofold invitation has enabled them to escape from a London winter: Helen's brother has lent her his villa at Santa Marina, a sleepy little resort on the South American Atlantic coast, while Willoughby Vinrace has offered to take them there on the *Euphrosyne* bound for the Amazon. Calling at Lisbon, Vinrace finds himself obliged to take on two passengers, the Dalloways. Their brief stay on board creates a tension in the atmosphere and has a revealing effect upon the two characters who occupy the foreground: Rachel is stirred to life by a casual kiss from Richard Dalloway, while Helen Ambrose, jealous of the interest taken by Rachel in the Dalloways and at the same time intrigued by her niece's emotional disturbance, feels herself irresistibly drawn to the girl and invites her to stay at

[13] AWD vii (vii)

Santa Marina. After three months of intimacy with Helen, of reading Ibsen, Meredith and unspecified modern writers, and of walking through the town at night to watch life, Rachel seems to have acquired a stronger, more definite personality. An incident then occurs in the shape of a picnic organized by a young intellectual staying at the hotel, Terence Hewett. Besides a number of eccentrics of both sexes, who are obviously mere walkers-on, this picnic brings into Rachel's and Helen's world Terence and his friend St John Hirst. The four people become involved in a relationship of mingled curiosity, sympathy, desire, tenderness and love. Dances, tea-parties, walks and discussions mark the successive stages of their exploration of themselves and of each other, which had begun on the day of the picnic. The last stage is an expedition down the river, during which Terence and Rachel at last acknowledge to each other and to themselves their mutual love. Yet they still have to elucidate it, to explore its growth, its existence and its potentialities—and perhaps too to discover its inadequacy (p. 370 (302)) and, beyond it, that second loneliness which is the very essence of man's state, a portent of the final separation that awaits them. Rachel, possibly during this expedition, contracts a malignant fever of which she dies. This pointless death brings for a moment a sense of pointlessness in its wake; but only for a moment—life flows on, or drifts on, except perhaps for Terence, Helen and Willoughby; but Virginia Woolf says nothing about it; that would be a different version of Rachel's story than the one she has chosen to tell us.

It is immediately obvious that the interest of this novel does not lie in its incidents. For a few pages at most the reader can share Helen's curiosity, and wonder which of the men, Terence and St John, is going to fall in love with Rachel and to win her love.[14] But the uncertainty is slight and is never exploited, any more than the possibilities of rivalry between the two young men. Even the final catastrophe, pointless and unnecessary as it is, represents a vicissitude in the order of things, but not in the human lives with which the book deals. It scarcely shocks; it surprises even less. It is the natural harbour in which this voyage had to end. One might quote about this first book a remark of

[14] "She had been thinking about Rachel and which of the two young men she was likely to fall in love with . . .", VO 242 (205).

Proust's which applies to all the rest and to which Virginia Woolf would certainly have subscribed: "The plot . . . the plot, my dear fellow, what is the plot? What is the plot of the *Divine Comedy* or of Shakespeare's *Sonnets*, or *Tristram Shandy*, or *Ecclesiastes?*"[15]

In fact, from the outset, we leave the world of events to enter into a world beyond their scope. Once the *Euphrosyne* has cast off its moorings, its passengers are set free from the bonds that connected them with society, with the ordinary succession of circumstances which seem to form an integral part of everyone's existence. On this boat, "an emblem of the loneliness of human life",[16] they escape from that setting of space and time within which events are inscribed and within which we inscribe our own lives, and become merely centres of feeling, consciousnesses reduced to what is purely inward. The port of Santa Marina has the same out-of-this-world character. It seems like a lost island, connected by ships and letters not to the rest of the planet but only to its faintest echoes. If a plot is an experiment set up by an author to arouse or to motivate the reactions and deviations of his characters, here the setting consists precisely in this exclusion of the outside world. This is what the title clearly indicates, among other things: a setting forth for the open sea.

This purifying of destiny is a postulate of all Virginia Woolf's novels. In *To the Lighthouse*, as in *The Voyage Out*, it is brought about by an outside agency; it becomes the inward principle of *The Waves*. *Mrs Dalloway* and *Between the Acts* attain it by subtler but no less effective means; *Jacob's Room* by a play of leit-motivs.

And if *Night and Day* and *The Years* appear to renounce it, we shall see that this is only on the surface. In *Orlando* the very exaggeration of the adventure leads finally to its negation, while incidents are swallowed up and lost in the timeless immobility of a human being.

It may seem paradoxical, then, that Winifred Holtby could define *The Voyage Out* as "the preparation of a naive young girl for maturity", preluding "not only life but death".[17] Such a formula at first sight implies too much action or at any rate too much activity, far more than is ever found in the novel. It suggests a making contact, an exploration of the self. David Daiches'

---

[15] Quoted by Clive Bell in *Proust* (1928), p. 71.
[16] VO p. 99 (87)
[17] W. Holtby, *Virginia Woolf*, p. 61.

expression seems more appropriate: "Development of the heroine from immaturity to maturity and death."[18]

Moreover, whereas Winifred Holtby attempts somewhat arbitrarily to connect the deeper meaning of the book to this apparent theme, Daiches is well aware that it is merely a pretext. The rarefied life of the characters is a means, an artificial one maybe, but effective, of concentrating their attention on what is essential. Liberated from the complex of chance circumstances, where the different orders of reality are superimposed, distracting the attention and demanding incompatible answers, the characters find themselves reduced to their inner life in relation to each other, and beyond that, to the sense of existence in all its purity and indeterminateness.

If the discovery and analysis of love assume in this novel an importance such that Blackstone considered it as the central theme, providing the unity of inspiration of *The Voyage Out* and *Night and Day*,[19] it is because Virginia Woolf identifies love with life. As she wrote of Christina Rossetti: "She starved herself of love, which meant also life."[20] To speak of development, of attaining maturity, is only justified if we give these terms a restricted meaning akin to the literal sense and not the figurative sense commonly applied to a personality. Basically, Rachel does not really change; her character is not enriched. Rather, she acquires precision and definiteness at the same time as, for her and for those around her in the novel, a more precise and definite answer emerges to the two questions which are the same question: "What is love? What is life?" And if this question is the subject that Virginia Woolf was really seeking to deal with, as I believe, the hesitations, the uncertainties, the heterogeneities of the novel fade away, its interruptions and incongruities take shape around this central theme to provide the dialectic display of question and answer which resolves itself in the closing harmony.

Thus the first chapter, which seems to place Helen Ambrose in the foreground and to introduce her husband Ridley, Mr Pepper, Willoughby and Rachel Vinrace, can only mislead the passive

---

[18] D. Daiches, *Virginia Woolf*, New Directions, p. 15; Nicholson & Watson, London, pp. 21-2.

[19] B. Blackstone, *op. cit.*, Introd. ch. i and ii, particularly pp. 11, 32

[20] AWD p. 1 (1)

and superficial reader who, relying on his habits, immediately assumes that these are the essential characters around whom the plot is going to be built up. Naturally he very soon begins to ask himself what was the point of Willoughby, Ridley and Mr Pepper?

Similarly he may be surprised, a few pages later, to see the Dalloways play so large a part in the life of the travellers on the *Euphrosyne*, only to disappear completely at some unnamed port of call. In fact, these figures are not meant to take part in any action. Their essential role is to represent a way of life, to give their answer to the question "What is life?" which, from two different points of view, is being asked by the two characters between whom the novel is unfolded rather than enacted. On the one hand, in the centre of the picture, Rachel, who is so to speak the living embodiment of the question, who assimilates the various answers that chance offers her, in the form of denial or acceptance, to extract or elaborate therefrom her own substance. On the other hand, at the periphery, Helen, chiefly an observer, and at the same time a kind of answering witness whose wisdom, partly detached, now serves as a mirror in which the consciousness of others is reflected and now presents a definite image with which they are contrasted. "Her eyes looked straight and considered what they saw."[21] It is she who asks about Mr Pepper the unexpected and yet crucial question: "Has he ever been in love?"[22] Rachel's reply, unfounded perhaps since she has never asked him,[23] serves to get rid of the character, whose interest is now exhausted.

People whose hearts are "a piece of old shoe leather"[24] are only included in the book to show the narrow limits within which they are confined: Mr Pepper with his little yellow books, Ridley with his Pindar, Miss Allan with her "Introduction to English Literature" and even St John Hirst in spite of his youth, his exceptional intelligence, and the relatively important place conferred on him by his friendship with Terence Hewett and his admiration for Helen, display, in contrast with the fluid world of the three protagonists, the rigidity of a sclerotic world, set in the mould of form: objects, words, gestures. The two worlds, the world of facts and of appearances, and the world of feelings and of reality, whose obsessive confusion is the common experience

[21] Cf VO p. 8 (14) [22] VO p. 14 (19)
[23] VO p. 14 (19) [24] VO p. 14 (19)

from which the heroes of the book try to escape, are symbolized by Terence and St John, as well as defined by them in their opening discussion[25].

The latter's static view of the world, apprehensible by reason, made up of juxtaposed circles within which human beings are confined, is contrasted by Terence with his own dynamic and irrational vision: "I see a thing like a teetotum spinning in and out—knocking into things—dashing from side to side—collecting numbers—more and more and more, till the whole place is thick with them. Round and round they go—out there, over the rim—out of sight."[26]

Their fellow-guests in the hotel, a set of grotesque and ungainly puppets, Mr and Mrs Hughling Elliot, Mr and Mrs Thornbury, Miss Warrington, Mr Arthur Venning, Mr Perrott, Evelyn Murgatroyd, if they introduce a jarring note into the novel do so on purpose. They justify St John's philosophy and at the same time the attempt of Terence, Rachel and Helen to escape from it. Sometimes even their solidity and quiet are threatened. Miss Warrington and Evelyn are also made to answer the question: what is love?

And if they do not go so far as to associate this problem with the one it implies, "what is life?" it is precisely because they remain on the plane of appearances, where people and things are separate fragments each confined within a chalk circle. The chapters in which these characters appear, which look like realistic interludes between the inward-looking analyses devoted to the so-called principals, would indeed jeopardize the unity of the novel if they were in fact intended as such. Neither are they a concession to a traditional genre or style. They represent the land, appearing intermittently to the travellers bound for the high seas, both to enable them to measure the progress of their journey and to strengthen their intention to escape.

To feel, to love, to live—what do they mean?

In the first place, they mean communicating, and eventually entering into communion, attaining fusion with what is other than oneself. Living means conquering loneliness, escaping from the circle within which everything conspires to confine one.

[25] Cf. VO p. 122 (106) ff. J. K. Johnstone points out resemblances between Lytton Strachey and St J. Hirst (*The Bloomsbury Group*, p. 127 ff.).
[26] VO p. 124 (108)

Here we recognize the central theme of all Virginia Woolf's work. And this first exploration leads perceptibly to the same results as all those that follow. Terence and Rachel live a few perfect moments, islets amid waste spaces of uncertainty and yearning. Their union is sealed in death, for nothing can disturb it any more: it escapes from the dissolving factors of time and space.

It was happiness, it was perfect happiness. They had now what they had always wanted to have, the union which had been impossible while they lived. . . . It seemed to him that their complete union and happiness filled the room with rings eddying more and more widely. He had no wish in the world left unfulfilled. They possessed what could never be taken from them.[27]

True, this peace is only a fleeting visitation, a moment in the life of the soul, experienced through a kind of prolonged anticipation. When the mind becomes once again aware of its body and of existence, the revolt and loneliness of the whole being burst forth in a vain, heartrending cry: "Rachel, Rachel!"[28]

And later on we have "Jacob, Jacob!"[29] and then "Mrs. Ramsay!"[30] and Bernard's sudden combative impulse on the last page of *The Waves*.[31] We may wonder then what is the meaning of this victory which is a defeat. Is it not that Rachel has accomplished her voyage out alone, has reached the haven of unity and peace while the others remain tossed on the ocean of division of multiplicity, of uncertainty and suffering? The final paragraph (450 pages after the first) calls up a chaos of impressions and appearance very like that which the Ambroses left behind them in London, thousands of miles away. The visions that flit across St John's drowsy gaze and consciousness echo those that were glimpsed through Helen's tears[32]: "Across his eyes passed a procession of objects, black and indistinct, the figures of people picking up their books, their cards, their balls of wool, their work-baskets, and passing him one after another on their way to bed"[33] —on their way to death too, if we remember how Terence has demonstrated the likeness between sleep and death.[34]

And just as the structure of the book does not depend upon its incidents, so the centre of interest is not provided by the charac-

[27] VO p. 431 (353-4)
[29] JR p. 176 (176)
[31] The W p. 211 (383)
[33] VO p. 458 (375)

[28] VO p. 432 (354)
[30] To the L p. 310 (300)
[32] VO p. 3 (9)
[34] VO p. 170 (146)

ters. If the successive revelations during which the principal characters are gradually defined remind one of Henry James's technique, this influence, which is not incompatible with Virginia Woolf's tastes, is purely on the surface of the writing. Basically, all the protagonists of *The Voyage Out* have the same uncertain and intermittent quality which prevents them from taking shape and making an impression on the reader. If the author had intended to achieve that solidity which gives concrete life to the heroes of traditional novels, we might blame her for the fluidity of her characters. But surely she meant them to be like that? Is not this why we find it harder to visualize Rachel than Evelyn M., and Terence than St John? The fluidity of the universe in which they are immersed is due above all to the fluidity of the beings in whose thoughts it exists. Whether this harmony results from a deliberate intention of the novelist's or simply from an unconscious unity of her point of view, we have no means of deciding. Whatever its origin, it displays an art which has one essential virtue: the power to resolve heterogeneous elements.

Not that this first book is free of faults, or more precisely of awkwardnesses. The most evident, that which perhaps more than anything else displays a certain lack of craftsmanship, is the insistence with which the two kinds of world are contrasted. It is deliberate to the point of clumsiness, and has shocked and disconcerted many critics.

There is such a distance between the subdued style of certain passages, full of echoes and reticences, and the contrasting angularity of certain others, that their relationship escapes more than one reader; which might incline one to think that the means employed go beyond the aim envisaged. Sometimes, as though the author were approaching her subject from too far off, a scene may begin with generalizations which introduce into this otherwise self-sufficient world a discordant alien voice: that of the author herself.[35]

Finally it would be easy to point out longueurs and superfluous details. But this is always a rash method of criticism. Thus we may be less interested than Terence in the description of Mrs Hunt,[36] a friend of Rachel's aunts; yet what may appear insipid, puerile or irrelevant in it, apart from the light it sheds on

[35] VO, esp. ch. I, p. i. par. i, and ch. XV, p. 230
[36] Cf. VO p. 257 (214)

Rachel's life, brings out more clearly Terence's veiled, unconscious declaration, thus causing the girl to shrink back, in one of those manifold alternations of refusal and acceptance that characterize the birth of sympathy, leading to love. Sometimes one could wish for greater conciseness in descriptions of the life of the hotel and its fauna. But who knows if the balance between the two opposing worlds would not thereby be destroyed; or indeed if some readers, with quite legitimate leanings towards realism, would not on the contrary prefer less subtlety in the psychological analysis of the inhabitants of the villa? The argument would then bear on the author's intentions, and would be out of place here.

Re-reading her work in 1920, five years after its publication, Virginia Woolf speaks of it more harshly than I have done:

If you ask me what I think I must reply that I don't know—such a harlequinade as it is—such an assortment of patches—here simple and severe—here frivolous and shallow—here like God's truth—here strong and free flowing as I could wish. What to make of it, Heaven knows. The failures are ghastly enough to make my cheeks burn—and then a turn of the sentence, a direct look ahead of me, makes them burn in a different way. On the whole I like the young woman's mind considerably. How gallantly she takes her fences—and my word, what a gift for pen and ink! I can do little to amend, and must go down to posterity the author of cheap witticisms, smart satires and even, I find, vulgarisms—crudities rather—that will never cease to rankle in the grave. Yet I see how people prefer it to *N. and D.* I don't say admire it more, but find it a more gallant and inspiring spectacle.[37]

Does this severity put a more indulgent critic to shame, and does it authorize the censure I have dismissed? I do not believe so. While appreciating the author's clearsightedness, one may question her right to self-criticism. For while she was re-reading *The Voyage Out*, Virginia Woolf—starting from *The Mark on the Wall*, *Kew Gardens* and *An Unwritten Novel*—had foreseen a new form of the novel, that which was to give birth to *Jacob's Room* and eventually to *The Waves*.

It is in the light of the work to which she is now aspiring that she ridicules the earlier book. And these lines, with which one author condemns another in the name of her own ideal, considered as an absolute, are rather a measure of the distance travelled by Virginia Woolf between 1913 and 1920 than an

[37] AWD p. 24 (23)

assessment of the value of her first novel. We need only dwell on the few words of praise that are included—the only ones that bear the mark of a genuinely critical attitude, that is to say implying an effort to coincide with the artist's point of view. Despite the objections that may be called forth by one or another aspect of the novel, *The Voyage Out* has the merit of being charged with meaning, of expressing in its totality, by the combined use of various means, a conception of the universe and of existence.

"Vague and universal",[38] it was thus characterized by E. M. Forster in contrast with *Night and Day*. This was doubtless one of those simple judgments that, unlike some others, he did not disdain to pronounce, and which had won him Virginia Woolf's respect and trust.[39] One is tempted to think that, on re-reading her MS in 1913, Virginia Woolf might have summed up her general impression in similar terms. The book needed a companion to correct and complete it. She had to strengthen its significance by re-writing it in terms of the precise and the particular, to treat once more in an everyday setting the problem she had treated vaguely and indirectly. The companion was to be *Night and Day*.

NIGHT AND DAY (1919)

Although the beginning of *A Writer's Diary* covers the period of composition of *Night and Day*, it reveals nothing about it; only a brief entry opposes the artist derived from writing it to the effort her first book cost her.[40] Are we then to conclude that she allowed her spontaneity to take precedence over studied intention? No doubt there is a certain amount of truth in this hypothesis, which Virginia Woolf does not examine. Nevertheless it would perhaps be a mistake to take ease and facility as the criteria for a more direct sort of activity, more faithful to the artist's innermost personality. It may be, indeed, that in *The Voyage Out* the effort of which the young novelist complains arose from the struggle with the stubbornness of her material—of all that makes up writing—rather than from an attempt to dam up

[38] AWD p. 20 (20)

[39] AWD p. 21 (20): "He says the simple things that clever people don't say; I find him the best of critics for that reason."

[40] AWD p. 11 (20): "I don't suppose I've ever enjoyed any writing so much as I did the last half of *Night and Day*. Indeed, no part of it taxed me as *The Voyage Out* did."

the natural flow of her deepest inspiration. This would imply that it was by a surrender to outside forces, to the weight of tradition and habit, that *Night and Day* avoided the obstacles that the earlier work had had to overcome. However that may be, the general impression left by this book is far less striking and original, though far clearer and more precise, than that made by *The Voyage Out*.

On the one hand, the setting of the book—London—although confined within the limits of the West End and Highgate, with Bloomsbury and the Inns of Court as a central meeting-ground, instead of transporting us out of life as a ship's deck or a distant port would do, evokes a whole familiar world, active and crowded, in which the protagonists and their adventures are involved. On the other hand, there is a genuine conflict between the characters which, although straightforward and devoid of surprises, gives a direction to the reader's curiosity and at the same time provides a framework to the novel.

Katharine Hilbery and Ralph Denham are introduced to us in the opening pages; they seem in every way contrasted; Ralph, a young lawyer who works for a solicitor and writes articles for Mr Hilbery's journal, is poor and unsociable; his ambitions are perhaps not disproportionate to his qualities, but they are stifled by his family duties—his mother, a tradesman's widow, and six or seven brothers and sisters are more or less dependent on him; Katharine, granddaughter of one of the greatest poets of the last century, has no responsibilities other than those of her social life, and the unexacting household duties imposed on her by a romantically minded mother and a father absorbed in his profession and in literature. However, she is obliged to collaborate with her mother in writing the biography of the famous ancestor, a task in which her mother displays more zeal and filial piety than talent or method. The vanity of this undertaking, predoomed to failure, symbolizes in Ralph's eyes the vanity and sterility of Katharine's existence. Meanwhile, despite her apparent passive acceptance, the girl suffers from a sense of maladjustment akin to Ralph's own. Just as the latter takes refuge in his room from the tyranny of domestic life, to work and to dream, so Katharine, in her own, escapes from the frivolities of society and literature to study mathematics—and to dream too. In Chelsea as in Highgate, they are both prisoners of two worlds which differ only in outward appearance, even if these appearances are as solid as the houses in which they live and as unyielding as the people who surround them. As a pendant to these two principal characters we soon meet another pair, Mary Datchet and William Rodney. Mary, a clergyman's daughter, has left her father's home in Lincolnshire to work in London for the women's movement. She is active, intelligent and likable, and clearly happy in the path she has chosen, to which she devotes the best of herself. She is a friend of Ralph's, who appreciates her honesty and strength of character. Rodney, a civil servant by profession and a poet by vocation, is supposed to be engaged to Katharine, although he seems scarcely capable of arousing much love in the girl, nor, apparently, does he consider her an ideal wife. Will the hazards of love and social life confirm the plans sketched in the opening chapters? Will Rodney marry Katharine, and through her win both wealth and fame? Will Ralph and Mary be drawn together by their common revolt against an unjust society, against those who lead idle lives and have money to spend? However, the book is more concerned with emotional than with social problems. The social setting, the teas and dinners in Cheyne Walk or at Stogdon House, at the Denhams', the meetings in the suffragettes' office or at Mary's, merely provide a background of illusory realism, against which, in the foreground, the human drama is played out between the four protagonists.

Resisting, with alternate success and failure, the tendencies of their social groups, each seeks to define his own natural tendency, to separate accidental and superficial sympathies and antipathies from deeper feelings. This search is the real subject of the novel, and the situations—for one can hardly speak of a plot—are both its occasion and its consequence. Through a series of duets during which the different partners face one another successively, interlaced with a series of solitary analyses, in which each of them assesses the situation and anticipates a fresh encounter, we witness an exploration in depth of love which, moving from makebelieve to indecision, from indecision to error, attains at last its essential purity. Katharine, after having broken off and then resumed her engagement to William, finally accepts the evidence of the passion that binds her to Ralph, while the latter, after offering marriage to Mary and then envisaging a life of solitude, ends by yielding to the true nature of his feelings. Mary, having refused

Ralph's offer, which was based on reason rather than on genuine passion, becomes the militant that was surely always latent in her. As for William, through a device which has an element of farce and which is quite in keeping with his ridiculous personality, he marries Cassandra Otway, a cousin of Katharine's who has herself organized this change of partners, like some dreadful children's game, in the respectable house in Cheyne Walk, to the great horror of Mr Hilbery, while Mrs Hilbery's Shakespearean romanticism confers on the denouement an air of fantasy which in no way detracts from the dramatic moments that gave rise to it.

Any attempt to judge this book by standards which are not those that Virginia Woolf wished to accept, involves one in the same difficulties to which such an attitude gave rise in the case of *The Voyage Out*.

If we choose to take it as a picture of social milieux or types, we are bound to find it superficial and, moreover, confused by the presence of heterogeneous elements, notably the long interior analyses. If on the contrary we look for rounded and convincing characters, we are disappointed at finding only aspects or moments in the life of beings whose outlines are blurred and whose total effect is indeterminate. If there is one weakness for which this novel can be condemned, it is not for failing to correspond with any type of the classical novel, but for letting the reader suppose that it attempts to conform to such a type. In that case, one can always blame the reader's judgment. None the less, the fact that so intelligent a reader and one so close to the author as E. M. Forster made this mistake inclines one to think that the weakness is a real one. The Denhams and Hilberys, for instance,[41] or the Datchets and the Otways,[42] are presented with an abundance and precision of details that imply an order of reality, a structure of the world apparently alien to those which the book attempts to work out. If the full-length portraits of the principal characters are less misleading, because it is easier to re-establish continuity between the different layers of their being, nevertheless they, too, from time to time, are drawn with vigorous strokes that detract from the homogeneity of one's impression. Basically, this amounts to accusing the novelist of a certain awkwardness or primitive stiffness, of covering the whole of her

[41] Cf. N & D chs. II, III, XII   [42] Cf. N & D chs. XV, XVII

canvas with a uniform touch and an equally sharp outline, without those heightenings and shadings-off that would have brought out the essential meaning of her picture.

The book errs by being too much worked over; a characteristic fault of the beginner, who has not yet learnt the art of understatement, abbreviation and omission. A fault moreover which one must have had and expiated, so to speak, before one can shed it; it is through excessive meticulousness that one acquires liberty and mastery of unselfconsciousness.[43] If this aspect is more striking in *Night and Day* than in *The Voyage Out*, so much so that E. M. Forster preferred the latter,[44] it is because the framework and the elements of the story tend to bring it out rather than to blur it. The deliberate escape from reality implicit in the subject of the earlier novel served to some extent to repel the temptation of realism, which in the second weighs on the author constantly, almost in spite of herself.

Moreover, as soon as we look beneath the surface to the deeper substance of the novel we see, as in *The Voyage Out*, that heterogeneity is fused in the unity of the internal design. Like the first book, and even more systematically and profoundly, this second is an attempt at the dialectical analysis of feelings, aiming at disentangling their essential nature from the foreign elements with which we tend to confuse them.[45]

Ralph, and particularly Katharine, resume Rachel's quest, no longer under the privileged circumstances of an experience skilfully prepared to eliminate the greatest possible number of factors alien to the central problem. Instead of the token image of the world of appearances, evoked intermittently, and as it were outside the world of the heroes, by the life of the Santa Marina hotel, that hollow reality, in this book, adheres to the characters themselves: their families, their prejudices, their traditions and habits weigh them down and enfold them. The very structure of the novel, which consists of a regular alternation—so rigidly regular indeed as to smack of artifice—between surface descrip-

---

[43] Cf. AWD p. 35 (34). Speaking of N. & D. to J. M. Keynes, V. W. says: "Oh, it's a dull book, I know, but don't you see you must put it all in before you can leave out."

[44] Cf. AWD p. 20 (19): "I understand why he [E. M. F.] likes it less than *V. O.*"

[45] Cf. N & D p. 331 (313): "To seek a true feeling among the chaos of the unfeelings or half feelings of life, to recognize it when found, and to accept the consequences of the discovery . . . it is a pursuit which is alternately bewildering, debasing, and exalting. . . ."

tion and interior analysis, stresses both the twofold aspect of the
book and the author's intention to contrast these two aspects.
From this opposition the book gains a rhythm and a tension
which *The Voyage Out* lacked. And these are not purely formal
qualities; they help, if not to make individual characters
more alive, at least to permeate the entire book with a certain
quality of life, of humanity perhaps, which makes it more
endearing, gives it a greater hold over the reader. This moreover
is not the only advance it shows over its predecessor. If it
endeavours to answer the same question: "What is love? What is
life?"[46] it replies not only in a far completer fashion, developing
certain points which were only elusively touched on in the earlier
book,[47] but it goes much further into the generalization of the
problem, including in it the relations between reality and the
imaginary and the attainment of truth. Love, "the thing that
matters most in life",[48] is precisely the crucial experience which
enables us, by way of sufferings and joys, to attain the summit
from which that universal chaos, which was our anxiety and our
torment, takes shape according to its successive planes in a
harmony the sign of which is a moment of illumination and
peace.[49] Katharine, and Ralph too, in his way, like Rachel, start
from the same inarticulate aspiration: "I want . . .".[50] That "I
want" means the whole world of dream: the dream that haunts
Ralph as he looks out at London from the window of his room,
the dream that Katharine follows in her refuge at the top of the
house in Cheyne Walk; the world of dream where dwell ". . . the
realities of the appearances which figure in our world".[51] But

[46] Cf. N & D pp. 107 (107), 137 (134), 265 (253), 284 (269), 290(275-6), 294 (279),
301 (287), 313-14 (298), 409 (386), 413 (390), 423 (398), 437-8 (412-3), 449 (423),
500-1 (472), 512 (484-5), 513 (487), 522 (493)

[47] Cf. for instance the coexistence of several loves and friendships, VO pp. 224 (190),
380 (312), N & D p. 103 (104); esp. Rodney's twofold attachment to Cassandra and
Katharine, ch. XXII, end of ch. XXIV and end of ch. XXIX.

[48] Cf. N & D p. 284 (269): ". . . people say this is the thing that matters most . . ."
and p. 315 (298): "It's become the thing that matters most in my life."

[49] Cf. N & D p. 273 (260): "Her vision seemed to lay out the lines of her life until
death in a way which satisfied her sense of harmony. It needed only a persistent effort
of thought . . . to climb the crest of existence and see it all laid out once and for ever."
Cf. also: ". . . love . . . a soothing word . . . a riveting together of the shattered
fragments of the world", N & D p. 512 (484).

[50] Cf. VO p. 65 (60): " 'I want—' She did not know what she wanted, so that she
could not finish the sentence; but her lip quivered."

[51] N & D p. 145 (141)

to recognize them under their material disguise requires both vigilance and determination and, even more, a sort of grace: "how to see the truth is our great chance in this world."[52]

In the rarefied reality that surrounded Rachel in *The Voyage Out*, everything was prearranged for this chance. In the confusion of lives involved with everyday reality and with the past, a ceaseless watchful consciousness is needed to bring it about. Rachel could wait and accept, passively. But without that tense resolution which, in Katharine, seems even more masculine than her passion for mathematics, and in Ralph, verges at times on the will to power, neither of them would have succeeded in their quest, which ends in the fusion of dream and reality and, at the same time, in the blending in a single symbol of the image of love with the image of life.[53] Yet despite this victory, the closing note is not without melancholy, for it is a fragile victory. The lovers know that the vision is intermittent; what they call their "lapses"[54] constitute the very rhythm of the inner life, oscillating ceaselessly between communion and solitude. The difficulty of communication between human beings is the shadowy theme of the book, which alternates constantly with its daylight theme. In the last pages these are so closely associated that the union of Ralph and Katharine which had seemed, for a moment, an unqualified goal, loses its importance:

She might speak to him, but with that strange tremor in his voice, those eyes blindly adoring, whom did he answer? What woman did he see? And where was she walking, and who was her companion? Moments, fragments, a second of vision, and then the flying waters, the winds dissipating and dissolving; then, too, the recollection from chaos, the return of security, the earth firm, superb and brilliant in the sun.[55]

Their hands part and a door closes between them, as though to indicate that nothing has been achieved. Then a few scattered phrases in the book assume their full significance:

[52] N & D p. 263 (251)
[53] Trying in vain to express his love, Ralph ". . . began to draw little figures in the blank spaces, heads meant to resemble her head, blots fringed with flames meant to represent—perhaps the entire universe" N & D p. 516 (487). When Katharine sees them " . . . it did not occur to her that this diagram had anything to do with her. She said simply, and in the same tone of reflection: 'Yes, the world looks something like that to me too' ", N & D p. 522 (493)
[54] N & D pp. 500 (472), 501 (473)
[55] N & D p. 45 (50)

". . . it's being and not doing that matters."[56]

"They *were*, and that's better than doing."[57]

"It's life that matters, nothing but life—the process of discovering—the everlasting and perpetual process, not the discovery itself at all."[58]

True, the stature of the heroes and the orderly civilization in which they move preclude any comparison with the Dostoevskyan world which this quotation hints at in the background.

Nevertheless the comments in the Diary, with a restraint akin to that of the novel, imbue the latter with a personal content which gives moving human significance to the lesson that emerges from it, aside from any aesthetic weaknesses:

L. finds the philosophy very melancholy. . . . Yet, if one is to deal with people on a large scale and say what one thinks, how can one avoid melancholy? I don't admit to being hopeless though: only the spectacle is a profoundly strange one; and as the current answers don't do, one has to grope for a new one, and the process of discarding the old, when one is by no means certain what to put in their place, is a sad one.[59]

If the pessimism of *The Voyage Out* was of the same nature and origin, it was more diffuse and more abstract. Without disavowing previous criticisms, one may subscribe to the author's opinion, that *Night and Day* "has more depth than the other",[60] "is a much more mature and finished and satisfactory book than *The Voyage Out*".[61] From more than one aspect, and in spite of the abundance of dialogue, and in fact by the very distance that lies between the remarks and the innermost reality of the interlocutors, *Night and Day* is that novel "about silence, the things people don't say"[62] that Terence Hewett wanted to write.

A novel about feelings,[63] she next suggests rather less boldly. Yet under the traditional dress that has been pointed out, two features may be noted as significant. On the one hand a certain Shakespearean structure, on the other a certain Proustian

[56] N & D p. 45 (50)

[57] N & D p. 117 (116)

[58] N & D pp. 132 (130), 138 (135)

[59] AWD p. 10 (10)

[60] AWD p. 20 (19)

[61] AWD p. 10 (10)

[62] "I want to write a novel about Silence, . . . the things people don't say", VO p. 262 (216)

[63] Cf. N & D, p. 150 (146): ". . . novels are all about feelings", and *ibid.*, p. 508 (480): ". . . it's what we feel that's everything."

quality.[64] *Night and Day* has its "Swann's Way" and its "Guermantes Way"; the Strand and the Thames, the path of reality and the path of dream, which the heroes take alternately.[65] Virginia Woolf guides them at will along one or the other; at will, too, she makes their ways cross or diverge, as mistress of their encounters, which happen with the same freedom as in one of Shakespeare's fantasies. A hint of a sub-plot—the love affair of one of Katharine's cousins—resumes the central theme in a simplified form, like a caricature. And finally, and particularly, Mrs Hilbery, who is both in the game and outside it, rational and eccentric at once, darts through the book like the Shakespearean fool to whom she compares herself.[66]

Far more than the influence of Jane Austen,[67] George Eliot or Meredith, which, though undeniable, is yet accidental and superficial, what gives *Night and Day* its imprint of originality is the emergence of these two streams, the modern and the Elizabethan. These are the deep, significant sources, those on which the author's thought and sensibility have fed to produce their own substance.

JACOB'S ROOM

Night and Day, finished on March 24, 1919,[68] came out on October 20th of the same year.[69] *Kew Gardens* was published earlier, on May 12th; and June of that year saw the second edition of *The Mark on the Wall*, of which 150 copies had already been printed by hand at the Woolfs' press in July 1917. Although

[64] Note, however, that V. W. did not read Proust until late in 1922. Cf. AWD p. 52 (50)

[65] Cf. N & D p. 284 (270): "... should she walk on by the Strand or by the Embankment? It was not a simple question, for it concerned ... different streams of thought. If she went by the Strand she would force herself to think out the problem of the future or some mathematical problem; if she went by the river she would certainly begin to think about things that didn't exist—the forest, the ocean beach, the leafy solitudes, the magnanimous hero."

[66] Cf. N & D p. 324 (306): "... I'm quite a large bit of the fool, but the fools in Shakespeare say all the clever things."

[67] Cf. AWD p. 22 (21) (Dec. 5, 1919): "But I had rather write in my own way of *Four Passionate Snails* than be, as K. M. [Katherine Mansfield] maintains, Jane Austen over again." If this sentence from a paragraph which also mentions George Eliot may be taken as acknowledging a debt, it entitles us, nevertheless, to ascribe only limited importance to such influences.

[68] Cf. AWD p. 10 (10)

[69] Cf. AWD p. 19 (18)

I propose to study the stories and sketches separately,[70] an exception must be made for these two sketches and for *An Unwritten Novel*,[71] since Virginia Woolf referred to these studies when she defined her third novel, as she had conceived it on January 26, 1920.

This page has already been quoted and analysed in connection with her creative activity and the way her mind worked.[72] I shall only refer here to what is relevant to the new novel she had begun to think about, which was to be *Jacob's Room*.

The chief novelty is the suppression of all that she called the "scaffolding",[73] facts, actions, events precisely situated in space and time, forming an itinerary and a chronology without gaps or breaks, a continuous milieu whose continuity is in our habits of thought, consubstantial with the continuity of life itself. What will result from such a renunciation of all that hitherto seemed to be an essential element of life and of its representation?

"Conceive *Mark on the Wall*, K.[*ew*] G.[*ardens*] and *Unwritten Novel* taking hands and dancing in unity."[74] Kew Gardens is well summed up by the opening phrase of its final paragraph:

Thus one couple after another with much the same irregular and aimless movement passed the flower-bed and were enveloped in layer after layer of green blue vapour, in which at first their bodies had substance and a dash of colour, but later both substance and colour dissolved in the green-blue atmosphere.[75]

It is the account of a moment of pure sensibility which refuses to be organized according to the habitual patterns of perception.

The flower-bed is reduced to a juxtaposition of elementary shapes and lines animated by shifting colours. This background, in which everything is fluid, absorbs in its flickering brightness everything that passes by, dissecting human beings into gestures and fragments of gestures, no longer organized into actions, and detaching a few words which are no longer welded into dialogue. This piece of garden with its flowers, its strollers, is shattered

---

[70] Cf. *infra*, ch V, p. 239 ff
[71] Published in the *London Mercury*, July 1920. Mentioned in the Diary, Jan. 26, 1920 (AWD p. 23 (22)), quoted *supra*, p. 73
[72] Cf. ch. III, pp. 73-5
[73] AWD p. 23 (22)
[74] AWD p. 23 (22)
[75] HH p. 38 (35)

into a thousand fragments and yet the countless cracks and lines that separate them have not entirely destroyed the accustomed pattern: we recognize all the familiar objects and elements, as we recognize a rabbit or a huntsman in the tangle of lines in a picture puzzle. But the outline, momentarily grasped, vanishes a minute later, swallowed up by a crack across a neighbouring object. Stability, solidity, permanence become dubious; as the eye traces an imagined arabesque through this mosaic, the mind regroups fresh wholes in this atomized universe, breaks habitual links and associations to form others, hitherto unnoticed or neglected. This moment in the garden becomes the meeting-point for several lives, which received from it a common content which they absorb, differentiating it in their various ways and thus defining themselves in relation to one another. This chance conjunction in space and its results as revealing human beings were what Virginia Woolf was to retain for the composition of *Jacob's Room*.

The Mark on the Wall and *An Unwritten Novel* may be considered as the reverse and complementary experiment: instead of exploiting the surface richness of a spectacle, of dividing it *ad infinitum* into all these fragments, perceptible to the senses, which belong to this moment and this place, these other sketches explore the other dimension of reality. Starting from a few surface impressions, a mark noticed on the wall, a woman sitting in a railway carriage, the artist attempts to go back through time to the origin—an object, a circumstance, an action—of which this appearance is the sign, the consequence, the ultimate manifestation. From this attempt there results a hesitant succession of hypotheses, the elaboration and the selection of which call into play all the faculties of the observer. The latter, struck by some sensation—a mark, a gesture, a look, a sigh—lets his net drop (to use a favourite image of Virginia Woolf's) into the inaccessible regions of the past and of the elsewhere, to capture that reality which has surfaced for a fleeting moment. This reality is not a concept, a piece of knowledge, something abstract and fleshless; it is not to be confirmed or invalidated by science, or history, or any irrefutable audit. For all such things are outside ourselves, consequently unintelligible and dead; they are nothing to us. The reality that matters is that effervescence of the imagination, as it fastens on to the sign perceived, leaving it only to return to it constantly, and which at the same time is animated by all the inner life from which it springs. It is this knowledge (in Claudel's sense, *connaissance = co-naissance*) that Virginia Woolf's two stories are trying to express.

They assert, with a humour which does not conceal its tragic underside, the blind loneliness in which we are confined. This attempt to see and to know beyond the "mark on the wall" to the nail, the rose-leaf, or the crack in the wood[76]; to see and to know the life behind the face, the thought behind the glance, the action behind the gesture, is cruelly disappointing; the mark on the wall is merely a snail; the unhappy woman is not called Minnie Marsh, is not consumed by remorse or regret, is not going to her sister-in-law's, does not know any Mr Moggridge: it is her son who is waiting for her on the station platform, and they go off, "Mysterious figures! Mother and son. Who are you?"[77] And yet, despite this uncertainty, despite the risk of almost unavoidable mistake, this is the only door we have open on to the world: this is all we can claim to know about that which is not ourselves. Combining this hypothetical elaboration of the inner life on the basis of sporadic manifestations and intermittent visions with the instantaneous impressionism of *Kew Gardens*, *Jacob's Room* attempts to communicate the reality of a human being, as conveyed through the immediate data of sensibility and consciousness.

After *Night and Day*, having learned her craft within the limits of a form handed down by the tradition of the novel, having experienced its resistance and undergone its restrictions, Virginia Woolf now sees what she wants to do.[78]

When, a few months later, she makes a clearer statement of her aim, such as I have just defined it, she still has no subject in mind.[79] Doubtless she conceived this subject during the early months of 1920. We cannot be sure, but it is not impossible that one moment in *Night and Day* might have been the germ of it, this thought of Katharine Hilbery's which is certainly a thought of Virginia Woolf's: "The dream nature of our life had never been more apparent to her, never had life been more certainly an

---

[76] HH p. 41 (39)
[77] HH p. 23 (21)
[78] Cf. AWD p. 19 (18): "But on the whole I see what I'm aiming at."
[79] Cf. AWD p. 23 (22): ". . . the theme is a blank to me. . . ."

affair of four walls, whose objects existed only within the range of lights and fires, beyond which lay nothing, or nothing more than darkness."[80] Katharine's room may have widened out to become Jacob's room: each of them contains both dream and life, in each the themes of light and fire alternate with themes of darkness. Moreover, in this same meditation of the heroine's—and she has many points in common with the author—we find another phrase which this time echoes *The Voyage Out*: "She [Katharine] heard them [voices] as if they came from people in another world, a world antecedent to her world, a world that was the prelude, the antechamber to reality; it was as if, lately dead, she heard the living talking."[81]

Is not that world the last port of the voyage on which Rachel set out, with this difference that Rachel had actually landed on the shores of the Beyond? This echo is merely parenthetical. As we approach Virginia Woolf's third novel, unanimously considered to be the first of the series which was to vindicate her claim to originality, as the first which really bears her mark, it seems not irrelevant to underline its inner connection with earlier works.

Having once found the theme, the material to be moulded in the form she had recently imagined, Virginia Woolf started work on April 16, 1920.[82] She began with ease and even with exuberance, but presently was writing in calmer fashion; after less than a month's work, the difficulties engendered by the new technique made writing arduous. If the aim was clear, the paths that led to it were full of shadows and encumbered with obstacles.[83] By the end of September, after a conversation with T. S. Eliot, the doubts that hitherto she had been able to set aside halted her. She no longer felt sure of either the value or the originality of her conception. She came to think that "what I'm doing is probably being better done by Mr Joyce".[84]

We may note incidentally that if this remark justifies possible comparisons between the two writers, it does not therefore substantiate the hypothesis of borrowed inspiration or direct

[80] N & D p. 373 (352)
[81] N & D p. 373 (352)
[82] AWD p. 25 (24): "April 10. I'm planning to begin *Jacob's Room* next week with luck" and *ibid.*, p. 40 (39): "Nov. 15, 1921 . . . having begun it on April 16, 1920."
[83] Cf. AWD p. 26 (25). Tuesday, May 11 (1920)
[84] Cf. AWD p. 28 (27), Sunday, Sept. 26th.

influence.[85] If Virginia Woolf had started from James Joyce she would not have stumbled across him half-way. Eliot and Joyce moreover are only pretexts, ghosts made responsible for the interruption of *Jacob's Room*, which was to last for probably over a month. The true cause was the physical and nervous depression that always threatened Virginia Woolf after each prolonged period of effort: melancholy, neurasthenia, a sense of tragedy, personal and universal pessimism. If during this painful experience she confirmed her view of existence as being absurd and "so tragic; so like a little strip of pavement over an abyss"[86] she first needed to recover the power of writing, for it was only in writing that she could regain her balance. During the summer of 1921 another illness was to interrupt the book, which she finished on November 4, 1921.[87]

From the fact that the book was not typed until June 1922[88] and not shown to Leonard Woolf until July 23rd of that year,[89] it may be concluded that after the first draft was completed it took another eight months to get the book in trim.[90] In September came the task of proof-reading,[91] and on October 27, 1922, *Jacob's Room* appeared, well enough received—by the reading public if not by the critics—for a second edition to be immediately embarked on.[92]

Jacob's room is made up of the four walls that circumscribe his immediate universe: the child's room in the little Cornish cottage, where a streak of light reveals the chest of drawers, the looking-glass, the sheep's jawbone that the little boy has picked up on the beach; outside there is nothing but darkness and the confusion of the storm, with one deserted witness—the child's bucket, in which the crab found in a hollow of the rock circles round and round vainly trying to get out. A child's room, a child's night, a

[85] E.g. Robert Peel, "Virginia Woolf", *The Criterion*, Oct. 1933, XIII, 50. (*JR* the least interesting of her books") "it is tempting to believe that the author has been reading Mr Joyce and had decided that her technique needed bringing up to date." For a fuller discussion of this problem of influence, cf. *infra*, p. 241-5.

[86] AWD p. 29 (27)

[87] Cf. AWD p. 40 (39): "I wrote the last words of *Jacob*—on Friday November 4th to be precise. . . ."

[88] Cf. AWD p. 46 (45): "*Jacob* is being typed by Miss Green. . . ."

[89] Cf. AWD p. 47 (45). "Wednesday, July 26th: On Sunday L. read through *Jacob's Room*."

[90] Cf. AWD p. 41 (39), Nov. 15, 1921: "Then I shall have to furbish up *Jacob*."

[91] Cf. AWD p. 49 (48), Sept. 6, 1922: "My proofs come every day. . . ."

[92] Cf. AWD p. 54 (52)

child's day, a child's world, the whole of little Jacob; this is the simplest and most complete of all the rooms to which after every excursion he returns, as though to his centre and the unity of his being. Because a small boy is simple and his world is limited to a few images, a few objects—at least that is what we believe. This first chapter of the novel presents the theme in its first development, with all its wealth and all its implications.

It is taken up again in a dozen variations which are juxtaposed to build, in space and time, that complex and mysterious whole of which we can never grasp more than the outline or the surface —a human being, impenetrable, whom a word might suffice to express if only one could find it[93]: the only valid word, and yet a useless one, is his name, Jacob. The adolescent's room, into which a collection of butterflies brings the whole of the surrounding countryside, is succeeded by the undergraduate's room at Cambridge, made up of books, discussions, friendships, immersed in the unreal light that hangs over the university town, opening, so to speak, both on to the river and on to the college dining-hall. Then comes the room in Lamb's Conduit Street in London, to which Jacob returns after his work, or an evening out, or an afternoon in the British Museum reading-room, or a visit to a friend of his mother's, or a day's hunting: where his letters await him, where he reads by himself, where he argues with Bonamy, or goes to bed with Florinda, or Laurette, or Fanny Elmer. After his travels in France, then Italy, then Greece, these four walls seem to enclose a space too small to hold him; he is no longer seen there; and yet with his letters strewn about in confusion, his wicker armchair, an old pair of slippers, it is all that is left of him —all, save a little dust somewhere in Flanders, and that name, that call, that ghost summoned by Bonamy: "Jacob! Jacob!"

This crude resumé contains and perhaps unduly exaggerates the structure of the novel, such as it is, or more exactly such as it lingers in the mind of an attentive reader. To give an exact idea of this book, which, as might have been expected from what has been said about the form which Virginia Woolf sought to give it, bears no resemblance to the traditional novel, I should have to complete this analysis by what might be called a description. If each of the fourteen chapters corresponds to one period in

---

[93] Cf. JR p. 69 (71): "... of all occupations this of cataloguing features is the worst. One word is sufficient. But if one cannot find it?"

Jacob's life, it is only very rarely and quite by chance that these periods are precisely stated.[94] They sometimes last a few hours, sometimes a few months; it is as though a spotlight had lingered here and there on the twenty-six years of the hero's life, or a camera's eye gazed at it intermittently. Thus the whole thing in fact produces the impression at which the novelist had aimed: "all crepuscular, but the heart, the passion, humour, everything as bright as fire in the mist".[95] Within each chapter there is the same discontinuity; a series of paragraphs successively reveal different points in space at the same moment: Mrs Flanders finishing her letter, the painter Steele hurriedly trying to fix the woman's figure on his canvas before she goes away, Archer calling his brother, Jacob exploring the beach; or else, after the same break—a two-line blank space—that served to transport us in space, we move forward in time: Mrs Flanders has found Jacob and gone home; and now it is ten o'clock at night; or else we had been at a service in King's College Chapel and now we are at Mr Plumer's, waiting for Jacob to come to lunch; or else, again, Jacob has been at the Countess of Rocksbier's in Grosvenor Square and now we see him, having lost the hunt, galloping over Essex, before another two-line gap reveals him at Bonamy's, talking politics. Such is the general principle according to which the material is cut up; in point of fact Virginia Woolf exploits her method with such flexibility and variety as to conceal its artifice and leave room for the irregularity, the complexity, the fluidity of outline that characterise real life. The gaze, or the consciousness, which is at the centre of every paragraph, is a cohesive force creating what one might call group-objects, bringing together various elements of reality which are normally separated, to underline their relationship. Thus at one point we have Mrs Flanders and the painter, then the painter and Archer; between these two groups, a single line introduces a close-up: Archer, all alone, calling Ja-cob! Ja-cob![96] Elsewhere, a series of images and thoughts called forth by a name, an object, a sensation fill the words or gestures or the momentary experience of a character with a whole section of the past.[97] Sometimes it is only a fragment

[94] Cf. JR p. 34 (36), we guess that he is 20; p. 71 (72): "I am twenty-two"; p. 153 (154), Jacob, in Greece, is 26.
[95] AWD p. 23 (22)
[96] Cf. JR p. 6 (8)
[97] Cf. JR pp. 30-1 (32-3), 116 (118-9), 175 (175)

of dialogue overheard on the river bank, in a restaurant, in a café . . . an isolated remark such as one might catch passing by an open window.[98] The focus of observation is everywhere and yet nowhere; it is at the disposal of the novelist, taking up her stand here or there, for a second or for an hour, according to whether a single word or gesture is needed or a whole scene. No obstacle impedes the author's godlike mobility, her changing moods; she stands beside her characters, listening to them, watching them; she is inside them, following their words and their thoughts simultaneously,[99] or the fantastic train of image-memories; and often she seems to forget them, letting her thoughts and imagination ramble at a tangent from the path, already quite unpredictable enough, that she is following: Cambridge and learning, the busy teeming life of London, Japanese flowers, the tragedy of life, letters—their messages and their lies—what we know about people, what we can know about them, what they are. . . .

And yet this multiplicity, this disorder or this imaginativeness —the word chosen tells us more about the individual reader's mind than about the nature of the book—do no more than reproduce the twofold discontinuity and disconnectedness of human beings: that which is native to them, and that which is inherent in the observer's vision of them. But in the very core of every being, as in the core of others' vision of him, an unremitting force, so discreet as to be generally invisible, gives direction to all these scattered fragments, so that lines emerge, a figure takes shape, Jacob suddenly appears and takes his place among the people that we know. The disconcerting strangeness of the novel is due to its presenting at the same time the object of our knowledge—the life of Jacob, enclosed within the four walls, real or symbolic, of his "room"—and our actual knowledge of this object. In one of these meditations, where the author-observer turns aside from watching the scene to examine herself, she defines her procedure:

The march that the mind keeps beneath the windows of others is queer enough. Now distracted by brown panelling; now by a fern in a pot; here improvising a few phrases to dance with the barrel-organ; again snatching a detached gaiety from a drunken man; then

---

[98] Cf. JR p. 41 (45)
[99] Cf. for example JR p. 71 (72): Jacob's interior monologue interspersed, in parentheses, between his remarks to Bonamy, whose answers are not given.

altogether absorbed by words the poor shout across the street at each other (so outright, so lusty)—yet all the while having for centre, for magnet, a young man alone in his room.[100]

This sentence asserts a victory over heterogeneity; a little further on comes the assertion of victory over discontinuity: "As frequent as street corners in Holborn are these chasms in the continuity of our ways. Yet we keep straight on."[101] If the heterogeneous and the discontinuous are the appearance, whereas their unity, the force that ensures their fusion and unites them, is the reality, we can recognize in this novel the same preoccupation that was already dominant in the two earlier ones. But this time the author has found modes of expression which seem to participate in the very nature of these two modes of being, which are so to speak coextensive with them. Instead of transcribing them in a single language which remains external to both of them, as was the case in *The Voyage Out* and *Night and Day*, Virginia Woolf has invented a form which has the same qualities as what it clothes. At the same time she eliminates all that was jarring, awkward and mechanical in the first two books— features which I sought to explain, without entirely excusing their weakness. The alternation between realistic descriptions and inward analyses gives way to a constant confrontation between impressions and the inaccessible, indescribable experience they conceal; the impression left by the world around Jacob, by the four walls of his room, is constantly set against Jacob's innermost and essential self, which is only a blank, a void.[102] And yet this blank, this void, is circumscribed with such precise lines, shapes and colours that mould him and cling so closely to him that he receives therefrom a kind of substance and solidity. Naturally, as with all voids, its content depends more on the reader who sounds it than on the author who created it. Some will only discover the blue eyes, the powerful build,[103] the awkwardness and the distinction,[104] which are the only features of the hero that

---

[100] JR p. 94 (95)

[101] JR p. 95 (96)

[102] Cf. Desmond MacCarthy, *Criticism*, p. 173: ". . . not the man himself but, so to speak, the impression of his body upon the bed where he has lain." On the whole he disapproves, and prefers VO and N & D ("two good ones").

[103] Cf. JR p. 28 (30-1)

[104] Cf. JR pp. 60, 69 (61, 70)

the author chooses to mention. Others, like Leonard Woolf, see him as a ghost.[105] As regards the first, we shall see elsewhere[106] the arguments that Virginia Woolf could bring against them. As for the others, surely what they see is exactly what she wanted to show them? For them, Jacob acquires that "semi-transparent" quality[107] which throughout the book denotes the way people appear to one.

In fact, we are well aware that beneath this semi-transparency there is a reality, "there is something . . ."[108] which neither the eye nor the mind can reach, which words only express metaphorically, and that in trying to take metaphors literally one runs the risk, humorously illustrated in *An Unwritten Novel*, of replacing one ghost by another, even more unsubstantial.

That Jacob is insignificant is another matter. Ralph, Katharine and even Rachel had more stuff in them. But that very quality contributed, perhaps, to making *The Voyage Out* and *Night and Day* more uncertain and undecided as novels, of obscuring their true aim. In fact, conceived from the point of view of character study, with the more or less conscious, more or less deliberate intention of undermining the foundations of character study, they were vitiated by an inner contradiction which the author could only resolve from outside, by artifices of structure and of style. *Jacob's Room* does not claim to create characters, or even a single character; and its superiority to its two predecessors lies precisely in excluding any possibility of misunderstanding in this direction. Who could suppose that Archer's desolate cry, "pure from all body, pure from all passion, going out into the world, solitary, unanswered, breaking against rocks"[109] could ever be answered? that this longing for another's presence could ever be satisfied? This depersonalized cry is universal; it sums up, in itself, all desire and all possession. It wells up in Clara's mind,[110] mute, but just as heartrending and as vain; the girl's love has

[105] Cf. AWD p. 47 (45): "he says that the people are ghosts."
[106] Cf. particularly ch. VI, 1, p. 353 ff
[107] Cf. JR p. 55 (57): "Opposite him were hazy, semi-transparent shapes of yellow and blue." *Ibid.*, p. 61 (62): "She looked semi-transparent. . . ." *Ibid.*, p. 70 (72): ". . . life is but a procession of shadows. . . ."
[108] Cf. JR p. 139 (140): " 'But mixed with the stupidity which leads him into these absurd predicaments,' thought Bonamy, 'there is something—something'—he sighed, for he was fonder of Jacob than of any one in the world."
[109] JR p. 7 (8-9)
[110] Cf. JR pp. 166 (166), 167 (167): "Jacob! Jacob! thought Clara."

not been able to overcome her own timidity nor the young man's awkwardness; they have passed close by one another without being able to communicate, one ghost beside another ghost. And, resounding on the last page in an echo of the first, Bonamy's cry confirms the vanity of this endeavour which is thwarted not by life, not by death, but by what we ourselves are. A cry of defeat and a cry of victory, at the same time, speaking of the inaccessibility and unknowableness of the Other and of irremediable loss, even while it tells of communion, of the inalienable, unique being one has within oneself, and which, in spite of everything, in spite of life and of death, is the most real of all realities.[111] If Jacob were made of more solid flesh, if he were more definite materially, if his inner being were more strongly drawn and more substantial, so that he existed in his own right and stood out from the book, like a character in Thackeray for instance, the very purpose of the novel would be destroyed. The vagueness, the lack of certainty, the disconcerting quality of this work, and the kind of uneasiness, insecurity and frustration it leaves with the reader, may perhaps be faults in relation to absolute standards in the art of fiction. But in relation to what the author had set out to express, it must be acknowledged that these characteristics are qualities.

In the moods of doubt that overcame her during composition or on the point of facing the public, Virginia Woolf, by acquiring a kind of dual personality, forgets her own point of view to adopt the common reader's, anticipates the censure that she will incur[112] and even, speaking for herself, judges her book "thin and pointless".[113] This criticism has a twofold interest. In relation to the novel, it points out weaknesses of which the author was not

---

[111] Cf. JR p. 70 (72). "In any case life is but a procession of shadows, and God knows why it is that we embrace them eagerly, and see them depart with such anguish, being shadows . . . why are we yet surprised in the window corner by a sudden vision that the young man in the chair is of all things in the world the most real, the most solid, the best known to us—why indeed? For the moment after we know nothing about him. Such is the manner of our seeing. Such the conditions of our love."

[112] Cf. AWD p. 46 (45): "If they say this is all a clever experiment . . . your fiction is impossible . . . you can't make us care a damn for any of your figures, I shall say read my criticism then. Now what *will* they say about *Jacob*? Mad, I suppose: a disconnected rhapsody; I don't know."

[113] Cf. AWD p. 49 (48): "The thing now reads thin and pointless; the words scarcely dint the paper; and I expect to be told I've written a graceful fantasy, without much bearing upon real life."

unaware. Although "quite intelligible"[114], as Leonard Woolf found it, it requires an effort at collaboration from the reader without which it misses its goal. This principle is of course valid for all works of art, but in varying degrees; the impressionistic, suggestive character of *Jacob's Room* makes it particularly imperative. As regards the novelist herself, her disappointment proved a source of progress, giving rise to important characteristics which were to differentiate her fourth novel, *Mrs Dalloway*, from her third.[115]

Meanwhile, however, the experiment was not purely a negative one: if Virginia Woolf asserts that "*Jacob* was a necessary step for me, in working free"[116] she also considers that the work has its own merits: "At last, I like reading my own writing. It seems to me to fit me closer than it did before. I have done my task here better than I expected."[117]

The reception given to *Jacob's Room* enables one to sum up its most striking characteristics. "This time the reviews are against me and the private people enthusiastic."[118] The critics, set in their habits and referring to the laws of fiction, condemned in the book whatever disturbed the former and did not respect the latter. Its originality was the thing they attacked. And it was this same originality that delighted her readers—some of them at any rate. Among these we may mention, quoting the author herself: E. M. Forster, Lytton Strachey, David Garnett, Violet Dickinson, Logan Pearsall Smith, Philip Morell.[119] We must put aside the thought, often suggested by the author's enemies, that their praise is merely a token of friendship and hence without value. Repeatedly, each of them showed that they could preserve their literary judgment from the influence of personal affection. But we must remember that they were artists and intellectuals, who shared with Virginia Woolf a certain number of ideas about art, its requirements, its relations with tradition. They were avant-garde readers, appreciating an avant-garde author and enjoying her work as such. If today, after thirty years of experiment and

---

[114] Cf. AWD p. 47 (46): ". . . he found it very interesting and beautiful, and without lapse (save perhaps the party) and quite intelligible."
[115] Cf. *infra*, p. 227
[116] AWD p. 52 (51)
[117] AWD p. 52 (50)
[118] AWD p. 54 (52)
[119] AWD p. 54 (52)

education, *Jacob's Room* may seem a ~~little pale~~ and moreover ~~extremely accessible~~ it was likely to shock and disconcert the public in 1922. Without being alone of its kind,[120] it may claim a distinguished place immediately after the work of Joyce and Proust, in the series of novels which attempted to free the genre from the forms that had been determined for it by the great writers of the nineteenth century.

MRS DALLOWAY (1925)

Mrs Dalloway is mentioned for the first time in *A Writer's Diary* on June 23, 1922,[121] when the final version of *Jacob's Room* had not yet been completely typed out. On August 16th of that year Virginia Woolf writes that she is working on it,[122] and on August 28th that she expects to finish it by September 2nd.[123] The reference, of course, is not to the novel which now bears that title, but only to a sketch whose possible developments the author did not yet envisage clearly. No doubt, ideas were proliferating[124] around these fifteen pages. Even a kind of sequel, or second chapter, is allotted a place in the writer's programme of work.[125]

The title, perhaps even the subject, is still uncertain. There are references to *The Prime Minister*, which she finished, ten days or so behind schedule, about October 21st.[126] In the meantime Virginia Woolf has been reading Homer, Plato, Ibsen, Racine, Marlowe, and finishing Joyce's *Ulysses*.[127]

Remember that *Jacob's Room* appeared on October 16th, greeted by the conflicting criticisms to which I have already referred, and which obsessed Virginia Woolf in spite of herself. It was at this period that out of *Mrs Dalloway* and *The Prime Minister* there emerged the idea of a book: "I adumbrate here a study of insanity and suicide; the world seen by the sane and

---

[120] Cf. ch II–1.

[121] Cf. AWD p. 46 (45).

[122] Cf. AWD p. 48 (46): "Now I break off . . . to write *Mrs. D.*"

[123] Cf. AWD p. 48 (47): ". . . *Mrs. Dalloway* finished on Saturday 2nd Sept."

[124] Cf. AWD p. 48 (46): ". . . *Mrs. D.* (who ushers in a host of others, I begin to perceive).

[125] Cf. AWD p. 49 (47): "And then?" (after Sept. 22nd) "Shall I write the next chapter of *Mrs. D.*—if she is to have a next chapter; and shall it be *The Prime Minister*? which will last till the week after we get back—say October 12th."

[126] Cf. AWD p. 53 (51): "I shall finish *The Prime Minister* in another week—say 21st.

[127] Cf. AWD pp. 47 and 49 (47-8)

the insane side by side—something like that."[128] But profiting by the lesson of *Jacob's Room*, which she blames herself for having written somewhat at random, solving problems as she met them, she determines to conceive this book as a whole, "to foresee [it] better than the others and get the utmost out of it".[129]

Owing to a gap of seven months in *A Writer's Diary*, we are reduced to pure conjectures: the most plausible being that she has only written a few pages, constituting studies for the book which is slowly maturing, and that she is devoting herself more particularly to reading and to the critical essays which she plans to collect into a volume. In June 1923, indeed, a fresh stage seems to have been reached and the theme is enriched with a further purpose: "I am a great deal interested suddenly in my book. I want to bring in the despicableness of people like Ott. [Lady Ottoline Morell]. I want to give the slipperiness of the soul. I have been too tolerant often. The truth is people scarcely care for each other. They have this insane instinct for life. But they never become attached to anything outside themselves."[130]

The structure of the novel seems to become clearer, as well as its intentions; that at least is what one may conclude from the mention of the new title, *The Hours*, still hypothetical in any case,[131] and of the difficulties she anticipates in casting its substance in the mould she has conceived: "I foresee, to return to *The Hours*, that this is going to be the devil of a struggle. The design is so queer and so masterful. I'm always having to wrench my substance to fit it. The design is certainly original and interests me hugely."[132]

The different themes, at first seen separately, are fused: "I want to give life and death, sanity and insanity; I want to criticise the social system, and show it at work at its most intense".[133]

[128] Cf. AWD p. 52 (51)

[129] Cf. AWD p. 54 (53): "I want to think out *Mrs. Dalloway*. I want to foresee this book better than the others and get the utmost out of it. I expect I could have screwed *Jacob* up tighter, if I had foreseen; but I had to make my path as I went."

[130] AWD p. 55 (54). According to Stephen Spender (*World within World*, p. 159) V. W. was not alone in giving one of her characters the features of Lady Ottoline Morell. He mentions D. H. Lawrence, Graham Greene, Aldous Huxley and "several others".

[131] Cf. AWD p. 57 (56): ". . . *The Hours*, if that's its name?"

[132] AWD p. 58 (57)

[133] AWD p. 57 (56)

During that summer, Virginia Woolf was simultaneously working at her novel and preparing the volume of essays which was to be the first *Common Reader*. This twofold activity in no way impaired the freshness and intensity of the interest which she felt for her novel, an interest stimulated by the difficulties it presented: "I've been battling for ever so long with *The Hours*, which is proving one of my most tantalising and refractory of books . . .; I'm much interested; can't stop making it up yet—yet."[134]

Only now, after over "a year's groping" and experiment had she discovered the "tunnelling process"[135] which was to enable her to achieve the effects she sought.[136] By mid-October she had already written a hundred pages, roughly half the book. At times the difficulties of this ambitious project were such that she almost gave it up.[137] Tackling an intractable scene of which she could barely write fifty words in a whole morning, she even came to doubt the value and originality of the great discovery on which she had set all her hopes.[138]

It is probable that the gradual enrichment of the subject, already referred to, was partly responsible for the difficulties with which she had to contend. Two remarks in the Diary, alluding to the breadth of her project. irresistibly recall André Gide's efforts to put the whole of his experience into *Les Faux Monnayeurs*[139]: "I am stuffed with ideas for it. I feel I can use up everything I've ever thought."[140] Seven months later, at the end of May 1924, stimulated by a magnificent spring, her mind full of her novel which she plans to have finished by the end of September, Virginia Woolf reverts to the idea of a *summa*, closely connected moreover with this new form: "I feel as if I had loosed the bonds pretty completely and could pour everything in. If so—good."[141] Moments of weariness,[142] unforeseen events such as an

---

[134] AWD p. 59 (58)

[135] AWD p. 61 (60): "It took me a year's groping to discover what I call my tunnelling process, by which I tell the past by instalments, as I have need of it."

[136] AWD p. 60 (59): "I think that gives exactly what I want."

[137] Cf. AWD p. 61 (60): "indeed I made up my mind one night to abandon the book." Cf. also AWD p. 79 (77)

[138] Cf. AWD p. 61 (60): "I've not re-read my great discovery, and it may be nothing important whatsoever."

[139] Cf. André Gide, *Journal*

[140] AWD p. 61 (60)   [141] AWD p. 62 (61)

[142] Cf. AWD p. 63 (62): "A feeling of depression is on me . . . being at a low ebb with my book. . . ."

article to be written on the occasion of Conrad's death,[143] barely delayed by a fortnight the completion of the first version of *The Hours*, now become *Mrs Dalloway* again. The final stages are reached: August 2nd, death of Septimus[144]; September 7th, the beginning of the last tableau, the party at Mrs Dalloway's[145]; October 9th, the book is finished.

After following the progress of the work from August 16, 1922, onwards, we may be somewhat surprised to read in the Diary on October 17, 1924, this summary of its history: ". . . in some ways this book is a feat; finished without break from illness, which is an exception; and written really in one year; and finally, written from the end of March to the 8th October without more than a few days' break for writing journalism."[146] From these assertions we should conclude that the book came into being not as a continuous growth, but in three successive stages, each characterized by very different states of mind and methods of work.

In the first place, it is perhaps premature to speak of "a book" prior to October 1923. In the wake of *Mrs Dalloway* and *The Prime Minister*, two sketches analogous to those that had appeared in *Monday or Tuesday*, there emerged ideas and scenes which Virginia Woolf treated as studies. No doubt she intended to make a novel out of them, but she had not yet conceived the "form" of it, that form which I have attempted to define earlier[147] and which for her was the active, fertilising element in writing. It is not unlikely that the discontinuity of *Jacob's Room*, its form symbolised by "*Mark on the Wall, Kew Gardens* and *Unwritten Novel* taking hands and dancing in unity", was the link which was to unite these fragments. In any case, in the very process of writing, Virginia Woolf discovered a new form, tried it out, perfected it, between August and October 1923. Only then did she consider that she had begun her novel.[148] For lack of precise data about the whole of the subsequent period, which completely covers the second stage of composition, we are reduced to a hypothesis supported by a single sentence. Without reconsidering

---

[143] Cf. AWD p. 64 (63), Friday Aug. 15th.
[144] Cf. AWD p. 63 (62)
[145] Cf. AWD p. 66 (65): "There I am now—at last at the party. . . ."
[146] Cf. AWD p. 68 (66-7)
[147] Cf. ch. III, p. 73 ff
[148] Cf. AWD p. 62 (61). Monday, May 26, 1924: ". . . since the crisis of August last, which I count the beginning of it. . . ."

what she had written previously, without examining more deeply
the validity of her formula Virginia Woolf pins her hopes to it[149]
and decides: "I am going on writing it now till, honestly, I can't
write another line."[150] How far had she gone thus, continuing a
novel which she had not really begun? We do not know. In fact,
it matters little whether she had reached the end of merely some
scene in the second half which still had to be written. All that
we can say with certainty is that March witnessed the end of this
second phase of writing, which was in one sense a definitive one,
since the author was in possession of the form of the book, but
also flawed by the heterogeneity of the first hundred pages,
which had not been written in the light of that form. At the end
of March, Virginia Woolf began again from the beginning and
wrote again in a little over seven months, at one sweep, what she
really considered to be the first version of *Mrs Dalloway.* Moreover, the way in which she envisaged the revision of this MS
allows one to assume that the process of recasting, in order to
integrate the first half with the second, was somewhat hurried:
". . . I have still to read the first chapters, and confess to dreading
the madness rather; and being too clever. However, I'm sure I've
now got to work with my pick at my seam. . . ."[151] Whether because
she was pressed by external circumstances—a delay in the preparation of *The Common Reader,* plans for a trip to France[152]—or
because she was uncertain of the extent of her task,[153] she did not
allow herself the three months' decanting which she had anticipated.[154] By November she was at work again, revising certain
parts of it.[155] Then in December she typed out the whole thing,
correcting it as she went: "a good method, I believe, as thus one
works with a wet brush over the whole, and joins parts separately
composed and gone dry".[156] At last, as a sort of New Year's gift,
she handed her manuscript to Leonard Woolf when they were
staying at Rodmell in January 1925.[157]

[149] AWD p. 61 (60)   [150] AWD p. 61 (60)   [151] AWD p. 66 (65)
[152] Journey to the South of France, visit to Cassis, spring 1925. Cf. AWD April
8th 1925, pp. 72-3 (71-2)
[153] Cf. AWD p. 68 (67): "I am going to skate rapidly over *Mrs D,* but it will take
time. No: I cannot say anything much to the point, for what I must do is to experiment next week; how much revision is needed, and how much time it takes."
[154] AWD p. 62 (61)   [155] Cf. note 153, AWD Nov. 1, 1924.
[156] AWD p. 69 (68)
[157] Cf. AWD p. 71 (70). Wednesday, Jan. 6, 1925: "I revised *Mrs D.* . . . L. read
it."

In May 1925 *Mrs Dalloway* came out simultaneously in England and in America.

The novel, within the framework of twenty-four hours in London, consists of two intertwined lines of development, having for centres of interest first Mrs Dalloway, outwardly the perfect London hostess, and secondly Septimus Smith, a shell-shocked ex-soldier. These two sets of characters and incidents develop alternately, coinciding momentarily at different points in space and time made concrete by objects, people and scenes which flash across the consciousness of the principal characters in both series. The Prime Minister's car, an aeroplane spelling out an advertisement in the sky, a little girl playing in Regent's Park, an old beggar woman singing by an Underground station, or a mere impression of kaleidoscopic changes due to the lights and shadows, or the passing of an ambulance. And each time the author abandons one series to follow the other. Thus on the one hand Clarissa Dalloway, going to buy flowers for her party, meets Peter Walsh who has been, and still is, in love with her. He roams aimlessly about London; Mr Dalloway, with another friend of his wife's, lunches with Lady Bruton who has invited them to put the finishing touches to a letter to *The Times*; Elizabeth Dalloway, Clarissa's daughter, goes shopping with Miss Killman, an old maid who gives her history lessons and tries to inculcate piety. That evening all these characters—except Miss Killman—forgather with many others at Mrs Dalloway's party. That same day Septimus Smith and his wife Rezia go for a walk in Regent's Park before visiting Dr Bradshaw, a specialist in nervous diseases who, after a brief consultation, advises sending Septimus to a mental home. When the latter is sent for that evening he throws himself out of the window. The Bradshaws, guests at the Dalloways' party, tell the story of this suicide, thus bringing together the two lines of fate in the idea of death. Originally Virginia Woolf had conceived of an even closer fusion by making Mrs Dalloway kill herself at the end of the party.[158]

Basically, this slight framework is only a pretext. What is actually revealed to us is the whole of Clarissa Dalloway's life and that of Septimus Smith, echoing one another, not just as

---

[158] Cf. Preface to 1929 American edition, quoted by D. Daiches, *Virginia Woolf*, New Directions, p. 75; Nicholson & Watson, London, p. 74. Cf. also E. M. Forster who, on first reading the book, believed Mrs. D. killed herself.

they have been lived of course, but as, accumulated in the protagonists' minds, they fill and colour and affect their present
existence, what they do and what they are. This integration of
past with present is the important discovery that has already
been referred to.[159] We have seen, in the case of the earlier novels,
how the analysis of form helped to disclose their secret; and,
setting what Virginia Woolf has divulged about her intentions
beside what she has achieved, we may try to bring out the
significance of this novel, which has remained one of her most
popular books.

In the first place, Virginia Woolf speaks of "my tunnelling
process, by which I tell the past by instalments, as I have need of
it".[160] So, in fact, by a succession of interior monologues, set off
by some sensation which brings back its homologue from the past
and, with it, an associated train of places and people, feelings and
thoughts, we discover in Clarissa on the one hand her parents'
summer home at Bourton, her 18-year-old self, her passionate
relationships with Peter Walsh and Sally Seton, her meeting with
and marriage to Richard Dalloway, and on the other Westminster, and her life as a mother and as the wife of a mediocre
politician. By the same process we know that Septimus, a promising clerk in an estate agent's, left his job to volunteer during the
war, made friends with an officer called Evans who was killed
just before the Armistice. We learn of his marriage to a Milanese
girl, Rezia, his return to his old job and his sudden collapse; the
local doctor finds absolutely nothing wrong with him, and when
Septimus begins talking to himself he scolds him like a small boy
and sends him to consult Bradshaw.

Even from this brief summary, which misrepresents the flashbacks by depriving them of their wealth of impressions and all the
intellectual reverberations that make them meditations in depth,
we can see the sort of selection the author makes in the lives of
her heroes. She retains only their loves and marriages and their
reactions to the life imposed on them by society. Another remark
in the Diary sheds light on the secret relation between Septimus
and Clarissa:

I should say a good deal about *The Hours* and my discovery: how I dig
out beautiful caves behind my characters: I think that gives exactly

[159] Cf. *supra*, p. 229
[160] Cf. AWD p. 61 (60)

what I want; humanity, humour, depth. The idea is that the caves
shall connect and each comes to daylight at the present moment.[161]

These caves, evidently, are the whole of this buried life: "... the
depths of that leaf-encumbered forest, the soul. . . ."[162] explored
by the unconstrained consciousness of the heroes. They lost
themselves in it in time, to find themselves in timelessness,
abandoning their outer appearance, the surface they present to
people and to things: Clarissa Dalloway, the happy and respected
wife, mistress of her house, dominating mother; Septimus Smith,
an odd and possibly dangerous man. Then they recover their
confused and mysterious wholeness in which loves and hates are
at once fleeting and eternal, aspirations are infinite, judgments
are contradictory, and loneliness is a prison peopled with ghosts.
It is in the most intimate depths that the "caves connect". The
casual and meaningless way in which the heroes' lives are recon-
structed—when the caves "come to daylight at the present
moment"—reveals the shallowness of apparent contacts, and on
the other hand emphasizes the profound unity that comes from
participation in the inward experience of life. In fact these
beings, Clarissa and Septimus, not only communicate with one
another through identical emotions but are superimposed on one
another to the point of identity. Indeed, "in the first version,
Septimus, who later is intended to be her double, had no existence".[163] Through his neurosis, moreover, he amplifies all
Clarissa's reactions, and plays in the novel the role of an echo
chamber. The explosion from the Prime Minister's car startles
Clarissa, who thinks of a pistol shot; for Septimus, "The world has
raised its whip; where will it descend?"[164] Life—things and
people—is for Clarissa something that one is constantly ". . .
making up, building . . . round one, . . . creating . . . every
moment afresh"[165] in its unique novelty. And the hallucinated
vision of Septimus, with its exaggerated yearning for love and
beauty,[166] is of the same nature. Identical, too, are their alternations of terror and joy which, in the form of loneliness and

[161] AWD p. 60 (59)
[162] Mrs D p. 15 (17)
[163] Preface written by V. W. for the 1929 American edition. Quoted by Daiches,
Virginia Woolf, p. 75.
[164] Mrs D p. 17 (20)
[165] Cf. Mrs D pp. 6 (5) and 134-5 (184-5)
[166] Cf. Mrs D pp. 75-7 (101-5)

love, apprehension of death and ecstatic delight in existence, mark the pulse of that awareness of life, whose keenness is the dominant trait of these protagonists. "What one feels"[167] has become for Clarissa the only thing that matters. And it is precisely the loss of the power to feel that terrifies Septimus[168] and leads him to envisage the suicide to which he is finally driven by the unfeelingness of society as typified by Bradshaw. By throwing away his whole life, now become meaningless, he consummates the symbolic sacrifice made by Clarissa when she threw a coin into the Serpentine.[169] Like Rachel, Katharine and Ralph, like the invisible spectator who tries to define Jacob, Clarissa, Peter Walsh and Septimus are involved in the pursuit of the reality behind appearances. Clarissa, by marrying Richard, has condemned herself to a compromise—as, too, has Sally Seton by marrying Lord Rosseter and his £10,000 a year. Peter Walsh, the solitary traveller,[170] half-way between Clarissa's surrender and the intransigence of Septimus, is doomed to social failure. As for Septimus, guilty of the unpardonable crime of "attaching meanings to words of a symbolical kind",[171] he is literally cast out by society. We see from this how the social criticism intended by the author[172] is grafted on to the psycho-metaphysical theme of the novel. Politics, money, religious intolerance, everything in our civilization which is built on ready-made ideas into which feeling does not constantly infuse fresh life and significance, creates around human beings a prison parallel to that in which our own nature confines us—so closely parallel indeed that, to Septimus's visionary mind, it becomes its concrete embodiment.[173]

Are we to conclude from the suicide of Septimus and Clarissa's participation in that suicide that Virginia Woolf sees no other deliverance than death? That her answer here echoes that of

[167] Cf. Mrs D p. 210 (292): "For she had come to feel that it was the only thing worth saying—what one felt."

[168] Cf. Mrs D pp. 97-8 (132-3): ". . . the appalling fear came over him—he could not feel . . . his brain was perfect; it must be the fault of the world then—that he could not feel."

[169] Cf. Mrs D p. 202 (280): "She had once thrown a shilling into the Serpentine, never anything more. But he had flung it away. They went on living. . . ."

[170] Cf. Mrs D pp. 63 (85), 64 (86), 65 (87). "The solitary traveller" mentioned six times.

[171] Mrs D p. 106 (145)

[172] Cf. supra, p. 228

[173] Cf. Mrs D p. 108 (148): "Once you fall, Septimus repeated to himself, human nature is on you. Holmes and Bradshaw are on you."

The Voyage Out and *Jacob's Room*? True, the themes of loneliness, of the impossibility of knowing other people or communicating with them, of the futility, frustration and renunciation inherent in existence recur constantly. Nevertheless, the obsessive burden they lay on human beings is lightened, and even vanishes completely, at certain privileged moments filled solely with the miracle of life. These perfect moments, as Sartre would say, these moments of vision, to use Virginia Woolf's own term, lift Clarissa, Peter, even Septimus, even Richard Dalloway on to the crest of a wave from which everything is made clear and orderly. At such moments, fugitive though they be, life becomes an exciting adventure whose poetry is overwhelming.[174] They make us cling to life in spite of all its bitterness and all its frustrations. Even Septimus, poised on the window-ledge, "did not want to die. Life was good."[175] And certain people carry within them a sort of power that renders them sensitive to the beauty of life and at the same time makes them mediums through whom other people are sensitized in their turn. Clarissa is one of these, despite her faults, her failings and lapses. This power is as nameless as it is indefinable. It can be summed up in a single word: being. We recognize here one of the leading ideas of *Night and Day*[176]; here, however, it is not merely asserted, it is embodied in the central character. The final sentence of the novel: "For there she was",[177] does not only assert Clarissa's material presence, it sums up her very present-ness, as defined by Peter Walsh:

. . . that extraordinary gift, that woman's gift, of making a world of her own wherever she happened to be. She came into a room; she stood, as he had often seen her, in a doorway with lots of people around her. But it was Clarissa one remembered. Not that she was striking; not beautiful at all; there was nothing picturesque about her; she never said anything specially clever; there she was, however; there she was.[178]

Finally, every individual, even those most utterly despised and rejected by existence, the Rezias and Ellie Hendersons or the old beggar woman singing by the Underground station, have one

[174] AWD p. 56 (55). June 13, 1923: "It is a general sense of the poetry of existence that overcomes me."
[175] Mrs D p. 164 (226)
[176] Cf. *supra*, p. 212 ff
[177] Mrs D p. 213 (296)
[178] Mrs D p. 84-5 (114-5)

ultimate resource against despair and defeat: memory. The aura of happiness which, throughout the book, surrounds the manifold returns to the past counteracts the pessimism that pervades the present. Life relived glows with delusive happiness; it is our escape, our victory over time and space—and perhaps over death.

But it must be admitted that this miracle of memory, and that gift of presentness, are merely beacons in the darkness. Septimus dies, the Bradshaws go home, competent and dignified; the old woman over the way goes to bed quietly, all alone; night has gathered round the little islet of light of the enchanted garden, created by Clarissa, the magician, as Mrs Hilbery says in her daft, gentle way,[179] like the Shakespearean fool she resembles.

There are so many doors, she goes on, such unexpected places that she could not find her way.[180] She makes only a transient appearance and says little more, but these few words take on the hope and despair of the book, when a page later Sally Seton compares life to a prison cell on whose walls one scratches in vain. The recourse to past happiness, where all the bitterness has now settled like lees, the love of life, love itself, an unfailing sensitivity, all those riches that are summed up in the intensity and keenness of existence, permit nothing more than an individual victory, even less, perhaps—an intermittent victory. The obscure and hostile forces of society and life remain intact; terror and death are still there. Septimus, visionary as he is, is no Christ but just a madman; and Clarissa, for all her charm and kindliness, is only a society woman. The small scale of her heroes, which we already noticed when considering *Night and Day*, is a weakness of which Virginia Woolf was not unaware. It was because she felt that Clarissa Dalloway was not big enough to bear all the human attributes with which she sought to burden her that she almost gave up the novel.[181]

Even after one admits the inadequacy of Virginia Woolf's answers to the problems she sets—or more exactly their incongruity to these problems, since the answers remain on the personal plane whereas the problems spill over on to the social plane,

---

[179] Cf. Mrs D pp. 209-10 (290-1) and *supra*, p. 214

[180] Mrs D p. 210 (291)

[181] Cf AWD p. 79 (77): ". . . I remember the night at Rodmell when I decided to give it up, because I found Clarissa in some way tinselly" and p. 61 (60): "The doubtful point is, I think, the character of Mrs Dalloway. It may be too stiff, too glittering and tinsely (*sic*)."

Mrs Dalloway is probably the one of all her novels which is the most universally human, the one that covers the widest field. Some readers prefer *To the Lighthouse*; the fantasy and liveliness of *Orlando* delight others more; *The Waves* is generally considered her masterpiece, although with reservations; *The Years*, which should have been an amplification of *The Hours*, remains perhaps an ambitious project which its commercial success scarcely redeems.[182] *Mrs Dalloway*, which at first was only moderately successful,[183] owes its lasting hold on the public, no doubt, to the balance it achieves between essentially "woolfian" qualities on the one hand and the traditional requirements of the novel, made flexible by the numerous experiments of the last three decades.

Starting from a sketch, Virginia Woolf sought to "keep the quality of a sketch"[184] in her novel. And in fact the lightness of touch, the way the colours shade off indefinitely, the precision of the anecdotes scribbled in the margin, so to speak, the slightness of the illusory present, the schematic, distilled flashbacks to the past, the fragmentary characters glimpsed through the consciousness of other characters, all this belongs to the novella rather than to the novel.

It all corresponds, too, to certain aspects of Virginia Woolf's temperament, to certain of her limitations, as also to her vivacity and spontaneity. The fact that the book cost her much effort and constraint is not incompatible with this harmony; it was against other resistances and other temptations that she had to struggle. By a curious paradox, it was by frankly exploiting these processes and potentialities that she achieved a novel of greater fulness than *Jacob's Room*, which attempted to inscribe a series of sketches within the broader framework of the novel. In any case, all this describes the charm of *Mrs Dalloway* rather than its specific qualities. And these can be defined more precisely if we start from *Jacob's Room*.

In spite of the praise that *Jacob's Room* won for her, Virginia Woolf, as we have seen, quite clearly foresaw the criticism this book was to arouse.[185] Her own criticisms are even more interest-

---

[182] Cf. AWD p. 282 (272). *The Years* was for six weeks the best selling novel in the U.S.A.

[183] Cf. AWD p. 79 (77): 1,250 copies sold in the first month, 250 in the second.

[184] AWD p. 66 (65)

[185] Cf *supra*, p. 225

ing, because of the direction they were to give to her next work. For one thing, she plans to be "more close to the fact"[186]; for another, she wants the book to be "tighter", more coherent, better composed.[187] However, these general aims could only be made effective by the intermediary of more precise principles and processes. In the discovery of these means of execution two contradictory forces can be distinguished: on the one hand, the resolute determination to continue along the path of which *Jacob's Room* marks the first stage[188]; on the other, the dread of having landed in a blind alley, of having achieved at one stroke in that novel, an imperfect one on the whole, all that her vision and her theories could ever beget. This apprehension crystallized around Murry's comment that "there's no way of going on after *Jacob's Room*",[189] to which Virginia Woolf refers three times in her Diary.[190] Her own dissatisfaction further fostered this obsession. Whether she liked it or not, adverse criticisms focussed on the problem of her characterization confined her thought within circumscribed limits. If she seemed still to believe that her article in *The Nation*[191] was sufficient answer, she was aware at heart that this answer was valid only for *Jacob's Room*, explaining it and justifying it with reference to its underlying intentions. But although she had broken the fetters that hindered the expression of life and reality as she conceived them, yet life and reality had to some extent eluded her; she knew she had grasped only ghosts in a twilight world. And she knew that the nub of the problem was in the characters.[192] To judge by a first impression, one is tempted to call *Mrs Dalloway* a compromise. Virginia Woolf seems to have abandoned the method of defining a character by

[186] AWD p. 52 (51). Cf. also p. 57 (56): "I daresay it's true, however, that I haven't that 'reality' gift . . . Have I the power of conveying the true reality?"

[187] Cf. AWD p. 54 (53): "I want to foresee this book better than the others. . . ."

[188] Cf. AWD p. 52 (50): "It is I think true, soberly and not artificially for the public, that I shall go on unconcernedly whatever people say", and p. 53 (52): "But I am perfectly serious in saying that nothing budges me from my determination to go on, or alters my pleasure."

[189] AWD p. 63 (62)

[190] Cf. AWD pp. 57 (57), 63 (62), 68 (67).

[191] Cf. AWD p. 57 (56): "My answer is—but I leave that to the *Nation*. . . ." The reference is to "Mr. Bennett and Mrs. Brown", *Nation & Athenaeum* 12/1/1923, first version of "Character and Fiction", a paper read to the Heretics at Cambridge on May 18, 1924, and finally reproduced under the original title "Mr. Bennett and Mrs. Brown" in CDB pp. 90-111 (94-119).

[192] Cf. AWD p. 57 (56): "It's a question though of these characters."

giving texture to its outline, and merely circumscribing the void that contains the mystery of personality. She fills this void with a substance consisting of her character's physical aspects, his thoughts, his motives, instead of dwelling on superficial sense impressions and gestures. But this is only an illusion, and the fact that we are taken in by it betokens the success of the method. In point of fact it is by her surface self, by the impression she makes and that which she receives, that we know Clarissa. Nevertheless, the nature of this peripheral self is no longer the same; instead of being inert, just a bombardment of atomic sensations simply chosen and organized by the author, these impressions are polarized and commented on by other minds. Scrope Purvis the neighbour, Peter Walsh, Richard Dalloway, Hugh Whitbread, Sally Seton, each in turn show us a different aspect, a different face, a different version of the heroine. But in each case the face, the aspect remain peripheral; their interpretation, their inner truth are hypothetical and at the same time belong rather to the person who has imagined them than to the person whom he is supposed to be completing and expressing. The only trait—true, it is an important one—which would entitle us to speak of a compromise, of a partial renunciation of the extreme position adopted in *Jacob's Room*, would be Clarissa's own tentative synthesis, her endeavour to compose her own character out of these manifold images. Her own interior monologue pours substance into that "insubstantised"[193] void which the author had deliberately created in Jacob. However, if by this means of presentation the reader makes contact with the character in a way that is more like what he is used to, he is bound to admit finally that Mrs Dalloway escapes him, that like Jacob she is reduced to a name flung out into the unknown: "Clarissa! Clarissa!" or to the little phrase that contains everything and states nothing precisely: "There she was." And he will have to confess that in fact she exists more in relation to others than as an autonomous reality. In this sense *Mrs Dalloway*, far from being a repudiation of *Jacob's Room*, takes up the problem from where that novel had brought it and, as we shall see, carries it to the point at which the following novel, *To the Lighthouse*, begins.

Before leaving *Mrs Dalloway*, it may perhaps be as well to

---

[193] Cf. AWD p. 57 (56): "I insubstantise wilfully, to some extent, distrusting reality —its cheapness."

clarify as far as possible a question of influences which has already been touched on in its general aspect[194] but which is particularly relevant as regards this novel. It is undeniable that a number of elements in *Mrs Dalloway* suggest comparisons with Joyce's *Ulysses* and Proust's *A la recherche du temps perdu*.

Like *Ulysses*, Mrs Dalloway aims at being a *summa*, and takes place in twenty-four hours in a capital city; the stream of consciousness, or interior monologue, plays an important part in both novels. One might even compare the passing of the Prime Minister's car with the Lord Mayor's procession. But as J. W. Beach, and after him David Daiches, have shown by close analysis,[195] these similarities are very superficial; in structure the two novels are not comparable, that of *Ulysses* being a transposition of the Odyssey and that of *Mrs Dalloway* being autonomous. Virginia Woolf's treatment of the interior monologue, again, is essentially different and far closer to Proust than to Joyce.[196] Particularly Proustian is the passage where Clarissa explores a sudden feeling of sadness and, after eliminating various possible causes, passing from simple facts to impressions, she eventually discovers the cause of her disquiet, guided in her enquiry by an object, a bunch of roses given her by her husband; and this discovery, in itself, satisfies her completely: "Now that she knew what it was, she felt perfectly happy."[197]

Is this sufficient to allow us to conclude, like Bernard Blackstone, that in search of "a form that would convey the movement of things under the surface—the free movement of thought, emotion, insight"[198] Virginia Woolf had gone to school to her contemporaries, Proust, Joyce, Dorothy Richardson? Or to assert even more boldly, like Robert Peel, that "it is tempting to believe that the author had been reading Mr Joyce and had decided that her technique needed bringing up to date"?[199] Without referring

[194] Cf. *supra*, ch. II, p. 29 ff, and esp. pp. 37-43

[195] Cf. J. W. Beach, *The Twentieth Century Novel*, XXXIII 2, pp. 428-32, and cf. David Daiches, *Virginia Woolf*, New Directions, pp. 70-1; Nicholson & Watson, London, pp. 69-70.

[196] James Hafley has particularly stressed the distance between V. W.'s version of the interior monologue and Joyce's. Cf. *The Glass Roof*, p. 73.

[197] Mrs D pp. 133-4 (183)

[198] Bernard Blackstone, *Virginia Woolf*, p. 13.

[199] Robert Peel, "Virginia Woolf", *The Criterion*, London, Oct. 1933, XIII, 50, p. 85. The comment is made about *Jacob's Room*, which Peel considers the least interesting of her books. Leon Edel's statement (*The Psychological Novel*, New York

once again to the pervading influences of the contemporary climate of ideas, I shall try to provide a precise statement of Virginia Woolf's reactions to Joyce and Proust.

That she knew Joyce's work is not in doubt; yet it seems desirable to specify the dates at which she read his books and the reactions these aroused in her. The *Portrait of the Artist as a Young Man* is mentioned only once, at the same time as *Ulysses*, in "Modern Fiction",[200] which appeared on April 10, 1919. The fact that on March 5th of that year Virginia Woolf had noted in her diary that she has got to read "the entire works of Mr James Joyce"[201] entitles one to assume that it was during that spring that she read *Portrait of the Artist* and, during the same period, ran through the first hundred pages of *Ulysses*, as far as the graveyard scene.[202] She had already had an opportunity to glance at the manuscript two years earlier when the Hogarth Press, then in its infancy, had been approached about publishing the novel.[203] But it was not until the summer of 1922 that she really read it, and then "not carefully and only once". [204]

These dates sanction the hypothesis of Joyce's general influence on her writing after 1919, and more specifically the influence of the *Portrait* on *Jacob's Room* and of *Ulysses* on *Mrs Dalloway*. In the latter case, which is more frequently quoted, it is tempting to suppose that her reading of *Ulysses* fertilized the sketch mentioned in the Diary under the titles of *Mrs Dalloway* and *The Prime Minister*,[205] and gave birth to the novel; supported by a few

---

p. 190 ff; London, p. 126 ff): "The influence of James Joyce upon her is much more profound than is generally believed" is only a hypothesis, proved by an arbitrary manipulation of the texts. As early as 1932 F. Delattre (*Le Roman Psychologique de V. W.*, p. 163) had set the tone: "In *Mrs Dalloway*, which came out in 1925, the influence of (Joyce) becomes clearly evident." James Hafley (*The Glass Roof*, 1958, pp. 72-3, seems to have been the first to contest this theory.

[200] Cf. CR I p. 190 (155): the article first appeared in the *TLS* of April 10, 1919, under the title "Modern Novels".

[201] AWD p. 8 (8), March 5, 1919: "But oh, dear, what a lot I've got to read! The entire works of Mr James Joyce, Wyndham Lewis, Ezra Pound . . ."

[202] Cf. CR I pp. 190-201 (155-6): while V. W. was writing her article *Ulysses* was coming out in the *Little Review* and she particularly mentions the graveyard scene.

[203] Cf. V. W. & Lytton Strachey, *Letters*, p. 73 (23/4/1918): "We've been asked to print Mr Joyce's new novel. . . .", and AWD p. 363 (349).

[204] Cf. AWD p. 50 (48) (Sept. 6, 1922): "I finished *Ulysses* and think it a mis-fire. . . . I have not read it carefully; and only once. . . ."

[205] Cf. *supra*, pp. 227, 230

resemblances, the hypothesis is taken to be an obvious fact, repeated by all Virginia Woolf's critics. No doubt she is herself partly responsible for this attitude: does she not associate Joyce's name with her own theory of the novel in "Modern Fiction"? Does she not single him out as the most notable representative of avant-garde novelists, and acclaim *Ulysses* as a masterpiece?[206] Nevertheless, as against this official opinion which, undoubtedly, remains valid and bears witness to her impartiality as reviewer to the *Times Literary Supplement*, it is surely indispensable to quote her more spontaneous, more intimate reactions, as author of *Mrs Dalloway*. The first contact with the manuscript of *Ulysses* seems to have left her cold: "First there is a dog that p's—then a man that farts, and one can be monotonous even on that subject— moreover, I don't believe that this method, which is highly developed, means much more than cutting out the explanations and putting in the thoughts between dashes."[207] There may have been other reasons behind the refusal of the Hogarth Press to assume responsibility for the publication of *Ulysses*. None the less we may safely conclude that for the moment Virginia Woolf seemed scarcely in the mood to profit by Joyce's lessons. True, she was quite conscious that his experiments were in the same direction as her own, and her praise in the 1919 article says so clearly; but it says nothing more. When, shortly after, in January 1920, she tries to define the form which was to be that of *Jacob's Room*, she refers to Joyce in the same breath as Dorothy Richardson, not as bearing out her own intentions, or in the hope of discovering from him what was still unclear in her own ideas,[208] but quite the contrary, to guard against the danger of egocentrism which narrows and restricts the work of her two predecessors. A few months later, in a moment of discouragement, she seems to recognize not indeed affiliation but a parallel between what she is writing and the *Portrait*. But her phrase: "what I'm

---

[206] Cf. CR I pp. 190-1 (155-6)

[207] V. W. & Lytton Strachey, *Letters*, p. 73. Cf. also the passage in the Diary where, on Jan. 15, 1941 (AWD p. 363 (349)), she describes Miss Weaver bringing the MS of *Ulysses*: "The indecent pages looked so incongruous: she was spinsterly, buttoned up. And the pages reeled with indecency."

[208] Cf. AWD p. 23 (22): "What the unity shall be I have yet to discover. . . . I suppose the danger is the damned egotistical self; which ruins Joyce and Richardson to my mind: is one pliant and rich enough to provide a wall for the book from oneself without its becoming, as in Joyce and Richardson, narrowing and restricting?"

doing is probably being better done by Mr Joyce . . ."[209] surely
indicates that she has no intention of making *Jacob's Room* into
another *Portrait*, but on the contrary wants to do as well as, if not
better than, Joyce in her own way. It is a simple admission of the
ineffectiveness, just then, of her method compared to Joyce's,
and it may be considered as showing a firm determination not
to borrow his. If there has been any influence at this date, it takes
the form of opposition rather than of imitation. True, the
similarity of the general principles underlying their works gives
this opposition a wholly different character from that which she
professes towards Bennett, Wells and Galsworthy. The fact
remains that it is difficult to see in the analogies between Virginia
Woolf and James Joyce anything more than common participation in an attitude of mind, a stock of ideas belonging to the
atmosphere in which they both developed.

Her reading of *Ulysses* in 1922 only strengthened Virginia
Woolf in her own position. She repeats, in her Diary, the accus-
ation of egotism and criticizes the book above all for being
"insistent, raw, striking and ultimately nauseating"—in short,
for its lack of art.[210] Just as the first summary condemnation
quoted earlier may have been somewhat exaggerated in order to
amuse Lytton Strachey, this fresh harsh verdict may be partly
due to a desire to contradict T. S. Eliot, who puts *Ulysses* "on a
par with *War and Peace*".[211] But this is merely a question of degree,
and does not alter Virginia Woolf's basic opinion. If she is aware
of the irrational factors which may have led her to take up an
extreme position, if she admits having read the book hastily and
"scamped the virtue of it", even if, reading a review in the *Nation*,
she seems prepared to reconsider her judgment, she none the less
asserts her loyalty to her first impression.[212] In view of such an

[209] AWD p. 28 (27): ". . . I reflected how what I'm doing is probably being better
done by Mr Joyce. Then I began to wonder what it is that I am doing."

[210] AWD p. 47 (46). Cf. *ibid.*, p. 49 (48): "The book is diffuse. It is brackish. It is
pretentious. It is underbred, not only in the obvious sense, but in the literary sense."

[211] Cf. AWD p. 47 (46): "And Tom, great Tom, thinks this on a par with *War and
Peace*! An illiterate, underbred book it seems to me." *Ibid.*, p. 50 (48): ". . . but it is
entirely absurd to compare him with Tolstoy." *Ibid*, p. 50 (49): ". . . I was over
stimulated by Tom's praises."

[212] AWD p. 50 (48): "I have not read it carefully; and only once; and it is very
obscure; so no doubt I have scamped the virtue of it more than is fair. . . . A very
intelligent review of *Ulysses* in the American *Nation* . . . certainly makes it very much
more impressive than I judged. Still I think there is virtue and some lasting truth
in first impressions; so I don't cancel mine."

attitude, it seems unlikely that a few months later she would have dreamed of borrowing from Joyce the slightest positive element to incorporate it in *Mrs Dalloway*.

It is quite evident, from all that has just been said, that the two novelists were temperamentally incompatible and impermeable to one another's influence.[213] It is easy to see what it was about Joyce that Virginia Woolf disliked so violently: his histrionic manner, his arrogance, his negativism, his love of indecency and ratiocination—all features which are reflected in his work and which could not fail to repel the author of *Mrs Dalloway*. If this novel is in any way indebted to *Ulysses* it is not for those features which are usually considered points of resemblance, but rather for the points wherein they differ. Far from borrowing anything whatever from Joyce, Virginia Woolf has striven to avoid what she considers as his weaknesses, faults or mistakes. It may be added furthermore that the parallel nature of their attempts and the similarity between their objectives only enhanced and sharpened the antagonism between their personalities. There exists a family feud between them which in some ways is sharper than a conflict between strangers, such as, for instance, that waged by both of them against the Edwardians.

About the period of *Mrs Dalloway* we find two references to Proust in *A Writer's Diary*. On October 4, 1922, Virginia Woolf finishes *Ulysses* and begins reading Proust.[214] She has just finished *Mrs Dalloway*, the sketch, and is about to start on *The Prime Minister*.[215] We do not know how much she read of *A la Recherche du Temps Perdu*, what her first impressions were, what she thought of it. All that can be asserted is that she resumed, or continued, her reading of the book in April 1923,[216] a few weeks before the publication of *Mrs Dalloway*. Then, either because she was struck by certain similarities, or because the memory of a letter from Jacques Raverat in which the painter, discussing and praising *Mrs Dalloway*, may have mentioned Proust,[217] leads her to make

---

[213] Cf. F. Delattre, *Feux d'Automne*, pp. 236-9. In this passage of the book he was preparing, the author of *Le Roman Psychologique de Virginia Woolf* makes important corrections and qualifications to what he had written in 1932 about the relations between V. W. and J. J. This latest position is akin to my own.

[214] AWD p. 52 (50)

[215] Cf. *supra*, p. 227

[216] Cf. AWD p. 72 (71)

[217] Cf. AWD p. 72 (71). Raverat's death reminds her of the letter he wrote her about *Mrs Dalloway*.

the comparison, she questions the value of her own novel, writing: "I wonder if this time I have achieved something? Well, nothing anyhow compared with Proust, in whom I am embedded now."[218] In this sentence we should read not only humility in front of genius, but also a certain disappointment resulting from the discovery of their kinship.[219] When, in June 1923, Virginia Woolf was trying to analyse her own literary processes, she considered herself in relation to Dostoevsky; she confessed her uncertainty about reality and wondered if she only wrote essays about herself.[220] If Proust had contributed in any way to the Proustian element in what she was writing, would she not have pointed it out in this long and scrupulous analysis? And when she speaks of her discovery—the "tunnelling process"[221]—which after all is only one form of the Proustian technique[222]—she first says that it has taken her a year of groping and then adds: "The fact that I've been so long finding it proves, I think, how false Percy Lubbock's doctrine is[223]—that you can do this sort of thing consciously. One feels about in a state of misery . . . and then one touches the hidden spring."[224] If it were to Proust that she owed this discovery, would she have made it by such devious ways? If Proust played any part, it is less as the author of *A la Recherche du Temps Perdu* than as a nameless influence, inseparably intermingled with all the shadowy influences buried in Virginia Woolf's subconscious. And if in the abstract it is tempting to trace the origin of her method to that of Proust,[225] as he himself describes it with reference to Elstir's painting, such an assertion, which might be valid for *Jacob's Room* as well as for *Kew Gardens* and *The Mark on the Wall*, is contradicted by the evidence of

[218] AWD p. 72 (71)

[219] Cf. *supra*, p. 244, a similar expression about Joyce when she was working on *Jacob's Room*.

[220] Cf. AWD p. 57 (56)

[221] Cf. AWD p. 61 (60) and *supra*, pp. 229, 233-4

[222] One might add: and the technique of Dorothy Richardson (*Pointed Roofs*, 1913; *The Tunnel*, 1919) so that the arguments here suggested against Proust's influence are also valid against D. R.'s influence. On this subject cf. also W. Holtby, *Virginia Woolf*, p. 108.

[223] Percy Lubbock, *The Craft of Fiction*, 1921

[224] AWD p. 61 (60)

[225] As does Dorothy M. Hoare, *Some Studies in the Modern Novel*, Chatto & Windus, London, 1938. Cf. p. 43. The passage of Proust quoted is from *A l'ombre des jeunes filles en fleurs*, *NRF*, vol. 2, p. 123.

chronology and by the later revelations of the Diary.[226]

To return to Virginia Woolf's judgment on Proust, in which every word speaks of a deep-seated kinship, we realise that this is not a matter of influence but of a complex coincidence, consisting on the one hand of the analogy between two temperaments (which was not the case with Joyce) and on the other of the exploitation of a common fund of ideas and theories which were in the air:

The thing about Proust is his combination of the utmost sensibility with the utmost tenacity. He searches out these butterfly shades to the last grain. He is as tough as catgut and as evanescent as a butter-fly's bloom.

Furthermore, her conclusion settles the question of influence with regard not only to Proust but to any author with whom one may be tempted to compare her: "And he will, I suppose, both influence me and make me out of temper with every sentence of my own."[227] This influence which she dreads is, fundamentally, the inevitable temptation of the thing done by one's *alter ego*, the attraction of the way shown by one who happens to have reached the aim pursued by oneself, or one closely similar. But this phrase, more than any other more direct assertion maybe, reveals to what extent Virginia Woolf is an artist of integrity, in short an artist. Instead of accepting the help of a pioneer, she strives with the utmost vigilance not to follow him, in order to be more wholly herself. In point of fact, can one not say that *Mrs Dalloway* is the most Proustian point in her career, just as *Jacob's Room* is its most Joycean point, and that having perceived the connection, which she had neither wished for nor sought, she resolutely turned aside to find a solitary path, her own.

[226] Delattre, in the chapter entitled: "The influence of Marcel Proust and James Joyce", speaks of "concordances", yet asserts unhesitatingly: "In making the characters of Jacob, Clarissa, Mrs Ramsay mere collections of psychological moments, V. W. *simply followed Proust's example*" (p. 149: my italics); and later: "Bergson's 'pure and integral memory', Proust's 'involuntary memory' are identical, for Virginia Woolf who follows them closely, with the soul" (p. 154); and p. 155: "following Proust's example . . ." Without denying the subtlety and justice of the *parallelism* established by Delattre, one of the first critics of Virginia Woolf, one cannot accept the thesis of *influence* and *models* present throughout his analysis; which is to a consider-able extent contradicted by the verdict of "personal originality" with which he con-cludes his chapter.

[227] AWD p. 72 (71)

TO THE LIGHTHOUSE (1927)

One afternoon in Tavistock Square, even before *Mrs Dalloway* had reached the public, Virginia Woolf thought out her fifth novel, *To the Lighthouse*.[228] It came to her, as most frequently happened, quite unexpectedly, with sudden urgency, between essays and sketches[229] whose brevity proved both restful and stimulating after the long labour of *Mrs Dalloway*. On May 14, 1925, we find it mentioned for the first time in *A Writer's Diary*, with its principal characteristics:

This is going to be fairly short; to have father's character done complete in it; and mother's; and St. Ives; and childhood; and all the usual things I try to put in—life, death, etc. But the centre is father's character, sitting in a boat, reciting We perished, each alone, while he crushes a dying mackerel.

Yet this was only a germ which must be allowed to develop, for she adds:

However, I must refrain. I must write a few little stories first and let the *Lighthouse* simmer, adding to it between tea and dinner till it is complete for writing out.[230]

Sketchy as this project is, it includes two points that are worth noting. On the one hand, the importance given to her characters as characters, if not in the traditional sense, at least in the sense implied in *Mrs Dalloway*; which leads one, from the start, to expect similarity of treatment with the book's predecessor.

On the other hand, the theme of loneliness in death: its importance is emphasized by its association with the central figure; resuming one of the obsessions that haunt *Mrs Dalloway*,[231] it promises an analogy of substance which combined with the analogy of form, will make this novel the natural sequel to the one she has just completed.

---

[228] Cf. AWD p. 106 (105): ". . . so I made up the *Lighthouse* one afternoon in the Square here."

[229] Cf. AWD p. 74 (73): Monday April 20 (1925): "I have now at least 6 stories welling up in me. . . ."

[230] AWD pp. 76-7 (75)

[231] Cf. *Mrs Dalloway*, p. 103 (140): "Besides, now that he was quite alone, condemned, deserted, as those who are about to die are alone, there was a luxury in it, an isolation full of sublimity...", and p. 202 (280-1): "Death was defiance. Death was an attempt to communicate, people feeling the impossibility of reaching the centre which, mystically, evaded them; closeness drew apart; rapture faded, one was alone. There was an embrace in death."

A month later, on June 14th, the broad lines of the novel are already laid down, somewhat too precisely perhaps for the author's liking,[232] since she dreads being confined within too narrow a framework which would not allow her latitude for the enrichments and excrescences which constitute the life of writing.[233] Between the superficial, bread-and-butter commitments of criticism consequent on the success of *The Common Reader*, the book takes shape in the depth of her mind,[234] surfacing indiscreetly at times to distract her from her writing.[235] The themes of death, solitude and memory intermingled, the sound of the sea in the background,[236] seem to steep these preliminary meditations in a very special colour, which impregnates the form in anticipation to such a point that Virginia Woolf realises the inadequacy of the word "novel" and seeks another to describe her work: "A new —— by Virginia Woolf. But what? Elegy?"[237] This sense of overflowing the limits of the genre is here explicitly expressed for the first time: it grew constantly more marked until the end of her career.[238] By July, a fortnight before leaving for Rodmell, where she hoped to begin her book and complete it during her two months' stay, the project has ripened[239]; the division into three parts is settled: ". . . father and mother and child in the garden; the death; the sail to the Lighthouse".[240] Among possible enrichments, those she already envisages are, first, a number of compressed character sketches, then the world of childhood.[241] Meanwhile, however, two problems preoccupy her. The first is the fear of lapsing into the sentimentality which the subject, compact of intimate memories, invites irresistibly.[242]

[232] Cf. AWD p. 78 (77): ". . . [I] have thought out, perhaps too clearly, *To the Lighthouse*."

[233] Cf. AWD p. 80 (79): "I think, though, that when I begin it I shall enrich it in all sorts of ways, thicken it; give it branches—roots which I do not perceive now."

[234] Cf. AWD p. 80 (78): ". . . slipping tranquilly off into the deep water of my own thoughts navigating the underworld. . . ."

[235] Cf. AWD p. 80 (78): "But while I try to write, I am making up *To the Lighthouse*."

[236] Cf. AWD p. 80 (78): ". . . the sea is to be heard all through it."

[237] Cf. AWD p. 80 (78)

[238] Cf. *infra*, p. 328

[239] Cf. AWD p. 80 (79): ". . . having a superstitious wish to begin *To the Lighthouse* the first day at Monk's House. I now think I shall finish it in the two months there."

[240] AWD p. 80 (79)

[241] Cf. AWD p. 80 (79): "It might contain all characters boiled down; and childhood. . . ."

[242] Cf. *infra*, note 244.

This apprehension is no doubt a highly personal one, the artist's reaction to the natural inclination of her sensibility—and also the origin of its antidote, her humour. But at the same time it is an echo of *Mrs Dalloway*, the discrimination between sensibility and sentimentality being one of the problems raised by the personality of Clarissa.[243]

For the moment she thinks of resorting to a classic remedy, catharsis; and she considers getting rid of this dangerous propensity by giving vent to it freely in a story.[244] The second problem is a positive one: it concerns "this impersonal thing, which I'm dared to do by my friends, the flight of time and the consequent break of unity in my design".[245] This idea involves not only the second chapter—"seven years passed" at the time, "Time passes" in the final version—but the whole structure of the novel: it was the basic problem corresponding to that which she had solved for *Mrs Dalloway* by her discovery of the "tunnelling process". The interest she takes in it reveals her determination to experiment and improve: "A new problem like that breaks fresh ground in one's mind; prevents the regular ruts."[246]

However, once at Rodmell, an attack of depression[247] not only renders her incapable of any steady work during the two months that were to have been devoted to *To the Lighthouse*, but confuses her ideas, undermines her powers of decision and raises doubts on the essential features of the book.[248] In point of fact, being deprived of her zest and energy, she realizes the danger of facile repetition: either a companion piece to *Mrs Dalloway*, a novel dominated by a single character, or else a "far wider slower book" in which she would "run the risk of falling into the flatness of *N. & D.* [*Night and Day*]".[249]

A partial improvement in her health and a brilliant start

---

[243] Cf. Mrs D p. 41 (53-4): "She owed him words: 'sentimental', 'civilised'; they started up every day of her life as if he guarded her. A book was sentimental. . . . 'Sentimental', perhaps she was to be thinking of the past." And p. 210 (292): was "Clarissa pure-hearted; that was it. Peter would think her sentimental. So she was."

[244] Cf. AWD p. 80 (79): "The word 'sentimental' sticks in my gizzard (I'll write it out of me in a story . . .). But this theme may be sentimental. . . ." The anxiety was to persist until the book was in print, cf. AWD pp. 100 (98), 101 (100), 107 (106).

[245] AWD p. 80 (79)   [246] AWD pp. 80-1 (79)   [247] Cf. *supra*, ch. III, p. 85 ff

[248] Cf. AWD p. 81 (79-80): "I am intolerably sleepy and annulled and so write here. I do want indeed to consider my next book, but I am inclined to wait for a clearer head. The thing is I vacillate between a single and intense character of father; and a far wider slower book. . . ."

[249] Cf. AWD p. 81 (80)

towards the end of August were short-lived.[250] Not until February 1926[251] do we find her writing with ease and fluency, immersed, save for a brief period in the afternoons, in her novel, the whole of which is now present in her mind.[252] By April 29th she has finished the first part and started on the second,[253] her pace and enthusiasm no whit diminished by the abstract and unusual character of this section, which is completed on May 25th.[254] She expects to finish by the end of July. Difficulties arising over the last pages, time wasted on an essay about De Quincey,[255] and perhaps also too fine and too busy a summer,[256] postpone the completion date to September 13th.

Having completed this task with considerably less effort than *Jacob's Room* and *Mrs Dalloway*,[257] she expresses her usual feelings of "relief and disappointment"[258]. However, the revision and retyping—three times over for certain passages—which took from October 25, 1926, to January 14, 1927,[259] left her fairly satisfied. She writes that "it is easily the best of my books: fuller than *J's. R.* [*Jacob's Room*] and less spasmodic, occupied with more interesting things than *Mrs D.* . . . It is freer and subtler, I think."[260] A second reading, shortly before publication,[261] confirms

[250] Cf. AWD p. 82 (80): "I have made a very quick and flourishing attack on *To the Lighthouse*. . . ."

[251] Cf. AWD p. 85 (84), Feb. 23rd: "I am blown like an old flag by my novel." She must actually have started in early January 1926, since, expecting to finish it by the end of July, she allows seven months: cf. AWD p. 89 (88).

[252] Cf. AWD p. 85 (84): "I live entirely in it, and come to the surface rather obscurely . . . Of course it is largely known to me. . . ."

[253] Cf. AWD p. 88 (87): "Yesterday I finished the first part of *To the Lighthouse*, and today began the second."

[254] Cf. AWD p. 89 (88): "I have finished—sketchily I admit—the second part of *To the Lighthouse*—and may, then, have it all written over by the end of July."

[255] Cf. AWD p. 100 (99): "I am exacerbated by the fact that I spent four days last week hammering out de Quincey, which has been lying about since June. . . ."

[256] Cf. AWD p. 99 (97): "For the rest, Charleston, Tilton, *To the Lighthouse*, Vita, expeditions . . . such an August not come my way for years; bicycling; no settled work done, but advantage taken of air for going to the river or over the downs."

[257] Cf. AWD p. 85 (84): ". . . after that battle *Jacob's Room*, that agony—all agony but the end—*Mrs Dalloway*, I am now writing as fast and freely as I have written in the whole of my life. . . ." And p. 89 (88): "Compare this dashing fluency with *Mrs Dalloway* (save the end).

[258] Cf. AWD p. 100 (99)

[259] Cf. AWD p. 103 (102): "Since October 25th I have been revising and retyping (some parts three times over) and no doubt I should work at it again; but I cannot."

[260] AWD p. 102 (101)

[261] Cf. AWD p. 104 (103), Feb. 12, 1927: ". . . I have to read *To the Lighthouse* tomorrow and Monday, straight through in print . . .", and March 21, p. 106 (105):

this judgment, which is scarcely shaken by some friends' criticism[262] or the coolness of a review,[263] amply made up for by the book's success with the public and the enthusiasm of her own circle.[264]

The lighthouse that shines out at night, in the offing from the island where the Ramsays are spending their holidays with a group of friends, is the vanishing point, both material and symbolic, towards which all the lines of *To the Lighthouse* converge. James Ramsay, six years old, cutting out an old catalogue as he sits at the feet of his mother, who is knitting by the window, is going to the Lighthouse tomorrow, thus realising his profoundest dream. He shall go if it's fine, Mrs Ramsay says. But it won't be fine, Mr Ramsay declares. The day draws to a close, a day like many other days, made up of nothing; the children play, Lily Briscoe paints, Carmichael dozes and dreams, Tansley argues with his master Mr Ramsay, Mrs Ramsay knits and James cuts out his catalogue. The dinner gong summons them all to table to enjoy *boeuf en daube*; the children go to bed, the young people go off to the beach, Mr and Mrs Ramsay read. It will rain tomorrow. The evening is as empty and yet as full—and almost as long—as Clarissa Dalloway's day. Whereas the latter took its rhythm from the hours struck by Big Ben, here only the changing light in the garden marks the flow of time, and the unchanging noise of the waves holds the evening motionless. The characters, though their physical closeness creates a multiplicity of contacts, meanwhile withdraw each into his haunted solitude.

Then everybody comes indoors, the lights go out; and that night, that few hours' withdrawal, blends with the darkness and withdrawal of ten years' absence that flow over the empty house in twenty-five pages in which marriages, births and deaths are inscribed in parentheses. This is the second part which, after the personal reign of Duration, asserts the impersonal triumph of Time.

And as morning dawns after these two nights merged into one,

"Dear me, how lovely some parts of the *Lighthouse* are!" She compares her impressions on May 1st, p. 106 (105): "... I was disappointed when I read it through the first time. Later I liked it."

[262] Cf. AWD p. 104 (103): "Roger [Fry] it is clear did not like 'Time Passes.'"

[263] Cf. AWD pp. 106-7 (105): "I write however in the shadow of the damp cloud of *The Times Lit. Sup.* review. ..."

[264] Cf. AWD, May 11 and May 16, 1927, p. 107 (106)

corresponding to the evening that had flowed into them, James starts off for the Lighthouse with his sister Cam and his father, while Lily Briscoe sets up her easel where it must have stood ten years ago and completes her painting, realising her vision at the same moment as James realises his dream. In the intensity of this second moment, Duration has revived and triumphed over Time, triumphed even over death since Mrs Ramsay—who has died, in parentheses, under the reign of Time—haunts these pages with a presence that echoes the material permanence of the lighthouse.

When describing the birth and growth of this novel[265] I pointed out those features in its conception which seemed to relate it to Mrs Dalloway. Even from the resumé given above, it is patent that this relationship has altered between the initial project and the final achievement. That Mrs Ramsay has usurped the place originally assigned to her husband is a point to which I shall return. What interests us here is rather the way in which the central character dominates the book. Behind the account of Mrs Ramsay's day we find no analysis of her feelings, no generalized interpretation of her attitudes; she is not the centre toward which all elements converge, as was the case with Mrs Dalloway, in order to define her and strengthen her autonomous personality in face of the conflicts that divide her and the contradictory impressions that she arouses around her. On the contrary, by a kind of centrifugal process, Mrs Ramsay radiates through the book, impregnating all the other characters.[266] And it is the relations that emanate from her personality, rather than the personality that emanates from these relations, that becomes the focus of interest in the book. This is an essential alteration of the initial project: in fact, Virginia Woolf has chosen the "wider slower book", thus escaping from the ghost of Mrs Dalloway and from the danger of repetition.[267] By this choice she has committed herself to the path that she envisaged at the same time, the attempt "to split up emotions more completely."[268] Freed from the requirements of cohesion involved in the working out of a

[265] Cf. *supra*, p. 249
[266] Cf. Lodwick Hartley, "Of Time and Mrs Woolf", *Sewanee Review*, XLVII, 1939, p. 235: "Change of tack. Instead of showing how many lives influence one character, it deals with the influence of one character on several lives."
[267] Cf. *supra*, p. 250
[268] Cf. AWD p. 81 (80)

single character, she finds herself closer to the "purely psychological" conception of D. H. Lawrence.[269] The newness of this material, and the subtlety and richness in it, have saved it from the other danger she apprehended: the flatness of *Night and Day*.[270]

On the other hand the obsession with solitude, originally associated with death, as in *Mrs Dalloway*,[271] loses its tragic character. Mr Ramsay's "We perished, each alone" retains under its declamatory exaggeration a grievous truth and the pain of defeat. But although the words become symbols, as the author is at pains to point out[272]—perhaps unnecessarily—they do not efface the memory of a different, triumphant solitude, that of Mrs Ramsay, the solitude and silence into which the human being withdraws in order to become "a wedge-shaped core of darkness", piercing to the heart of things in peace and eternity.[273] This meditation of Mrs Ramsay's, when she is alone for a moment, the only time in the whole evening, seems to be the happiest peak to which Virginia Woolf's thought ever attained. It corresponds on the plane of sensibility and life to Lily Briscoe's vision,[274] which completes it on the plane of rational and aesthetic thought. This enables one to say that *To the Lighthouse*, deriving from *Mrs Dalloway*, not only continues it but replies to the questions it asked. Septimus died in solitude, and one guessed that Clarissa's sense of communion might be a victory over that solitude and that death—but one could only guess it. Clarissa answered the riddle that she asked by her mere presence, which was unexplained except by the words "she was". Mrs Ramsay is the

[269] Cf. D. H. Lawrence, Letter to Edward Garnett, June 5, 1914. Quoted by A. Huxley in *Stories, Essays and Poems*, Dent, London 1938, pp. 342: ". . . You must not look in my novel for the old stable *ego* of the character. There is another *ego*, according to whose action the individual is unrecognisable, and passes through, as it were, allotropic states which it needs a deeper sense than any we've been used to exercise, to discover are states of the same single radically unchanged element (Like as diamond and coal are the same pure single element of carbon)."

[270] Cf. *supra*, p. 250, note 249

[271] Cf. *supra*, p. 248

[272] Cf. To the L pp. 227-8 (219): ". . . like everything else this strange morning the words became symbols, wrote themselves all over the grey-green walls."

[273] Cf. To the L ch. I, section II, pp. 99-104 (95-100), particularly p. 99 (95): "To be silent; to be alone. All the being and the doing, expansive, glittering, vocal, evaporated; and one shrunk, with a sense of solemnity, to being oneself, a wedge-shaped core of darkness, something invisible to others."

[274] Cf. To the L pp. 244-5 (235-6), 249 (240), 278-9 (269-70), 296-7 (288), 309-10 (299-300)

explicit expression of such a presence. And at the same time the survival of that presence beyond death, the dramatic character of which is relegated to the domain of literature that obtrudes in Mr Ramsay's declamations, abolishes solitude and brings about the communion that Clarissa had only suggested. Without denying those two ineluctable truths, solitude and death, *To the Lighthouse* makes of them the two fundamental experiences through which the human being, aspiring towards a single truth, a single light, reaches these and fulfils himself.

This progress from one book to the next is the result neither of literary artifice nor of abstract speculation. We have seen that Virginia Woolf had really begun her novel in January 1926,[275] and it is on February 27th of that year that she writes in her diary the important analysis of her "moments of vision".[276] The essential thing that lies behind the appearances and the superficial individualities of Lily Briscoe and Mrs Ramsay is derived not from Julia Stephen or the painter Vanessa,[277] but from Virginia Woolf herself. Does this mean that this "elegiac" book[278] which inevitably drew its substance from memories—even at the risk of becoming "sentimental"—slips into that "self-centred dream" to which, at this period, the author was accused of succumbing?[279] The boundary between one's present self and one's past is so imprecise that they inevitably merge into one another. Moreover, these two complementary realities are not mutually exclusive; the first envelops and conceals the second. Virginia Woolf had to pass through the present moment in order to recover time past, without betraying either aspect of reality in her painting of it. Her sister's opinion is reliable evidence:

Nessa enthusiastic—a sublime, almost upsetting spectacle. She says it is an amazing portrait of mother; a supreme portrait painter; has lived in it; found the rising of the dead almost painful.[280]

Thus, in addition to whatever else it has become, the novel actually is that evocation of the past that it sought to be. The

[275] Cf. *supra*, p. 251
[276] Cf. *supra*, ch. III, pp. 111-12
[277] Leonard Woolf has suggested that the analysis of the painter's processes in Lily Briscoe is based on Vanessa Stephen, who married Clive Bell.
[278] Cf. *supra*, p. 249
[279] Cf. *supra*, ch. III, p. 65, and AWD pp. 120-1 (118-9)
[280] AWD p. 107 (106)

close involvement of the author's whole being with that past is further confirmed by the liberating function ascribed by Virginia Woolf to her book, when on the ninety-sixth anniversary of her father's birth she writes:

I used to think of him and mother daily: but writing the *Lighthouse* laid them in my mind.[281]

The Ambroses,[282] the Hilberrys,[283] Mrs Dalloway were too sketchy, too much mingled with foreign elements to free her from the burden of all that she inherited from father and mother; only the completion of their portraits could exhaust both the feeling that clung to them and the literary temptation that gave a parasitical life to their memories.

It remains to be asked why the respective positions of Mr and Mrs Ramsay have been inverted. *A Writer's Diary* says nothing about this alteration, which seems significant enough to justify some comment, even if the reasons adduced remain mere hypotheses.

Mr Ramsay, it must be admitted, is not a sympathetic character; his originality, his anxiety and loneliness, his need for admiration and sympathy do not suffice to redeem his intransigent positivism, his selfishness and brusquerie. No doubt it is of the unflattering side of her portrait that Virginia Woolf is thinking when she writes: "People will say I am irreverent. . . ."[284] The picture of Leslie Stephen in her *Times* article of 1932[285] is certainly recognizable as Mr Ramsay, but in a gentler and more lovable form. If we compare these two portraits with the one that emerges from Annan's book[286] we realize that both are true. Their difference is that which separates an intimate relationship from a more impersonal acquaintance. Mr Ramsay is the father figure which had to be exorcised; it was his despotism in all its forms, over mind and heart, that had to be overthrown. And no doubt the domination he exercised over his entourage gave rise to the initial idea that he should dominate the book. But the

[281] Cf. *supra*, ch. III, p. 62, and AWD p. 138 (135)
[282] In *The Voyage Out*.
[283] In *Night and Day*.
[284] AWD p. 106 (105)
[285] "Leslie Stephen", published in *The Captain's Death Bed*, pp. 67-71 (69-75)
[286] Noel Annan, *Leslie Stephen*, Macgibbon & Kee, London, 1951, and Harvard University Press, 1952.

element of antagonism between the author and her protagonist
eclipsed their affinities, and would have condemned the book
to a certain externality, acceptable perhaps for the short, swift
book originally planned, but incompatible with the longer, slower
book eventually chosen.

Of Virginia Woolf's relations with her mother we know little.
Yet from the violence of the shock which the 13-year-old girl felt
at her loss[287] we may conclude that between mother and daughter
there were certain deep affinities which became fixed and ideal-
ized at the same time through this premature death. *To the
Lighthouse*, being an elegy, could only have as its central figure
a being wholly and unreservedly loved. Moreover, if Leslie
Stephen could represent that rational quest of truth and that
feeling of solitude which the author sought to express, only Julia
Stephen could represent that unfailing intuition, that sensibility,
that gift of sympathy which, for Virginia Woolf, are the supreme
human qualities, those which give a person that intensely radiant
power that illuminates our darkness like a lighthouse beam.
Finally, in this novel which is above all an analysis of the relations
that connect and mingle human beings beneath the words and
gestures whose value as communication is so inadequate, a
medium was needed who could scarcely be imagined save as a
woman endowed with "some secret sense, fine as air".[288] No doubt
Virginia Woolf would be the first to protest against the artificial
element in the traditional opposition between men's and women's
natures. Yet she usually respects their broad lines, and in *To the
Lighthouse* she stresses the opposition and exploits it.[289] And one
can even see in this exploitation a certain bias which reflects
tendencies that were strongly marked in her: on the one hand,
her feminism, in the broad sense of the word, which might be
defined as a defiant belief in woman's superiority in the quest for
truth and the almost occult knowledge of life: on the other hand,
a kind of nostalgic yearning for a relation between women,
opposed to love between man and woman. I have tried to define,
with all the prudence necessitated by the lack of precise docu-

[287] It was following the death of her mother that V. W. had her first nervous
breakdown and tried to commit suicide. Cf. Rantavaara, *V. W. and Bloomsbury*, 1953,
p. 106.
[288] To the L p. 303 (294)
[289] Cf. Mary Electa Kelsey, "V. W. and the She-condition", *Sewanee Review*,
Oct.-Dec. 1931, esp. pp. 433 and 442.

ments, Virginia Woolf's conception of love[290]; Ruth Gruber[291] has pointed out the interest she showed in Lesbianism, as witness the relations between Sally Seton and Clarissa Dalloway, Elizabeth and Miss Kilman, and the ambiguity of *Orlando*. While writing *Mrs Dalloway*, she drops a hint in her diary:

Yesterday I had tea in Mary's room and saw the red lighted tugs go past and heard the swish of the river Mary: in black with lotus leaves round her neck. If one could be friendly with women, what a pleasure —the relationship so secret and private compared with relations with men. Why not write about it? Truthfully?[292]

Without seeking to extract from this passage more than it contains, one cannot help being aware of the emotional burden it betrays and the uneasiness that emanates from it. No doubt it is merely something instantaneous, as fleeting as Sally's kiss on Clarissa's lips or Lily Briscoe's impulse of affection for Mrs Ramsay. No doubt, these lines only express aspiration and longing, but at the same time they admit concealment and tabu. In the summer of 1926, when *To the Lighthouse* was nearing completion, Virginia Woolf saw a great deal of Victoria Sackville-West,[293] as she did again the following summer, when the idea of *Orlando* occurred to her.[294] In January 1927 she went to Knole.[295] And it was in September 1928, after the publication of *Orlando*, that the two friends went to France together, by themselves.[296] The biographical enigma posed by these facts, these allusions, these literary transpositions can only be answered—apart from the *Orlando* frolic which has already been referred to[297]—by Mrs Ramsay's reflection: "Love had a thousand shapes."[298] And this

---

[290] Cf. *supra*, ch. III, pp. 66-70

[291] Ruth Gruber, *V. W. A Study*, (Kolner Anglist Arbeiten XXIV, Leipzig, Tauchnitz, 1935, pp. 100). Quoted by Rantavaara, p. 148.

[292] AWD pp. 68-9 (67)

[293] Cf. AWD p. 99 (97) (quoted *supra*, p. 251, note 256)

[294] Cf. AWD pp. 110 (108), 113-14 (112)

[295] Cf. AWD p. 103 (102), Jan. 23, 1927

[296] Cf. V. Sackville-West in *Horizon*, May 1941, Vol. III, no. 17, pp. 318-24, and AWD p. 133 (131): "I went to Burgundy with Vita ... on 26th September when I went to France."

[297] Cf. *supra*, ch. III, p. 79.

[298] To the L, p. 295 (286). The phrase occurs in Lily Briscoe's interior monologue and is both personal and reminiscent of Mrs Ramsay's words; it echoes Mrs Ramsay's thought, p. 162 (157) "... one of those unclassified affections of which there are so many."

assertion, while it answers our enquiry, however inadequately, also replies to the doubt that flashed through Rachel twenty years earlier, when she thought about her feeling for Helen Ambrose, about Richard Dalloway's kiss, or about any other man she might meet later on: "...she could not possibly want only one human being."[299] *Orlando* and *The Waves*, later, assert the same conviction, which moreover is complementary to those intermittences of the heart to which Virginia Woolf's psychology allotted so important a place.

The analysis of the married relation which Blackstone, for instance, tends to consider the chief focus of interest in *To the Lighthouse*,[300] is in fact only one particular case of the instability and complexity of our feelings. The paragraph in her Diary on "The married relation",[301] written in the summer of 1926, suggests that by then, after fourteen years of marriage, Virginia Woolf had decided to take her bearings. However, if certain elements of personal experience have unquestionably been transposed into the novel, this has a significance that goes far beyond what it can tell us about the Ramsays or the Rayleys, and it is at least as plausible to take the Diary paragraph as a hybrid comment, scribbled in the margin of the book and of life, rather than as the sign of a dominant preoccupation underlying the book.

Since I propose to study the problem of Time[302] and the question of structure[303] elsewhere, I shall merely allude to the importance of these two points, which I have tried to bring out in my summary of *To the Lighthouse*. I shall only mention that the change of tone, of style, of movement in the second part caused the author some anxiety.[304] Perhaps Roger Fry's disapproval[305] was partly responsible; unless it was her awareness of the audacity represented by this technical process and the inevitable hostility it would arouse among critics and readers. It is not surprising to find Arnold Bennett condemning this second part.[306] There is no doubt that the virtuosity of these pages

---

[299] Cf. VO p. 370 (302)

[300] Cf. Bernard Blackstone, *V. W.* pp. 100 and 113

[301] Cf. *supra*, ch. III, p. 70

[302] Cf. *infra*, ch. VI, section 3

[303] Cf. *infra*, ch. VI, section 5

[304] Cf. AWD p. 107 (105): "I am anxious about 'Time Passes'. "

[305] Cf. AWD p. 104 (103): "Roger it is clear did not like 'Time Passes'."

[306] Cf. A. Bennett in *The Evening Standard*, June 23, 1927. "... The middle part does not succeed. It is a short cut, but a short cut that does not get you anywhere. ..."

emphasizes their strangeness. Yet they are neither irrelevant ornament nor a purely technical device. Their aim is precisely to set in the very centre of the book, in a significant fashion, the essential, ambiguous protagonist: Time-Duration. Whereas under the aspect of Duration it plays its role in the two other sections, discreetly merged into the consciousness of the *dramatis personae*, in this second part, under the aspect of Time, it achieves its inhuman task as cosmic agent.

No doubt Virginia Woolf implicitly admits a heterogeneity, the dangers of which she did not minimize: "The lyric portions of *To the Lighthouse* are collected in the 10-year lapse and don't interfere with the text so much as usual." But declaring in the next sentence that the book fetched its circle pretty completely this time,[307] she asserts thereby that its heterogeneity, far from interrupting the line of the work, is an integral part of it. Without contesting that the dual nature of the tone is evidence of a duality in the author's personality, what has been called (by R. Las Vergnas) her androgynousness, I should like to suggest that *To the Lighthouse*, by its structure, its movement, as also by its essential subject, attempts to resolve that duality, and that *The Waves* only develops and carries to the limits of their potential the resources of style and composition which are exploited here.[308]

Such as it is, retaining enough traditional elements and characters and a semblance of a plot to satisfy the common reader, yet brimming with inward life and with a lyricism which give it a density characteristic of Virginia Woolf, *To the Lighthouse*, by the synthesis which it achieves and the balance it maintains between contradictory tendencies, won the favour of the reading public[309] and at the same time, if it did not gain unanimous approval from the critics, was at least granted indulgence by some who unhesitatingly condemn her other novels.[310]

I doubt the very difficult business of conveying the idea of the passage of a very considerable amount of time can be completed by means of a device . . . (it) has to be conveyed gradually without any direct insistence—in the manner of life itself."

[307] AWD p. 100 (98)

[308] Cf. *infra*, ch. V, pp. 282-302

[309] In 1951, 11 editions of To the L as against 7 of Mrs D and JR and 6 of VO, N & D and The W.

[310] Cf. Conrad Aiken, "The Novel as a Work of Art", *Dial*, July 1927; Orlo Williams, "*To the Lighthouse*", *The Monthly Criterion*, July 1927, vol. VI, 1, p. 28; D. M. Hoare, *Some Studies in the Modern Novel*, 1933, p. 61; Robert Peel, "Virginia

SYNTHESIS AND FICTION

ORLANDO (1928)

When attempting to reconstruct the genesis of a work, taking *The Waves* for my example, I showed how *Orlando* had interrupted the stream of inspiration which was to lead to *The Waves* and had, in some sort, taken possession of the author to its own advantage and at the expense of this other book, which had been envisaged before it, even before the completion of *To the Lighthouse*.[311] Without dwelling on the conflict of tendencies displayed by this intrusion, it is none the less indispensable, for a just appreciation of a book which has most frequently been taken either too seriously or too lightly,[312] to look back at various passages in the Diary which render possible a clear definition of its intentions and its significance.

On December 20, 1927, two and a half months after she has started on *Orlando*, the first half of which has already been drafted, Virginia Woolf writes in the Diary:

> How extraordinarily unwilled by me but potent in its own right, by the way, *Orlando* was! as if it shoved everything aside to come into existence. Yet I see looking back just now to March that it is almost exactly in spirit, though not in actual facts, the book I planned then as an escapade; the spirit to be satiric, the structure wild. Precisely.[313]

One must note in this passage the three characteristics of *Orlando* (mentioned moreover in various terms in almost every paragraph of the Diary that refers to it) which yield the whole secret of that work, disconcerting enough in other respects and full of pitfalls for an unwary reader. First and foremost, it is a book which was "unwilled"; it willed itself. Although the element of artifice and tension in Virginia Woolf's novels has often been exaggerated or misinterpreted, it is difficult to deny it entirely. *Orlando*, on the contrary, is essentially spontaneous. But here again one must not confound spontaneity with externality, as the

---

Woolf", *The Criterion*, Oct. 1933, vol. XIII, 50, p. 91; Martin Turnell, "Virginia Woolf", *Horizon*, VI, July 1942, pp. 53-4. Among critics generally favourable to V. W., E. M. Forster (*Virginia Woolf*, The Rede Lecture, Cambridge Univ. Press, 1941, p. 14), David Daiches (*Virginia Woolf*, New Directions, 1942, pp. 95-6; Nicholson & Watson, London, pp. 92) and I. Rantavaara (*Virginia Woolf and Bloomsbury*, Helsinki, 1953, p. 116) assert their preference for *To the Lighthouse*.

[311] Cf. *supra*, ch. III, p. 76 ff

[312] Irma Rantavaara, *op. cit.*, pp. 132-6, a good résumé of the principal interpretations offered by various critics.

[313] AWD p. 120 (118)

author herself frequently invites us to do.[314] The externality is entirely superficial, it lies in the manner not in the matter; it is a refusal to go deep, which is not the same thing as a rejection of depth. *Orlando* is spontaneous, in so far as it imposed itself upon her, its necessity lay within itself, that is to say it was not the fruit of a deliberate purpose or an idea, but an inevitable gesture, an urgent need of the whole being.[315]

One might refer here to that "summa" which Virginia Woolf, like all great artists, constantly dreamed of writing, from *Mrs Dalloway* to *Between the Acts*.[316]

Yet it is not true to say that the author has poured all her experience into it, but rather that all her experience underlies it and sometimes comes to the surface. We can see here a reversal of the creative process which demands a reversal of the method of interpretation. Instead of seeking in this work the final stage of a train of thought, the result of a working out process, which should be if not a conclusion at least the ultimate term of a pursuit, we should see in it the immediate data, in their simplest form, the fund of ideas, interests and preoccupations which constitute the manifold starting-points for those explorations in depth, her other novels.

As a joke Virginia Woolf labelled *Orlando* a "biography".[317] Among those composite titles with which she was always trying to define her books, when she felt them overflowing the framework of the novel, perhaps the one that best suits *Orlando* is, as we shall see, "Essay-novel".[318] For the time being we might suggest "Conversation piece" or "In confidence". Indeed, through that kind of spontaneity I have defined, these three hundred pages are one long rambling discussion in which the author confides in us, now inspired by some chance remark, now

---

[314] "I am writing *Orlando* half in a mock style very clear and plain . . .", AWD p. 117 (115). " . . . I like these plain sentences; and the externality of it for a change", AWD p. 118 (116). ". . . too frivolous for a serious book", AWD p. 124 (122). "People say this [O] was so spontaneous, so natural. . . . But those qualities were largely the result of ignoring the others. They came of writing exteriorly; and if I dig, must I not lose them?", AWD p. 139 (136).

[315] Cf. *supra*, ch. III p. 80, another assertion of this need.

[316] Cf. *supra*, ch. V p. 229

[317] Cf AWD p. 133 (130): ". . . the fun of calling it a biography."

[318] Cf. *infra*, p. 271. "Essay-novel" is moreover applied by V. W. to *The Years*, which book she compares to *Orlando*: "Everything is running of its own accord into the stream, as with *Orlando*", AWD p. 189 (184).

in a long development where fanciful wit does not preclude seriousness, now with an exaggeration which is sometimes playful, sometimes provocative, sometimes ironical, sometimes a hypothesis and sometimes a disguise for sincerity, and sometimes all these together. In this respect *Orlando* offers a wealth of revelations—and it is also extremely difficult and risky to make use of in this respect. Its tone requires a constantly alert attention. After all it is only a book, but we have to re-create in it the author's total presence: the inflexion of the voice, the liveliness of the eyes, and even the gestures and attitude of the whole body. We need to confirm every sentence, almost every word, with some sign that would guarantee its "truth". A book can only be read that way—if "reading" is the right word—if one is intimately acquainted with its author. And even considering that Leonard Woolf himself took *Orlando* "more seriously than [she] had expected"[319]—should one add, than she took it herself?—I would go so far as to say that only the person to whom it was dedicated, for whom, actually, it was written—Vita Sackville-West—can solve the riddle of it. She was its point of departure[320]: in her alone it reaches its destination. For her it has its meaning; for us it offers only signs. Let us admit straight away that this is certainly a weakness, the chief weakness of *Orlando*. If its author, for all her usual lucidity, never discovered this clearly, she none the less felt and expressed it indirectly. In the first place, it is "a writer's holiday"[321]—a release for the artist who, essentially, speaks to the general public—and for this Virginia Woolf felt some reluctance before she finally yielded to it. Then the terms "farce", "joke" recur constantly in her descriptions of the book.[322] But while farces and jokes are never purely such, and this is certainly the case with *Orlando*, they are always to some extent a closed book to the uninitiated.

However, although this deep seated hermetic quality makes any systematic interpretation dubious and therefore invalid, the novel has characteristics which ensure for it an honourable, if a rather special, place among the author's works. These are the

[319] AWD p. 128 (125)

[320] Cf. AWD p. 114 (112): "Vita should be Orlando, a young nobleman" and AWD p. 117 (115): "It is based on Vita, Violet Trefusis, Lord Lascelles, Knole etc."

[321] Cf. *supra*, ch. III, pp. 79, 80

[322] Cf. AWD pp. 117 (115), 124 (122), 126 (124), 128 (125)

two aspects stressed in the passage quoted above: the spirit of satire, whose verve, combined with the lively pace of the story and the brio of the fantasy, carries the reader along through the paths of history and literature and the mazes of the human soul, all so entangled and at the same time so vigorously drawn that he is continually losing his way and then finding it again, without really being sure of anything. These two traits, satire and fantasy, fun and freedom, comprise the surface but also the whole bearing of the book; they confer on it that vigour and that somewhat turbulent charm that distinguish it from the other novels and yet cannot be dismissed as mere accident, artifice or caprice. Dense and polyvalent beneath the clarity and apparent lightness of its style, *Orlando* is, both in detail and taken as a whole, more ambiguous and elusive than its hero-heroine. Its complexity can best be suggested by applying to it those lines with which Virginia Woolf tries to prepare a reader for the mysteries of another fantasy which, beneath obvious dissimilarities, is related to her own by manifold and close links:

In reading *The Faery Queen* the first thing, we said, was that the mind has different layers. It brings one into play and then another. The desire of the eye, the desire of the body, desires for rhythm, movement, the desire for adventure—each is gratified. And this gratification depends upon the poet's own mobility. He is alive in all his parts. He scarcely seems to prefer one to another.[323]

From what we have just said, it is easy to imagine that, in this supposed "Defoe narrative", the essentially picaresque story which the author pretends—without deceiving herself or anyone else—to tell without allowing herself to be distracted from her purpose, is only a pretext and an occasion. And it would be even more pointless to summarize it than in the case of the other novels. I shall only do so in order to emphasize that extravagance which is the deliberately chosen aspect of the book, and to specify the elements of that baroque edifice which I intend to discuss.

Orlando, born of a noble and illustrious family about 1570, is 16 years old on the first page; in his dress, his actions, his feelings and thoughts he represents the perfect type of those "strange

[323] *The Moment*, p. 27 (27). She was reading *The Faery Queen* in January 1935; cf. AWD p. 238 (230).

Elizabethans" who yet "had a face like ours".[324] His biographer follows him up to his thirty-sixth year, that is to say until 1928. Thus crudely reported, the fact that the centuries sit as lightly on the hero as the decades may cause some surprise. But when we follow him from the court of Elizabeth to that of James I, from the banks of the Thames to the shores of the Bosphorus, from a love affair with Sasha, the passionate Muscovite lady, to marriage with the romantic adventurer and, eventually, highly modern aviator, Marmaduke Bonthrop Shelmerdine—for in the mean-time Orlando has changed sex—we realise, in fact, that time has impaired neither his youth nor his beauty nor his zest for life. All that one can say is that this hero-heroine takes part in the life of each century with an admirable flexibility and openminded-ness: that is no doubt the secret of his perpetual youth; violent and passionate in the Elizabethan atmosphere, under James I he blossoms forth at court and then, in disgrace, retires to his estate to brood like Hamlet or Sir Thomas Browne; in Turkey he is more Turkish than the Turks; and when he, or rather she returns to the London of Addison, Dryden and Pope, the interest she takes in these figures is fully equal to that taken by other people of her class. Just as the young man Orlando frequented the court when this was the only place where life seemed worth living, so the young woman Orlando frequents salons under Queen Anne, still in pursuit of the same treasure—life—which at that time is only to be found there. Under Victoria, how can she live? By putting on a large number of petticoats and, eventually, getting married: let us add, "by loving nature, and being no satirist, cynic or psychologist".[325] Luckily this is only a brief interlude: the twentieth century arrives and Orlando collects her thoughts before venturing at last into the maelstrom of trains, cars, shops and society lunches; and she asserts her unity and her continuity in a last symbolic gesture by publishing *The Oak Tree*, a poem on which she has been working since her Elizabethan adolescence.

It is pointless to dwell on the fantastic character of the hero

---

[324] Cf. CR II p. 23 (16): "The Strange Elizabethans."

[325] Cf. O, p. 329 (266): "She had just managed, by some dexterous deference to the spirit of the age, by putting on a ring and finding a man on a moor, by loving nature and being no satirist, cynic, or psychologist . . . to pass its examination successfully."

and the story. It can only disconcert us if we forget that we have here simultaneously a biography, a narrative à la Defoe, contemporary memoirs, a satire, and finally, a fantasy or joke in which the author's verve, imagination and humour are given free rein without any further aim than the fun of writing. Thus *Orlando* cannot be confined within any of the genres in which it participates, and whatever certain critics may say[326] we have to recognize it as a novel of the same type, if not in the same vein, as the rest of Virginia Woolf's novels. Like them, it rejects literary conventions, and like them it seeks, with apparent casualness but in all sincerity, to grasp the essence of a fluid and complex reality which our habits of speech, confused with our habits of thought, have unduly solidified and simplified. And this is because this search is Virginia Woolf's sole problem and because even in fun, even when playing truant, she cannot give it up. Indeed, *Orlando* provides the soundest possible argument against those who accuse Virginia Woolf of artificiality and accuse her of wearing herself out in Byzantine refinements of form and technique at the expense of the real and living content of her work. Even when she casts off all concern for form and technique, indeed when she makes fun of them in herself as in others, we see that her object remains the same, and the fundamental subject of her book remains the same; which allows one to assert that both of these represent the essence of her being, the direction of her entire inner life, and not simply the superficial curiosity of a sterile intellectual.

Orlando is a biography in so far as the hero's life is consubstantial with history; in other ways it is no more of one than any novel in which a historical character plays a leading part. The Preface leaves no doubt about the element of parody in the work, and moreover the so-called biographer loses no opportunity of pointing out the obstacles that frustrate her scholarship and the pitfalls that ensnare her art. Indeed, she takes a mischievous delight in displaying and exploiting the weaknesses of that literary genre which, being neither art nor science, is only a technique, as she explains more seriously elsewhere.[327] The destruction of some essential documents, the dubious character of certain others, the respect for propriety, and even more far-

[326] Winifred Holtby and Irène Simon.
[327] Cf. "The Art of Biography", in DM pp. 119-26 (187-97)

fetched reasons—such as the simple fact that Orlando starts to think—are constantly referred to by the author as excuses for her lacunae, her flights of fancy, her digressions, and even the blank spaces which, in imitation of Sterne, she leaves us free to fill as we choose. And in fact *Orlando* reminds one of *Tristram Shandy* rather than of *Robinson Crusoe* or *Moll Flanders*. It is not a story any more than a biography. That "on with the story" with which Virginia Woolf summed up the brisk movement of *Moll Flanders*[328] recurs constantly, either in these very terms or disguised in other forms; but far from preventing interruptions, it merely closes them. If certain episodes, particularly at the beginning when her enthusiasm was overflowing and her pen racing along,[329] flow with the same swift rhythm as the action described, the movement in general comes from elsewhere, being less a consequence of the adventure than a characteristic of the hero. In fact, it is not so much the story as the protagonist that reminds us of Defoe, and one might say of Orlando what Virginia Woolf said of Moll Flanders: ". . . life delights her, and a heroine who lives has us all in tow."[330]

Another project of the author's was to write the memoirs of her contemporaries. The Diary even specifies certain names; the keys are there, but are we therefore entitled to play the parlour game they suggest? The sight of the manifold changes undergone by the principal character is discouraging. Did the author even follow up her original intention? Before starting the book she talks about Lytton (Strachey), Roger (Fry), Duncan (Grant), Clive (Bell), Adrian (Stephen)[331]; and since none of these lives is "related", as promised in the same passage, one may assume that this aspect was discarded. A fortnight after the book was begun—that is to say, at most, when she was finishing the first chapter—Virginia Woolf notes that "it is based on Vita, Violet Trefusis, Lord Lascelles, Knole etc."[332]

"Based on" is already vaguer than the biographical narratives announced a month previously. The fact that subsequently we

[328] Cf. Defoe, in CR I p. 125 (92); written in 1919.
[329] Cf. AWD p. 117 (116): "I write so quick I can't get it typed before lunch" (Nov. 20, 1927), but contrast: ". . . I miss the fun, which was so tremendously lively all October, November and December" (AWD p. 123 (121), Feb. 11, 1928).
[330] CR I p. 126 (93)
[331] AWD p. 114 (112): "Their lives should be related."
[332] AWD p. 117 (115)

do not read of any names in connection with her remarks about Orlando, may be due to judicious cutting by Leonard Woolf. I believe, however, that it can be explained simply by a change of orientation in the book. The fantasy which, partly to make fun of History, had plunged the author's friend into remote historic distances, was now caught up in the trammels of its own artifice; History had taken its revenge by asserting its authority, and Nick Greene and Pope had ousted from the stage the friends whom Virginia Woolf had thought of introducing on to it. Nick Greene, indeed, appears as a typically twentieth-century figure, and "this gentleman, so neat, so portly, so prosperous",[333] with such definite ideas about literature, is surely some influential critic from the author's circle. But even admitting that this may be so, this portrait which may have amused the Woolfs and their friends by reference to its original has enough comic virtue as an un-named type to render unnecessary any curiosity about the model that inspired it. Even if he owes to that model his way of pro-nouncing "Glory"—Glawr—and other characteristics, his fic-tional identity with the Nick Greene of the second chapter is far more important that his actual status. The hunt for keys may have a historic interest and may sometimes shed light on the process of literary creation; in the case of *Orlando* it is doubtful whether it presents either advantage, and even whether the data for the sport exist. Later, when studying *Orlando* as a fantasy, I shall examine the relations between reality and the imaginary world, of which the problem of keys, rightly understood, is only one particular aspect. For the moment I must conclude that, starting from the project of writing the memoirs of her contem-poraries, Virginia Woolf quickly dropped this scheme in favour of what one might sub-title "the memory of contemporaries". And the pun reveals the whole distance between a subject which, all things considered, was alien to the author, since memoirs belong to the order of facts and actions,[334] and an essentially Woolfian subject. But before approaching the content of the

[333] ". . . this gentleman, so neat, so portly, so prosperous, with a cane in his hand and a flower in his button hole, with a pink, plump face, and combed white mous-taches . . .", O p. 248 (276). Stephen Spender declares (*World within World*, p. 152, that Nick Greene's ingratitude towards his host reflects that of a poet who repaid the Nicolsons' hospitality with a satire against them.

[334] Cf. *supra*, ch. IV, pp. 150, 159, on the reasons for, and the nature of, V. W.'s interest in Memoirs.

book, let us finish examining the form under which it is disguised.

Satire and fantasy, inseparable, since they are derived from one another, are the dominant features of *Orlando*. They define the humour which gave rise and constant sustenance to this "half laughing, half serious"[335] work. In that passage written in March 1927, to which the author refers, half-way through her task, to observe the identity of her achievement with her conception, we read: "Satire is to be the main note—satire and wildness. . . . My own lyric vein is to be satirised. Everything mocked."[336] We have already seen that the story-teller's art and that of the biographer are imitated only to be parodied. Yet considering that Virginia Woolf believes neither in the continuity of a story,[337] nor in the unity of a personality circumscribed in space and time, a postulate essential to the biographer, there is nothing surprising about her mockery. But she is too lucid and too intelligent to stop short at irony; she dares to be humorous. Her habitual state of tension may make us forget her capacity for this amused detachment; yet all her favourite heroines, from Mrs Ambrose to Mrs Ramsay, have had this gift, relieving their essential seriousness. If Lord Orlando is somewhat lacking in it—no doubt because it is rarely a masculine virtue—Orlando has enough of it to reduce her impulses of enthusiasm and passion to their right proportions. But it is above all the story-teller's humour that compels our attention. It is shown throughout in the mischievous glance that deflates fine sentiments, diminishes grand gestures, trips up a flight of eloquence with an aside, breaks the lyrical flow of a description with an incongruous detail or simply a dissonant word. At every line the writer makes fun of writing, she parodies herself page after page, indicts her own habits—her use of symbols, her exaggerated concern with detail and her excess of imagination, her fondness for interior analysis and her love of words. Even traits which are characteristic of her as a person rather than as a writer are not spared: her changing moods, her alternate fits of self-confidence, enthusiasm and discouragement,[338] the way she oscillates between love of society and love of solitude, between zest for life and despair, between a taste for

[335] Cf. AWD p. 120 (118)
[336] AWD p. 105 (104)
[337] Cf. *supra*, ch. III, p. 76
[338] Cf. particularly O p. 77

action and a passion for literature and the contemplative life, even the conflict between her masculine and feminine sides. The manifold oppositions of her nature are an inexhaustible storehouse: set side by side, they prove mutually destructive by ridicule.[339] This play of contrasts is one of the forms that fantasy takes in *Orlando*; the other is exaggeration.[340] This pervades the book, in its totality as in its detail, in action as in speech, in its characters and in its objects. It might almost be set down in figures: Orlando's age is multiplied by ten, and everything, roughly, is in proportion. The list of furnishings for the great house with its 365 bedrooms[341] is shorter than that which inspired it, in Vita Sackville-West's *Knole and the Sackvilles*[342]: but the figures are inordinately swollen: the Spanish blankets are increased from two to fifty, and so are the chandeliers; the stools from three to sixty, the walnut-tree tables from two to sixty-seven, and so forth. The great frost in James I's reign, the mists of the Romantic period, the Victorian damp, Orlando's love affairs, his slumbers, Nick Greene's vanity and spite, the devastating effect of Pope's wit, Marmaduke's courage, are all enlarged to gigantic, extravagant proportions. One is inevitably reminded of Cervantes, Rabelais, Sterne, Swift; Virginia Woolf borrows from all these masters of the heroic-comic vein. But if the book has the charm and the defects of a pot-pourri, it possesses a twofold unity, external and internal, which fuses imitations and tones down artifice. Exaggeration cannot destroy its proportions; here things and places, time and events are on the same scale as the human beings involved with them. The expansion of a moment or the shrinking of centuries, the spreading panoramas and the spectacular transformations, the ephemeral love affairs and the enterprises that are part of history, all are so perfectly in keeping that fantasy takes on the look of reality—too much so, perhaps, so that one forgets and ceases to be astonished. And on the surface, the same voice is constantly heard, in a self-parody that some-

---

[339] The scepticism and agnosticism revealed in the process corresponds to many passages in the Diary: cf. *supra*, p. 110 and pp. 121-3 and also AWD p. 141 (138), Jan. 4, 1929, and p. 144 (141): "I shall make myself face the fact that there is nothing—nothing for any of us."

[340] Cf AWD p. 120 (118): ". . . with great splashes of exaggeration."

[341] O p. 101 (108)

[342] V. Sackville-West, *Knole and the Sackvilles*, Heinemann, London, 1922, pp. 95-6.

times seeks to parody others. The writing in *Orlando*, swift, easy and yet vigorous, remains—throughout all the vicissitudes of the subject—faithful to its spontaneity, to its playful tone, constantly obliterating the stroke it has just set down, asserting only to deny the moment after, creating and destroying its own creation in a rhythm which is perhaps the most profound expression of her whole personality ever given us by Virginia Woolf.

Yet if the style of Orlando, in the most general sense of the term, reproduces the essential personal style of Virginia Woolf, that way of being and acting that is displayed in every aspect and action of an individual, the teeming wealth of ideas, hinted at or exploited to the full, in the form of witty paradox or argument, transposed into images or embodied in dramatis personae, makes this book an authentic repository of the author's thought.

Orlando: courtier, diplomat, poet; Orlando: man, woman; three centuries, thirty years; the culture of a whole nation, the experience of an individual; a family tree, a single being; Orlando is either, or both, as you like. As you like it, not merely because Orlando was born in Shakespeare's day, but because the complexity of a personality is an elusive and incommunicable mystery to which there is no other answer. That is the essence of this book, which is everywhere in it and nowhere in particular; the versatility of the form and that of the hero, the fantastic train of events, the intermittence of the commentary. It is each of these elements and none of them in particular, for they all hold together to express a vision of a human being. And this vision is expressed both through the hero and through his story—which gives us the novel; and also through the digressions and asides that accompany it: which gives us the essay. And I have suggested essay-novel to characterise this book, for its two aspects are not simply juxtaposed, although it is easy to distinguish the limits of each; they react profoundly on one another; thought has stylized the novel, and the novel lends its fantasy to the essay. This explains, furthermore, apart from the other reasons that she may have suggested, the satisfaction that Virginia Woolf found in writing it: her intelligence and her sensibility found equal vent.

Already in *The Voyage Out*, the human personality was seen as overflowing the narrow bounds within which Hirst sought to confine it. What line could circumscribe the "two thousand and fifty-two" different personalities within each of us?[343] And how can one follow or disentangle the "seventy-six" kinds of time "all ticking in the mind at once"? Here, humorously expressed, we recognize preoccupations with which the earlier novels had already made us familiar. The fantastic, changeable, ambiguous and irrational character of Orlando[344] is merely the diversity that lies within each of us, given that intensification which is at the base of the novel.

The relations of this hero with people and things are disconcerting not only because they emanate sometimes from one self, sometimes from another, but also because they oscillate constantly between the behaviour dictated by the conventions (or as Virginia Woolf would say, the spirit of the time) and that to which his essential nature impels him. One may wonder, as with Mrs Dalloway, if he really is his superficial or his deeper self. And as with Clarissa, the answer is that he is neither one nor the other, but the fusion of both in a rhythm that makes him shift constantly from one to the other—or more simply still, that "he is".

The problem of time will be considered elsewhere.[345] I shall merely mention here that in *Orlando* it provides both the structure of the book and part of its substance. It is approached now in the form that was characteristic of *Mrs Dalloway*,[346] now in that with which Virginia Woolf had experimented in *To the Lighthouse*.[347] Space, as well as time, is compressed within one individual's consciousness; and the inward eye that can look back through tens and hundreds of years has the same power of spanning space, from the English Channel to Snowdon,[348] or calling forth the greenness of an English landscape on the arid slopes of Mount Athos, and vice versa.[349] Faced with such confusion (a crossing of the lines) one asks, like Orlando: "What is appearance, what is reality amidst all this?" The riddle that

[343] Cf. O p. 277 (308): "For if there are (at a venture) seventy-six different times all ticking in the mind at once, how many different people are there not—Heaven help us—all having lodgment at one time or another in the human spirit? Some say two thousand and fifty-two."

[344] Cf. esp. O pp. 69, (73), 73-4 (77-8), 160-1 (175-6)

[345] Cf. ch. VI, pp. 382-398

[346] Cf. esp. O p. 274 (305)

[347] Cf. esp. O p. 91 (98)

[348] Cf. O p. 20 (23)

[349] Cf. O pp. 137-8 (150-1) and 293 (326)

haunts Orlando's mind, and his creator's, is the same as that for which the heroine of *The Voyage Out* had sought an answer. Here, the cruise is replaced by a dream-journey, but the same instinctive aspiration inspires this illusory quest, this pursuit of phantom figures[350]—love, friendship, truth.[351] And when all is said and done, "is this . . . what people call life?"[352] And what is life?[353] And does not this fruitless quest recur in each of Virginia Woolf's books? Surely it is the dominant aspect of her own being?[354] The phantom, "the great fish who lives in the coral groves",[355] the "wild goose", the impossible, inaccessible truth, seems to have been grasped by the end of the book,[356] but its capture fails to elucidate its mystery. As in the earlier books, it is an incommunicable experience, the presence of a being wholly comprised within a name, a call, a cry: "Rachel, Rachel!" "Clarissa!" "Mrs Ramsay!" and now "Shel!" And as the whole book has merely catalogued that disparate collection of "scraps of torn paper tumbling from a sack"[357] that each of us is, without ever discovering "the Key self, which amalgamates and controls them all"[358] the answer can only be another, final invitation to further search. Orlando's ecstasy brings us to the same point as Lily Briscoe's vision. Both leave us on the threshold across which no word can take us: yet if we can learn to see and to love, we may perhaps be granted our own "vision", our own revelation.

This central problem involves an infinity of others. Amongst those most closely associated with personality, we should consider memory, which, in Orlando's case, combines with heredity to make him transcend time and space; and above all, sexual ambiguity. Since the brief reference to Sapphism[359] made on March 14, 1927, when Virginia Woolf was planning *The Jessamy*

[350] Cf. O p. 281 (313): "There flies the wild goose. It flies past the window out to sea. Up I jumped . . . and stretched after it. But the goose flies too fast. I've seen it, here—there—there—England, Persia, Italy."

[351] Cf. O p. 92 (99): ". . . What is love? What friendship? What truth? . . ."

[352] Cf. O p. 177 (195): "Lovers she had in plenty, but life, which is after all of some importance in its way, escaped her. 'Is this,' she asked . . . 'what people call life?'"

[353] Cf. O p. 243 (270): "Life, it sings, or croons rather, like a kettle on a hob, Life, life, what art thou? Light or darkness? . . ."

[354] Cf. *supra*, ch. III, pp. 150, 159 ff

[355] "But never the great fish who lives in the coral groves", O, p. 282 (313)

[356] Cf. O p. 295 (329)

[357] Cf. O p. 276 (307)

[358] Cf. O p. 279 (310)

[359] Cf. AWD p. 105 (104): "Sapphism is to be suggested."

Brides, this aspect had gained considerable importance. Standing between the feminist preoccupations of *Night and Day* (1919) and the pamphlet *A Room of One's Own*,[360] *Orlando* reveals the living substance that fed Virginia Woolf's feminism. If *Orlando's* bisexuality is due to the resemblance between Vita Sackville-West and the Hon. Edward Sackville, whose portrait by Cornelius Nuie[361] serves as frontispiece to the original edition; if it is also due to certain characteristics of Vita herself, yet one may safely assert that it is chiefly due to the author's own dual nature. Without entering the field of biographical hypotheses, unconfirmed at the present time by any evidence, and restricting oneself to questions of character and temperament, it is undeniable that Virginia Woolf was compact of elements which an oversimplified conception, largely obsolete today but still prevalent in 1927, would have divided between the two sexes.[362] And the whole of her dual nature gives weight to her assertion of human ambisexuality:

Different though the sexes are, they intermix. In every human being a vacillation from one sex to the other takes place, and often it is only the clothes that keep the male or female likeness, while underneath the sex is the very opposite of what it is above.[363]

The energy and vitality of the hero-heroine suffice, with the aid of the author's verve, to solve the difficulties to which this ambiguity gives rise. In this Orlando really plays the role of a hero, the creator of an attitude. He proves and affirms by being and living. *A Room of One's Own*, and later, *Three Guineas* deal with the problem from a logical point of view without being any more convincing.

The difficulty of communicating with another person and of understanding human beings is only a direct consequence of the complexity of the individual. The gulf seems deepened, at times, by differences which extend beyond the individuals themselves and spring from a whole network of circumstances which can be summed up by the word "culture". Such is the case in Orlando's relations with Sasha, the Russian girl, or with the Greek gipsies,

---

[360] Note that AROO, in its final form of Feb.-May 1929, seems a remodelling of fragments written in 1928, immediately after *Orlando*. Cf. AWD pp. 141-2 (138-9). Cf. *supra*, ch. IV, pp. 167-8

[361] It is also on p. 106 of *Knole and the Sackvilles* by V. S-W.

[362] Cf. *supra*, ch. III, pp. 66-8

[363] O p. 171 (189)

but in fact he is equally remote from Nick Greene, whether in his seventeenth- or his twentieth-century form, or from the Archduke.

A special sort of communication, but one which assumes capital importance both for the poet-hero and still more for his biographer-novelist, is the problem of literary expression. The vicissitudes of inspiration, the pitfalls of language, those of imitation, the influence of the period, the bondage of technique, are so many aspects of literary activity which, although the tone and treatment are playful, are none the less described with a penetration and authenticity which are reinforced by many parallel passages in the Diary. We may note, on the one hand, the conclusion that emerges from Orlando's literary experience and, on the other, that which emanates from the book itself, and which is expressly formulated. The first brings out the identity of motive between artistic creation and action: both are directed towards reality, they are the two convergent ways taken alternately by the human being in his pursuit of an inexpressible and inaccessible truth. When he suffers a setback on one path, Orlando starts off along the other. This is surely the same rhythmical alternation we noticed in Virginia Woolf herself.[364] If the motives are identical, so too are the results. Action leaves us disappointed and dissatisfied; and the paths of art do not lead us to the secret that we are seeking:

Having asked then of man and of bird and the insects, for fish, men tell us, who have lived in green caves, solitary for years to hear them speak, never, never say, and so perhaps know what life is—having asked them all and grown no wiser, but only older and colder (for did we not pray once in a way to wrap up in a book something so hard, so rare, one could swear it was life's meaning?) back we must go and say straight out to the reader who waits a-tiptoe to hear what life is— alas, we don't know.[365]

Nevertheless, disappointment and frustration do not mean despair; they are the condition of life itself, its torment but also its driving impulse.[366]

Knowledge, revelation, communication can only be attained

---

[364] Cf. *supra*, ch. III, pp. 120-121
[365] O p. 244 (271)
[366] On this dynamic scepticism, see *supra*, ch. III, p. 81, and also *infra*, The W.

in silence.[367] And we remember both that book of silence that Hewett in *The Voyage Out* wanted to write, and Mrs Ramsay's longing "to be silent, to be alone . . ."[368]

Every age, in its own way, tries to *be* and to formulate its being. The masterly portrayals of successive periods in *Orlando* express the success and failure of these attempts. Shakespeare and Sir Thomas Browne, Pope, Addison and Swift survive not through what they found but because they sought, and because we follow their footsteps on man's eternal quest. We should note in passing the almost total omission of the writers of the nineteenth century, very characteristic of Virginia Woolf's dislike of this period, which in her view was not moved by human anxiety and did not "seek".

One evident consequence of this conception of literary creation is the inadequacy of that criticism which distributes praise and blame in accordance with some textbook rules, and even more of that which studies the author rather than his work.[369] If we can recognize, in the figure of Nick Greene, the attitude of some of Virginia Woolf's detractors, yet her satire goes far beyond these. Basically criticism and all other subsidiary aspects of literature, from the patronage of former days to modern commercialization, including literary fame and that apparently ineluctable phase, the public fate of the printed work, are unrelated to art. For the work of art is a profoundly personal gesture, at most "a secret transaction, a voice answering a voice".[370]

If the relations between one human being and another, and those more special relations between an artist and his public, are neither easy nor satisfying, how much less so are social relations in general. If Orlando, like Virginia Woolf, was for a while seduced by fashionable life, like her he plumbed its emptiness; the evening endured at Lady R.'s[371] bears a curious likeness to the luncheon party described by the author in her diary, November 30, 1927.[372]

[367] Cf. O p. 282 (314): ". . . when communication is established" people fall silent.

[368] Cf. To the L p. 99 (95): "To be silent; to be alone . . . a wedge-shaped core of darkness. . . ."

[369] Cf. O p. 190 (209)

[370] Cf O. p. 292 (325): "Was not writing poetry a secret transaction, a voice answering a voice?" And also p. 252 (280)

[371] Cf. O p. 182 (200)

[372] Cf. AWD p. 118 (116)

Thus, despite Orlando's numerous love affairs and the crowds with which he mingles, loneliness is his lot. Not the solitude in which he sometimes chooses to withdraw and which gives him the opportunity to try out those great themes beloved of Virginia Woolf, the Sea, the Air, the Forest, the Earth, in a vein of parody to be sure, yet not without a secret enjoyment—but the basic loneliness of the Outsider. I may be accused of unjustifiably and anachronistically annexing Virginia Woolf for Existentialism. And yet the absurd, atomized world into which she plunges her hero and to which he cannot give any unity but his own, without even being certain of his own unity, is singularly akin to that of Camus.

I have tried to elucidate this book which, under a style that is "very clear and plain, so that people will understand every word"[373] has indubitably a hidden meaning, because it is at the same time a book, a mask and a confidential message, and one is never quite sure with which of the three one is dealing. However, whereas I have frequently pointed out its connection with the author's personal experience, and even insisted on the hero's kinship with his creator, there remains one point on which a scrupulous reader is entitled to demand enlightenment: the faithfulness of the portrait to its model. Even if the fantastic nature of the treatment and the general trend of modern art may lessen the importance of this problem, they cannot wholly deprive it of meaning.

In an earlier section I reported the little that is known about the friendship between Virginia Woolf and Vita Sackville-West.[374] It scarcely enables one to establish any deeper connection between the novel and reality.[375] Vita's books should not be neglected: *Knole and the Sackvilles*, already mentioned,[376] from which Virginia Woolf borrowed certain details, and the poem *The Land*, a few lines of which are quoted as being part of Orlando's *The Oak Tree*.[377] And it should also be mentioned that certain other characters may, from time to time, have come

---

[373] Cf. AWD p. 117 (115)

[374] Cf. ch. V, p. 258

[375] Cf. AWD p. 117 (115): "But the balance between truth and fantasy must be careful." When we consider the scale on which things are magnified or exaggerated here we may justly wonder what the author meant by this balance.

[376] Cf. *supra*, pp. 270, 274

[377] *The Land* by V. S-W. won a prize in 1927; quoted in O p. 238 (265).

between the painter and her model, mingling their features with the latter's. Sir John Harington for instance, whom Lytton Strachey sketches in a few pages; a great favourite with the ladies, who welcomed Queen Elizabeth for a day in that vast Somerset manor to which periodically, when out of the royal favour, he would retire to seek consolation with his dog and to translate Ariosto's *Orlando Furioso*.[378] But these are merely superficial elements. We are forced by our ignorance of the facts to return to the work itself. Beneath the ideological pessimism we discovered in it, it is a paean to life, it speaks of joy. And this joy is not only derived from the artist's sense of deliverance, as she relaxes in easy creativity; it is a feeling that springs from a deeper source; it is the whole of that "singularly happy autumn"[379] of 1927. In the whole of the Diary, this is the only time we find so wholly unclouded a statement, such a completely expansive note. Three months spent writing *Orlando*, living *Orlando*, living in him—in her. And one may venture the hypothesis that Virginia Woolf found in her model, and put into her book, not only herself, as we have seen, but her complement: all that was lacking in herself, and to which she aspired—vigour and robustness, a sort of unselfconsciousness and a sort of greatness which her fragility and introspectiveness forbade her. Whereas "twilight and firelight were her own illumination"[380] she gave Orlando a solar brilliance. She loved Vita for all that they had in common, she admired her for the qualities she would have liked to have; she made Vita her hero-heroine, which was one way of fulfilling herself through her friend. If, as is likely, Vita Sackville-West was thinking of *Orlando* when she defined Virginia's penetration and the use she made of it for her art, this passage confirms the truthfulness of the portrait, unaffected by the embellishments of fancy and the glow of inward vision:

She could also create fabulous tapestries out of her peculiar vision of her friends, but at the same time, I always thought her genius led her by short cuts to some essential point which everybody else had missed. She did not walk there: she sprang.[381]

[378] Cf. Lytton Strachey: *Portraits in Miniature*, "Sir John Harington", pp. 1-9. Previous to the publication of this book (1931) the article had appeared in *The New Statesman and Nation*.

[379] Cf. AWD p. 120 (118): ". . . a very happy, a singularly happy autumn."

[380] V. Sackville-West in *Horizon*, May 1941, vol. III, no. 17, p. 320.

[381] *Ibid.*, p. 320

How, then, are we to judge this book, so intimate and yet so external? If we remain on the purely literary plane we shall see nothing but the artifice, the "fabulous tapestries". And *Orlando*, considered thus, is too contrived a book. If the author follows her whim, its wayward wanderings are too cunningly traced, and it seems deliberately devised to mystify the reader, even though it frequently instructs while it entertains him. In general, when *Orlando* first appeared, critics did not go below the surface of the book. Indulgent or sarcastic, they tempered their disapproval by praising either its satire[382] or its fantasy.[383]

Others, at a later date, considering it in its proper perspective, in relation to the rest of her work, have probed its ideological implications, stressing this or that according to their own temperament and thus reaching what might be called the middle strata of the work. Thus they have admitted its serious significance and a certain value which their predecessors had denied it. One might feel justified in going no further, by Virginia Woolf's own comments. Once she had got the book out of her system, her own judgment, as almost always, anticipates with great soundness that of her critics:

. . . I think it lacks the sort of hammering I should have given it if I had taken longer; is too freakish and unequal, very brilliant now and then. As for the effect of the whole, that I can't judge. Not, I think, "important" among my works.[384]

This last phrase is a revealing one; it stresses the particular, unique character of *Orlando*, while the inverted commas limit the sense of the word *important*. If *Orlando* is thus diminished, not to say condemned as a "work", it may perhaps have "importance" of another sort—that which I have attempted to bring out, which is only to be discovered by probing below the middle strata. But in that case it must be admitted that *Orlando* becomes an esoteric work which can only yield its whole secret to a handful of initiates. Without claiming to be one of these, I have approached it with all the circumspection required by an obscure document, lacking the context of notes, appendices and references which would have shed full light on it.

[382] Cf. J. C. Squire: "*Orlando*", in *The Observer*, Oct. 21, 1928.
[383] Cf. *Times Lit. Sup.*, Oct. 11, 1928, and Desmond McCarthy: "Fantasmagoria", in *Sunday Times*, Oct. 14, 1928. Cf. also *Cambridge Review*, no. V.
[384] AWD p. 128 (125)

Reproaching herself for the futility of *Orlando*, the author seems to forget that she has been on holiday. Or was it because Virginia Woolf never took a holiday? Already on November 20, 1927, in the middle of that marvellous period of unconstrained writing, she asks herself: "Do I learn anything?"[385] For the time being she experiences only the delight of this unbridled style, and she promises herself to hand over her pen to the artist anxiously whispering over her shoulder, who must shape all this random chatter into a work of art. We have just seen that Virginia Woolf was later to consider this recasting as hastily and inadequately done. In any case, not until a year later does she reply to the question put by her more exacting self: "*Orlando* taught me how to write a direct sentence; taught me continuity and narrative and how to keep the realities at bay."[386] This formal gain, however, fails to satisfy her (yet another argument against those who accuse her of being exclusively preoccupied with form and technique): ". . . I did not try to explore. And must I always explore? Yes I think so still."[387] Exploring, for her, means that research in depth through which form and substance are fused in indestructible unity, and which, as I have pointed out, was lacking in *Orlando*: that research in depth which, for Virginia Woolf, is the very essence of artistic creation and which alone entitles a work to be called "important". After this momentary abdication, her essential exactingness revives, as with new strength and greater intensity than ever she pursues the boldest of her explorations, *The Waves*.

THE WAVES (1931)

Having taken *The Waves* as an example for my study of the genesis of a work, I shall refer the reader to that analysis for all that concerns the circumstances of its composition and the relations that may be established between that point in Virginia Woolf's work and her personality, her inmost preoccupations, her artistic purpose.[388] In the following pages I shall merely study

---

[385] Cf. AWD p. 118 (116): "Do I learn anything? Too much of a joke perhaps for that; yet I like these plain sentences; and the externality of it for a change. It is too thin of course; splashed over the canvas; but I shall cover the ground by January 7th (I say) and then re-write."

[386] AWD p. 136 (133-4)

[387] AWD p. 136 (133)

[388] Cf. ch. III, pp. 75-95

The Waves in the light of what has already been said, supplementing this however with certain passages from the Diary directly referring to the form or content of the book.

Although *The Waves* is classified among the novels and described as such on its cover, it would be rash and futile to approach it without defining the term more precisely. From the beginning, even before she has formed more than a vague suggestion of the work, Virginia Woolf describes it as "a new kind of play, prose yet poetry, a novel and a play".[389] A little later, she drops the word novel and speaks of a "play-poem".[390] We read elsewhere of a "serious, mystical poetical work",[391] and an "abstract mystical eyeless book".[392] This must be our starting-point, rather than the label "novel" attached primarily for commercial reasons to *The Waves*.

One has only to open the book to realize immediately that the label "play" seems equally unjustified. None the less, certain italicized paragraphs at the head of the various sections suggest stage directions. And if there does not appear to be any dialogue, in the sense of remarks called forth by one another, the text in inverted commas does represent the speech of the six protagonists. The narrator has stepped aside: there is only a setting—and we shall see what it is—where an anonymous herald announces the voices with a uniform formula: "Bernard said, Susan said, Rhoda said . . ." But before this neutral voice introduces the characters, so quietly that one scarcely hears it and indeed almost forgets the name it has uttered, a scene appears, or rather a background unfolds, the same for the nine tableaux, the nine episodes in the play. The sky, the sea, the shore, the garden, the house provide the outlines and planes amidst which the ballet of light and sound takes place uninterruptedly. From the grey silence of dawn, the sun, that alchemist transmuting nothingness into life, will create, at every stage of his course, by the magic power of light, colour and shadow, outlines ever sharper, objects ever more solid, which then after the autumnal glory of twilight will fade and dissolve into the greyness of evening and finally return to the chaos of darkness. The song of the birds, the sounds of life

[389] Cf. *supra*, p. 76
[390] Cf. *supra*, p. 78 and AWD **p.** 108 (107)
[391] Cf. *supra*, p. 77, and AWD p. 105 (104)
[392] Cf. *supra*, p. 82, and AWD p. 137 (134)

swell and decrease with the light. The noise of the waves, like the birds' song and the human sounds and the light itself, speaks with a wide variety of rhythms until at last, when everything is swallowed up in night, when all the voices are hushed, it becomes the one monotonous and ageless voice that beats out time on the shore of eternity.

I spoke of a setting, a background, to keep to the terms of the theatre. Yet I deliberately introduced the word ballet. For in fact these italicized interludes contain a movement so powerful that their plastic qualities, those colours and shapes that suggest a stage setting, soon become secondary. Their essential character is even more quickly grasped when they are read consecutively—as they seem to have been written in the second version.[393] They are heard, then, as what I believe they really are, the overture to an opera, presenting all the essential motifs in compressed form and in their mutual relationship. Divided into sections corresponding to each of the nine scenes, this prose poem may lose part of its effect and value—or rather it requires of the reader an unusual effort of memory and concentration. Yet this way of presentation proves amply justified. The interludes become so many partial overtures, and their symbolism defines the general sense of each scene while determining its position in the course of the day and of life. Moreover the nature of the book is such that there is nothing heretical about re-reading these scattered passages at one go.

Having thus watched the background shift and dissolve into the body of the work, we may furthermore be surprised to find the characters not speaking to one another, but merely speaking. The obvious conclusion to be drawn is that they are soliloquizing, and most if not all critics have promptly assumed that *The Waves* is composed of six interlaced interior monologues. This definition is a tempting one because it is short and simple—too short and too simple to sum up so complex and so dense a work. The six characters, three boys: Bernard, Louis and Neville, and three girls: Susan, Rhoda and Jinny, speak in turn; at first with a single sentence expressing a single sensation, then, gradually, as the world awakens around them and as they awake to the world, sensations accumulate till whole scenes are evoked and complex

---

[393] Cf. AWD p. 162 (158): "Then, as I think, I shall make one consecutive writing of *The Waves* etc.—the interludes—so as to work it into one. . . ."

impressions are rendered. The single sentence is replaced by the paragraph. As long as they are together, in the country house of their early childhood, at the boys' school or at the girls', the voices frequently speak alternately: they relay one another in expressing the same reality which binds them together. Then, except for Neville and Bernard who, for a while, go to the same University, the band scatters. Louis works in an office, Susan lives on her father's farm, Jinny and Rhoda in London. Then each separate voice, for several consecutive pages, explores its own universe. It is only when they reassemble to say goodbye to Percival—the seventh character, who is never heard—and at their final meeting, with the confrontation of what they were, what they have become and what they have never ceased to be, that the alternation of monologues is resumed. Finally, the last hour of that day which the sun has travelled through the heavens, the last day of this journey, is left to Bernard, the story-teller, the craftsman in words, who "sums up" or picks up again the threads of all these destinies and tries to unravel them. One phrase in the Diary allows us to suppose that originally this summing-up must have been divided between the various sections, concluding each and thus balancing each overture. The author rightly felt that a single finale had the advantage of "absorbing all those scenes and having no further break".[394]

Hitherto, for lack of a better term, I have used the word "monologue" or "voice" to describe what the characters say; I must point out, however, that neither of these words is satisfactory. These are not voices, in the sense that they are not differentiated. But for the "Bernard said" or "Jinny said" that introduces them, they would be indistinguishable; they have the same texture, the same substance, the same tone. Only apparently has a herald replaced the narrator; it would be truer to say that the poet has replaced the characters. Thus we come to that other aspect of *The Waves*, the poem, and a study of this will enable us to define not only the language, but the true nature of these so-called monologues.

Each time she attempted to picture clearly to herself the still uncertain aspect of her new book, Virginia Woolf invariably

---

[394] Cf. AWD p. 162 (159): "It occurred to me last night . . . that I would merge all the interjected passages into Bernard's final speech . . . thus making him absorb all those scenes and having no further break."

mentioned its poetic character. Yet since she speaks of her previous novels as "these serious poetic experimental books..."[395] the adjective by itself tells us little. We must seek other references: "Away from facts"[396]; "the idea of some continuous stream"[397] "Something abstract poetic..."[398]; "an abstract mystical eyeless book...."[399] If we remember what Virginia Woolf means by abstract,[400] not only do we realize that there is no contradiction between abstraction and poetry, but we begin to see in what sense the latter term must be understood; and at the same time the substance, as well as the form, of *The Waves* becomes clearer. The word "mystic", moreover, leads us in the same direction, implying a direct contact between sensibility and intelligence fused in a single act, that of apprehending a truth and a reality which eludes our ordinary awareness. And when Virginia Woolf contrasts this mystical aspiration with what words give us—"what I say, what people say"[401]—we realise that the verb *say* ("he said, she said") introducing each speaker in *The Waves* does not bear its ordinary meaning, that the voice it refers to speaks through no mouth, has no individual timbre, does not use the language of everyday. And to define that voice is to solve the whole problem of *The Waves*—for the reader, as it was for the author.

On one of her various attempts to get started, Virginia Woolf writes: "... several problems cry out at once to be solved. Who thinks it? And am I outside the thinker? One wants some device which is not a trick."[402] This thinker is to become Bernard, Neville or Susan—but not entirely, since they are not detached from one another as their separate names and bodies and apparent destinies might suggest. And this effacement of their individuality, of the differences between them, only increases the temptation, for the author to mingle with them, to become part

[395] Cf. AWD p. 105 (104)

[396] Cf. AWD p. 104 (103)

[397] Cf. AWD p. 108 (107): "... the idea of some continuous stream, not solely of human thought, but of the ship, the night etc., all flowing together...."

[398] Cf. AWD p. 128 (126)

[399] Cf. AWD p. 137 (134)

[400] Cf. *supra*, ch. III, pp. 112, 113

[401] Cf. AWD p. 137 (134): "... that is my temperament, I think, to be very little persuaded of the truth of anything—what I say, what people say—always to follow, blindly, instinctively with a sense of leaping over a precipice—the call of—the call of —now, if I write *The Moths* I must come to terms with these mystical feelings."

[402] AWD p. 146 (143)

of them. Already, faced with the same problem, she has let slip the word "autobiography"[403]; which indicates that these are not six voices in search of characters, but a single being in search of voices. Moreover, these voices, originally merged in one single voice—the thinker, She—as, basically, they still remain, behind the literary convention which has divided them, ought to be anonymous: "I don't want a Lavinia or a Penelope; I want a She."[404] It might almost be said that the problem comes down to "placing" these voices, almost in the physical sense of the expression, so that while preserving a certain individuality, while remaining faithful to the basic differences from which they emanate and which their purpose is to express, they do not rise above the submerged level at which they communicate in an undifferentiated tone and where they are as yet uncontaminated by the surface of things, of people, of life.[405] To define this position and to hold it, that was the vital task: "I am convinced that I am right to seek for a station whence I can set my people against time and the sea—but Lord, the difficulty of digging oneself in there, with conviction."[406] This region is not governed by those conjunctions of space and time which give solidity to thought and being; it lies at a level of consciousness which may justify the use of the term "interior monologue". But it should be clearly understood that this interior monologue has nothing in common with what the term usually implies—the verbal transcription of the stream of consciousness, to a greater or lesser depth according to each author.

At this point, poetry has to be brought in. What we find in *The Waves* is neither the transcription nor even the translation into words of the inner life at the conscious or subconscious level defined above, but what might be called, borrowing a formula

---

[403] Cf. AWD p. 143 (140): "Autobiography it might be called", and also p. 156 (153): "As this morning I could say what Rhoda said. This proves that the book itself is alive. . . ."

[404] Cf. AWD p. 143 (140): "But who is she? I am very anxious that she should have no name. I don't want a Lavinia or a Penelope: I want 'she'."

[405] J. K. Johnstone is one of the critics who have best appreciated this special character of the "monologues" in *The Waves*. Cf. *The Bloomsbury Group*, p. 367: "The subdued, uninvolved, almost halting sentences of the monologue, which do not change in style as we move from one character to another, give a uniform texture to the novel and remind us that we are beneath the layer of the mind which expresses itself fluently in speech."

[406] AWD p. 149 (146)

from T. S. Eliot, its poetic correlative. By this I mean a way of writing, a style, which is essentially that of the writer, freed from any preoccupation with realism, calling on all his resources, knowledge and skill with words to obtain an equivalent to the sort of reality he is trying to express. What Bernard, Rhoda, Louis etc. "say" is just, in fact, what they do not say, it is not even what they think or what they feel, whether clearly or confusedly, but what will affect the reader's sensitivity and intelligence so as to make him conceive and feel, as though by direct experience, the conscious or subconscious reality which might form the stuff of their true interior monologue, in the usual sense of the term.[407] Bernard, in his final summing-up, considers his own mental attitude, and incidentally provides a definition: ". . . that which is beyond and outside our own predicament; to that which is symbolic, and thus perhaps permanent, if there is any permanence in our sleeping, eating, breathing, so animal, so spiritual and tumultuous lives."[408]

Simultaneously, this interpretation sheds light on the epithet "mystical" which Virginia Woolf often uses about this book. It refers to that direct access to "reality", to what is true and essential, which is the result of poetry. And this invalidates all criticism of these monologues, made from the point of view of realism, on the grounds of their generalized character, their lack of verisimilitude—which is particularly striking in the early pages, where the speakers are children—or of the monotony of these voices, distinguished by no individual accent.

If the formal characteristics of *The Waves* seem thus, on the one hand, to correspond to the author's intentions and, on the other, to be justified by their logical consistency, this may be attributed to the author's mastery and virtuosity; but it is only by examining the reality which has been cast in this form and which is revealed by it that we can judge whether the form itself came from a compelling need, or was merely a display of technical skill.

We can readily recognize in *The Waves* that favourite subject of Virginia Woolf's: the unity and multiplicity of personality, in its

[407] J. W. Beach (cf. *The Twentieth Century Novel*, p. 495) has given a good analysis of this monologue's complex content, though he fails to emphasize its originality.

[408] The W p. 176 (349). Cf. also this statement where, in 1927, the form of *The Waves* is adumbrated though not clearly envisaged: ". . . [The Novel] will give the relation of the mind to general ideas and its soliloquy in solitude", G & R, p. 19 (19).

relations with the outside world of things and other people. The originality of this work, the undoubted advance shown over its predecessors, are due to the total elimination of elements alien to that "reality" which the author is seeking to express:

. . . what I want now to do is to saturate every atom. I mean to eliminate all waste, deadness, superfluity: to give the moment whole; whatever it includes. Say that the moment is a combination of thought; sensation; the voice of the sea. Waste, deadness, come from the inclusion of things that don't belong to the moment; this appalling narrative business of the realist: getting on from lunch to dinner: it is false, unreal, merely conventional.[409]

This statement, made on November 28, 1928, while the novelist was still only at the groping, exploratory stage, sums up fairly well what she wants to eliminate and what she is seeking to convey. The sparse landmarks defining certain events in space and time, and those events themselves, which, from *Jacob's Room* to *To the Lighthouse*, had served as support, as scaffolding,[410] and also as boundaries, to that transparent, fluid, shifting edifice in which Virginia Woolf tries to seize the essence of the inner life, these have disappeared.

Places have no longer any reality, even the sketchiest reality, outside the consciousness of the individuals, who both create them and assimilate their substance in a single act of perception. The house, the garden, the school, Louis' office, Jinny's room, Susan's farm, the restaurant at Hampton Court, are at no point, by no word, integrated into spatial reality or even co-ordinated with space. They do not exist *in* space; no path leads to them, no map could reproduce their topography; they exist only in relation to the consciousnesses on which the novelist-poet concentrates exclusively. Time, too, is abolished. If it seems to have slipped in furtively in the hour of a rendezvous, between the pages of a calendar, compressed in a reference to someone's age, it is as if by accident, like some frontier incident occurring at the extreme limits between time and duration, when the mind loosens its hold on the moment and seeks to get its bearings from that remote, external line on which the minutes are marked out uniformly. But in fact we must beware of the traps laid by the ambiguity of

[409] AWD p. 139 (136). Cf also *ibid.*, p. 143 (140) where, one month later, after a meditation that completes this one, the author concludes: "Also I shall do away with exact place and time."

[410] AWD p. 23 (22): ". . . no scaffolding; scarcely a brick to be seen. . . ."

language. Most frequently such expressions as "eight o'clock", "May or June", "twenty-five years", even if the reader deduces therefrom an implicit chronology, are charged with an emotional content which denatures them and reintegrates them into the world of consciousness from which they seem to have been detached. This is not part of a day or a year or a human life; it is the point at which emotions converge—the eagerness of friends about to meet, a longing for the countryside or for freedom, a whole part of one's life compressed in a figure so as to be grasped in its entirety. In the same way, the fleeting references to points in space, such as London or Hampton Court, are no more part of ordinary space than is the imaginary Elvedon. This is not the London, or the Hampton Court, that may be as familiar to us as it is to the characters in the book, but one which exists only in the mind that is aware of it and which is really only a single bundle of sensations, images and thoughts, hastily tied up and labelled.

Events, the material of a story, have disappeared also. They were still to be found, however sparsely, in the earlier novels, where, despite their simplicity and ordinariness, they seemed to be connected with the characters. Here there are only events of such a general nature—school, university, profession, town life, country life, marriage or celibacy, that they no longer count as incidents or accidents, as things that happen. They melt into the texture of the whole of life. What we are given is only the cluster of impressions on which the psyche has fed; all that has remained external to it, all that might constitute an event, strictly speaking, is eliminated.

What is left, then, for these voices to utter, if time no longer exists to give order to their speech, if space no longer exists to contain them and the things around them, to separate or bring them together, if events no longer exist to form a story or stories in which they might play their part and become characters?

"The Waves" is a poetic title, charged with complex potency as well as with a multiplicity of meanings, and is thus mysterious. It stresses the continuity—and also the eternity—of the discontinuous; the conflict between time and duration, parallel to that between the transitory and the permanent; it evokes cosmic forces that submerge the frail voices of mankind, and intermittences that echo those of the human heart. The eternal tide of reality, moving forward from the remote horizon to beat and break on the shores of consciousness, the deep unity underlying apparent plurality, these and a thousand other things are suggested in turn by the waves at each of their appearances in the novel. An equally characteristic, though less fascinating, title would have been "Here and Now", which Virginia Woolf at one time considered giving to the book that became *The Years*. The fact that she says in her diary "*The Waves* is also here and now"[411] may entitle us to read a valuable hint into this variant. Moreover, apart from this statement, which is an afterthought, we can refer to the recurrence of the phrase in the book itself.[412]

It is the here-and-now, or (to use an equivalent and neater expression of Virginia Woolf's) the moment, that this play-poem, in my opinion, explores and strives to express. I have already noted the importance of "the moment" for Virginia Woolf, in her life[413] as well as in her work.[414] I have stressed the capital importance of this experience, which is the centre of her psychological and intellectual life, and moreover the point on which all her work is focussed. *The Waves*, after the not unrelated interlude of *Orlando*, marks her return to this fundamental preoccupation. Its originality and its value are due to the fact that it springs solely from this source, and that it exploits in a coherent manner all the data and all the consequences of that inner adventure which hitherto had provided only the culminating points, or indeed the starting-points, for her novels.

Before seeking a fuller definition in *The Waves* itself, we may turn to the sketch *The Moment: Summer's Night*[415] in which certain phrases formulate in brief abstract fashion the essential lines of the complex whole we are striving to grasp: "...everybody believes that the present is something, seeks out the different elements in this situation in order to compose the truth of it, the whole of

---

[411] AWD p. 215 (208); Jan. 16, 1934.

[412] Cf. for instance The W pp. 90 (262), 100 (271), 121 (293), 159 (331) (twice), 214 (377).

[413] Cf. *supra*, ch. III, p. 110 ff

[414] Cf. *supra*, ch. V, p. 253 ff

[415] Published for the first time in *The Moment and Other Essays*. It is interesting to note that Leonard Woolf's preface tells us that this was the first draft, a typescript copiously corrected by hand. Although no precise data entitle one to make the assumption, considering the affinities between this sketch and *The Waves* it is tempting to suppose that they date from the same period, and even that this is one of those little "sketches" that she wrote every morning "to amuse" herself while brooding over her novel (cf. AWD, p. 142 (139).)

it."[416] This is the postulate that must be accepted before venturing on *The Waves*, and without which the book has no meaning. "To begin with: it [the present moment] is largely composed of visual and of sense impressions."[417] The words "I see", "I hear", "Look", in the opening lines of *The Waves* fling pure sensations at the reader; but more than this, they are incantatory formulae which awaken his sensibility to the world of impressions into which he is entering. True, we immediately recognize the "myriad impressions" received by the mind "from all sides . . . an incessant shower of innumerable atoms" which, as early as 1919, Virginia Woolf had declared it the novelist's task to convey "with as little mixture of the alien and external as possible".[418] But this was the first time she was going to follow literally, in a novel, her own critical suggestion and to concentrate unremittingly and uncompromisingly on rendering life as she had conceived it: "a luminous halo, a semi-transparent envelope surrounding us from the beginning of consciousness to the end".[419] Moreover, the 1919 formulation is a general one; it expresses an intuition without, however, analysing it. The phrases are often quoted, on account of their concentration and their startling newness at the time. But they are only a point of departure; I have quoted them in order to stress the unity of Virginia Woolf's thought. We must return to *The Moment* to follow that thought to the final stages of its development.

"But this moment is also composed of a sense that the legs of the chair are sinking through the centre of the earth, passing through the rich garden earth; they sink, weighted down."[420] Sense impressions were the surface of the moment; here we have its depth, its relation with the rest of the universe, its roots in the darkness. That rich garden soil, that centre of the earth with which the moment brings us into contact, are all those forms of reality which, through the different layers of the concrete, lead us to the heart and essence of things. And our participation in this essence, our rootedness, is fate itself weighing us down.

Finally, the moment includes a third component, of a different nature: "Here in the centre is a knot of consciousness; a nucleus divided up into four heads, eight legs, eight arms, and four separate bodies."[421] The other elements, whether peripheral or

[416] The M p. 9 (3)   [417] *Ibid.*, p. 9 (3)   [418] CR I p. 189 (154)
[419] *Ibid.*, p. 189 (154)   [420] The M p. 9 (4)   [421] The M p. 10 (4)

290

central, were detached and, so to speak, unsupported; they made up the multiplicity, the heterogeneity, the discontinuity of the moment. Perhaps this is the world of *Jacob's Room*, circumscribing a void in which something could be sensed, something had to be postulated: that something was the third element of the moment, this integrating power, this nucleus of consciousness. It may seem surprising that Virginia Woolf took so long to make so simple a discovery. But then its simplicity is only apparent. What is this consciousness? It is one and yet manifold; and it has always haunted Virginia Woolf. Remember that Septimus Smith was Clarissa Dalloway's "double"; and the inextricable multiplicity of Orlando may be only an arabesque scribbled in the margin of the research that led up to *The Waves*. These separate consciousnesses, which, released from the prison of single bodies to which centuries of rationalist and pragmatic thought had confined them, are fused in the moment, are to be the central element in *The Waves*. And inversely, the succession of moments that makes up the book organize themselves around these consciousnesses, while merging with them to become their very substance.[422] That dateless morning in the garden of their childhood means for each of the six protagonists what he is *for* and *through* the other five, as well as what he is *for* and *through* himself. On this first layer all later experience will settle; their shared years at school, their meetings in youth and in maturity. And even in the inevitable separation imposed upon them by their individual destinies, the six consciousnesses will constantly adhere to one another. If each of them becomes a centre: Susan on her farm, Rhoda in her solitude, Jinny in her sensual adventures, Neville amongst his books, Louis at his office and Bernard in his social life, one or other of the rest is constantly appearing as though to ensure a relief or to make a contribution.

Naturally, this synthesis attains perfection on the two occasions when the six friends meet. On the first, when they are saying goodbye to Percival, the latter—a mythical figure through his silence, a symbol through his name—becomes the kingpin of this multiple consciousness. The others' love for him is the catalytic agent that gives rise to this perfect moment, "the thing we have

---

[422] Cf. The W p. 158 (330): "... I perceived, from your coats and umbrellas, even at a distance, how you stand embedded in a substance made of repeated moments run together ...".

made, that globes itself here . . .". To tell the content of "this globe whose walls are made of Percival"[423] one would have to quote the whole page. The moment holds all human things, all space, the happiness of a secluded life, of ordinary life, of fields and seasons, of the future which is still to be created and which they will create. This richness justifies Bernard's phrase: "The moment was all; the moment was enough."[424]

Does Percival's death mean the disintegration of this multiple consciousness? Does it bring to an end the eager quest which, through him, they all pursued? The twenty-fifth year, his departure and his death are perhaps only one and the same event. To measure the extent of this catastrophe, listen to Bernard, who has a gift for words, some twenty years after, at their final gathering:

It was different once. . . . Once we could break the current as we chose. How many telephone calls, how many post cards, are now needed to cut this hole through which we come together, united, at Hampton Court? How swift life runs from January to December! We are all swept on by the torrent of things grown so familiar that they cast no shade; we make no comparisons; think scarcely ever of I or of you; and in this unconsciousness attain the utmost freedom from friction and part the weeds that grow over the mouths of sunken channels.[425]

Once, that's to say in their youth, when Percival was alive and their communion was a living thing, their intermingled consciousnesses, made keen by mutual contact, could grasp the profound reality of the universe and of life. Each in his own way and according to his individual tendencies, but stimulated and enriched by the differences between them, they went from one moment to the next, and each moment was fullness and knowledge and shared rebirth. The here-and-now, which was a miracle, has become a routine: it has been consciousness, voice and communion; it has become unconsciousness, silence and solitude.[426]

Yet, for all the note of despair in this last moment, recovered

---

[423] ". . . the thing that we have made, that globes itself here. . . . Let us hold it for one moment . . . this globe whose walls are made of Percival, of youth and beauty, and something so deep sunk within us that we shall perhaps never make this moment out of one man again", The W p. 104 (276).

[424] The W p. 197 (369). Cf. also AWD, p. 139 (136): ". . . to give the moment whole; whatever it includes. . . ."

[425] The W p. 153 (326)

[426] Cf. particularly The W p. 159 (332)

against all reason by an act of will which is also an act of faith, Bernard—and doubtless the others too, since he is their mouthpiece—refuses to abdicate, and turns defeat into victory. From the universal current which has swept him away and broken his impetus, he takes fresh impetus. Since everything goes too fast for the moments to expand, since life now consists of actions and events, to fit oneself into the new rhythm is the only possible solution; by accepting and willing it, one can dispel its evil power, subjugate it, recover the initiative, become central once again: the quest assumes its other aspect, that of a fight; the first was turned towards life, the second faces death: "Against you I will fling myself, unvanquished and unyielding, O Death!"[427]

Hitherto, by analysing the blended voices and the content of that poetic utterance which unfolds the single substance of which the speakers are made, I have in some sort followed the path traced by the novel. However, if I quoted its final phrase, it was only on account of its forcefulness. Actually I have not yet considered the final section, the long monologue in which Bernard sums things up.

Bernard, indeed, has always loved words and stories, and by dint of turning everything, himself included, into words and stories, he has even anticipated, as it were, his ultimate role: "I conceive myself called upon to provide, some winter's night, a meaning for all my observations—a line that runs from one to another, a summing up that completes."[428] Yet, even if there was a slight affectation about his voice, if it tended rather more than the rest to be abstract and prosaic, it was not essentially different: it was just a man's voice. And yet he is not heard in the sixth section, nor is Rhoda. Neither the one who has the gift of communication, Bernard, the sociable, talkative one, nor the other who, on the contrary, has no gift for making contact, Rhoda, the timid, lonely one, takes part in this song of life. Rhoda's abstention is due no doubt to her being too deeply and intimately involved with her own inner reality to break the silence essential to her being, even by some inward melody. But Bernard? Must it be admitted that his voice was too clear and too shrill? That he

---

[427] The W p. 211 (383). The last sentence in the book. Cf. also p. 166 (338), where in the acceptance of life we feel a tragic tension that shows how far the two attitudes are complementary.

[428] The W p. 83 (255). Cf. also p. 135 (306-7)

would have lapsed from the intense level of the moment and, seduced by his evil genius, would have talked about life instead of expressing it? Thus it is quite natural that when the time comes to sum up and explain he, who was mute in the sphere of life and action, becomes the narrator, enabled, through words, to make solid what is in process of becoming, to circumscribe people and things; enabled by means of phrases to shape life into groups and sequences and constructions. Yet we must not forget that Bernard repeatedly doubts himself: "But what are stories? Toys I twist, bubbles I blow, one ring passing through another. And sometimes I begin to doubt if there are stories."[429] Age and experience have increased his doubts, which have even become a negative certainty by that winter evening when he renders his account: "Of story, of design I do not see a trace then."[430] Thanks to this doubt which, perhaps, destroys something essential to Bernard but which brings him closer, *in extremis*, to his friends, his voice follows quite naturally on the other voices: his summing-up sounds no jarring note, and is all the more truthful for it.

"In the beginning, there was the nursery, with windows opening on to a garden, and beyond that the sea."[431] Everything came from there, as from the Word, everything is rooted there, everything will return there. Faced with the riddle of the world, faced with the enemy, the first impulse is the urge to explore. And Bernard's repeated cry: "Let's explore!"[432] defines the movement that carries youth forward, and the quest which, throughout the book, is symbolized by Percival. But inevitably the impulse dies away: "And what to explore? The leaves and the wood concealed nothing."[433] Yet, however weary, however numbed by habit a human being may be, the universe incessantly confronts him with its riddle; and the relentless contact of that grindstone forces a spark from him, a quiver, and the cry: "Fight. Fight."[434] The battle is the victory of order over chaos, of truth

---

[429] The W p. 103 (275). Cf. also *ibid.*, p. 134 (306): "But why impose my arbitrary design?"

[430] The W p. 169 (342), concluding a long speech that includes such remarks as: "How tired I am of stories, how tired I am of phrases ... Also, how I distrust neat designs of life that are drawn upon half sheets of notepaper."

[431] The W p. 169 (342)

[432] The W pp. 170 (343), 191 (363)

[433] The W p. 191 (363)

[434] The W p. 191 (363). Cf. AWD pp. 147-8 (144) (Oct. 11, 1929): "... what I like is to flash and dash from side to side, goaded on by what I call reality. If I never

over the unknown, of Being over Nothingness. But the battle brings no triumph, it is inexpressible. No word can describe the moon, nor love, nor death; a howl, a cry are enough; reality itself speaks, piercing us through.[435] And Bernard, sociable, talkative Bernard, having done with phrases and with men, retreats into silence and solitude, that silence and solitude into which Louis, Neville, Susan, Jinny and Rhoda have gone, to fight, like them, against death.

Meanwhile, above the quest and the battle, ordinary life— tolerable, good, even pleasant—the life of Monday, Tuesday and every day, the life that can be told by one's biographer, flows on with orderly precision. But it is only a convenient lie, and Bernard speaks of it only to denounce it as a tempting illusion.[436] And the "I", whether Bernard's or anyone else's, with which we connect such a life, that too is "a mistake, a convenience, a lie". If life (real life, that is) "is not susceptible perhaps to the treatment we give it when we try to tell it", neither can the human being be grasped by our primitive methods. We have already seen how Orlando made fun of this problem—but then he made fun of everything. Here we are in earnest. "... who am I? ..." Susan once asked.[437] "I . . . what am I?" Bernard once wondered[438]; and before actually asking himself the question he had found it strange to be "contracted by another person into a single being ...".[439] The answer he suggests later, in his conclusion, does not surprise one; it is the outcome of the whole book, and its foundation: "I am not one person; I am many people...."[440] And on the occasion of their last meeting, they have a fleeting vision of this symbiosis: "We saw for a moment laid out among us the body of the complete human being whom we have failed to be, but at the same time, cannot forget. All that we might have been we saw; all that we had missed. . . ."[441]

---

felt these extraordinarily pervasive strains—of unrest or rest or happiness or discomfort—I should float down into acquiescence. Here is something to fight; and when I wake early I say to myself Fight, fight."

[435] The W p. 209 (381)   [436] The W p. 181 (355)   [437] The W p. 70 (242)
[438] The W p. 84 (256)   [439] The W p. 64 (236)
[440] ". . . I am not one person; I am many people; I do not altogether know who I am—Jinny, Susan, Neville, Rhoda, or Louis: or how to distinguish my life from theirs", The W p. 196 (368). Cf. also *ibid.*, p. 199 (372): "For this is not one life; nor do I always know if I am man or woman, Bernard or Neville, Louis, Susan, Jinny or Rhoda—so strange is the contact of one with another."
[441] The W p. 196 (369)

This sentence certainly sheds light on *The Waves*, but while it makes clearer the relation of the characters to one another it also reveals the relation between the author and her characters, which almost every page of her diary confirms. On one occasion Virginia Woolf asserts her identity with Rhoda.[442] In fact, she might be identified with each of the six protagonists—or rather, one might say that she has something of each of them, and their sum total is her whole being, as I tried to define it in Chapter III. She is in love with words, like Bernard: in love with books, like Neville: a lover of action, like Louis: like Susan feminine, earthy, nature-loving: like Jinny sensual and sociable; like Rhoda hypersensitive and solitary—must one anticipate and say that like Rhoda she was to kill herself? She is all this, and now one aspect, now another predominates. And Percival, who has not had to acquire reality, who has remained purely possible, incarnates in his unfinished life, his premature death, all these possibilities intact. Thus he is the perfect being, towards whom all the others' love converges.

One is tempted at times to believe that this inextricability, growing more complex and richer throughout the course of existence, is the very essence of life, or of the moment through which we grasp life: but that would be to reckon without Virginia Woolf's anxiety, nay her anguish, that rhythm that drove her constantly from one extreme to the other. And the contrary hypothesis is suggested, in an unexpected fashion indeed but, actually, in perfect keeping with her versatility, her spirit of doubt and of exploration: was that manifold mobility, that flowing out to mingle with Susan, Neville, Rhoda, Jinny and Louis, in itself a sort of death? A new assembly of elements? Some premonition of what was to come?[443] Although Bernard does not answer, he harks back to his fundamental question, "Who am I?", constantly trying to go further in his reply: "Am I all of them? Am I one and distinct? I do not know." Yet against these two abstract hypotheses, which, on the plane of logic, are mutually exclusive, he can put forward an experience of the senses which reconciles them: "We sat here together. But now Percival is dead, and Rhoda is dead; we are divided; we are not here. Yet

---

[442] Cf. AWD p. 156 (153), and *supra*, p. 285, note 403.
[443] The W pp. 203-4 (376-7)

I cannot find any obstacle separating us. There is no division between me and them."[444]

Pursuing his exploration, facing the material universe, he finds himself confronted with the same sort of contradictory hypothesis: Something—Nothing. Direct experience, as in the case of "Who am I?" confirms both. But an incident occurs which calls everything into question again and, at one blow, denies, for both problems, one of the two solutions. Bernard, "walking bang into a pillar-box", is forced to opt for the reality of the outside world and the limited unity of the human being. But what force could constrain us to believe one intuition rather than another? And Bernard, like Mrs Ramsay, retreats beyond the reach of body and soul into the heart of an obscure solitude, facing the ultimate dilemma of life and death, for which there is no solution: he exists, and to accept that is what we call living.

The foregoing analysis will allow critical comment to be considerably curtailed. *The Waves* is unquestionably Virginia Woolf's masterpiece, if such a term describes the creation that most faithfully conveys its author's conception of the world, and in which she includes the most completely what she thinks, feels and is. The hostile comments, the objections called forth by *The Waves* are all connected with this completeness; they have nothing to do with literary criticism properly speaking, but are a matter of temperament or metaphysical attitude. A believer can only condemn an assertion of disbelief, a materialist an assertion of idealism. This brings us back to the argument about principles which I mentioned at the beginning of this study. Nevertheless there are two points which deserve attention.

To begin with, the everlasting question of "characters". It is suggested by two contradictory remarks in the Diary. As she is finishing the first version, Virginia Woolf notes: "What I now think ... is that I can give in a very few strokes the essentials of a person's character. It should be done boldly, almost as caricature."[445] And when the book is out, assessing her reviews, she writes: "Odd, that they (*The Times*) should praise my characters when I meant to have none."[446]

This contradiction recalls the sort of hesitation and intellectual

[444] The W p. 205 (377)
[445] AWD p. 157 (153), April 9, 1930
[446] AWD p. 175 (170), Oct. 5, 1931

uncertainty that I analysed in *Mrs Dalloway*.[447] Here, the novel-ist's theories being pushed to their extreme consequences, the problem emerges far more clearly. The contradiction be-tween the two passages just quoted is due solely to the use of the same word in two different senses.[448] It is not difficult to identify the characters which she draws in a few bold strokes. The six protagonists are clearly outlined, and if we do not know in detail what they do, we none the less know quite well what they are—with the possible exception of Neville, who remains slightly blurred. These are the "characters" that the *Times* critic praises, taking them for something they are not, namely complete and self-sufficient individuals deliberately drawn and brought alive for us as such by the author. Enough has been said on this subject for further comment to be needless. But if she refuses autonomy and completeness to her characters, if she rejects this aspect of their reality, Virginia Woolf does not deny that every being consists of a perfectly definite bundle of tendencies and faculties. This collection of fundamental individual traits constitutes the "character" according to the first passage quoted. But far from being the whole of a person, far from representing the human being in his living complexity, it is only one element in him. That we can distinguish Susan from Jinny proves that Virginia Woolf was entitled to be satisfied with her skill; that we are aware of the mutual intermingling, the deep-rooted participation in each other's being of the six protagonists, the reality of that "six-petalled flower made of six lives" proves that she was equally justified when she wondered at the critics' lack of under-standing.

The second point I wish to touch on is the effectiveness of the style of *The Waves*. I have already tried to define it[449]: its poten-tialities and its limitations may be deduced from that definition. Renouncing the basic characteristics of prose, this style escapes the bondage that these imply, and in particular what might be called figurative realism. Thus it is no longer subject to the tyranny of objects and the relations between them, the unreality of which the author justly seeks to denounce while, at the same time, she seeks to dissolve them. In this respect her style is

---

[447] Cf. *supra*, pp. 239-40
[448] This ambiguity will be examined in detail in ch. VI, 1, p. 353 ff
[449] Cf. *supra*, p. 285 ff

perfectly adapted to her ends; at the same time, however, it loses universality. Like all poetry, it derives its justification and its value solely from its power of suggestion. That *The Waves* possesses such suggestive power, no critic will deny. However, since a sensitivity to poetry and suggestion is not considered to be a faculty conforming to fixed standards, nor like "intelligence" included among the essential elements qualifying one to be a reader, it is obvious that any appreciation of this aspect of *The Waves* is bound to remain a controversial matter. All that can be asserted, without taking into account the degree of sympathy that may be established between the reader and the book, is that this world of images, of sensations, of impressions, has such consistency that it cannot fail to impress those who remain outside it, as well as those who enter into it. Sentences, now incisive as a sharp sensation, now fluid as reverie, take on the very rhythm of the inner life they suggest. But above all a whole network of echoes, of evocative reminders, creates around every image, every phrase, every paragraph an aura of accumulated meanings which gives the book its weight and density. True, this accumulated wealth only reveals itself fully and clearly in the course of successive readings; and even then, it demands the active participation of the reader. But is not this the characteristic of any great work, which, like a living person, becomes fully known only after long intimacy?

Although there is a certain risk in stressing the interludes, one can scarcely discuss the poetry of *The Waves* without mentioning them. Their tenor and function have already been specified; to this it should be added that they provide, as it were, a repertory of the forms and substance of Virginia Woolf's poetic imagination.

From the varied play of assonance and alliteration to the most complex rhythmical combinations, all the musical resources of the language are exploited. The virtuosity of these pages is all the more striking when we look through their apparent luxuriance to the sobriety of their component elements. Since the landscape and objects are identical throughout the series, the same words and kindred images recur. But the artist plays on these with such skill and mastery that she draws from them an infinite number of effects, and succeeds in condensing into these few pages not merely all the moments of the day, with which are blended the succession of the seasons and the evolution of the cosmos itself, but all the emotions of human life. Thus in the first interlude, the first verse, heavy with polysyllables, adverbs, present participles, displays the confusion of chaos on the eve of the creation. The same parts of speech, the same slow, brooding syntax are dominant throughout the second verse, which only lifts and brightens with its closing sentence: "An arc of fire burnt on the rim of the horizon, and all round it the sea blazed gold" (p. 5 (8)). This is the transition heralding the shortened rhythm, interspersed with silence and space, of the last verse, in which each little sentence creates, like light, an object emerging out of immensity. In the final interlude, steeped in the same darkness after sunset as before sunrise, the landscape, objectively, presents the same spectacle: yet a quite different tonality is rendered by a variation in the structure: two homologous phrases enable one to appreciate the effectiveness of this style: "The sea was indistinguishable from the sky . . ." (p. 5) from the first interlude becomes, in the last: "Sky and sea were indistinguishable" (p. 167).

Separate objects, as yet uncreated in the original inorganic chaos, are ready, nevertheless, to spring into existence. On the contrary, they glide into the final confusion that swallows them up, the elements dissolve into one another to return to undifferentiated unity, while at the same time a sort of quiet harmony settles over all, expressed by the fluidity of the three following lines, that pulse with the waves of which they tell:

The waves breaking spread their white fans far out over the shore, sent white shadows into the recesses of sonorous caves and then rolled back sighing over the shingles.

Whereas on the contrary in:

The sea was indistinguishable from the sky, except that the sea was slightly creased as if a cloth had wrinkles in it. . . ."

the roughness and hesitation which, moreover, characterize the whole of the following verse, suggest the efforts of a world in travail.

But, brilliant and effective as is their form, these pages derive their poetic power from the treasury of images they call forth. They contain the whole universe that Virginia Woolf loved: the ocean with its everlasting waves, over which the ships pass, the cliff, the shore strewn with driftwood, the sky alive with birds, with winds and squalls, with shifting light, clouds and smoke, the hills patterned with meadows and cornfields, in their tragic winter desolation or their ecstatic summer splendour; the house with its familiar homely objects, its sounds, its smells; the garden where petal, flower, leaf, fruit, dewdrop or raindrop play, on their own scale, the leading parts in the universal drama of life and death. But if this is the essence of the world as St Ives and Rodmell had distilled it in Virginia Woolf's mind and as it reappears scattered throughout all her novels, she succeeds, in these poetic pages, in conveying it to us with such precision, with so many polyvalent resonances, that it awakens within each of us echoes of his own St Ives or Rodmell, of all those moments of contact with nature which, from childhood to maturity, deposit within each of us, like a sediment, a capacity for universal poetic reactions.

Many critics,[450] while recognizing the merits of the book, have none the less condemned it, claiming that the convention on which it is based is as rigid, and moreover as remote from reality, as the realistic conventions that Virginia Woolf rejected and sought to replace. The comparison suggested by Daiches between the mask theory of Yeats and O'Neill and the voices of *The Waves* is interesting.[451] Yet it is difficult to accept it, save as shedding special light on the art of Virginia Woolf, revealing therein certain expressionist features. Still less can we extend the mask theory to criticism of the whole of her work, even by ricochet as does Daiches at the close of his study of a book which he evidently does not like:

[450] Cf. Joan Bennett, *Virginia Woolf*, p. 98; Gerald Bullitt, "Virginia Woolf Soliloquizes: *The Waves* by V. W.", *New Statesman & Nation*, Oct. 10, 1931; David Daiches, *Virginia Woolf*, New Directions, p. 111; Nicholson & Watson, pp. 105; Irène Simon, *Formes du Roman Anglais de Dickens à Joyce*, p. 385

[451] In "O'Neill's Own Story of *Electra* in the Making" (reproduced in Barrett H. Clark, *European Theories of the Drama*, p. 534) we read: ". . . have strong feeling there should be much more definite interrelationship between characters' masks and soliloquies, that *soliloquies should be arbitrarily set in a stylized form that will be the exact expression of stylized mask symbol*". The passage in italics justifies Daiches's comparison; this sentence might in fact serve as text for my own analysis of the monologues in *The Waves*, so much so that source-hunters would doubtless have found this a vein worth exploiting, did not the dates forbid it categorically: on July 19, 1930, when O'Neill wrote the words, Virginia Woolf was working on the second version of *The Waves*; and when they were printed in the *New York Herald Tribune* of Nov. 8, 1931, *The Waves* had been published for over a month (Oct. 8, 1931).

. . . (The mask) is itself so rigid and inflexible that unless you have
seen its meaning beforehand you can never be persuaded of it by
watching the mask. The Mask is most effective as a means of communication between those who have the same insights. But Virginia
Woolf *in her novels* tried to convey unique insights.[452] (My italics.)

If a certain community of vision is undoubtedly necessary for
the understanding of *The Waves*, we must not forget that to
bring us to the meaning concealed within their stylized form,
Virginia Woolf's masks have at their disposal all the resources of
poetry. And all things considered, the only reproach that can be
levelled at *The Waves, A Novel*, is that it is neither the "novel"
that it promises nor even the "lyrical novel" that Delattre saw in
it, but that "play-poem" which Virginia Woolf had longed to
write.

THE YEARS (1937)

In 1932, the year that followed the publication of *The Waves*,
Virginia Woolf brought out the second volume of *The Common
Reader*, without indeed seeming to attach much importance to
this collection,[453] on which she had worked for over six months
without great enthusiasm, considering this recasting of old
articles as a piece of drudgery that she hoped never to have to
repeat.[454] Yet, if the critic and the novelist in her conflicted to
the point of endangering her mental stability,[455] the creative
forces none the less pursued their underground work. The sequel
to *A Room of One's Own*, planned in January 1931, had no doubt,
by the beginning of 1932, split up to produce, on the one hand,
A Tap on the Door (later *Three Guineas*), and on the other, the book
that was to be *The Years*. Although she gives no precise details,
we have every reason to believe that it was in view of this novel
that she was practising dialogue.[456] During the whole of this
preparatory work the project remained very vague, since on

[452] D. Daiches, *Virginia Woolf*, New Directions, p. 111; Nicholson & Watson,
London, p. 105.

[453] Cf. AWD p. 187 (182): "My *C. R.* doesn't cause me a single tremor."

[454] Cf. AWD, p. 182 (177): "There is no sense of glory; only of drudgery done. . . .
I doubt that I shall write another like it all the same."

[455] Cf. AWD p. 181 (176): "I tried to analyse my depression: how my brain is
jaded with the conflict within of two types of thought, the critical, the creative. . . ."

[456] Cf. AWD p. 178 (173): "Things I dashed off I now compress and re-state.
And for purposes which I need not go into here, I want to use these pages for dialogue
for a time."

May 25, 1932, we find her wondering: "... shall I write another novel? ..."[457] She was considering a new form, in sharp contrast to *The Waves*, and with some such experiment in mind set to work seriously on October 11, 1932. But on trying it out, and with the concentration required by sustained effort, she modified her initial plan after a few weeks, and on November 2nd we find the first reference in the Diary to that book which was to take over four years' laborious work:

And I have entirely remodelled my "Essay". It's to be an Essay-Novel, called *The Pargiters*—and it's to take in everything, sex, education, life etc.: and come, with the most powerful and agile leaps, like a chamois, across precipices from 1880 to here and now. ... Everything is running of its own accord into the stream, as with *Orlando*. What has happened of course is that after abstaining from the novel of fact all these years—since 1919—and *N & D* is dead—I find myself infinitely delighting in facts for a change, and in possession of quantities beyond counting: though I feel now and then the tug to vision, but resist it.[458]

In this brief sketch we recognize ambitions and tendencies with which we are by now familiar: the wish to include everything in the novel, to make a *summa* out of it,[459] the concern with mastering time by an original treatment of the discontinuous: and above all the longing for a change[460] which, after an "ecstatic" work, urges her towards realism. We must note, however, what she calls the "tug to vision" which, from the first, betrays a latent conflict to which I shall refer again.[461] None the less, the first months of work were characterized by an ease and euphoria which in no way suggested the anguish to come. Scenes and dialogues crowded into her mind, distracting her from *Flush*, which she was trying to finish,[462] and even set her talking to

---

[457] AWD p. 180 (175)

[458] AWD p. 189 (183-4)

[459] Cf. *supra*, p. 229

[460] Cf. also AWD p. 191 (185): "I took it [*Flush*] up impetuously after *The Waves* by way of a change ..." and also *ibid.*, p. 194 (188-9): "No critic ever gives full weight to the desire of the mind for change. Talk of being manysided—naturally one must go the other way. ... Looming behind *The Pargiters* I can just see the shape of pure poetry beckoning me."

[461] Cf. *infra*, p. 314

[462] Cf. AWD p. 193 (187): "Ah but my writing *Flush* has been gradually shoved out, as by a cuckoo born in the nest, by *The Pargiters*." Cf. also *ibid.*, p. 194 (188), for the same image.

herself on her walks.[463] However, despite the inward necessity that stimulated her writing, the élan that kept her going and the pleasure that went with it, it seems as if from the beginning she found herself at grips with difficulties which she does not specify but which we can guess from certain passages in the Diary. We have already seen how at the end of autumn 1932 she dropped the "essay" for an "essay-novel"; on December 19th of the same year she announces that she has written 60,320 words since October 11th; now, although she claims simultaneously to have "secured the outline and fixed a shape for the rest"[464] and seems, from various allusions in the Diary, to be going forward, by April 6, 1933, there are only 50,000 words.[465] Even taking into account the revision of the first chapter, undertaken and completed at the beginning of the year,[466] this re-writing and the compression it involves do not adequately explain the contradiction between the two figures. We must assume significant recasting and even the elimination of a considerable part of the work done during these five months. The kind of problems that confront one in attempting to define the stages of the first version give indirect evidence of her indecision about the whole, as well as about details. The names of some of the characters are not those we find in the novel: Martin and Sara seem to have begun as Bobby and Elvira,[467] North as George or John.[468] Except for the first and the last section, it is difficult to establish any reliable correspondence between the "chapters" mentioned in the Diary and the definitive sections of the book. Are the "straight narrow passages of narrative"[469] referred to on January 5, 1933, which

[463] Cf. AWD pp. 189 (184), 193 (187), and esp. 226 (219): "Lord how many pages of *Sons and Daughters*" (a provisional title for *The Years*) "I made up, chattering them in my excitement on the top of the down, in the folds."

[464] Cf. AWD p. 190 (184)

[465] Cf. AWD p. 195 (190): "50,000 words written in 5 months—my record."

[466] Cf. AWD p. 195 (189): "Today [Feb. 2, 1933] I finished—rather more completely than usual—revising the first chapter."

[467] Cf. AWD p. 212 (205): "No, my head is too tired to go on with Bobby and Elvira—they're to meet at St. Paul's—this morning." There is, in the book, only one meeting at St Paul's—between Martin and Sara. Although on p. 222 (214) of the Diary a remark ascribed to Elvira is, in the book, made by Eleanor, it is more than likely that the Elvira of the Diary is Sara. Cf. in this connection AWD p. 238 (230): "Get as far from T[heresa] (so called after my Sarah and Elvira provisionally)."

[468] Cf. AWD p. 218 (211): "Elvira and George, or John, talking in her room."

[469] Cf. AWD p. 193 (187): ". . . a series of great balloons, linked by straight narrow passages of narrative."

are to connect the different episodes, the same as the "interludes" of February 2nd,[470] which, after that date, disappear as such and are incorporated in the text? And in the symbolic descriptions introducing each section of the novel, like the "overtures" in *The Waves*, what is there left of these connecting recitatives? The scene which was to be "the turn of the book"[471] seems to have become just a year, 1907, like any other, before the great turn of The Present. If on April 25, 1933, Virginia Woolf notes: "I think I begin to grasp the whole"[472] what are we to make of the similar declaration noted above, which is dated December 19, 1932? One begins to have doubts about the orientation of the intervening effort and of the unity of what had been written with what was to follow. And even so, does not this assertion contradict the questions the author has just asked herself, and left unanswered?

It should aim at immense breadth and immense intensity. It should include satire, comedy, poetry, narrative; and what form is to hold them all together? Should I bring in a play, letters, poems?[473]

Finally, the different titles successively considered by Virginia Woolf might be set out in a graph, showing the oscillation between the two tendencies, realistic and abstract, which the author wanted to conciliate: *The Pargiters, Here and Now*,[474] *Music* or *Dawn*,[475] *Sons and Daughters* or *Daughters and Sons*,[476] *Ordinary People*,[477] *The Caravan*[478] and finally *The Years*.[479] Of course we must not forget that during the year 1933 Virginia Woolf had finished *Flush*, and had spent May in France and Italy; but these were only superficial distractions; moreover the first version progressed, reaching 80,000 words by September 2nd, and what the author calls the fourth part, perhaps corresponding to 1914 or even 1917 in the final version, by December 17, 1934,[480] began promisingly, but towards the end of

---

[470] Cf. AWD p. 195 (189): "I am leaving out the interchapters—compacting them in the text. . . ."

[471] Cf. AWD p. 196 (190): "I've brought it down to Elvira in bed. . . . It's the turn of the book."

[472] AWD p. 198 (191)

[473] AWD pp. 197-8 (191). Cf. also p. 208 (201)

[474] Cf. AWD pp. 211 (204) and 212-14-15 (205)

[475] Cf. AWD pp. 222 (214), 223 (216)

[476] Cf. AWD p. 226 (219)   [477] Cf. AWD p. 234 (227)

[478] Cf. AWD p. 237 (229)   [479] Cf. AWD p. 253 (244)

[480] Cf. AWD p. 214 (207): "I finished part 4 of *Here and Now* yesterday. . . ."

January illness interrupted her work for three weeks[481]; and another month was lost in the same way, from May 18th to June 11th.[482] There remained only the last chapter to write: Present Day, which "must equal in length and importance and volume the first book: and must in fact give the other side, the submerged side of that."[483] We must assume, none the less, that over six weeks were devoted to research and first drafts, for Virginia Woolf was not ready to tackle this last chapter until July 27th.[484] On August 17th the end was in sight,[485] but not until September 30th, nearly two years after beginning work, could she set down in her Diary: "The last words of the nameless book were written 10 minutes ago, quite calmly too. 900 pages: L. says 200,000 words."[486]

At the close of this long effort, Virginia Woolf found herself in much the same state as after finishing her other books: her mind blank, exhausted, depressed, on the brink of despair.[487] The death of her friend Roger Fry on September 9th made recovery slower and more difficult.[488] Not until November 14, 1934, could she start re-reading the book with an eye to revision. In this, she was guided by three principles: to condense, in order to reduce this enormous mass to reasonable proportions; to dramatize and bring out contrasts; to introduce some connecting thread which should integrate discontinuous and heterogeneous elements. It is noticeable that the same expressions recur constantly each time she speaks of the book in her Diary.[489] These preoccupations, indeed, confirm what I have said about the

---

[481] Cf. AWD p. 215 (208): "And I began *Here and Now* again this morning, Sunday, at the point where I left off all but three weeks ago for my headache."

[482] Cf. pp. 218-19 (211-2)

[483] AWD p. 219 (212)

[484] Cf. AWD p. 220 (213): ". . . I'm free to begin the last chapter. . . ."

[485] Cf. AWD p. 220 (214): ". . . I think I see the end of *Here and Now*. . . ."

[486] AWD p. 225 (218)

[487] Cf. AWD p. 229 (222): "I looked up past diaries . . . and found the same misery after *Waves*—after *Lighthouse*. . . ."

[488] Cf. AWD pp. 226 (217) and 230 (222): "This time Roger makes it harder than usual."

[489] Cf. AWD p. 232 (224-5): "The thing is to contract: each scene to be a scene: much dramatised: contrasted: each to be carefully dominated by one interest . . . compacting the vast mass . . ."; *Ibid.*, p. 234 (227): "My idea is to contract the scenes; very intense, less so; then drama; then narrative"; *Ibid.*, p. 237 (229): "I make out that I shall reduce *The Caravan* . . . to 150,000"; *Ibid.*, p. 239 (231): "What I want to do is to reduce it all. . . . And the most careful harmony and contrast of scene . . . has also to be arranged"; *Ibid.*, p. 242 (234): "Oh that scene wants compacting."

conditions under which the first version was written. With her usual optimism, unless maybe by an effort at mental discipline, to counteract her discouragement, Virginia Woolf envisaged finishing her task in three months at a rate of ten pages a day.[490] But already by January 1935 she had come to realize that it would take her longer: the Diary speaks of May.[491] On April 1st, although she had only done about two-thirds,[492] she expected to finish before leaving for a journey to Holland, Germany, Italy and France. But it was only on her return in June that she tackled the final section.[493] On July 17th, four months later than anticipated, she completed this first revision which, although many passages had been re-written and the whole thing cut down by a quarter, still seemed to her very imperfect.[494]

She immediately got to work on it again, "typing out again at the rate, if possible, of 100 pages a week, this impossible eternal book".[495] Once again she had overestimated her strength: weariness,[496] the preparation of Roger Fry's biography,[497] an irresistible wish to begin the pamphlet she had long been considering,[498] all this held her up, and not until December 29, 1935, did she complete the second revision—and envisage a third, for which she dared not fix a completion date:

And is it good? That I cannot possibly tell. Does it hang together? Does one part support another? Can I flatter myself that it composes; and is a whole? Well there still remains a great deal to do. I must still condense and point: give pauses their effect, and repetitions, and the run on. . . . Yes, it needs sharpening, some bold cuts and emphases. That will take me another—I don't know how long.[499]

---

[490] Cf. AWD p. 232 (224): ". . . I've started re-writing the *Ps*. Lord, Lord! Ten pages a day for 90 days."

[491] Cf. AWD p. 237 (229): ". . . and shall finish re-typing in May."

[492] As far as "1917", the air raid chapter. Cf. AWD p. 243 (234): "But I shall finish it before I go away."

[493] Cf. AWD p. 250 (242): "It's beginning this cursed dry hand empty chapter again in part."

[494] Cf. AWD p. 252 (243): ". . . I think I can shorten: all the last part is still rudimentary and wants shaping. . . ."

[495] Cf. AWD p. 253 (244): ". . . typing out again at the rate, if possible, of 100 pages a week, this impossible eternal book."

[496] Cf. AWD pp. 253 (244-5), 257 (247).

[497] Cf. AWD pp. 257 (247-8), 258 (247-8).

[498] Cf. AWD p. 239 (231): "an anti-Fascist pamphlet"; p. 245 (236): "*On Being Despised*", and p. 257 (248): ". . . *The Next War* . . . I couldn't resist dashing off a chapter. . . ."

[499] AWD p. 261 (252)

Whereas after each of her books she questions the value of what she has just written, we must note that here, contrary to her usual habit, she is preoccupied by one very precise aspect: composition and unity. In the middle of this third revision, in April, she had already noted: "It's not the writing but the architecting that strains."[500] In fact, physical and mental lassitude are apparent in every reference to her book throughout this third revision: apart from a few spurts of energy, a few scenes re-attempted—such as that of the air-raid, worked over for the thirteenth time[501] —she seems to be giving up, and resigning herself to surface pruning and polishing.[502] Hoping to have finished by March 10th, she worked without respite, in spite of headaches.[503] But when March 10th came the book was not ready: she then decided, with her husband, to start printing before completing it—a thing she had never done before.[504] A week later, about two-thirds still remained to be done, and the book seemed to her so bad that she thought of throwing it away.[505] Mechanically, she stuck to her task, and then confidence revived, and on April 8th the last batch was sent off to the printers.[506] She had only been waiting for this deliverance to set to work on her pamphlet, now called *Two Guineas*.[507] But she had driven herself too hard, and was overcome by a depression only equalled, in her memory, by that of 1913.[508] Barely out of convalescence, and still under observation, on June 11, 1936, she took up the proofs of *The Years* again for a fourth and final revision[509]; dominated, yet again, by the need to

[500] AWD p. 246 (238)

[501] Cf. AWD p. 265 (256)

[502] Cf. AWD p. 264 (255): "Further work must be merely to tidy and smooth out."

[503] Cf. AWD p. 265 (256): "I work all the morning: I work from 5 to 7 most days. Then I've had headaches ... I have sworn that the script shall be ready, typed and corrected, on 10th March."

[504] Cf. AWD p. 266 (256): "We have decided to take this unusual course—that is to print it in galleys before L. sees it. . . ."

[505] Cf. AWD p. 267 (257-8): ". . . there I was, faced with complete failure. . . . Then I set to: in despair; thought of throwing it away: but went on typing."

[506] Cf. AWD p. 268 (258-9): "April 9th. . . . The last batch was posted to Clark at Brighton yesterday."

[507] *Ibid.*: "No sooner have I written that, than I make up the first pages of *Two Guineas*. . . ."

[508] Cf. AWD p. 268 (259): ". . . two months dismal and worse, almost catastrophic, illness—never been so near the precipice to my own feeling since 1913. . . ."

[509] Cf. AWD p. 269 (259): ". . . home yesterday for a fortnight's trial. . . . Wrote 1880 this morning."

condense and unify.[510] But her recovery was still incomplete and, before a fortnight was up, she had collapsed again under a fresh attack which was to last four months. After this relapse, on November 1st, having re-read everything except the final chapter, she felt ready to burn her work;[511] however, she let herself be persuaded by her husband's admiration and, with his encouragement, finished the job in a month.

By December 31st the proofs were corrected. Over four years' work, five successive versions, some passages re-written twenty times, six months' nervous depression—"the worst summer in my life, but at the same time the most illuminating . . ."[512]—a long patience and a long battle, one might say a martyrdom; such, in brief, is the story of the composition of this novel *manqué*, whose failure is perhaps the most significant symptom we have of the disequilibrium that made Virginia Woolf's originality and greatness—and which led to her undoing.

Is *The Years* a chronicle of three generations of Pargiters? By no means. If the death of Mrs Pargiter is the focal point of the first hundred pages ("1880") this is only a chance coincidence. Besides, this death occurs, so to speak, in the wings, or more precisely in a room into which we scarcely enter. But anxiety, expectation, indifference even, like so many threads fastened to a single point, connect the various members of the family: Abel Pargiter, the father, and the children: Eleanor, Delia, Milly, Rose, Martin, Morris and Edward. Subsequently, deaths, marriages and births occur, so to speak, in parenthesis, without the typographical abruptness of "Time Passes" in *To the Lighthouse*, but otherwise in just as unexpected a fashion, being merely referred to. Love, ambition, undertakings, conflicts, successes or failures take a purely marginal place: Eleanor takes up housing and politics, Morris is called to the Bar, Martin becomes a Captain and Edward an Oxford don; of their nephews and nieces, North lives for a long time on an African farm and Peggy is a doctor; their cousins Peggy and Sara live Bohemian existences

---

[510] Cf. AWD p. 270 (260): "I am trying to cut the characters deep in a phrase: to pare off and compact scenes: to envelop the whole in a medium."

[511] Cf. AWD p. 270 (261): "I made myself yesterday read on to Present Time. When I reached that landmark I said, 'This is happily so bad that there can be no question about it. I must carry the proofs, like a dead cat, to L. and tell him to burn them unread.' This I did."

[512] AWD p. 278 (268)

in unfashionable districts. . . . But all this is only hinted at, and remains as insubstantial as the bill boards indicating an Elizabethan stage set. The years are made up of something very different—1891, 1907, 1908, 1910, 1911, 1913, 1914, 1917, 1918 —as by chamois leaps, to use the author's term, they bring us to the present day. While the figures age, yet their gestures remain unaltered; while the families increase, yet the living children are not more present than the dead parents; while the years are marked by the death of kings, the beginning and the end of wars, yet these historic events are no more than newspaper headlines and the howl of sirens. A string of encounters, most frequently by chance: a tea-party, a dinner, an evening gathering; a door opens, someone comes in; the place and the hour expand like a bubble; and people carry on their usual behaviour, their usual train of thought, which belong to the past and the future as much as to the present: of the twelve months or twelve years that separate two meetings, we know practically nothing; yet they are that indefinable substance that clings to human beings to produce something that cannot be grasped or described[513]: life. In the opinion of sensible, clear-headed Kitty, who has chosen Lord Lasswade's fortune rather than Edward's love, "The years changed things; destroyed things; heaped things up—worries and bothers; here they were again".[514] This, formulated as prosaically as possible, is what the novel is trying to show, what the constantly changing, constantly renewed sea of *The Waves* has already told us with its infinitely more mysterious, more moving voice, and surely with far more truth diffused through its poetic imprecision. Half knowing others, half known by them[515]—and half known by readers—the characters are pivots around which is coiled the thread of days, events, things and other people.[516] As a result of the crossing of these threads, of their momentary coincidence, each individual comes to wonder, like Maggie: "Am I that, or am I this? Are we one, or are we separate? . . ."[517] The thread or threads conceal the pivot, that " 'I' at the middle of it, . . .

---

[513] Cf. The Y p. 395 (366): "My life. . . . And I haven't got one, she thought. Oughtn't a life to be something you could handle and produce? . . ."
[514] The Y p. 292 (271)
[515] The Y p. 337 (313)
[516] Cf. The Y p. 110 (104): Eleanor's reflections.
[517] The Y p. 150 (140)

a knot; a centre . . .",[518] "the fountain, the sweet nut"[519] covered by the carapace under which we shelter. The last evening party brings them all together. "Let me see," says the hostess, Delia, "there's all your uncles and aunts. . . ." And she adds somewhat vaguely, but thus suggesting indirectly the essence of the gathering and at the same time that of the book: "Only all the generations in our family are so mixed: cousins and aunts, uncles and brothers—but perhaps it's a good thing."[520] A good thing no doubt in this sense: that each of them is enriched by all the rest, that each life overflows in space and time to become, eventually, part of this crowd, this enduringness, these memories, hopes and nostalgic longings which, from the basement to the attics of the house—as strange and impersonal as society and everyday life—represent the sole reality, fragmentary and compact at the same time, ephemeral as the night that contains it and yet, in its instantaneous richness, participating in the absolute and the eternal.

The Years, the story of the Pargiters, or more exactly stories about Pargiters. "What could be more ordinary?"[521] as Rose remarks. Just so: insignificant incidents, gestures, words that might be anybody's. If each moment in itself constitutes a perfect sketch in which, faithful to her genius, Virginia Woolf admirably conveys all that lies between the surface of human beings and their depths, between the expressed and the unexpressed, the sequence as such is wearisome and disappointing. The realism of the dialogue and of the general treatment, approaching the characters from the outside, sends us in a wrong direction, so to speak: one is constantly expecting these stories to become a story. True, this was not the author's intention, but by concentrating on facts, by writing from the outside, she leads us, against her will, on a false trail. Rose is very human when she makes the remark quoted above, and all the Pargiters undoubtedly think as she does, "And yet she felt that she had been herself very interesting."[522] The distance that divides the interest one takes in oneself

[518] The Y p. 395 (367): "Perhaps there's 'I' at the middle of it, she thought; a knot, a centre. . . ."
[519] The Y p. 444 (412): "What I mean is . . . underneath there's the fountain; the sweet nut. The fruit, the fountain that's in all of us . . . so why caparison ourselves on top?"
[520] The Y p. 393 (364)
[521] The Y p. 181 (168)
[522] The Y p. 181 (168)

and one's family reminiscences from the interest that strangers take in them indicates the distance between *The Years* and a good novel. No doubt, beyond and beneath the futility of speech, gestures and incidents, Virginia Woolf has tried to reach something else: "It's not ordinary" is Sara's reply to Rose. "The Pargiters ... going on and on ... until they come to a rock...."[523] Their number, their continuity, their collective will, their solidity, which are indeed extraordinary since on the surface one sees only individuals, the stillness and discontinuity of scattered moments, the passivity and fragility of single beings: such is the true subject, Virginia Woolf's eternal subject; but it must be admitted that the synthesis of the two orders of reality, that of facts and that of vision, to use the author's own terms, remains insecure and intermittent and consequently fails to convince the reader. The latter loses his way and grows weary, between 1880 and "Today". If the dates which stand at the head of each section serve to replace the chronological appendix which the author at one point considered adding,[524] one frequently regrets not being able to refer to a genealogy: which is as much as to say that, in spite of herself, Virginia Woolf reminds us of Galsworthy. True, the last section to some extent fulfils the requirements of the author's plan and, as she intended, sums up and integrates what has gone before, reveals the unity of the deep stream which surface eddies had concealed from us.[525] But if this retrospective explanation enables us to get at the meaning of the novel, it is powerless to inject that meaning, and the connecting-link this would provide, into the earlier chapters as we read them. One might almost say that "Today" is self-sufficient; all the detailed facts from which its abundance of allusions emanates, and to which it seems to refer one back, add nothing to it; they are a useless preparation or scaffolding, the very thing that hitherto Virginia Woolf had striven to eliminate from her novels, and which here she vainly tries to reintegrate into them.[526]

[523] The Y p. 181 (169)

[524] Cf. AWD p. 195 (189): "... project an appendix of dates. A good idea?" It is interesting psychologically that the rest of the paragraph is obsessed by Galsworthy.

[525] Cf. AWD p. 211 (204): "... I thought of *Here and Now* as a title for the Pargiters. I think it better. It shows what I'm after and does not compete with the Herries Saga, the Forsyte Saga and so on."

[526] Cf. AWD p. 219 (212): "The last chapters must be so rich, so resuming, so weaving together...." And *supra*, p. 311

Yet this attempt at integration was too deliberately made, too lucidly and stubbornly carried on, to be summarily dismissed as a failure. Certain resemblances with *The Waves* have already been noted[527]; and it is to that book that one should refer, rather than to *Night and Day* as most critics have done, if one wishes to understand both what Virginia Woolf wanted to do and why she failed. In fact, there is no question here of a return to her pre-1919 "realism". Many pages in *The Years* may perhaps suggest such a hypothesis, although the resemblances are very superficial, but the whole structure of the book refutes it; moreover, such a return would introduce an inexplicable interruption in the author's development and might even call in question the fundamental principles governing her artistic creation.

Before turning to those revelations in the Diary which were inaccessible to those critics who were baffled by *The Years*, a brief examination will serve to bring out the continuity of this novel with *The Waves*. The central idea, the manifold variety of human beings brought together by life and whose personalities are fused into a whole of uncertain nature and limits, is the same. So, too, are the elements and the structure: a group of individuals, here joined by family connections, who have been formed by the same experience due to their shared childhood; a succession of meetings during which their fusion takes place as though by alchemy, while at the same time they are revealed as different and yet one, original and yet coinciding; and finally, a general confrontation in which is incorporated the summing-up, the commentary or explanation which in *The Waves* was detached and entrusted to a single character. The overtures are no longer italicized and their lyricism is less metaphorical, yet as in *The Waves* they present a whole sheaf of motifs which reappear in the sections they introduce.

If I have stressed the kinship between the two novels, it is in reaction against certain critical tendencies; I do not wish to suggest that they are identical but to point out clearly that *The Years*, returning to ideas and methods of which *The Waves* had made use, far from being a retrograde step is surely, like all Virginia Woolf's books, an essentially new attempt to express with greater truth and force that Reality which, indefatigable seeker that she was, she unremittingly pursued. I have already

[527] Cf. *supra*, p. 305

noted that at each stage of this quest, apart from the mental therapy and the rhythm which impelled her to alternate between deep, concentrated writing and a looser, more external form, the excesses as well as the deficiencies of each book decided the direction of the next, leading her to tone down temerities and to fill gaps, in short to revise and perfect what seemed to her to be successful and to modify or complete what seemed to her inadequate. And it is surely this form of progress that we recognize here. Its failure is no condemnation of the method, which bears witness to Virginia Woolf's ambition and probity, but it will enable us to define the limits of her genius.

With *The Waves*, she had taken the novel to the extreme limits of abstraction and poetry, realizing, no doubt, as closely as she could her vision of 1920.[528] If, when she embarked on *The Years*, as when after *To the Lighthouse* she had flung herself into *Orlando*, she seems to be following the opposite trend in her nature, she did not thus indulge herself for long. The attraction of "vision", which she was striving to resist,[529] the appeal of pure poetry, to which she only intended to respond later on,[530] became so imperious that she could not avoid them, and thus found herself involved in a synthesis whose achievement seemed problematical:

I must be bold and adventurous. I want to give the whole of the present society—nothing less: facts as well as the vision. And to combine them both. I mean, *The Waves* going on simultaneously with *Night and Day*. Is this possible? . . . How am I to get the depth without becoming static?"[531]

All the difficulties which she was to encounter, and which were to make the composition of this book like a long and painful childbirth[532] are merely different facets of this same problem. To begin with, she is well aware that what is needed is a profound fusion, which is essentially a matter of artistic creation: ". . . how give ordinary waking Arnold Bennett life the form of art?"[533] Then gradually she accepts the solution of simple alternation:

[528] Cf. *supra*, pp. 73, 215
[529] Cf. AWD p. 189 (184), quoted *supra*, p. 303
[530] Cf. AWD p. 195 (189): "Looming behind *The Pargiters* I can just see the shape of pure poetry beckoning me."
[531] AWD p. 197 (191)
[532] Cf. AWD p. 273 (263): "I wonder if anyone has ever suffered so much from a book as I have from *The Years*. . . . It's like a long childbirth."
[533] AWD p. 208 (201)

"I have a good excuse for poetry in the second part, if I can take it."[534] And meanwhile, still aspiring to the ideal of fusion, she is constantly seeking for some equivalent to it: "... how to make the transition from the colloquial to the lyrical, from the particular to the general?"[535] Her attempt to introduce ideas without propaganda, preaching or philosophy shows the same desire to embrace a wider field, to include more material without falling back on traditional formulae.[536]

Contemporaneous with the first draft and suggested by the work she was doing on the first revision, three roughly identical entries in the Diary shed light on the book's failure:

The lesson of Here and Now is that one can use all kinds of "forms" in one book.[537]
The discovery of this book, it dawns upon me, is the combination of the external and the internal. I am using both, freely.[538]
... in this book I have discovered that there must be contrast; one strata or layer can't be developed intensively, as I did I expect in The Waves, without harm to the others. Thus a kind of form is, I hope, imposing itself, corresponding to the dimensions of the human being. ...[539]

This shows that Virginia Woolf seems to be attaining to a new conception of "reality" and at the same time to a new conception of the work of art destined to express this reality. Without renouncing the idealist position she had taken up as against the Edwardians, she has moved in a direction which might have been foreseen from her keen sense of the concrete, and discovered, through art no doubt as much as through direct experience, several degrees of idealism; in other words, that the surface of things, the world of matter and of facts in its exterior aspect, in its appearance, is also part of "reality" and cannot be excluded from the work of

[534] AWD p. 211 (209)
[535] AWD p. 221 (214)
[536] Cf. AWD p. 194 (188): "I'm afraid of the didactic ...", and p. 198 (191) "And there are to be millions of ideas but no preaching ...", also p. 239 (230): "And the burden of something that I won't call propaganda. I have a horror of the Aldous novel: that must be avoided." And p. 245 (236): "... one can't propagate at the same time as write fiction. And as this fiction is dangerously near propaganda, I must keep my hands clear."
[537] AWD p. 222 (215)
[538] AWD p. 237 (229)
[539] AWD p. 258 (248)

art. Her intuitions of the different levels of consciousness,[540] of the different layers of the mind,[541] seem to have crystallized, not into a theory, which would imply too much precision and too much logic, but into a complex vision which *The Years* tries in vain to unify in the sweep of artistic creation. This new position, far from marking a retrogression which would imply renunciation and impoverishment, constitutes a step forward, even if for the moment Virginia Woolf has not succeeded in exploiting its aesthetic consequences:

It struck me tho' that I have now reached a further stage in my writer's advance. I see that there are four? dimensions: all to be produced, in human life: and that leads to a far richer grouping and proportion. I mean: I; and the not I; and the outer and the inner—no I'm too tired to say: but I see it. . . . This will be my next novel, after *The Years*.[542]

In fact, whereas to "produce" and express the "I" and the inner, she had perfected a form whose power of suggestion, despite all the reservations I have already made, had proved itself in *The Waves*, yet for these other dimensions, these other strata which she sought to include in her work she had no means at her disposal. The "narrative"[543] or "representational"[544] part of which she speaks, and which she had deliberately accepted, failed to attain the end she had set them. If they convey the surface, the appearance of the "not I" and "the outer", they miss its solidity, its hardness, its constraint and cohesion. This profoundly impressionistic form has no grip on its material. And the choice of that material, of these facts that lack weight, of these events that lack consequence, of these gestures that do not connect up into action, is rather significant. It might be said that Virginia Woolf, aware of the limits of her means of expression, only entrusted to them her most immaterial material; it seems

[540] Cf. AWD p. 75 (74): ". . . people have any number of states of consciousness . . . etc.", *Ibid.*, p. 216 (209): "This is working out my theory of the different levels in writing and how to combine them: for I begin to think the combination necessary.", and particularly p. 230 (223): "About novels: the different strata of being: the upper, under. This is a familiar idea partly tried in the Pargiters."

[541] Cf. *supra*, note 323, quoted from The M p. 27 (27); also AWD p. 257 (248).

[542] AWD p. 259 (250); cf. also AWD p. 283 (273): "I'm trying to get the four dimensions of the mind. . . ."

[543] Cf. AWD p. 219 (212): "There's no longer any need to forge ahead, as the narrative part is over."

[544] AWD p. 225 (218): "The representational part accounts for the fluency."

more probable that these other strata of reality constituted for her an aspect of the universe and of life to which she was not insensitive, but which she was powerless to penetrate, to master, to organize, and which thus remained beyond the reach of her art. Is it not symptomatic that it was in the middle of composing *The Years* that she wrote that sentence which I quoted earlier, referring to the conflict that divided her between life and art, between the world of everyday reality and the inner world from which she created her art: "The difficulty is the usual one—how to adjust the two worlds."[545] She was doubtless as well equipped as anyone to live in the ordinary world, and I have stressed the intense zest which she brought to the concrete realities of existence.[546] On the other hand, *The Waves* shows how far her sensibility, allied with patient technical experiment, could take her in the exploration of the strata submerged in the depths of the human consciousness. But although she had come to realise that everything was connected, that the reality she was pursuing embraced all the levels of experience, her nature was both too fragile and too sensitive to succeed in embracing this whole. Was the psychological unbalance which underlay her attacks of depression responsible for this incapacity, or was it the result of it? In this matter, clinical documents about her illness—which are unfortunately lacking—would shed light on certain aspects of her genius. Be that as it may, the failure of *The Years* remains significant. In fact, Virginia Woolf only had the illusion that she was making use of several forms; and it is not so much its lack of unity that weakens the novel as the dilution and degeneration of the form she had already mastered. When she declares that she is "breaking the mould made by *The Waves*"[547] she thinks of this as a victory; in fact, she is pronouncing her own condemnation. The "form corresponding to the dimensions of the human being . . ." did not come of its own accord—for the simple reason that the dimensions were not Virginia Woolf's. She had realised what was incomplete about her work, but for all her clear-sightedness she did not associate this limitation, which moreover proved fertile in many respects, with the peculiarities of her own nature.

The picture of society is far vaguer in *The Years* than in any

---

[545] AWD p. 215 (208), quoted *supra*, ch. III, p. 59
[546] Cf. *supra*, ch. III, p. 111 ff
[547] AWD p. 220 (213)

other of her books. Avoiding any exploration in depth of these moments, in order to convey their externality, she has only succeeded in whittling them down to the point of indistinctness. Undoubtedly, she conveys the insignificance of what she condemns as insignificant; but her picture itself, grown insignificant, fails to hold our interest.

If for a brief while she allowed herself to be persuaded by a few favourable criticisms,[548] the severity of Scott James and Edwin Muir summed up her own doubts and turned them into convictions; basically, she accepts their verdict: ". . . E. M. says *The Years* is dead and disappointing. So in effect did S. James. All the lights sank; my reed bent to the ground. Dead and disappointing —so I'm found out and that odious rice pudding of a book is what I thought it—a dank failure."[549] Hugh Walpole "came and said nothing about *The Years*",[550] and his silence is put on the debit side of the novel. On its credit side must be allowed its success in America[551] as well as compliments from Sally Graves and Stephen Spender.[552] But how was the account to be interpreted? Virginia Woolf did not know what to think, but if, by way of therapy, she accepted this encouragement, her refusal to consider the problem more closely[553] seems to indicate that she had no more illusions. Moreover, the proofs of *The Years* had scarcely been corrected when she set to work on *Three Guineas*,[554] and in that same month, June 1937, when she definitely put out of her mind any further thought of *The Years*, "that awful burden",[555] she contemplated writing "a dream story about the top of a mountain. . . . About lying in the snow; about rings of colour; silence; and the solitude".[556] The same nostalgic longing, perhaps, as with *The*

[548] Cf. AWD p. 279 (268-9): ". . . 'they' say almost universally that *The Years* is a masterpiece . . . The praise chorus began yesterday. . . ."

[549] AWD p. 280 (270)

[550] AWD p. 281 (271)

[551] Cf. AWD p. 282 (272): "*The Years* is the best-selling novel in America . . . at the head of the list in the *Herald Tribune*. They have sold 25,000. . . ."

[552] Cf. AWD p. 283 (272): ". . . in private Sally Graves and Stephen Spender approve: so, to sum up, I don't know, this is honest, where I stand; but intend to think no more of it."

[553] Cf. *supra*, note 552

[554] Cf. AWD p. 275 (265): ". . . January 28, 1937 . . . began *Three Guineas* this morning. . . ."

[555] AWD p. 287 (276). Cf. also pp. 294-321 (284-309) and 359 (345)

[556] AWD p. 283 (273). This project referred to again much later, Nov. 23, 1940, at the same time as she notes that she has finished *Between the Acts*, AWD p. 360 (345)

Waves? But since she considered all repetition futile, it was to be something different—and even if there is no mountain-top, nor snow, nor rings of colour in *Between the Acts*, the origin of that book may perhaps be traced back to this vague desire.

BETWEEN THE ACTS (1941)

The dream, the nostalgic longing were to remain pure dream and pure desire, symbolically compensating for her arid struggle with facts. Virginia Woolf was working at *Three Guineas*, which she was to finish at the beginning of January 1938, and at her biography of Roger Fry; her novelist self was disengaged:

Will another novel ever swim up? ... The only hint I have towards it is that it's to be dialogue: and poetry: and prose; all quite distinct. No more long closely written books. But I have no impulse; and shall wait; and shan't mind if the impulse never formulates; though I suspect one of these days I shall get that old rapture.[557]

We shall see to what extent *Between the Acts* fulfilled these expectations. For the time being, at the end of 1937, Virginia Woolf found sufficient relief in writing short stories. One of these, *The Shooting Party*, she thought of working into "the form of a new novel" in which "all the scenes . . . radiate towards a centre."[558] She kept the idea in reserve, but does not appear ever to have made use of it. One point is worth noting, however: she comments that this "would admit of doing it in short bursts".[559] *Three Guineas* was presumably absorbing her too much for these vague projects to take clearer shape. But as soon as she had got her pamphlet out of the way, even before correcting the proofs, she began the first draft of *Roger Fry*, which was to provide her with a regular, solid, sometimes arduous but perhaps essential task for the next two years, while leaving her "free for fresh adventures",[560] in other words for the novel which would mean that exploration, that spontaneity, that were so essential to her as an artist. On April 11, 1938, she notes: "Last night I began making up again: summer's night: a complete whole: that's my

[557] AWD p. 285 (275)

[558] Cf. AWD p. 287 (276-7): ". . . I saw the form of a new novel. It's to be first the statement of the theme: then the restatement: and so on: repeating the same story: singling out this and then that, until the central idea is stated . . . all the scenes must be controlled and radiate to a centre."

[559] AWD p. 286 (277)

[560] AWD p. 288 (278): ". . . on April 1st I think, I started *Roger* . . . I'm quit of that [*Three Guineas*]: free for fresh adventures. . . ."

idea."[561] Nothing else, for the moment, but a time of day: but it was the time of day that opens *Between the Acts*: "It was a summer's night and they were talking . . .", and above all it was a favourite time of day for Virginia Woolf, the moment of respite when, in peace and silence, everything seems about to shrink back into darkness and there lose its appearance, to recover its truth. A summer's night did indeed mean for Virginia Woolf an interlude, an *entr'acte*, and even if this is only a brief instant, a few pages of the work that was being born, it seems indeed to owe its atmosphere and its innermost meaning to this opening, written almost by chance. A fortnight later we read in the Diary a long passage which is worth quoting in its entirety, although it does little more than sketch the setting and movement of *Between the Acts*, and although if one took it literally one might be tempted to reproach the novel for not fulfilling all the promises of the initial project:

... here am I sketching out a new book; only don't please impose that huge burden on me again, I implore. Let it be random and tentative; something I can blow of a morning, to relieve myself of *Roger*: don't, I implore, lay down a scheme; call in all the cosmic intensities; and force my tired and diffident brain to embrace another whole—all parts contributing—not yet awhile. But to amuse myself, let me note: Why not *Poyntzet Hall*: a centre: all literature discussed in connection with real little incongruous living humour: and anything that comes into my head; but "I" rejected: "We" substituted: to whom at the end there shall be an invocation? "We" . . . the composed of many different things . . . we all life, all art, all waifs and strays—a rambling capricious but somehow unified whole—the present state of my mind? And English country; and a scenic old house—and a terrace where nursemaids walk—and people passing—and a perpetual variety and change from intensity to prose, and facts—and notes; and—but eno'![562]

The need for relaxation and freedom is what strikes us most here; the mood recalls that of *Orlando*, but tempered with reserve or lassitude. And this substitution of "we" for "I" betokens a certain renunciation or detachment as though the author were afraid of a return to the tension and intensity inseparable from that focus to which everything converges and from which everything radiates.

Of all the books whose genesis the Diary enables us to follow, this one seems to have been written with the greatest ease: no arduous problems to be solved, no exhausting struggle against a recalcitrant form or material. Settled in "the airy world of

[561] AWD p. 288 (278). Cf. B the A p. 7 (3)   [562] AWD p. 289 (279-80)

Poyntz Hall",[563] Virginia Woolf allows this "fantastic" novel[564] to take shape as though of itself. If sometimes she cannot write for more than an hour,[565] or if excess of concentration makes her head ache,[566] she shows neither irritation nor despondency. The most frequent note is that of satisfaction and pleasure.[567]

By the end of 1938 about half of the book was written.[568] From spring 1939 until spring 1940, preoccupation with the war and the finishing of *Roger Fry* seem to have considerably slowed down, or even interrupted, the writing of *Between the Acts*. On May 29th, Virginia Woolf writes that she is starting work on it again,[569] but although she had only about thirty pages to write, the book remained unfinished until November 23rd.[570] The war, the sense of futility it introduced into life, the uncertainty and the difficulties to which it gave rise,[571] were no doubt responsible for the many interruptions[572] which explain this delay. It is probable, moreover, that Virginia Woolf, faithful to her desire to let the book expand freely, sketched out the successive scenes as the spirit moved her and then went over them, not to correct them, which would mean revision properly so-called, but to enrich them with important additions; at any rate that is what is suggested by a comparison between an early manuscript and the final text.[573]

[563] AWD p. 292 (282) [564] AWD p. 291 (281)

[565] Cf. AWD p. 304 (293): "I'm taking a frisk at *P. H.* at which I can only write for one hour."

[566] Cf. AWD p. 303 (292): "I've been rather absorbed in *P. H.*, hence headache."

[567] Cf. AWD p. 299 (289): "Rather enjoy doing *P. H.*"; similar remarks on pp. 304 (293), 309 (298), 311 (300), 344 (331), particularly 359 (345).

[568] Cf. AWD p. 309 (298): "I've written too 120 pages of *Pointz Hall*. I think of making it a 220 page book."

[569] Cf. AWD p. 334 (321): "Began *P. H.* again today. . . ." Probably not a complete re-writing, since two days later V. W. quotes "Scraps, orts and fragments" from p. 219 (188) of B the A.

[570] Cf. AWD p. 359 (345): "Having this moment finished the Pageant—or Poyntz Hall? . . ."

[571] Cf. AWD pp. 316 (304), 318 (305), 332 (319), 336 (321), 337 (334), 339 (342). In August 1939 the Woolfs left their flat in Tavistock Square for Mecklenburg Square. In September 1940 this new flat was damaged in an air raid and the press was then evacuated to Letchworth; in October of the same year their former flat in Tavistock Square was completely destroyed.

[572] Cf. AWD pp. 356 (341), 358 (343)

[573] This first version is divided into short scenes, each having a title: (The Grove, The love corner, the House . . .); certain scenes are only half their eventual length. This division into scenes with titles seems to have been V. W.'s method at the time, certain references in the Diary suggesting that it was also followed for *Mrs D* (AWD pp. 48 (46), 49 (47), 52 (50) and 53 (51)) and *The W* (AWD p. 152 (151)'

When the first version was finished, Virginia Woolf immediately envisaged not one but two new books, which she would compose simultaneously, as she had done with *Roger Fry* and *Between the Acts*: one as discipline and drudgery, the other as escape, based solely on spontaneous inspiration.[574] From the two brief mentions in the Diary during the following months[575] we may conclude that the polishing of *Between the Acts* raised no important difficulty; it was completed on February 26, 1941. On March 28th, Virginia Woolf committed suicide.

Between the Acts, to give it its final title,[576] had originally been *Pointz Hall* and then *The Pageant*. These three successive titles define the three aspects, or rather the three levels of the work. The novel begins on a summer's evening in an old country house, Pointz Hall, on the eve of the village fête which is to take place in the garden. This is to be *The Pageant*, a synthetic, theatrical and poetic version of *Orlando*, retracing through a series of tableaux the evolution of the British consciousness, from Chaucer's time to the present day. During each interval, the owners of the manor, their guests and the village people resume the thread of their thoughts, preoccupations and feelings, on which the scene they have been watching has left its trace. And when the play is over, as the evening falls, recalling that of the opening pages, we realise that they are each returning to his habitual ways, slipping back into his everyday self, after this interlude which gradually fades into the past to merge with the stuff of which each life is made: acts and entr'actes, dream and reality.

If the unity of time and place, the long drawn out lapse of a few hours, remind us of *Mrs Dalloway* or the first chapter of *To the Lighthouse*, while the pageant suggests the theme of *Orlando*, this latest novel has none the less an accent all its own, and thereby constitutes a new and final stage in that eternal quest in which

---

[574] Cf. WD p. 359 (345-6): "Having this moment finished the Pageant—or Poyntz Hall? . . . my thoughts turn well up, to write the first chapter of the next book (nameless) Anon, it will be called . . . I've enjoyed writing almost every page. This book was only (I must note) written at intervals when the pressure was at its highest, during the drudgery of *Roger*. I think I shall make this my scheme: if the new book can be made to serve as daily drudgery—only I hope to lessen that— anyhow it will be a supported on fact book—then I shall brew some moments of high pressure. I think of taking my mountain top—that persistent vision—as a starting point." [575] Cf. AWD pp. 362 (348) and 364 (350)

[576] Cf. AWD p. 365 (351): "Finished Pointz Hall, the Pageant; the play—finally *Between the Acts* this morning."

the art of Virginia Woolf consisted. What strikes one particularly is the lightness of touch. Nothing is stressed, nothing is probed, nor exploited. Half a dozen characters catch our attention in turn, without holding it: Isa Oliver, her husband Giles, her father-in-law Bartholomew Oliver, her aunt Lucy Swithin, their guests Mrs Manresa and William Dodge, each in turn attain certain moments of intensity that reveal them and yet leave them incomplete, without solidity; only an occasional reference, by association, fills out their slender present with a fragment of the past; but this is no more than a flash, nothing comparable to the "caves" that were dug behind the lives of Clarissa Dalloway or Septimus Smith. Nor is there in the fleeting evocation of their feelings any of the sustained analysis which gave the portrait of Mrs Ramsay such richness and significance. These are faces glimpsed for a few hours, and they do not live beyond this brief encounter. When the book is closed, what we remember is not so much one or other of them as the whole group and the fluctuations of atmosphere caused by their mutual relations. No doubt this is the result of that abandonment of the "I" already mentioned.[577] No one character attempts to explore himself nor invites exploration. Not that the problem is completely eliminated; it remains as the underside of these surface fluctuations, these varied judgments passed by the characters on one another; but this instability, the flickering multiplicity of the "we" is what the author shows us, merely allowing us to guess at the mystery it conceals.

There is the same change of viewpoint in the historical panorama of the pageant, which serves, in the novel, as a "play within a play", as in *The Taming of the Shrew* or *Hamlet*, or rather like the Masque in *The Tempest*. The collective experience of a whole culture, instead of being concentrated into an individual consciousness as in *Orlando*, remains spread out in historic time and is only introduced into the present from outside, so to speak, by means of the landscape, the actors, the reactions of the audience. From this shattering of the centre of reference, this dispersal of the points of view, there undoubtedly results a certain obscurity, as Lord David Cecil points out.[578] The reader

---

[577] Cf. *supra*, p. 320
[578] Cf. *The Spectator*, July 18, 1941: "Virginia Woolf's last novel" by David Cecil. "However it must be confessed that Mrs Woolf does not make her meaning altogether clear. . . . Confusion of convention leaves the reader confused. . . ."

may ask, like Mrs Swithin, "What did it mean?" and conclude, like old Bartholomew, "Too ambitious . . . considering her means!"[579]

Perhaps *Between the Acts* is fully intelligible only to a reader prepared by long familiarity with Virginia Woolf's writings. He alone can recognize her characteristic themes under the faint outlines, and amplify a mere allusion with a full context from elsewhere; the conflict between appearance and reality, between aspirations and realisations, between time and duration, between being and action, between what is manifold and discontinuous in personality and what is one and continuous, between order and absurdity, between the beauty and horror of existence, its fragility and its enduringness. With these, another theme must be included, somewhat unexpected in its frankness: physical desire and the element of antagonism implicit in sexual relationship. No doubt the hatred that is the underside of love was already apparent in the relations between Ralph Denham and Katherine Hilbery; the same mixed feelings were present in *Orlando*, and both *To the Lighthouse* and *The Waves* develop this duality, but on the plane of feeling, whereas here, attraction and repulsion are shown as animal reactions. Are we to see this as a belated manifestation of the author's affinities with D. H. Lawrence,[580] which her recent reading of Freud[581] had encouraged her to express? Or is it simply the rendering in concrete terms, since she wanted the concrete to be continually present in this book, of a side of life which she had hitherto only approached from the psychological angle? However that may be, this note strikes one as much by the sense of discomfort and disquiet it introduces throughout the book as by the emphasis which is laid upon it in the closing page. It stands beside that constant assertion of loneliness that weighs over Virginia Woolf's world. It is amid the solitude and silence of night that Isa and her husband, face to face, meet with their hatred and their love, stripped of all pretence, having shed that mask of words and gestures that are the convention of the world of appearances, the convention of that stage on which we play out our life, thinking we are living it,

[579] B the A p. 249 (213)

[580] Cf. AWD pp. 187-8 (182): "I am also reading D. H. L. with the usual sense of frustration: and that he and I have too much in common. . . ."

[581] Cf. AWD p. 326 (314): "Now I'm going to read Freud", and p. 322 (310): "I read Freud on Groups. . . ."

whereas it is in the darkness, in what we call "between the acts", that the essential things take place, that the miraculous drama of life and death is ineluctably acted out.

And thus the enigmatic phrase that closes the book: "Then the curtain rose. They spoke",[582] is open to a host of interpretations. The interval which was brought to an end by the rising of the curtain, and which the book has just shown us, is none other than everyday life, the life of Monday and Tuesday, with all those familiar gestures which, from morning till night, we perform according to a constantly repeated ritual and rhythm. The manor house, the garden, the barn are none other than the theatre of the world, which with an imperceptible wave of her wand Virginia Woolf has gradually broadened out to its true dimensions. Spectators, actors, the author, stage hands and costumiers jostle one another, look for one another, find and then lose one another, talk of trivial matters, of their minor and major worries, while each pursues, more or less obscurely, his inner dream. Meeting at random, they improvise those scenes and interrupted dialogues in which they act, half as themselves and half as the characters they have assumed, torn between being and playing a part. But all this matters little however much importance we attach to it; a vain, ridiculous surface agitation, born afresh each day and dying every night. It is only a barely perceptible, insignificant tremor in the immensity of the cosmic process. Old Bartholomew, rising from his armchair to go to bed, only repeats the movement of prehistoric man standing upright at last.[583] These two identical gestures, separated by millions of years, are equally insignificant if considered individually; it is only in their infinite repetition that they acquire meaning, become real gestures and find their place in the history of the world. In the same way the love between Isa and Giles, the flaws and failings of which have seemed of paramount importance all day, dwindles to a purely animal reaction and takes its place in the universal scheme of things, just as this twentieth century night becomes one with the nights of the Stone Age.

The ceaselessly repeated round of the hours and days, the eternal cycle; true, there is something of this in *Between the Acts*,[584] as in the other novels, particularly from *Orlando* onwards. But I feel that a more disillusioned note, perhaps even a bitterer one,

---

[582] B the A p. 256 (219)   [583] Cf. B the A p. 255 (218)   [584] B the A p. 256 (219)

sounds here. After "Time Passes", with its indifference and its absurdity, Lily Briscoe finished her painting, and James Ramsay, despite his disappointment, did reach the lighthouse; Bernard faced time and death, although the waves went on breaking on the shore; and dawn, in *The Years* as in *The Waves*, did bring a gleam of hope into the closing pages. Here, the curtain rises on a sky "drained of light, severe, stone cold".[585] True, this heart of darkness[586] may recall the ultimate retreat in which Mrs Ramsay recovered her integrity, and the comparison is not a misleading one. After voyaging through illusion, we must seek to land on the shores of truth; after the meaningless interval, we must resume the thread of the drama, recover the Word. But when we are faced with the imminence of that decisive gesture, despite the fascination of the sky and the free immensity with which it fills the window,[587] the night remains threatening: the house has lost its protective power, and the visceral terror that the cave man felt, staring out into the darkness, grips one's being on the threshold of mystery and shadow—on the threshold of death.

From these final pages a deep disillusionment, akin to despair, spills over on to the whole book, dimming its brightness, sapping its joy. The pageant had at first appeared a parody; now it grows bitterly ironic. It had seemed to be playing with past and present in the vein of *Orlando*, establishing unity under diversity, the permanent under the transitory. The confusion of the signs of reality and appearance, life and play-acting which it introduced into the novel, which had seemed a piece of mischievous fun, now wears a baleful aspect. We had not been very sure what was real and what was fiction, or rather a representation of reality; the play represented life, but in its movement, its force, its permanence and richness, this representation was more convincing, true and more real than the insipid reality of the intervals between the acts. But at the same time these, in spite of their fugitive insignificance, were after all more authentically life than the pageant was. This uncertainty, these cross-purposes were just a witty pastime, stimulating and refreshing. And then suddenly as the curtain rises on a different scene we are roused from our somnambulism: play and setting, actors and audience, Queen

---

[585] B the A p. 255 (218)
[586] B the A p. 256 (219): ". . . in the heart of darkness, in the fields of night."
[587] Cf. B the A pp. 255 (218), 256 (219)

Elizabeth and the shopkeeper who played her, history and the present day, appearance and reality—all topple over into the wings: this midsummer afternoon's dream vanishes, leaving before us only the abyss.

Never had Virginia Woolf expressed her pessimism so categorically. Her doubt had always been accompanied by a belief in life and in the beauty of the world, fragile though both of these might be. And it is symptomatic that, until its final pages, the book encourages our illusion. It is an elegy, a hymn to love, to the earth, to men, to the life that has vanished. If I may have been mistaken about the irony that tinges *Between the Acts*, the error is surely slighter than it appears. Virginia Woolf herself probably wrote this last book in a mood of ambiguity; towards the ghosts that she knew to be ghosts, towards the illusions that she knew to be illusions she still retained that passionate love that had helped her to live. But at the end of this reminiscent reverie, she was forced to awaken; after the pilgrimage was over, she had to admit to herself, to acknowledge that the gods were dead and that nothing was to be found here below save the unchanging earth and the suffering, mortal flesh of man.

In this sense, *Between the Acts* assumes a sort of testamentary value. Virginia Woolf breaks off her book on the threshold of that moment of truth, on those unutterable words which for thirty years she had been trying to interpret, using every artifice to give transparency to what was opaque, to break up by means of art the artificialities and inadequacies of language. We have seen that her state of health was the determining cause of her suicide, and the projects over which she was brooding a few weeks before her death make it rash to advance any hypothesis involving reasons of another order. And yet what does one know of the sum total of thoughts that lead up to any act? Did she entrust to her Diary any feelings that her husband's discretion may have concealed? What secret or even unconscious obsession had prepared her for this abdication, which a physical accident served to precipitate? Had she, too, found herself at the end of that play, or rather of that *entr'acte* which we call life, ready to see the curtain rise on a stage lit up, at last, by that light to which she aspired?

In this respect one entry in the Diary, associating suicide with the absurdity of existence, seems to anticipate the irruption of

aircraft, symbol of violence and unreason, into the serene afternoon sky, and enables one to imagine the slow, hidden working
of some fundamental obsessions:

A saying of Leonard's comes into my head in this season of complete
inanity and boredom. "Things have gone wrong somehow." It was
the night C. killed herself. We were walking along that silent blue
street with the scaffolding. I saw all the violence and unreason crossing
in the air: ourselves small; a tumult outside: something terrifying:
unreason—shall I make a book out of this? It would be a way of
bringing order and speed again into my world.[588]

This was in 1932: the book, or books, for *The Years* and *Three
Guineas* share in this vision just as much as *Between the Acts*, are all
directed towards the same exorcism. Must we conclude that,
when this proved ineffective, Virginia Woolf found herself alone
and powerless, struggling with her demons, and succumbed?

But in itself, quite apart from any biographical context and
from the rest of her works, *Between the Acts* does not, perhaps,
entirely succeed in yielding all its secrets. The fact that the author
describes this novel as "more quintessential than the others"[589]
does not necessarily imply that its richness is self-evident. For the
reader, whose view takes in the play and the spectators both at
once, the play lacks the concentration it would gain on the stage,
while the spectators fall short of the everyday reality they should
acquire. Without accepting L. P. Hartley's verdict that the book
marks a return to an earlier manner, one can agree with him that
the characters are presented with a certain objectivity[590]; it
remains none the less true that they are merely sketched in, too
lightly to constitute the essential interest of the book which, in
fact, lies elsewhere. If, as the *Guardian* critic suggests, "*Between the
Acts* contains three books in one—a novel, a book of poems and a
play"[591]—this mixture of genres, after which Virginia Woolf had
hankered for so long,[592] is indeed effectively achieved, too effectively perhaps, so that the reader remains divided between

[588] AWD p. 181 (175-6) (May 25, 1932)
[589] AWD p. 359 (345): "I think it's more quintessential than the others. More
milk skimmed off."
[590] L. P. Hartley, "The Literary Lounger", *The Sketch*, Aug. 13, 1941: "*Between
the Acts* marks a return to Mrs Woolf's earlier manner, before individuality had
become soluble in the crucible of timelessness. . . . There is more objective characterization. . . ."
[591] Cf. *The Guardian*, Aug. 15, 1941: "Virginia Woolf's Last Novel."
[592] Cf. *supra*, pp. 249, 281, 303-4

various possible attitudes. One is tempted to conclude, like the author: "... it's an interesting attempt in a new method."[593] The variety and perfection of each page are more striking than the general design and the meaning of the whole, which the structure is insufficient to elucidate. I can subscribe only to the first part of Edwin Muir's twofold judgment: "*Between the Acts* is one of her most ambitious and most perfect novels."[594] One is reminded both of the merits and of the imperfections of *Jacob's Room*. Now, in full mastery of her genius, Virginia Woolf attacked a new form; this last book is, like *Jacob's Room*, a brilliant experiment in synthesis, but it it is only an experiment. We may wonder what *Mrs Dalloway*, what *To the Lighthouse* she would have had to write to bring to fruition the masterpiece that lies in germ in this her final endeavour.

2. STORIES AND SKETCHES

With the exception of "A Society" and "Blue and Green" (originally published in March 1921, in the only collection to appear in her lifetime, *Monday or Tuesday*), Virginia Woolf's sketches and stories, eighteen in number, were collected by Leonard Woolf in a small volume, *A Haunted House and other short stories*, published in 1944. In his preface, Leonard Woolf indicates how Virginia Woolf wrote these pieces, thus suggesting the place they should be allotted in her work:

All through her life, Virginia Woolf used at intervals to write short stories. It was her custom, whenever an idea for one occurred to her, to sketch it out in a very rough form and then to put it away in a drawer. Later, if an editor asked her for a short story, and she felt in the mood to write one (which was not frequent), she would take a sketch out of her drawer and rewrite it, sometimes a great many times. Or if she felt, as she often did, while writing a novel that she required to rest her mind by working at something else for a time, she would either write a critical essay or work upon one of her sketches for short stories.[595]

Without questioning the fact that these brief compositions were sometimes considered by Virginia Woolf merely as inter-

[593] AWD p. 359 (345)
[594] Edwin Muir in *The Listener*, July 24, 1941
[595] HH Foreword, p. 7 (v)

ludes, and that the chance requirements of her profession induced her to write some particular story at one moment rather than another, if we looked no further than this statement of Leonard Woolf's we should be liable to neglect one important aspect of several of these writings: their experimental character. This is stressed in the Diary,[596] and furthermore chronology provides an argument in favour of this hypothesis, which a study of the texts will confirm. In fact, the publication of the stories falls into three brief periods: 1917-1921, 1927-1929 and 1938-1940.[597] Although these dates only enable one to give a rough estimate of the time of writing,[598] they correspond too closely to the periods of exploration in Virginia Woolf's career for the coincidence to be a fortuitous one.

The first group in particular, which includes at least four stories prior to the composition of *Jacob's Room* and three that are contemporary with it, represents unquestionably an exploratory path which was to lead to that novel.[599] With the other two groups, although the relations between the sketches and the novels of the same period are less clear, and as we shall see are confused by other links with earlier works, one of them coincides with the point when, feeling her way towards *The Waves*, Virginia Woolf lingered over *Orlando*, and the other with the point when, at the end of that long labour *The Years*, she was turning in the direction of *Between the Acts*. Written between 1927 and 1929,

[596] Cf. AWD p. 31 (30). Speaking of *Monday or Tuesday*, she writes: ". . . they don't see that I'm after something interesting", and p. 33 (32): "And then there was Roger [Fry] who thinks I'm on the track of real discoveries. . . ." Cf. also AWD p. 23 (22), quoted *supra*, ch. III, pp. 72-3.

[597] Dates of publication of the stories:

    I. 1917-1921: 1917, The Mark on the Wall; 1919, Kew Gardens; 1920, An Unwritten Novel; Solid Objects; 1921, A Haunted House; Monday or Tuesday; The String Quartet; Blue and Green; A Society.

    II. 1927-1929: 1927, The New Dress; 1928, Moments of Being; 1929, The Lady in the Looking Glass.

    III. 1938-1940: 1938, The Shooting Party; The Duchess and the Jeweller; 1939, Lappin and Lapinova.

    IIIa. Posthumously published: The man who loved his kind; The Searchlight; The Legacy; Together and Apart; The Summing up.

[598] "The Duchess and the Jeweller", published in April 1938, seems to have been finished by August 1937 (cf. AWD p. 286 (275)); "The Shooting Party", published in March 1938, seems to have been finished by October 1937 (cf. AWD p. 287 (276)); "Lappin and Lapinova", recast in November 1938, had been sketched in 1918 (cf. AWD p. 308 (297)). We have only internal evidence about the five last stories (IIIa) which will be discussed in due course.

[599] Cf. *supra*, ch. V

"The New Dress", "Moments of Being" and "The Lady in the Looking Glass" are each in its way studies of those special moments which reveal the truth about a human being; in this, they link up with *Mrs Dalloway* and, more, with *To the Lighthouse*; but they are less concerned with repeating Lily Briscoe's vision than with developing its potentialities and trying to go beyond these. Finally, in the last stories, the endeavour to combine poetry with realism, social satire with psychological analysis, an aspiration imperfectly satisfied in *The Years*, seems to anticipate *Between the Acts*.

On the strength of these observations, I might have divided my study of the sketches between these three periods. However, I felt this would mean unduly stressing a single aspect of them which, though not unimportant, was secondary or at any rate supplementary; it would also mean neglecting their autonomous character. If, indeed, they may have served as exercises, they are something more than that. And I have chosen therefore to classify them according to other criteria, more appreciative of their individual character and thus more apt to encourage a just assessment of their merits.

Without reverting to my earlier analysis of "Kew Gardens", I shall associate with it four other impressionist studies, "Blue and Green", "A Haunted House", "Monday or Tuesday" and "The String Quartet". These five sketches are characterized by their lack of any dramatic framework and by their attempt to present, in a contiguity which creates continuity, the disparate elements of consciousness, made homogeneous by uniformity of tone and the absence of any precise reference to place or time. We have here moments snipped out of existence, without any "before" or "after"; the close of day between two flights of a heron through the sky ("Monday or Tuesday"), the space of time between the moment of taking one's seat in a concert hall and the moment of parting at the door ("The String Quartet"). The consciousness through which there flit sensations, perceptions, fragments of thought, images from the past and from elsewhere, fancies, words heard or spoken, has no face and no body. It does not exist in itself; it exists in what passes through it, making and unmaking it constantly, leaving the reader with the contradictory reality of this possession and this transience. One is tempted to speak of pure atmosphere. "A Haunted House", with its opening phrase:

"Whatever hour you woke there was a door shutting"[600] might incline one to do so. But the ambiguity by which the inhabitants of the haunted house become one with the ghosts that haunt it is evidence of a different intention. The atmosphere, strictly speaking, is only one element in these stories. What they are trying to convey is, at the same time, the way in which it pervades the being who is immersed in it, and the way in which it emanates from him. For basically, the real subject is one moment of his existence, and it is in this respect that these sketches are on the way that leads to *Jacob's Room*, *Mrs Dalloway* and *The Waves*. And indeed their failure, or at least their uncertain character, can be explained when we set them beside the comparable moments that make up the later novels, for which they prepared the way. It is the accumulation and interconnectedness of such moments that brings to life Jacob or Clarissa, Susan or Bernard. If we isolate one moment, its resonances remain dead; cut off from its whole it becomes pale and lifeless; all that remains is a wonderful shimmering background where the human being is lost. Only "Kew Gardens", perhaps on account of its greater complexity and the solidity of its structure, is fully successful; the others delight the eye and ear without satisfying the mind. The most extreme example, "Blue and Green", goes outside the realm of reality to lose itself in the world of dream, where images are connected only by a slender thread. This arbitrary universe was not the one Virginia Woolf sought to explore, and that is doubtless why she proposed leaving it out of the later editions which she envisaged.[601]

Of the same type as "An Unwritten Novel" are three other stories: "Moments of Being," "The Lady in the Looking Glass" and "The Shooting Party". Despite differences of treatment and style, the general plan is the same. All four show the writer in quest of "Mrs Brown", according to the methods set forth in the 1923 article. In fact, Minnie Marsh in "An Unwritten Novel" is elder sister to Mrs Brown, and Virginia Woolf undoubtedly bore in mind the sketch—written in 1919-1920, when elaborating the typical figure on whom she based her theory.[602]

---

[600] HH p. 9 (3)

[601] Cf. HH Foreword, p. 7 (vi)

[602] The first article entitled "Mr Bennett and Mrs Brown" appeared in the *New York Evening Post*'s Literary Review on Nov. 17, 1923; it was then incorporated

SYNTHESIS AND FICTION

"The Shooting Party", although the last in date of the series, is outwardly the closest to its prototype. As in "An Unwritten Novel", the anonymous observer-narrator, sitting opposite an unknown woman in a railway carriage, reconstitutes from a few signs a whole section of the stranger's life, complete with settings and companions. At the end of the journey, the construction breaks down before a touch of reality: the son waiting on the platform relegates into the world of fancy Minnie Marsh, the maiden aunt with her unhappy love affairs and her miserly relations. In the same way, under the glare of the station lights Milly Masters, the poor tailor's daughter who has been seduced by the squire, turns into a very ordinary woman visiting London on some trivial errand. But whereas in "An Unwritten Novel" the makebelieve story keeps referring back to the real character for confirmation and impetus, in "The Shooting Party" it flows on uninterruptedly and thus gains an autonomy which seems a guarantee of authenticity, so that at the *dénouement* this para-reality withstands the corrosive power of facts. The author does not feel compelled to justify it, as she had done in the last paragraph of "An Unwritten Novel". Even if all that really existed was "M. M.", the woman with the suitcase and the brace of pheasants, while the Squire, the manor and the shooting party were mere phantasms, these convince us and remain in our minds when the slender reality from which they were born has vanished into the past and oblivion.[603]

In "Moments of Being" the observer, Fanny Wilmott, constructs out of fragments—gestures, appearances, words—the life and personality of her piano teacher, Julia Craye: her family circumstances, her manifestations of avidity, independence and frustration, all contribute to confirm the hypothesis of a narrow, disappointed life. Then suddenly Julia Craye takes Fanny in her arms and kisses her mouth. This revelation, without completely destroying the image Fanny had formed, reorganizes it around a different centre. The stress which had been laid on loneliness and pathos now falls on independence and will-power: what had seemed semi-failure becomes semi-victory.

into "Character in Fiction", which appeared in *The Criterion* in July 1924; after various other appearances under the title "Mr Bennett and Mrs Brown" it was included, under this title, in CDB.

[603] The experimental aspect of The SP is suggested in AWD p. 287 (276-7).

Unlike "An Unwritten Novel" and "The Shooting Party", "Moments of Being" contains a certain dramatic element closely linked to the general theme of the exploration of a personality. Although Fanny chooses unhappy solitude, the possibility of voluntary solitude is never absent, and a sort of tension arises which is only resolved in the final paragraph. Moreover, the conflict between the real and the imagined is not what is most essential in this story: the title indicates that it is more specifically concerned with the revelation which replaces this conflict and solves it by integrating the contradictory elements. The moment of being is at the meeting of the two worlds where, during the space of a privileged moment, we catch a glimpse of truth. This moment, defined here by the commonplace sentence "Slater's pins have no points",[604] recalls Joyce's "Epiphanies", whose characteristic is the liberation of the revelatory power latent in an insignificant word or gesture.[605]

"The Lady in the Looking Glass" might have been called "An Unwritten Novel". In fact, in the effervescent mood that was to produce *Orlando*, Virginia Woolf notes in her Diary:

But I can think of more books than I shall ever be able to write. How many little stories come into my head! For instance: Ethel Sands not looking at her letters. What this implies. One might write a book of short significant separate scenes. She did not open her letters.[606]

The story ends on practically the same sentence. If the mere fact that these letters were bills explains the indifference of Isabella Tyson, alias Ethel Sands, the revelation implied by this gesture is made dramatic by the slow preparation at cross-purposes, the misunderstanding which is the theme of the story. "The Lady in the Looking Glass", however, combines the psychological enquiry of "An Unwritten Novel" and the rich impressionism of "Kew Gardens". This alliance is perhaps not

---

[604] Cf. HH p. 89 (103): the phrase, which opens the story and reappears in its closing lines, was the title it originally bore on its publication in *The Forum* (N. Y.) in January 1928; it serves as sub-title in HH.

[605] Cf. AWD p. 99 (98): "As usual, side stories are sprouting in great variety as I wind this up: a book of characters; the whole string being pulled out from some simple sentence, like Clara Pater's 'Don't you find that Barker's pins have no points to them?' I think I can spin out all their entrails this way; but it is hopelessly undramatic."

[606] Cf. AWD p. 114 (112).

unconnected with the exploration which Virginia Woolf was then undertaking for *The Waves*. That reality is distinct from our image of it is suggested, from the beginning, by the distinction between the real scene and its reflection in the looking glass. And paradoxically, as one might have expected from Virginia Woolf, the reflected image, with its precision and fixity contrasted with the confusion and movement with which real space is filled by the light and shadows, the air, the flowers, captures the essence of reality and reveals it. Isabella has disappeared into the garden; the observer's conception of her is suggested by her delightful home, her luxuriant garden. Her wealth implies happiness and success; her silence, mystery and passion, and the bundle of letters the postman has just flung on to the marble table bears witness to this. But when Isabella reappears in the mirror, the light that surrounds her figure reveals a very different truth: loneliness, indifference, emptiness, age—and the letters are only bills. The same emptiness, the same sterility in social relations are similarly conveyed in the final pages of *Between the Acts*, where the heroine, another Isa, again has "only bills" by the evening post.[607]

The mirror which thus separates accessories from essentials, appearances from reality, and as if by magic dissipates that myth engendered by imagination which is alien both to the observer and the observed, is surely of a different nature from the incident that invalidates the imaginary character foisted on Mrs Brown or Minnie Marsh, Milly Masters or Julia Craye. There, the direct impact of reality had burst the iridescent bubble blown by a self-indulgent fancy; here, we have a second reality, reflected in the light. This light, indeed, shines again in "The Shooting Party": it is the glare from a station lamp, substituting an ordinary woman for that romantic figure Milly Masters. Does this common factor between the two last stories in the same vein entitle us to suppose that Virginia Woolf meant to give significance to this detail, that between the flesh and blood figure, opaque, unknown, and the character elaborated by imagination on the strength of certain details, an autonomous reality inter-

---

[607] Cf. B the A p. 252 (216): "Isa had only bills." Note also that we find a Mrs Sands in *Between the Acts*, and also a scene of Isa at her looking glass where the relations between the character and her reflection are considered (pp. 19-23 (13-16)).

venes, dazzling and far purer, the reality of artistic creation, identical with the revealing vision? Such a hypothesis, although not certain, seems not impossible. But it may be, too, that the sort of abstraction of the mirror's truth-revealing function aimed at in this story was suggested to the author by the theme of the looking glass which, two years earlier, she had used chiefly for psychological ends in "The New Dress".[608]

With "The New Dress" we come to the stories which form part of what one might call the *Mrs Dalloway* saga, which comprises also "The Man who loved his Kind", "Together and Apart" and "The Summing Up". In this group, "The New Dress" stands apart. From its date, 1927, as well as from several pieces of internal evidence, it seems to be a reject left over from the novel. We see the famous party through the eyes of Mabel, a humble acquaintance of the Dalloways. Like the other guests in the novel, she is greeted in the cloakroom by Mrs Barnet, who sizes up each visitor's class and dress. The perspicacity of the old servant, already mentioned in the novel,[609] lies at the root of Mabel's misfortunes; Mrs Barnet's attitude makes her aware of the unsuitability of her dress, and this feeling isolates her during the whole party, making her conscious, amidst all these rich people, of her own poverty, then of the failure of her life, and revealing to her, moreover, the vanity and sterility of such social contacts. After having endured the hypocrisy, indifference and selfishness of others and her own humiliation, she makes her retreat with a polite lie: "I have enjoyed myself enormously." This lie synthesizes all the lies, all the treacheries not merely of these few hours but of the whole of existence. We see from this that its setting is not the only factor that connects "The New Dress" with *Mrs Dalloway*. The satirical implications of the story are akin to those of the novel; at an even deeper level, through her pessimism, Mabel recalls Septimus, while like him she is connected with Clarissa by "a divine moment" of sea and sand

---

[608] Cf. G & R p. 16 (16). In "The Narrow Bridge of Art", published under the title of "Poetry, Fiction and the Future" (*N. Y. Herald Tribune*, Aug. 14, 1927), a few months after the publication of "The New Dress", we read: "There trips along by the side of our modern beauty some mocking spirit which sneers at beauty for being beautiful; which turns the looking-glass and shows us that the other side of her cheek is pitted and deformed." It is this reverse side that the mirror shows in both these stories.

[609] Cf. Mrs D p. 183 (253)

and sun.[610] Apart from the recurrence of this theme we may note also, as though referring to Peter Walsh and his life-story, Mabel's youthful daydream: she had pictured herself living in India, married to a hero, whereas Hubert, her husband, has a dreary subordinate job in the Law Courts. Finally, perhaps she was intended to form a parallel to Ellie Henderson,[611] or else to take her place at the party. Like Ellie, in fact, Mabel is an outsider, reluctantly invited at the last minute, and is too poor to spend money on her dress. The distance that divides her from this world allows it to be seen, through her, from a different angle to that of the other characters. Nevertheless, Mabel's viewpoint is as unlike Ellie's as is their way of dressing: Ellie is natural and sweet-tempered, whereas Mabel is timid and embittered. Perhaps Virginia Woolf was rightly reluctant to alter the atmosphere of the closing pages of her novel by this corrosive ingredient, and therefore relegated this character into the drawer where she kept her rough sketches.

In spite of all the links that can be found between the short story and the novel, "The New Dress" is none the less a perfectly self-contained narrative, with its own progress and peripeteia. Mabel, having gone through the hell of her shame and loneliness, reaches the safe shore of happy memories, which reconcile her to herself and her life; she acquires new strength and resolution; but is it through having looked in the mirror, having once again encountered the same Mabel that the others see? She can merely mumble a conventional falsehood, and goes back to her own truth.

The three other stories which take their setting from Mrs Dalloway's party, written considerably later, it seems, even if the idea of them occurred to Virginia Woolf while she was writing her novel, reflect the latter only indirectly. The atmosphere of a social gathering is conducive to the development of the theme which, like the setting, is common to all three. They are variants on the difficulty of communicating with other people. In "The Man who Loved his Kind" Prickett Ellis and Miss O'Keefe, both

[610] Cf. HH p. 50 (55): "... or down by the sea on the sand in the sun, at Easter— let her recall it—... and then the melody of the waves—'Hush, hush', they said ... yes, it was a divine moment, and there she lay, she felt, in the hand of the Goddess who was the world ...". Cf. "Fear no more", Mrs D, pp. 34 (44), 45 (59), 154 (211).

[611] Cf. Mrs D p. 185 (256) ff.

philanthropists in different ways, try in vain to tell each other of their common love for humanity, while exasperated by the sight of the frivolity and indifference around them. All that they are able to express, or to feel, is hatred! The same impossibility of mutual understanding divides the two characters of "Together and Apart". Just as Prickett Ellis and Miss O'Keefe failed to meet on the common ground of philanthropy, so Mr Serle and Miss Anning fail to make contact in their common recollections of Canterbury which, for a brief second, had given them a sense of closeness; but it was for a second only. They go back each to his solitude and separate, indifferent to each another. Whereas in "The New Dress" and "The Man who Loved his Kind" Virginia Woolf had given free rein to her sense of caricature and had got her effects by exaggeration, here she works in half-tones, suggesting the submerged world which she knows so well, where she can here and there use her characters for a meditation on her favourite themes. The same atmosphere recurs in "The Summing Up", where a man and a woman are talking in Mrs Dalloway's garden. The woman, indeed, listens more than she speaks; she listens and thinks about something else, spell-bound by the perfection of the place and the moment. From this advanced point in our civilization she looks back, vaguely, to the primitive times when marshes lay where London stands, for the two extremes are the very substance of the soul, although the riddle of nature and man remains insoluble. This Sasha Latham is akin to Mrs Swithin in *Between the Acts* in her sense of cosmic continuity as well as in her calm, wondering acceptance of things human.

"Lappin and Lapinova" and "The Legacy" are abridged dramas of married life. They show, the first in a vein of heroic-comic fantasy, the second with a tension which is sustained from beginning to end with the help of dramatic irony, the deterioration of relations between a married couple, gradually slipping into what, in her note on the married relationship written in 1926, she called "the automatic customary unconscious days on either side".[612] Since Virginia Woolf wrote a first version of "Lappin and Lapinova" in 1917 or 1918[613], returned to the theme and even wrote another story of the same subject towards the end

---

[612] AWD p. 98 (97)

[613] Cf. AWD p. 308 (297) (Nov. 22, 1938): ". . . a story written I think at Asheham 20 years ago or more; when I was writing *Night and Day* perhaps."

of her life, we may assume that her opinions on this point never altered. Moreover, from the hesitancies of Rachel and Terence in *The Voyage Out* to the more concrete hostility between Isa and Giles in *Between the Acts*, every one of her novels touches on this problem. It is a common enough problem, no doubt, but with Virginia Woolf it acquires freshness through its implications. It is just a special case of the difficulty all human beings have in understanding and knowing one another, an example of the ignorance and loneliness from which we try in vain to escape.

The protagonists of "Lappin and Lapinova" triumph for a while, thanks to the artifice of a personal and secret world in which they take refuge. Their escapades into the new Forest of Arden into which Rosalind has led her solemn sensible Ernest, where he becomes King Lappin and she, the little silver-grey hare with big protuberant eyes, a little crazy but none the less a Queen, bring them together while separating and protecting them from everyday life—their own and that of others. But there comes a day when the spell will not work. King Lappin dies first, and when Rosalind mourns his loss, Ernest, who had reassumed for good his sensible man's skin, calls his wife a fool. It only remains for Lapinova to die in her turn. But Rosalind cannot repudiate Rosalind, so that this moment marks the end of their love.

Virginia Woolf dreaded sentimentality too much not to have realised that there was an excess of sentiment in this story: no doubt owing to the author's youth, as is the discreet reference to *As You Like It*. These characteristics stamp it as contemporary with *Night and Day*. But it is also contemporary with *The Years* and *Three Guineas*. Lacking the original version, we may suppose that the author sought to redeem her youthful weaknesses by introducing the satiric verve of her later books: the portraits of the Thorburns of Porchester Terrace and their worthy descendant, Ernest, might have come straight out of *Marriage à la Mode*.

In "The Legacy" Gilbert Clandon, after the death of his wife Angela, gives their secretary Sissy Miller a brooch that Angela has left her, and reads through the diary she had left on purpose for him. He discovers from this how Angela had passed gradually from love, admiration and enthusiasm into lukewarmness, indifference and bored loneliness; how she had flung herself into social work, and met a certain B. M. with whom she seemed to have fallen in love. She had refused to go away with him; he committed suicide, and the last sentence in the diary reveals that she herself had died not as the result of an accident, but having deliberately chosen to give up a life that had lost its meaning and to join the man she loved—the brother of Sissy Miller—in death. Can we trace the origin of this story to "C's" suicide mentioned in the Diary of May 25, 1932,[614] and are we to imagine Virginia Woolf working out the dramatic story from one action, as she worked out a whole life from one face in "An Unwritten Novel" and "The Shooting Party"? This is merely a hypothesis, unsupported by any document. None the less, just as I referred to this passage in the Diary in connection with *Between the Acts*,[615] so it is tempting to derive both the novel and the story from the same disturbing real life incident. The relations between Isa and Giles, surely, have suffered the same deterioration as those between Angela and her husband. And does not the immemorial night on which the curtain rises at the close of *Between the Acts*, a symbol of absolute time and space which alone would render possible communication between human beings and explain the absurdity of existence, prefigure the death in which Angela has chosen to join B. M.? And, when the catharsis of literary creation failed to work, after a season of emptiness and boredom, who, or what, did Virginia Woolf herself seek to find by means of her own suicide? Are we to add, furthermore, to these sources the accident related in the Diary on April 8, 1925? Two factors favour this hypothesis: the impression that the sight made on Virginia Woolf: "A great sense of the brutality and wildness of the world remains with me",[616] and the fact that she connects this event with an accident to her niece Angelica, whose name would thus, by suggestion, have provided that of her heroine.

Independently of the echoes which it awakens, "The Legacy" is Virginia Woolf's most dramatic story, in the sense that the

---

[614] Cf. AWD p. 181 (175-6): "A saying of Leonard's comes into my head in this season of complete inanity and boredom. 'Things have gone wrong somehow.' It was the night C. killed herself. . . . I saw all the violence and unreason crossing in the air: ourselves small; a tumult outside: something terrifying: unreason—shall I make a book out of this? It would be a way of bringing order and speed again into my world."

[615] Cf. *supra*, p. 328

[616] Cf. AWD p. 71 (70-1). She notes that Vanessa, not having seen the incident, could not share her feeling, "though she made some effort to connect it with Angelica's accident last spring".

riddle towards whose solution it moves with a sure art of suggestions and partial revelations, is connected with action rather than with a personality. The chain of events leading up to the *dénouement* provides a solid basis for the accompanying characterization, and confers on the whole more firmness and clarity of outline than is generally found in these stories.

The other four, while they bear the imprint of their author in detail of execution and in the suggestion of certain themes, seem to be, each in its way, incursions into less familiar fields. "Solid Objects" (1920) is a philosophical tale[617] where, after an opening reminiscent of *Jacob's Room*, Virginia Woolf portrays a man who, having found a piece of glass brought in by the waves, fascinated by this "solid object"—truth, concealed and misunderstood—abandons a promising political career in order to devote himself to an eccentric search for other specimens of this reality. "The Duchess and the Jeweller" is a satirical portrait in the same vein as *The Years*. "The Searchlight", which is not easy to label, is at the same time perhaps the least successful of all the stories and the most profoundly typical of Virginia Woolf. In the flash of a searchlight, a woman glimpses a fragment of the past—not even of her own past but of her grandmother's youth. The meaning of this fragmentary and fleeting revelation only appears in the closing lines: "The light . . . only falls here and there."[618] The symbol of the telescope thanks to which the narrator's grandfather discovered the woman who was to become his wife links the story, after a fashion, with the searchlights that are raking the sky. But the whole thing remains vague; the moment of vision loses its special flavour in the long drawn out narrative that is needed to clarify or communicate it. As for "A Society", Virginia Woolf was surely right in wishing to exclude it from later editions. This social fable tells of the imaginary enquiry undertaken by a group of women into the basis of civilization, in order to decide whether it is worth while perpetuating the race. The general design is uncertain, the irony often clumsy. None the less this failed venture into militant literature, which Virginia Woolf had the good taste to cast aside, marks an interesting stage in her development. It contains the germs of *A Room of One's Own* and

617 Cf. Louis Gillet, "Virginia Woolf et le Conte Philosophique", *Nouvelles Littéraires,* Jan. 26, 1935.
618 HH p. 106 (125)

Three Guineas; it shows that her feminist attitude remained constant as regards education, marriage, literature and the liberal professions, as did her opinions about men of law, academics, soldiers and politicians. But it was to take another ten years, the experience of writing *Orlando* and perhaps too, the self-confidence that came from success to sharpen her verve. When the ideas of "A Society" had been developed and satisfactorily set forth in her pamphlets, this somewhat feeble story could be put aside as a rough draft. It contains, incidentally, a certain biographical interest by its account of the visit made to one of His Majesty's ships by Virginia Woolf and her friends disguised as Ethiopians.

It is difficult to formulate any general judgment on such dissimilar pieces. If "The Legacy" and "The Duchess and the Jeweller" correspond, more or less, to the traditional conception of a short story, the rest can only be described as sketches or studies. In this field, as in that of the novel, Virginia Woolf refused to be bound by ready made formulae. Granted her hostility to any sort of "story", to the organization of events within a rigid framework of time and space, it might be said that short story writing was a challenge to her. Yet just as certain novelists have used the short story to emphasize and epitomize their vision of the world, Virginia Woolf sought to render in a few pages the essence of her universe. "Moments of Being" might serve as sub-title for each of these fragments. They attempt, indeed, to convey the unique quality of an instant when the world of our senses and the inner world, the present and the past, the here and the elsewhere, like the different elements in a solution, suddenly combine to form that solid body, reality—which, a moment later, once glimpsed, is again dissolved into its elements. From this very nature of her reality, Virginia Woolf was able to extract a principle of composition which may be considered a rule of the genre as she conceived it and through which, moreover, she carries on a tradition.

She always starts from something mysterious or, at least, perplexing and disturbing, to which the closing lines provide an answer, most frequently an unexpected one. Only the group I have described as impressionist sketches cannot be thus characterized. The fact that these were all written between 1919 and 1921, in a period of experiment and exploration, after which Virginia Woolf wrote no more atmospheric sketches of this sort, inclines one to believe that she was aware of the limitations of the genre. If "Kew Gardens" remains a masterpiece, it is none the less true that it could not be safely imitated or reproduced. If many pages of *The Waves* show that Virginia Woolf put to good account its teaching and its potentialities, after the three attempted variants of 1921 she returned to the trail blazed by "The Mark on the Wall" and "An Unwritten Novel". Supplementing her longer journeys through the world of appearances and through the years, these stories each represent a brief excursion from which, in her unremitting quest for reality, Virginia Woolf brought back some slight quarry—slight indeed but revealing of the depths in which it was discovered.

3. THE BIOGRAPHIES

The classification of Virginia Woolf's works into three categories—Fiction, Biography, Criticism etc.—involves a margin of uncertainty. "The Mark on the Wall", for instance, at first classified under "Criticism etc.", figures in the collection *A Haunted House and other stories*, which is included in the "Fiction" group. *Orlando*, sub-titled A Biography, has never been considered under this heading, which covers only Flush and Roger Fry. I have chosen to study these two works separately, not so much out of passive acceptance of the labels proposed by their author, as in consideration of the special characteristics of these two books, which, profoundly though they differ from each other, are akin both in the circumstances of their composition and through the author's attitude towards them.

Although *Orlando* is based on reality it never submits to the restrictions of reality. The author remains constantly in control, is absolute creator. This is not the case with *Flush* and *Roger Fry*. Even filtered through the eyes of Flush, the spaniel, the events, actions, words and thoughts determined by documents assign to the biographer limits which have to be respected—and which are scarcely compatible with the genius of Virginia Woolf. Although she deliberately chose to write *Flush*, whereas *Roger Fry*, without being strictly speaking commissioned, was written in response to various requests, and although she devoted as much patient and meticulous care to these biographies as to her novels, she considered them as secondary works, as chores, forming an integral part of her professional task no doubt, but basically uncongenial to her; never, while she was writing them or once they were published, did they procure her really deep satisfaction. When, late in 1938, after several months spent on *Roger Fry*,[619] she expressed her opinion on biography as a literary form, while recognizing its merits and its still unexplored possibilities, she nevertheless considered it as a matter of technique rather than of art, and described it as work on a lower plane.[620] Although at the time she based her arguments on an estimate of the work of Lytton Strachey, it is clear that to a large extent her own experience provided the real substance of this article.

These considerations, which have led me to treat *Flush* and *Roger Fry* by themselves, require the critic to adopt a different attitude towards these books than towards the novels.

FLUSH (1933)

Long before *The Waves* was finished, on April 20, 1930, the tension of that "ecstatic book" had already aroused a wish for a work whose lightness[621] would ensure that relief of genius by talent which *Orlando* had provided after *To the Lighthouse*.[622] True, there is some incompatibility between the "something imaginative" of which she dreamed and that life of Duncan Grant, the sketch for which haunted the depths of her mind. But when she corrects herself to suggest: "no, something about canvasses glowing in a studio" we see a first attempt to reconcile these incompatibles, a foretaste of the synthesis proposed in *Flush*. Duncan Grant retires behind his canvasses, his studio, which none the less reveal him while leaving more freedom to the play of imagination, just as Elizabeth Barrett Browning was to allow Flush to play the hero. This literary form, in the line of *Orlando*—and also of *Jacob's Room*—corresponds no doubt to a deep-seated tendency of the author, one might even say to her angle of vision about human beings. When *Flush* was just about to appear, indeed, she

[619] Cf. AWD p. 309 (298)

[620] Cf. DM "The Art of Biography", pp. 119-26 (187-97), particularly section IV, pp. 125-6 (195-7)

[621] Cf. AWD p. 158 (155): ". . . I must hastily provide my mind with something else . . . something imaginative, if possible, and light; for I shall tire of Hazlitt and criticism after the first divine relief; and I feel pleasantly aware of various adumbrations in the back of my head; a life of Duncan; no, something about canvasses glowing in a studio. . . ."

[622] Cf. *supra*, ch. III, pp. 80-1

was contemplating writing a "fantasy on the theme of Crabbe"[623] which resulted in the few pages in *The Captain's Death Bed* about the clergyman with a passion for flowers, fossils and seaweed. Moreover, such embryonic projects were still premature. *The Waves* still absorbed all the novelist's energy and at the same time fostered the longing for "some swifter slighter adventure—another *Orlando* perhaps".[624] Nevertheless, what took shape a few days later was not the idea of *Flush* but the germ of *Three Guineas* and *The Years*.[625] However, when *The Waves* was finished at last, we see Virginia Woolf taking up *Flush* "impetuously . . . by way of a change", and that is all we know about the origins of the book.[626] How long did the initial enthusiasm last? *A Writer's Diary* does not tell us. Other interests, other projects seem to have filled up the fifteen or sixteen months following the first mention of this biography: the publication of *The Waves*, reactions to criticism, depression, *Three Guineas*, revision of articles for the second *Common Reader*, *The Years*. . . . Where are we to place the "four months of work and heaven knows how much reading"[627] which resulted in thirty thousand words of *Flush*—practically the eventual length of the book? This question, which must remain unanswered for the moment, is only of interest as displaying the secondary character of the work, which got pushed aside by more urgent tasks to which the writer devoted herself, driven by some irresistible inner force.[628] True, after the tension of *The Waves*, humour in the vein of *Orlando*, which is very noticeable in the opening pages of *Flush*, found a more favourable field for free expansion in *Three Guineas* and above all in a voluminous sixty-thousand-word first draft of *The Years*. One feels that Virginia Woolf had launched into this biography without forethought and consequently found herself tethered to a failure on which she was to labour without enthusiasm in the intervals of *The Years*. From December 23, 1932, to January 26, 1933, she devoted five

[623] Cf. AWD pp. 211-12 (204): "Why not, one of these days, write a fantasy on the theme of Crabbe?—a biographical fantasy—an experiment in biography."

[624] Cf. AWD p. 165 (161): ". . . I shall fling off, like a cutter leaning on its side, on some swifter, slighter adventure—another *Orlando* perhaps."

[625] Cf. AWD pp. 165-6 (161-2)

[626] AWD p. 191 (185)

[627] Cf. AWD p. 191 (185): "Oh what a waste—what a bore! Four months of work and heaven knows how much reading—not of an exalted kind either—and I can't see how to make anything of it."

[628] AWD p. 190 (184)

weeks almost exclusively to "that abominable dog *Flush*"[629] whom she finally "despatched"[630] without ever escaping from the obsession of her novel. She managed to finish "that silly book *Flush*"[631], however, and corrected the proofs towards the end of April before setting off for a three weeks' journey through France and Italy.

To picture Elizabeth Barrett, the recluse of Wimpole Street, her passion for Robert Browning, their runaway marriage, their life in Italy, the democratic excitement of Florence in 1848, the birth of their son Robert, their journey to England in 1851 and the influence of spiritualism on Elizabeth Barrett Browning, by taking the poetess's spaniel as centre of observation and reference, was an exercise in virtuosity which, in anyone but the author of *Orlando* and *Jacob's Room*, would verge on the preposterous. It must indeed be admitted that for the reader, as for the author herself, the *tour de force*, although successful enough at times, is somewhat overlong.[632] These "human minutes and hours" dropped "into a dog's mind"[633] are curiously refracted there, in keeping with the theory that Virginia Woolf was to develop later in her article on biography: "Biography will enlarge its scope by hanging up looking glasses at odd corners." Flush's mind and sensibility are indeed a looking glass of this sort, odd and oddly placed; but it is the only one, and the images it reflects are all of the same quality, as the author must have realized, since she uses the plural, "looking glasses", and adds: "And yet from all this diversity it will bring out, not a riot of confusion, but a richer unity."[634] Thus put into practice in an extreme particular case, the theory of the point of view reveals its inadequacy, and it was no doubt with this failure in mind that Virginia Woolf at one point considered that Roger Fry's life "should be written by different people to illustrate different stages".[635] Moreover, although Vanessa Bell's cover drawings stress the likeness which the spaniel's ears and Elizabeth's ringlets reveal between the

[629] AWD p. 192 (185)

[630] AWD p. 194 (186)

[631] AWD p. 199 (188)

[632] Cf. AWD p. 191 (185): "It's not the right subject for that length; it's too slight and too serious."

[633] Cf. *Flush* p. 119 (134): "And when we take . . . human minutes and hours and drop them into a dog's mind. . . ."

[634] Cf. DM p. 125 (195)

[635] Cf. AWD p. 230 (222)

two heroes, the distance between them remains considerable, and divides the reader's attention, inflicting a constant strain on his mind as if he were striving not to see more than Flush sees, or beyond what Flush sees. This divided interest, which is due, fundamentally, to Flush's incapacity either to interest us in his own story or to tell us his mistress's effectively, leads one to wonder why Virginia Woolf chose this subject and this point of view. Although she does not enlighten us on this matter anywhere, a comparison between *Flush* and the article "Aurora Leigh" may provide the elements of an explanation.

Elizabeth Barrett represents, first and foremost, woman as the victim of the Victorian ideal; her sequestration is a symbol and her liberation through the love that brings her back to life is no less symbolic. Her story is a general illustration to *A Room of One's Own,* and also to more than one passage of *Three Guineas,* which Virginia Woolf conceived at the same time as *Flush.* It should also be noticed that many comments in the chapter "Whitechapel", suggested by Thomas Beames's *The Rookeries of London,* scrupulously noted among the sources, show something of the same spirit of social satire to which she gives full vent in the pamphlet. But the author of *Aurora Leigh*[636] has other claims to the interest shown in her by the author of *The Waves*; had not she, too, long fostered the intention of "writing . . . a sort of novel-poem",[637] and was there not in the recluse of Wimpole Street more than one characteristic which entitled her biographer to see in her a kindred spirit? Elizabeth Barrett Browning with her "lively and secular and satirical" mind[638] was sister to Orlando and to Virginia Woolf, while her tendency to magnify the inner life, leading her to declare that the artist, to express life, must take "the soul itself"[639] for stage entitled our novelist to consider her as a forerunner. It was precisely this exaggeration of sensibility, this unusual quality of vision, that Virginia Woolf attempts to convey through her witness-protagonist, Flush. With his instinct, his flair, the spaniel picks up the slightest signs that betray his mistress's feelings and thoughts. And by his very nature, he avoids the temptation to analyse them and discuss them, thus

[636] Cf. CR II pp. 202-13 (182-92)

[637] Cf. CR II p. 203 (183)

[638] *Ibid.,* p. 207 (187)

[639] *Ibid.,* p. 208 (187): ". . . magnifying what was within . . .", and p. 209 (190): ". . . our stage is now the soul itself . . .".

impelling the author to a kind of immediate expression: "Not a single one of his myriad sensations ever submitted itself to the deformity of words."[640]

The attraction of such an experiment for Virginia Woolf need not be stressed, but its difficulties are immediately apparent. Flush's inarticulate and primitive reactions, however penetrating, are incompatible with the resources of literature. After all, this was never meant for dogs, and through not wanting to betray Flush Virginia Woolf was reduced to sacrificing Elizabeth.

This little book is interesting chiefly by reason of the limits it seems to set to the author's theories, and as a study of sensations. Occasional traces of Virginia Woolf's favourite preoccupations— the contrast between time and duration, the enigma of reality and personality, solitude, the difficulty of communication—are too fugitive to enrich it; they amount only to a matter of style, the writer's personal imprint. Unlike *Orlando*, which had matured and expanded into a major work, *Flush* was a work of fantasy which had developed beyond its true potential. There was stuff in it for a "study" like the sketches in which Virginia Woolf found relief after writing her novels, while experimenting in the field of technique. No doubt the vitality and success of *Orlando* were responsible for the unjustified ambition of *Flush*—which might have been a delightful story and only succeeds in being a partial biography, whose originality is swamped by artifice. If Virginia Woolf was aiming at that effect of caricatural exaggeration and compression that she recognizes in Lytton Strachey's *Eminent Victorians*,[641] she achieves it only intermittently. She tried to be too complete, and no doubt she expected too much from what she may have conceived of as a method, but which in practice proved to be merely a device.

ROGER FRY (1940)

Virginia Woolf hesitated for a considerable time before yielding to the wish of Margery Fry and Helen Anrep to see her write a life of Roger Fry. Not that she did not feel tempted; here, surely, was "the chance of trying biography; a splendid, difficult chance—better than trying to find a subject".[642] Her hesitation,

---

[640] *Flush*, p. 125 (140)   [641] Cf. DM p. 122 (189)
[642] Cf. AWD p. 232 (224): "If I could be free, then here's the chance of trying biography. . . ."

moreover, was due to considerations unconnected with literature; would she be free to write the book as she chose? Would not Roger Fry's relatives insist on reticence, discretion?[643] If in addition to the bondage of facts she must endure that of propriety and convention, what was the point? Virginia Woolf always considered independence as a fundamental condition which a writer must under no circumstances renounce. And yet, having just finished the first version of *The Years*, she felt herself more uncommitted than she was ever, in fact, to be. In the subsequent months, she was to be obsessively recasting *The Years* while, in addition, *Three Guineas* clamoured to be written. On the other hand, the shock of Roger Fry's death[644] fostered the wish to perpetuate his presence. Even more than a token of friendship, such a book would be a way of salvaging that part of herself that had died with her friend. And this closeness, verging on identity, is probably what gave rise to the puzzling remark in the Diary that concludes the first reference to the *Roger Fry* project: a remark of whose origin and consequences she was herself not clearly conscious: "I must now do biography and autobiography."[645] Thus, she seems to put down as a New Year's resolution an anticipatory definition of the book.[646] On July 12, 1935, an opening address for a Roger Fry Exhibition at Bristol[647] served as a sort of prelude—not an encouraging one, indeed[648]— for the work, the materials for which were accumulating. If in October of that same year the work was taking shape,[649] it was still only in the writer's mind. She had not reached the point of writing, as she had reckoned on doing earlier in the year, but only of using the preparatory work as a relief from the effort required by the final polishing of *The Years* and the composition of *Three Guineas*.[650] The serious breakdown which she underwent in the summer of 1936 completed the disruption of her projects, and it was not until April 1, 1938, that, without zest or illusion,

[643] Cf. note 642, also AWD p. 233 (225)

[644] Cf. AWD pp. 223-4 (216-7). Roger Fry died on September 9, 1934.

[645] AWD p. 230 (223)

[646] AWD Jan. 1, 1935, p. 236 (228)

[647] Published in *The Moment*, pp. 83-8 (99-105): "Roger Fry".

[648] Cf. AWD p. 251 (242): "A curious sense of complete failure."

[649] Cf. AWD p. 259 (250): "Yes that book shapes itself. . . . Suppose I finish *The Years* in January: then dash off the *War* [i.e. *Three Guineas*] . . . in six weeks: and do Roger next summer?"

[650] Cf. AWD p. 257 (248)

she started on the book whose innermost life had gradually faded away since 1934. And so, instead of being the anticipated relaxation, *Roger Fry* became the chore, whereas *Pointz Hall*—later *Between the Acts*—conceived about the same time, provided rest and escape.[651] On March 10, 1939, a first version was completed,[652] but the book did not acquire its final form for another year or more.[653] It was only to be expected that its publication on July 24, 1940, during a particularly agonizing stage of the war, made little impression on the public or on the author herself, owing to the historic intensity of the hour.[654] As usual, however, the two contradictory trends took shape: on the whole, Fry's friends liked the book; but the reticent attitude of E. M. Forster, Leonard Woolf and Vanessa Bell left Virginia Woolf in two minds about the real value of her work.

In fact, the unconscious combination of biography and autobiography explains both the faults and qualities of this book. This ambiguity did not escape the author.[655] When she wonders whether her book is not "too like a novel"[656] one immediately thinks of *Orlando* and *To the Lighthouse*, in which, on a framework of objective data, of facts, Virginia Woolf embroidered the arabesques of inner lives which say as much or more about herself than about the half-fictitious, half-real characters she has chosen for her heroes. Reflecting on the first reactions of her critics, on July 25, 1940, she finds a particularly felicitous phrase to express the inextricable relation of painter and model:

What a curious relation is mine with Roger at this moment—I who have given him a kind of shape after his death. Was he like that? I feel very much in his presence at the moment; as if I were intimately connected with him: as if we together had given birth to this vision of him: a child born of us.[657]

On the whole, Leonard Woolf's severe criticisms are wholly

---

[651] Many passages in the Diary express with a consistency unusual in V. W. the same feelings about the three books: cf. AWD pp. 288-9 (278-9), 291 (281), 299 (288-9), 309 (298) ("I rush to it [*Pointz Hall*] for relief after a long pressure of Fry facts"), 311 (300), 314 (302), 315 (304), 316 (306).

[652] Cf. AWD p. 311 (300): "I set the last word to the first sketch of *Roger*."

[653] Cf. AWD p. 331 (319), April 6, 1940.

[654] Cf. AWD p. 340 (325)

[655] Cf. AWD p. 313 (301): "I finished my first 40 pages of [R.] . . . —childhood etc.—well under the week; but then they were largely autobiography. . . ."

[656] AWD p. 313 (302)

[657] AWD p. 339 (326-7)

SYNTHESIS AND FICTION

justified. The character is analysed, rather than described[658]; the
wealth of quotations gives us the colour and movement of his
thought and sensibility from the inside, but in scattered discontinuity, with no synthetic vision uniting them. Anyone who
had known Roger Fry could supplement this lack of a centre by
the polarizing force of a living memory; but the stranger is
confronted with the evocation of an inner life that lacks inwardness, lacks that profound cohesion which belongs to living beings
and works of art, and which is an indefinable sign of authenticity,
or reality; while no external convincingness compensates for this
weakness in the psychological texture; the portrait lacks the
material solidity which a figure drawn from the outside might
have attained.

Do not these defects imply that, basically, Virginia Woolf's
conception of personality is incompatible with biography, which
requires more "realism" in the philosophical sense of the word,
than our novelist could admit? When she attributes the severity
of her husband's judgment to "lack of interest in personality"[659]
one must specify: for personality as she conceived it. The primacy
of the inner life, the importance of "moments", the inter-
penetration of human beings—and particularly the inter-
penetration of the biographer and her subject—all these
assumptions explain, though they do not justify, the inadequacies
of the book, its hesitation between novel, biography and autobiography. This polyvalence is synonymous with failure; but the
failure is a richly revealing one. Virginia Woolf has preserved
what she and Roger Fry had in common, in temperament and in
ideas. The painter-critic's adolescent rebelliousness, his youthful
timidities, the struggles of his maturity and his assertion of fulfilment are a transposition of the author's own destiny. And this
being, divided between an external life of bustle and distraction
and an inner life of stillness and slow concentration, is just as
much the alter ego of Orlando—who, like Roger Fry, is Virginia
Woolf plus another—as the twin of Virginia Woolf herself. And
furthermore, the essential problems whose urgency appears as the
mainspring of this personality: the quest for the "vision" of
reality and for the means of expressing it are Virginia Woolf's
own problems *par excellence*. In so far as one can speak of her
sources, there is no doubt that to Roger Fry must be ascribed an

[658] Cf. AWD p. 328 (316)   [659] Cf. AWD p. 328 (316)

351

important role in the development of his biographer's art and thought. What we find in *Vision and Design*, or in *Transformations*, many echoes of which occur in other documents of which Virginia Woolf made use, represents the whole substance of their discussions together.[660] The enduring friendship and the deep affection that united Virginia Woolf and Roger Fry were based on a similarity of nature and a community of interests which ranged from the paintings of Manet to the *bœuf en daube* that Fry enjoyed in his retreat at St Rémy. The fact remains, however, that one cannot help suspecting that some process of screening has eliminated from the portrait such features of the model as were too foreign to the painter. This may seriously diminish the general and historic interest of this biography; in exchange, it becomes an illustration of human relationships as they governed the life and art of Virginia Woolf, and thus it brings yet another convincing argument against those who choose to see in her work merely artifice and futile formal experiment.

[660] Cf. John Hawley Roberts, "Vision and Design in V. W.", *PMLA*, vol. LXI, no. 3, Sept. 1946, p. 835-47.

CHAPTER VI

BASIC PROBLEMS:
THE APPREHENSION OF REALITY
AND THE SEARCH FOR A FORM

1. CHARACTERS AND HUMAN RELATIONS

IT can be said without exaggeration that critics have unanimously reproached Virginia Woolf with a certain inability to
create characters.[1] None of her heroes or heroines, not even
Clarissa Dalloway or Mrs Ramsay, impress the reader's imagination with that precision, richness and vitality which ensure an
independent and convincing existence for characters in fiction.
It is moreover significant that the heroes of her first two novels,
and the secondary figures in her more original works, are those
that stand out most sharply. Helen Ambrose, St John Hirst, the
four protagonists of *Night and Day* particularly, Mrs Flanders,
Bonamy, Sandra Wentworth Williams, Sir William Bradshaw,
Sally Seton, Charles Tansley, Carmichael, Mrs Swithin, Mrs
Manresa and a score of other silhouettes, sketched in with a few
gestures, attitudes and phrases, thanks to their manageable simplicity, leave a lively and living impression on the reader. But
except for the heroes of the two early novels, these figures are
obviously caricatures rather than portraits. Their slightness, and
the restricted place they occupy in the books, makes it difficult if
not impossible to base on them a study of Virginia Woolf's
characterization. None the less, the contrast they present with
figures like Clarissa Dalloway or Mrs Ramsay, and even more
with the protagonists of *The Waves*, provides an opportunity for
preliminary comments which are surely essential to any discussion of this side of Virginia Woolf's art.

The primary quality of all these characters, the one which
ensures for them a convincing presence in the novels and the
power of surviving in our memories, is their very limitedness. They
are fixed, static, in every respect. They have a history, a profes-

[1] Apart from various authors of reviews, F. Delattre is the first to have stressed
this aspect of Virginia Woolf's art (cf. *op. cit.*, p. 121). Among more recent criticisms,
that of D. S. Savage is particularly harsh (cf. *The Withered Branch*, p. 95).

353

sion, a passion or a mania, a gesture, an attitude or a turn of phrase that defines them; and their fidelity to themselves is unfailing; thus they are, and thus they remain. Around them the author has, like St John Hirst, traced the chalk circle which gives them being but which also confines them. They correspond exactly to the traditional notion of personality, made of a bundle of more or less complex tendencies and manifested by constant reactions. All the characters named above are of the same nature. Between a Katherine Hilbery and a Sally Seton, a Ralph Denham and a Bonamy or a Charles Tansley, there is only a difference of degree or, if you like, of richness and complexity. The diversity of the situations, the detail of the analyses that give the heroes of *Night and Day* a different stature (which does not mean a different density) from the figures in the later novels, should not deceive us. The accumulation of circumstances, the multiplicity and complication of events involving multiple and complicated reactions, arouse our curiosity, foster our interest in the characters and may even lead us to believe that this description is the essential part of the novel. We have seen that this is not so. This traditional painting of characters of traditional type is here merely the survival of a technique which was inadequate to the author's intention and which she used for lack of a better, still undiscovered one. The following books, just as much as the essays on the art of fiction, amply prove that Virginia Woolf had other ambitions. The fact that she retained this mode of characterization for her secondary figures, for Dr Crane in *The Waves* or Mrs Manresa in *Between the Acts*, far from being a concession to the method, or a residue from it, is on the contrary an implied criticism of it, and brings out the more sharply the essential features of the method by which she intended to replace it. In fact, these figures have no reality, no existence of their own; they make a momentary appearance in the field of vision of the chief protagonists, and it is the two-dimensional image which they leave as they pass, in the latters' accumulated experience, that the novelist reproduces. They may have colour and movement enough to give the illusion of life, but it is merely an illusion. They lack two essential traits to attain human reality as Virginia Woolf perceived it from the very first and as she tried to express it later: imprecision of outline and an infinite potentiality for renewal and creation. There is no indeterminate zone around their desires, their will, their feelings or ideas which might leave room for hesitation, doubt, and in the final analysis anguish. None of these walkers-on could say, like Louis in *The Waves*, "I am conscious of flux, of disorder; of annihilation and despair."[2] Enclosed within their security, their certitude, they are immune to questioning from without or within. They are clockwork figures, wound up once and for all, functioning in season and out of season with equal blindness and self-confidence. They are never taken by surprise and can never surprise anyone else. They have the solidity and permanence of material objects. It is owing to this, no doubt, that they leave a vivid and enduring impression in the reader's mind. But quite obviously Virginia Woolf never believed in the effectiveness or value of so crude a method of representation. From *The Voyage Out* to *The Years*, through the medium of Hewett[3] and North, to quote only these two, she never ceased to say so: "These little snapshot pictures of people left much to be desired, these little surface pictures that one made, like a fly crawling over a face, and feeling, here's the nose, here's the brow."[4] If these characters exist, it is only for the superficial, hasty observer, used to this convenient formulation of his fellows, which has the backing of a whole literary and psychological tradition. Though they seem substantial, and acquire importance from the foreground position they occupy, the four heroes of *Night and Day* have no more than this elementary reality. From our first encounter with them, we know them. Nothing that happens to them, at whatever place or time, really enriches them, or opens up any unknown prospect into the shadowy depths of their past or the mystery of their future; it merely provides an occasion for them to react according to their predetermined nature. As far as they are concerned, the novel is the development, the unfolding, in the spatial sense of the term, of what they have within them, compactly collected within the limits of their body and as definite and definable as that body. The subtlety of the analysis, the coherence of the character, the verisimilitude of the situation serve to provide the whole with that appearance of truth or reality which the reader is entitled to expect from a "good novel". The adventure and the heroes having nothing particularly remarkable, the book suffers from their mediocrity in so far as we judge it in function of these

[2] The W p. 67 (239)   [3] Cf. VO p. 264 (220)   [4] The Y p. 341 (317)

elements; but as we have seen, its interest lies elsewhere. If we consider that Terence Hewett and above all Rachel Vinrace in *The Voyage Out* are far less sharply outlined, blurred by their mutual contacts, which make them part of one another, and at the same time by the multiple points of view from which they are presented, we are tempted to see in *Night and Day* a deliberate application of the traditional technique and psychology, being tried out by Virginia Woolf in order to test their possibilities and ascertain her own resources and limitations. It is basically the least characteristic of her novels, but a necessary experiment in order to exorcise any temptation to follow the beaten path. E. M. Forster admirably defined the difference between his friend's first two novels when he told her that *Night and Day* being "a strictly formal and classical work" the reader felt the lack of heroes, whereas in *The Voyage Out* he did not feel the need to consider the characters as such.[5] A little later, Virginia Woolf writes in her diary: "But I had rather write in my own way of *Four Passionate Snails* than be, as K. M. [Katherine Mansfield] maintains, Jane Austen over again."[6] What she wrote about Jane Austen[7] later entitles us to see in this declaration an assessment of her own personal genius, the discovery that she had wandered into a blind alley, and one of the first premonitions of the path along which, a few weeks later, she was to venture.[8]

"Vague and universal" was E. M. Forster's verdict on *The Voyage Out*; "vague and inconclusive" Virginia Woolf had written a few months earlier to sum up her impression of one of Chekhovs' stories, which seemed to her characteristic of those elements in Russian literature that exerted a revivifying influence on the contemporary English novel.[9] This is the aspect, at first sight a

---

[5] Cf. AWD p. 20 (20): ". . . *N. and D.* is a strictly formal and classical work; that being so one requires, or he [E. M. Forster] requires, a far greater degree of lovability in the character than in a book like *V.O.* which is vague and universal. None of the characters in *N. and D.* is lovable. . . . Neither did he care for the characters in *V.O.*, but there he felt no need to care for them." If my interpretation of the terms "lovability", "lovable", "care for" seems an extension of Forster's judgment, yet it surely does not distort his meaning.

[6] AWD p. 22 (21)

[7] Cf. "Jane Austen at Sixty", *Nation & Athenaeum*, 15/12/1923, incorporated in "Jane Austen" in CR I, particularly pp. 181-3 (146-9).

[8] Cf. *supra*, ch. III, p. 72 ff

[9] Cf. "Modern Novels", *TLS*, April 10, 1919 (E. M. Forster's comment is mentioned in the Diary on Nov. 6, 1919); under the title "Modern Fiction in CR I". See p. 193 (157); also *ibid.*, p. 223 (180), in "The Russian Point of View".

negative one, which may be considered the essential weakness of Virginia Woolf's characters, not only in her first novel where she unconsciously followed her own bent, but in those of her maturity where she tried out all the resources of writing in turn in order to convey that haziness without which any representation of that essential object of the artist's quest, "whether we call it life or spirit, truth or reality",[10] is merely a vain and disappointing counterfeit.

The specific question of characters and their function in the novel, of the way of portraying them and conveying their personality, is not tackled directly in the article of 1919. We have to wait until 1924 for "Character in Fiction", better known under the title "Mr Bennett and Mrs Brown",[11] to find, if not the solution, at any rate a precise analysis of the data of the problem:

I believe that all novels begin with an old lady in the corner opposite. I believe that all novels, that is to say, deal with character, and that it is to express character—not to preach doctrines, sing songs, or celebrate the glories of the British Empire, that the form of the novel, so clumsy, verbose, and undramatic, so rich, elastic, and alive, has been evolved.[12]

Winifred Holtby, who usually offers interesting interpretations of the novels, seems not to have taken into account the context when she quotes this phrase to assert that "Mrs Woolf holds that in novel writing, character creation is the all-important quality".[13] She thus ignores that essential reservation that follows this apparent concession to the traditional laws of the genre[14]:

To express character, I have said; but you will at once reflect that the very widest interpretation can be put upon these words. . . . You see one thing in character, and I another. You say it means this, and I that. And when it comes to writing each makes a further selection on principles of his own. Thus Mrs Brown can be treated in an infinite variety of ways, according to the age, country, and temperament of the writer.[15]

[10] Cf. CR I p. 188 (153): "Whether we call it life or spirit, truth or reality, this, the essential thing, has moved off, or on. . . ."

[11] Published in *The Criterion*, July 1924, pp. 409-30, then in CDB. See above, p. 239, note 191.

[12] CDB pp. 96-7 (102)

[13] Winifred Holtby, *Virginia Woolf*, p. 151

[14] Other critics have made the same mistake, whether or not they realized that this assertion of the novelist's did not correspond to the basic meaning of her work. Cf. for instance John Graham, in the opening paragraph of his article "Time in the Novels of Virginia Woolf" (*Univ. of Toronto Quarterly*, Jan. 1949, pp. 186-201).

[15] CDB p. 97 (102-3)

Moreover, despite the effort at elucidation to which Virginia Woolf was driven, first by her difficulties in the composition of *Jacob's Room*, then by her researches for *Mrs Dalloway* and her controversy with Arnold Bennett, it is clear[16] that at this period she had not yet completely broken free from that central convention of the novel which forms an essential part of any definition of the genre. She had only cast off its formal restrictions, the method of creation, those tools so skilfully handled by the Edwardians and yet, to her mind, so inadequate.[17] If the failure of Wells, Bennett and Galsworthy to satisfy her, if her sense that the stuff with which such figures as Dr Watson and Hilda Lessways are padded out is irrelevant and external incited her to discover something else, at the same time the example of the great novels —*War and Peace, Vanity Fair, Tristram Shandy, Madame Bovary* . . . —maintained, alive and active, the fascination of that element which seems to distil and transmit the essence of these masterpieces: their characters. The result of this conflict between what she rejects and what she accepts is particularly noticeable in *Jacob's Room* and *Mrs Dalloway*, and, to a lesser degree, in *To the Lighthouse*. Without seeking to minimize the wish to make something new, nor the originality of the means employed to attain her ends, the fact remains that the presentation of one or several beings, the creation of characters, is one of the determining factors in the composition of these three novels. The very titles of the first two are significant in this respect. As regards the third, remember how, at its inception, Virginia Woolf envisaged this book: "This is going to be fairly short; to have father's character done complete in it; and mother's. . . ."[18] In connection with each of these novels I examined how this conflict had been settled,[19] and I stressed particularly the author's determination to break free from the traditional framework, in order to bring out the active ferment of her work and the course of her development. Considering these works at a little distance, we can now see how, from one to the next, the lure of character diminishes. *Jacob's Room* is dominated by the desire to present character as she conceives it, in opposition to the conceptions and

---

[16] Cf. *supra*, ch. V, pp. 239-40
[17] Cf. CDB pp. 104 (110) and 106 (112)
[18] AWD p. 76 (75); quoted earlier, ch. V, p. 248.
[19] Cf. *supra*, ch. V; for JR p. 221 ff; for Mrs D pp. 239-40; for To the L p. 253 ff

methods of her contemporaries. She takes her hero almost from the cradle and follows him to his death. She eliminates any sort of plot, to devote herself solely to portraiture. Even if this elimination is, in itself, rich with other implications as to the theory of the novel, it none the less contributes to concentrating our interest on the portrayal of her hero. Jacob may have become discontinuous, but he remains chronological. But after all, if discontinuity is an essential part of reality, which is blurred to the point of being destroyed in the traditional type of narrative, it may on the other hand be only an inevitable condition of the literary art: an exhaustive chronicle is an impossibility; and by one of its distinctive features, *Jacob's Room* conforms to type.[20]

If the figure of Clarissa Dalloway dominates Virginia Woolf's fourth novel and, on the whole, leaves a clearer impression than Jacob, it is because she seems to be concentrated in a single day and place; a concentration which has a synthetic power akin to that of the plot in the traditional novel. This result, which is repeated with Mrs Ramsay in *To the Lighthouse*, is to the credit of Virginia Woolf's art. But what matters to us here is the profound nature of these characters, who, while remaining autonomous individuals, reveal a dependence and a diffusion which *Jacob's Room* had described from the outside without succeeding in integrating it. Around Jacob there were other figures, which like mirrors or the walls of his room showed us his reflection or his shadow, his reflections or his shadows; it was through these reflections and shadows that he existed, and to a large extent he *was* them—whence his difficulty in being Jacob. On the contrary, with the figures that surround Clarissa and Mrs Ramsay, even the flimsiest, or to use E. M. Forster's term the flattest of them, such as Richard Dalloway or Mr Bankes, the function of reflector is only a secondary one. In fact, they are essentially a part of the central figure. They converge towards her to mingle and blend with her substance, in the case of Clarissa. Inversely, in the case of Mrs Ramsay, she turns towards them and is diffused into them.[21] In either case, this blurring of outlines and this fusion of beings reveals an order of reality entirely different from that

[20] Cf. Edwin Muir, *The Structure of the Novel*, p. 115: "*Jacob's Room* (with *Sons and Lovers* and *Portrait of the Artist as a Young Man*) is perhaps the best chronicle that has appeared in recent years." In *Transition*, in 1926, Muir asserts that, unlike Joyce and Lawrence, "Mrs Woolf accepts her characters as ends" (p. 42).

[21] Cf. *supra*, ch. V, p. 253

which the terms character, personality, hero normally imply. What we have here is no longer somebody or something, it is not a person or an object which, though more or less complex or composite, is nevertheless determined, difficult as it may be to trace its outline; what we have is a nexus of relations, a manifold participation in all that lies around, absorbing it all into his own substance, which is constantly altered by this contact. It no longer *is*; it *becomes*. This profound alteration of the nature of a character, which Virginia Woolf achieved in three stages, was already implicit in what she wrote of the heroes of the great novels:

... if you think of these books, you do at once think of some character who has seemed to you so real (I do not by that mean so lifelike) that it has the power to make you think not merely of it itself, but of all sorts of things through its eyes—of religion, of love, of war, of peace, of family life, of balls in country towns, of sunsets, moonrises, the immortality of the soul. . . . And in all these novels all these great novelists have brought us to see whatever they wish us to see through some character.[22]

However, although these lines show that Virginia Woolf does not consider characters as the end of the novel but only as a means, if we compare this text with the one from which it was derived, published six months earlier, we see that she did not reach this position all at once. Referring to the same heroes, she had then written:

They love, they joke, they hunt, they marry, they lead us from hall to cottage, from field to slum. The whole country, the whole society is revealed to us through the astonishing vividness and reality of the characters.[23]

"The astonishing vividness and reality of the characters" which brought about this revelation and which consequently were deemed essential features are relegated to the background in the later text; moreover, Virginia Woolf is careful to distinguish what seems real from what is merely lifelike. Besides, in the paragraph where she contrasts the Russian novel with the Victorian novel, although she only defines a negative aspect of these characters that fascinate her, she uses an image which, echoing that in which a few months previously she had described the method used in

[22] "Mr Bennett and Mrs Brown", CDB, originally "Character in Fiction", *Criterion*, July 1924.

[23] "Mr Bennett and Mrs Brown", *New York Evening Post*, Literary Review, Nov. 17, 1923, reprinted in *Nation and Athenaeum*, Dec. 1, 1923.

Mrs Dalloway,[24] suggests an unexplored wealth of visions and presentiments: "These are characters without any features at all. We go down into them as we descend into some enormous cavern."[25] True, what I have called the lure of the character, exerted by figures like Natasha, Becky Sharp or Emma Bovary, remains. But, following the evolution we have just examined, which occurred during the last months of 1923, this lure loses its restrictive power. With figures whose realism has dissolved away and whose finality has been rejected, Virginia Woolf can henceforward take liberties. She can bend them to her intentions, give them the form which would hold the content she seeks to put into her work, and the transparency which would reveal the essence she wishes to communicate.

I shall not dwell upon that essential reality, with its manifold names, which constitutes the true subject of Virginia Woolf's books; I shall only stress the progressive adaptation of her characters to the aim that the novelist assigns to them. ". . . all the usual things I try to put in—life, death, etc.,"[26] she says, elliptically, when envisaging *To the Lighthouse*. In other words—more detailed if not more precise—she means, by this, that vision of the universe which each one of us has, and which is made up of the relations which the "I", that central enigma where everything happens and from which everything emanates, maintains with what lies around it: individuals, society, events, nature. From the traditional point of view, at least from that of those she called "materialists", all these elements, circumscribed in their definition, solid with conviction, can be juxtaposed and set out like so many objects. But for Virginia Woolf reality, life, are not like that: they form a luminous halo, condensed around our impressions, and they can only be expressed by means of these sensations. And it is only because human beings are the seat of these that they remain the medium to which the novelist must have recourse. To reduce them to this function, deprive them of the opacity and

[24] Cf. AWD pp. 60-1 (59), quoted *supra*, ch. V, pp. 233-4

[25] "Mr Bennett and Mrs Brown", *Nation & Athenaeum*, Dec. 1, 1923, p. 342. Since V. W. speaks in her diary on June 19th of her answer to Bennett (AWD p. 57 (56) we may assume that the article was written during that summer. The similarity of expression noted here inclines one to think that it might be more profitable to seek for the artistic sources of *Mrs Dalloway* in the Russian novel than in James Joyce.

[26] AWD p. 76 (75)

rigidity which makes masks and puppets of them instead of the filters, the living beings that they are, such is the goal towards which Virginia Woolf slowly gropes her way, from *Jacob's Room* to *To the Lighthouse*, finally reaching in *The Waves* the elimination of all that is alien and heterogeneous to this pure sensibility. I should point out here that by the term sensibility, used somewhat loosely, I mean all the activity of the psyche that extends from sensation to thought, but in which the predominance of receptivity, of the whole phase of contact and absorption, is such that the word seems preferable to any other. The progress in the three novels that may be described as preparatory or experimental can be defined by an increased inwardness of impressions and of expression. The surface contacts which mould Jacob are combined, in *Mrs Dalloway*, with inner resonances, the exploration of deep caverns.[27] In this region what had been mere contiguity, juxtaposition, becomes fusion and connectedness. And it is to the constant shift from one to the other, the balance between the outer and the inner, between the periphery and the centre, the object and the subject, that Clarissa owes the firmness and clarity of outline which the heroes of the later novels lack. Mrs Ramsay retains something of it, but to a lesser degree. The first pages of *To the Lighthouse* are characteristic in this respect. Recollections of her walk with Charles Tansley, and Charles Tansley himself, are inextricably fused in Mrs Ramsay's mind: the landmarks of time and space which mark out people and events are practically obliterated. Yet, slender as they have become, the book still retains a scaffolding of events and circumstances which, even when they are only in parentheses, guarantee a certain integrity to individuals, keep them separate from one another and from the outside world. It is only in *The Waves* that Virginia Woolf achieves absolute homogeneity. Instead of preserving on the one hand a centre of apprehension, *Mrs Dalloway's* "unseen part of us, which spreads wide",[28] even if reduced to the abstract form of a kind of figurative symbol like Mrs Ramsay's "wedge-shaped core of darkness",[29] and on the other hand all that comes to it from the universe and from existence, there remains only pure apprehension: the subject-object duality which had proved a

---

[27] Cf. *supra*, ch. V, pp. 229, 233-4
[28] Cf. Mrs D p. 232 (232)
[29] Cf. To the L p. 99 (95)

stumbling block to Mr Ramsay and Lily Briscoe in their different ways[30] is finally reabsorbed in a monism which is also a phenomenologism. These terms, which suggest rationally constructed systems, contrary as they may be to the spirit of our author and thereby risky to use, are none the less useful if we wish to penetrate fully the meaning of her work. In spite of the hesitations and uncertainties of vocabulary,[31] it is this metaphysical attitude that underlies Virginia Woolf's vision as revealed in her finest work.

The elimination of plot and of spatio-temporal determinations is complementary to the disintegration of the character. They are all ways of denying matter, whether the material nature of objects which petrifies their qualities, or that of our bodies which limits the infinite potentialities of human beings for expansion and participation. In the centre of the universe—we may say, too, at the beginning and at the end, so as not to lay more stress on the spatial than on the temporal, both moreover being symbolic and conventional—at its heart and always, there is what we call "I", without being able to state its nature more precisely. It is the sole and ultimate sum of everything, and it is, itself, the whole world reflected in itself. But these two terms, the I on the one hand and the Universe on the other, are beyond our grasp; no definition can circumscribe them, no description can account for them. This is what Virginia Woolf gradually discovered, between *Jacob's Room* and *To the Lighthouse*. The only reality accessible between these two phantoms is the relationship between them, that function of the "soul", the inner life, or just *life*, which is sensation, emotion, feeling, desire, will, ideas, to use words which are not quite accurate, since they have acquired, by their use through the ages and in various philosophies, a variety of meanings. All the moments and all the aspects of this activity have an essential common character; they are appearances, phenomena, phantasms; they arise, they alter, they remain, they disappear, they arise once more, and we can neither control nor account for these metamorphoses: this is reality, this is truth—the only ones to which we have access, all the rest being only a mode of representation, a convention, an algebra, convenient perhaps but illusory.

This power of absorption and transmutation is what we find in its purest state in *The Waves*. Whatever critics may have said for

[30] Cf. To the L p. 40 (38)   [31] Cf. *supra*, ch. V, pp. 297-8

or against it, whatever they may have looked for or found in it, Virginia Woolf sought neither to create nor to present characters.[32] Many expressions, noted during an attempt to summarise the intentions of this novel, point to the same refusal. And at the same time Virginia Woolf was realising her ambition to express life, love, nature, death, conveyed through this consciousness which is one and yet many, faceless and nameless. It seems futile to criticise *The Waves* by suggesting, as Daiches and other critics have done, that the novelist has merely substituted one convention for another. Such an attitude implies that this convention is arbitrary, a mere artifice. For one thing, throughout this study I have striven to show that such a critical attitude is incompatible with the artist's temperament and with her conceptions. For another, if we look closely at the meaning of the work, we immediately realise that this convention is the actual answer to the question which haunts and dominates all Virginia Woolf's writing: *What* are we? *Who* are we? From Rachel to Bernard, none of her characters has hitherto brought a satisfactory solution to this riddle. But beyond all the hypothetical and approximate formulae they may offer, either directly through being as their creator made them, or indirectly through what they say, the form of *The Waves* asserts that man is essentially a consciousness, that is to say a potential of relations, whose centre is everywhere and whose circumference is nowhere, and which creates itself at the same time as it creates the universe.

I shall examine separately the notions of time and space which are closely connected with the notion of being. I am only concerned here with one aspect of Virginia Woolf's work, which may be considered the direct consequence of her conception of character as I have defined it: the relations between human beings.

I have intentionally dwelt on *The Waves* in this attempt to formulate Virginia Woolf's theory, and if I have not referred to *Orlando*, it is because, while perfectly consistent with the conceptions that underlie *The Waves*, it only gives their reverse side, so to speak. We see all the framework, all the seams. The element of fantasy, of discursiveness and caricature in *Orlando* is indeed not without its explanatory value, but thereby deprives the book of the atmosphere and the resonances essential to a reality which is

---

[32] Cf. AWD p. 175 (170), quoted *supra*, ch. V, p. 297.

better conveyed by half tones, blurred contours and suggestion than by sharp outlines and colours, or by formulae.

On the other hand it seems to me that Virginia Woolf's two last novels can be considered as attempts to exploit, in a generalized fashion, the principles put into practice in a state of purity, so to speak, in *The Waves*. In *The Years* we have not so much a return to realism, as some critics have thought, realism of the external world and realism of character, as a concern with expressing the same manifold relations, the same obscure intermingling of consciousnesses with one another and with the universe. None of the Pargiters, and none of their satellites, despite appearances, can claim more individuality, autonomy or precision than Rhoda or Louis. Like these, each is a focus of irradiation of that nebula, their inextricably intermingled consciousness. Eleanor, Milly, Delia, Rose, Martin, Morris, Edward alternate like the voices in *The Waves*, separate, meet, scatter and come together again through chronological vicissitudes that permeate them and cling to them in the same fashion. They go through childhood, schooldays, professional and family life and love, just like the characters in the previous novel. Delia gathers them all together, moved by the same impulse as Bernard. She takes the same rose to consider its ephemeral brilliance.[33] The speech which is to sum things up, the final assessment, is never uttered; but is it needed? The summing-up is there: confusion and fusion, separation and unity, despair and resolution—and the riddle which had baffled all Bernard's dialectic is expressed only in the sibylline song of the two children who appear at the party in the first light of dawn.[34]

The difference of treatment between Bernard's monologue and the party in "Present Day" reflects the difference between *The Waves* and *The Years*. Whereas in the first we had the concentration of a laboratory experiment, in the second Virginia Woolf has tried direct observation. Instead of the deliberately arranged voices of her faceless protagonists, she has sought to preserve "the human voice at its natural speaking level"[35] and, by gradual steps, around these voices, the whole complex of space and time in which they sound, and in which words take on their immediate and superficial meaning. This attempt in no way contradicts her

---

[33] Cf. The Y p. 431 (399), and The W p. 210 (383)
[34] For other connections between The W and The Y, cf. *supra*, ch. V, p. 313 ff
[35] The Y p. 445 (411)

vision of beings nor her vision of reality. If, from the point of view of aesthetic success, it is ill-fated, it nevertheless confirms her theories by its very failure. To express the one on the level of the many, to express a relation on the level of the extremes which this relation is intended to bring together, means restoring material- ism and dualism. All the skill, all the artifice intended to reabsorb these heterogeneous elements are used in vain; the recurrence of analogous situations, the duplication of characters by one another, the dislocation of an event in the various consciousnesses that apprehend it, the contrast between words and thoughts in simple juxtaposition, the whole system of echoes, leitmotivs, subtle intertwinings, do not penetrate the real substance of the novel. These characters, being too ponderous, betray their voca- tion and their essence, while their vocation and their essence dissolve away the garment of flesh they have tried to put on.

The bareness of *Between the Acts* brings us back to a more homogeneous vision. If the intermittent emergence of a few clearly drawn secondary figures, such as Mrs Manresa and Mr Streatfield the clergyman, or even the sharpness of outline in which the apparently central figures of Isa and Giles are some- times held stationary, may suggest that Virginia Woolf was trying out a compromise analogous to that of *The Years*, this hypothesis will not stand up to examination.[36] The rudiments of physical presence and personal history attached to their names are not intended to define them, to set them up against one another, but solely to outline those superficial contacts from which their deeper relations spring and spread in an obscure tangle, all that open system of attractions, repulsions and participations which Virginia Woolf sought to substitute for the closed system of contiguity and the reactions of personality. The first scene, which brings together the Haineses, Bartholomew and Isa, is charac- teristic in this respect. A few touches seem to promise portraits: Mrs Haines's protruberant eyes, Isa's curls, the haggard face of the gentleman farmer. But in fact this shorthand is only super- ficially, or rather parenthetically, characterological. It is focussed entirely on the feelings, in the broadest sense of the term, that these people experience for one another: the repulsion and contempt inspired by Mrs Haines; the suggestions of youth, care- lessness, intimacy and sensuality that emanate from Isa; Haines's

[36] Cf. *supra*, ch. V, pp. 322-4

rough, inarticulate masculinity. These physical details are not meant to distinguish the characters, any more than the details of their status (Mr Oliver of the Indian Service, retired . . . her husband, the stockbroker . . ."[37]) but to provide implicit causes and reasons for the atmosphere of jealousy, contempt, tenderness and desire that pervades these four pages.

The extreme simplification of the general plan, the elimination of the circumstantial, lead here to a result analogous to that obtained in *The Waves* by different means. The pageant provides under a symbolic form the wealth of events, of facts, that broadens the setting and gives substance to those one-day relations without arousing the uncertainty and ambiguity which the direct angle of approach had introduced into *The Years*.

If I have made some reservations as to the success of this novel taken as a whole,[38] I believe none the less that from this restricted point of view it constitutes the end of Virginia Woolf's quest, integrating all her successive discoveries, realising that novel of silence dreamed of by Hewett in *The Voyage Out*—the novel of all that which, not yet having reached the level of speech, has been preserved from the treachery and sclerosis of words. It is only when the reality of behind the scenes, the flow of life between the acts, in a word all that true reality of which we are granted a glimpse through and beyond the world of people and things, has been expressed that the curtain rises to let the characters appear and speak; it is time then for the novelist to stop, for neither these words nor these appearances are her reality.

The walls of Jacob's room had flung back to us a single name, that echoed through the years to the seaside childhood of the ghostly hero. Percival, invisible and mute, had remained a myth in the inner lives, inextricably interconnected, of the voices in *The Waves*. "What need have we of words to remind us? Must I be Thomas? You Jane?" is the question asked in *Between the Acts*.[39] The answer lies in the totality of the novel, which denies the validity of a sign whose meaning the earlier novels had sought in vain. There are no personalities; there are no characters; there is only the inner life, a centre of fusion and assimilation whose individuality and autonomy are only apparent and usurped.

The analysis of the means to which Virginia Woolf successively resorted to express this inner life will enable us to follow in closer

[37] B the A pp. 8 (4) and 10 (5)   [38] Cf. *supra*, ch. v, pp. 328-9   [39] B the A p. 222 (190)

detail the evolution and solution of that conflict, which we have already witnessed with regard to her characters, between the heritage of tradition and the original vision of the author. It will moreover provide an opportunity to bring out what may be called, since Virginia Woolf often uses the term in this sense, the dramatic character of her work.

2. THE EXPRESSION OF THE INNER LIFE

From all that has been said so far, it emerges clearly that the expression of the inner life was always Virginia Woolf's dominant preoccupation. As with the portrayal of characters, we shall see how she gradually moved away from the conceptions and techniques inherited from the tradition of the psychological novel to forge her own method, the tools capable of expressing reality as she conceived it. In this evolution, we shall recognize the same conflict between the influence of the masters of the novel and the wish, not to be original, but to respect reality. This conflict, although important, is a secondary one. Far more important to my mind, since it goes outside the field of technique to encroach on that of metaphysics, is the multiple paradox that confronted Virginia Woolf from the very beginning and which was to remain the centre of her preoccupations and the hallmark of her art: how to express the inward by the outward, depth by surface, silence by words, the abstract by the concrete.

I shall not dwell on the two earliest novels, in which we find full-length portraits, mingling with judicious balance physical descriptions, the psychological conclusions to be drawn from these, biographical circumstances and their consequences; dialogues, with commentary, complete the complex pattern of physical and mental habits which forms the framework for the inner adventure which the novel is to unfold. This is determined by a series of circumstances of extreme simplicity: meetings and separations contrived by the author in a sort of void where nothing interrupts the well-ordered ballet; and is presented in the classic form of psychological analysis, punctuated by the traditional "he felt, he thought, he was aware, it seemed to him . . .". The author is constantly present, narrating the sequence of thoughts, impressions and feelings, and with the aid of indispensable adverbs and epithets describing gestures and attitudes, intonations and facial expressions, following her characters' glances to take in the surrounding scene. Sometimes, very rarely, the character seems to push the author aside and take it upon himself to set forth his thoughts. Most frequently this changeover is occasioned by a question or exclamation, springing directly from the character's consciousness; but it is no more than a flash—in fact, simply a device for economy and variety. At no moment does this consciousness cease to be an object which the novelist scrutinizes, noting all its aspects, according to the divisions and terminology of a well ordered system of psychology. Long dialogues in which the protagonists reveal themselves to one another and at the same time to the reader complete this exploration, while formulated as well as unformulated thoughts are commented on by the author.

It is hard to discover anything particularly original in this method. On rare occasions only does discursive analysis dissolve into symbolic images whose poetic suggestions concretely evoke the tonality of emotions.[40] Here can be seen the first hint of the lyrical transposition which was to reach its full development in *The Waves*. The only other aspect worthy of interest is the constant maintaining of contact between the outside world and the characters under the searchlight that probes their consciousness. The flow of their sense impressions accompanies the flow of their feelings and thoughts, so that a certain density from the outside world seems constantly to cling to these self-centred beings. Impressions of interior scenes or of nature thus become part of themselves, in a somewhat mechanical way, which does not achieve complete fusion but which is evidence of the author's unmistakable trend.

If I have elsewhere stressed the unity of Virginia Woolf's work, it was partly by way of reaction against the general tendency to distinguish periods at the risk of concealing the continuity of her inspiration. But it is chiefly because, convinced of the secondary importance of technique, I did not wish to attribute to surface interruptions a priority which seemed contrary to the artist's intentions and thus prejudicial to a correct interpretation of her writings. The change in method in the expression of the inner life which we notice when passing from the first two novels to *Jacob's Room* is precisely one of those breaks which, spectacular though it is, must be considered from the

[40] Cf. N & D pp. 108 (107), 418 (394-5)

point of view of form, without forgetting that form is the servant of substance.

In her pursuit of the essence and content of the soul, Virginia Woolf, after having tried out the tools handed down to her by the predecessors that she admired—Jane Austen and Thackeray in particular—discovered, in practice, that they were unsuitable for grasping reality as she saw it. She abandoned them in favour of others which seemed better adapted to her aims. She renounced the artist's privilege of getting inside his characters to make an inventory of their emotions, feelings and thoughts. By a sort of radical preliminary decision, she rejected the whole of that hypothetical construction by which the novelist attributes to himself divine ominiscience. Now she takes up her position where all of us, readers and author alike, are ineluctably condemned to remain: outside, equipped with only our senses to apprehend the aspects of things and of people. All she tells us about Jacob—and about the other figures in the book too—is what surrounds him; or, more precisely, what enters into his field of perception and how he himself, as part of the perceptible world, appears to others. She will go no further than what is in his face: "Whether we know what was in his mind is another question".[41] She deliberately refrains from using that knowledge that seems to her dubious or at best hypothetical. Whence the disappearance of those "interior analyses" which I have referred to in the two earlier novels. The stratum of sense impressions, which had been only a "luminous halo", a marginal zone of transition between the self and the non-self in the characters in *The Voyage Out* and *Night and Day*, has become the only reality which the novelist allows herself to express. The principle underlying this technique is apparently a kind of sensationalism, which enables Chastaing to place Virginia Woolf in the tradition of Hume. But in fact this is a retreat from one convention to another, due less to any metaphysical conviction than to her sense of the artifice and inadequacy of the conventional line taken by the Edwardians and their predecessors. The whole system of feelings, of their combinations, their reactions, their evolution, as described by these novelists and by herself after them, is nothing but an abstraction, a system of reference and notation, practical perhaps in daily life but valueless when one is attempting to convey

[41] JR p. 93 (94)

reality. By using the words love, hate, jealousy, joy, sorrow, despair, by examining the nuances and the development of what they really represent, she discovered that, having as many meanings as the contexts in which they appear and as the consciousnesses in which they arise, they have, strictly speaking, no longer any valid meaning. One can juggle with them as with algebraical signs, and by respecting their laws of combination one can trace an arabesque which, since it conforms to what we are accustomed to, satisfies us. But to see in that a representation of life, of reality, is another matter. The elements of psychical life lie on the hither side: sounds, colours, shapes are the only reality that words can express and thus communicate with a sufficiently reduced margin of uncertainty, with a low enough coefficient of individual variation to supply the solid, universally valid material required for a work of art. It is out of this periphery of sense impressions that Jacob, or rather, as the title indicates, Jacob's "room", is to be made. The terms that spring to one's mind: immediate data of consciousness, impressionism, suggesting Bergsonism and the Grafton Gallery exhibition, bring the art of *Jacob's Room* into line with a whole movement.[42] But it is not so much the assimilation of these currents of thought as the personal striving for discovery, through successive experiments where, in each case, assets balanced liabilities—certain formulations being rejected and others retained—that explains the development of Virginia Woolf's genius. However, if Bergson and Cézanne form part, as it were, of Virginia's house rather than of Virginia's room, if the distance between herself and them, the transposition required by the shift from philosophy or painting to fiction safeguards the liberty and originality of the artist, the problem is rather different as regards works of literature, where the treatment may have influenced our author more directly, may have helped her to find answers to the questions she was asking herself. We learn from *A Writer's Diary* that at the very time when she was conceiving the form that was to produce *Jacob's Room*, she had the examples of Dorothy Richardson and Joyce in mind.[43] On the basis of what she wrote then and later, I rejected the popular theory that she was influenced by Joyce.[44]

[42] Cf. *supra*, ch. II, p. 30 ff
[43] Cf. AWD p. 23 (22)
[44] Cf. *supra*, ch. II, pp. 40-1, and ch. V pp. 241-5

It may be that texts hitherto kept from the public by her family may eventually shake this position. It may be slightly disquieting not to find the reviews of Dorothy Richardson's books in the various collections published to this day, particularly in *Granite and Rainbow*. The appreciation and understanding our novelist manifested there towards the author of *Pilgrimage* may lead to suppose that, consciously or unconsciously, the protectors of Virginia Woolf's fame feared this homage could bring the critics to question her originality. The reviews of *The Tunnel*[45] and *Revolving Lights*,[46] listed in Kirkpatrick's *Bibliography* published shortly before *Granite and Rainbow*, may have escaped Leonard Woolf's notice, or more probably been considered as outside the scope of the collection which, as all others previously published, did not include criticism of contemporary authors. These two reviews show that Virginia Woolf had read Dorothy Richardson before writing *Kew Gardens*, "An Unwritten Novel" and *Jacob's Room*, and had recognized in her a pioneer of the novel, like herself in reaction against the Edwardians, and like herself in quest of "Life itself",[47] which they could not or would not attempt to grasp. What strikes one in the first article is a sketch of the analysis which was to be resumed and developed in "Modern Novels",[48] published two months later, so that one may legitimately wonder at not finding the name of Dorothy Richardson mentioned after those of Joyce and Hudson, if not beside Hardy's and Conrad's. No document at present available justified the slightest hypothesis regarding this omission. Moreover, it would be rash to draw any precise conclusions, on the basis of the similarity of dates and texts I have noted, about the nature and importance of Virginia Woolf's debt to her two immediate predecessors. Her desire for a renewal of form is clearly enough expressed in *The Voyage Out* to dismiss the idea that *Pointed Roofs* (1915) and *A Portrait of the Artist as a Young Man* (1916) might have had a decisive influence on her orientation. In order to draw up, not indeed a strict statement of credits and debits, but

---

[45] Cf. *TLS*, Feb. 23, 1919 ("The Tunnel")

[46] Cf. *Nation & Athenaeum*, May 19, 1923 ("Romance and the Heart").

[47] The phrase appears in neither of the two 1919 articles, although in both the critic tries to define "life". "Life itself" is both in "Romance and the Heart" (*Nation & Athenaeum*, May 19, 1923, p. 229) and in "Mr Bennett and Mrs Brown" (*ibid.*, 12/1/1923; cf. CDB p. 111 (119).

[48] Otherwise "Modern Fiction", CR I

a mere table of priority which, interesting as it might be from the point of view of literary history, would teach us nothing about the individual development of the artists in question, we should have to embark on a textual comparison which would be outside the scope of this study. I shall merely state that the analogies or parallels that I have been able to discover have not seemed to contribute anything precise or important enough to be worth quoting in the present discussion.

Virginia Woolf having written, about *The Tunnel*,

Sensations, impressions, ideas and emotions glance off her unrelated and unquestioned, without shedding as much light as we had hoped into the hidden depths,[49]

it may seem surprising that *Jacob's Room*, from certain aspects, lays itself open to similar criticism. Neither the concentration of chosen moments, nor their interrelatedness by means of structure and tone, nor the network of leitmotivs quite succeed in expressing that indescribable centre which the author has deliberately forbidden herself to formulate. The extremism, the purity of her method should probably not be ascribed solely to the radicalism of an innovator. The fear of being seduced by "the damned egotistical self; which ruins Joyce and Richardson"[50] is, I believe, responsible for the ban she so scrupulously respects; she has sought to avoid the trap by staying outside, instead of getting to the centre where all the threads meet. As if this exercise in austerity had immunized her against the temptation she feared, she eventually felt strong enough to risk the ordeal of the "I" and to try to get inside her characters' consciousness. True, the relative failure of *Jacob's Room* impelled her in this direction; but it was necessary to have been through this to draw the lesson from it, to reject its excesses and turn its discoveries to good account.

One has only to read the first page of *Mrs Dalloway* to be immediately aware of the principal features of the new technique: "Mrs Dalloway said she would buy the flowers herself." The novelist, standing for a moment by the heroine's side, hears her words and repeats them to us; then, without warning us, she becomes identified with her creation, directly transcribing the content of her consciousness: "For Lucy had her work cut out for her. The doors would be taken off their hinges; Rumpelmayer's men were coming." Then once again, without further preparation, the author stands back, reporting the character's thought, this time indirectly: "And then, thought Clarissa Dalloway, what a morning—fresh as if issued to children on a beach."[51] The dash, indeed, marks a break which is more than grammatical; as if the reader, disconcerted by the change of interlocutor, had turned his head; and in that moment of hesitation the two voices have united: the author is still speaking, but it is Clarissa whom we hear. Two more discreet asides: "What a lark! What a plunge? *For so it had always seemed to her*" where the logical connecting-link—recurring constantly and often reduced to "so"—is ambiguous in function, as if the author were suggesting it to her character: and: "when, with a little squeak of the hinges, *which she could hear now*, she had burst open the French windows . . .".[52] Then we have once more the flow of impressions directly transcribed, where the dual personality is no longer that of the character plus the author, but the character plus the image of herself which she watches and refers to in the third person. This closeness of the author to her character, the constant shift from one to the other, is the essential thing about this new manner, which combines the resources of the interior monologue and of indirect analysis. It thus enables the excesses inherent in each of these to be neutralized. Analysis, forever on the point of slipping into interior monologue, acquires, through contiguity and as it were through overlapping, some of its inward quality; its very substance is modified; it readily accommodates imagery and lyricism, which thus no longer seem superimposed, artificial and rhetorical, but carry on the flow of recollection and reverie. . . . And in its turn the interior monologue, held in check by analysis, avoids the diffuseness, the rambling character, that lavish running to seed that borders on sterility. The meticulous rendering of surface impressions that was characteristic of *Jacob's Room*, always with strict reference to a consciousness that governs their choice and determines their tonality, not only disciplined the writer but above all led her to define "her" reality. But instead of leaving it scattered, as she had left it around Jacob, she gave it an inward direction—and in so doing unified it to make of it Clarissa's very substance. The scenes of her past, the images of

<hr />

[51] Mrs D p. 5 (3)   [52] Mrs D p. 5 (3)

people she knows, concentrated within a single day, are at the same time compressed within the limits of her inner life instead of being scattered through the course of her existence. Duration has absorbed time, and simultaneously consciousness has absorbed the whole of the universe.

From *Mrs Dalloway* to *To the Lighthouse*, there is no noticeable difference in the expression of the inner life. Only the slower rhythm, the broader sweep, enable each moment to expand more and at greater leisure. But the method remains the same. Nevertheless the significance of what is revealed is not identical. Whether this alteration is due to the stillness, bordering on immobility, in which beings and things are steeped, or to the permanence of the contact between the protagonists, it is difficult to say. It may simply be the result of a decision, on the part of the novelist, to lay increasing stress on the relation between people and to substitute it for what had been merely contact or acquaintance. Objects and people were a sort of content in Mrs Dalloway's consciousness; they appeared there in the form of sensations, images, gestures, words and scenes, coloured, it is true, by feelings and emotions. When Peter Walsh thinks of Clarissa, or Clarissa of Peter Walsh, in either case only one is thinking of the other. In *To the Lighthouse* we can take up a position *between* individuals and follow the currents of communication and interference which, at every phrase, affect their inner development. Tansley or Bankes or Mr Ramsay never stand still to be looked at by Mrs Ramsay; at each instant, what they see, what they hear, and what they say or feel, modifies the moment, destroys the autonomy of their interlocutor's consciousness. This perhaps necessitates the more frequent intervention of the author as analyst, but by the constant use of that process, previously described, whereby analyses slips into interior monologue and *vice versa*, any impression of arbitrariness, of psychology for psychology's sake, is avoided. The gain in depth and subtlety involves no excess of abstraction, no loss of contact with the reality of human beings. This closeness, which enables the author to coincide with her characters so that her presence is not noticed, seems to be the result of a sort of rhythm. Constantly, the exploration of the stream of consciousness alternates between surface and depth, between what is immediate, present and perceptible to the senses and what is remote, past or obscure. When Lily

Briscoe is painting, or Mrs Ramsay knitting while she reads, their immediate gestures, the attention they pay to the world around them is always rather like the story of the Fisherman and his Wife read by Mrs Ramsay to James, "like the bass gently accompanying a tune, which now and then ran up unexpectedly into the melody".[53] The fisherman's story carries Mrs Ramsay's thoughts to the conflict of wills in marriage, thence to Minta Doyle and Paul Rayley, to the Doyle parents and her relations with them; then James's presence beside her recalls the mother to her own children, to their happiness, present and to come, to her own happiness, into which there intrudes the unwelcome shadow of a fifty-pound bill to be paid; then the story draws to an end, while night falls, reminding her of the children and young people who are out on an expedition. However far we have wandered, we seem not to have left the window from which, now, can be seen the beam from the lighthouse, now lit up.[54]

The same characteristics, the same devices recur in *The Years* and *Between the Acts*. However, in *The Years*, the use of dialogue, the multiplicity of scenes and the desire to integrate a large number of facts and incidents prevents us, too often, from getting inside the characters. These consciousnesses, more ordinary so to speak, less meditative and more dispersed, are possibly more real, or rather more lifelike; but they lack the concentration which gives *To the Lighthouse* and *Between the Acts* their charm and their success. If certain moments in the lives of Maggie, Sara and Eleanor have as much density as those of Mrs Ramsay or Isa, they absorb too much of the outside world without really assimilating it, without converting it into their inner lives. This is the very problem that Virginia Woolf had set herself in this book, this conflict between facts and the content of consciousness, which she did not succeed in solving perfectly.

The Waves, through its originality and through the extreme character of the solution it offers for the expression of the inner life, deserves special attention. I have already pointed out that the poetic character of the monologues involved a certain transposition, an oblique approach. But these are only general traits. Detailed analysis reveals characteristics, directly derived from these general traits, which enable us to contrast Virginia Woolf's technique with kindred experiments. The interior monologue,

[53] To the L p. 91 (87)   [54] Cf. To the L pp. 88-99 (84-94)

whether it be realistic in inspiration, diffuse as in *Pilgrimage* or concentrated as in *Ulysses*, or else breaking out into poetry as in *The Sound and the Fury* or *As I Lay Dying*, remains closely linked— as does the psychical life which it serves to express—to a precise circumstancial context, from which it emanates, so to speak. In *The Waves*, the circumstancial context is still there, but it has been subjected to the same process of abstraction and compression as the stream of consciousness. Instead of the weft of facts and events, whether close or slack in texture, whether woven by chance or tightly and deliberately fastened off by the author, we have circumstances that are epitomes, recomposed by the novelist outside space and time. Instead of a German pension, Molly's room or the Bundrens' farm, on some particular day at some particular point in the protagonists' lives, we have the garden of childhood, school with its rules, maturity with its occupations, without any fixed place or day, without any action being performed. Villages, streets, dates and duties belong to the outside world, and as such would be alien to that universe without dimensions or landmarks in which the author places us. If at certain moments we seem to glimpse a school corridor, a restaurant dining-room, or Louis's office, or to recognize an hour or a day, we immediately perceive that the walls are not solid or opaque, that the moments are marked on no clock face, on no calendar. These words which seem to belong to a "story", or to a fragment of a story, have no narrative purpose; they belong to a language of symbols; the image they call forth is connected with reality only through the medium of the mind in which it arises and which chooses it as representative, as laden with multiple meanings, with personal allusions. Even the two dinner parties at which the friends foregather are only apparently circumstances. As soon as we look for some detail which might characterize and define the situation we find nothing, except perhaps a door[55]—which is scarcely a door, but is chiefly expectation, the threshold to be crossed before meeting others and oneself.

This purifying process, whereby the content of consciousness is freed from anything contingent, has the advantage, no doubt, of confronting us with a perfectly homogeneous universe; but if there is a gain in artistic purity, there is the constant risk of lapsing into the artificial and the arbitrary. The spatio-temporal

[55] Cf. The W pp. 88-99 (84-95)

setting did not only provide a framework for the unfolding of Clarissa's inner life, or Mrs Ramsay's, but at the same time controlled this and prevented it from straying; it provided the novelist with boundaries that restrained her fantasy, her imagination, and held in check the tendency to lyricism. I would not go so far as to indict *The Waves* of such excesses, but it avoids them only by what one might call the miracle of genius. This novel recalls certain analogous achievements in painting, which only their absolute mastery saves from failure. This precarious balance, inimitable even by the author herself, is surely the hallmark of a masterpiece.

We may wonder, however, whether the unique character of such an achievement does not imply that this convention, which Virginia Woolf substituted for those she had used hitherto, and to which, albeit with certain enrichments, she was to return, was less effective than she believed? In fact, the paradox of the inner life, which the very different monologues of Mrs Ramsay, Eleanor Pargiter, Molly Bloom and Darl Bundren all succeed in conveying, is the simultaneous apprehension of the order of time and the order of duration, or in other words, the integration of the totality of the subject's experience with his experience of the present moment. By stripping the present moment of its anecdotic or historic character and creating moments that are epitomes, syntheses of manifold present moments, Virginia Woolf has, if not dodged the problem, at least partially solved it at the start. The here and now which must be integrated with the anywhere and at any time, in spite of all the concrete elements of which it is made up, has lost the heterogeneity and externality that separate it from the latent content of consciousness; and at the same time the tension between the two elements no longer has the familiar aspect it wears in our common experience. True, there remain a conflict and a tension, acute and tragic, but they do not belong to any particular instant or situation; we might describe them as transcendental; they are the essence of the soul, not its existence. Which amounts to saying that *The Waves* is less an expression of the inner life than an attempt to formulate Being. This would suffice to justify the abandonment— as far as this aspect is concerned—of a technique which, given the object to which it is applied, could not be employed twice without resulting in repetition pure and simple. The limits within which the method can be used, far from invalidating it, emphasize its relevance. I have already replied to certain critics' complaint that Virginia Woolf replaces one convention by another with no appreciable advantage.[56] After what I have just said, I dare assert more positively that the difference of point of view, and of the aim pursued, makes nonsense of the idea of substitution. The classic type of interior monologue is a convention that may legitimately be compared with interior analysis, because both tend to express the same reality: the content of a consciousness in a given situation. "... that which is *beyond* and *outside* our own predicament ...,"[57] says Virginia Woolf. Yet one question remains: is not such a situation an essential part of the novel? The moment, taken out of its context, suspended in duration, once the threads are broken and the connections lost that bound it to space and time, surely becomes a theme for poetry rather than for the novel? But Virginia Woolf was well aware of this. The only conventional thing she did was to affix the label "novel" to a book which is no such thing.

If we consider the desire for purification which always haunted Virginia Woolf and which directed all her efforts in her quest for reality, the degree of abstraction (which of course does not affect the style) attained in *The Waves* is a natural conclusion and, on the whole, a success. Having gradually disengaged her characters from material contingencies, having filtered the complex product that is life and kept back only what she called "the soul", namely that which is consciousness and that which the consciousness contains at any given moment, it seems natural that she should have wished to attempt an even more radical purification. In *Mrs Dalloway*, and to a lesser degree in *To the Lighthouse*, there still remained foreign or external elements. Their degree of externality can be measured by the possibility we have of reconstructing with these elements, however vaguely, an objective universe, namely one that exists for the reader as well as for the protagonists. Nothing of the sort in *The Waves*: everything is turned inward. But while this result is in conformity with the author's intentions, and is a positive achievement, it may be asked whether the suppression of the outside world in which,

[56] Cf. *supra*, ch. V, pp. 301-2
[57] The W p. 175 (349). My italics. This is part of Bernard's final monologue (cf. *supra*, ch. V, p. 293 ff). I have referred to certain existentialist aspects of V. W. Here she obviously diverges from this line of thought.

after all, our lives take place, the suppression of that which is relative and against which we pit what is absolute in ourselves, does not denature the very truth that has to be expressed. While remembering that the relations between the self and the non-self are the subject of the book, and expressed with all the suggestive resources of poetic writing, it is possible that the desubstantiation of the non-self may have its repercussions on the self. Deprived of its point of support and its point of reference, its effort is enfeebled. We sometimes have the impression that these beings are playing at life, or acting out their lives rather than living them, even if the play be a tragic one.[58] David Daiches accused Virginia Woolf of "keeping her characters on holiday",[59] and David Cecil asserts that in the vision she pursues there is no place for drama.[60] I am only in partial agreement with these critics. For them, the words "holiday" and "vision" imply a limitation, which no doubt is quite a legitimate interpretation. But what seems a limitation to them may not be one to Virginia Woolf. Whereas the freedom of holidays is for Daiches something artificial, on the fringe of life, whereas vision for David Cecil implies a kind of static epipheno-menon or a gratuitous flowering, that is not how the novelist envisages them. When she gives her characters a holiday setting, whether at Santa Marina, on the island of Skye or in the geo-graphical, historical and social vacuum of *The Waves*, it is not in order to isolate or protect them from life, but rather to isolate and protect them from what, according to her, is only the illusion of life: a vain agitation and a sterile dispersion—and thus to enable them to concentrate themselves on the life which is within them, which is their own; which is themselves. And their vision, far from being a mirage or a phantom, is the actual perception of reality. Moreover, if we consider the word "drama" and kindred terms, as used constantly by Virginia Woolf both in her Diary and in her essays, we notice that it hardly ever implies action or movement. It is always used of the inward drama, the awareness of the tensions, the conflicts and contradictions that dwell within us. She is not concerned with the struggle against events, against

---

[58] Cf. David Cecil, *Poets and Story Tellers*, p. 171.

[59] Cf. David Daiches, *The Novel and the Modern World*, p. 160. After ascribing the superiority of To the L to Mrs D to the fact that V. W. had shown her characters on holiday, he adds: "But no novelist can keep his characters on holiday throughout his whole career as a writer."

[60] David Cecil, *op. cit.*, p. 168.

other people, against the universe, with the attempt to bring order into a chaos over which, on the whole, we have little power —none, perhaps. These tasks, this labour, or this game, which belong to history, or which provide the material for stories, are men's business. All such things merely serve to distract and entertain us, in Pascal's sense of the words; the essential thing is to win order within oneself, to preserve the constantly threatened balance between unity and multiplicity, between fear and hope, between the instinct of life and the lure of death. The change of accent, the altered stress which Virginia Woolf requires the novel to realise, which she unremittingly sought to achieve herself, is nothing other than this. For her, the inner life is not, perhaps, what we commonly understand by the words. It is something unmixed, silent and still, like the ideal novel that she conceived to express it. She called *The Waves* "that mystical eyeless book".[61] And surely it conveys a mystical experience, although its mystery consists in created things rather than in a Creator. Although François Mauriac's words are not completely true: "She appears to have lived at once outside the world and remote from God",[62] they do suggest the isolation that, under the stress of meditation, developed into a fundamental solitude, through which the mind pursued its odyssey. "That is the suicides' way," adds Mauriac. And indeed one can hardly believe that the psychological disturbance which affected Virginia Woolf was in no way responsible for that excessive withdrawal, that piercing sense of the mystery of existence which, in better balanced natures, is allayed by action and movement and easy going trust in life. The unique character of her experience, which pervades her work, may diminish its universal quality; but on the other hand it enhances its interest, makes of it an exploration into a realm where we are not entitled to venture. And since, in fact, the boundaries between the normal and the abnormal, between neurosis and health are more or less arbitrary, easily and frequently crossed, Virginia Woolf's expression of the inner life is of a more general value than is commonly believed. In the intermittences of everyday existence, it happens to all of us to catch a glimpse of those submerged abysses that she plumbed.

---

[61] Cf. *supra*, ch. III, p. 82, and ch. V, p. 260
[62] François Mauriac, Bloc-Note, May 5, 1958, *L'Express*, May 1958.

3. TIME AND SPACE

"Whatever is most valuable in modern literature is a meditation on the nature of time, on the mystery of memory and personality," Louis Gillet wrote in 1929 in an essay on Virginia Woolf.[63] A few months later, J. J. Mayoux published an article: "Le Roman de l'Espace et du Temps: Virginia Woolf",[64] which opened the long series of studies devoted to this problem in the works of our author.[65]

Dealing with a question on which philosophers usually disagree, it was inevitable that critics should be led to discuss it in terms of systems setting forth a theory of space and time akin to that which may be extracted from the work of Virginia Woolf. This method has the twofold advantage of profiting by the analytical efforts of those who may be called specialists, and on the other hand of placing the novelist in the current of thought, of inserting her in a tradition. To refer to Bergson's distinction between time and duration, and to his theory of memory, when analysing *Mrs Dalloway* or *Orlando*, helps to throw light on many of these novels' characteristics, whether as regards their composition, their psychology or their metaphysical implications. It reveals a richness which they genuinely possess, since no alert reader can fail to subscribe to the comparison; it also enriches them with a whole ideological context which the novel form conceals and, so to speak, holds in reserve. But when, after Delattre, we see Wiget and Chastaing taking an opposite line and discovering in Virginia Woolf the climax of the Anglo-Scottish tradition, and considering her novels as a generalized application of Locke's associationism, we begin to wonder if this process of pathfinding by the philosophical map is not a risky one, and possibly less fruitful than it seems. Our doubts are further increased by Jean-Claude Sallé, who assigns to Addison rather than to Locke the responsibility for the distinction between time

---

[63] Louis Gillet, "Virginia Woolf", *La Revue des Deux Mondes*, Sept. 1, 1929; developed in *Esquisses Anglaises*, Firmin Didot, Paris, 1930, pp. 214.

[64] *Revue Anglo-Américaine*, April 1930, pp. 312-26.

[65] Apart from the discussion of this aspect in general studies, particularly in those of Delattre, Daiches, Chastaing, Edwin Muir and James Hafley, one should also note: Lodwick Hartley, "Of Time and Mrs Woolf", *Sewanee Review*, April-June 1939; James Southall Wilson, "Time and Virginia Woolf", *Virginia Quarterly Review*, Spring 1942; John Graham: "Time in the Novels of Virginia Woolf", *University of Toronto Quarterly*, Jan. 1949, pp. 186-201; Erik Wiget, *Virginia Woolf und die Konzeption der Zeit in ihren Werken*.

and duration . . . which is to be found in certain passages of *Tristram Shandy!*[66] I shall not repeat what I said earlier when sketching the intellectual climate in which Virginia Woolf matured.[67] By this stage, I think I have defined the author's temperament and interests, her preoccupations, the process of her thought and her methods of work sufficiently to justify the point of view from which I propose to study her idea of time and space. Instead of projecting such and such a theory on to the text, pointing out coincidences whose true origin and nature are unknown to us and whose true significance with regard to the author remains, in consequence, problematical, I shall confine myself to her writings themselves, which shed mutual light on one another, and I shall only have recourse, in support of my hypothetical interpretations, to such revelations as Virginia Woolf herself may have left, to the theories she sketched out and the axioms scattered throughout her writing.

Space being of a more concrete nature, being a simpler notion, easier to represent and capable of being defined in a convenient way without necessarily presupposing a whole metaphysical system, let us begin with space. We shall see moreover that this choice is not only dictated by reasons of clarity and convenience, but that the analysis of Virginia Woolf's concept of space will provide factors essential to the analysis of her concept of time.

In *The Voyage Out* and *Night and Day*, we have the classic concept of space, in which beings and things are set out; it determines their closeness or distance, their contact or separation. Its solidity, its fixedness, enable it to include and define movement, and consequently temporal succession. The characters go from London to Lisbon and to Santa Marina, from the villa to the hotel, from Cheyne Walk to Highgate, from the vicarage to Lincoln; and each stage of a character's journey is also a moment in his life, which thus develops according to a simple curve, fixed according to equally simple co-ordinates. In this Euclidian universe, space enjoys undoubted priority, having all its own qualities and furthermore providing the means of representing and measuring time, which is coextensive with it. It is the true

[66] Cf. Jean Claude Sallé: "Sterne's distinction of Time and Duration", *The Review of English Studies*, vol. VI, no. 22, April 1955, pp. 180-2. He traces a passage of *Tristram Shandy* (World's Classics, III, 18, pp. 160-71) to a passage in No. 94 of *The Spectator*.

[67] Cf. *supra*, ch. II

form of reality, in which and according to which human life unfolds and organizes itself—as does the novel which tells of it. True, the solidity and rigidity of this space and of this spatialized time seem to dissolve away in the mind; imagination and memory have the power of calling up the elsewhere and the past to the point of obliterating the here and the now—without, however, destroying them. This is merely an illusory excursion which in no way interrupts the course of the voyage, an inventory or a recapitulation which do not disturb the regular succession of night and day. The fact is that two orders of reality are concerned, which have nothing in common but their name. The vision of England which may be attributed to the passengers on the Euphrosyne,[68] the picture of Mrs Parry's drawing-room called forth simultaneously in the minds of Mrs Ambrose and Mrs Thornbury by a remark of Hughling Elliott's,[69] or Katherine's house, as Ralph returns to it in his daydream,[70] or the Italian hills that flash into Katherine's mind as she reads "Isabella and the Pot of Basil",[71] all these fragments, with their emotional and temporal connotations, bear the same relation to reality as a picture postcard to the landscape it represents. The mind imagines places and moments with the same characteristics of structure and quality as if it were actually perceiving them, but at the same time it refers them to the real place, and this operation serves to empty the image of its reality. In short, time and space exist independently of ourselves and constitute the setting of the universe, within which our lives unfold.

In consequence, as soon as the reality of this universe of juxtaposed objects and successive moments is called in question, the space and time essential to their contiguity and to their separation, to the delimitation and autonomy of all these objects and beings so neatly laid out on a chessboard, are also threatened. "The Mark on the Wall", "Kew Gardens", "An Unwritten Novel" are so many attempts to disintegrate reality, are as it were the first blows struck at the objectivity of space and time.

This thing, the little black mark on the wall which turns out to be a snail, this minute fraction of space, this point on the line of time, undergoes, between the sensation that reveals it and thus brings it into being, and the identification that detaches it from

[68] Cf. VO, pp. 28-9 (32)   [69] Cf. VO p. 172 (147)
[70] Cf. N & D p. 21 (28)   [71] Cf. N & D p. 109 (109)

mind and restores it to the outside world, to what we call its reality, but stripped of its substance and meaning, a vital operation whose process, on this reduced scale, enables us to grasp the essence of Virginia Woolf's vision.

"How readily our thoughts swarm upon a new object, lifting it a little way, as ants carry a blade of straw so feverishly, and then leave it. . . ."[72] From the start, she asserts the primacy of the mental operation, of the content of mind, over that element of the outside world which is merely its occasion. This little mark, this spot, is to be inflated in all dimensions until it evaporates to leave room for the free play of thought, memory, feelings and emotions. We may be tempted to confuse this arousing of mental functions with the classic concept of the process of perception, namely the projection of hypotheses on sense data in order to reduce them to known universal groupings, and to discover behind them the familiar configuration of the material world in which we are immersed. But actually, the absurdity of this conclusion is shown by the sudden ending of the sketch. The fact that the mark was a snail—and it was only necessary to get up and correct the visual data by the tactile data to make sure of this—is both ridiculous and unimportant. The coincidence between the original sensation and this object is, basically, purely accidental. What is essential is all that came into the mind between sensation and perception: this content is reality, it is the mark on the wall. And whether we consider the mark, or the woman in "An Unwritten Novel"—Minnie Marsh, who is not Minnie Marsh—it is exactly the same: "the mystery of life",[73] "mysterious figures . . .".[74] All the mystery lies in the impenetrability of the non-self, of all that lies around us and the reality of which is only a postulate—in fact, a pure nothingness by the side of that inner effervescence aroused by the activity of our senses.

This assertion of subjectivity or idealism is pregnant with consequences as regards space, which is both setting and attribute of the universe; it loses its reality at the same time as that universe; it no longer exists, save in the sensibility that apprehends it and in the mind that thinks it. It had been that which contained; it has become a content. This solid area on which it was possible to

[72] HH p. 36 (37)
[73] HH p. 36 (38)
[74] HH (Unwritten Novel), p. 23 (21)

depict the world, to locate movements, to follow the course of a person's destiny—and to lay out a novel—is now shattered into a thousand fragments, now flung higgledy-piggledy into that sack we call mind or consciousness, the self, or "I". Things that had been separate are superimposed and entangled, things that had been contiguous are dissociated, divided sometimes for ever. In that solid, ordered universe, time had found its own solidity and order; succession, with its references to past, present and future, had fitted neatly therein; and time is shattered and overthrown by this catastrophe. Nothing remains of that fine ordered system we lived in, save the "scraps, orts and fragments"[75] with which Miss La Trobe bewilders her audience. "Kew Gardens" is a handful of these floating debris, adrift beside a flowerbed, "enveloped in layer after layer of green blue vapour, in which at first their bodies had substance and a dash of colour, but later both substance and colour dissolved in the green blue atmosphere".[76] In this setting, which is a complex of sensations imbued with emotion: colours, light, heat, air, sounds,—no smells— satisfaction, desire, nostalgia, every sort of space and time, are juxtaposed and intermingled, so that obviously the use of such terms is only an approximation. The irregular quadrilateral formed by the father, mother and two children walking is none other than the separation of their thoughts and interests; the figure flattens into a straight line ("now walking four abreast")[77] when the mother has allayed her husband's anxiety and imposed her will on the children. The snail, the thrush, the insect, the butterflies, each moves within a space made to its own measure, crowded or free, vertical or horizontal, rectilinear or irregular according to its nature. As for time, it may be a few minutes, fifteen years, or centuries ago, or the imminent moment when the waitress will have to be paid. We must not be misled by the expressions of measure which are dotted about the text; they are there to assess heterogeneity, not to provide a homogeneous canvas. Each centre of life is a centre that creates its own space and time, having no common measure with any other. All these characteristics can be summed up in two words: relativity and subjectivity.

[75] B the A pp. 220 (189), 251 (215)
[76] HH p. 34 (35)
[77] HH p. 30 (30)

But "The Mark on the Wall", "An Unwritten Novel" and "Kew Gardens" are merely sketches, bearing on a single detail; they elucidate only a fragment of space and time, and if on this scale the experiment has been successful, much has of course been gained, but the discovery has still to be given general application, transferred from the laboratory to the whole of life. Could the achievement which had been simplified and made possible by the narrow setting of a room, a flowerbed, a railway carriage, the selection of a few moments separated from before and after, be repeated for a city, a country, the whole earth, a life, or lives?

Jacob's Room is a first attempt in this direction. The novel is made up of juxtaposed fragments like those in the sketches, complex unities which J. J. Mayoux suggests calling "space-moments",[78] a suggestive term, provided one remembers that the time and space concerned are manifold and shifting within a multiplicity of consciousnesses. In the opening pages, for instance, we have those of Betty Flanders, Charles Steele, Archer and Jacob, so many circles covering different areas, different periods, whose overlappings mark hatchings, as it were, on a common zone and thus make it stand out from the arabesques in which it was concealed: the bay in Cornwall, this evening. Shall we say: space and time regained? One can scarcely recognize them, so shapeless and insubstantial are they. This is not the solid framework of a univers: this is only the fortuitous and inconsequential residue of the different autonomous creations that have emerged in each consciousness, floating in an ether, a vacuum, to which we usually attach the label "space" and "time" but which is nothing of the sort.

What is true of the elements of one section is also true of the different sections, considered as elements of the book. They leave a deposit in which, according to our habits, we recognize vestiges of Scarborough, Cambridge, London . . . as Jacob passes through them; and from Jacob's passing, as well as from his gestures, the content of his vision and a few brief parentheses of the author's, we infer the passing of time. But this space and this time, like the brief and rare comments referring to them, are marginal to the book. If we extract them from the book for ourselves, by super-

[78] J. J. Mayoux, "Le Roman de l'Espace et du Temps", Virginia Woolf, *Revue Anglo-Americaine*, vol. 7; April 1930, p. 316

imposing our vision of things on the text, or if here and there a sentence of the author's provides a helpful landmark, that is something accessory, a survival, an alien factor.

This element of impurity, which also implies incongruity, is one aspect of the partial failure of *Jacob's Room*. In order for the attempt to succeed, this marginal element should either have been completely banished or completely integrated. As things stand, Jacob's room proves too vast, and Jacob stays in it too long; and above all, he himself lacks the presence and the substance needed to absorb his universe, to make it solely his own; in the gaps formed by his absence and his discontinuity, time and space have surreptitiously crept in.

One single day, one single place, Clarissa, Septimus: the two foci of the ellipse to be explored; are these different data, simpler and closer to the original experiment of the sketches, going to produce a better result? The two protagonists each carry with them their own space and time, intensely and profoundly personal. But instead of being suspended in the void, they are rooted in the city, its streets, its parks, its houses; and in the day, which flows gently from hour to hour, to the rhythm of Big Ben. And these hours, these moments, seem very real and solid, since we lean on them as we turn now towards Clarissa, now towards Septimus. And immediately the counterpoint, Time/Duration, real space/experienced space, provides the critic with a rich store of Bergsonian variations. But is this really what Virginia Woolf wished to achieve, or what she did achieve? It is not irrelevant to note that during its composition, for about a year, the title of *Mrs Dalloway* was *The Hours*,[79] and that this title is echoed by *The Years*, which was almost *Here and Now*,[80] which also fitted *The Waves*.[81] But these hours belong to no clock, any more than the years (from *Jacob's Room* to *Between the Acts*) belong to any calendar; nor do they correspond to anything real, which could be divided thus into homogeneous and successive sections. It is surely characteristic that "the leaden circles dissolved in the air".[82]

[79] Cf. AWD p. 57 (56) (June 19, 1923) and p. 62 (61) (May 26, 1924). The title *Mrs Dalloway* only reappears on Aug. 15, 1924. Cf. p. 65 (63)

[80] Cf. AWD p. 211 (204), 212 (205), 214 (207), 215 (208), and *supra*, ch. III, pp. 305, 312

[81] Cf. AWD p. 215 (208), and *supra*, ch. III, p. 289

[82] Mrs D p. 6 (5): "First a warning, musical; then the hour, irrevocable. The leaden circles dissolved in the air . . . For Heaven only knows why one loves it so,

Only a Bradshaw could believe in that sort of time, cut it up into three-quarter-of-an-hour lengths and charge for it like so many yards of cloth. The sound of bells that rings out periodically throughout the book, throughout the day, does not superimpose physical time upon duration; it both sounds the knell of an illusion and recalls that sole reality that contains all realities, the moment: "First a warning, musical, then the hour, irrevocable."[83] And a little later: "For heaven only knows why one loves it so. . . ."[84] And the conclusion of the paragraph leaves one in no uncertainty: "life; London; this moment of June."[85] Can it be more clearly stated that life is identical with the apprehension of the moment, of the "here and now", that time and space are coextensive and consubstantial with consciousness? As James Hafley suggests when he contrasts *Mrs Dalloway* with *Ulysses*, Virginia Woolf has shown "that there is no such thing as a single day".[86] And there is no such thing as a city, in spite of Westminster, Hyde Park, Regent's Park, Bond Street and Piccadilly, Harley Street or Buckingham Palace. Clarissa's shopping expeditions, the walks taken by Peter Walsh or Septimus Smith, the route of the bus on which Elizabeth travels, or of the ambulance, or of the Prime Minister's car bear no reference to the points of the compass; they are only the transient disturbance that arises in some individual consciousness, whose ripples reach greater or lesser depths[87]; the lines one can trace from this point to that are as unsubstantial as the letters traced by the aeroplane, which dissolve in the air[88] like the eleven strokes of the clock.

If *Mrs Dalloway* marks an advance on *Jacob's Room*, and indeed scores a triumph, it is precisely because the illusion of time and space is preserved, to the point of taking one in. But to be taken in is the mistake made by the Bradshaws and Holmes, who "mix

---

how one sees it so, making it up, building it round one, tumbling it, creating it every moment afresh; . . . in the triumph and the jingle and the strange high singing of some aeroplane overhead was what she loved; life; London; this moment of June."

[83] Cf. *supra*, n. 82
[84] Cf. *supra*, n. 82
[85] Cf. *supra*, n. 82
[86] Cf. James Hafley, *The Glass Roof*, p. 73: "(Virginia Woolf) used the single day as a unity (. . .) to show that there is no such thing as a single day."
[87] Cf. Mrs D pp. 20-1 (25-6), particularly the last sentence of the paragraph: "For the surface agitation of the passing car as it sunk grazed something very profound."
[88] Cf. Mrs D pp. 24-5 (29-30)

the vision and the sideboard",[89] taking the material for the real, sense-appearances for the essence of things. It matters little that this conception lacks, maybe, the consistency of the Bergsonian theories that critics have sought to recognize in this novel. As Virginia Woolf says in her preface: "In the present case it was necessary to write the book first and to invent the theory afterwards"[90]—which assuredly she never bothered to do, leaving that pastime to us, for her own greater amusement no doubt. The only clear and conscious elements that we can find as the source of *Mrs Dalloway* are a few intentions and intuitions. In particular, "to be more close to the fact" than in *Jacob's Room*,[91] that is to say to convey reality more adequately, to catch hold of things that had slipped through its slack mesh, to "keep the quality of a sketch",[92] that is to say to take advantage of "Mark on the Wall", "Kew Gardens" and "An Unwritten Novel"; and finally the "tunnelling process", the "underground caves" full of the past and of elsewhere.[93] The nature and content of these caves deserves to be examined. They will enable us to define those "space-moments". Immediate space, dense with manifold sensations, fills their luminous centres. No doubt Edwin Muir was referring to the suggestive force of these sensations when he described *Mrs Dalloway* as the most skilful spatial picture of life in contemporary literature. To justify such a description, these sensations should on the one hand be pure, and on the other, should be effectively projected in space. Now they are frequently, if not always, laden with impressions which proliferate into notions and thoughts, which certainly shows that they are moved by a centripetal rather than by a centrifugal force, that they are not dispersed in space around the characters but sink deep into them to arouse the life buried within. These impressions, with all the wealth of images and thoughts that unfold around the sensations of the moment, illuminate the darkness of the cave with innumerable lights of varying intensity and duration; and these new lights, in the background, dim the brilliance of those from which they had sprung, until they have extinguished them.

[89] Cf. Mrs D p. 163 (225): ". . . yet judges they were; who mixed the vision and the sideboard; saw nothing clear. . . ."

[90] Cf. J. Hafley, *op. cit.*, p. 61.

[91] Cf. *supra*, ch. V, p. 239

[92] Cf. *supra*, ch. V, p. 238

[93] Cf. *supra*, ch. V, pp. 233-34

The "here and now" has become elsewhere and another time. The spatio-temporal notions of contiguity and simultaneity, of distance and succession, are of no avail for inventorying the content of these moments, simply because everything happens there outside space and time, in a quite different setting: the consciousness, the soul, the sensibility, whatever we choose to call it. It might be thought that the distinction, within the moment, between the here and elsewhere, between now and another time, postulates that space and time whose presence I deny. It postulates them only according to the Bergsonian viewpoint, which I cannot accept. For Virginia Woolf, as she says in *The Waves*, the moment is all, the moment is nothing[94]; there lies the problem, there lies the anguish, not in the reconciliation of time and duration. The word "moment" is misleading, for it is borrowed from our language which accepts time. But Virginia Woolf's "moment" has no before, no afterwards: it is, as we are, instantaneously and totally. Hence the static character of the novels, of which no critic seems to have taken account, and which is perhaps the strongest argument in favour of the present interpretation. That which, like others before me, I have called discontinuity in *Jacob's Room*, is basically only an elementary form of that static quality. From the fact that the moments of that book fail to unite into any sort of time or duration, we can see what difficulty Virginia Woolf experienced in conceiving this notion. And the later novels show that she replaced this heterogeneous link, these "moments" still coloured by traditional notions of space and time, by the cohesive force of consciousness. It is evident that the "moments" lived by Clarissa, Peter Walsh or Septimus—or by Mrs Ramsay or Lily Briscoe—constitute neither a sequence, nor a true process-of-becoming. None of the words: progress, advance, forward movement, passage, or decline can properly be applied to them, nor to those collections of moments, the June day in *Mrs Dalloway*, the dateless day in *To the Lighthouse*. The failing of the light in the landscape, which seems to play the same part as Big Ben in marking the so-called passage of time, has no other meaning or function than the bells. It is a mere quality of the moment, one amongst many others. Nevertheless, Big Ben is a man-made machine; it forms part of that huge apparatus that ensures order and proportion for the

94 Cf. The W, particularly p. 197 (369)

universe of Bradshaw and his like. We have seen that it is used for other ends by Clarissa and all the real human beings around her. The atmospheric quality of the moment, which may also serve to measure time, is on the contrary a natural phenomenon; it is a reality, that is to say that through the sensation we have of it, we reach something essential. Beyond their similarity, there is a primordial difference between these two elements: the bell of Big Ben, essentially made to measure time, is diverted from its purpose to become merely a gong-like sound calling one's attention to the instant. The modification of light, essentially a quality of the instant, is diverted from its purpose if it is used to measure time. And the unwarranted character of such a diversion is strikingly illustrated in "Time Passes", in the interludes of *The Waves*, and the prologues of *The Years*, where we find the very essence of Virginia Woolf's concept of time, which hitherto we have only grasped negatively.

The fact that Virginia Woolf inserted "Time Passes" between those two moments, "The Window" and "The Lighthouse", confirms the immobility of these moments. But then, it may be said, the very title of this intermediary section seems to assert that apart from these moments—between them, around them, or parallel with them, so many spatial images whose value is of course purely metaphorical—there is time, and time passing. Ten years, in fact. This particular is furnished, incidentally, on the fifth page of the following chapter,[95] and not in this one, which is, significantly, concerned more with the weather than with the passing of time.

At the beginning of the reign of "Time" we see all the lights go out,[96] which implies that all consciousness abdicates, all sensibility is suspended, letting the universe sink down into the mysterious nothingness of darkness. In that night, where all is confusion, a sort of original chaos, an infinite number of forces, an innumerable army of elves with bodies of air and water, earth, heat and cold—the elements of ancestral cosmogonies—attack the substance which the abdication of light had deprived of form. The field of their action is limited to matter; they have no power over the sleeping beings, despite the latters' apparent

[95] Cf. To the L p. 229 (220-1): "Yes, it must have been precisely here that she had stood ten years ago."
[96] Cf. To the L p. 195 (189): "So with the lamps all put out, the moon sunk. . . ."

vulnerability.[97] This time, this force has no hold on us: we do not know it. Even if the moment of truth, the vision of timeless reality lasted only a second,[98] this disintegration and destruction affect only appearances, that phantom, futile universe where an otiose causality reigns. The real world of "what and why and wherefore" remains intact, in its wonder and mystery.[99] Thus the passing of Time, as Virginia Woolf has sought to show it in this chapter,[100] is only the qualitative modification of the universe: day, night, summer, winter, the rain, the sun, the blossoming of violets and daffodils, the poppies invading the bed of dahlias, the slender bough that beat against the window growing into a tree, casting its green shadow into the room, the rust on the stove, the mould on the carpet, the flaking plaster. . . . The passing of time is a substanceless expression, a metaphor and an allegory; there is only the futility and insensibility of nature, its life where, as in our own, *before* and *after* have no meaning, where the duplication of days, seasons, blossomings and fadings, like the duplication of our own sensations, thoughts and gestures, makes nonsense of them both, inextricably entangling the sequence till it becomes unintelligible. There is only what is present—presence —and what is different—difference. In the interludes of *The Waves* and the prologues of *The Years*, we find nothing other than this. What we call the moments of our life, the years that we count and number, are merely the presence in our consciousness of the unique quality of a bit of landscape where the light, the wind, the heat give to the tree, the rock, the wave, the bird, a colour and line, a voice and a tactile quality which are superposed on one another without obliterating each other, which remain themselves although becoming other. It is this diversity in permanence, this endless repetition, endlessly incurring loss and yet endlessly enriched with fresh spoils, that we call "time".

Must we call it spatialized time because it seems to adopt the rhythm, to identify itself with the nature, that we conceive under the form of space? There seems no justification for the term. This pseudo-space in which Nature, according to Virginia

[97] Cf. To the L p. 197 (191): ". . . here you can neither touch nor destroy."

[98] Cf. To the L pp. 198-9 (192-3)

[99] Cf. To the L p. 199 (193): "Almost it would appear that it is useless in such confusion to ask the night those questions as to what, and why, and wherefore, which tempt the sleeper from his bed to seek an answer."

[100] Cf. *supra*, ch. V, pp. 259-61

Woolf's conception, unfolds itself, having neither dimensions nor coordinates, does not deserve its name. It is so foreign to space as we conceive it, so indeterminate, that to treat it as a determinant of time seems futile. The only epithet that seems to me capable of helping one to define it is "sensationalized". Sensationalized time, because there is nothing to be found in it beside sensations; rather, indeed, it is nothing but sensations for the mind that apprehends it. There indeed, lies its paradox: one might say its nothingness, for sensation is timeless.

Orlando and *Between the Acts* deny time in a casual and apparently arbitrary manner; but if one may hesitate to take these negations seriously, it is difficult not to yield to the corrosive vision of *To the Lighthouse*, *The Waves* and *The Years*. But before examining the consequences of this disintegration of the reality of time, it seems apposite to take advantage of the preceding analysis to deal with space, expelled like its fellow by the same revolution.

Although no special chapter provides a key to Virginia Woolf's thought on this point, a glance at the novels that follow *Mrs Dalloway* is enough to convince one that in the interim, space, which had been a mere ghost, has lost even its skeleton. Just as no real time really elapsed between the mid-September of the first chapter of *To the Lighthouse* and the mid-September of the third, so no real space surrounds its characters. What we have in its stead, what looks like space—but only looks like it without being it, just as Mrs Dalloway's London only looks like London—is filtered through the "window". The window, that is to say the entry into consciousness which purifies it of all its traditional attributes and retains, as in the case of time, only sensations. These are actually there, in reality, as they are repeated on Lily Briscoe's canvas as a representation of reality: these greens, these blues, these lines in all directions, this effort and this aspiration, this attempt at something, which would be hung up in the attics or destroyed.[101] Space is even more unrecognizable in *The Waves*, where union and separation are achieved without its aid on every page, in every line. And if we imagine we find it again in *The Years*, it is through the same illusion that made us fancy we found time there; there is only the shadow of space, as though to persuade us that space is merely a shadow. *Orlando*, in fantastic

[101] Cf. To the L pp. 310-20 (301-10)

vein, kills space by caricature. From Russia to England, from Turkey to Cape Horn, it is too extravagant to exist. It is stretched out like a circus hoop, and going through it is a game. Like Orlando's great house with its three hundred rooms, it might be said to have three hundred dimensions: which is like saying it has none.

But this time and this space, reduced, like all reality, to the timeless and spaceless content of a consciousness, if they are stripped of all "real" or "material" attributes, of all those that conferred existence on them apart from and independent of the apprehension we have of them, acquire their own qualities, not to be measured or represented, which result from their being objects of consciousness and consequently "realities" in the Woolfian sense of the word. This apprehended time and space, as such, cannot be defined in the language of physics, but only in the language of mind. If we consider the "here and now", the moment apprehended with the intensity and sharpness of Virginia Woolf's "vision"—whether we are concerned with Clarissa, Mrs Ramsay, Lily Briscoe, any of the characters in *The Waves*, or Eleanor Pargiter, we realise that it means a sense of peace and plenitude. It is thus because in it, life and the feeling of life attain perfect harmony. Everything is included and understood. Totality, union, communion, possession, this moment satisfies the demands of the whole being, who has mastered his life, who lives it and contemplates it in a single act, which is existing, feeling and thinking at once. But this moment is an ephemeral victory, a precarious integrity. On the reverse side of its unity, its cohesion and certitude, it carries all the germs of its own destruction. The past which it has summoned up from its depths and coloured with the present until the two are indistinguishable retains, nevertheless, its own weight and colour: it is that which is lost, the irrevocable: "Jacob! Jacob!" "Mrs Ramsay! Mrs Ramsay!": the call rings out, unanswered. Something has slipped in between ourselves and that fragment of ourselves that we had salvaged: something that is commonly called time, but which is simply a sense of separation, of loss, of heart-rending bereavement. That which we had gathered together across space, all the "elsewhere", is scattered by some invincible force which affects us in the same way: "Jacob! Jacob!" is Archer's cry, too, on the deserted beach; and the scattered characters of *The Waves* feel distance slipping in and stretching out between them, distance which is also loss and heart-rending bereavement. When J. J. Mayoux pointed out that in *Night and Day* space "tends to take the romantic shape of distance, which is akin to time"[102] his phrase anticipated the whole of that development of Virginia Woolf's conception which I am trying to clarify here. She can be said to have replaced time and space, which she denies, by the apprehension of what we call time and space: that apprehension which is a sense of distance, of separation. And when a human being envisages that other direction of time, the future, the threat, although apparently different, has the same inner repercussions. Tomorrow is mysterious, but only as regards its detail, its modalities; experience tells us that tomorrow will be like today, Tuesday like Monday. That is to say, the moment we possess now will have slipped into the past and will be lost; little James Ramsay will have grown; who else, besides Rhoda and Percival, will have died? Although we do not know which fragment of our lives will have been torn from us, we know that there will be a tearing away, separation, loss. And, mentally adding up these successive losses, we come to the final stage of deprivation, which is death—the ultimate loss and the ultimate separation against which Bernard summons up all his energy.

From all this we gather that for Virginia Woolf the problem was not the reconciliation of time and duration, any more than of physical space and mental space. She only encounters it incidentally, by way of words so to speak—just as I have had to make use of an ambiguous terminology which constantly threatens my analysis with deviation and confusion. We must give up referring to Bergson. Nor is this the search for lost time, for although time is here so often regained it is so only incidentally; we must give up referring to Proust. The central problem, which recurs through all the vicissitudes of technique, the accidents of success or failure, the various stages towards maturity of craftsmanship and thought, from *The Voyage Out* to *Between the Acts*, is the analysis of anguish. Anguish is precisely that feeling of the threat that hangs around the moment, of the precarious nature of vision which extends to the whole being, since the whole being is basically that

[102] J. J. Mayoux, "Le Roman de l'Espace et du Temps: Virginia Woolf", *Revue Anglo-Américaine*, vol. 7, p. 314.

vision. Anguish is the reverberation within ourselves of the imminence of that dispersion and loss which, wherever we look— in front or behind, before or after—oppresses the whole of what we are, the things and beings that make up our own being. This anguish is inherent in our being, since it is the very sense, the revelation of our existence, based on its reverse, its negation, nothingness. The solitude which haunts the heroes of Virginia Woolf is the most expressive aspect of this anguish. It is what remains when everything is lost, when everything has sunk beneath the horizon of time and space, when no power can reduce the distance or rejoin what is separate. It is at this zero point of life, which coincides with the zero point of space and time, that Bernard faces death, and the question is asked: will death irrevocably swallow up all our losses, or will it be the ultimate recovery? the access to fusion, communion, unity to which we aspire. The answer remains uncertain. Rachel, Terence, Clarissa and Septimus, Bernard, Isa seem to allow a glimpse of hope. The death of Jacob allowed none; and Bernard's hope is so intentional that it seems more of an aspiration than a belief. "The waves broke on the shore."[103] Does this mean nothingness sanctioning the victory of time and space, our enemies and our defeat, or does it mean eternity sanctioning our victory over their vain and illusory opposition? Dare one take into account Virginia Woolf's own suicide, to incline the answer in one direction or another? Scarcely; all that this reveals is the reality, the power of that anguish which, for her, meant the sensation and also the essence of time and space—an anguish which alternated, in her, with a joy no less intense.[104] All that one can say is that on the threshold of an attack in which she knew her integrity to be imperilled, in which she would find herself dispossessed of that which was life itself for her: closeness, participation and communion, then what was left to her— physical life and ghost-haunted solitude—was meaningless and valueless.

If there is one trend of thought with which one can associate Virginia Woolf, in which, apart from any question of sources or

[103] The W p. 211 (383). Cf. "The sun rose", which concludes *The Years*; apparently more positive, this is only the stressed beat of the same rhythm in which the breaking of the waves is the unstressed beat.

[104] Cf. *supra*, ch. III, p. 112 ff

influences, she can most readily be inscribed, it is probably existentialism, to which I have already referred repeatedly. Surely Jean Wahl's comment on Kierkegaard can be aptly applied to the author of *The Waves*? "The person who exists is he who will not rest satisfied with ready-made truths, but who, maintaining a negative attitude towards himself, lives through effort amidst uncertainty, in Becoming. He will know that the only important thing is subjectivity, and that what matters is less the truth than the way in which one reaches it and feels it. But he will also know that subjectivity is error. Torn between these two affirmations about existence, he will exist through the very fact of being so torn, through this wound."[105]

4. SYMBOLISM

An exhaustive study of Virginia Woolf's use of symbols would require a second commentary on her novels from a fresh point of view, and one as voluminous as that which I have already devoted to them. There is material here for a work of analysis and synthesis which would exceed the limited scope of the present chapter, whose only purpose is to shed light on certain aspects of our author's art and thought.

All critics have recognized the importance of symbols in the writing of Virginia Woolf, a corollary to its poetic nature, which they may praise or condemn but cannot fail to acknowledge. *Mrs Dalloway*, *Orlando*, and above all *To the Lighthouse* and *The Waves* have proved profitable ground for symbol-hunters. I have myself ventured certain inescapable suggestions where relevant. However, the most pertinent comments have been made in studies of a more general nature, and the interest shown in Virginia Woolf by specialists in symbolism invites one to examine the problem not incidentally, in connection with any particular novel, but as a whole. From the various writings of Gaston Bachelard[106] can be gleaned a whole series of analyses showing the wealth of symbols relating to the elements and to nature in general. While one must make certain reservations, in so far as the poetic imagination of the philosopher has outstripped the

[105] Jean Wahl, "Kierkegaard, L'Angoisse et l'Instant", *NRF*, April 1932, vol. 38, p. 635.
[106] Cf. particularly: *L'Eau et les Rêves*, *L'Air et les Songes*, *La Terre et les Rêveries du Repos*.

poetic imagination of the novelist, these studies bring together groups of meanings and images which open up vistas throughout the whole of Virginia Woolf's work, revealing the continuity of her inspiration. William York Tyndall in *The Literary Symbol*, while providing helpful interpretations,[107] devotes particular attention to the mechanism of symbolization, to what he calls "the passage from discourse to symbol".[108] While taking advantage of these studies, I shall approach the question from a different point of view. I shall simply seek to draw up a list of images—that is to say of objects, or groups of objects, apprehended by the imagination of the author and communicated to the imagination of the reader—whose obsessive character on the one hand and whose wealth of implication on the other entitle us to consider them as key elements in Virginia Woolf's world. The word "vision" has recurred so frequently that I need not stress yet again to what extent it implies, for Virginia Woolf, essential contact with, and penetration of, reality. The special images I propose to study correspond to that vision, and thus communicate what in Virginia Woolf's experience is the most substantial reality, that to which she returns constantly when the ephemeral, the apparent, the contingent and the futile have fled.[109]

I am well aware of the twofold risk involved in such an undertaking. To begin with, the danger which is inherent in any interpretation, any development of what is merely suggested or implied: that of reading too much into it. This is the snare in all studies of symbolism, which I have sought to avoid by deliberately refraining from interpretation, however tempting. I shall confine myself to the surface of the vision, to the world of images this vision offers, without attempting to psychoanalyse the waking dream it presents. The other danger is that of an illusory screen interposed by art between ourselves and the real, or private, world of Virginia Woolf. May not that world, which we seek to discover in her work, be obscured and contaminated by "literature"? And may not all that art—which some call artifice

---

[107] Cf. particularly *op. cit.*, the analysis of the symbolism of *To the Lighthouse*, pp. 158-63.

[108] Cf. *op. cit.*, p. 203.

[109] Cf. AWD p. 144 (141), where, discussing her project for *The Waves*, she writes: "The unreal world must be round all this—the phantom waves . . . there must be great freedom from 'reality'. . . . Well all this is of course the 'real' life; and nothingness only comes in the absence of this."

—that she put into her novels, that concern for structure for rhythm, that play of echoes and leit-motivs, confuse the issue and lead us to mistake the expression for the impression itself? I shall try to take this disturbing factor into account, to allow for a certain sum of art so as to strike a just balance. It should be immediately understood, however, that this amount is so slight as to be negligible. For one thing, the artist in Virginia Woolf is at the service of reality: her resources and her skill are devoted to stressing reality, not to distorting or concealing it. True, in her diary she calls "reality" all the "unreality" with which she fills her work[110]; but when, after a metaphor, she writes: "This metaphor shows how tremendously important unconsciousness is when one writes",[111] she is recognizing the authenticity of origin of what might appear superimposed decoration. The comments she makes on *The Waves*, the novel in which the symbolic meaning is densest while the art is most deliberate, are reassuring:

What interests me in the last stage was the freedom and boldness with which my imagination picked up, used and tossed aside all the images, symbols which I had prepared. I am sure that this is the right way of using them—not in set pieces, as I had tried first, coherently, but simply as images, never making them work out; only suggest. Thus I hope to have kept the sound of the sea and the birds, dawn and garden subconsciously present, doing their work under ground.[112]

And with reference to *The Years*, she sums up that process of writing which allows the act of literary creation to be considered like any other act, as perfectly expressive and revealing of the being from whom it emanates: "Who was it who said through the unconscious one comes to the conscious, and then again to the unconscious?"[113]

The rhythms of nature, as we have seen, may be taken as a manifestation, perceptible to the senses, of the process of Becoming, and thus as the very essence of Virginia Woolf's concept of time. Their constant presence in the novels, even before their meaning and metaphysical content are clearly envisaged by the

---

[110] Cf. AWD p. 144 (141), quoted *supra*, p. 399, note 109.

[111] AWD p. 213 (205-6)

[112] AWD p. 169 (165)

[113] AWD p. 239 (230-1). On the same page, dated a week earlier, we find creation identified with the subconscious, and contrasted with rational thought: "But ideas are sticky things: won't coalesce: hold up the creative, subconscious faculty. . . ."

author, reveals a singularly acute sensitivity to these phenomena, which is at the root of the developments we have traced. Even in *The Voyage Out*, where the setting and the natural phenomena are often associated with dramatic moments in a way that recalls the "pathetic fallacy" of the Romantics, it happens that the seasons of the year, the different times of day, take on the substance and meaning which pervade them increasingly with each new novel. That marvellous autumn like a lingering summer,[114] prolonged by the eternal sunshine of Santa Marina, where London fogs are unknown,[115] already represents that period of respite and blossoming, that suspension of the course of things and of lives, that holiday season for the soul, which it so emphatically becomes in *Mrs Dalloway*, in *To the Lighthouse*, at the beginning of *The Waves*, in three chapters of *The Years* and finally in *Between the Acts*. We know nothing about the summers of Virginia Woolf's childhood, except through their reflection in *To the Lighthouse*, enriched no doubt by the nearer glow of her Sussex summers; on the other hand, the Diary discloses the intensity with which she lived during the summers amid the Downs at Rodmell.[116] Here there is no question of "literature" or the pathetic fallacy. What we have here is a profound physical harmony, gradually communicated to the whole sensibility and to the mind, procuring that plenitude which it identifies with knowledge, with direct contact with reality.

But if in the interlude, the fixed time, of *The Voyage Out*, "the change of season from winter to spring had made very little difference",[117] this is not the case elsewhere. We can leave aside the winter of *Night and Day*, with its uncertainties and doubts, its misunderstandings, its estrangements, and the too early spring that follows it, where passions burst forth purified of their shadows at the same time as the buds in Kew Gardens: these are only twopence-coloured pictures, backgrounds for pairs of lovers. It is in *Jacob's Room* that we find the first representation of the true Woolfian winter[118]: the immobility and silence of the hard earth, swept by icy blasts; the night of the year; the season when life, driven from outside, retires within itself, and in its withdrawal, amid the threats that surround it, experiences a foretaste of death. It is the season of the old servant Crosby and the air raid in *The*

---

[114] Cf. VO p. 28 (31)   [115] Cf. VO p. 103 (90)   [116] Cf. *supra*, ch. III
[117] VO p. 108 (95)   [118] Cf. JR pp. 97-8 (98-9)

Years; it is the season of Bernard's "summing up",[119] the season of hopeless disillusionment.[120] Can the Great Frost in *Orlando*, with its carnival and its love making, its brilliance and its vitality, efface this vision of winter? Surely not. That would mean forgetting both the Elizabethan fantasy of the chapter and the irony of the whole book. This frozen revelry is akin to the Dance of Death; before the courtiers begin to tread their measures, death has littered the fields with corpses, and the apple woman under the ice on the Thames has a blueness about the lips that hints at the truth.[121] Spring and autumn, on either side of summer, are moments of turbulence: wind, rain, buds bursting, dead leaves drifting, clouds and birds flying, the sky and the temperature both unstable; these are essentially seasons of change, heavy with hope or with the nostalgia of leave taking. But if Virginia Woolf renders all their latent mutability and richness, they are not *her* seasons. They are moments of passage, strictly speaking. They represent variety and entertainment, indeed, and she welcomes them eagerly, but with a certain anguished reserve: they lack serenity; they make one aware of the lapse of time and of life; even spring's fertility heralds maturity and decay. At bottom, these are hostile seasons, the destructive equinoxes. It was in spring that Virginia Woolf would break off work and go abroad; it was in April and October that she suffered from influenza, headaches and depressions—it was in April that she killed herself.

The alternation of day and night, the manifold meanings of which can be fitted to the different pairs of balanced forces in *Night and Day*, recur in all the novels. Even more than the succession of seasons, this brief rhythm, more accessible to immediate consciousness, provides at every instant, so to speak, the image of the mind's constant rhythmical alternation between darkness and light, concentration and dispersal, attention to itself and attention to the outside world. Day with its light, giving shape and colour to objects, is the creative presence of the universe, reborn at every dawn.[122] For Jacob, Clarissa, Mrs Ramsay, Orlando, the characters in *The Waves*, those of *The Years* and

[119] Cf. *supra*, ch. V, p. 293
[120] Cf. The W p. 202 (375)
[121] Cf. O pp. 35-6 (35-6)
[122] Cf. particularly the end of The W and of The Y.

Between the Acts, it is the marvellous fantasmagoria of life. The interludes in *The Waves* depict this continuous, constantly changing creation; they are a hymn to the daily world revealed to our eyes. And the dazzling sun which, in the margin of that book, calls forth the cosmos out of chaos, is surely connected with Percival. That hero, silent though omnipresent, also stands, as it were, in the margin of the book; and he, too, is a centre of reference and a source of creative light. As Nelli says, "It is all too easy to see in Percival simply a figuration of the sun"[123]; and we have no reason to believe that Virginia Woolf sought in the learned history of the Grail[124] a confirmation of the intuition that led her to make parallel use of these two symbolic themes. Their association is none the less significant. But if day represents life in its richness and splendour, the dazzlement which accompanies it and the multiplicity which it imposes represent disorder and confusion. Night, obliterating one colour after another, one form after another, the whole of the visible world, leaving us alone with what faint afterglows of vanished light are left within us, will restore our integrity, our self-control, the power of understanding after having felt: the vision, which sight had concealed from us. Ralph and Katherine had asked night, romantically indeed yet sincerely, to help them clarify their uncertainties. On the threshold and at the close of *Jacob's Room*, the scattered fragments of the day in one case, of Jacob's destiny in the other, assume order and harmony. It is in the heart of darkness that Clarissa's world and that of Mrs Ramsay take on meaning. By night, too, Bernard and Eleanor collect all the tangled threads of the days, the years, the human beings that made up their lives. And finally it is in a still deeper, darker, more silent and lonelier night, "night before roads were made, or houses",[125] that Isa and

[123] Nelli, *Lumière du Graal*, p. 24 (Cahiers du Sud, Paris, 1951, 336 pp.).

[124] More convincing are the arguments of Fr. Wiersma-Verschaffelt (Quelques réflexions au sujet de l'iconographie du Graal): "I cannot say whether the Greek cross" (shown on the cover of the Grail in medieval representations) "stood for Christ or for the Sun. What is certain is that solar images are found in great number: for instance, certain Knights of the Round Table wore the solar wheel on their helmets and shields and even on their horses." A little later, with reference to Lancelot's vision, we read: "Because he is not pure enough, he can only see the Grail from afar and in a dream; but what he sees is not a chalice but the Greek cross surmounting the mountain of the world. In my opinion this is the cosmic or elemental Grail. It is the sun, or the light, united to the world, or matter" (p. 325).

[125] B the A p. 256 (219): "It was night before roads were made, or houses. It was the night that dwellers in caves had watched from some high place among rocks."

Giles attain to the truth that no word can speak, no light illuminate.

Day: sensation, contact; night: consciousness, fusion—the two complementary modes of existence; they are the rhythms of Virginia Woolf's books as they are of her life. Their contradiction, their antagonism are within her: her passion for both was equal, and this divided loyalty is perhaps not unconnected with her anguish. There is always something exhausting about this miracle of the world, which has to be made afresh every day and thought over afresh every night; even more exhausting is the effort of conciliation. One cannot help thinking of those moths, night creatures flying in to burn themselves in the light, which, in the beginning, were to have given its title and its symbolic motif to what became *The Waves*. Another symbol of rhythm took their place, which is probably the most constant and the richest symbol in Virginia Woolf's writing.

Since I offered a brief analysis of the symbolism of the waves when discussing the book that bears that name, I shall not revert to its manifold possible meanings. Moreover, since another symbolic element merges with it, our list of its implications will soon be complete. The storm that tosses the Euphrosyne whips up mere masses of water, ordinary unsymbolic waves. And at the end of the book, as Rachel is dying,[126] we have only an almost commonplace image, like a theme borrowed from an anonymous ageless song; a fleeting appearance, and its interest is purely historical. In fact, it is only in *Jacob's Room* that the waves begin to awaken echoes beyond the shores on which they break. To begin with, amid the din of wind and rain that rage around the sleeping child[127] they pass unnoticed. But in the radiant peace that reigns about the boat when Jacob and Timmy go sailing, "the waves slapped the boat, and crashed, with regular and appalling solemnity, against the rocks".[128] The mysterious force with which these words are charged is intensified by the reminder, on the next page, of the perennial nature of the sea swell: "Very lonely it must be in winter, with the wind sweeping over those hills, and the waves dashing on the rocks".[129] Then we have their strength again, their menace, their regularity, their infinite succession, associated with the wind, the fury, the sudden bursts

[126] Cf. VO p. 423 (344) [127] Cf. JR p. 12 (14)
[128] JR p. 51 (52) [129] JR p. 51 (53)

of enthusiasm by which life is briefly shaken, arising without apparent cause between two scenes, between the opening and shutting of two doors—between a coming and a going, a beginning and an end.[130] At every instant life is being lifted up, dropped again, threatened, while the whisper and the sigh of the waves remains; but on the last page it swells to merge into the sound of guns, with the stroke of destiny that kills Jacob.[131] The essence of the theme is there; we might follow analogous developments in *Mrs Dalloway* and *To the Lighthouse*. In *Mrs Dalloway* the image, most frequently associated with "Fear no more", suggests peace, even if this peace is a forewarning of death.[132] The waves are the movement of life carrying us towards the shore, irresistible but on the whole beneficent. In *To the Lighthouse*[133] they assume their dual aspect, while identifying themselves more closely with existence, in its alternating serenity and anguish:

... the monotonous fall of the waves on the beach, which for the most part beat a measured and soothing tattoo to her thoughts and seemed consolingly to repeat over and over again as she sat with the children the words of some old cradle song, murmured by nature, "I am guarding you—I am your support", but at other times suddenly and unexpectedly, especially when her mind raised itself slightly from the task actually in hand, had no such kindly meaning, but like a ghostly roll of drums remorselessly beat the measure of life, made one think of the destruction of the island and its engulfment in the sea, and warned her whose day had slipped past in one quick doing after another that it was all ephemeral as a rainbow—this sound which had been obscured and concealed under the other sounds suddenly thundered hollow in her ears and made her look up with an impulse of terror.[134]

The lives of the characters in *The Waves* are tossed on the same sea. And yet, in *To the Lighthouse*, while the first part is punctuated by the echo of these waves, an opposing force rises up against them: the beam of the lighthouse cuts across the waves.[135] The perfection of the moment prevails over mutability[136]; and in the

[130] Cf. JR p. 119 (120)
[131] Cf. JR p. 175 (176)
[132] Cf. Mrs D pp. 16 (19), 26 (32), 34 (44), 44 (59), 154 (211), 162 (224), 191 (264)
[133] Cf. To the L pp. 14 (12), 29-30 (27-8), 36 (34), 65 (61), 97 (93), 103 (99-100), 119 (115), 220 (214), 244 (236), 293 (284), 317 (307)
[134] To the L p. 29 (27-8)   [135] Cf. To the L p. 98 (94)
[136] Cf. To the L p. 163 (158)

third part, which is dominated by the lighthouse and by Lily Briscoe's creative act, the waves lose both their force and their meaning. Moreover, it was for Mrs Ramsay that they had a meaning: for Mr Ramsay, the rationalist, they were not a force but merely an obstacle which man's will and intelligence must surmount.[137] So that in spite of the story of the shipwreck, these waves seem no more than inoffensive ripples, dominated by the solidity and permanence of the lighthouse.

There are several possible explanations for the absence of the waves in *Orlando*. For one thing, this book, conceived, as we have seen, at the same time as *The Waves*, and written while the latter was maturing, is complementary to it on more points than one, and particularly in the matter of symbols. It is the novel of the earth as opposed to the novel of the sea. Moreover the waves, being the inward sign of time-space and of anguish, belong to the lyrical vein: humour is alien to them. The tumultuous oceans crossed by the adventurous and romantic Marmaduke are the only touch of parody that the author dares to introduce.

Nor are there any waves in *The Years*: the rhythm of the seasons takes the place of their rhythm; it is more diffuse, more concrete, and better fitting to this novel, which deliberately eschews the abstraction of *The Waves*.

They reappear at last in *Between the Acts*, but so to speak only in the wings: ". . . one can hear the waves on a still night. After a storm, they say, you can hear a wave break".[138] In the pause between the acts, time is suspended. When the storm gathering over Europe breaks out, the noise of the rollers will reach Pointz Hall. Moreover, the sea, as space-time, is a frontier, implies separation[139]; now the interlude which, at the close of Virginia Woolf's work, acts as a "summing up", like the closing chapters of *The Waves* and *The Years*, essentially represents fusion, undefined unity: "It seems from the terrace as if the land went on for ever and ever."[140] The waves have retreated to let us glimpse the truth,[141] and it is only when Miss La Trobe leaves the deserted stage that we are aware of their return: "From the earth

[137] Cf. To the L p. 254 (245)
[138] B the A p. 37 (28)
[139] Cf. B the A p. 115 (96): "The wave has broken. Left us stranded, high and dry. Single, separate on the shingle."
[140] B the A p. 38 (29)
[141] Cf. B the A p. 221 (189): "As waves withdrawing uncover. . . ."

green waters seemed to rise over her. She took her voyage away from the shore. . . ."[142] And thus, through its symbolic themes of a sea journey and of silence, this last novel rejoins the first. The undivided space and time of *Between the Acts* is shot through, moreover, with movements and rhythms by the swallows: "Year after year they came."[143] They used to come in prehistoric times; they are real amidst the artificiality of the setting[144]; they skim "the grass that had been the stage"[145]; and Swinburne's poem, echoing sporadically through the book,[146] contributes, with its popular nostalgia, to give a universal appeal to Virginia Woolf's symbol.

The waves, the swallows are images that convey pure movement, manifestations of mysterious forces whose motives and designs escape us; to these must be added birds, butterflies and fishes. These are secondary themes, but they recur constantly like so many reminders of a primordial aspect of reality, like the sudden emergence of truth. . . . The gull rocked by the wave or tossed by the storm against the glass of the lighthouse, the cloud of rooks or starlings dropping on to a tree like a net and rising the moment after to spread its meshes against the evening sky. The butterflies clinging to flowers or beating against window panes, mysteriously going to their fate: a lamp lost in the darkness of the forest. The fish crossing pool or pond as swift as an arrow, exploring submerged worlds: the fin cleaving the surface of the water like some obscure sign breaking into consciousness. Moreover, the symbolic value of wave, fish, butterfly and bird is completed and enriched by their participation in two elements: these being so dominant in what one might call Virginia Woolf's cosmogony that they have constantly provided the vocabulary used by critics to define her work. Water and air are everywhere, not to provide setting or atmosphere but to reveal the nature of things, as a concrete sign that lets the abstract show through it.[147]

The waves, as we have seen, expressed one aspect of the sea—

---

[142] B the A p. 246 (210-11)

[143] B the A p. 129 (108): also pp. 80 (65), 120 (100), 121 (101), 122 (102), 123 (103), 129 (108) . . .

[144] Cf. B the A p. 192 (164): "Rather prettily, real swallows darted across the sheet."

[145] Cf. B the A p. 242 (207)   [146] Cf. B the A pp. 130-9 (109-18)

[147] Cf. *supra*, ch. III, pp. 112-13

its form. But other aspects are, as it were, its substance: it is one and eternal, it is transparency combined with mystery, and this contradictory duality is resolved in its depths. It conceals treasures of submerged life, all the underside of the visible world, all that, being inaccessible, fascinates us—and also the drowned lives of shipwrecked sailors, who attain there the eternity of legend and, perhaps, eternity itself. It represents the lure of travel and adventure—not so much that which attracted Elizabethan sailors, although their journeys have their own symbolic value, but that which led Rachel to her death and took James to the lighthouse. The river plunging deep into the tropical forest represents the universe closing in at the conclusion of a life, like the Thames at Hampton Court, bringing memories to Bernard.[148] Still water, in ponds or in the Serpentine, if it loses the immensity and power that add to the fascination and terror of the ocean, being more on our human scale assumes a familiar, almost harmless aspect. It is none the less that other world of silence and death. You may just throw a coin into it, like Clarissa; but the lady in *Between the Acts* drowned herself in bitter earnest, "in that deep centre, in that black heart".[149]

All the images that Virginia Woolf constantly borrows from the world of water: nets, lines, diving, flotsam and jetsam, boats and sails, suggest a profound intimacy, a sort of harmony between her nature and water. The fact that she chose death by drowning rather than any other may be only illusory evidence; it is difficult, however, not to consider it as an act that rounds off and gives sudden meaning to that universe within her own universe: it removes from all these symbols and images, these metaphors and motifs, any literary taint, and makes them pregnant with her own destiny.

Air is complementary to water in the representation of the universe. These are the two fluidities between which we maintain our permanence.[150] And if air, like water, is one aspect of space, and like it an irreducible destructive element,[151] if it serves as auxiliary to storms, yet its physical and spiritual lightness relegates it to a minor role. ". . . the stir in the air is the indescribable

[148] Cf. The W pp. 165-7 (337-9)

[149] B the A p. 55 (44)

[150] Cf. B the A p. 239 (204): "Above, the air rushed; beneath was water. She stood between two fluidities, caressing her cross."

[151] Cf. particularly "Time Passes" in To the L.

agitation of life"[152]—agitation, not development or change, implying fantasy and impulse, mere surface confusion. Air is the unpredictable animator that provokes the play of emotion on the earth's face, that now sets grass and leaves shivering, corn rippling, now shakes and twists the trees, tosses the rain against the window, lashes the pane with a branch. It is in *The Years*, following in the wake of the seasons, that its incoherent turbulence is most manifest, an authentic image of the incoherence of our lives. But here we are dealing with the wind rather than with the air; unless it should be called "air as wind" in contrast with the "air as sky" suspended over all creation: vertical distance made perceptible to the senses, just as the sea outstretched at the horizon, hiding abysses, was horizontal distance and depth. Should these words imply that space has been reintegrated into the world of Virginia Woolf? By no means; all this brings out, on the contrary, the concrete character of that apprehended space which is hers, and which she has substituted for abstract space. This air as sky is the region of aspiration and dream: this vertical dimension implies peace or exaltation; the smoke rises straight up into it, above the houses, above life, to dissolve not into nothingness but into identification with the loftiness to which it aspires. The sky's loftiness has a liberating quality, a remoteness that bestows harmony and peace on everything. Terence, shattered by Rachel's imminent death, takes refuge "in an unvexed space of air, on a little island by himself".[153] Katherine takes refuge thus, seeking for the cryptic meaning of the stars. For Jacob on his voyage, even if the threat of the waves mingles with it, the sky spreads piety, peace and ecstasy over the landscape.[154] In Clarissa's final meditation, the sky absorbs the tragedy. True, night plays its part in this peace; but it is air that dissolves all hardness, all hostility, all divergence.[155] Even in the burlesque vein, in the closing pages of *Orlando*, it is from the sky that peace descends.[156]

It is akin to the creative light of dawn at the close of *The Waves* and *The Years*. The peace, the exaltation that the sky symbolizes, the feeling of serene mastery of all conflicts that goes with it, recall an image which, gradually taking root in Virginia Woolf's

[152] JR p. 162 (163)   [153] VO p. 418 (342-3)
[154] Cf. JR p. 47 (49)   [155] Cf. Mrs D pp. 204-5 (282-4)
[156] Cf. O pp. 294-5 (327-9)

mind, was to have provided her with the theme of a book she never wrote—which instead of writing she doubtless endeavoured to live: what in her Diary she calls her "mountain top".[157] The features she sketches first in 1937: "silence; and the solitude",[158] and then in 1938: "looking out at peace from a height"[159] seem not only to sum up, but also to spring from, the attributes of the air as sky vanishing into infinite height, as she climbs a hill in a dream.[160] This vision, indeed, which gave rise to the symbol and fostered it to the point of creating a potential book, is much earlier than the dates just mentioned. It occurs in the Diary as far back as February 1926[161]; and even before that, this imaginary mountain, a region of solitude and peace, figured in *Night and Day*.[162] It is associated with the act of going upstairs: Clarissa leaving her guests, or Mrs Ramsay climbing an imaginary tree: "she was ascending, she felt, on to the top, on to the summit. How satisfying! How restful!"[163]

In contrast with the fluid elements akin to life, to being, to thought, we find the earth. Not the fertile earth, but rock—hard, permanent, not to be assimilated, the obstacle against which consciousness stumbles, against which the waves break. Jacob discovers the world, and disillusionment, there.[164] And to James, as he reaches the lighthouse on its rocky island, the undifferentiated bareness of matter comes as a sudden revelation.[165] Needless to say this is the aspect of the universe most alien to Virginia Woolf. In fact, she has recourse to it only to mark out the frontiers of mobility and change. The fourth element, fire, seems not to assume any special significance: I shall venture no conjecture about this absence, leaving this point to psychoanalysts or to my critical successors, who may be better supplied with documents

[157] Cf. AWD p. 360 (346): "I think of taking my mountain top—that persistent vision—as a starting point."

[158] Cf. AWD p. 283 (273): "I would like to write a dream story about the top of a mountain. Now why? About lying in the snow; about rings of colour; silence; and the solitude."

[159] Cf. AWD p. 307 (296): "There are very few mountain summit moments. I mean looking out at peace from a height. I made this reflection going upstairs. That is symbolical."

[160] Cf. The W p. 146 (319): "Now I climb this Spanish hill. . . ."

[161] Cf. AWD p. 86 (85), quoted *supra*, ch. III, p. 111

[162] Cf. N & D pp. 66 (67) and 447-8 (442)

[163] To the L p. 186 (181)

[164] Cf. JR, pp. 7 (9) and 8 (10)

[165] Cf. To the L pp. 311-12 (301-2)

than myself. But if fire as such has no place in Virginia Woolf's work, on the other hand light is everywhere. Light is identical with day, is the very soul of day, and yet, as if by some basic need of human nature it is infinitely multiplied: firelight in the hearth, candle light, lights in lonely windows in the countryside, innumerable lights in cities by night. The way they flash on, dim or brighten, and die out suggests the flickering nature of life itself; while each point of light seems a focus of consciousness, unstable and fascinating. The lighthouse naturally presents the symbol at the peak of its development, as lodestar and distant guide, intermittent and yet enduring, identical with Being.[166]

One last symbol borrowed from nature must be mentioned, the tree with all its derivatives: leaves, roots, the forest. The forest, that concentration of mysterious life in whose exuberance there is something oppressive, features significantly in *The Voyage Out*. It is associated with the Elizabethans,[167] with the sea,[168] it shelters the love affair of Terence and Rachel, and is indeed a manifestation of that vital impulse which, as James Hafley shows, is always present in the work of Virginia Woolf. But it is in *Mrs Dalloway* that the tree becomes a truly symbolic motif; it stands for Clarissa's life,[169] for that of Septimus,[170] for Rezia's.[171] It is the beauty and strength of creation, standing firm against all assaults.[172] Yet even here, as in *The Voyage Out*, the tree's life consists in its shivering and swaying, which suggest the waves, just as the green gloom of its shade suggests undersea depths. With *Orlando*, the Oak Tree, as poem and as real tree, to which Orlando periodically returns, represents the two lines of development of life: that of nature and that of art. True, the land, from which both spring, is not immune from the generalized ambiguity of the novel: it represents earth, the fertility of nature, but it is also "The Land", Vita Sackville-West's poem, prototype of "The Oak Tree".[173] Throughout *The Waves*, trees are like the foam of life on the surface of the earth, surviving the eternal flux[174]; they are the first to catch the light, and from them rises the birds' song of joy. This conjunction of trees and birds is also one refrain

[166] For the many interpretations of the Lighthouse symbol, see J. Hafley, *op. cit.*, pp. 79-80.
[167] Cf. VO p. 328 (268)
[168] Cf. VO p. 331 (271-2)
[169] Cf. Mrs D p. 11 (12)
[170] Cf. Mrs D p. 26 (32)
[171] Cf. Mrs D pp. 77 (104), 163 (224)
[172] Cf. Mrs D p. 90 (122)
[173] Cf. O p. 291 (324)
[174] Cf. The W pp. 176-7 (350-1)

of *The Years*; it recurs in the final pages of *Between the Acts*.[175] It is banal maybe, but it is saved from literary banality by the context, which inspires it afresh with a forgotten meaning.

We have seen[176] how Virginia Woolf delighted in the bustle of cities and could recognize reality there, just as in the solitude of the Downs. Town and country provided the alternate settings for her novels. In *The Voyage Out*, nature is dominant, in *Night and Day*, London; then comes *Jacob's Room*, where the two are equally important. The setting of *Mrs Dalloway* is essentially urban, that of *To the Lighthouse* exclusively natural. *Orlando* and *The Waves* shift constantly from town to country, and whereas *The Years* is predominantly urban, *Between the Acts* returns to nature. It is not surprising, then, that civilized life in general, and town life in particular, also provided our author with symbolic motifs.

The whole city itself, with its intensity, its variety, its movement, its rhythms, its confusion is expressive of life. There is scarcely one of Virginia Woolf's heroes, from the Mrs Dalloway of *The Voyage Out* to Bernard or Eleanor Pargiter who, watching the London scene from the top of a bus, by day or night, or mingling with the crowd in the street, does not experience a sense of contact with something essential and significant. Whereas the forces of nature, in so far as they govern our destinies, are revealed in certain special manifestations, city life reveals man as a social, civilized being. Without even taking into account the pamphlets, *A Room of One's Own* and *Three Guineas*, we could find enough sociological material in the novels to disprove the myth of an ivory tower Virginia Woolf, preoccupied only with art for art's sake.

These streets, through which her characters drift with the human tide, or where, standing outside it on the bank, they feel the mysterious transient contact of the crowd with its countless eddies and ripples, are the very image of the anonymity and mystery of all these lives, so close and yet so distant, in which they share without knowing them. Solitude[177] and solidarity are the

---

[175] Cf. B the A p. 254 (218)

[176] Cf. *supra*, ch. III, pp. 115-16

[177] Or rather *loneliness*, in contrast with Mrs Ramsay's *solitude*; a negative feeling, implying a conflicting desire for communion, whereas Mrs Ramsay's "solitude" is a deliberate withdrawal, a victory over dispersion and multiplicity; "loneliness" is the victory of dispersion and multiplicity over the human being.

two extremes that meet there in an insoluble dilemma. And the being who experiences them both together sees them as two divergent ways to knowledge, a goal only reached when they converge once more in some privileged experience. From this point of view, one might say that *Mrs Dalloway* is the urban novel *par excellence*.

There are other elements borrowed from civilized life which, by their close connection with the individual and the mutual impregnation which ensues take on manifold meanings, now hidden, as though buried under appearances, now explicit, breaking through their concrete envelope to shed light on the text.

Thus, a house is so closely associated with the life it shelters that it serves to define certain features of that life, which cling to it through agelong association. In "Time Passes", in *To the Lighthouse*, it is significant that the house stands at the heart of change, enduring and at the same time revealing it. Permanent and yet vulnerable, it retains the imprint of human gestures and thoughts without completely saving them from an erosion which gradually blurs their outlines, sparing only what is essential: the atmosphere of certain privileged moments. It is as though stones and rafters had become a memory where life accumulates and remains visible to all. Sometimes the house is merely a far-off white mark on the coast, with its thread of smoke, telling Jacob and Timmy that human beings are there, rooted in these hills.[178] Sometimes it is a profusion of roofs and windows, the three hundred and sixty-five bedrooms of Orlando's Great House[179]—on a later page there are four hundred and seventy-six of them,[180] for after all, years vary in length and distance blurs the view and confuses numbers. A house, like life, is now brilliantly lit up, full of people and bustle, and now plunged in darkness and silence, with only an uncertain glimmer roaming from one room to another. And the regions that surround a house, whether bounded by garden fence or park walls, or else stretching as far as the lighthouse, or to the other end of England, are the familiar horizon of both the outer and the inner eye, what the gaze or the imagination takes in, and they are, like one's body, like one's room, an integral part of oneself. They are the universe reduced to the scale of an individual, in which he rescues himself from

[178] Cf. JR p. 47 (48)   [179] Cf. O pp. 103 (108), 135 (148)   [180] Cf. O p. 137 (149)

the distintegration with which the greater universe threatens him: "The body must contract now, entering the house. . . ."[181] This contraction is the first phase of that closing-in process which gradually brings Mrs Ramsay to the "wedge-shaped core of darkness" in which her whole being is concentrated. The dream cottage imagined by Mary Datchet, which suggests to Ralph Denham the image of perfect happiness, is characteristic in that it gathers together in a vignette of extraordinary density and simplicity the chief elements of Virginia Woolf's symbolism:

Two rooms are all I should want . . . one for eating, one for sleeping. Oh, but I should like another, a large one at the top, and a little garden where one could grow flowers. A path—so—down to a river, or up to a wood, and the sea not very far off, so that one could hear the waves at night. Ships just vanishing on the horizon.[182]

In *The Waves*, the children's house, Susan's home, and Elvedon, the dream manor, represent three aspects of life, whose features, thus made concrete, take on a richness in the imagination that no abstraction could evoke. Already in *The Voyage Out*, the Ambroses' house and that of Rachel's aunts had their representative significance. And right at the end, Pointz Hall—less fantastic than Orlando's mansion, more generalized than the Ramsays' house—symbolizes continuity, rootedness, the shared life of successive generations. The difference between these houses and those depicted in the work of realists, Bennett and Galsworthy particularly, might serve to differentiate the art of these novelists from that of Virginia Woolf, and to illustrate their characteristic points of view, as sketched in "Modern Fiction" and "Mr Bennett and Mrs Brown".[183]

But even more than the house, the room, which enfolds the individual almost as closely as his own body, has a special place in Virginia Woolf's work and in her world. I shall not repeat what I said with reference to *Jacob's Room* and *A Room of One's Own*, whose titles show the importance of this symbolic theme. Whereas the house represents the integration of a person with a family, a line of forebears or a group of contemporaries, facing

[181] Mrs D p. 181 (250)
[182] N & D p. 353 (334)
[183] Cf. particularly: "There is not so much as a draught between the frames of the windows, or a crack in the boards" (CR I p. 186 (152)) and ". . . we can only hear Mr Bennett's voice telling us facts about rents and freeholds and copyholds and fines" (CDB p. 103 (109)).

out on to the world so to speak, the room, on the contrary, represents protection and intimacy; it is turned inwards towards its centre, the person who dwells in it and who absorbs it in order to define the limits of his inviolable self. Rachel's cabin, then her bedroom, have this intimate character.[184] Then there are the rooms of the four protagonists of *Night and Day*, whose seclusion, so propitious to intensified self-awareness, foreshadows all those rooms, those shells[185] into which Virginia Woolf's heroes retreat in quest of themselves. Threatened by the intrusion of Holmes into his room, Septimus, by committing suicide, asserts the inviolability of that retreat, that sanctuary, which is the first requisite of any individual life deserving that name. The room can be defined by its content, by familiar individual things: the skull Jacob picked up on the shore, and the one hanging on Cam Ramsay's bedroom wall; Rachel's musical scores and Katharine's mathematics. . . . But these are particular and contingent. General traits, by their recurrence, stamp the symbol with the imprint of universality. First, warmth and light; then the walls, dividing and enclosing. And when Katharine realises that "never had life been more certainly an affair of four walls",[186] her intuition provides the key to the symbolism of the room as well as to the secondary symbols associated with it: doors and windows.

It is a truism that one has to pass through a door when going in or out of a room, and that one can only see out by looking through a window. So that if countless doors open to let Virginia Woolf's characters pass, and countless windows look on to the street or the countryside, it is of necessity and not of the author's choice. But the use to which she puts this is too personal for any possible misunderstanding of the importance and significance of these familiar actions. If life is an affair of four walls, of boundaries which are partly impassable and of protection which is partly precarious, it is livable and tragic precisely in proportion to its precariousness and to the possibility of getting through. If it was in her own room that Virginia Woolf felt happiest,[187] we must not forget that the world of men and things beyond the four

184 Cf. VO p. 142 (123)

185 Cf. B the A p. 250 (214): "Within the shell of the room" (cf. p. 252 (216): "Sitting in the shell of the room").

186 N & D p. 373 (352)

187 Cf. AWD p. 258 (249)

walls had for her a reality as wonderful and as magnetic as her inner world: a monad without doors or windows would have been inconceivable to her.

The door is the crack in the wall of our loneliness, through which other beings reach us. No doubt we must attribute to Virginia Woolf's feminine passivity the fact that her doors open almost exclusively inward; a door, for her, does not suggest a going away but an arrival, expected with hope or with apprehension. We find Mary Datchet thus apprehensive before her party[188] and above all when she hears an unknown step on the stair[189]; her anguish and her reactions anticipate in a curious way those of Septimus when he hears Dr Holmes coming and imagines him about to break down the door.[190] Katharine knocking on Rodney's door brings with her reality, which interrupts the conjectures aroused by expectation in the young man's mind.[191] "But there were so many doors..." exclaims Mrs Hilbery as she is leaving Clarissa's house.[192] It is standing in a doorway that Peter Walsh remembers Clarissa most vividly,[193] and it is when she comes back into the drawing-room that he recognizes her before seeing her.[194] The full meaning of the symbol breaks out in *The Waves*, when the six characters foregather to say goodbye to Percival; their eyes fixed on the door, which keeps opening, they wait for their hero, for his coming, for the coming of their reality.[195] And the final meeting takes place in the doorway; the door has no further purpose, now that Percival is not coming.

If the door is the way in for other people, the window is our own outlook on to the world. It is characteristic that almost all Virginia Woolf's windows are uncurtained, from the Ambroses' house to Pointz Hall. And half way between these two, we have the title of the first chapter of *To the Lighthouse*, set down like a transparent but separating sheet of glass between reality and Mrs Ramsay's mind. In all the novels we see a character standing in front of a window, gazing at the street, at the sky, at the landscape, and experiencing, as by some catalytic phenomenon, the mingling of his own being with the outer reality which he beholds. These are moments of both revelation and integration:

---

[188] Cf. N & D p. 44 (50)
[189] Cf. N & D p. 282 (268)
[190] Cf. Mrs D p. 164 (226); also *ibid.*, p. 45 (59)
[191] Cf. N & D p. 296 (281)
[192] Mrs D p. 210 (291)
[193] Cf. Mrs D p. 85 (114-15)
[194] Cf. Mrs D p. 213 (296)
[195] Cf. The W pp. 85-8 (257-60)

they are most often marked by a sense of peace which is mysterious and sometimes mystical, as with Mrs Dalloway and Mrs
Ramsay. That Virginia Woolf chooses, unconsciously no doubt,
to interpose a screen between reality and consciousness and to
restrict reality by a framework, may be considered a sign of her
hypersensitivity and an instinctive desire to filter the experience
of her senses, which in its natural state was too violent, too
tumultuous for her; also to an obscure need for structure and
form, corresponding to that primacy of the mind that apprehends
over the reality which is apprehended. The window reduces the
pageant of the world to the scale of the being who contemplates
it. And finally, this window, which for all its transparency serves
to screen reality, is the very symbol of the imperfection of our
contact and our knowledge. An imperfection which ends perhaps
with death—that is only a hope, not a certainty—with death
which may immerse the soul in reality once more, beyond that
surface where the two extremes are only tangential. And
Septimus's action is related to that of the lady who drowned
herself in the lake, that of Rhoda who, haunted by death, flings
her violets into the sea,[196] then imagines herself like them, floating
for a while then tossed by the waves, submerged,[197] that of
Clarissa, throwing her shilling into the Serpentine—that of
Virginia Woolf, finally, drowning herself in the Ouse. In every
case the surface is penetrated that separated the being from the
depths to which it returns.

There is another sheet of glass, another transparency that
constantly recurs in Virginia Woolf's writing: the looking-glass.[198]
Each character gazes therein at his own image, which is nothing
but an image, like all those reflected in the minds of all those
who know him; an image familiar and yet strange, reassuring
and yet disquieting, where the real and the imaginary mingle
inextricably, but are both so patent that the miracle of their
unity and their duality is made perceptible to the senses. The
mirror is another fragment of the universe, displaying the paradox of surface/depth, absence/presence, nothingness/being.

This partial list may be completed by another object which is

[196] Cf. The W p. 117 (289)

[197] Cf. The W p. 147 (319)

[198] Cf. VO p. 371 (303); Mrs D pp. 41-2 (54-5); To the L p. 200 (194); O
p. 27 (26); The W p. 157 (330); The Y p. 64 (61); B the A p. 60 (48); cf. also *supra*,
ch. V, section 2.

actually more metaphorical than real: the globe of life. It combines so many diverse attributes already present in the symbols enumerated above, and it reappears so constantly in Virginia Woolf's work, that it cannot be ignored. Imagine it made of that translucent substance that envelops us: glass, water, sky, luminous halo blown out in volume. It is the iridescent and fragile bubble which contains the wonder of our reality and of our dream and also the reality and unreality of the world. At intense moments the consciousness around which it has englobed itself like a pearl breaks free of it, to contemplate it; it represents the perfect vision, perfect in form and in substance; a concrete object and an abstract figure. It is the room whose walls have thinned down so as to become both window and mirror; it is the last, finished design drawn by the soul in answer to the questions: what is life? who am I?

I have mentioned only the clearest and most frequently used symbols. Of course, with a being as sensitive and as imaginative as Virginia Woolf, for whom "everything was partly something else",[199] symbolization was latent everywhere. Not only things, but gestures and people assume meanings which often may pass unnoticed and only reveal themselves in the wider context of the author's work and even of her life. I have referred to the action of going upstairs, particularly of going to one's room, of knocking at the door, of throwing, of sinking, of dissolving. . . . Among such gestures and many others, there is one which takes on poignant resonance from Virginia Woolf's suicide: going down to the sea. In *To the Lighthouse*,[200] this lure of the wave-battered shore grows more explicit, seems to herald some revelation on the confines of the two elements. Septimus, envisaging his suicide, imagines that scene on the shore[201] which had already occurred in Clarissa's reverie: "Fear no more, says the heart, committing its burden to some sea. . . ."[202] Mary Datchet's cottage had its path leading down to the sea; and in *Between the Acts*, the story of Crabbe's capricious ride[203] is told of a legendary ancestor: "Hearing the waves in the middle of the night he saddled a horse and rode to the sea."[204]

[199] Cf. O p. 290 (323): ". . . everything was partly something else . . ." and p. 131 (143): "Everything, in fact, was something else."
[200] Cf. To the L pp. 199 (193) and 203 (197-8)
[201] Cf. Mrs D p. 103 (140)   [202] Mrs D p. 45 (59)
[203] Cf. CDB p. 34 (30)   [204] B the A p. 37 (28-9)

There is, finally, one heroic figure who stands at the beginning and at the end of Virginia Woolf's work: Antigone, who appears in *The Voyage Out*[205] and in *The Years*,[206] is referred to incidentally in "On Not Knowing Greek" and quoted as an example in *Three Guineas*.[207] True, many literary figures make transient appearances in Virginia Woolf's work. Orlando of course, Hamlet,[208] Othello,[209] Tom Jones,[210] mingled with the shades of Ann Hathaway,[211] Shelley, Byron,[212] Dostoevsky[213] and many others; but these are only glimpses, as fleeting and accidental resemblances are suggested between some character and these historic figures. Whereas Antigone, the incarnation of a whole ideal of passion, poetry, heroism and fidelity,[214] piously attached to her brother, proud and independent, passionately alive and yet fascinated by death, appeals to Thoby Stephen's devoted sister like a double whose fate haunts her. If we combine the figures of Antigone and of Percival in *The Waves*—impossible love, purity, the quest for the Grail—we have an intuition of all the reserved feelings and veiled impulses that are perhaps the essence of Virginia Woolf's mysterious personality. Perhaps her affection for Thoby was her real love, and her loneliness, her anguish, the fascination of death sprang from this hopeless passion? It is tempting to associate Virginia Woolf with Antigone in the same way that Clarissa was associated with Septimus; the parallel being not between sanity and madness but between reality and legend. And amid this universe of waves, beaches, trees and birds, of teeming cities, successively brought into being by day and obliterated by night, shaken by equinoctial storms, frozen by winter's cold or glowing in summer's peace, there she stands, within the house, within the room waiting for the door to open, listening to the bough striking against the window-pane, shut in there—Antigone.

[205] Cf. VO p. 46 (45)
[206] Cf. The Y pp. 54 (51), 144-6 (135-6)
[207] Cf. Three G pp. 148 (81-2) and 301-13 (138)
[208] Cf. The W p. 177 (349)
[209] Cf. Mrs D pp. 39 (51) and 202 (281)
[210] Cf. JR pp. 121 and 123 (122-4)
[211] Cf. N & D p. 454 (427)
[212] Cf. The W pp. 62-4 (234-6)
[213] Cf. The W p. 177 (349)
[214] Cf. CR I p. 44 (28)

5. STRUCTURE AND MOVEMENT

When Virginia Woolf wrote in 1919, having unquestionably in mind her own experience as novelist and particularly *Night and Day*, which she had just completed:

... we go on perseveringly, conscientiously, constructing our two and thirty chapters after a design which more and more ceases to resemble the vision in our minds.[215]

this implicit condemnation of the traditional forms of composition should not lead us to believe that she rejected any sort of structure. We must take into account the dissatisfaction and the revolutionary mood of the author of "The Mark on the Wall" and "Kew Gardens". And against this declaration and others, equally extreme, from the same article ("Life is not a series of gig lamps symmetrically arranged",[216] for instance) we should set certain less uncompromising comments:

Can we not discover even in the vortex and whirlpool of Victorian fiction some constraint which the most ebullient of novelists forced himself to lay on his material, to reduce it to symmetry?[217]

she was to write in 1922, admitting a necessity she had seemed to dismiss. And in 1926 those deplorable chapters which she had condemned in 1919 are rehabilitated: "The thirty-two chapters of a novel ... are an attempt to make something as formed and controlled as a building. . . ."[218] In fact, despite her constant concern with conveying life, despite her acute sense of the complexity of existence and its fluidity, at no time did Virginia Woolf believe that the novel, as a work of art, could free itself from certain aesthetic requirements which she considered fundamental. And now, early in 1919, even while she was criticizing the Edwardians for clinging to outmoded forms, and extolling the experiments of some of her contemporaries, in her review of *The Tunnel*, after praising the originality of the method and proclaiming the value of such an endeavour, she concludes: "We . . . require that Miss Richardson shall fashion this new material into something which has the shapeliness of the old

[215] CR I p. 188 (153) (first published as "Modern Novels", *TLS*, April 10, 1919)

[216] CR I p. 189 (154)

[217] The M p. 131 (161-2) (appeared in *TLS*, July 20, 1922)

[218] CR II p. 259 (235) ("How should one read a book?", first published in *Yale Review*, Oct. 1926.)

accepted forms."[219] Proportion, symmetry, architecture are thus still deemed basic needs, implicit in the general term "form" which the novelist constantly uses in her diary and in her critical essays. And it is that "form" which, as we have seen, takes so important a place in Virginia Woolf's work, which is sometimes even pre-existent to any other elements in the conception of her novels, that I now propose to examine.

If the first two novels, constructed according to accepted pattern, scarcely deserve examination in themselves, they none the less constitute landmarks which enable us better to appreciate the development of the novelist. We can trace there, moreover, mingled with the anonymous texture, the first signs of more individual tendencies.

The composition of these novels is closely dependent on the story, slender as this may be, which they relate. Rachel's voyage and her stay at Santa Marina, her discovery of love and her death, in *The Voyage Out*; the emotional hesitations and fluctuations which eventually settle into new and more stable positions, in *Night and Day*. The succession of chapters, twenty-seven for *The Voyage Out*, thirty-four for *Night and Day*, follows the temporal sequence of events, grouped in scenes which are determined by the time, the place, the grouping of the characters. In both novels, we can discern a regular alternation between the various centres of interest, which thus react on each other and complete one another: life in the Ambroses' villa and at the hotel; the respective homes of Katharine, Mary, Ralph and William. Common to both novels, too, is the presence of a certain dramatic line. In *The Voyage Out*, Rachel's destiny and her meeting with Terence reach a crucial stage towards the middle of the book (ch. xvi). Their duologue at this point leaves no doubt about the subsequent development of their mutual relations. Their hesitations represent only a psychological time lag, their growing awareness of a destiny whose curve was an already determined fate. Thus, too, in Night and Day, the Christmas interlude in Lincolnshire (chs. xv-xix), in spite of the apparent reserve, the superficial abdication of will and feeling, allows us to glimpse the truth that it only remains for each protagonist to elucidate his position for the final clarification to be reached. It should be noted, however, that in *Night and Day* the sequence of duets and

[219] *TLS*, Feb. 13, 1919

the changes of partner constitute a regular pattern, which might be described as abstract and which may seem arbitrary, into which reality has been cast. Symptomatic, too, of the same trend is the suppression of transitional passages between the different scenes: the novelist no longer tells us what has happened during blank periods. Certain details also show her taking liberties with traditional cohesion and indivisibility. Thus, immediately after William's talk at Mary's, we hear Ralph and one of his friends discussing philosophy, some way behind Katharine and William; during a moment's inattention Ralph loses sight of this couple, who have turned towards the riverside; without any transition, the novelist abandons Ralph and his interlocutor to follow Katharine and William.[220] In the same way, at the sound of an explosion, or at a mere glance, she will shift from Clarissa to Septimus[221] or from Septimus to Peter Walsh,[222] Even more abrupt is the break at the end of Chapter XI where, after a scene between Katharine and William, illustrating the distance between them, we have an extract from a letter from Mrs Hilbery dealing with the same subject.[223]

Throughout this study I have stressed the continuity of Virginia Woolf's work, maintained by the permanence of certain fundamental traits: I was forced to admit, however, that *Jacob's Room* formed a turning-point. As I have pointed out, in agreement with all other critics, this turning-point is most spectacular as regards form. From the point of view of structure, the eleven sections of this novel have nothing in common, either as a whole or in detail, with the chapters of the two preceding novels. Although it was only in January 1920 that Virginia Woolf first envisaged the "form" of what was to be *Jacob's Room*,[224] what she had written in the spring of 1919 in "Modern Novels" heralds the abandonment of those elements that provided the structure of her earlier novels: ". . . if a writer were a free man . . . there would be no plot, no comedy, no tragedy, no love interest, or catastrophe in the accepted style. . . ."[225] All these elements, in so far as they marked out the progress from one scene to another and connected the scenes together, have disappeared. The only link remaining between the sections is Jacob's name: the only sign of progression,

---

[220] Cf. N & D p. 62 (64)
[222] Cf. Mrs D p. 79 (106)
[224] Cf. *supra*, ch. III, p. 73

[221] Cf. Mrs D p. 16 (19)
[223] Cf. N & D p. 146 (142)
[225] Cf. CR I p. 189 (154)

an evasive chronology. Instead of an action, in the broadest sense of the word, made up of a sequence of connected phases, we have a discontinuous series of moments proliferating round a single being. Does the uncertain presence of this character, now in the foreground, now in the wings, suffice to supply cohesion to the set of vignettes that make up the novel? If by cohesion we understand connections that are as precise and apparent as the terms of a syllogism, it is obvious that they cannot emanate from a character as intermittent, inarticulate and inactive as Jacob. Only an old illusion of permanence and existence to which Jacob's name and his appearances have given rise in our mind can make us believe, for a single moment, that it is he who connects these scattered fragments. That this is the case implies that the book is not such a failure as some people say. But it also implies that we must look elsewhere for the secret of its structure. Having shattered "the story" into a series of moments separated by indeterminate intervals, by "blanks", Virginia Woolf links them not formally, from outside, but through their very substance, making them so to speak mutually permeable. Thus the cry "Ja—cob! Ja—cob!" uttered by Archer on the shore,[226] echoed by Johnny on the hill at Scarborough,[227] then by Clara Durrant[228] and finally by Bonamy,[229] link together, by means of their emotional identity, not only those years, from the hero's childhood to his death, in which these cries were uttered, but also other scenes which gave rise to them: meetings between Clara and Jacob, talks or fights between Bonamy and Jacob,[230] Mr Floyd's meeting with Jacob, referred to as a recent event[231] in an account of the relations between the vicar and the Floyd family, which belongs to Jacob's childhood and is in fact told shortly before his death,[232] brings together moments some fifteen years apart, almost the whole extent of the novel. And on the same page, the start that Clara gives on catching sight of Jacob in a crowd serves to reintroduce the forgotten theme of her unrequited love. Many other examples might be quoted: the moth hunt, suddenly

[226] Cf. JR pp. 6-7 (8)
[227] Cf. JR p. 17 (19)
[228] Cf. JR pp. 166-7 (166-7)
[229] Cf. JR p. 177 (176)
[230] Cf. JR pp. 42 (44), 71 (72-3), 101 (102), 164 (164-5) . . .
[231] Cf. JR p. 20 (22)
[232] Cf. JR pp. 173-4 (173-4)

remembered in the middle of a service at Cambridge; or, like a refrain, Jacob's return to his room in Cambridge[233] or in London.[234] But it is above all these other characters, such as Mr Floyd, Clara and Bonamy, apparently suspended in the void and in fact only existing through and for the sake of Jacob, who, every time they appear, despite their own intermittence, serve to renew Jacob's continuity and cement his impalpable substance. And between these landmarks, the years stretch out, measured by the way they change: Jacob, while retaining his timidity, awkwardness and distinction, moves from adolescence to the threshold of manhood.

Thus, instead of the regular progress and rigid architecture of a story, we have a succession which, though apparently syncopated, has in fact its own inner, thematic continuity. And the final chapter, uniting the main themes in a sort of résumé, gives that impression of a closed circle which we shall meet again in all the subsequent novels.

Even if we qualify the criticisms made of *Jacob's Room*, we must admit that the system of echoes, recurrences, superposition of parallel images, is not wholly successful, especially on a first reading. The content overflows the vessel and swamps the design. But before condemning the method, one should make sure that it alone is responsible. Allowing for the difference in scale, and for its debt to the technique of *The Waves*, *The Years* is constructed like *Jacob's Room*: a series of periods, separated by blanks; within each period, a series of vignettes without explicit links. However, the network of internal echoes—the fragments of setting, character or gesture—intended to create permanence and continuity under the shifting discontinuous surface, is more closely woven, more skilful and more effective. The fact remains that despite its greater art, this novel suffers from the same weaknesses as *Jacob's Room*. And since, like the latter, it embraces a long succession of years, it seems probable that there is a certain incompatibility between the material and the treatment it has received, as though the excess of empty spaces over full ones in so vast a field resisted any attempt at assimilation. This hypothesis seems confirmed by the success of Virginia Woolf's other experiments.

Of her five other novels, only two cover a long stretch of years: *Orlando* and *The Waves*. Let us, for the moment, leave aside *To*

[233] Cf. JR p. 45 (46)   [234] Cf. JR p. 94 (95)

the Lighthouse, which offers a special solution to the problem that concerns us. *Orlando,* in spite of the peculiar nature and longevity of its hero and the Sternean vagaries of his biographer, naturally finds its unity and its progression in the personality, development and adventures of Orlando, and also in the historic setting.[235] These elements, which are not usually treated by Virginia Woolf, are here reinforced by the devices which were used in *Jacob's Room,* and which help to make of this novel, apparently picaresque, something very different. But the composition of *Orlando* having certainly set no particular problem to its author, we need dwell on it no further. *The Waves,* on the contrary, as we have seen,[236] demanded long efforts and much rewriting, particularly as regards its structure. In certain respects, the crucial problem was the same as with *Jacob's Room*: to connect, without the help of a story or of any character kept in the foreground, periods or significant moments stretching out over several decades of a life, and separated by considerable blank spaces. The interludes transform discontinuity into continuity.[237] They characterize each moment or period, while through the permanence of cosmic elements underlying the mutability of their aspects, they bind these moments tightly together into a day, into a life. We have seen[238] that Virginia Woolf rewrote these passages to perfect their continuity and their unity. The structure might be criticized for being superimposed on the novel and for providing only a set of compartments by way of framework. This criticism, in my opinion, would be valid if the content of *The Waves* was of the same nature as that of *Jacob's Room,* for instance; the heterogeneity between the structural elements and the substance for which they provide structure would create an impression of artifice and would detract from the effectiveness of the method. This is, to some extent, the case with the "overtures" in *The Years* where, despite the internal echoes that link them with the main body of the sections, these lyrical passages remain extrinsic.

---

[235] From casual references to dates and historic events, and rare direct indications, we can establish the chronology of the novel as follows: Ch. I: 1585-1625; Ch. II: 1625-1680; Ch. III: 1680-1702; Ch. IV: 1702-1800; Ch. V: 1800-1900; Ch. VI: 1900-1928.

[236] Cf. *supra,* ch. III, pp. 81-2

[237] Cf. AWD p. 153 (150): "The interludes are very difficult, yet I think essential; so as to bridge and also give a background. . . ."

[238] Cf. *supra,* ch. V, p. 282

On the contrary, in *The Waves*, the homogeneity of tone, duplicated at the beginning by homogeneity of substance, helps to fuse the two series into one. It should be remembered, too, that Bernard's "summing-up" only appears in the second version.[239] In the first version, it seems that a partial summing-up by Bernard must have followed each section, forming a pendant to the overture. Lacking the text of this version, it is difficult to imagine the result; we must accept the judgment of Virginia Woolf[240] who, when she suppressed these intermediary passages and combined them all in the final section, meant to suppress any sort of break, to absorb discontinuity into one continuous movement. Moreover, thanks to Bernard's summing-up, this novel, which follows the parabolic curve I noted in *The Voyage Out* and *Night and Day*, rising to the catastrophe of Percival's death which occurs between sections four and five, and then dropping to the parting of the six friends after their final gathering at Hampton Court (section 8) comes round full circle, thus conforming to the twofold pattern which we also find in *Mrs Dalloway*, *To the Lighthouse* and *Between the Acts*: a parabola surmouting a circle at a tangent to its branches. This pattern provides a graphic symbol of drama superposed on endless repetition, which, combining movement and immobility, is identical with the paradox of existence as Virginia Woolf conceived it.

The division into monologues is another discontinuity which had to be reabsorbed. The permanence of the themes characteristic of each character ensures the connection between these six respective sequences, within each section and also throughout the whole novel. More interesting from the point of view of composition is the use made by Virginia Woolf of the rhythm of succession of the voices, on which she plays as a virtuoso in verse might play on the infinite resources of prosody. When the characters are together, in their childhood home, at school, at the two dinner parties, the rapid alternation of voices expresses their participation in a common experience; on three occasions we even find a dialogue transposed to that inner, abstract level to which, as I showed in an earlier analysis,[241] the voices belong; Susan and Bernard in the first section, Louis and Rhoda, the

---

[239] Cf. *supra*, ch. III, p. 89, and ch. V, p. 283
[240] Cf. AWD p. 163 (159), quoted *supra*, ch. III, p. 89
[241] Cf. *supra*, ch. V, pp. 283-6

lovers, during the two reunions.[242] Akin to these dialogues, and to the intensity of communion in childhood, is the evocation of old memories, introduced by Louis: "Now let us issue from the darkness of our solitude."[243] Exchange of feeling, and shared feeling, are expressed by the same accelerated rhythm: in two pages we have nineteen voice changes, as against only fifty-two for the other twenty-six pages of the same section. When school separates the children into two groups, it naturally follows that the boys' and the girls' voices are separate too. But it is noticeable too that, with one exception, the series are opened respectively by Susan and Louis, the two strongest and best-balanced characters. In the third section, except for Bernard and Neville, who are at the university together and whose voices alternate again in the opening pages, the others speak once only, as again in sections 5, 6 and 7. An apparent break in the pattern may seem surprising; why, in section 5, do we find only Neville, Bernard and Rhoda, and in section 6 only Louis, Susan, Jinny and Neville? The reason is that Percival's death does not touch them all to the same degree. For Neville, the homosexual, it means passionate grief, as also for Rhoda, and if the after-effects are different in each case the intensity is equal. For Bernard, it means the loss of a very deep friendship, revealing the absurdity of existence. Whereas for the other three, this physical catastrophe is absorbed in the general flux of existence. For Louis, Percival dies almost in parentheses, like Mrs Ramsay, Prue and Andrew in *To the Lighthouse*; Susan, whom he loved[244] but who was probably not in love with him, merges his remembered but unnamed image in the reality of her child's, and the lullaby she sings to the baby is also a requiem for Percival.[245] As for Jinny, the most sensual and inconstant, she does not distinguish Percival from her other, anonymous lovers: "Some will never come into this room again. One may die tonight,"[246] and that is all. And if Neville "speaks" again after her, thus framing the two sections that are centred on the death of the hero, it is because his physical passion and his anguish impel him, like Jinny, like Susan too in a way, to pursue his reality and his dream through other realities.

[242] Cf. The W pp. 100-1 (272-3) (where the dialogue is in brackets) and pp. 162-5 (335-7)

[243] The W p. 88 (260)

[244] Cf. The W p. 112 (285)

[245] Cf. The W pp. 122-3 (294-5)

[246] The W p. 125 (297)

This perfection of arrangement, this meticulous disposition of material to which reality could contribute no support, no organization, displays both the importance and the triumph of artistic form, which here actually creates a new substance. This formal perfection, crowning all the reasons already adduced, surely justifies a preference for *The Waves*. The artistic success unquestionably achieved by *Mrs Dalloway*, *To the Lighthouse* and *Between the Acts* is due, I feel, less to the genius of the artist than to a skilful simplification of the problem. The spread and discontinuity of the successive periods, the fluctuating dispersed character of the centre were difficulties which *Jacob's Room* had not solved in satisfactory fashion. By the restriction of the novel within the unities of time and place, and by the concentration of its centre, *Mrs Dalloway* triumphs where *Jacob's Room* had failed. The term "unities of time and place", although suggestive, is not quite correct. It should be emended by reference to what has already been said about Virginia Woolf's concept of time and space. To be accurate, one should speak of "unity of the moment". "This June day, in the evening of which Clarissa is giving a party, in a great city where parks alternate with residential districts and crowded streets." There is scarcely as much matter here as in the slightest section of *Jacob's Room*. The concentration and homogeneity of the moment immediately bring together the most extreme and divergent points: contiguity is the first factor of cohesion, an external factor no doubt but one which functions. And for centre, instead of the volume that has to be filled out by Jacob, two points only: Clarissa and Septimus, acting as focus on the one hand, and on the other maintaining between themselves the distance which will allow of a changing viewpoint, of varied spot-lighting, of relativity. However, this simplification does not solve everything. On the scale of the moment, the gaps remain, even if, considered absolutely, they are infinitesimal compared to those which separate the phases of Jacob's life. And although in the reader's mind this relativity scarcely has a mathematical value, we none the less feel the need of an organizing formula.

The novel as a whole can be considered as the alternate succession of Clarissa's moments and those of Septimus. Superficially, it is at the intersection, in space or time, of the two series that we part company from one to follow the other: at the Bond

Street florist's,[247] then when Clarissa wonders what people are staring at in the sky,[248] when the little girl whom Peter is watching runs into Rezia's legs,[249] at a quarter to twelve when Peter, leaving the park, passes in front of Septimus and his wife,[250] at the cross roads where Peter and Rezia hear the beggar woman singing,[251] etc. However, this interlacing of their respective routes provides only a material framework, a structural device borrowed from the physical world and, actually, a mere illusion. The fact that at twelve o'clock precisely Clarissa lays down her sewing, just as the Smiths are walking along Harley Street to visit Bradshaw, contributes only in a remote and not very significant fashion to bringing their destinies together. If the structure of *Mrs Dalloway* consisted in nothing more than this not only would the novel seem to be made of bits and pieces, but moreover it would have no meaning. This clear-cut pattern in space and time is only a substitute for the plot on to which *The Voyage Out* or *Night and Day* were hung. It is artificially brought out by analysis. In reality it should be allotted a very minor place and importance, as providing material landmarks for the various stages of the book. The true structure is of another nature: it is homogeneous with the content, and that is why the restriction of the book's substance to precisely defined moments and centres of reference is of capital importance. What allows us to shift without a jar from Clarissa to Septimus, in front of the flower shop, is not their spatial contiguity, nor even the explosion that rings out in the ears of both. It is the contiguity of their thoughts. The monstrous threat of the "spectres who stand astride us and suck up half our life-blood, dominators and tyrants", against which Clarissa protests, is the same that Septimus apprehends when he hears the explosion, and against which Rezia wants to call for help. And beside their reactions to surprise and mystery we witness the manifold anonymous reactions of the crowd. In the same way, the second meeting between Septimus and Clarissa is brought about not by the fact of their both looking at the aeroplane at the same time, but by the feeling of beauty and peace, of mingled awe and exaltation, of religious revelation which both

[247] Cf. Mrs D p. 16 (18)
[248] Cf. Mrs D p. 33 (42)
[249] Cf. Mrs D p. 73 (97-8)
[250] Cf. Mrs D p. 79 (106)
[251] Cf. Mrs D p. 90 (122)

experience—as do, each in their way, Mrs Dempster and the unknown man pausing on the steps of St Paul's. If the little girl helps to link Rezia's recollections with Peter's it is not because the latter sees her stumble against the legs of the Italian girl; it is because the child's tears caricature the grief with which Peter has just recalled his loss of Clarissa: "It was awful, he cried, awful, awful . . ." echoed by Lucrezia's: "It's wicked; why should I suffer?"[252] It is pointless to pursue this analysis further; the few examples which have been quoted, and which might be multiplied indefinitely, are sufficient proof that the structure of *Mrs Dalloway* does not lie on the level of time and space, of the distance travelled by its characters or the hours struck by the city's clocks. If it were so, how could there be any communication in the present between those underground caves tunnelled out in the characters' past? What meaning would this have, if it were merely a material coincidence? This is not a relay race through London between the Dalloway team and the Smith team. The two apparently distinct lines have to be reduced to one—and this is in conformity with the intention of the author, who had originally conceived of Septimus as deprived of real existence. This single line is defined on the opening page:

How fresh, how calm, stiller than this of course, the air was in the early morning; like the flap of a wave; the kiss of a wave; chill and sharp and yet (for a girl of eighteen as she then was) solemn, feeling as she did, standing there at the open window, that something awful was about to happen. . . .[253]

In this atmosphere of calm, joy, exaltation, maintained throughout the book until the evening party, whose civilized brilliance crowns the gaiety of this June day, the threat grows, from that first explosion to the catastrophe, Septimus's suicide. And as the ringing of the ambulance bell gradually fades into the distance, the terror and threat fade away or rather, like the chime of the bell, are absorbed into the moment; they remain subjacent, cropping up here and there: Aunt Helena's death recalled[254]— and after all she is not dead, but turns up like a ghost at the party[255]—and the death of an old vicar of Bourton[256]; the mere

---

[252] Mrs D p. 72 (98). On the following page "Why should she suffer" recurs twice.

[253] Mrs D p. 5 (3) [254] Cf. Mrs D p. 178 (246)

[255] Cf. Mrs D p. 195 (271) [256] Cf. Mrs D p. 185 (256)

appearance of old Mrs Hilbery serving as a reminder that "it is certain we must die"[257]; the possibility of Sally's death[258]; while terror and threat break out finally, and this time with inexorable directness, when Clarissa hears of Septimus's suicide: "in the middle of my party, here's death . . .".[259] One has only to read the three pages[260] devoted to Clarissa's reflections to grasp the composition of the novel, its manifold variations on a single theme, summed up in Peter's words: terror, ecstasy.[261]

Thus considered, all falls into shape, all the elements are integrated in a continuous movement: Clarissa, Peter, the episodic figures surrounding Clarissa; Septimus and Rezia; their memories; the supernumeraries in the crowd. And the recalling of the various themes, the gathering together of all the characters in a sort of finale, followed by their departure which leaves Clarissa standing in the doorway, alone with Peter in the background, reproducing the picture in the opening page, thus bringing the book round full circle to where it began and suggesting the figure composed of circle and parabola which, as I have shown, is that of *The Waves*.

From this point of view, the hypothesis of a relationship between *Mrs Dalloway* and *Ulysses*, which I have already rejected for other reasons, becomes even less plausible. One can always find a cloud in any sky, and in any capital some procession or official carriage. And if there are two heroes, in one city, they are presumably going to meet. I cannot see that on account of such details, as commonplace as they are insignificant, one need assume indebtedness, or that there is any point in such an assumption. Why not say, for instance, that *To the Lighthouse* is inspired by the *Odyssey* because Mrs Ramsay knits, just as Penelope wove, while Mr Ramsay, as realistic and yet chimerical as Ulysses, pursues his egotistical quest for truth like Ulysses on his wanderings? As I have already pointed out, if Virginia Woolf was anywhere influenced by the example of Joyce, it is more probably in the cut-out technique of *Jacob's Room*, which recalls that of *A Portrait of the Artist*. The use of the device and its development through the work not to mention other factors,

[257] Cf. Mrs D p. 193 (267)
[258] Cf. Mrs D p. 199 (277)
[259] Mrs D p. 201 (279)
[260] Cf. Mrs D pp. 202-4 (280-4)
[261] Cf. Mrs D p. 213 (296): "What is this terror? what is this ecstasy?"

are so different however that to mention them serves to emphasize Virginia Woolf's originality rather than to suggest any sort of debt.

To the Lighthouse might be considered as an attempt to apply the form perfected in *Mrs Dalloway* to a wider field: "The Window" and "The Lighthouse", offering material analogous to that of the previous novel, are, roughly, treated in the same way. However, analysis reveals certain differences. Whereas "The Lighthouse", by its movement and the twofold line of interest— Lily and the group in the boat—bears a certain resemblance to *Mrs Dalloway*. "The Window", by its static character, is wholly different. We may thus expect to find original characteristics in this first section, and in the third a structure analogous to that which we have just studied. Lily Briscoe, painting on the lawn, from time to time casts a glance towards the bay to watch the boat on which Mr Ramsay, James and Cam are sailing.[262] But this link, like the paths that cross in *Mrs Dalloway*, is purely external; the real unity of the sections lies in the coincidence of projects and thoughts: the completion of Lily's canvas, the fulfilment of James's plan. It is purely fortuitous that Lily sees the sail fill and flap; what matters is their common immobility: "Life stands still here,"[263] and "The boat made no motion at all".[264] And further on, the mixture of charm and tyranny in Mr Ramsay occupies now Cam's thoughts, now Lily's; and so on to the end, where Mr Ramsay's unexpressed vision is identified with Lily's— his defeat and his triumph,[265] Lily's defeat and triumph.[266] The brackets enclosing the brief sections 7 and 10 (four lines, ten lines) irresistibly recall the events inserted in the same fashion in "Time Passes". Like these, they are hard kernels of a different nature to the flux out of which they emerge without rhyme or reason, absurdities of existence: the mutilated fish interrupting Lily's tragic cry,[267] the sea having apparently swallowed up the little boat and obliterated the lives of the passengers while, all the

[262] Cf. To the L pp. 250-1 (241-2), 262 (253-4), 280 (271), 293 (284), 310 (300), 318-19 (308-9)

[263] To the L p. 249 (240)

[264] To the L p. 251 (242)

[265] Cf. To the L p. 318 (308): ". . . he might be thinking, We perished, each alone, or he might be thinking, I have reached it."

[266] Cf. To the L p. 320 (309-10): "It would be hung in the attics, she thought; it would be destroyed . . . It was done; it was finished . . . I have had my vision."

[267] Cf. To the L pp. 277-8 (268-9)

time, James, Mr Ramsay and Cam pursue their own train of thought. But heterogeneous as they are, these observations, like the events in "Time Passes", have a secret relationship with the context that they seem to interrupt. The mutilation and survival of the fish is, at the same time, the survival of Mrs Ramsay and the mutilation of Lily's universe expressed by her cry and her tears; the feelings of distance and peace evoked by the scene she is contemplating emphasize the remoteness of the past which the occupants of the boat are remembering, and the feeling of reconciliation which is dawning amongst them at this moment.

In the first part, where there are no coherent events, no coherent movement to provide continuity and progression, these are obtained by a complex play of echoes enriched by variations. The few remarks exchanged about the probability of the expedition to the lighthouse provide a framework for the flux of emotions and thoughts they liberate, canalising them, directing them, enabling them to pass from one character to another; then a brief dialogue in indirect style gathers up all the threads: Tansley the disciple, Mr Ramsay's irritating irony, James's hatred of his father, thoughts of the child's future; Mrs Ramsay's knitting and the sail to the Lighthouse; finally the conflict between feeling and reason.[268] Mr Ramsay's comings and goings, the chance passage of some character or another give a new direction to Mrs Ramsay's thoughts, or replace them by those of Mr Ramsay, Lily, or Mr Bankes. But just as in *Mrs Dalloway*, these changes in the centre of reference alter only the form and tonality of the meditation, the basis of which remains the same: the mutual relations of all these human beings. We have a foretaste of the alternating voices of *The Waves*. As the substance is fined down, so is the structure simplified and schematized.

As regards the novel as a whole, I have already referred to the problem of the break made by "Time Passes" between the two panels of the triptych. The consummate art with which the transitions are accomplished[269] surely silences all criticism. The reign of night, of the absence of life, the abdication of the human element, between the end of one day and the dawn of another distant day, is not only legitimate but essential. The continuity between this chapter and those on either side of it is moreover ensured not only by sections 1, 2 and 10 but by many other

[268] Cf. To the L p. 53 (50)   [269] Cf. *supra*, ch. V, pp. 252-3

factors scattered throughout the chapter: the dilapidation of the house, to which Mrs Ramsay had frequently referred, the doors and windows banging in the wind, the waves, the beam from the lighthouse, the vain efforts of a single person—Mrs Macnab—to keep the place in order. Even the deaths of Prue and Andrew are the sudden and ironic reply of fate to the hopes Mrs Ramsay had built on their future, their success and their happiness.[270]

If the arrival at the lighthouse and the completion of Lily Briscoe's picture complete the circle of the book, and if "Time Passes" forms a sort of landing between the upward movement of "The Window" and the downward, resolving movement of "The Lighthouse", we find here the same structural design. It should be noted, however, that the first part, taken by itself, conforms to this design to some extent. Section 11, when the fairy tale is finished and James has gone, a perfect moment, rich with solitude and revelation, certainly forms a peak that communicates its exaltation to the second half of the chapter, which however never reaches the same intensity as this moment. In other respects the closing pages, while they show the differences between the Ramsays being resolved, bring us back to the starting-point, the projected journey. In one sense, the circle is completed here too. Nevertheless the postponement of the plan, the frustration of James's hopes, introducing the possibility of a later realization, leave the way open for the third part.

Between the Acts, at the close of Virginia Woolf's literary career, provides confirmation of these hypotheses about the problems of composition which the author had been seeking to solve ever since *Jacob's Room*: the finding of a formula which would enable her to include in her presentation of the moment—her chosen field, because it coincides with her vision of reality—the dispersed elements of all experience, spreading beyond the bounds of personal experience to include the course of history. This final novel, a sort of marriage between *Mrs Dalloway* and *Orlando*, aims, by superimposing one theme on another, at fusing together, in a single summer's day, the transient feelings of a few characters, English history, the story of the world and the feelings of all mankind. The two planes on which the book develops are connected in various ways. The most obvious, and also the most superficial, is the audience's commentary on the pageant. Stage

[270] Cf. To the L pp. 110 (106) and 170 (164-5)

directions, and the descriptions which complement what is happening in the play, constantly translate the historical or universal nature of the events represented in terms of contemporary life. The ambiguity of the setting, which serves both for the stage and for reality, and the ambiguity of the characters, whose actual identity shows under the disguise of their speech and costume, contribute most effectively to this translation, while revealing its deficiencies.

But under these apparent links, Virginia Woolf has woven a whole network of correspondences, which a few examples will serve to illustrate. From the very first page, the incongruity between the beauty of the moment and the discussion about the cesspool foreshadows the generalized incongruity of the audience's reaction, first displayed by their confusion between the nightingale and some daytime bird.[271] The Haines's claim to a remote ancestry, like old Oliver's allusion to local historic remains, state the theme of the continuity of past and present. At the beginning of the interval, we have the theme of the procession "Follow, follow"[272] interwoven with the opposing theme: "Dispersed are we. . ."[273] enacted by the feelings and behaviour of the characters for some thirty pages. This is moreover only a variation on the central theme, which is clearly set forth in the closing notes of the pageant: "*Unity-Dispersity*".[274] If in the last twenty pages we find once again that return to the starting-point with which this book, like the others, comes full circle, it is difficult to trace a clearly defined curve of progression. Does its peak come in the middle of the book, at the first interval, where the relations between the characters seem the most tense, or else at the end of the pageant, when Mr Streatfield's summing-up is followed by the summing-up of all the explanatory hypotheses of the audience? This twofold possibility may correspond to the two lines of development—the summer's day at Pointz Hall, and the pageant —the slight gap between which allows of the insertion of a correspondingly slight thread of reality. Moreover, if we turn back to *Mrs Dalloway*, we can distinguish a similar pattern there. If we divide the Septimus theme from the Clarissa theme, Septimus's suicide marks the apex of the first line; the news of his suicide, reaching Clarissa much later, almost at the close of

---

[271] Cf. B the A p. 7 (3)

[272] B the A pp. 115-16 (96)

[273] B the A p. 115 (96)

[274] B the A p. 235 (201)

the book, may be considered as the culminating point of this second line. The absence of any catastrophe, strictly speaking, of any crucial event, the preparation for which and the results of which would determine the progress and the solution of the whole, is responsible for a kind of uncertainty, of hesitancy in the movement and accentuation of *Between the Acts*. However, before assuming any weakening or retrogression of Virginia Woolf's art, we must remember that her ambition was, in fact, to free the novel from that framework—that straitjacket, in her opinion—the plot, the story, a purely external factor of organization, and to replace it by inner cohesion. One might go so far as to say that the coexistence, already clearly apparent before *Between the Acts*, of the parabolic and circular patterns, betokens the obscure and tenacious survival of a traditional element.

Her increasing mastery of the play of echoes and associations, becoming richer the deeper one penetrates into the novel, which grows like a crystal formation, tells us in what the essential element of her composition consists. It is dangerous, of course, to criticize one art by means of the vocabulary of another. A novel is neither a painting nor a symphony. However, the structure of any work of art is merely an abstraction, and as such lacks the special characteristics of any particular material or means of expression. Structure is a system of relations, which is not profoundly affected by the nature of the related elements, whether words or colours, forms or sounds. I took the plot as starting-point to study Virginia Woolf's composition, precisely because at the beginning of her career as novelist she took the novel as she found it, an art-form still bound up with representative realism, mingling heterogeneous elements with its own proper substance. I have shown, I hope, how she gradually achieved its liberation, its purification. I realize that there is something arbitrary about the figures with which I have tried to illustrate the movement of Virginia Woolf's novels, and the relations between their different parts, yet I believe that such a figuration is in keeping with the mental attitude of an author whose use of the term "pattern" is so constant. I have used the image of a circle to describe the globe of life, or the moment; but actually, have we any means other than metaphor to express structure, whether that of a book or of an atom? Similarly, I have been unable to avoid the terms overture, theme, variations, echoes, which have a more precise meaning in music than they can have in literature; they correspond to an aspect of Virginia Woolf's work whose importance it is easy to exaggerate. But if we were purists enough to reject any transposition of terms from one art to another, we should leave out of account an essential quality of Virginia Woolf's writing, which, as we have seen, invariably tended towards an integration of those genres that literary tradition keeps separate, and which was based on the identity and unity of art underlying the multiplicity of its forms and of its methods.

Painting, too, through Vanessa and Clive Bell, Duncan Grant and Roger Fry, played a vital role in Virginia Woolf's aesthetic formation and development. If I have stressed the movement of her novels, that is because it is of so unusual a character as to have been frequently overshadowed by a certain static quality, for which the author has been blamed. This static character, this use of the tableau form, particularly striking in *To the Lighthouse* and *Between the Acts*, this tendency to symmetry and balance and strong lines suggests that the novelist's method has been affected by the technique of painting.[275] I have not mentioned the cinema, of which *Jacob's Room* in particular reminds one with its cuts and close-ups, its fade-outs, its "travellings". It is highly questionable whether Virginia Woolf borrowed these devices from the seventh art. From what she wrote in 1926,[276] the films of that period do not seem to have helped her much. It is remarkable, on the contrary, that she was struck, rather, by the lack of maturity and experience of this new means of expression and by its subservience to literature. The developments she envisages in the cinema are inspired rather by her own experiments[277] than by the achievements of the time. If the resources of cinematographic technique offer a method of analysis easily and effectively applicable to the novels of Virginia Woolf, it is rather because these novels share with the screen a problem fundamental to both forms of art: the reduction of discontinuity to continuity. And thus we see, once again, that there is nothing arbitrary about Virginia Woolf's researches into artistic form, and that they are in no way derived from a belief in art for art's sake.

---

[275] Cf. AWD pp. 69 (68) and 171 (166), quoted *supra*, ch. III, p. 93 note 175.

[276] Cf. CDB "The Cinema", pp. 166-71 (180-6). Pub. in *Arts*, N.Y., June 1926.

[277] Cf. particularly CDB p. 170 (185)

6. HUMOUR AND LYRICISM

I have chosen to conclude my study of the various aspects of Virginia Woolf's art by an examination of her humour and her lyricism, not only because these two tonalities of style are dominant in her writings, but above all because they seem to me to express on the formal level the contradictory duality which characterizes her personality. On the one hand, the love of fun, a gaiety that derives sustenance from the pageant of life, a lightness that skims the surface of things and of beings, a carelessness that does not look beyond the moment; and on the other hand, anxiety, doubt, a keen sense of the tragedy of man's state, the anguish of a being dedicated to solitude, at grips with the forces of destruction. Just as in life she shifted from one mood to the other, so in her books she shifts from the comic vision to the tragic vision, from the detached tone of mockery to the passionate, poetic expression of meditative rapture. But such an alternation is too common to serve, in itself, to characterize Virginia Woolf. It is the form in which she expresses these two moods that distinguishes her. As we shall see, her comic sense almost exclusively takes the form of humour, while her tragic sense, essentially inward, is not expressed in the shape of actions or events but in expansive lyricism.

From the very first page of her first novel Virginia Woolf shows her awareness of the twofold aspect of human beings, who are comic and tragic at the same time. Ridley Ambrose, swinging his walking-stick and reciting Pindar along the banks of the Thames, is Bluebeard to the small boys in the street. But if he seems to them merely a ridiculous eccentric, he is shown to us as a man full of tenderness and compassion, a kind father and husband in whose very awkwardness there is something touching. Similarly, if Mrs Ambrose's tears and sobs are slightly grotesque, they none the less express a mother's grief that is genuine and violent. The very way in which these two aspects of reality are superimposed on one another clearly reveals the two points of view which the novelist assumes alternately, according to whether she wishes to make us laugh—or rather smile—or to move us. A detached spectator, keeping her distance, seeing only surfaces and lines, she notes what is ridiculous about the clumsy and mechanical gestures of her shadowy actors. But a moment later, abandoning her indifference, she draws closer: the shadowy figures take on substance; the grotesque effect derived from telescoping different planes is replaced by the moving complexity of a new world from which neither author nor reader can remain detached. Behind these faces and words and gestures we discover thoughts and feelings, life itself, which we cannot go on merely watching, but which demand our participation, our sympathy. We realize moreover that the shifting point of view characteristic of the first pages of *The Voyage Out* is only a temporary hesitation, reflecting the uncertainty with which contact is made with the characters: the attempts at intimacy, the alternatives of indifference. The choice soon becomes clear, between friends and mere acquaintances, between heroes and walkers-on. On one side the Peppers, the Willoughbys, the Dalloways, the fauna of the Santa Marina hotel; on the other Helen, Rachel, Terence. The former remain superficial, and as such are fated to be laughed at and despised. As for the others, we are so deeply involved in their inner lives that we no longer see the absurdities, the eccentricities, the awkwardnesses which might impair the emotion that sustains our understanding and our interest. That partiality towards those who are like herself for which Virginia Woolf sometimes blames herself is manifest in her first two novels. She establishes a division between two sorts of people, whom her attitude rather than their real nature, perhaps, confines within two ways of life, two disparate worlds. Nevertheless certain characters give one an inkling that the distinction between puppets and living beings, between the comic and the tragic, is less absolute than it seems, that the amusing absurdity of appearances may conceal a heart-rending absurdity of thought or feeling. St John Hirst in *The Voyage Out*, William Rodney and Mrs Hilbery in *Night and Day* display, in varying degrees, an ambiguity like that of the figures in the later novels who, freed from conventional characteristics, are more essentially Woolfian in their contradictory complexity.

These three characters are of very different importance in the novels in which they appear. William, without being a foreground figure like Ralph and Katharine, is nevertheless an essential one; St John merely serves to set in sharper relief, by contrast, the figure of Terence; and the somnambular presence of Mrs Hilbery in *Night and Day* is connected with the other characters, with the plot, with the whole novel, by the loosest of links, whose subtlety conceals their importance. The common feature to be noted is a certain antagonism between the author and these characters: towards William's conception of life, St John's type of intelligence, Mrs Hilbery's attachment to certain prejudices. This feeling obtrudes repeatedly, so as to sap sympathy and understanding, in a word to prevent the author's identification with the beings she has created. But this momentary indifference and detachment are quite unlike the cold remoteness which withholds all indulgence from such figures as the Peppers, the Dalloways, the Flushings, Miss Allan, Cassandra or Miss Milvain, leaving them defenceless against scathing censure and ridicule. On these three, she bestows an almost affectionate interest which, although superficially intermittent, surrounds them with an imperceptible aura, something indefinable which seems to assert the undisclosed aspects of their being, the mysterious presence of a complex whole not entirely incompatible with the black-and-white simplicity of their outward behaviour. This shadowy zone is their refuge, and protects them from the hostility of critical judgment and of laughter, which affect only the mask and the gesture, leaving the face and the action intact. This immunity which they enjoy, in contrast with the vulnerability of those characters who are caricatures, indicates the essential factors which will help us to define the nature of Virginia Woolf's comedy in general, and to bring out its relationship with the dominant tragic vein in her writings.

After *Jacob's Room*, we find no more essentially comic figures, such as those referred to above in *The Voyage Out* and *Night and Day*. Their presence in these novels, which is mainly of literary origin, was based on aesthetic conventions and more general postulates which Virginia Woolf later came to reject. She was already aware that such beings, confined within some definition as if within St John Hirst's chalk circle, exist only in novels. She had retained them, as she had retained other elements in the novel, while making use of them for her own ends.[278] But if people are not like that, why persist in depicting them under such misleading appearances? And furthermore, the very concepts of what is comic and what is tragic, as applied to human beings, are far from being as homogeneous and distinct as our wish for clarity and our mental laziness incline us to believe. These emotional complexes are, like love and hate, forms of our relations with

[278] Cf. *supra*, ch. V, pp. 203-4

other people, and like love and hate they are primarily relations, and above all, unstable relations: their exclusive antagonism is a Cartesian myth. In her effort to rediscover reality Virginia Woolf was to give up these simplified outlines which after all only make us laugh because we do not really understand them; so superficial and imperfect a contact had no interest for her. She did not, however, give up the right to exercise her perspicacity, to see the extravagance, the grotesqueness and absurdity in man; but this point of view was not self-sufficient; superimposed on a deeper knowledge which softened its edge, it reveals itself in that form, that attitude which has so often been tentatively, but never satisfactorily, defined: humour.

I shall not endeavour, after so many others,[279] to offer a general definition of humour as a starting-point for my study. The essentially personal nature of this way of writing, which is also a way of thinking, makes any attempt of this sort a disappointment. All that I can hope to do is, starting from a few examples, to pick out the factors which characterize this aspect of the art and personality of Virginia Woolf.

The first page of *Jacob's Room*, which, like the first pages of *The Voyage Out*, depicts a woman trying to keep back her tears, enables us to measure the distance between traditional comic effects and what one might call typically Woolfian humour. In both cases we see, in an appropriate setting, a character overwhelmed by grief at separation; tears rise to her eyes and distort her vision. As outside observers we see Helen Ambrose's tears blur the sight of the Thames and then fall into the river. The presence of a narrator apparently establishes the same relationship of observer to observed between ourselves and Betty Flanders; but here the narrative is whispered from so close by Betty's side that we are drawn thither, and lose our externality; it is through Betty's eyes that we see the bay quiver, the lighthouse wobble; and even when the narrator declares: "she had the illusion that the mast of Mr Connor's little yacht was bending like a wax candle in the sun"[280] there is not time for the form of

---

[279] E.g. Raymond Las Vergnas, *W. M. Thackeray, l'homme, le penseur, le romancier,* Champion, Paris, 1932, pp. 330-41, and Louis Cazamian, *L'Humour de Shakespeare,* Aubier, Paris, 1945, pp. 11-20 and 215-28.

[280] Cf. JR p. 5 (7). The objective statement: "The entire bay quivered; the lighthouse wobbled" ensure our identification with Betty and weaken the detachment implicit in "and she had the illusion", etc.

the comment, asserting the difference between our own dry-eyed vision and that of Betty's tear-dimmed eyes, to separate us from her: her fear of an accident, which she tries to avert by fluttering her eyelids, keeps us close beside her, within her. And indeed this distorted seascape, together with the tear-blot on the letter to Captain Barfoot, is even funnier than the picture of Mrs Ambrose weeping into the Thames. But although at this point in the story we know no more about the sources of one heroine's grief than about the other's, and have no reason to sympathize with one more than with the other, we do not smile at the first page of *Jacob's Room* with the same sheer, surprised amusement as at the opening of *The Voyage Out*. Indeed, whereas the whole description of the street laid before us a scene in which Helen Ambrose was only one factor among many others, while her feelings, objectively related, added no concrete reality to those outward manifestations which claimed all our attention, the four lines which introduced Betty Flanders to us have already, despite their obscurity or insignificance, set us not beside her, as the narrative form had done, but within her. The whole doom of parting is in the sentence she is writing—and in the way she drops her pen and reflects on that doom; the reader has an obscure sense of sharing in a melancholy destiny, while he looks through the heroine's eyes, and thus a vague, compassionate anxiety mingles with his smile.

The proximity, or even the identification, of narrator and hero —leading up to the reader's proximity and identification—are in fact only a means, a technical device towards the achievement of humour, which here seems to attenuate the surface comedy by the evocation of a profound, antagonistic emotion. This attenuation, indeed, is only a superficial result. The duality, in this case the contrast between grief and its manifestations, profoundly alters the quality of the reaction it engenders. Humour, with Virginia Woolf, is neither a weakened nor a reticent form of comedy; it is the simultaneous presentation of two aspects of reality: the outer and the inner, the surface and the depths, and the comic element consists in the anomaly, the incongruity or the contradiction between them; but this element cannot be separated from the other emotions, feelings and ideas that spring from this double vision. It is on this account that identification with the hero is essential; without it, the vision of inner reality would remain an abstraction and could not merge with the vision of

outer reality. The two aspects would remain separate, in juxtaposition, one after the other, as in the opening of *The Voyage Out*.
Such a division is favourable to an ordered presentation of
experience; it is, in itself, a classification. But precisely on this
account, it is incompatible with Virginia Woolf's turn of mind;
rather than such implicit analysis, she chooses humour which,
by its synthesis, restores the complexity and confusion that better
befit the immediate data of experience.

Other examples may be quoted in favour of this interpretation.
When, in *To the Lighthouse*, Mrs Ramsay reflects on Minta's
extraordinary good luck in marrying a man with a wash-leather
bag for his watch,[281] the absurdity of her thought, which brings a
smile to her lips[282]—and to the reader's—owing to all that we
know about Mrs Ramsay and her relations with her husband,
carries on the reverse side of its humorousness all the uncertainty,
all the possible disillusionment of the future. Further on, when
Lily admires Mr Ramsay's boots,[283] if the unexpectedness of her
comment and its effects dissipates the tension which had accumulated between these two interlocutors, beneath the comic
effect of the scene we are aware of the melancholy, indeed the
tragic element in these lives, doomed to solitude through their
incapacity to communicate. Even when the attitude hardens and
a certain critical content brings us to the verge of irony, this is
held in control by a movement of sympathy, the admission of a
weakness so universally human that those who are its victims can
hardly be condemned as guilty. Thus the Prime Minister,
arriving at Mrs Dalloway's, is after all more to be pitied than
censured.[284] It is in *Orlando* that this form of Virginia Woolf's
humour occurs most frequently. Sasha, Shelmerdine, Nick
Greene, even when their extravagance assumes a malicious form,
are treated with indulgence simply because they cannot escape
the common condition of mankind. While studying that novel[285]
I quoted most of the expressions in the Diary which bear witness
to the author's intentional mockery and playfulness. Nevertheless,
in this respect as in many others, ambiguity is the chief characteristic of *Orlando*, which was written "half in a mock style"[286] and
intended to be "half laughing, half serious".[287] Underlying the

[281] Cf. To the L p. 180 (175)   [282] Cf. To the L p. 181 (176)
[283] Cf. To the L p. 237 (229)   [284] Cf. Mrs D p. 189 (261)
[285] Cf. *supra*, ch. III, pp. 79-80 and ch. V, pp. 262-3 and 269
[286] AWD p. 117 (115)   [287] AWD p. 120 (118)

comic absurdity of its incidents, situations and characters we sense the agonizing absurdity of man's nature and destiny. Thus, the association of clumsiness and love of solitude in the hero becomes a dig against the arbitrary deductions of psychologists: "Having stumbled over a chest, Orlando naturally loved solitary places, vast views. . . ."[288] Yet, for all the criticism implicit in the word "naturally", one might discover deep-seated associations which would, in fact, connect these two attributes of the hero's, whereas the expression merely stresses their incongruity. Similarly, on the following page, one word serves to unsettle, if not to dissolve into thin air, the huge landed estates of Orlando's family:

The heath was theirs and the forest; the pheasant and the deer, the fox, the badger, and the *butterfly*.[289]

All problems, small and great: fashion and love, amusement and death, literature and life, politics and the nature of personality, thus carry their own pettiness on the reverse side of their greatness. "My own lyric vein is to be satirised",[290] Virginia Woolf declared, thus authorizing us to see in Orlando a pastiche of the writer by herself. But a singular sort of pastiche, combining the two possible aspects of the genre: the satiric pastiche which brings out the most superficial element in the processes of form and thought, accentuates gestures till they become mannerisms and attitudes till they become poses. But no intentional mockery, no deliberate exaggeration can induce the author to mimic herself, still less to repudiate herself. Under the veil of parody we find that authentic pastiche which is simply the ineluctable fidelity to oneself that ensures to every artist his individual accent and aspect, recognizable among all others. To realize the closeness of her lyrical vein and its parody, one has only to compare the second section of "Time Passes" with the opening of Chapter V of *Orlando*. In these two passages the author treats of her favourite theme, "this impersonal thing, . . . the flight of time".[291] She has recourse to the same cosmic elements which bring about change: water, wind, light, shade, conceived of as mysterious powers, as an army of goblins attacking objects one by one to corrode them, transform them, disintegrate them. Whether night is invading the

Ramsays' house, or rainy gales assaulting the whole of England, the change of scale is scarcely noticeable, for the proportions of the opposing forces remain the same: man and his world on the one hand, and on the other the elfin army, unseen and immeasurable. The vision is the same in both cases. Parody and satire creep in gradually, almost surreptitiously, between the lines of *Orlando*: here a turn of phrase: "…beards were grown…",[292] there an audacious logical inference: "… as coffee led to a drawing-room in which to drink it, and a drawing-room to glass cases . . . the home . . . was completely altered."[293] Then condensation of phrase leads to aphorism, exaggeration becomes extravagance, and we are back in the fantastic world of Orlando. I have chosen these two passages for comparison since, by Virginia Woolf's own admission, "Time Passes" is particularly representative of her lyric vein.[294] It can therefore serve as starting-point for an attempted definition of that lyricism.

What is immediately striking, and to some extent disconcerting, is the deliberately impersonal nature of these pages. There is no character, no individual consciousness, no voice uttering the poetic words. There is only a scene taking place independent of any spectators, life pursuing its course independent of any living being. Is this depersonalization not antagonistic to the very essence of lyricism? If by lyricism we mean the expression of exalted feelings, as in Shakespeare's sonnets, the *Immortality* Ode, *Epipsychidion* or *La Tristesse d'Olympio*, it obviously becomes difficult to use the term of "Time Passes". Nevertheless the presence of an "I", of an individual consciousness as the seat of such feelings, is perhaps only an accidental element in lyricism, a literary convention and, all things considered, a superficial characteristic. In the poems above mentioned, we are scarcely concerned with the "I", which has no distinct features and is only the transparent support for the emotion—love, anguish, nostalgia, aspiration— which is the real substance of the poem. That Virginia Woolf did away with this support is not surprising; it follows logically from her principles. When, shortly after *To the Lighthouse*, she writes in her Diary, thinking of *The Waves*: "I mean to eliminate all waste, deadness, superfluity: to give the moment whole; whatever it

[292] O p. 206 (228)   [293] O p. 206 (228)
[294] Cf. AWD p. 100 (98): "The lyric portions of *To the Lighthouse* are collected in the 10-year lapse. . . ."

includes. Say that the moment is a combination of thought; sensation; the voice of the sea",[295] she not only anticipates the austerity of the novel she wishes to write, but she also defines the complex content of its most intense pages which, precisely at this period, seem to her the ideal at which she is aiming.

"Time Passes", as a whole, does indeed correspond to this expression of the moment in its purity, stripped of any particular or anecdotic element, and even of any consciousness which, apprehending it, might impair its absolute and universal character. Facing the cosmos, thinking about it and enduring it, we have only the anonymous human being: "we", "one", "whoever", the indefinite subject of an infinitive verb. This degree of abstraction appears to me characteristic of one aspect of Virginia Woolf's lyricism. It attempts to render directly, without passing through the intermediary of any individual experience, the relations between man and the universe. These are thus reduced to their most elementary form. The themes of traditional lyricism, nature, love and death are convenient labels for those fundamental complexities of which each poet creates his characteristic variant or blend. They are, in fact, so many questions without intelligible answers, whose mystery the artist tries to probe obliquely by means of a whole system of transpositions, whose evocative value and whose load of symbolism are destined to act on the sensibility and intelligence of the reader, so as to convey to him the inexpressible reality. The two questions which obsessed Virginia Woolf and provided the material for her lyric outbursts are the same as those which she asked and tried to answer under all the forms with which her art experimented in turn: time and personal identity. We shall see, moreover, that they are complementary, to such an extent that one cannot be contemplated without the other. None the less one may be dominant, while the other merely provides the accompaniment.

In "Time Passes" it is relatively easy to follow the way in which Virginia Woolf succeeds in translating what words betray, in giving body and substance to what abstract thought has devitalized. She apprehends time in the form of the changes it brings about, just as an artist is recognized through his creation. But change is also an abstraction; to make it concrete and perceptible to the sense, it is necessary to expand the present until it contains

[295] AWD p. 139 (136)

the past too, and to insert, between its two limits, mobility, or rather mutation, which includes permanence within change. The openings of sections 3 and 9 are particularly characteristic:

But what after all is one night? A short space, especially when the darkness dims so soon, and so soon a bird sings, a cock crows, or a faint green quickens, like a turning leaf, in the hollow of the wave. Night, however, succeeds to night. The winter holds a pack of them in store and deals them equally, evenly, with indefatigable fingers. They lengthen; they darken.[296]

The house was left; the house was deserted. It was left like a shell on a sandhill to fill with dry salt grains now that life had left it. The long night seemed to have . . . triumphed. The saucepan had rusted and the mat decayed. Toads had nosed their way in. Idly, aimlessly, the swaying shawl swung to and fro.[297]

There is not a verb here, either standing alone or modified by an adverb, which fails to indicate some alteration; yet at the same time, under the change of aspect, of colour, of texture, we feel the enduring nature of night, of the house, of the wave, of the breeze, the saucepan or the shawl. This seems to be a description, although distended by time and undermined by mutability; but that which is described and describable, that which is seen, is only a means of expressing the indescribable, the invisible, that is contained within it. Surely this is precisely that abstract-concrete reality so necessary to Virginia Woolf, which, shortly after writing these pages, she considered one of the revelations experienced during her summers at Rodmell.[298] These images and sensations, merging together in the synthesis of an inner landscape, over and above their plastic value have a symbolic power which makes them linger in the mind. Almost all the words in these passages have a double aspect: night, the wave, the grain of salt, the wind, the toad, rust—these are agents of decay and destruction, the forces of time warring against the forces of life: the bird, the leaf, the house, the shawl. . . . And so such passages expand into abstraction without a break, imperceptibly: the words ruin, corruption, oblivion, insensibility of nature, which occur later are associated with so many images and sensations that they take on fresh life, an almost physical content. Meditation is superimposed on the thing seen, and it does not obliterate it, rather

[296] To the L p. 198 (192)
[297] To the L p. 212 (206-7)
[298] Cf. AWD p. 132 (130), quoted *supra*, ch. III, p. 112

recalls it constantly. A few lines, indeed, can give no idea of the richness and artistry of these pages, in which words invoke and answer one another from one paragraph to the next, while awakening distant echoes from the book's furthest horizons. Their music, moreover, adds to their incantatory power and perfects their poetic character.

In the interludes in *The Waves* we find the same traits of style and the same symbolic landscape, composed of the same elements: sea, light, garden, house. . . . In the overtures to *The Years*, however, while the author has sought to make the passage of time perceptible to the senses through the same recourse to cosmic elements, she has replaced symbolic concentration by a unanimistic dispersion which slackens the lyric tension. Description prevails over meditation, through the survey of space with its geographical precision, its deliberately identified details and characters. Even if, as the book progresses, such passages become less lavish, the human and the cosmic elements—or rather the everyday and the timeless—remain in juxtaposition. The result is rather a potentially lyrical atmosphere than true lyricism.

However, although I have taken as my starting-point these outstanding pages in the work of Virginia Woolf, they are far from representing all that may be described as lyrical in her work.

The Waves, that "mystical" book as she called it, is lyrical through and through. Each of the voices utters a song about the world, life, time, love and death, from the alternating verses of the opening pages to Bernard's lengthy meditation. The reappearance of the "I", taking into account the nature of the voices in *The Waves*, which I defined earlier,[299] confirms what I have said about the secondary character of that element in lyricism. There is no fundamental difference between the first section with its multiple centre and the last with its single centre. The polyvalence of each consciousness, the participation of all in each and of each in all by means of the dispersion of identity, confers a general and abstract quality on the central consciousness, which becomes pure consciousness, that anonymous and faceless "she" that Virginia Woolf had at one point sought to represent.[300]

Apart from the symbolic value both of the elements of the universe and of each particular experience, which form, as it

[299] Cf. *supra*, ch. V, pp. 283-6   [300] Cf. AWD p. 143 (140)

were, the material of this book, the implicit feeling that all this is the essence of life is what moulds its form, and forms its lyricism. The wonder, the mystery, the anguish conveyed by the movement of a sentence, by the choice of its verbs, are identical with the sense of life itself; they are the basic emotions of consciousness in a state of exaltation, suddenly illuminated by contact with "reality". The splendour of nature, from the fragile beauty of a flower to the majestic and eternal power of the ocean, the fascination of human beings which, apart from any question of speech or silence, of gesture or stillness, of presence or absence, remains inexplicable: the agonizing mystery of the self, both one and many, permanent and in process of becoming; the even more agonizing mystery of time, which contains us and which we contain, which creates and destroys us, and which we create and destroy at will—which is eternity, but which is also entirely confined within our birth and our death: such is the lyrical aura which surrounds that long flow of images—and which emanates from them—whether its apparent style be that of litany or meditation, of elegy or of hymn to the present.[301]

The very concentration of lyricism in *The Waves*, the multiplicity of its themes and forms, helps us to recognize the same vein in its countless recurrences throughout the work of Virginia Woolf. It is remarkable that the first two novels are practically devoid of lyrical moments. In *The Voyage Out*, one brief evocation of London by night, seen from the deck of the Euphrosyne (p. 11 (17)), of an English autumn (pp. 27 (31), 28 (31)) and of the boat, island like amidst the solitude of the sea (p. 29 (32)) give an inkling of what Virginia Woolf can put into a description, over and above what is actually seen: of how much she can include of that reality "dwelling in what one saw and felt".[302] Moments which one would have thought favourable to lyrical expression, such as Rachel and Terence's walk in the forest, and even more the death of Rachel,[303] are treated analytically. This restriction—or discipline—voluntarily accepted, is even more noticeable in *Night and Day*, where a rigorous introspection patiently traces out the maze of particular circumstances. Only

---

[301] Long before clearly envisaging the form *The Waves* was to take, V. W. seems to have anticipated it. Cf. G & R p. 19 (19) (1927): "[The novel] will give the relation of the mind to general ideas and its soliloquy in solitude."

[302] Cf. VO p. 35 (37)

[303] Cf. VO pp. 420-1 (442-4)

half way through the novel, and more frequently towards its end, is analysis relaxed to allow, here and there, a sentence or a paragraph to break forth transcending the instant or the individual, to express a pure emotion stamped with the impress of the universal.[304]

The break with the traditional form of the novel and its conventions, which stood as a screen between herself and reality, was to liberate Virginia Woolf's vision and at the same time to allow full expansion to her lyricism, which coincides with the expression of that vision and is, in fact, an attempt to convey the essence of reality. Already in "The Mark on the Wall" she had touched on the nature of knowledge (pp. 41 and 42) and evoked the indistinct dream of an afterlife (p. 37). And the final page of "Kew Gardens" blends together all the sensations of one moment into a picture where the richness of her palette and the delicacy of her drawing only form the surface; underneath lies the quivering sense of a reality, and of the mystery of existence, which makes itself felt through the shimmer of colour, the diversity and movement of form.

In subsequent novels, constantly, a paragraph or merely a phrase in the course of the narrative, the description or the interior analysis, suddenly ring out with a different tonality. The restricted framework of time and place fades, and expands to the proportions of the universe, while the identity of the character becomes confused and behind the "he" or "she" or even the "one" which often takes their place only the essential human being remains. Thus at the close of the first section of *Jacob's Room*, the storm, from being a mere incident, becomes the unleashing of maleficent elements against frail, stubborn humanity.[305] A little further on (p. 14 (16)) the mysterious permanence of beings lost in the living universe which endures after their death, extends far beyond the fleeting recollection of Seabrook in Betty Flanders' mind (p. 14 (16)). In Jacob's youthful reverie, in the memories of butterfly hunting, between the concrete and circumstantial details there are inserted, here and there, phrases

---

[304] Cf. N & D, p. 204, Katharine's perplexity at the thought of a *tête-à-tête* with William or Ralph; also pp. 330, 332, 338; and during Ralph's interview with Katharine in Kew Gardens: pp. 353, 358; Ralph's reverie, p. 373; Ralph and Katharine in search of one another across London: pp. 417-18, 465; Mrs Hilbery recalling her past: pp. 511-12; the uncertainties of love: pp. 502-37.

[305] Cf. JR p. 11, last paragraph, and p. 12, last paragraph (12-14).

that take us beyond the particular instant of day or night into a universal nostalgia for time, space, inaccessible beauty (pp. 21-2 (23-4)).

Again, there is the scene where Mrs Jarvis on the moor seems to vanish like a ghost, leaving behind only a passionate, anxious love of life (pp. 25-6 (26-7)). Throughout the novel, comparable examples might be quoted. The same is true of *Mrs Dalloway*. Yet on account of the general difference in technique, the bursts of lyricism take a slightly different form. Since, as we have seen, Jacob is approached from the outside, the lyrical element in this novel develops in the same way, centripetally, from the universe to man. The landscape becomes cosmos, while its relations with humanity are revealed. In *Mrs Dalloway*, on the contrary, since the point of view, the centre of reference is the consciousness of the characters—Clarissa, Septimus, Peter—the lyrical element develops in the same direction, from man outward to the universe. "What a lark! What a plunge!" thinks Clarissa,[306] and it is from there that, by way of Bourton and her memories, we go back to the wonderful beauty and promise of that morning, of all mornings, of her youth and of all youth. Fascinated by the shimmer of light and shade, of blue and green in the leaves, Septimus feels the trees coming to life (p. 26 (32)); their rhythm is their life, life which is everywhere rhythm: it pervades his own body, absorbing and effacing it, until nothing remains but this harmonious arabesque of sounds and lines "which all taken together meant the birth of a new religion". A little later (p. 77 (104-5)), emerging from lethargy or hallucination, Septimus again experiences a revelation which, springing up within him, pervades him and seems to extend through all creation independent of any human consciousness; the feeling of beauty and truth is identified with the beauty and truth of things. Elsewhere, the multi-coloured, multi-formed richness of life is experienced in contrast with the hollow rigour of abstract thought, by Peter on his way to Clarissa's party. But Peter is only an intermediary here: true, it is through him that the aspect and meaning of the town by night are disclosed; but there is no "he" nor "Peter" in the paragraph; only passives and present participles, impersonal and indefinite pronouns. And the poor woman singing by the Tube station seems to dissolve into her wordless song, which

[306] Mrs D p. 5 (3)

itself dissolves into a timeless longing for eternal love and youth (pp. 90-1 (122-3)). Lyricism in *Mrs Dalloway*, a diversion or alteration of the stream of consciousness, pierces through at the intensest moments of that day; but the most commonplace of them are affected by its emanation. The conjunction of life and death, the impossibility of love and knowledge, the irremediable loss and the undying presence of the past, form, through a close network of connected and echoing images, a sort of lyrical accompaniment to the whole book. The same is true of *To the Lighthouse*. The orchestration of the lyrical themes in the central section disguises or muffles the scattered elements in the other two panels of the triptych. Yet what could be more lyrical than Mrs Ramsay's long meditation (pp. 99-104 (95-100)) or that of Lily Briscoe which corresponds to it (p. 249 (240-1)), and many other paragraphs in the third part?

In fact, Virginia Woolf was gradually groping her way towards the expression of that essential reality which, to her, was the very stuff of the novel, that essential reality which was none other than the content of moments of vision, and the ineffable illumination which could only be rendered in lyrical form. What was an accompaniment in Mrs Dalloway becomes the whole movement of *To the Lighthouse*; it constitutes the very substance of *The Waves*, where all the elements of recitative, anecdote or action have disappeared, leaving only song. Reality has found its form at last: "the mystical eyeless book".

Through attempting to restore its everyday context to poetry, through seeking to reintegrate it with the word spoken, the gesture, the object—table, house or street—which gave rise to it within us, Virginia Woolf stifled it. Deliberately, indeed, and for the sake of something else; but to those who find in the abstract intensity of *The Waves* a singularly felicitous and original expression, *The Years* is lacking in resonance. One has only to read Eleanor's reverie, where the presence of waves and moths recalls the themes of *The Waves* and allows one at the same time to assess the altered quality of the poetry, the change of register from one book to another. A mark on the ceiling, a sign of the wear and tear of time, decides Eleanor not to take another house:

Again the sense came to her of a ship padding softly through the waves; of a train swinging from side to side down a railway-line. Things can't go on for ever, she thought. Things pass, things change, she thought, looking up at the ceiling. And where are we going? Where? Where? . . . The moths were dashing round the ceiling . . . [307]

The image of the train and the boat which, two pages before,[308] had been partly a memory of Eleanor's recent journey, partly evocative of our perpetual transit through places and people, is here supposed to be no more than a symbol, and the dance of the moths is the answer to Eleanor's question. But the particularization of the scene, the insistent individualizing of the thought, keep us on the plane of psychological analysis. We remain spectators, we do not share in the anguished process of change in which the pure juxtaposition of images in *The Waves* involved us. And when later Eleanor, grown old, echoes Bernard's meditation on life:

Oughtn't a life to be something you could handle and produce? . . . Millions of things came back to her. Atoms danced apart and massed themselves. But how did they compose what people called a life?[309]

emotion and impulse are held in check by all the circumstancial details—a dozen lines which have been omitted here—intended to anchor feeling to the realists' reality, or to integrate the two. But the fusion will not work; the atoms of concrete and abstract remain separate. The catalysis achieved in the case of Bernard by music, movement and freedom from the contingent fails to operate here.

Between the Acts, where the atmosphere is that of an interlude, fantastic and unconstrained, and which deliberately avoids expressing certain forms and aspects of reality, admits of a return of the lyrical element. More fugitive, lighter and more elusive than in *The Waves*, although not parodied as in *Orlando*, it is disguised; there is no excess; it slips by almost unnoticed. Isa at her dressing table catches a glimpse of the terrace where her little boy and two nursemaids are walking; she taps on the window to catch their attention; they do not hear.

The drone of the trees was in their ears; the chirp of birds; other incidents of garden life, inaudible, invisible to her in the bedroom, absorbed them.[310]

[307] The Y, p. 229 (213)   [308] The Y, p. 227 (211)
[309] The Y p. 395 (366-7)   [310] B the A p. 20 (14)

The two adjectives implying separation and incommunicability condense the mist of reverie which surrounded Isa at her looking glass, and a single sentence with ascending rhythm unfolds immensity around our isolation:

Isolated on a green island, hedged about with snowdrops, laid with a counterpane of puckered silk, the innocent island floated under her window.[311]

And the longing to get free of the bondage of space gradually takes shape: Isa, turning once more to her looking glass and to her love, murmurs broken scraps of verse:

Where we know not, where we go not, neither know nor care.[312]

And if, hesitating between one rhyme and another, she mechanically picks up the telephone to order fish, this down to earth interlude, far from interrupting the flow of feeling, gives it greater pathos. And even the conversation of which we hear only half: the number rung, the names of fish, sound like mysterious formulae. In the pageant, this lyricism breaks out here and there in the general ferment, between the fragments of conversation, appearing and disappearing amid the variegated crowd like one guest among many, one colour among many.

There . . . would the dead leaf fall, when the leaves fall, on the water. Should I mind not again to see may tree or nut tree? Not again to hear on the trembling spray the thrush sing, or to see, dipping and diving as if he skimmed waves in the air, the yellow woodpecker?[313]

Or again, in the narrow path leading to the greenhouse, with William Dodge following her, Isa hums:

Fly then, follow . . . the dappled herds in the cedar grove, who, sporting, play, the red with the roe, the stag with the doe. Fly, away. I grieving stay. Alone I linger, I pluck the bitter herb by the ruined wall, the churchyard wall, and press its sour, its sweet, its sour, long grey leaf, so, twixt thumb and finger. . . .[314]

Later on, picking a rose and then letting it drop, and repeating the last words of her reverie as she resumes her train of thought, she goes on:

[311] B the A p. 20 (14) [312] B the A p. 21 (15)
[313] B the A p. 124 (104) [314] B the A p. 134 (112)

Where do I wander? . . . Down what draughty tunnels? Where the eyeless wind blows? And there grows nothing for the eye. No rose. To issue where? In some harvestless dim field where no evening lets fall her mantle; nor sun rises. All's equal there. Unblowing, ungrowing are the roses there. Change is not; nor the mutable and lovable; nor greetings nor partings; nor furtive findings and feelings, where hand seeks hand and eye seeks shelter from the eye.[315]

In their brevity, their simplicity, their fantasy and also in their use of words, these passages have an archaic quality reminiscent of the Elizabethan lyric and of folk song and befitting the elementary nature of the characters' emotions. They lack the richness and vigour of *The Waves*, but have a compelling power as of magic formulae. Here, beyond the anguish and aspiration with which Bernard's or Susan's mind and heart are tormented, Virginia Woolf touches that mysterious, uncertain ground of physical emotion, which can only be expressed stammeringly. As the summer evening fades into the silence of night, they tell of a vague uneasiness fading into the night of time.

It is undoubtedly in Virginia Woolf's sensibility that we shall find the common source of her humour and of her lyricism. That sensibility which threatened her independence and jeopardized her autonomy, which led her to conceive so clearly and so persistently the complex participation of human beings in one another, could not find room for the comic element, properly so-called. The outbursts of violent hostility which are displayed in *A Room of One's Own*, and still more in *Three Guineas*, represent exceptional moments when the artist in her abdicated to give free rein to that caustic turn of mind which all her friends admitted, and sometimes deplored. But from the dominant tone of her work, we must conclude that this was a secondary quality, an aspect of her nature fit for everyday life, in which, however, she found no positive elements capable of fertilizing her art. Passivity, vulnerability are the most constant traits revealed by her diary. Moreover, we find her continually on guard against sentimentality. Humour was precisely the way to keep in check that tendency of the more feminine side of her personality; it offered her a safeguard involving neither mutilation nor renunciation; the lightning flash of reason, veiled just enough not to deaden passion. For a passion for human beings, a passion for life—

[315] B the A pp. 181 (154-5)

however disturbing, however agonizing—just because it was agonizing—was for Virginia Woolf the essential thing in existence, and the essential thing in her own work. She seems to have been incapable of any average states of mind; at all events she considered such states as wholly unimportant. For her, only intensity mattered. All her quest, all her efforts were devoted to the elimination of wasted time, to the expression of pure intensity; and that is the way that leads to poetry. The shower of atoms, the myriad impressions that struck her, always called forth, sooner or later, that lyric note mingling wonder and anguish, and striving, through the opacity of language, to render the emotion of a human being at grips with the obsessive mysteries: life, love and death—and time and space, which are the forms under which we apprehend them.

Paradoxically, this lyricism, through which Virginia Woolf's novels part company with the traditional novel and enter the sphere of poetry, is also the element that connects them with the origins of the novel,[316] and through which her work may well recover, for many readers, an attraction it may have lost in other ways. Edouard Dujardin, being an interested party, is perhaps an unreliable authority; nevertheless that "triumphal entry of poetry into the novel"[317] without being as absolutely characteristic of contemporary literature as he declares, is a phenomenon which has been pointed out by other critics.[318] For a wide public, these great lyric themes with their universal character may well provide the interest, and the fundamental

[316] Cf. Richard Church, *The Growth of the English Novel*, p. 1: ". . . the general reader today tends to forget that the novelist is a poet, a bard, or at least a kinsman of those first beguilers. We see the relationship, and often the very identity coming up again and again as a valuable reminder of the genesis of the novel, and of the obsolescent literary forms (such as the epic) which it contrives to replace".

[317] Cf. E. Dujardin, *Le Monologue Intérieur*, p. 106: ". . . from 1885 dates the liberation of poetry, the new meaning given to poetry, and that triumphal entry of poetry into the novel which is the characteristic of contemporary literature."

[318] Cf. for instance Richard Church, *The Growth of the English Novel*, p. 2: "But at times a novel appears (such as *Wuthering Heights* by Emily Brontë, *Green Mansions* by W. H. Hudson, *The Waves* by Virginia Woolf, *The Body* by William Sansom) to remind us that the novelist is more, and of a nobler heredity, than the mere recorder of births, deaths and marriages; that he is concerned with the mystery of words and their music and with events as representing something larger than our social comprehension can envisage." A little later, speaking of the poet and the novelist, he writes: "Their approach to life, their sensuous apprehension, their interpretation in terms of significant symbols, may be different in degree, but they are the same in kind" (p. 4). Cf. also p. 213, where he speaks of Virginia Woolf's lyricism.

elements of communication, that the plot contributed to novels of classical type. Although Virginia Woolf's best novels are much read by the younger generation, this is only a hypothesis. If it were proved right, this convergence between the altered taste and habits of the reading public and the aims achieved in *To the Lighthouse,* that elegy, and *The Waves* and *Between the Acts,* play-novels or play-poems, would be the artist's revenge, the justification of her intuition and of her effort.

CONCLUSION

THE critical attitude defined at the outset of this study and, I trust, maintained throughout it, precludes any estimate of value by way of conclusion. Moreover, even if this were not undesirable on principle, my long familiarity with the work would make it impossible. I could not make abstraction of a whole network of elements: circumstances, intentions, reasons, with which from now onwards every book of Virginia Woolf's is involved for me, and which would prevent me from considering it as a finished product, an object of art to be classified in the museum of literature.

Hitherto I have avoided apologia, since my judgments have borne only on the relations between the work and the intention underlying it. It is in this connection that I spoke of the success of *The Waves* and the failure of *The Years*, for instance. This in no way implies that, from an absolute point of view, the former novel is better than the latter. To decide that, it would be necessary to judge the artist's intentions with reference to standards which could only be personal and, as such, arbitrary.

I have given cautious consideration, in the appropriate place, to Virginia Woolf's intentions, basing my opinions less on what might be called the laws of the genre than on general aesthetic principles.

I do not think I can go any further in this direction, nor am I entitled to generalize these particular comments. All that it seems legitimate to attempt is to gather together, in a quick sketch, the dominant features of the artist's work, just as at the end of Chapter III I endeavoured to sketch the artist herself.

In the light of these characteristics it will then be possible to risk a hypothesis about the possible future of that work. But it will only be a hypothesis; works of art go on living, under our very eyes, in as mysterious a fashion as human beings. And if there is some truth in Virginia Woolf's vision, as I believe there is, the complex way in which every work mingles with all those that surround it, obscurely and ceaselessly, alters their aspect and fashions their destiny.

CONCLUSION

As I embark on my "summing-up" I find myself in the position of Bernard, at the outset of that meditation that concludes *The Waves*. Like him, I have the illusion that "something . . . has roundness, weight, depth, is completed . . ." and can be grasped and handed over like a solid object: a globe in which the artist and her work are enclosed and made one.

But it is merely an illusion: Virginia Woolf herself has convinced us of that. Here are only fragments and stories: gestures, attitudes, words and thoughts have been collected; the story of one book and then of another has been told, the story of a vocation, of friendship and of passion, the story of non-existent characters and of non-temporal time—and none of these stories is true; the neat drawings with which we represent life on small squares of paper are not to be trusted. And yet that habit of mind must be satisfied which requires this handy picture, to be classified among all the rest.

No doubt, as the shifting and entangled realities I have tried to suggest grow dim in the memory, this picture will gradually lose its force as a magical formula and become merely an arid, cryptic arabesque. Without envisaging too clearly so unfortunate a fate, I hope that for the time being these few pages will reflect something of the life that I strove to awaken in the chapters that precede it.

Beneath the apparent variety of her writings, Virginia Woolf's work possesses remarkable unity. The fact that her novels represent less than half her production should not mislead us. Her reviews, her portrait sketches of literary figures, her general criticism, even her biographies, even *A Room of One's Own* betray a single preoccupation: the novel.

These writings are only a prolonged commentary in the margin of the various manifestations of that form of art to which she devoted her genius; thus she devoted her talent to it too, seeking, by setting her own experience against that of her predecessors, a definition, a formula for that literary genre which cannot be defined and knows no laws. She acquired, in this field, a fame which none will dispute.

Her analyses are consulted by every critic. But we must not forget that such research was never for Virginia Woolf an end in itself; it was at once a preparation for her work as novelist and a residue of that work. However interesting, however highly esteemed these critical writings may be—and some attribute to them a surer and more enduring value than to her novels—they should be relegated to the secondary place and the accessory role that Virginia Woolf ascribed to them. By considering them from this point of view, moreover, we shall avoid the common error of believing that she took an interest in technique for its own sake, and that her perpetual experimenting with new forms was merely an aesthete's game, intended to compensate for or to disguise certain deficiencies in her creative genius.

Enough has been said, surely, to show that nothing is further from the truth. Finding earlier formulae—Defoe's and Jane Austen's as well as Bennett's—unsuitable for her purpose, she rejected them, as a craftsman rejects tools or materials which would falsify his intentions and distort his conceptions. Those outmoded forms which the masters of the novel had used successfully before her could not contain or express her vision of reality. To dispute the validity of this argument, invoking against it the fruitful merits of discipline and constraint, seems futile. Virginia Woolf did not take the easiest path. On the contrary: in the way she chose, down which she ventured alone and where she remained alone, in spite of the similarities that may be discovered in the parallel attempts of Dorothy Richardson, James Joyce, Proust and Faulkner, she had to invent everything, matter and form.

So much stress has been laid on her so-called formal experiments that this double aspect of her originality has escaped notice. It is fundamental, none the less. Virginia Woolf is less an artist in quest of a form than a consciousness in quest of reality, a human being in quest of herself. Reality, the self: problems for a philosopher, not for a novelist, it may be said, or futile preoccupations of drawing-room intellectuals whom a harsher contact with everyday life would have torn from their egocentric meditations and at the same time would have provided the answer they sought.

Neither of these two interpretations is valid in the case of Virginia Woolf. Bergsonians, relativists, empiricists, associationists, idealists, existentialists, may each in turn claim her as an adept: she belongs to none of these philosophical schools, and she participates in all of them. She has no pretensions to abstract thought: her domain is life, not ideology. Her reality is not a factor to be specified in some equation of the universe: it is the Sussex downs, the London streets, the wave breaking on the shore, the woman sitting opposite her in the train, memories flashing into the mind from nowhere, a beloved being's return into nothingness; it is all that is not ourselves and yet is so closely mingled with ourselves that the two enigmas—reality and self—make only one. But the important thing is the nature or quality of this enigma. It does not merely puzzle the mind; it torments the whole being, even while defining it. To exist, for Virginia Woolf, meant experiencing that dizziness on the ridge between two abysses of the unknown, the self and the non-self.

The hypersensitivity, the temperamental instability, the intense zest for life that kept her constantly keyed up to the highest pitch, were no doubt the physiological and psychological sources of this obsession. I mention this again in order to reaffirm that this was no purely intellectual activity, but a dramatic involvement of the whole personality.[1] This total commitment is what makes the novels of Virginia Woolf vibrate with the pulse of that human experience from which they spring. All the artist's virtuosity, all her efforts are bent towards the faithful expression of that experience. It is true that they ended by substituting one literary convention for another. But this convention (and all expression requires some such support) offered her, instead of that opaque screen which she rejected, the transparency that she sought. It is easier to feel or even to describe this transparency than to define it. It is the transposition into writing of that attribute of the inner life which Virginia Woolf held essential.

It does away with time and space and makes possible the telescoping of past and present, of the here and the elsewhere, the self and the non-self; it disintegrates objects and personalities and replaces them by that universal participation which Virginia Woolf's vision so disturbingly reveals. And this disintegrated world harbours and gives rise to anguish. Here the scattered personality, in search of self, experiences nothingness. But, as against this ultimate liability, we must count as an asset the quest

[1] Cf. George Whalley, *The Poetic Process*, p. xxxiv. Although condemning certain excesses of narcissistic art, the critic asserts: "So intricate, and delicate, and impossible is the making in art that it absorbs the whole of the artist's energy and attention; the virtue of humility and disinterestedness are forced upon him by the nature of his activity. But that does not mean that his work is amoral or powerless to communicate and influence."

itself; along the path that leads to the abyss, it oscillates between despair and joy, between solitude and communion; although it ends in doubt, yet the trail is blazed with certainties.

All these contradictions form a challenge to reason. They also preclude any possibility of finding an ethical system, strictly speaking, in Virginia Woolf's work. Yet if the interpretation of life which she offers cannot be matched with universally valid and practically useful rules of conduct, there emerges from it, none the less, a lesson whose significance exceeds that of any formula. It can be summed up in a single word, of which the whole of her work is the explanation, the definition, re-examined constantly and ever more searchingly: "Being." Being as opposed to seeming, believing, thinking, wanting, doing.

The exemplary value of this lesson is due, no doubt, to the compelling suggestive power of a style and form which are, on the whole, perfectly adapted to their object, but also to the nature of the lives portrayed. "Astonishingly ordinary lives" of "people on holiday", we might say, combining the expressions of J. J. Mayoux and David Daiches. No inner or outer upheaval uproots them from the familiar ground of everyday, or impels them to spectacular or memorable attitudes of heroism.

In the catastrophic world of today, they may appear unworthy of our attention or interest. Such characters may seem to belong to another period, almost to another planet. Must we conclude from this that they, and what they represent, and the work of art in which they exist, are doomed to sink into oblivion? Surely not. For beneath our characteristic and bewildering agitation, beneath the threats that obsess us and that take on a new name every year, our daily life is still the same accumulation of insignificant doings, of unsensational feelings, of memories and aspirations, of anxieties and distress that survive unchanged through the centuries. The present-day fashion for the abnormal, or a more permanent love for the romantic, may deter the general public from appreciating Virginia Woolf.

But this is surely only an ephemeral phenomenon. In the novel, as in the theatre, there are many works today that shed an unfamiliar light on common experience, that show it as disturbing, fantastic or horrible, in a word that reveal excitement in regions to which the most timid, the humblest and the most dispossessed have access. Who knows if the ever-increasing ease with which we move about and uproot ourselves in the modern world may not bring about a renewed interest in the literature that deals with the stillness of the inner life, of which Virginia Woolf's novels are signal examples? One can picture a day when, blasé with his conquest of space, the reader may turn towards the conquest of time, and seek escape in Jacob's room or by the window where Mrs Ramsay sits, or in the deserted restaurant which is the scene of Bernard's meditation. Such an escape would bring him back to the elementary truths.

The density of the moment, its polyvalence, its weight of existence, which can only be felt in contemplative stillness, in silence and solitude, these are the realities most seriously jeopardized by our civilization. Those for whom they have been obliterated by the demands of productivity and the bondage of a herd existence can learn them anew from the author of "The Moment." And just because her characters are not bound to a social or historic context that would have dated them and rendered them outmoded, they will reveal with ever-increasing clarity (once the ephemeral trappings that still disguise them have worn away) more and more of the integral humanity which is their substance.

The fact that they belong to a social minority, and one in process of disappearing, will then no longer seem a flaw liable to alienate the sympathy or interest of readers. What does it matter to us today if Mme de Clèves was a princess or Catherine Earnshaw a landed proprietor, and if neither of them took any interest in the economic, social or political problems of her day, although these were as acute and exciting as those of our own? The burning questions of the day are forever passing into history, and once they are no longer being dealt with in the newspapers we turn to historians to read about them, not to novelists.

The controversy aroused by what some have called "the clerks' betrayal" and others "commitment" was fostered by historic circumstances: it became thereby the more impassioned, the less rational or pertinent. The only commitment which confers weight and authenticity on a work of art is not its commitment to some particular cause as against some other cause, but the artist's commitment to life. The intensity with which he experiences the human condition, not some particular condition of existence, is the basic deposit which, in his work, will survive all kinds of erosion.

It is not because of her attack on the Holmeses and Bradshaws of the world, the Lord Mayors, the Church or the Army, commercialism, patriotism or fascism, that Virginia Woolf will survive the test of time. I have stressed these examples of "commitment" to contemporary issues, not because they add any virtue to her work—I should be inclined to assert the contrary—but because they betoken a vitality, an awareness of the world, an infinitely richer kind of interest and contact than has commonly been ascribed to her. The figure of Antigone, which she evokes more than once with a sense of kinship, Antigone with her passion for truth, independence and integrity, holds undoubted fascination and wins our sympathy.

True, it must be admitted that this fascination and the sympathy we feel are not wholly pure. This Antigone is too much of a political or moral heroine, and as such she is subject to the vicissitudes of history and ethics. But she is more than that: her particular passions derive their determination and their violence from an unconditional and unconditioned passion that can be identified with the instinct of life.

It was by this untamed ardour, and not by the struggle against Creon which was only a sign of it, that Virginia Woolf recognized *her* heroine. The "What am I?" and the "What is life?" that echo constantly throughout the Diary are her cries of revolt against the false or one-sided affirmations that conspire to enslave and degrade us. It matters little that she left these questions without any answer other than the eternal sound of the waves breaking on the shore. It is the special attribute of works of art, the secret of their permanence and of the need for their perpetual renewal, that they bring us only a reflection, an echo, a symbol of that reality of which the artist has been granted a glimpse during a moment of vision.

BIBLIOGRAPHY

I. BOOKS BY VIRGINIA WOOLF

With the exception of Hogarth Press pamphlets, only works published in book form are included in this list. For other pamphlets and for articles, prefaces, essays and other writings the reader is referred to B. J. Kirkpatrick's *Bibliography of Virginia Woolf*, the Soho Bibliographies, Hart-Davis, London, 1957.

The Voyage Out, London, Duckworth, 1915.

The Mark on the Wall, Hogarth Press, Richmond, 1917 (also in *Monday or Tuesday* and *A Haunted House*).

Kew Gardens, Hogarth Press, Richmond, 1919 (also in *Monday or Tuesday* and *A Haunted House*).

Night and Day, London, Duckworth, 1919.

Monday or Tuesday, Hogarth Press, Richmond, 1921 (all the stories in this collection except "A Society" and "Blue and Green" were reprinted in *A Haunted House*).

Jacob's Room, Hogarth Press, Richmond, 1922.

Mr Bennett and Mrs Brown, Hogarth Press, London, 1924 (also in *The Captain's Death Bed*).

The Common Reader, Hogarth Press, London, 1925.

Mrs Dalloway, Hogarth Press, London, 1925 (Only the American edition, in The Modern Library, 1928, has an introduction by V. W.).

To the Lighthouse, Hogarth Press, London, 1927.

Orlando: A Biography, Hogarth Press, London, 1928 (in the Uniform Edition of 1933 and later editions the 8 illustrations were omitted).

A Room of one's Own, Hogarth Press, London, 1929.

On Being Ill, Hogarth Press, London, 1930 (also in *The Moment*).

The Waves, Hogarth Press, London, 1931.

A Letter to a Young Poet, Hogarth Press, London, 1932 (also in *The Death of the Moth*).

The Common Reader: Second Series, Hogarth Press, London, 1932.

Flush: A Biography, Hogarth Press, London, 1933.

Walter Sickert: A Conversation, Hogarth Press, London, 1934 (also in *The Captain's Death Bed*).

The Years, Hogarth Press, London, 1937.

Three Guineas, Hogarth Press, London, 1938.

Reviewing, Hogarth Press, 1939 (also in *The Captain's Death Bed*).

Roger Fry: A Biography, Hogarth Press, London, 1940.
Between the Acts, Hogarth Press, London, 1941.
The Death of the Moth and Other Essays, Hogarth Press, London, 1942.
A Haunted House and Other Short Stories, Hogarth Press, London, 1943 (actually published January 31, 1944).
The Moment and Other Essays, Hogarth Press, London, 1947.
The Captain's Death Bed and Other Essays, Hogarth Press, London, 1950.
A Writer's Diary, Hogarth Press, London, 1953.
Virginia Woolf and Lytton Strachey: Letters, edited by Leonard Woolf and James Strachey, Hogarth Press and Chatto & Windus, London, 1956.
Granite and Rainbow: Essays, Hogarth Press, London, 1958.

Translations, in collaboration with S. S. KOTELIANSKY:

Stavrogin's Confession (F. M. Dostoevsky), Hogarth Press, London, 1922.
Tolstoi's Love Letters, Hogarth Press, London, 1923.
Talks with Tolstoi (A. B. Goldenveizer), Hogarth Press, London, 1923.

II. BOOKS ON VIRGINIA WOOLF

The works briefly discussed on pages 15-24 of the Introduction are marked with an asterisk.

BADENHAUSSEN, Ingebord, *Die Sprache Virginia Woolf's: Ein Beitrag zur Stilistik des modernen englischen Romans*, Marburg, 1931.

*BENNETT, Joan, *Virginia Woolf: Her Art as a Novelist*, Cambridge University Press, 1945, 131 pp.

*BLACKSTONE, Bernard, *Virginia Woolf: A Commentary*, Hogarth Press, London, 1949, 256 pp.

*BLACKSTONE, Bernard, *Virginia Woolf*, Longmans Green, London, 1952, 38 pp.

BREWSTER, Dorothy, *Virginia Woolf's London*, Allen & Unwin, London, 1959, 120 pp.

BREWSTER, Dorothy, *Virginia Woolf*, Allen and Unwin Ltd, London, 1963, 184 pp.

*CHAMBERS, R. L., *The Novels of Virginia Woolf*, Oliver & Boyd, Edinburgh, London, 1947, 102 pp.

*CHASTAING, Maxime, *La Philosophie de Virginia Woolf*, Presses Universitaires de France, Paris, 1951, viii, 200 pp.

*DAICHES, David, *Virginia Woolf*, New Directions, Norfolk, Conn., 1942, 169 pp.; Nicholson & Watson, London, 1945, 151 pp.

*DELATTRE, Floris, *Le Roman Psychologique de Virginia Woolf*, J. Vrin, Paris, 1932, 268 pp.

BIBLIOGRAPHY

FINKE, Ilse, *Virginia Woolf's Stellung zur Wirklichkeit*, Marburg, 1933.

*FORSTER, E. M., *Virginia Woolf* (The Rede Lecture, 1941), Cambridge University Press, 1942, 27 pp.

GRUBER, Ruth, *Virginia Woolf: A Study*, Tauchnitz, Leipzig, 1935, 100 pp.

*HAFLEY, James, *The Glass Roof*, University of California Press, 1954.

*HOLTBY, Winifred, *Virginia Woolf*, Wishart, London, 1932, 205 pp.

*KIRKPATRICK, B. J., *A Bibliography of Virginia Woolf*, Rupert Hart-Davis, London, 1957, 180 pp.

LOHMULLER, Gertrude, *Die Frau im Werk von Virginia Woolf*, Universitätsverlag von Robert Noske, Leipzig, 1937, 102 pp.

MOODY, A. D., *Virginia Woolf*, Writers and Critics Series, Oliver & Boyd, Edinburgh and London, 1963, 119 pp.

*NATHAN, Monique, *Virginia Woolf par elle-même*, Editions du Seuil, Paris, 1956, 192 pp.

*NEWTON, Deborah, *Virginia Woolf*, Melbourne, University Press, 1946, 79 pp.

*PIPPETT, Aileen, *The Moth and the Star: A Biography of Virginia Woolf*, Little, Brown & Co., Boston and Toronto, 1955, 368 pp.

*RANTAVAARA, Irma, *Virginia Woolf and Bloomsbury*, Helsinki, 1953, 171 pp.

WEIDNER, E., *Impressionismus und Expressionismus in den Romanen Virginia Woolf's*, Greifswald Diss., 1934, 115 pp.

WIGET, Erik, *Virginia Woolf und die Konzeption der Zeit in ihren Werken.* Abhandlung zur Erlangung der Doktorwürde der Philosophischen Fakultät der Universitat's Zurich, Juris, Zurich, 1949, 125 pp.

III. ARTICLES ON VIRGINIA WOOLF

AIKEN, Conrad, "The Novel as a Work of Art", *Dial*, July 1927.

—— "Orlando", *Dial*, February 1929, pp. 147-49.

ANNAN, Noel, "The Legacy of the Twenties", *The Listener*, March 22, 1951.

ARROWSMITH, J. E. S., "The Waves", *Mercury*, December 1931, pp. 204-5.

BEACH, Joseph Warren, "The Novel from James to Joyce", *Nation*, 132, June 10, 1931, pp. 634-6.

—— "Virginia Woolf", *English Journal*, October 1937, pp. 603-12.

BECK, Warren, "For Virginia Woolf", in: *Forms of Modern Fiction*, edited by William Van O'Connor, University of Minnesota Press, Minneapolis, 1948, pp. 243-54.

BELL, Clive, "Virginia Woolf", *Dial*, December 1924, pp. 451-65.

BENNETT, Arnold, "Virginia Woolf's *To the Lighthouse*", *The Evening Standard*, June 23, 1927.

BENNETT, Joan, "Le Journal inédit de Virginia Woolf", *Roman*, janvier 1951, pp. 6-8.

BLANCHE, Jacques-Emile, "Entretien avec Virginia Woolf", *Nouvelles Littéraires*, 13 août 1927.

—— "Un nouveau Roman de Virginia Woolf" (*Orlando*), *Nouvelles Littéraires*, 16 février 1929.

BOWEN, Elizabeth, "*Between the Acts*", *The New Statesman and Nation*, July 19, 1941.

—— "The Achievement of Virginia Woolf", *New York Times*, Book Rev., June 26, 1949, pp. 1-21.

—— "The Principle of her Art was Joy", *New York Times*, Book Rev. Vol LIX, No. 8, February 21, 1954.

BRACE, M., "Worshipping solid Objects: The Pagan World of Virginia Woolf", *Accent Anthology*, Harcourt Brace, New York, 1946, pp. 489-95.

BRADBROOK, M. C., "Notes on the Style of Virginia Woolf", *Scrutiny*, May 1932, pp. 33-8.

BROOKS, B. G., "Virginia Woolf", *Nineteenth Century and After*, No. 130, December 1941, pp. 334-40.

BULLETT, Gerald, "*Mrs Dalloway*", *Saturday Review*, May 30, 1925, p. 588.

—— "*Orlando*", *English Journal*, December 1928, pp. 793-800.

—— "Virginia Woolf soliloquises", *New Statesman*, October 10, 1931.

BURGUM, E. B., "Virginia Woolf and the Empty Room", *Antioch Review*, No. 7, December 1943, pp. 596-611.

BURRA, Peter, "Virginia Woolf", *Nineteenth Century and After*, No. 115, January 1934, pp. 512-25.

CANTWELL, Robert, "The Influence of James Joyce", *New Republic*, No. 77, December 27, 1933, pp. 200-1.

CAREW, Dudley, "Virginia Woolf", *The London Mercury*, May 1926.

CAZAMIAN, Louis, "L'Œuvre de James Joyce", *Revue Anglo-Américaine*, décembre 1924.

—— "La Philosophie de Virginia Woolf" (Review of the essay by Maxime Chastaing), *Etudes Anglaises*, oct.-déc. 1952.

CECIL, Lord David, "Epitaph on Virginia Woolf", *Times Lit. Supp.*, April 12 and 19, 1941.

CHEVALIER, Jacques, "Le continu et le Discontinu", *Cahiers de la Nouvelle Journée*, 1929.

CHURCH, Margaret, "Concepts of Time in Novels of Virginia Woolf and Aldous Huxley", *Modern Fiction Studies*, vol. 5, No. 2, May 1955, pp. 19-24.

BIBLIOGRAPHY

CLUTTON-BROCK, Alan, "Vanessa Bell and Her Circle", *The Listener*, May 4, 1961.

COLLINS, H. P., "The Common Reader", *Criterion*, July 1925.

COWLEY, Malcolm, "England under Glass", *New Republic*, 105 October 6, 1941, 440 pp.

CRAVEN, Thomas Jewell, "Mr Roger Fry and the Artistic Vision", *Dial*, July 1921, vol. LXXI.

CUSTANCE, John, "Wisdom in Madness", *Listener*, April 10, 1952.

DATALLER, R., "Mr Lawrence and Mrs Woolf", *Essays in Criticism*, VIII, No. 1, January 1958.

DELATTRE, Floris, "La Durée Bergsonienne dans le Roman de Virginia Woolf", *Revue Anglo-Américaine*, déc. 1931, pp. 97-108.

—— "Le nouveau Roman de Virginia Woolf" (*The Years*), *Etudes Anglaises*, juillet 1937, pp. 289-96.

—— "Un Roman lyrique de Virginia Woolf: *The Waves*", *Impressions*, Paris, No. 19-20, janv.-févr. 1938.

—— Review of: *Les Vagues*, by Virginia Woolf, translated by M. Yourcenar, *Etudes Anglaises*, avr.-juin, 1938, pp. 201-2.

—— Review of: *Three Guineas*, by Virginia Woolf, *Etudes Anglaises*, avr.-juin 1939, pp. 177-8.

DERBYSHIRE, S. H., "An Analysis of Mrs Woolf's *To the Lighthouse*", *College English*, III, January 1942, pp. 353-60.

DOTTIN, Paul, "Les Sortilèges de Mrs Virginia Woolf", *Revue de France*, 1er avril 1930 (also in *Revue de l'Enseignement des Langues Vivantes*, juin 1930).

ELIOT, T. S., "Ulysses, Order and Myth", *Dial*, 1923 (see O'Connor, *Forms of Modern Fiction*).

—— "Les Lettres Anglaises: Le Roman Contemporain", *NRF*, 1er mai 1927.

—— "On Virginia Woolf's *Monday or Tuesday*", *Dial*, vol. LXXI, August 1928.

—— "On Clive Bell's *Civilization*", *Criterion*, vol. VIII, September 1928.

—— "Virginia Woolf", *Horizon*, May 1941, vol. I, pp. 313-16, II, No. 17.

EMPSON, William, "Virginia Woolf", *Scrutinies II*, Wishart, 1931.

FAIRLEY, Margaret, "Symbols of Life", *The Canadian Forum*, January 1932.

FORSTER, E. M., "The Novels of Virginia Woolf", *New Criterion*, No. 4, April 1926, pp. 277-86.

—— "The Art of Virginia Woolf", *Atlantic*, 170, September 1942, pp. 82-90.

FULTON, A. R., "Expressionism: Twenty Years after", *Sewanee Review*, vol. 52, 1944.

"Galahad, Sir", "Virginia Woolf", *Neue Schweizer Rundschau*, 1948, pp. 528-41.

Gillet, Louis, "Virginia Woolf et le Conte Philosophique", *Nouvelles Littéraires*, 26 janv. 1935.

Gould, Gerald, "*The Waves*", *The Observer*, October 11, 1931.

Graham, John, "Time in the Novels of Virginia Woolf", *University of Toronto Quarterly*, January 1949, pp. 186-201.

Grant, Duncan, "Virginia Woolf", *Horizon*, II, June 1941, pp. 402-6.

Gregory, Alyse, "A Fanfare from Bloomsbury", *Dial*, vol. LXXXII, June 1929 (On Clive Bell's *Civilization*).

Hartley, Lodwick, "Of Time and Mrs Woolf", *Sewanee Review*, vol. XLVII, April-June 1939.

Hartley, L. P., "New Novels", *The Week End Review*, October 24, 1931.

—— "The Literary Lounger", *Sketch*, August 13, 1941.

Hartman, G. H., "Virginia's Web", *Chicago Review*, XIII, 1960, pp. 20-32.

Havard-Williams, Peter and Margaret, "Bateau Ivre: The Symbol of the Sea in Virginia Woolf's *The Waves*", *English Studies*, XXXIV, 1953, pp. 9-17.

—— "Mystical Experience in Virginia Woolf's *The Waves*", *Essays in Criticism*, IV, 1954, pp. 71-84.

—— "Perceptive Contemplation in the Work of Virginia Woolf", *English Studies*, XXXV, 1954, pp. 97-116.

Hawkins, Desmond, "Virginia Woolf's *The Waves*", *The Twentieth Century*, January 1932.

Hoare, D. M., "Virginia Woolf", *The Cambridge Review*, October 16, 1931.

Holtby, Winifred, "Novels of the Year", *The Bookman*, December 1931.

Hughes, Richard, "Virginia Woolf", *Spectator*, November 20, 1953.

"*Impressions*", "Hommage à Virginia Woolf", janv.-févr. 1938, 5e série, nov. 19-20.

Isherwood, Christopher, "Virginia Woolf", *Decision*, May 1941.

Jaloux, Edmond, "*Les Lauriers sont coupés*, d'Edouard Dujardin", *Nouvelles Littéraires*, 17 janv. 1925.

Josephson, Matthew, "Virginia Woolf and the Modern Novel", *New Republic*, 66, April 15, 1931, pp. 239-41.

Kelsey, Mary Electra, "Virginia Woolf and the She Condition", *Sewanee Review*, October-December 1931.

Kenyon Review, "Unities of Modern Fiction", Spring 1955.

Kronenberger, Louis, "Virginia Woolf as Critic", *The Nation*, No. 155. October 17, 1942, pp. 382-5.

BIBLIOGRAPHY

LEAVIS, F. R., "After *To the Lighthouse*" (review of *Between the Acts*), *Scrutiny*, 10, January 1942, pp. 295-8.

LEAVIS, Q. D., "Caterpillars of the Commonwealth Unite" (in connection with *Three Guineas*), *Scrutiny*, September 1938, p. 203 *et seq.*

—— "Leslie Stephen: Cambridge Critic", *Scrutiny*, March 1939, pp. 404-15.

LE BRETON, Maurice, "Problème du Moi et Technique du Roman chez Virginia Woolf", *Journal de Psychologie*, 40ᵉ année, janv.-mars, 1947.

LEHMANN, John, "Working with Virginia Woolf", *The Listener*, January 13, 1955.

LOGÉ, Marc, "Quelques Romancières contemporaines", *Revue Politique et Littéraire*, 21 nov. 1925.

LYND, Sylvia, "Mrs Woolf's Experiment", *News Chronicle*, October 14, 1931.

MACAULAY, Rose, "Virginia Woolf", *Horizon*, May 1941, vol. III, No. 17.

MACCARTHY, Desmond, "Phantasmagoria", *Sunday Times*, October 14, 1928.

—— "Le Roman Anglais d'Après Guerre", *Revue de Paris*, 1932, tome III, pp. 129-52.

MACNEICE, L., "A Poet's View", *The Observer*, September 29, 1954.

MANN, Thomas, "The Artist and Society", *The Listener*, June 5, 1952.

MARCEL, Gabriel, "*Les Vagues* par Virginia Woolf", *NRF*, févr. 1932.

MAUROIS, André, "Première rencontre avec Virginia Woolf", *Nouvelles Littéraires*, 19 janvier 1929.

MAYOUX, Jean-Jacques, "A propos d'*Orlando* de Virginia Woolf", *Europe*, 15 janv. 1930, nᵒ 85, tome XXII, pp. 117-22.

—— "Le Roman de l'Espace et du Temps: Virginia Woolf", *Revue Anglo-Américaine*, avr., 1930, pp. 312-26.

—— "Sur un livre de Virginia Woolf", *Revue Anglo-Américaine*, juin, 1938.

MELLERS, W. H., "Mrs Woolf and Life" (review of *The Years*), *Scrutiny*, 6, June, 1937, pp. 71-5.

—— "Virginia Woolf: The last Phase", *Kenyon Review*, 4, Autumn 1942, pp. 381-7.

MONROE, N. E., "The Inception of Mrs Woolf's Art", *College Bookman*, 2, December 1940, pp. 217-30.

MORTIMER, Raymond, "Mrs Woolf and Mr Strachey", *American Bookman*, February 1929.

MUIR, Edwin, "Virginia Woolf", *Nation & Athenaeum*, April 17, 1926.

—— "Virginia Woolf's Last Novel", *The Listener*, July 24, 1941.

MUIR, Edwin, "The Decline of Imagination", *The Listener*, May 10, 1951.

—— "Some Conclusions", *The Observer*, September 26, 1954.

NICOLSON, Harold, "The New Spirit in Literature, VII", *The Listener*, November 18, 1931.

—— "Is the Novel Dead?", *The Observer*, August 29, 1954.

O'BRIEN, Justin M., "La Mémoire involontaire avant Proust", *Revue de Littérature Comparée*, XIX, 1939, pp. 19-36.

OCAMPO, Victoria, "Virginia Woolf, Orlando y Cia", *Sur*, Buenos Aires, 1938.

OVERCARSH, F. L., "Virginia Woolf", *Accent*, 10, Winter 1959, pp. 107-22.

PEEL, Robert, "Virginia Woolf", *The Criterion*, October 1933, vol. XIII, No. 50, pp. 78-96.

PHELPS, G. H., "Virginia Woolf and the Russians", *Cambridge Review*, October 17, 1942, vol. LXIV.

PINGAUD, Bernard, "Six Personnages en Quête d'un Héros", *L'Express*, 23 janvier 1958.

PLOMER, William, "Virginia Woolf", *Horizon*, May 1941, vol. III, No. 17, pp. 323-7.

PRITCHETT, V. S., "*The Waves*", *The Christian Science Monitor*, November 21, 1931.

PRYCE-JONES, Alan, "The Novelist's Fault", *The Observer*, September 26, 1954.

RALEIGH, John Henry, "The English Novel and the three Kinds of Time", *Sewanee Review*, Summer 1954, pp. 428-40.

RANSOM, John Crowe, "The Understanding of Fiction", *Kenyon Review*, No. 12, Spring 1950.

RILLO, Lila E., "Katherine Mansfield (1885-1923) and Virginia Woolf (1882-1941)", English Pamphlets Series, No. 7, Buenos Aires, 1944.

ROBERTS, John Hawley, "Towards Virginia Woolf", *Virginia Quart. Rev.*, 10, October 1934, p. 587-602.

—— "End of the English Novel", *Virginia Quart. Rev.*, 13, 1937, pp. 437-9.

—— "Vision and Design in Virginia Woolf", *PMLA*, September 1946, vol. LXI, pp. 835-47.

ROBERTS, R. Ellis, "Virginia Woolf", *The Bookman*, January 1928.

—— "Virginia Woolf", *The Bookman*, February 1930.

—— "Virginia Woolf, 1882-1941", *Saturday Review of Literature*, April 1941, XXIII, No. 25.

ROMAIN, Yvonne (de), "L'Evolution du Roman anglais", *Revue de Politique et de Littérature*, 3, janv. 1931.

ROUSSEAUX, André, "Le premier Roman de Virginia Woolf", *Figaro Littéraire*, 3 janv., 1953.

BIBLIOGRAPHY

RUSSELL, H. K., "Virginia Woolf's *To the Lighthouse*", *Explicator*, 8, March 1950.

SACKVILLE-WEST, V., "The Future of the Novel", *The Week-End Review*, October 18, 1930, p. 535.

—— "Virginia Woolf", *Horizon*, March 1941, vol. III, No. 17, pp. 318-23.

—— "Virginia Woolf and *Orlando*", *The Listener*, January 27, 1955.

ST JEAN, R. (de), "*Mrs Dalloway*", *Revue Hebdomadaire*, 16 mars 1929.

SALLÉ, Jean-Claude, "Sterne's Distinction of Time and Duration", *The Review of English Studies*, vol. VI, No. 22, April 1955.

SANDERS, C. R., "Lytton Strachey's Conception of Biography", *PMLA*, June 1951.

SAVAGE, D. S., "The Mind of Virginia Woolf", *South Atlantic Quart.*, 46, October 1947, pp. 556-73.

SCHORER, Mark, "The Chronicle of Doubt", *Virginia Quart. Rev.*, 18, Spring 1942, pp. 200-15.

—— "Fiction and the Matrix of Analogy", *Kenyon Review*, Autumn 1949.

SEGURA, Celia, "The Transcendental and the Transitory in Virginia Woolf's Novels", English Pamphlets Series, No. 4, Buenos Aires, 1943.

SIMON, Irene, "Some Aspects of Virginia Woolf's Imagery", *English Studies* (Holland), vol. XLI, No. 3, June 1960, pp. 180-96.

SMART, J. A., "Virginia Woolf", *Dalhousie Review*, 21, 1921, pp. 37-50.

SPENCER, Theodore, "Mrs Woolf's Novels", *New Republic*, 113, December 3, 1945, p. 758.

SQUIRE, J. C., "*Orlando*", *The Observer*, October 21, 1928.

SUTHERLAND, J. R., "Virginia Woolf", *The British Weekly*, October 24, 1929.

SWINNERTON, Frank, "Marionette Shows", *Evening News*, October 9, 1931.

TATE, Allen, "Techniques of Fiction", *Sewanee Review*, 52, Spring 1944.

Time and Tide, "Virginia Woolf", April 12, 1941.

Times Literary Supplement "The Air of Bloomsbury", August 20, 1954.

—— "The Perpetual Marriage", July 4, 1958.

TINDALL, William York, "Many-Leveled Fiction: Virginia Woolf to Ross Lockridge", *College English*, 10, November 1948, pp. 65-71.

TOYNBEE, Philip, "Virginia Woolf: A Study of Three Experimental Novels", *Horizon*, 14, November 1946, pp. 290-304.

—— "The Defense Brief", *The Observer*, September 5, 1954.

TREVELYAN, R. C., "*Roger Fry*, by Virginia Woolf", *The Abinger Chronicle*, April 1941.

TRILLING, Lionel, "The Life of the Novel", *Kenyon Review*, 12, Autumn 1946.

TROY, William, "Virginia Woolf, The Novel of Sensibility", *Symposium*, January-March 1932, pp. 53-63, and April-June 1937, pp. 153-66; also in *Profils*, January 1954, with the addition of a commentary of 1952 (cf. Zabel M. D.).

TURNELL, Martin, "Virginia Woolf", *Horizon*, July 1942.

VALERY-LARBAUD, "James Joyce", *NRF*, avril 1922.

VERGA, Ines, "Virginia Woolf's Novels and their Analogy to Music", English Pamphlets Series, No. 11, Buenos Aires, 1945.

VETTARD, Camille, "Proust et Einstein", *NRF*, 1er août 1922, tome XVIII, p. 385.

WAHL, Jean, "L'Angoisse et l'Instant", *NRF*, avril 1932, vol. 38.

WALPOLE, Hugh, "Virginia Woolf", *New Statesman and Nation*, June 14, 1941, p. 2.

WEST, Rebecca, "With a Secret Flowering", *New York Herald*, November 1931.

WILLIAMS, Orlo, "*To the Lighthouse*", *The Monthly Criterion*, July 1927, vol. VI, No. 1, p. 28.

—— "*The Waves*", *National Review*, December 1931.

WILSON, Angus, "Diversity and Depth", *Times Literary Supplement*, August 15, 1958.

—— "Sense and Sensibility in Recent Writing", *The Listener*, August 24, 1950, vol. XLIV, No. 1126.

WILSON, James Southall, "Time and Virginia Woolf", *Virginia Quarterly Review*, Spring 1942, vol. XVIII, pp. 267-76.

WRIGHT, Nathalie, "*Mrs Dalloway:* A Study in Composition"; *College English*, 5, April 1944, pp. 351-8.

ZABEL, Morton Dauwen, "The Victorian Ethos" (review of Noel Annan's *Leslie Stephen*), *The Nation*, March 1, 1952.

IV. GENERAL WORKS

Listed are works which either contain chapters on Virginia Woolf or which cast light on her work or character.

ALDRIDGE, John W., *Critiques and Essays on Modern Fiction, 1920-1951*, Ronald Press, New York, 1952, pp. xx, 610.

AUERBACH, Erich, *Mimesis*, A. Fracke, Berne, 1946, and Princeton University Press, 1953, 563 pp.

BIBLIOGRAPHY

ALLEN, Walter, *The English Novel: A Short Critical History*, Phoenix House, London, 1954 (partic. ch. 7: "1914 and After", pp. 327-348).

ANNAN, Noel Gilroy, *Leslie Stephen: His Thought and Character in Relation to his Time*, McGibbon & Kee, London, 1951, and Harvard University Press, 1952, viii, 342 pp.

BACHELARD, Gaston, *L'Eau et les Rêves*, José Corti, Paris.

—— *La terre et les Rêveries du Repos*, José Corti, Paris, 1948, 407 pp.

BEACH, Joseph Warren, *The Twentieth Century Novel: Studies in Technique*, p. 569, Appleton Century Crofts, New York & London, 1932 (pp. 485-500).

BELL, Clive, *Since Cézanne*, Chatto & Windus, London, 1922, pp. 229.

—— *Marcel Proust*, Hogarth Press, London, 1928, p. 88.

—— *Civilization* (1928), Penguin Books, 1947, 157 pp.

—— *French Impressionists*, with an introduction by Clive Bell, Phaidon Press, London, 1951 [1952], 18 pp.

—— *Old Friends, Personal Recollections*, Chatto & Windus, London, 1956, 200 pp.

BENNETT, Arnold, *The Savour of Life: Essays in Gusto*, Cassell, London 1928 (pp. 47-49 *et passim*).

BERESFORD, J. D., *Tradition and Experiment in Literature*, Oxford, 1929.

BOWEN, Elizabeth, *English Novelists*, Collins, London, 1942, 47 pp.

—— *Collected Impressions*, Longmans, Green, London, 1950, 245 pp.

BRACE, M., *Accent Anthology:* "Worshipping Solid Objects: The Pagan World of Virginia Woolf", Harcourt Brace, New York, 1946, pp. 489-95.

BREWSTER, D. & A. BURRELL, *Adventure or Experience* (pp. 77-116: "The Wild Goose: Virginia Woolf's Pursuit of Life"), Columbia Univ. Press, New York, 1930.

BROWER, R. A., *The Fields of Light: An Experience in Critical Reading* (Ch. on *Mrs Dalloway*), Oxford Univ. Press, New York, 1951.

BROWN, J. K., *Rhythm in the Novel*, University of Toronto Press, 1950.

BULLETT, Gerald, *Modern English Fiction: A Personal View*, London, 1926.

BURGUM, E. B., *The Novel and the World's Dilemma*, Oxford Univ. Press, New York, 1947, 352 pp.

CARRUTHERS, Joseph, *Scheherazade or The Future of the English Novel*, London, 1927.

CATTAUI, Georges, *T. S. Eliot*, Classiques du xxᵉ siècle, No. 29, Editions Universitaires, Paris, 1957, 143 pp.

CECIL, Lord David, *Poets and Story Tellers: A Book of Critical Essays*, Constable, London, 1949 (pp. 160-80).

CHEVALLEY, Abel, *Le Roman Anglais de notre Temps*, Oxford University Press, London, 1921, 256 pp.

CHURCH, Richard, *Growth of the English Novel*, Home Study Books, Methuen, London, 1951, 220 pp.

CLIFFORD, James L. (ed.), *Biography as an Art: Selected Criticism 1560-1960*, Oxford University Press, London and New York, 1962, xx, 256 pp.

COLLINS, Joseph, *The Doctor Looks at Literature: Psychological Studies of Life and Letters*, Allen & Unwin, London, 1923, 317 pp.

COMFORT, Alex, *The Novel and our Time*, Phoenix House, London, 1948, 80 pp.

CONNOLLY, Cyril, *Enemies of Promise*, Routledge & Kegan Paul, London, 1938, viii, 340 pp.

CORNWELL, Ethel F., *The Still Point: Themes and Variations in the Writings of T. S. Eliot, Coleridge, Yeats, Henry James, Virginia Woolf and D. H. Lawrence*, Rutgers Univ. Press, New Brunswick, 1962 (pp. 159-207).

COX, C. B., *The Free Spirit, A Study of Liberal Humanism in the Novels of George Eliot, E. M. Forster, Virginia Woolf, Angus Wilson*, Oxford Univ. Press, London, 1963 (pp. 103-16).

CUNLIFFE, J. W., *English Novelists in the Twentieth Century*, Macmillan, London, 1932 (*v.* pp. 201-58).

DAICHES, David, *The Novel and the Modern World*, Univ. of Chicago Press, 1938, x, 228 pp.

—— *The Present Age from 1920* (Introduction to English Literature, vol. V), The Cresset Press, London, 1958, x, 376 pp.

DELATTRE, Floris, *Feux d'Automne*, Didier, Paris, 1950 (pp. 226-47).

DOBREE, Bonamy, *The Lamp and the Lute: Studies in six Modern Authors*, Clarendon Press, Oxford, 1929, xvi, 133 pp.

—— *Modern Prose Style*, Oxford University Press, 1934.

DREW, Elizabeth, *The Modern Novel: Some Aspects of Contemporary Fiction*, Jonathan Cape, London, 1926, viii, 274 pp.

DUJARDIN, Edouard, *Les Lauriers sont coupés*, with preface by Valéry-Larbaud, Messein, Paris, 1924.

—— *Le Monologue Intérieur, son apparition, ses origines, sa place dans l'œuvre de James Joyce et dans le roman contemporain*, Albert Messein, Paris, 1931, 126 pp.

EDEL, Leon, *The Psychological Novel: 1900-1950*, J. B. Lippincott, New York and Philadelphia, 1955, 222 pp., also Rupert Hart-Davis, London, 1955, 147 pp.

EDGAR, Pelham, *The Art of the Novel: From 1700 to the Present Time*, Macmillan, London, 1934.

ELIOT, T. S., *Selected Essays 1917-1912*, Faber & Faber, London, 1932, 454 pp.

—— *Notes Towards the Definition of Culture*, Faber & Faber, London, 1948; Harcourt, Brace, N. Y., 1948, 128 pp.

ENRIGHT, D. J., *The Apothecary's Shop*, Secker, London, 1957, 236 pp.

EVANS, Ifor, *English Literature between the Wars*, Methuen, London, 1948, 133 pp.

FORSTER, E. M., *Aspects of the Novel*, Edward Arnold, London, 1927, 224 pp.

—— *Abinger Harvest*, Edward Arnold, London, 1936 (pp. 104-12: "The Early Novels of Virginia Woolf", 1925); also in a Pocket Edition, E. Arnold, 1940.

—— *Two Cheers for Democracy*, (pp. 280-90: "English Prose between 1918 and 1939" dated 1944) Arnold, London, 1951. This collection also contains "Virginia Woolf", The Rede Lecture 1941, and "On Anonymity", pp. 87-97.

FREEDMAN, Ralph, *The Lyrical Novel: Studies in Hermann Hesse, André Gide, and Virginia Woolf* (pp. 185-270), Princeton Univ. Press, Princeton, N. J., 1963.

FRIEDMAN, Melvin, *Stream of Consciousness: A Study in Literary Method*, Yale Univ. Press. New Haven, 1955, xi, 280 pp.

FRIERSON, W. C., *The English Novel in Transition, 1885-1940*, University of Oklahoma Press, Norman, 1942, xvi, 333 pp.

FRY, Roger, *The Artist and Psycho-Analysis*, Hogarth Press, London, 1924, 19 pp.

—— *Transformation*, Chatto & Windus, London, 1926, viii, 230 pp.

—— *Vision and Design*, Chatto & Windus, London, 1928, 302 pp.

GALLAND, René, *George Meredith, les cinquante premières années*, Paris, 1923 (pp. 296-8: portrait of Leslie Stephen).

GARNETT, David, *The Flowers of the Forest*, Chatto & Windus, London, 1955, 466 pp.

GILLET, Louis, *Esquisses Anglaises*, Firmin Didot, Paris, 1930 ("Virginia Woolf, 1er septembre 1929", pp. 209-24).

—— *Stèle pour James Joyce*, Sagittaire, Marseille, 1941, pp. 187.

GOULD, Gerald, *The English Novel of To-Day*, John Castle, London, 1924, 224 pp.

GRABO, C. H., *The Technique of the Novel*, Scribner's, New York, 1928.

HALEVY, Elie, *A History of the English People*, vol. V (vol. II of *Epilogue*), Ernest Benn, London, 1934 ("The Feminist Revolt", pp. 478-518).

HAMILL, Elizabeth, *These Modern Writers: An Introduction for Modern Readers*, Georgian House, Melbourne, 1946 (partic. ch. 8).

HENDERSON, Philip, *The Novel Today*, Lane, Bodley Head, 1936 (partic. pp. 87-91).

HOARE, Dorothy M., *Some Studies in the Modern Novel*, Chatto & Windus, London, 1938 (partic. pp. 36-67), 154 pp.

HUMPHREY, Robert, *Stream of Consciousness Technique: A Study of James Joyce, Virginia Woolf, Dorothy Richardson, William Faulkner and Others*, University of California Press, Berkeley and Los Angeles, 1954, and Cambridge University Press, vii, 129 pp.

ISAACS, J., *An Assessment of Twentieth Century Literature*, Secker & Warburg, London, 1951, 188 pp.

JALOUX, Edmond, *Au Pays du Roman*, Paris, 1931, 261 pp.

—— *D'Eschyle à Giraudoux*, Egloff, Fribourg, 1946 (pp. 251-60, "Mort de Virginia Woolf", April 20, 1941).

JAMESON, Storm, *The Writer's Situation and other Essays*, Macmillan, London, 1950, 200 pp.

JOHNSTONE, J. K., *The Bloomsbury Group: A Study of E. M. Forster, Lytton Strachey, Virginia Woolf and their Circle*, The Noonday Press, New York, 1954.

JONES, E. B. C. (See VERSCHOYLE).

KETTLE, Arnold, *An Introduction to the English Novel*, vol. 2: "Henry James to the Present", Hutchinson's University Library, London, 1953 (Ch. on *To the Lighthouse*).

KRONENBERGER, Louis, *The Republic of Letters: Essays on Various Writers* ("Virginia Woolf as Critic"), Knopf, New York, 1955.

KRUTCH, Joseph Wood, *Five Masters: A Study in the Mutation of the Novel*, Cape & Smith, New York, 1930.

LAWRENCE, Margaret, *The School of Femininity*, New York, 1936 (As: *We Write as Women*, London, 1937).

LEAVIS, F. R., *The Common Pursuit*, Chatto & Windus, London, 1952, 307 pp.

LEAVIS, Q. D., *Fiction and the Reading Public*, Chatto & Windus, London, 1932, xvi, 348 pp.

LEHMANN, John, *The Open Night*, Longmans, London, 1952, 248 pp.

—— *The Whispering Gallery*, Longmans, London, 1955, 342 pp.

LEWIS, Wyndham, *Men Without Art*, Cassell, London, 1934 (ch. 5 on V. W.).

LIDDELL, Robert, *A Treatise on the Novel*, Jonathan Cape, London, 1947, 168 pp.

—— *Some Principles of Fiction*, Jonathan Cape, London, 1953, 162 pp.

LINDNER, Gladys Dudley, *Marcel Proust, Reviews and Estimate in English*, Stanford Univ. Press, Cal., 1942.

LUBBOCK, Percy, *The Craft of Fiction*, Jonathan Cape, London, 1921, p. 276.

MACCARTHY, Desmond, *Memories*, Macgibbon & Kee, London, 1953 (*v.* "Bloomsbury: An unfinished Memoir", 1933).

—— *Criticism*, Putnam, London, 1932, xii, 311 pp.

—— *Leslie Stephen*, Cambridge Univ. Press, 1937, 46 pp.

McCormick, J., *Catastrophe and Imagination: An Interpretation of the Recent American and English Novel*, Longmans, London, 1957, xl, 327 pp.

McGehee, Edward Glenn, *Virginia Woolf: Experimentalist within Tradition* (Abstract of Thesis), Vanderbilt University, 1942.

Maitland, F. W., *The Life and Letters of Leslie Stephen*, Duckworth, London, 1906, viii, 510 pp.

Mansfield, Katherine, *Novels and Novelists*, Constable, London, 1930, 308 pp.

Maurois, André, *Quatre Etudes Anglaises*, Paris, 1927 (ch. IV, "La Jeune Littérature Anglaise", pp. 253-93).

—— *Mrs Dalloway*, French translation, Stock, 1929 (Preface).

Mayoux, Jean-Jacques, *L'Inconscient et la vie intérieure dans le Roman anglais: 1905-1940*. Centre Européen Universitaire, Nancy. Etude des Civilisations, fascicule 4, 1952.

—— *Vivants Piliers: le roman anglo-saxon et les symboles*, Julliard, Paris, 1960, pp. 296 (Partic.: "V. W. et l'Univers féminin", pp. 201-27).

Melchiori Giorgio, *The Tightrope Walkers: Studies of Mannerism in Modern English Literature*, pp. ix, 278, Routledge & Kegan Paul, London, 1956.

Mendilow, A. A., *Time and the Novel*, Peter Nevill, London, 1952, viii, 245 pp.

Meredith, George, *The Egoist*, 1879.

Meyer, K. R., *Zur erlebten Rede im englischen Roman des zwanzigsten Jahrhunderts*, Bern, 1957.

Meyerhof, Hans, *Time in Literature*, Univ. of California Press, Berkeley, 1955, xiv, 160 pp.

Monroe, N. Elizabeth, *The Novel and Society: A Critical Study of the Modern Novel*, Univ. of North Carolina Press, Chapel Hill, 1941, vi, 282 pp. (partic. pp. 188-224).

Moore, George Edward, *Principia Ethica*, Cambridge Univ. Press, 1903, xxvii, 232 pp.

Morrow, C., *Le Roman irréaliste dans les littératures contemporaines de la langue française et anglaise* (Thesis), Université de Toulouse, Didier, Paris, 1941.

Muir, Edwin, *Transition: Essays on Contemporary Literature*, Hogarth Press, London, 1926, ix, 218 pp.

—— *The Structure of the Novel*, Hogarth Press, London, 1928, 151 pp. (pp. 131-3).

—— *The Present Age from 1914*, Cresset Press, London, 1939, 309 pp. (pp. 129-54).

Muchnic, Helen, *Dostoiewsky's English Reputation: 1881-1936*, Northampton, 1938.

MULLER, Herbert J., *Modern Fiction: A Study of Values*, pp. 447, Funk & Wagnalls, New York, London, 1937 (ch. on: "Virginia Woolf and Feminine Fiction", pp. 317-28).

MURRY, John Middleton, *Countries of the Mind*, Oxford University Press, London, 1931, vi, 192 pp.

NICOLSON, Harold, *The Development of English Biography*, Hogarth Lectures on Literature, No. 4, Hogarth Press, London, 1927, 157 pp.

NELLI, René, *Lumière du Graal*, Cahiers du Sud, Paris, 1951, 336 pp.

O'CONNOR, William Van, *Forms of Modern Fiction*, Univ. of Minnesota Press, Minneapolis, 1948.

O'FAOLAIN, Sean, *The Vanishing Hero: Studies in the Novelists of the Twenties*, Little, Brown and Co., Boston, 1957, xliii, 210 pp.

PHELPS, Gilbert, *The Russian Novel in English Fiction*, Hutchinson, London, 1956.

PREVOST, Jean (editor), *Problèmes du Roman*, "Confluences", 21-24, 3e année, juillet-août 1943, 415 pp.

PRITCHETT, V. S., *The Living Novel*, Chatto & Windus, London, 1946, xi, 260 pp.

QUENNELL, Peter, *A Letter to Mrs Virginia Woolf* (Reply to "A Letter to a Young Poet"), Hogarth Press, London, 1932, 24 pp.

RAHV, Philip, *Image and Idea*, New Directions, 1949 (*v.* pp. 139-43); Weidenfeld & Nicolson, London, 1957.

READ, Herbert, *Reason and Romanticism*, Faber & Gwyer, 1926 (partic. ch. 11).

RICKWOOD, C. H., *Towards Standards of Criticism*, Wishart, London, 1935 ("A Note on Fiction", also in O'CONNOR: *Forms of Modern Fiction*).

ROUSSEAUX, André, *Littérature du XXe siècle*, Albin Michel, Paris: Tome I (1949); Tome VI (1958) and Tome VII (1961).

RUSSELL, Bertrand, *The Philosophy of Bergson*, in *The Monist*, July 1913, and Cambridge Univ. Press, 1914.

SACKVILLE-WEST, Vita, *Knole and the Sackvilles*, London, Heinemann, 1922, xvi, 230 pp.

—— *The Land, A Poem*, William Heinemann, London, 1926.

SAVAGE, D. S., *The Withered Branch: Six Studies in the Modern Novel*, Eyre & Spottiswoode, London, 1950 (*v.* pp. 70-105).

SCOTT-JAMES, R. A., *Lytton Strachey*, Longmans, Green, 1955, 39 pp.

—— *Fifty Years of English Literature: 1900-1950, with a Postscript: 1951 to 1955*, Longmans, Green, London, New York and Toronto, 1956, xi, 282 pp.

Scrutiny, The Importance of Scrutiny. Edited with an Introduction by Eric Bentley, The Grove Press, New York, 1948, 470 pp.

BIBLIOGRAPHY

SIMON, Irène, *Formes du Roman Anglais de Dickens à Joyce*, Faculté de Philosophie et Lettres, Liège, 1949, 464 pp.

SITWELL, Edith, *Aspects of Modern Poetry*, Duckworth, London, 1934 (ch. VIII: "Notes on Innovation in Prose").

SPENDER, Stephen, *The Destructive Element: A Study of Modern Writers and Beliefs*, Jonathan Cape, London, 1935, 284 pp.

—— *World within World: The Autobiography of Stephen Spender*, Hamish Hamilton, London and Harcourt Brace, New York, 1951, ix, 349 pp.

—— *The Making of a Poem*, Hamish Hamilton, London, 1955, (*v.* ch. V: "Two Landscapes of the Novel"), 192 pp.

STEPHEN, Karin, *The Misuse of Mind: A Study of Bergson's Attitude to Intellectualism*, Kegan Paul, Trench, Trubner, 1922, 106 pp.

STEPHEN, Leslie, *Hours in a Library* (1874), 4 vols., Smith Elder & Co., London, 1909.

—— *Studies of a Biographer* (1898), vol. I, in the New Reader's Library, Duckworth, London, 1929.

—— *Some Early Impressions* (1903, in *The National Review*), L. and V. Woolf, London, 1924, 192 pp.

—— *English Literature and Society in the 18th Century* (Ford Lectures, 1903), Duckworth, London, 1947.

STRACHEY, Lytton, *Books and Characters, French and English*, Chatto & Windus, London, 1922, 264 pp.

—— *Portraits in Miniature and Other Essays*, Chatto & Windus, London, 1931, 218 pp.

—— *Biographical Essays*, Chatto & Windus, London, 1948, 288. pp.

STRACHEY, Ray, *The Cause: A Short History of the Women's Movement in Great Britain*, G. Bell & Sons, London, 1928, 429 pp.

SWINNERTON, Frank, *The Georgian Literary Scene: 1910-1925*, William Heinemann, London and Toronto, 1935, x, 548 pp.

TINDALL, William Y., *Forces in Modern British Literature: 1885-1946*, Knopf, New York, 1947 (also Vintage Books, K. 35, vii, 316, pp. New York, 1956), vii, 278 pp..

—— *The Literary Symbol*, Knopf, New York, 1955.

TRILLING, Lionel, *The Liberal Imagination*, Secker & Warburg, London, 1951, 303 pp.

TURNELL, Martin, *Modern Literature and Christian Faith*, Darton, Longman & Todd, London, 1961, 81 pp.

VERSCHOYLE, Derek (ed.), *The English Novelists*, Chatto & Windus, London, 1936 (essay by E. B. C. Jones: "E. M. Forster and Virginia Woolf", pp. 259-76), 293 pp.

WAGENKNECHT, Edward, *Cavalcade of the English Novel*, Holt, 1945 (pp. 505-32).

WARD, A. C., *Twentieth Century Literature: The Age of Interrogation 1901-1905*, Methuen, London, 1928, xii, 266 pp.

—— *The Nineteen Twenties: Literature and Ideas in the Post-War Decade*, Methuen, London, 1930, x, 222 pp.

WEST, Ray B. Jr., *The Art of Modern Fiction*, 1949.

WEST, Rebecca, *Ending in Earnest*, Doubleday Doran, 1931 (pp. 208-213).

WIERSMA-VERSCHAFFELT, "Quelques Réflexions au sujet de l'Iconographie du Graal" (see René Nelli: *Lumière du Graal*).

WILSON, Edmund, *Axel's Castle: A Study in the Imaginative Literature of 1870-1930*, Scribner, New York and London, 1931, 319 pp.

—— *The Shores of Light*, Farrar, Straus & Young, New York, 1952; W. H. Allen, London, 1952 ("V. W. and the American Language").

WOOLF, Leonard, *Hunting the Highbrow*, Hogarth Essays, Second Series, No. 5, London, 1927, 51 pp.

—— *Essays in Literature, History, Politics, etc.* Hogarth Press, London, 1927, 255 pp.

—— *Sowing: An Autobiography of the Years 1880 to 1904*, Hogarth Press, London, 1960, 206 pp.

—— *Growing: An Autobiography of the Years 1904 to 1911*, Hogarth Press, London, 1961, 256 pp.

—— *Beginning Again: An Autobiography of the Years 1911 to 1918*, Hogarth Pr ess, London, 1964, 260 pp.

INDEX OF VIRGINIA WOOLF'S WORKS

GENERAL INDEX

INDEX

Books by Virginia Woolf
available in paperback editions
from Harcourt Brace Jovanovich, Inc.

The Voyage Out (HB 151)
Night and Day (HB 263)
Jacob's Room *and* The Waves (HB 37)
The Common Reader: First Series (HB 10)
Mrs. Dalloway (HB 81)
To the Lighthouse (HB 82)
Orlando (HB 266)
A Room of One's Own (H 020)
The Second Common Reader (HB 24)
Flush (HB 348)
The Years (HB 166)
Three Guineas (H 021)
Roger Fry: A Biography (HB 338)
Between the Acts (HB 189)
The Death of the Moth and Other Essays (HB 294)
A Haunted House and Other Short Stories (HB 105)
The Moment and Other Essays (HB 295)
The Captain's Death Bed and Other Essays (HB 253)
A Writer's Diary (HB 264)
Granite and Rainbow (HB 318)
Contemporary Writers (HB 347)
Mrs. Dalloway's Party (HB 279)